Encyclopedia of the
FIFA World Cup

Encyclopedia of the FIFA World Cup

Tom Dunmore

with Andrew Donaldson

ROWMAN & LITTLEFIELD
Lanham • Boulder • New York • London

Published by Rowman & Littlefield
4501 Forbes Boulevard, Suite 200, Lanham, Maryland 20706
www.rowman.com

Unit A, Whitacre Mews, 26-34 Stannary Street, London SE11 4AB

British Library Cataloguing in Publication Information Available

Library of Congress Cataloging-in-Publication Data

Dunmore, Tom.
  Encyclopedia of the FIFA World Cup / Tom Dunmore with Andrew Donaldson.
    pages cm
  Includes bibliographical references.
  ISBN 978-0-8108-8742-8 (cloth : alk. paper) — ISBN 978-0-8108-8743-5 (electronic)
1. World Cup (Soccer)—Encyclopedias. 2. World Cup (Soccer)—History—Chronology.
3. Fédération internationale de football association. I. Donaldson, Andrew. II. Title.
  GV943.49.D86 2015
  796.334'668—dc23

                                                                  2014000966

Printed in the United States of America

Contents

Chronology of the World Cup

1904   22 May: The foundation of world soccer's governing body, the Fédération Internationale de Football Association (FIFA), takes place in Paris, France. Robert Guérin is elected as the first president of FIFA.

1930   13–30 July: The first FIFA World Cup takes place in Uruguay. Thirteen nations compete, including seven from South America, four from Europe and two from North America. It is won by the host nation Uruguay, who defeats Argentina 4–2 in the final. The Uruguayans are awarded the Jules Rimet Trophy, named after the FIFA president. The United States takes third place and Yugoslavia fourth. Guillermo Stábile scores eight goals to win the Golden Shoe as the tournament's top scorer.

1934   27 May–10 June: The second FIFA World Cup is held in Italy. Defending champion Uruguay refuses to travel to Europe for the competition. Twelve European nations take part, along with two South American teams, one North American team and the first team from Africa to compete, Egypt. In the final, the host nation defeats Czechoslovakia 2–1 after extra time. Germany finishes in third and Austria fourth. Oldřich Nejedlý of Czechoslovakia is the Golden Shoe winner, scorer of a competition-leading five goals.

1938   4–19 June: In France, 15 teams play in the third World Cup: 12 from Europe and one each from Asia, North and Central America and South America. Italy wins the third FIFA World Cup, beating Hungary 4–2 in the final. Brazil wins the third-place play-off 4–2 over Sweden. Brazil's Leônidas is the Golden Shoe winner with seven goals.

1950   24 June–16 July: After a 12-year hiatus due to World War II, the FIFA World Cup resumes play and takes place outside Europe for the first time since 1930, in Brazil. Thirteen teams compete, with six from Europe, five from South America and two from North and Central America. Uruguay wins the decisive final round-robin game against Brazil to become a world champion for the second time, with the host nation finishing second, Sweden third and Spain fourth. Ademir of Brazil is the Golden Shoe winner, scoring eight goals.

1954   16 June–4 July: The World Cup returns to Europe, hosted by Switzerland. Twelve teams from Europe, two from South America and one each from Asia and North and Central America comprise the 16 nations taking part. West Germany claims the trophy, beating Hungary 3–2 in the final. Austria takes third place and Uruguay fourth. The total of 140 goals scored remains the highest number scored in a World Cup on a per-game basis. Hungarian Sándor Kocsis tallied 11 of those goals to claim the Golden Shoe.

1958   8 June–29 June: Sixteen teams participate in the sixth World Cup, held in Sweden. Twelve of those countries are European, three South American and one each from North and Central America. Brazil wins a first World Cup title, defeating the host nation, Sweden, 5–2 in the final. France takes third place and Germany fourth. France's Just Fontaine wins the Golden Shoe with 13 goals in the competition, a record haul for a single tournament that still holds today.

1962   30 May–17 June: The World Cup heads to South America for the second time. Sixteen teams compete: ten from Europe, five from South America and one from North and Central America. Host nation Chile finishes in third place, as Brazil claims its second World Cup title, beating Czechoslovakia 3–1 in the final. Yugoslavia finishes fourth. The Golden Shoe is claimed jointly by five players, all with four goals: Hungary's Flórián Albert, the Soviet Union's Valentin Ivanov, the Brazilian pair of Garrincha and Vava, and Yugoslavia's Dražan Jerković.

1966   11 July–30 July: The World Cup is hosted by England for the first time. Sixteen teams take part, with European nations comprising ten of the contenders, South America four and one each from Asia and North and Central America. England wins the World Cup for the first time, beating Germany 4–2 in the final at Wembley Stadium. Portugal wins the third-place match 2–1 over the Soviet Union. Eusébio's nine goals for Portugal give him the Golden Shoe.

1970   31 May–21 June: In Mexico, Brazil wins a third World Cup title and was thus allowed to keep the Jules Rimet Trophy forever as a result. Ten European teams, three South American teams, two North and Central American teams and one African team take part. The Brazilians, led by Pelé, defeat Italy 4–1 in the final. West Germany finishes in third place and Uruguay fourth. Red and yellow cards are used for the first time in the World Cup. The Golden Shoe is claimed by Gerd Müller of West Germany, with 10 goals in the competition.

1974   13 June–7 July: In the year that Brazilian João Havelange is elected as the seventh president of FIFA, West Germany wins the World Cup on home soil, beating the Netherlands in the final 2–1. Poland wins the third-place play-off over Brazil 1–0. The field of 16 teams is comprised of nine European nations, four South American nations and one representative each from Asia, Africa and North and Central America. Poland's Grzegorz Lato wins the Golden Shoe with seven goals.

1978   1 June–25 June: Argentina hosts the World Cup and wins it for the first time, defeating the Netherlands 3–1 in the final after extra time. Brazil wins the third-place play-off 2–1 over Italy. Sixteen teams take part, with five continents represented for the first time: ten nations from Europe, three from South America and one each from Africa, Asia and North and Central America. With six goals, Argentina's Mario Kempes claims the Golden Shoe award.

1982   13 June–11 July: The World Cup is expanded to 24 teams, with fourteen European countries, four South American countries, two African countries, two North and Central American countries and one Asian country making up the field in Spain. Italy takes a third world championship, fired by six goals from Golden Shoe winner Paolo Rossi. The Italians defeat West Germany in the final, 3–1, while Poland finishes in third place and France fourth.

1986   31 May–29 June: Mexico hosts the World Cup for the second time, with Diego Maradona's Argentina defeating West Germany 3–2 in the final after extra time to win a second world championship. France beats Belgium 4–2 in the third-place play-off. Twenty-four teams participate: fourteen from Europe, four from South America and two each from Africa, Asia and North and Central America. England's Gary Lineker earns the Golden Shoe award for his six goals in the competition.

1990   8 June–8 July: Italy hosts the FIFA World Cup for the second time, 56 years after the first occasion. West Germany wins the tournament, beating Argentina 1–0 in the final. Italy wins the third-place play-off 2–1 over England. Twenty-four teams take part, with fourteen European nations, four South American nations and two nations each from Africa, Asia and North and Central Europe comprising the field. Salvatore Schillaci's six goals for Italy give the striker the Golden Shoe award.

1994   17 June–17 July: The United States hosts the World Cup for the first time. Records that remain unbroken are set for both aggregate and average attendance at the competition, with 3,587,538 spectators attending at an average of 68,991 per game. The final is decided by a penalty shoot-out for the first time after a scoreless draw, with Brazil prevailing over Italy. Sweden wins the third-place play-off match 4–0 over Bulgaria.

1998   10 June–12 July: Joseph "Sepp" Blatter is elected as the eighth president of FIFA in the same year France hosts the World Cup for the second time and wins it for the first time, beating Brazil 3–0 in the final. Croatia wins the third-place play-off 2–1 over the Netherlands. An enlarged field of 32 teams takes part: fifteen from Europe, five each from South America and Africa, four from Asia and three from North and Central America. Davor Šuker of Croatia scores six goals to win the Golden Shoe.

2002   31 May–30 June: The World Cup is held in Asia for the first time, with South Korea and Japan acting as cohosts. Brazil wins a record fifth World Cup title, beating West Germany 2-0 in the final. Turkey takes third place after beating South Korea in a play-off. Fifteen European nations, five South American nations, five African nations, four Asian nations and three North and Central African nations comprise the 32-team lineup for the competition. The Golden Shoe is won by Brazilian Ronaldo, scorer of eight goals.

2006   9 June–9 July: Germany hosts the World Cup, won by Italy, who defeats France in a penalty shoot-out after the final ends in a tie. Germany wins the third-place play-off, beating Portugal 3–1. Thirty-two teams take part: fourteen from Europe, five each from Africa and Asia and four each from South America and North and Central America. Germany's Miroslav Klose is the Golden Shoe winner, with five goals.

2010   11 June–11 July: The FIFA World Cup takes place on the African continent for the first time, hosted by South Africa. It is won by Spain, claiming the nation's first World Cup title. The Netherlands finishes in second place, Germany in third and Uruguay in fourth. Thirteen European nations, six African nations, five South American nations, four Asian nations and three North and Central American nations comprise the field of 32 teams. Five goals and three assists earn Thomas Müller the Golden Boot award.

2014   12 June–13 July: The FIFA World Cup is held in Brazil for the second time (1950) and is won by Germany, their fourth overall title, when they beat Argentina 1–0 in the final at the Estádio do Maracanã in front of 74,738 fans. Host Brazil ends the tournament in embarrassing fashion, losing 3–0 in the third-place game to the Netherlands, one game after their record defeat in the semifinals, a 7–1 loss to Germany. Again, 32 teams made up the field: 13 from Europe, 6 from South American, 5 from Africa and 4 each from Asia and North and Central America; 24 of the 32 teams are returning nations from the 2010 World Cup in South Africa. With six goals and two assists, the Golden Boot was awarded to Colombia's James Rodríguez.

Introduction

In the United States—a country not historically known for its obsession with soccer—over 26 million people tuned in to their televisions to watch the 2014 World Cup final between Germany and Argentina held at the Maracanã in Rio de Janeiro, Brazil. Another 750, 000 tuned in online. FIFA's press release after the event proudly trumpeted that the World Cup, which had featured 32 teams from every continent, had been broadcast "in every single country and territory on Earth, including Antarctica and the Arctic Circle."

Eighty-four years previously, the very first World Cup final between Uruguay and Argentina held at Estadio Centenario in Montevideo, Uruguay, attracted far less global attention. The *New York Times* offered a three-paragraph recap of the game, noting that "Uruguay today won world supremacy in soccer football for the third time." The newspaper's count of the host nation's world titles referred to Uruguay's wins at the 1924 and 1928 Olympic Games—seen as the precursor to FIFA's newly established World Cup. Only 13 nations had traveled to Uruguay, with just 3 coming from Europe on long voyages by sea. The country where soccer had been founded in the 19th century, England, refused to take part (and wouldn't do so until 1950).

In the intervening 84 years between Uruguay in 1930 and Brazil in 2014, the World Cup was transformed from a buccaneering global sporting event developing in the nascent years of professional soccer to a hyper-commercialized event drawing billions of dollars of sponsorship and investment to bring it to a globalized television audience. The World Cup's popularity rests on its global appeal from the passion generated by international sporting conflict and the performances on the biggest stage by legendary players and teams who have left indelible marks on the competition. Pelé was one of the most famous people in the world in the 1960s and 1970s, and that stardom largely came from his role in Brazil's three World Cup victories between 1958 and 1970, broadcast on international television and for the first time in Technicolor at the 1970 World Cup in Mexico. Moments of magic on the playing field, such as those Brazil produced in its 4–1 victory over Italy in that tournament's final, continue to illuminate a tournament that has done more than any other event to make soccer the most popular sport in the world. It is a tournament that has also been marked by controversy on and off the field, and as millions of dollars have flowed around the competition, it has become criticized for its commercialism and the corruption that has at times eked into its organization.

The key development in the rise of the World Cup came with the formation of FIFA, soccer's world governing body, in 1904. Organized soccer had begun decades earlier in Great Britain, where the first national governing body, the Football Association (FA) in London, was formed in 1863. The FA played a key role in normalizing rules across the British Isles and introduced a wildly successful single-elimination competition, the FA Cup, in 1871. National associations soon formed in the rest of the British Isles (in Scotland, Wales and Ireland), and as British sailors, merchants and industrialists spread out across the formal and informal British Empire, around the world, soccer took hold from Austria to Argentina. Representative national teams of all-star players began playing each other in Britain in the 1870s, with England and Scotland staging the first official international game in 1872. As other countries around the world began to play each other, it became rapidly apparent that a global governing body was needed to oversee this play, to organize competitions and to ensure the same rules were followed around the world. The British nations' associations, however, were not interested in working to grow the game's organization outside the British Isles. Their administrators saw little to be gained by playing other countries, who they felt were far below their own playing standards. Overtures from French administrators to the Football Association to help form an international governing body went nowhere in the early years of the 20th century. Ultimately, continental European associations decided to form a world governing body for soccer themselves. FIFA was founded by seven founding member nations in Paris in 1904, initially composed of Denmark, France, Germany, the Netherlands, Spain, Sweden and Switzerland. The first president of FIFA was a Frenchman, Robert Guérin. England's FA joined the following year, though it would for decades have a topsy-turvy relationship with FIFA. FIFA's membership expanded in the following years, with new continents represented by South Africa's membership in 1909, Argentina and Chile joining in 1912 and the United States and Canada coming onboard in 1913. The inclusion of nations from Europe, Africa, South America and North America made FIFA a true global governing body for the sport within a decade of its formation.

As well as its geographic breadth giving it legitimacy, FIFA also claimed special rights: upon its founding, the organization claimed an exclusive right to organize a soccer world championship. This immediately raised the question of the validity of the international soccer competition held every four years at the Olympic Games. The sport had been first played at the games in 1904, in St. Louis, where a team of Canadians beat a team of Americans for the gold medal. With the Games returning to Europe in 1908, taking place in London, the question was whether FIFA would recognize the competition and, if not, whether it would be able to take action against any national teams or players who took part without its consent. In the end, FIFA proved to be too weak in both international authority and resources to organize its own independent world championship during its early years of existence. FIFA instead worked with the International Olympic Committee (IOC) to develop soccer's world championship as part of the Olympic Games. FIFA laid down the rules for the tournaments in London in 1908 and Stockholm in 1912, both won by British teams made up of English amateurs, with professionals banned from Olympic competition.

Following World War I, FIFA's membership rapidly grew in the 1920s alongside the spread of soccer globally—and the sport's growing professionalism raised a new, serious issue for the world championship at the Olympic Games. Many of the best players in the world were now either officially or unofficially paid by their clubs, a situation that contravened the Olympic Games' statutes and ethos of pure amateurism, doggedly defended by the IOC. Meantime, the improving quality of play in professional soccer and its genuinely global nature in the 1920s encouraged FIFA in the belief that an independent international competition could stand on its own feet. Separated from the mix of other sports at the Olympic Games, soccer could—FIFA president Jules Rimet asserted—thrive further with its own independent global event. Unlike most other sports that continued to accept the Olympic Games as the peak of its global competition, soccer did soon have its own competition of unrivalled prominence as Rimet led FIFA's commitment to holding a World Cup on its own in 1930.

The question was now where to hold the inaugural competition and how many nations would take part. Europe was the obvious choice for a location: it was, after all, the continent where FIFA had been founded and where the majority of its members resided, facilitating travel to the tournament in an era long before rapid jet transit. FIFA, though, made the brave decision to host the competition several thousand miles from its Paris headquarters: in Montevideo, the capital of Uruguay. The South American nation presented a compelling case to host the first World Cup. Uruguay had stunned international soccer circles by winning both the 1924 and 1928 Olympic Games' tournaments, with clever teamwork and individual brilliance awing global observers. Fueled by an export boom, Uruguay also had the financial resources to back a competition whose ability to break even financially was entirely unknown. Uruguay promised to build a grand, new stadium for the event and pay for the expenses of all traveling teams. Such lavish expenditure on hosting the competition served more than a sporting purpose for Uruguay: 1930 would also mark a centenary since the country's first independent constitution was promulgated, thus meaning the inaugural World Cup could showcase the country on the international stage as part of its elaborate and expensive centennial celebrations.

The decision to award Uruguay the World Cup immediately conferred on the competition global legitimacy. By contrast, a tournament hosted in FIFA's home nation, France, may have been seen as parochially European. There was a downside to FIFA's faith in Uruguay, though. Several nations who had hoped to host the tournament felt jilted, including Italy, a leading team who refused to travel to South America for the competition. Despite Uruguay's offer of financial assistance for traveling teams, the trip around the world also required a substantial commitment by European associations and their players and coaches: the journey by sea would alone take two weeks. FIFA was ultimately only able to coax four European nations—Belgium, France, Romania and Yugoslavia—into making the journey to South America. No African or Asian teams made the trip, while two countries from North America, Mexico and the United States, headed south. Along with 7 South American nations, Argentina, Bolivia, Brazil, Chile, Paraguay, Peru and host nation Uruguay, a field of 13 nations was set for the first World Cup.

FIFA now faced the question of how to organize the competition. Most cup competitions had traditionally been single-elimination affairs, including those held at the Olympic Games, but FIFA determined it did not want nations that had traveled around the world to potentially play one game and then depart. A first-round group stage was thus established: the 13 teams split into one group of four teams and three groups of three teams each. Uruguay lived up to its promise to build a new stadium as the main venue for the competition, but not in time for the opening games: the magnificent Estadio Centenario was unfinished by the time the tournament kicked off, forcing the first set of games to be played at two smaller stadia in Montevideo, Estadio Parque Central and Pocitos. Uruguay and its neighbor across the Rio de la Plata, Argentina, proved to be the strongest teams in the competition, confirming that the South American supremacy in the Olympic Games during the 1920s had been no mirage. Only one European nation made it to the semifinal stage, Yugoslavia, crushed 6–1 at that stage by Uruguay. In the other semifinal, Argentina defeated the United States, also by the one-sided score of 6–1. The final between Argentina and Uruguay was the grand affair for world soccer that Jules Rimet had dreamed of for decades. Thousands of traveling Argentinean fans poured across the Rio de la Plata by ferry, and Montevideo itself came to a standstill. Though Argentina led at halftime 2–1, Uruguay scored three times in the second period to claim the first World Cup, raising aloft the goddess of victory trophy designed by Frenchman Abel Lafleur.

The World Cup headed to Europe for the next competition in 1934 in Italy and remained there in France in 1938. The competition was not immune to the extreme politics that defined Europe that decade; the 1934 competition was held as a showcase for Benito Mussolini's fascist regime, who reveled in the victory of the home nation, who defeated Czechoslovakia 2–1 in the final in a competition that some suspected had featured refereeing dubiously favorable to the Italians. The Italian triumph, played out in a tournament spread across eight host cities that required qualification for the tournament to take place, was broadcast on the radio for the first time. Four years later, the 1938 World Cup was held under the shadow of war, with Austria—one of the strongest teams at the 1934 competition—a country no longer in existence by the time the tournament kicked off in June 1938, its players along with the nation subsumed into Germany months before. Italy triumphed again in a competition that fielded only 3 non-European nations among the 15 that took part.

With Europe still recovering from the intense devastation across the continent during World War II, the World Cup returned to South America in 1950, hosted by soccer-crazy Brazil and featuring 13 participating nations. Like Uruguay two decades previously, Brazil showed its commitment to the competition by building the Maracanã stadium, the world's largest with almost 200,000 spectators crammed in for the last game of the tournament. That game saw one of the greatest upsets in the history of the competition, as the host nation fell to Uruguay, who claimed a second world title, to the intense agony of the Brazilian nation. The World Cup was raised again by the Uruguayans, the trophy having survived World War II under the bed of FIFA Vice President Ottorino Barassi and now renamed in honor of FIFA President Jules Rimet.

The World Cup then returned to Europe for two more competitions in the 1950s, held in Switzerland in 1954 and Sweden in 1958, countries that today would be deemed far too small to host the tournament alone. The tournament remained far from a globally balanced contest in terms of its participants: in Sweden, 12 of the 16 nations taking part came from Europe, with just 3 from South America (Argentina, Brazil and Paraguay) and 1 from North America (Mexico), with Asia and Africa entirely unrepresented. After West Germany claimed a surprising win at the 1954 World

Cup in Switzerland, defeating favorites Hungary in the final, Brazil then triumphed in Sweden, led by the brilliance of a 17-year-old known as Pelé. Brazil thus became the first nation to win a World Cup outside of its own continent. It was a display carried on international television for the first time, a development that would soon transform the event into a global media phenomenon and make stars such as Pelé known the world over. The 1962 World Cup in Chile saw Brazil and Pelé triumph again, though he missed most of the competition with injury, and Pelé was limited once more by injury in England four years later, as the home nation—and the birthplace of organized soccer—won the competition for the first time.

In 1970, color television broadcast the first World Cup held in North America, in Mexico, and helped make global stars out of Pelé and a Brazilian team that romped to a famous third World Cup victory, allowed to keep the Jules Rimet Trophy forever for becoming the first team to lift it three times. In 1974, a new trophy, the 11-pound 18-carat gold FIFA World Cup Trophy, was awarded to host nation West Germany, whose team, led by the imperious Franz Beckenbauer, surprisingly defeated the favorites—Johan Cruyff's Dutch team—in the final. The Dutch also lost in the 1978 final to the host nation, Argentina, in a tournament covered by ticker tape on the field and no little controversy off it, with the World Cup used for political propaganda purposes by the South American country's ruling military regime. FIFA did not seem concerned; as an organization, its bottom line under President João Havelange had become the bottom line on the balance sheet above all else. Yet while the World Cup became more commercial, it also became less Eurocentric. Havelange's leadership, secured in a 1974 FIFA presidential election victory over Englishman Sir Stanley Rous, rested on his promise to expand the competition to include more African and Asian nations. In 1966, the two continents had shared one place in the finals; by the end of Havelange's tenure, in 1998, nine nations from Africa and Asia took part at the World Cup in France.

The World Cup's expansion, along with broader trends of globalization led by multinational companies, meant that by the 1980s sponsors such as Adidas or Coca-Cola were willing to pour hundreds of millions of dollars into what had become the only rival to the Olympic Games as an event for global sporting visibility. From 20 teams in 1978, the World Cup expanded to 24 for the competitions in 1982 in Spain, 1986 in Mexico and 1990 in Italy, won by Italy, Argentina and West Germany respectively. That period also saw another great bestride the stage, Diego Maradona, who took his country to its second World Cup win in 1986 and another final in 1990, before exiting ignominiously from the 1994 World Cup after failing a drug test. That competition saw the World Cup on American soil for the first time. Many had feared the United States—a nation traditionally with relatively little interest in soccer—would not adopt the World Cup enthusiastically, but those fears proved unfounded as record attendances watched Brazil claim a fourth world title, thanks mainly to its brilliant pair of forwards, Romário and Bebeto. The Brazilians won on penalty kicks in the final over Italy, the first time this method had been used to decide the decisive game, though it had first been introduced in 1982 to negate the need for replayed games following ties.

The World Cup expanded again to 32 teams in 1998, as the competition returned to France, who claimed a first world title, a victory orchestrated from midfield by the magisterial Zinedine Zidane. The size of the World Cup meant it was no longer possible for midsized nations to host the competition alone, due to the scale of infrastructure needed to cope with 32 teams, 64 games and huge contingents of visiting fans. This encouraged a joint South Korea/Japan bid for the 2002 World Cup, as the competition headed to Asia for the first time. It was familiarly won by a Ronaldo-fired Brazil, claiming a fifth title. The World Cup returned to Germany in 2006, with huge crowds lining fan fests in German cities, giving the competition a festive atmosphere and sponsors a captive audience outside of stadiums with the games additionally broadcast on huge video screens. Those screens broadcasted a dramatic finale, France's Zinedine Zidane sent off in extra time during the final for headbutting Marco Materazzi after an insult by the Italian, whose team won the World Cup for the fourth time on a penalty shoot-out. FIFA's drive to continue growing the World Cup, now under the stewardship of Havelange's controversial handpicked successor, Sepp Blatter, saw the competition reach another new continent in 2010, with the finals held in South Africa. There was another European triumph, the hypnotic passing of Spain driving the Iberian nation's first World Cup title.

As qualifying for the 2014 World Cup in Brazil took place, Blatter's reign continued amid controversy over corruption in the halls of FIFA—with multiple FIFA vice presidents stepping down or suspended following alleged bribery during the voting contest for the hosting of the 2018 and 2022 World Cups, awarded to Russia and Qatar respectively. The scale of the World Cup's success—a billion-dollar industry now revolving around it—had made FIFA's far from transparent governance vulnerable to the lure of the dollar, with the now honorary president Havelange himself forced to stand down in spring 2013 following further revelations about financial malfeasance under his tenure as FIFA president.

The World Cup manages to flourish despite FIFA's much-criticized oversight of the competition, with the naked corruption and commercialism surrounding it damaging its sporting integrity. Yet despite that, the tournament's appeal remains unmatched by any other single global sporting event. The World Cup is steeped in decades of magical memories for fans, players and coaches from Algeria to the Americas that give it a luster unique in world sport. A remarkable 207 nations entered qualifying for the 2014 tournament in Brazil, with the ultimate glory of lifting a trophy coveted by billions continuing to inspire the growth of soccer the world over.

Tournament Recaps

Abbreviations used in the tables: P: played; PTS: points; W: won; D: draw; L: lost; GF: goals for; GA: goals against; AET: after extra time; PSO: penalty shoot-out

1930 WORLD CUP

Host Nation: Uruguay
Dates: 13 to 30 July 1930
Teams: 13
Matches: 18
Winner: Uruguay
Runner-Up: Argentina
Third Place: USA
Fourth Place: Yugoslavia
Golden Shoe: Guillermo Stábile (Argentina), 8 goals

Thirteen teams representing their countries traveled to Uruguay for the inaugural World Cup held in July 1930, the realization of FIFA President Jules Rimet's vision of organizing a worldwide international tournament for national teams. Several countries had offered to host the competition, but Uruguay's promise to pay the travel and accommodation expenses was an important factor in FIFA's selection of them as hosts, with the tournament's financial viability unknown.

Uruguay celebrated its centenary as an independent nation that year and finished the tournament as the first World Cup champions, beating neighbors Argentina 4–2 in the final held at Estadio de Centenario in the Uruguayan capital, Montevideo. The spectacular new stadium had been specially built for the competition, though it was not completed in time for the first few games of the competition to be played there, with the initial matches staged elsewhere in Montevideo instead. Unlike in later World Cup tournaments, all 18 games of the competition were staged in a single city, Montevideo, at this World Cup.

A total of 70 goals were scored in the tournament, at an average of 3.9 per match, a healthy figure, though many of the goals came in lopsided games that showed the gulf in class between the world's two strongest teams, Argentina and Uruguay, and the rest: though the latter two teams also had to travel least, with the European competitors facing long boat trips that saw many teams pull out long before the tournament began. The eventual 13 competitors were divided into four groups for the initial stage of the competition, with one group of four teams and three groups of three teams, the top team in each group after each had played each other once going through to the final stage of single-elimination games: Argentina, Yugoslavia, Uruguay and the United States.

The semifinals demonstrated the two strongest teams' abilities to crush opponents who had traveled long distances, along with a divide in quality: Argentina destroyed the United States 6–1, with Uruguay taking care of Yugoslavia by the same score. The final of the tournament between Argentina and Uruguay was a closer affair than the 4–2 result in favor of the hosts indicates: Argentina in fact led 2–1 at halftime, thanks to goals from Carlos Peucelle and tournament top scorer, Guillermo Stábile, before a partisan crowd at Estadio de Centenario roared on Uruguay to score three unanswered second-half goals and become the first-ever World Cup champions.

FIRST ROUND							
Group 1							
13 July		France	4–1	Mexico			
15 July		Argentina	1–0	France			
16 July		Chile	3–0	Mexico			
19 July		Chile	1–0	France			
19 July		Argentina	6–3	Mexico			
22 July		Argentina	3–1	Chile			
Team	**P**	**PTS**	**W**	**D**	**L**	**GF**	**GA**
Argentina	3	6	3	0	0	10	4
Chile	3	4	2	0	1	5	3
France	3	2	1	0	2	4	3
Mexico	3	0	0	0	3	4	13
Group 2							
14 July		Yugoslavia	2–1	Brazil			
17 July		Yugoslavia	4–0	Bolivia			
20 July		Brazil	4–0	Bolivia			
Team	**P**	**PTS**	**W**	**D**	**L**	**GF**	**GA**
Yugoslavia	2	4	2	0	0	6	1
Brazil	2	2	1	0	1	5	2
Bolivia	2	0	0	0	2	0	8
Group 3							
14 July		Romania	3–1	Peru			
18 July		Uruguay	1–0	Peru			
21 July		Uruguay	4–0	Romania			

Team	P	PTS	W	D	L	GF	GA
Uruguay	2	4	2	0	0	5	*0*
Romania	2	2	1	0	1	3	5
Peru	2	0	0	0	2	1	4
Group 4							
13 July			United States	3–0	Belgium		
17 July			United States	3–0	Paraguay		
20 July			Paraguay	1–0	Belgium		
Team	P	PTS	W	D	L	GF	GA
United States	2	4	2	0	0	6	0
Paraguay	2	2	1	0	1	1	3
Belgium	2	0	0	0	2	0	4
SEMIFINALS							
26 July			Argentina	6–1	United States		
27 July			Uruguay	6–1	Yugoslavia		
FINAL							
30 July			Uruguay	4–2	Argentina		

1934 WORLD CUP

Host Nation: Italy
Dates: 27 May to 10 June 1934
Teams: 16
Matches: 17
Winner: Italy
Runner-Up: Czechoslovakia
Third Place: Germany
Fourth Place: Austria
Golden Shoe: Oldřich Nejedlý (Czechoslovakia), 5 goals

The second World Cup took place in Europe for the first time, with the competition won for the second consecutive time by the host nation, this time Italy. Seventeen matches were played in the competition from 27 May to 10 June 1934, in a substantially larger format than four years previously. The prestige of the World Cup had grown since the first edition in 1930, with 32 teams applying to FIFA to take part, leading to the organization of a preliminary qualifying competition to cut down the contenders to 16 nations for the final tournament. Italy themselves had to take part in the qualifying competition, successfully so, though all future hosts would receive automatic qualification to the finals tournament. Defending World Cup champions

Uruguay refused to travel to Italy and defend their title, partly in retaliation for Italy's refusal to travel to Uruguay for the previous World Cup competition.

The expansion of the tournament meant more stadiums needed to be used in the tournament than the first World Cup in 1930, with eight Italian cities hosting games. The 16 teams played in a straight knockout format, with hosts Italy defeating the United States 7–1 in the first round, the highest scoring game of the tournament. The advantages of playing close to home were demonstrated by the semifinals lineup, with all four teams coming from Europe: Czechoslovakia defeated Germany 3–1, and Italy beat an excellent Austria team 1–0. The final, held in Rome, proved to be a tightly fought game, hosts Italy coming out on top 2–1 over Czechoslovakia after extra time, with the score tied at 1–1 at the end of regulation. Angelo Schiavio scored the winning goal in the 95th minute, giving Europe its first World Cup champion, Italy.

FIRST ROUND			
27 May	Sweden	3–2	Argentina
27 May	Austria	3–2 AET	France
27 May	Germany	5–2	Belgium
27 May	Spain	3–1	Brazil
27 May	Hungary	4–2	Egypt
27 May	Switzerland	3–2	Netherlands
27 May	Italy	7–1	United States
27 May	Czechoslovakia	2–1	Romania
QUARTERFINALS			
31 May	Czechoslovakia	3–2	Switzerland
31 May	Germany	2–1	Sweden
31 May	Italy	1–1 AET	Spain
31 May	Austria	2–1	Hungary
1 June	Italy	1–0	Spain
SEMIFINALS			
3 June	Italy	1–0	Austria
3 June	Czechoslovakia	3–1	Germany
THIRD-PLACE GAME			
7 June	Germany	3–2	Austria
FINAL			
10 June	Italy	2–1 AET	Czechoslovakia

1938 WORLD CUP

Host Nation: France
Dates: 4 to 19 June 1938
Teams: 15
Matches: 18
Winner: Italy
Runner-Up: Hungary
Third Place: Brazil
Fourth Place: Sweden
Golden Shoe: Leônidas da Silva (Brazil), 7 goals

The third World Cup was the second to be hosted in Europe, just a year before the outbreak of the Second World War; it was held in France from 4 to 19 June 1938. Eighteen matches were played in 10 different French venues, with a total of 376,177 spectators attending at an average of 20,898 fans per game. A total of 87 goals were scored, at an average of 4.7 per game, and the result of the tournament saw Italy claim their second successive World Cup title, defeating Hungary 4–2 in the final. A preliminary qualifying tournament featuring 37 countries had determined the 15 finalist countries, with defending champions Italy and host France automatically qualifying. There were notable absentees from the tournament with Argentina and Uruguay both refusing to play because they believed South America had been snubbed in favor of Europe to host the tournament. Meanwhile, the stormy political situation in Europe prevented Austria and Spain from competing and cast a pall over the tournament as a whole, with antifascist demonstrations timed on the streets of France to coincide with games featuring Germany and Italy.

This World Cup was uniquely structured with three rounds of single-elimination games leading up to the final, starting with a first round featuring 14 of the 15 teams, Sweden receiving a bye to the second round. Switzerland and Germany tied in the first game 1–1, a replay five days later determining who would go through, the Swiss winning 4–2. The Dutch East Indies made their only appearance in a World Cup, losing 6–0 to Hungary. France beat Belgium comfortably by three goals to one. Cuba and Romania tied 3–3 and also played a replay, won by Cuba 2–1. Italy won a close game with Norway 2–1, their winning goal in extra time coming from Silvio Piola. The game of the tournament came on 5 June, with Brazil beating Poland 6–5 in a thrilling encounter. Leônidas da Silva scored three goals for Brazil, and Poland's Ernst Wilimowski remarkably ended up on the losing team despite scoring four of his team's five goals. In the final first-round game, Czechoslovakia won by the deceptively comfortable scoreline of three goals to none over the Netherlands, all three goals coming in extra time after a 0–0 tie at the 90-minute mark.

In the first game of the second round, on 12 June, Brazil tied with Czechoslovakia 1–1, needing a replay to go through with a 2–1 win in the second game two days later. Hungary beat Switzerland 2–0 in Lille, while in Antibes, Cuba was thumped 8–0 by Sweden, including a hat trick for Tore Keller. Host France lost 3–1 to Italy, with two more goals for Italian Silvio Piola. In the semifinals held on 16 June,

Hungary registered an emphatic victory over Sweden: despite conceding a goal in the first minute, they scored five unanswered goals to win 5–1, Gyula Zsengellér scoring three goals. In the other semifinal, Brazil, who had sauntered through to that point with the brilliant Leônidas da Silva lighting up the tournament, made the curious decision to rest their star so he would be fresh for the final, presumably expecting an easy win over Italy. But the defending champions were not to be taken so lightly, going 2–0 up early in the second half thanks to goals from Gino Colaussi and Giuseppe Meazza, and a late goal from Romeu that made it 2–1 was little consolation for the beaten South Americans.

Leônidas went on to score two more as Brazil won the third-place play-off with Sweden on 19 June, taking his total for the tournament to seven goals, the best in the competition. The final was held the same day, and Italy outclassed the Hungarians, with Meazza their creative hub, assisting on the Italians' first three goals as they ran out 4–2 winners. Silvio Piola and Gino Colaussi both scored twice. Italy's two successive championship victories in the World Cup had been masterminded by their coach Vittorio Pozzo. Due to the Second World War, it would be 12 years before the next World Cup took place.

FIRST ROUND			
4 June	Switzerland	1–1 AET	Germany
5 June	Hungary	6–0	Dutch East Indies
5 June	France	3–1	Belgium
5 June	Cuba	3–3 AET	Romania
5 June	Italy	2–1 AET	Norway
5 June	Brazil	6–5	
AET	Poland		
5 June	Czechoslovakia	3–0	
AET	Netherlands		
9 June	Cuba	2–1	Romania
9 June	Switzerland	4–2	Germany
QUARTERFINALS			
12 June	Brazil	1–1 AET	Czechoslovakia
14 June (Replay)	Brazil	2–1	Czechoslovakia
12 June	Hungary	2–0	Switzerland
12 June	Sweden	8–0	Cuba
12 June	Italy	3–1	France

SEMIFINALS			
16 June	Hungary	5–1	Sweden
16 June	Italy	2–1	Brazil
THIRD-PLACE GAME			
19 June	Brazil	4–2	Sweden
FINAL			
19 June	Italy	4–2	Hungary

1950 WORLD CUP

Host Nation: Brazil
Dates: 24 June to 16 July 1950
Teams: 13
Matches: 22
Winner: Uruguay
Runner-Up: Brazil
Third Place: Sweden
Fourth Place: Spain
Golden Shoe: Ademir (Brazil), 9 goals

The Second World War prevented the World Cup from taking place in 1942 and 1946, but it returned in 1950, staged in South America for the first time since 1930, in soccer-crazy Brazil from 24 June to 16 July 1950. A vast new stadium, the Maracanã, was specially built in Rio de Janeiro for the tournament. Despite the poor economic conditions following the war, six European teams traveled to Brazil to make up almost half the odd-numbered field of 13 teams for the tournament. Hosts Brazil qualified automatically, but a number of leading countries withdrew from the tournament, including Argentina and France, and at the last minute, Scotland, India and Turkey. The format for the tournament was changed from the straight knockout setup of the previous World Cup in 1938 to a two-stage group format—the teams were first divided into four groups, with the winners of each group advancing to a final round-robin format in a single group.

Due to the late withdrawals of several teams, the first-round groups were awkwardly divided into two groups of four teams, one group of three teams and one group containing just two teams. Brazil, Spain, Sweden and Uruguay each topped their groups. The biggest surprise came on 29 June 1950, in a result still remembered today: the United States upset England 1–0 in Belo Horizonte, Joe Gaetjens scoring the winning goal in a scrappy game. The result shocked England, appearing in the World Cup for the first time and still presuming that as the leading force in the development of the game since the 19th century they would easily beat an upstart soccer nation like the United States.

The final round of the tournament, the only time in World Cup history that the competition did not lead to a single-game final, contained a further surprise: heading into the final game of the round-robin, four-team group that would determine the winner of the competition, Brazil was in prime position to claim its first title, favored on home soil. It had crushed both Sweden (7–1) and Spain (6–1), while its opponent, Uruguay, had tied with Spain and just eked out a win over Sweden 3–2. The final game between the two was played at the Maracanã stadium in Rio de Janeiro, in front of a crowd officially registered at 174,000 but probably over 200,000, almost all of them cheering on the host nation. To the shock of all of Brazil, Uruguay won the game despite going down 1–0 to a goal by Friaça in the 47th minute, thanks to a strike by Juan Alberto Schiaffino in the 66th minute and the winning effort by Alcides Ghiggia in the 79th minute. Language itself changed, such was the momentous impact of the game: a new word in Spanish, *Maracanazo*, was coined to refer to such a blow at the home stadium of Brazil, the Maracanã. For the second time, Uruguay received the World Cup Trophy, which had been renamed that year in honor of FIFA president Jules Rimet's 25 years in charge of the global governing body of the sport, and was thus now known as the Jules Rimet Trophy.

FIRST ROUND

Group 1

24 June			Brazil	4–0	Mexico		
25 June			Yugoslavia	3–0	Switzerland		
28 June			Brazil	2–2	Switzerland		
28 June			Yugoslavia	4–1	Mexico		
1 July			Brazil	2–0	Yugoslavia		
2 July			Switzerland	2–1	Mexico		

Team	P	PTS	W	D	L	GF	GA
Brazil	3	5	2	1	0	8	2
Yugoslavia	3	4	2	0	1	7	3
Switzerland	3	3	1	1	1	4	6
Mexico	3	0	0	0	3	2	10

Group 2

25 June			England	2–0	Chile		
25 June			Spain	3–1	United States		
29 June			Spain	2–0	Chile		
29 June			United States	1–0	England		
2 July			Spain	1–0	England		
2 July			Chile	5–2	United States		

Team	P	PTS	W	D	L	GF	GA
Spain	3	6	3	0	0	6	1
England	3	2	1	0	2	2	2
Chile	3	2	1	0	2	5	6
United States	3	2	1	0	2	4	8

Group 3							
25 June			Sweden	3–2	Italy		
29 June			Sweden	2–2	Paraguay		
2 July			Italy	2–0	Paraguay		
Team	P	PTS	W	D	L	GF	GA
Sweden	2	3	1	1	0	5	4
Italy	2	2	1	0	1	4	3
Paraguay	2	1	0	1	1	2	4
Group 4							
2 July			Uruguay	8–0	Bolivia		
Team	P	PTS	W	D	L	GF	GA
Uruguay	1	2	1	0	0	8	0
Bolivia	1	2	0	0	1	0	8
FINAL ROUND							
9 July			Uruguay	2–2	Spain		
9 July			Brazil	7–1	Sweden		
13 July			Brazil	6–1	Spain		
13 July			Uruguay	3–2	Sweden		
16 July			Sweden	3–1	Spain		
16 July			Uruguay	2–1	Brazil		
Team	P	PTS	W	D	L	GF	GA
Uruguay	3	5	2	1	0	7	5
Brazil	3	4	2	0	1	14	4
Sweden	3	2	1	0	2	6	11
Spain	3	1	0	1	2	4	11

1954 WORLD CUP

Host Nation: Switzerland
Dates: 16 June 1954 to 4 July 1954
Teams: 16
Matches: 26
Winner: West Germany
Runner-Up: Hungary
Third Place: Austria
Fourth Place: Uruguay
Golden Shoe: Sándor Kocsis (Hungary), 11 goals

The 1954 World Cup, the fifth time the competition was contested, returned the tournament to Europe for the first time since the outbreak of World War II, with neutral Switzerland the safe choice selected by FIFA as hosts, especially as the country also was the home base of FIFA. It was the first World Cup to be broadcast on television, taking the games to a new audience. The tournament ended with a surprising winner, West Germany, who defeated the favorites, Hungary, 3–2 in the final. Forty-five teams entered the initial qualifying stage to become one of the sixteen countries taking part in the finals competition in Switzerland that lasted from 16 June 1954 to 4 July 1954, with the 26 games played in six different Swiss stadiums. The format of the tournament changed from the previous event in 1950. The first stage saw the 16 teams divided into four groups of four teams each, a complicated format meaning the two "seeded" teams in each group only played the non-seeds, with the top two in the group going through to the next round. From there, it would be a knockout round of single-elimination games.

The elimination rounds were full of high-scoring affairs: the hosts, Switzerland, lost by five goals to seven to Austria in the quarterfinals, with Uruguay, favorites Hungary and West Germany progressing to the semifinals. There, Hungary became the first team to beat Uruguay in any World Cup finals tournament, defeating them 4–2 after extra time. West Germany comfortably disposed of Austria 6–1 and would now face Hungary in the World Cup final. The two teams had played each other in the first-round group stage, Hungary having demolished the West Germans 8–3; they also beat the Republic of Korea 9–0 and were in the midst of a remarkable unbeaten run that stretched to 31 games, playing a form of free-flowing soccer never before seen, centered on their brilliant captain and creative star, Ferenc Puskás. Puskás, however, was injured in the first match against West Germany; though he returned for the final, held at Wankdorf Stadium in Bern and scored the opening goal in the game in the sixth minute, he was short of his best. Hungary scored a second goal in the eighth minute, but then what became known to West Germany as the "Miracle of Bern" began: the West Germans quickly tied up the game with goals from Max Morlock in the 10th minute and Helmut Rahn in the 18th minute. Inspirational leadership from the West German captain, Fritz Walter, saw them keep the usually rapacious Hungarians at bay for the rest of the game, and in the 84th minute, Rahn scored a winning goal for West Germany that shocked the world and gave them their first World Cup triumph.

FIRST ROUND							
Group 1							
16 June		Yugoslavia	1–0	France			
16 June		Brazil	5–0	Mexico			
19 June		Brazil	1–1 AET	Yugoslavia			
19 June		France	3–2	Mexico			
Team	**P**	**PTS**	**W**	**D**	**L**	**GF**	**GA**
Brazil	2	3	1	1	0	6	1
Yugoslavia	2	3	1	1	0	2	1

| France | 2 | 2 | 1 | 0 | 1 | 3 | 3 |
| Mexico | 2 | 0 | 0 | 0 | 2 | 2 | 8 |

| Group 2 | | | | | | | |

17 June		Germany	4–1	Turkey			
17 June		Hungary	9–0	Korea			
20 June		Hungary	8–3	Germany			
20 June		Turkey	7–0	Korea			
23 June		Germany	7–2	Turkey			

Team	P	PTS	W	D	L	GF	GA
Hungary	2	4	2	0	0	17	3
Germany	3	4	2	0	1	14	11
Turkey	3	2	1	0	2	10	11
Korea	2	0	0	0	2	0	16

| Group 3 | | | | | | | |

16 June		Austria	1–0	Scotland			
16 June		Uruguay	2–0	Czechoslovakia			
19 June		Uruguay	7–0	Scotland			
19 June		Austria	5–0	Czechoslovakia			

Team	P	PTS	W	D	L	GF	GA
Uruguay	2	4	2	0	0	9	0
Austria	2	4	2	0	0	6	0
Czechoslovakia	2	0	0	0	2	0	7
Scotland	2	0	0	0	2	0	8

| QUARTERFINALS | | | | | | | |

26 June		Austria	7–5	Switzerland			
26 June		Uruguay	4–2	England			
27 June		Hungary	4–2	Brazil			
27 June		Germany	2–0	Yugoslavia			

| SEMIFINALS | | | | | | | |

| 30 June | | Hungary | 4–2 AET | Uruguay | | | |
| 30 June | | Germany | 6–1 | Austria | | | |

| THIRD-PLACE GAME | | | | | | | |

| 3 July | | Austria | 3–1 | Uruguay | | | |

| FINAL | | | | | | | |

| 4 July | | Germany | 3–2 | Hungary | | | |

1958 WORLD CUP

Host Nation: Sweden
Dates: 8 June to 29 June 1958
Teams: 16
Matches: 35
Winner: Brazil
Runner-Up: Sweden
Third Place: France
Fourth Place: West Germany
Golden Shoe: Just Fontaine (France), 13 goals

The World Cup was played in Europe for the second successive time in 1958, this time in the Swedish summer, with international television coverage broadcasts of the games shown for the first time. The tournament is best remembered as the international coming out of a 17-year-old star called Pelé and his Brazil team that would dominate the next 12 years of international soccer as they won their first World Cup title. Sixteen teams took part in the final tournament, from an original field of 45 teams that entered the qualifying stage, with 35 matches played from 8 to 29 June 1958 across 12 Swedish stadiums, a then record number of host stadiums for a World Cup. Another record was set by France's Just Fontaine, whose 12 goals scored remains the most a single player has ever scored in the World Cup.

The 16 teams in the tournament were divided into four groups of four teams each for the first stage, each team playing each other once, with the top two teams in each group qualifying for a single-elimination knockout phase. Of the eight qualifiers to this stage, free-scoring France and Brazil impressed most. The latter, lining up in an innovative 4-2-4 formation, had not only Pelé but also the mercurial dribbling genius Garrincha and the experienced Didi, the team's elegant creative force in midfield. These two teams met at the semifinal stage, and goals galore flowed: Brazil won 5–2, inspired by a hat trick from Pelé that revealed France's defensive frailties. In the other semifinal, defending champion West Germany was comprehensively beaten by hosts Sweden three goals to one, despite taking an early lead in the game. The final, held in front of 51,000 spectators at Råsunda Stadium in Solna (just north of the Swedish capital, Stockholm), was another high-scoring affair, with Brazil's class eventually telling. Sweden struck first, though, through Nils Liedholm in just the fourth minute, but Brazil quickly equalized in the ninth minute with a goal from Vava, who then scored again in the 32nd minute to give Brazil the lead 2–1 at halftime. Pelé gave Brazil further breathing space with their third goal in the 55th minute. Mário Zagallo, who would later coach Brazil to further World Cup glory, scored Brazil's fifth in the 68th minute to make it 4–1. Sweden pulled one back through Agne Simonsson in the 80th minute, but Pelé fittingly had the final word with a fifth and final goal for Brazil in the 90th minute, his country claiming the first of what would become many World Cup triumphs.

FIRST ROUND

Group 1

8 June	Argentina	1–3	Germany
8 June	Northern Ireland	1–0	Czechoslovakia
11 June	Argentina	3–1	Northern Ireland
11 June	West Germany	2–2	Czechoslovakia
15 June	Czechoslovakia	6–1	Argentina
15 June	West Germany	2–2	Northern Ireland
17 June	Northern Ireland	2–1 AET	Czechoslovakia

Team	P	PTS	W	D	L	GF	GA
Northern Ireland	4	5	2	1	1	6	6
West Germany	3	4	1	2	0	7	5
Czechoslovakia	4	3	1	1	2	9	6
Argentina	3	2	1	0	2	5	10

Group 2

8 June	Yugoslavia	1–1	Scotland
8 June	France	7–3	Paraguay
11 June	Yugoslavia	3–2	France
11 June	Paraguay	3–2	Scotland
15 June	Paraguay	3–3	Yugoslavia
15 June	France	2–1	Scotland

Team	P	PTS	W	D	L	GF	GA
France	3	4	2	0	1	11	7
Yugoslavia	3	4	1	2	0	7	6
Paraguay	3	3	1	1	1	9	12
Scotland	3	1	0	1	2	4	6

Group 3

8 June	Sweden	3–0	Mexico
8 June	Hungary	1–1	Wales
11 June	Mexico	1–1	Wales
12 June	Sweden	2–1	Hungary
15 June	Sweden	0–0	Wales
15 June	Hungary	4–0	Mexico
17 June	Wales	2–1	Hungary

Team	P	PTS	W	D	L	GF	GA
Sweden	3	5	2	1	0	5	1
Wales	4	5	1	3	0	4	3
Hungary	4	3	1	1	2	7	5
Mexico	3	1	0	1	2	1	8

Group 4

8 June	Soviet Union	2–2	England
8 June	Brazil	3–0	Austria
11 June	Soviet Union	2–0	Austria
11 June	Brazil	0–0	England
15 June	Brazil	2–0	Soviet Union
15 June	England	2–2	Austria
17 June	Soviet Union	1–0	England

Team	P	PTS	W	D	L	GF	GA
Brazil	3	5	2	1	0	5	0
Soviet Union	4	5	2	1	1	5	4
England	4	3	0	3	1	4	5
Austria	3	1	0	1	2	2	7

QUARTERFINALS

19 June	Brazil	1–0	Wales
19 June	France	4–0	Northern Ireland
19 June	West Germany	1–0	Yugoslavia
19 June	Sweden	2–0	Soviet Union

SEMIFINALS

24 June	Sweden	3–1	West Germany
24 June	Brazil	5–2	France

THIRD-PLACE GAME

28 June	France	6–3	West Germany

FINAL

29 June	Brazil	5–2	Sweden

1962 WORLD CUP

Host Nation: Chile
Dates: 30 May to 17 June 1962
Teams: 16
Matches: 32
Winner: Brazil
Runner-Up: Czechoslovakia
Third Place: Chile
Fourth Place: Yugoslavia
Golden Shoe: Tied—Flórián Albert (Hungary), Valentin Ivanov (Soviet Union), Dražan Jerković (Yugoslavia), Leonel Sánchez (Chile), Vava (Brazil) and Garrincha (Brazil), 4 goals

The World Cup returned to South America after the two previous championships in 1954 and 1958 had been held in Europe, with Chile selected as hosts. Their ability to stage the tournament was cast into severe doubt by a massive earthquake in the country on 22 May 1960, with a magnitude of 9.5, the most powerful ever recorded anywhere in the world to date, with thousands killed and widespread physical disaster. The Chilean authorities, though, encouraged a national spirit of rebuilding in time to stage the World Cup despite this. New venues, including the sparkling Estadio Nacional in Chile's capital, Santiago, were built to provide fitting homes for the 32 matches played from 30 May to 17 June 1962, with the final seeing Brazil claim their second successive World Cup title.

The format of the tournament was the same as that of the 1958 World Cup, with a first-round stage featuring the 16 competing teams divided into four groups of four teams each, and the top two qualifying for the single-elimination knockout phase. The backdrop to many of the games, the stunning Andes mountain range, was often far more beautiful than the soccer played on the field: one infamous game in the first round, between Italy and Chile, became known as the "Battle of Santiago," with the game degenerating into vicious foul play, with two players sent off. Brazil's Pelé, meanwhile, tore his thigh muscle in their second game, against Czechoslovakia, and did not appear in any further games in the tournament. But, armed with plenty of other remarkable talent, including the flamboyant Garrincha at the height of his powers, Brazil soon proved to be the class of the competition: in the quarterfinals, they easily disposed of England by three goals to one, Garrincha scoring twice.

In the semifinals, Brazil faced hosts Chile, a game they comfortably won 4–2 in front of 76,500 spectators in Santiago, with two more goals coming from Garrincha, who was proving to be the star of the tournament. It was an all-European affair in the other semifinal, with Czechoslovakia defeating Yugoslavia 3–1 thanks to two goals late in the game by Adolf Scherer. In the final, the Czech underdogs surprisingly took an early lead through a goal in the 15th minute by Josef Masopust, their captain and outstanding player. But Pelé's replacement, Amarildo, equalized just two minutes later, and Brazil took control of the game in the 69th minute with Zito scoring from an Amarildo pass. A third goal by Vava in the 78th minute sealed the game for Brazil, who claimed their second World Cup title.

FIRST ROUND

Group 1

30 May	Uruguay	2–1	Colombia
31 May	Soviet Union	2–0	Yugoslavia
2 June	Yugoslavia	3–1	Uruguay
3 June	Soviet Union	4–4	Colombia
6 June	Soviet Union	2–1	Uruguay
7 June	Yugoslavia	5–0	Colombia

Team	P	PTS	W	D	L	GF	GA
Soviet Union	3	5	2	1	0	8	5
Yugoslavia	3	4	2	0	1	8	3
Uruguay	3	2	1	0	2	4	6
Colombia	3	1	0	1	2	5	11

Group 2

30 May	Chile	3–1	Switzerland
31 May	West Germany	0–0	Italy
2 June	Chile	2–0	Italy
3 June	West Germany	2–1	Switzerland
6 June	West Germany	2–0	Chile
7 June	Italy	3–0	Switzerland

Team	P	PTS	W	D	L	GF	GA
West Germany	3	5	2	1	0	4	1
Chile	3	4	2	0	1	5	3
Italy	3	3	1	1	1	3	2
Switzerland	3	0	0	0	3	2	8

Group 3

30 May	Brazil	2–0	Mexico
31 May	Czechoslovakia	1–0	Spain
2 June	Brazil	0–0	Czechoslovakia
3 June	Spain	1–0	Mexico
6 June	Brazil	2–1	Spain
7 June	Mexico	3–1	Czechoslovakia

Team	P	PTS	W	D	L	GF	GA
Brazil	3	5	2	1	0	4	1
Czechoslovakia	3	3	1	1	1	2	3
Mexico	3	2	1	0	2	3	4
Spain	3	2	1	0	2	2	3

Group 4							
30 May		Argentina	1–0	Bulgaria			
31 May		Hungary	2–1	England			
2 June		England	3–1	Argentina			
3 June		Hungary	6–1	Bulgaria			
6 June		Hungary	0–0	Argentina			
7 June		England	0–0	Bulgaria			
Team	P	PTS	W	D	L	GF	GA
Hungary	3	5	2	1	0	8	2
England	3	3	1	1	1	4	3
Argentina	3	3	1	1	1	2	3
Bulgaria	3	1	0	1	2	1	7
QUARTERFINALS							
10 June		Brazil	3–1	England			
10 June		Chile	2–1	Soviet Union			
10 June		Yugoslavia	1–0	West Germany			
10 June		Czechoslovakia	1–0	Hungary			
SEMIFINALS							
13 June		Czechoslovakia	3–1	Yugoslavia			
13 June		Brazil	4–2	Chile			
THIRD-PLACE GAME							
16 June		Chile	1–0	Yugoslavia			
FINAL							
17 June		Brazil	3–1	Czechoslovakia			

1966 WORLD CUP

Host Nation: England
Dates: 11 to 30 July 1966
Teams: 16
Matches: 32
Winner: England
Runner-Up: West Germany
Third Place: Portugal
Fourth Place: Soviet Union
Golden Shoe: Eusébio (Portugal), 9 goals

England, where professional soccer had first developed in the 19th century, played host to the World Cup for the first time from 11 to 30 July 1966, with 16 teams taking part and 32 matches played in the eighth edition of the competition. England won the tournament for the first time, defeating West Germany 4–2 in a controversial final. The competition was not without controversy or incident, beginning with the qualifying competition: though a record 70 countries entered the preliminary stage, 16 African nations withdrew to protest a FIFA ruling in 1964 that meant the African champion had to compete in a play-off against either the Asian or Oceanic zone winners to qualify for the finals tournament, requesting an automatic qualifying place. Further controversy followed when just months before the tournament, the Jules Rimet Trophy was stolen from an exhibition; it was, bizarrely, recovered by a dog named Pickles a week later, hidden under some bushes in London.

Once the tournament got underway, the first-round group stage saw the 16 teams divided into four groups of four teams. In group one, England did not impress with a cautious approach in the first round despite topping their group, starting with a dour 0–0 draw with Uruguay, who also qualified from the group, before some improvement with 2–0 wins over Mexico and France, both eliminated. Group two saw Argentina and Spain progress comfortably at the expense of a disappointing Spain and an outclassed Switzerland. Three of the world's strongest teams featured in group three, with defending champion Brazil joined by Portugal and Hungary, along with Bulgaria, who lost all three games. But Bulgaria did have some impact: vicious foul play in their first game against Brazil injured Pelé, ruling him out for the second game and limiting him in their third against Portugal. In that game, Portugal's star Eusébio scored twice as Brazil was defeated by three goals to one, eliminating them from the tournament, with Portugal and Hungary progressing. Group four also sprung a surprise: two-time World Cup winners Italy lost twice, first against group winners the Soviet Union and then, most shockingly, losing to reclusive North Korea and eliminated from the competition, finishing only above Chile.

In the quarterfinals, England won a bitter, brawling game against Argentina 1–0, West Germany easily brushed aside Uruguay 4–0 and the Soviet Union won a close encounter with Hungary 2–1, inspired by the goalkeeping of Lev Yashin. The most exciting game of the round saw North Korea briefly threaten a massive upset over Portugal after leading 3–0 after just 25 minutes, before eventually losing 5–3, the Portuguese comeback inspired by Eusébio's four goals. The semifinals were both close affairs. West Germany edged out the Soviet Union 2–1 after a surprisingly poor game by star Russian goalkeeper Lev Yashin. Meanwhile, Bobby Charlton scored twice as England played their best game of the tournament to beat a talented Portuguese team 2–1, with Portugal's Eusébio scoring again and ultimately ending up as the leading goal scorer in the competition with nine goals.

England had now found their rhythm under coach Sir Alf Ramsey, having switched to a formation without wide wingers in a 4-4-2 formation favoring hard-working players with their cool, dominant central defender and captain Bobby Moore leading from the back. West Germany, though, was a formidable foe in the final: their own captain and star defender Franz Beckenbauer was revolutionizing the role a defensive player could perform, roaming forward to spray passes around the field with incisive vision and even scoring four goals in the tournament. The game at Wembley Stadium proved to be controversial. The Germans took an early lead through a goal by Helmut

Haller, but English forward Geoff Hurst soon equalized, and the score was tied 1–1 at halftime. England took the lead when Martin Peters scored in the 78th minute, but Wolfgang Weber tied the game again just before full-time, with the game going to extra time. In the 101st minute, the controversy came: Geoff Hurst struck the ball off the underside of the crossbar; the ball then bounced down onto the line as most observers saw it. The assistant referee (then known as the linesman), Tofiq Bahramov, though, adjudged the ball to have crossed the line and awarded a goal. England did not look back, and Hurst completed his hat trick with England's fourth goal in the 120th minute. England had won their first World Cup title.

FIRST ROUND

Group 1

11 July		England	0–0	Uruguay			
13 July		France	1–1	Mexico			
15 July		Uruguay	2–1	France			
16 July		England	2–0	Mexico			
19 July		Uruguay	0–0	Mexico			
20 July		England	2–0	France			
Team	P	PTS	W	D	L	GF	GA
England	3	5	2	1	0	4	0
Uruguay	3	4	1	2	0	2	1
Mexico	3	2	0	2	1	1	3
France	3	1	0	1	2	2	5

Group 2

12 July		West Germany	5–0	Switzerland			
13 July		Argentina	2–1	Spain			
15 July		Spain	2–1	Switzerland			
16 July		West Germany	0–0	Argentina			
19 July		Argentina	2–0	Switzerland			
20 July		West Germany	2–1	Spain			
Team	P	PTS	W	D	L	GF	GA
West Germany	3	5	2	1	0	7	1
Argentina	3	5	2	1	0	4	1
Spain	3	2	1	0	2	4	5
Switzerland	3	0	0	0	3	1	9

Group 3

| 12 July | | Brazil | 2–0 | Bulgaria | | | |
| 13 July | | Portugal | 3–1 | Hungary | | | |

15 July			Hungary	3–1	Brazil		
16 July			Portugal	3–0	Bulgaria		
19 July			Portugal	3–1	Brazil		
20 July			Hungary	3–1	Bulgaria		
Team	*P*	*PTS*	*W*	*D*	*L*	*GF*	*GA*
Portugal	3	6	3	0	0	9	2
Hungary	3	4	2	0	1	7	5
Brazil	3	2	1	0	2	4	6
Bulgaria	3	0	0	0	3	1	8

Group 4

12 July			Soviet Union	3–0	North Korea		
13 July			Italy	2–0	Chile		
15 July			North Korea	1–1	Chile		
16 July			Soviet Union	1–0	Italy		
19 July			North Korea	1–0	Italy		
20 July			Soviet Union	2–1	Chile		
Team	*P*	*PTS*	*W*	*D*	*L*	*GF*	*GA*
Soviet Union	3	6	3	0	0	6	1
North Korea	3	3	1	1	1	2	4
Italy	3	2	1	0	2	2	2
Chile	3	1	0	1	2	2	5

QUARTERFINALS

23 July	England	1–0	Argentina
23 July	West Germany	4–0	Uruguay
23 July	Soviet Union	2–1	Hungary
23 July	Portugal	5–3	North Korea

SEMIFINALS

25 July	West Germany	2–1	Soviet Union
26 July	England	2–1	Portugal

THIRD-PLACE GAME

28 July	Portugal	2–1	Soviet Union

FINAL

30 July	England	4–2 AET	West Germany

1970 WORLD CUP

Host Nation: Mexico
Dates: 31 May to 21 June 1970
Teams: 16
Matches: 32
Winner: Brazil
Runner-Up: Italy
Third Place: West Germany
Fourth Place: Uruguay
Golden Shoe: Gerd Müller (West Germany), 10 goals

Brazil, dazzling in their yellow jerseys in the ninth edition of the World Cup and the first to be broadcast in Technicolor around the world, won their third World Cup title in the tournament hosted by Mexico from 31 May to 21 June 1970. It was the first time the tournament had been hosted in North America; all previous competitions had been held in either Europe or South America. FIFA rule changes introduced some new elements to the play, including the introduction of red and yellow cards and an allowance of two substitutes per game per team.

The first round of the competition divided the 16 teams into four groups of four teams each, with the top two from each group progressing to the quarterfinals. In group one, host Mexico qualified for the next round, finishing behind the Soviet Union, with Belgium and El Salvador both eliminated. Italy topped a tightly contested group two, Uruguay also qualifying and Sweden and Israel going out of the tournament. Group three was perhaps the strongest, with Brazil winning all three games and defending champions England qualifying to the next round in outstanding form as well, beating both Romania and Czechoslovakia. Brazil beat England 1–0 in a classic game, with Jairzinho scoring the winning goal, though the game is often recalled mainly for a remarkable save by England goalkeeper Gordon Banks from a close-range Pelé header. In group four, 1966 World Cup finalist West Germany impressed with victories over all three opponents, Bulgaria, Morocco (the first African contestant since the Second World War) and Peru, who also qualified to the next round after surprising many with their potent attacking style of play.

In the quarterfinals, an open and exciting contest between Peru and Brazil saw the latter prevail by four goals to two, thanks to goals by Rivelino, Tostão (two) and Jairzinho. Italy began to show their quality as they eliminated hosts Mexico 4–1. Uruguay won a close game that went to extra time over the Soviet Union 1–0, thanks to a goal in the 116th minute by Víctor Espárrago. The game of the round was a rematch of the 1966 World Cup final between West Germany and England. The defending champions, led by the stylish Bobby Moore and the attacking midfielder Bobby Charlton, ran out to a 2–0 lead with goals from Alan Mullery in the 31st minute and Martin Peters in the 49th minute. But the West German captain and outstanding creative force Franz Beckenbauer pulled a goal back for his country in the 68th minute, and with England missing goalkeeper Gordon Banks through illness, they quickly crumbled defensively, conceding a second to Uwe Seeler in the 76th minute and then succumbing to a winning goal from Gerd Müller in extra time. Müller, a lethal striker, was on his way to becoming the tournament's top scorer with 10 goals.

In the first semifinal, Uruguay took a surprise early lead over Brazil, but the best team of the tournament reasserted their superiority, playing a brand of skillful, attacking soccer rarely seen before in the World Cup. Brazil came out 3–1 winners to advance to their fourth World Cup final. There they would face Italy, who had beaten West Germany 4–3 in the other semifinal. That game was tied at 1–1 at the end of 90 minutes, then followed by a frenetic extra-time period that saw six goals scored, with a winning goal for Italy coming in the 111th minute. The final proved to be a classic in front of an official attendance of 107,412 at the Estadio Azteca stadium in Mexico City. It was announced that the winner out of Italy and Brazil, with two World Cup titles each, would be allowed by FIFA to keep the Jules Rimet Trophy for their third triumph. Brazil was at their brilliant best, with potent passing moves that even the smooth defensive efficiency of Italy could not cope with. Pelé opened the scoring with a header from a Rivelino cross in the 18th minute, and though Roberto Boninsegna equalized for Italy in the 37th minute, Brazil was unstoppable in the second half: goals from Gérson in the 66th minute, Jairzinho in the 71st minute and Carlos Alberto in the 86th minute sealed a 4–1 win. That final goal epitomized Brazil's flair and fluid passing, the ball passed around almost the entire Brazilian team before Pelé languidly laid it off for the final scoring shot. Brazil took home the Jules Rimet Trophy for good and earned a reputation as one of the greatest teams in World Cup history.

FIRST ROUND							
Group 1							
31 May		Mexico	0–0	Soviet Union			
3 June		Belgium	3–0	El Salvador			
6 June		Soviet Union	4–1	Belgium			
7 June		Mexico	4–0	El Salvador			
10 June		Soviet Union	2–0	El Salvador			
11 June		Mexico	1–0	Belgium			
Team	**P**	**PTS**	**W**	**D**	**L**	**GF**	**GA**
Soviet Union	3	5	2	1	0	6	1
Mexico	3	5	2	1	0	5	0
Belgium	3	2	1	0	2	4	5
El Salvador	3	0	0	0	3	0	9
Group 2							
2 June		Uruguay	2–0	Israel			
3 June		Italy	1–0	Sweden			
6 June		Uruguay	0–0	Italy			

7 June			Sweden	1–1	Israel		
10 June			Sweden	1–0	Uruguay		
11 June			Italy	0–0	Israel		
Team	P	PTS	W	D	L	GF	GA
Italy	3	4	1	2	0	1	0
Uruguay	3	3	1	1	1	2	1
Sweden	3	3	1	1	1	2	2
Israel	3	2	0	2	1	1	3

Group 3

2 June			England	1–0	Romania		
3 June			Brazil	4–1	Czechoslovakia		
6 June			Romania	2–1	Czechoslovakia		
7 June			Brazil	1–0	England		
10 June			Brazil	3–2	Romania		
11 June			England	1–0	Czechoslovakia		
Team	P	PTS	W	D	L	GF	GA
Brazil	3	6	3	0	0	8	3
England	3	4	2	0	1	2	1
Romania	3	2	1	0	2	4	5
Czechoslovakia	3	0	0	0	3	2	7

Group 4

2 June			Peru	3–2	Bulgaria		
3 June			West Germany	2–1	Morocco		
6 June			Peru	3–0	Morocco		
7 June			West Germany	5–2	Bulgaria		
10 June			West Germany	3–1	Peru		
11 June			Bulgaria	1–1	Morocco		
Team	P	PTS	W	D	L	GF	GA
West Germany	3	6	3	0	0	10	4
Peru	3	4	2	0	1	7	5
Bulgaria	3	1	0	1	2	5	9
Morocco	3	1	0	1	2	2	6

QUARTERFINALS

| 14 June | | | Brazil | 4–2 | Peru | | |
| 14 June | | | West Germany | 3–2 AET | England | | |

14 June		Italy	4–1	Mexico
14 June		Uruguay	1–0 AET	Soviet Union
SEMIFINALS				
17 June		Brazil	3–1	Uruguay
17 June		Italy	4–3 AET	West Germany
THIRD-PLACE GAME				
20 June		West Germany	1–0	Uruguay
FINAL				
21 June		Brazil	4–1	Italy

1974 WORLD CUP

Host Nation: West Germany
Dates: 13 June to 7 July 1974
Teams: 16
Matches: 38
Winner: West Germany
Runner-Up: Netherlands
Third Place: Poland
Fourth Place: Brazil
Golden Shoe: Grzegorz Lato (Poland), 7 goals

The 10th staging of the World Cup was held in West Germany from 13 June to 7 July 1974 and was won by the host nation, defeating the Netherlands in the final. The new World Cup Trophy, still used now, was awarded to West Germany, as the previous one, the Jules Rimet Trophy, had been given permanently to Brazil in recognition of their achievement in becoming the first country to win three World Cup titles in 1970. The force behind those triumphs, Pelé, had now retired from international soccer, but there was a magisterial replacement as the star of the tournament with the Netherlands' Johan Cruyff shining on the biggest stage in world soccer.

The format of the tournament changed substantially in 1974 from the previous edition of the World Cup in 1970, even though the same number of teams (16) took part. An initial group stage saw the 16 teams divided into four groups of four teams each, with the top two teams in each group progressing to the next stage. That was followed by a second group stage of four teams each, playing each other once, with the winner of each group progressing to the final. West Germany, though starting shakily, progressed into the second stage along with East Germany from group one in the first round. Yugoslavia and Brazil went through from group two, with Scotland eliminated despite not losing a game and Zaire losing all three games they played. In group three, the Netherlands impressed with two wins and a draw against Sweden, who also qualified, with Bulgaria and Uruguay exiting from the tournament. The best first-round performance came from Poland in group four, as they won all three games, and Polish forward Grzegorz Lato started a scoring spree that would see him end the World Cup as its top scorer with seven goals. Argentina also qualified from group four, with 1970 World Cup finalists Italy and tournament first-timers Haiti bowing out.

The second group stage that would determine the finalists began with a statement of the Netherlands and their coach Rinus Michels's commitment to open, attacking soccer that became known as Total Football, crushing Argentina 4–0 with Johan Cruyff scoring twice to open play in group A. Brazil won close games over both East Germany and Argentina, and which team out of Brazil and the Netherlands would reach the final came down to a game between the two teams on 3 July. Defending champions Brazil, not the power they had been in 1970, were no match for the Dutch, Johan Neeskens and Johan Cruyff scoring twice in the second-half to send the Netherlands to their first World Cup final. There they would face hosts West Germany, who had topped group B in a battle with Poland, after both had won their games against Sweden and Yugoslavia, setting up a decisive game between teams with a rivalry that extended deep into the history of the two nations. West Germany prevailed through a goal by Gerd Müller for a 1–0 win in pouring rain, with several outstanding saves from West German goalkeeper Sepp Maier proving to be the difference between the two teams.

The Netherlands entered the final as favorites due to the fantastic play that they had shown throughout the tournament, despite the home advantage for West Germany in front of an official crowd of 75,200 in Munich's Olympic Stadium. The Dutch scored early from the penalty spot after Cruyff had been fouled, Johan Neeskens scoring the penalty. The Netherlands controlled possession for much of the first half, but Paul Breitner scored a penalty to tie it up for West Germany after Bernd Hölzenbein was taken down by Wim Jansen. With the ever-elegant Franz Beckenbauer at the heart of the West German team and Berti Vogts tightly playing Johan Cruyff defensively, Dutch frustration grew, and Müller snatched a goal for the host nation in the 43rd minute that the Netherlands could not answer, giving West Germany its second World Cup title.

FIRST ROUND							
Group 1							
14 June		West Germany	1–0	Chile			
14 June		East Germany	2–0	Australia			
18 June		West Germany	3–0	Australia			
18 June		Chile	1–1	East Germany			
22 June		Australia	0–0	Chile			
22 June		East Germany	1–0	West Germany			
Team	**P**	**PTS**	**W**	**D**	**L**	**GF**	**GA**
East Germany	3	5	2	1	0	4	1
West Germany	3	4	2	0	1	4	1
Chile	3	2	0	2	1	1	2
Australia	3	1	0	1	2	0	5

Group 2

13 June			Brazil	0–0	Yugoslavia		
14 June			Scotland	2–0	Zaire		
18 June			Scotland	0–0	Brazil		
18 June			Yugoslavia	9–0	Zaire		
22 June			Scotland	1–1	Yugoslavia		
22 June			Brazil	3–0	Zaire		
Team	**P**	**PTS**	**W**	**D**	**L**	**GF**	**GA**
Yugoslavia	3	4	1	2	0	10	1
Brazil	3	4	1	2	0	3	0
Scotland	3	4	1	2	0	3	1
Zaire	3	0	0	0	3	0	14

Group 3

15 June			Sweden	0–0	Bulgaria		
15 June			Netherlands	2–0	Uruguay		
19 June			Netherlands	0–0	Sweden		
19 June			Bulgaria	1–1	Uruguay		
23 June			Netherlands	4–1	Bulgaria		
23 June			Sweden	3–0	Uruguay		
Team	**P**	**PTS**	**W**	**D**	**L**	**GF**	**GA**
Netherlands	3	5	2	1	0	6	1
Sweden	3	4	1	2	0	3	0
Bulgaria	3	2	0	2	1	2	5
Uruguay	3	1	0	1	2	1	6

Group 4

15 June			Italy	3–1	Haiti		
15 June			Poland	3–2	Argentina		
19 June			Argentina	1–1	Italy		
19 June			Poland	7–0	Haiti		
23 June			Poland	2–1	Italy		
23 June			Argentina	4–1	Haiti		
Team	**P**	**PTS**	**W**	**D**	**L**	**GF**	**GA**
Poland	3	6	3	0	0	12	3
Argentina	3	3	1	1	1	7	5
Italy	3	3	1	1	1	5	4
Haiti	3	0	0	0	3	2	14

SECOND ROUND							
Group A							
26 June	Netherlands	4–0	Argentina				
26 June	Brazil	1–0	East Germany				
30 June	Brazil	2–1	Argentina				
30 June	Netherlands	2–0	East Germany				
3 July	Argentina	1–1	East Germany				
3 July	Netherlands	2–0	Brazil				
Team	**P**	**PTS**	**W**	**D**	**L**	**GF**	**GA**
Netherlands	3	6	3	0	0	8	0
Brazil	3	4	2	0	1	3	4
East Germany	3	1	0	1	2	1	4
Argentina	3	1	0	1	2	2	7
Group B							
26 June	West Germany	2–0	Yugoslavia				
26 June	Poland	1–0	Sweden				
30 June	Poland	2–1	Yugoslavia				
30 June	West Germany	4–2	Sweden				
3 July	West Germany	1–0	Poland				
3 July	Sweden	2–1	Yugoslavia				
Team	**P**	**PTS**	**W**	**D**	**L**	**GF**	**GA**
West Germany	3	6	3	0	0	7	2
Poland	3	4	2	0	1	3	2
Sweden	3	2	1	0	2	4	6
Yugoslavia	3	0	0	0	3	2	6
THIRD-PLACE GAME							
6 July	Poland	1–0	Brazil				
FINAL							
7 July	West Germany	2–1	Netherlands				

1978 WORLD CUP

Host Nation: Argentina
Dates: 1 to 25 June 1978
Teams: 16
Matches: 38
Winner: Argentina

Runner-Up: Netherlands
Third Place: Brazil
Fourth Place: Italy
Golden Shoe: Mario Kempes (Argentina), 6 goals

The 11th staging of the World Cup took place in Argentina from 1 to 25 June 1978. The host nation, led by a tournament-leading six goals from forward Mario Kempes, won their first World Cup title, with the Netherlands losing their second successive World Cup final. The tournament returned to South American soil for the first time since the 1962 World Cup in Chile, with 38 matches played across six venues in Argentina. There had been controversy leading up to the tournament due to the military coup in Argentina in 1976 that resulted in considerable political repression in the country. Some countries considered boycotting the competition, but in the end, no country withdrew. Two of the stars from the previous 1974 World Cup were missing, though, with both Johan Cruyff of the Netherlands and Franz Beckenbauer of West Germany failing to make the trip with their countries. A young Diego Maradona was also snubbed by Argentina's coach Cesar Luis Menotti, who preferred to rely on the experienced and considerable talents of captain Daniel Passarella, the creative midfielder Ossie Ardiles and the striking prowess of Mario Kempes.

The tournament was structured in the same way as the 1974 edition. The 16 teams were divided into four groups of four teams, playing each other team in the group once, with the top two teams advancing. The second stage divided the remaining eight teams into two groups of four teams each, again each team playing each group member once, with the top team in the group going on to the final. The second team in each group would play for the third-place play-off. For the first time, FIFA introduced the penalty shoot-out into the World Cup rulebook to break ties after extra time, though no game in this World Cup actually needed to be decided this way.

Surprisingly, in the first round, hosts Argentina did not win their group, finishing behind Italy, who defeated them 1–0 thanks to a goal by Roberto Bettega. The hosts did qualify in second place, however, after beating Hungary and France, who were both eliminated. One issue that caused some controversy came with Argentina kicking off every game in the evening following the other games in the group, meaning they had the advantage of knowing where they stood in the group each time. Poland won group two, finishing ahead of West Germany in second place, with Tunisia and Mexico going out of the tournament. Tunisia did, though, become the first African team to win a game at the World Cup, beating Mexico 3–1. Group three saw a surprise as Austria won the group with three-time World Cup champions Brazil coming in second place, perennial World Cup underachievers Spain coming in third place and Sweden last. Peru impressed by winning group four, comprehensively beating both Scotland and Iran, who both went out of the tournament, with an underwhelming start by the Netherlands seeing them finish in second but still progressing on to the next round.

In the second-round group phase, the Netherlands found their feet in group A, destroying Austria 5–1, tying with West Germany and then beating Italy 2–1 despite going a goal down early on, a long-range strike from Arie Haan ensuring they topped the group and qualified for the final for the second consecutive World Cup. Group B was a tight battle between Brazil and Argentina. Both won their opening games, Brazil 3–0 over Peru and Argentina 2–0 over Poland, before playing each other to a 0–0 stalemate in the second game. Brazil then beat Poland 3–1 in their final group game, meaning Argentina, who had the advantage of playing their game after Brazil, knew they needed to beat Peru by at least four goals to advance in first place over Brazil due to a better goals for and against differential, the tie-breaking mechanism. Argentina easily achieved this by winning 6–0, with conspiracy theorists questioning the effort of Peru ever since. Brazil beat Italy in the play-off to finish in third place, ensuring they ended the tournament unbeaten but unhappy at failing to make the final.

The final took place on 25 June 1978 between Argentina and the Netherlands, with an official crowd of 71,483 spectators in attendance at Estadio Monumental Antonio Vespucio Liberti in Buenos Aires, a shower of pregame blue and white confetti from Argentine fans marking out the partisan support for the host country. Argentina was slow to come out as the atmosphere built, the Dutch later claiming the hosts had deliberately delayed the game. When the game got underway, Argentina struck first through Mario Kempes in the 38th minute, but substitute Dick Nanninga struck an equalizer with his head for the Netherlands in the 82nd minute. The Dutch had a glorious chance to win the game and their first World Cup in the last minute of normal time, as Rob Rensenbrink struck the post with his shot. In extra time, Argentina took charge of the game, with Kempes scoring his sixth of the tournament to put them in the lead in the 105th minute and Daniel Bertoni making it 3–1 and confirming a first World Cup title for Argentina with his goal in the 116th minute. A controversial World Cup ended with the hosts as champions, and the Netherlands left embittered after a second consecutive defeat in the World Cup final.

FIRST ROUND							
Group 1							
2 June		Italy	2–1	France			
2 June		Argentina	2–1	Hungary			
6 June		Italy	3–1	Hungary			
6 June		Argentina	2–1	France			
10 June		France	3–1	Hungary			
10 June		Italy	1–0	Argentina			
Team	**P**	**PTS**	**W**	**D**	**L**	**GF**	**GA**
Italy	3	6	3	0	0	6	2
Argentina	3	4	2	0	1	4	3
France	3	2	1	0	2	5	5
Hungary	3	0	0	0	3	3	8

Group 2

1 June		West Germany	0–0	Poland	
2 June		Tunisia	3–1	Mexico	
6 June		Poland	1–0	Tunisia	
6 June		West Germany	6–0	Mexico	
10 June		West Germany	0–0	Tunisia	
10 June		Poland	3–1	Mexico	

Team	P	PTS	W	D	L	GF	GA
Poland	3	5	2	1	0	4	1
West Germany	3	4	1	2	0	6	0
Tunisia	3	3	1	1	1	3	2
Mexico	3	0	0	0	3	2	12

Group 3

3 June		Sweden	1–1	Brazil	
3 June		Austria	2–1	Spain	
7 June		Austria	1–0	Sweden	
7 June		Brazil	0–0	Spain	
11 June		Brazil	1–0	Austria	
11 June		Spain	1–0	Sweden	

Team	P	PTS	W	D	L	GF	GA
Austria	3	4	2	0	1	3	2
Brazil	3	4	1	2	0	2	1
Spain	3	3	1	1	1	2	2
Sweden	3	1	0	1	2	1	3

Group 4

3 June		Netherlands	3–0	Iran	
3 June		Peru	3–1	Scotland	
7 June		Scotland	1–1	Iran	
7 June		Netherlands	0–0	Peru	
11 June		Scotland	3–2	Netherlands	
11 June		Peru	4–1	Iran	

Team	P	PTS	W	D	L	GF	GA
Peru	3	5	2	1	0	7	2
Netherlands	3	3	1	1	1	5	3
Scotland	3	3	1	1	1	5	6
Iran	3	1	0	1	2	2	8

SECOND ROUND							
Group A							
14 June	West Germany	0–0	Italy				
14 June	Netherlands	5–1	Austria				
18 June	Italy	1–0	Austria				
18 June	West Germany	2–2	Netherlands				
21 June	Netherlands	2–1	Italy				
21 June	Austria	3–2	West Germany				

Team	P	PTS	W	D	L	GF	GA
Netherlands	3	5	2	1	0	9	4
Italy	3	3	1	1	1	2	2
West Germany	3	2	0	2	1	4	5
Austria	3	2	1	0	2	4	8

Group B							
14 June	Brazil	3–0	Peru				
14 June	Argentina	2–0	Poland				
18 June	Poland	1–0	Peru				
18 June	Argentina	0–0	Brazil				
21 June	Brazil	3–1	Poland				
21 June	Argentina	6–0	Peru				

Team	P	PTS	W	D	L	GF	GA
Argentina	3	5	2	1	0	8	0
Brazil	3	5	2	1	0	6	1
Poland	3	2	1	0	2	2	5
Peru	3	0	0	0	3	0	10

THIRD-PLACE GAME							
24 June	Brazil	2–1	Italy				

FINAL							
25 June	Argentina	3–1 AET	Netherlands				

1982 WORLD CUP

Host Nation: Spain
Dates: 13 June to 11 July 1982
Teams: 24
Matches: 52

Winner: Italy
Runner-Up: West Germany
Third Place: Poland
Fourth Place: France
Golden Shoe: Paolo Rossi (Italy), 6 goals

The 12th iteration of the World Cup was hosted by Spain from 13 June to 11 July 1982, with a record 52 games taking place, as the tournament was expanded from its previous number of 16 teams to 24 teams, allowing in more qualifying countries from Asia and Africa. Italy claimed their third World Cup title, defeating West Germany in the final, inspired by the tournament's top scorer, the Italian surprise-package striker Paolo Rossi. Attendance at the tournament's games topped two million for the first time, with 2,109,723 showing up for the games held in 14 Spanish stadiums.

A record 109 teams had entered the qualifying stage, with the Netherlands—finalists in the previous two World Cup tournaments, in 1974 and 1978—the most surprising failure to make it to Spain. The 24 finalist teams were organized into a new format, with a first round of six groups of four teams, the top two in each group progressing to a second stage with four groups of three teams, with the top team only in each moving on to the semifinals, followed by the final.

In the first stage, Poland and Italy qualified from group one, though the Italians did not impress, drawing all three games and only edging past Cameroon, who they tied with on points, because they had scored one more goal than the African team. Controversy dogged group two: Algeria upset defending champions West Germany 2–1 in their first game but ultimately exited from the competition when the West Germans beat Austria 1–0 in their final game, played after Algeria's last game had been, a result that sent them and Austria through at the expense of Algeria and appeared to observers to be a conveniently arranged result. As a result, in future World Cups, the final round of games in the same group would be played at the same time. Group three saw Belgium and defending World Cup champions Argentina advance, Hungary exiting despite a record 10–1 win over hapless El Salvador. England dominated group four with three wins, France also qualifying, with Czechoslovakia and Kuwait eliminated. In group five, Northern Ireland surprised by qualifying in first place ahead of hosts Spain in second place, Yugoslavia and Honduras bowing out. Brazil played some fantastic soccer to roll through group six with three wins, the Soviet Union also qualifying with them, Scotland and New Zealand—the latter competing in their first World Cup—exiting the tournament.

In the second stage, Poland topped group one, advancing at the expense of Belgium and the Soviet Union. An all–Western European group two was won by West Germany, edging out England and Spain. Group three brought the surprising demise of Brazil, who continued their superb form with a 3–1 trouncing of Argentina before their World Cup ended in disaster as a Paolo Rossi hat trick gave Italy a 3–2 win over the Brazilians and a berth in the semifinals. They were joined there by France from group four, who beat both Austria and Northern Ireland to qualify with ease, their midfield spark Alain Giresse in superb form.

In the first semifinal at the Camp Nou in Barcelona, Italy strolled to victory over Poland, winning 2–0 with Paolo Rossi scoring two more goals in his sensational run of form. The second semifinal in Seville proved to be one of the most memorable and controversial games in World Cup history. Pierre Littbarski opened the scoring with a goal for West Germany in the 17th minute, soon matched from the penalty spot by Michel Platini for the French. The match exploded when a brutal clattering challenge by West German goalkeeper Harald Schumacher on substitute Patrick Battiston left the Frenchman unconscious, a clear foul that to French astonishment was not called by the referee. The score remained tied at 1–1 at full-time, but four goals followed in extra time, France going two up from goals by Marius Trésor and Giresse before a remarkable West German comeback, tying the game through goals from Karl-Heinz Rummenigge in the 102nd minute and Klaus Fischer in the 108th minute. After 120 minutes, the score was tied at 3–3, and the game became the first in World Cup history to be decided by a penalty shoot-out. France seemed set for victory when Uli Stielike had West Germany's third penalty saved, but misses by Didier Six and Maxime Bossis for the French saw them exit and Harald Schumacher end the game a West German hero despite his earlier violent challenge. An exhausted France lost the third-place play-off to Poland 3–2 in Alicante.

The final, held in front of a crowd of 90,000 fans at Estadio Santiago Bernabéu in the Spanish capital Madrid, was a tepid game, with West Germany drained from the semifinal exertions. Three second-half goals from Paolo Rossi in the 57th minute, Marco Tardelli in the 69th minute and Alessandro Altobelli in the 81st minute put Italy in full control, with only a late consolation strike coming for West Germany from Paul Breitner in the 83rd minute. Italy held on to win 3–1 and claim their second World Cup title and first since 1934. Paolo Rossi won the Golden Shoe as top scorer and the Golden Ball for best player of the tournament.

FIRST ROUND							
Group 1							
14 June		Italy	0–0	Poland			
15 June		Peru	0–0	Cameroon			
18 June		Italy	1–1	Peru			
19 June		Poland	0–0	Cameroon			
22 June		Poland	5–1	Peru			
23 June		Italy	1–1	Cameroon			
Team	**P**	**PTS**	**W**	**D**	**L**	**GF**	**GA**
Poland	3	4	1	2	0	5	1
Italy	3	3	0	3	0	2	2
Cameroon	3	3	0	3	0	1	1
Peru	3	2	0	2	1	2	6

Group 2

16 June		Algeria	2–1	West Germany		
17 June		Austria	1–0	Chile		
20 June		West Germany	4–1	Chile		
21 June		Austria	2–0	Algeria		
24 June		Algeria	3–2	Chile		
25 June		West Germany	1–0	Austria		

Team	P	PTS	W	D	L	GF	GA
West Germany	3	4	2	0	1	6	3
Austria	3	4	2	0	1	3	1
Algeria	3	4	2	0	1	5	5
Chile	3	0	0	0	3	3	8

Group 3

13 June		Belgium	1–0	Argentina		
15 June		Hungary	10–1	El Salvador		
18 June		Argentina	4–1	Hungary		
19 June		Belgium	1–0	El Salvador		
22 June		Belgium	1–1	Hungary		
23 June		Argentina	2–0	El Salvador		

Team	P	PTS	W	D	L	GF	GA
Belgium	3	5	2	1	0	3	1
Argentina	3	4	2	0	1	6	2
Hungary	3	3	1	1	1	12	6
El Salvador	3	0	0	0	3	1	13

Group 4

16 June		England	3–1	France		
17 June		Czechoslovakia	1–1	Kuwait		
20 June		England	2–0	Czechoslovakia		
21 June		France	4–1	Kuwait		
24 June		France	1–1	Czechoslovakia		
25 June		England	1–0	Kuwait		

Team	P	PTS	W	D	L	GF	GA
England	3	6	3	0	0	6	1
France	3	3	1	1	1	6	5
Czechoslovakia	3	2	0	2	1	2	4
Kuwait	3	1	0	1	2	2	6

Group 5

16 June		Spain	1–1	Honduras		
17 June		Yugoslavia	0–0	Northern Ireland		
20 June		Spain	2–1	Yugoslavia		
21 June		Honduras	1–1	Northern Ireland		
24 June		Yugoslavia	1–0	Honduras		
25 June		Northern Ireland	1–0	Spain		

Team	P	PTS	W	D	L	GF	GA
Northern Ireland	3	4	1	2	0	2	1
Spain	3	3	1	1	1	3	3
Yugoslavia	3	3	1	1	1	2	2
Honduras	3	2	0	2	1	2	3

Group 6

14 June		Brazil	2–1	Soviet Union		
15 June		Scotland	5–2	New Zealand		
18 June		Brazil	4–1	Scotland		
19 June		Soviet Union	3–0	New Zealand		
22 June		Soviet Union	2–2	Scotland		
23 June		Brazil	4–0	New Zealand		

Team	P	PTS	W	D	L	GF	GA
Brazil	3	6	3	0	0	10	2
Soviet Union	3	3	1	1	1	6	4
Scotland	3	3	1	1	1	8	8
New Zealand	3	0	0	0	3	2	12

SECOND ROUND

Group 1

28 June		Poland	3–0	Belgium		
1 July		Soviet Union	1–0	Belgium		
4 July		Poland	0–0	Soviet Union		

Team	P	PTS	W	D	L	GF	GA
Poland	2	3	1	1	0	3	0
Soviet Union	2	3	1	1	0	1	0
Belgium	2	0	0	0	2	0	4

Group 2

29 June		West Germany	0–0	England		
2 July		West Germany	2–1	Spain		
5 July		Spain	0–0	England		

Team	P	PTS	W	D	L	GF	GA
West Germany	2	3	1	1	0	2	1
England	2	2	0	2	0	0	0
Spain	2	1	0	1	1	1	2

Group 3							
29 June			Italy	2–1	Argentina		
2 July			Brazil	3–1	Argentina		
5 July			Italy	3–2	Brazil		

Team	P	PTS	W	D	L	GF	GA
Italy	2	4	2	0	0	5	3
Brazil	2	2	1	0	1	5	4
Argentina	2	0	0	0	2	2	5

Group 4							
28 June			France	1–0	Austria		
1 July			Austria	2–2	Northern Ireland		
4 July			France	4–1	Northern Ireland		

Team	P	PTS	W	D	L	GF	GA
France	2	4	2	0	0	5	1
Austria	2	1	0	1	1	2	3
Northern Ireland	2	1	0	1	1	3	6

SEMIFINALS			
8 July	Italy	2–0	Poland
8 July	West Germany	3–3 AET 5-4 PSO	France

THIRD-PLACE GAME			
10 July	Poland	3–2	France

FINAL			
11 July	Italy	3–1	West Germany

1986 WORLD CUP

Host Nation: Mexico
Dates: 31 May to 29 June 1986
Teams: 24
Matches: 52

Winner: Argentina
Runner-Up: West Germany
Third Place: France
Fourth Place: Belgium
Golden Shoe: Gary Lineker (England), 6 goals

Mexico became the first country to host the World Cup twice, the 1986 competition heading to Mexican soil just 16 years after its previous staging there in 1970. This only happened, though, because the originally chosen host nation for the 1986 competition, Colombia, pulled out of hosting the World Cup due to economic reasons in late 1982. Mexico was chosen as the replacement host by FIFA in May 1983. The run-up to the tournament was disrupted by a major earthquake in Mexico during September 1985, killing an estimated 20,000 people, but the tournament went forward as planned. It was Argentina who emerged as victors for their second World Cup title just eight years after claiming their first in 1978 as hosts, with Diego Maradona announcing himself as the world's best player, with five goals and five assists in the competition.

As in the 1982 World Cup, the 1986 tournament featured 22 teams who had qualified from 121 entrants to the preliminary competition along with the hosts Mexico and World Cup title holders Argentina, who received an automatic berth in the final tournament to make up the field of 24 countries. The first round followed the 1982 format of six groups of four teams each, but the previous second-round group phase was scrapped, replaced by a straight knockout from the 16 teams to qualify from the first round to the final. Along with the top two finishers in each group from the first round, the four teams with the best records who finished in third place in their group in that stage also progressed to make up the 16 teams for the second round. The groups in the first round were seeded into four pots, with the hosts (Mexico), reigning World Cup champions (Italy) and the second- through fifth-placed teams from the 1982 World Cup (West Germany, Poland, France and Brazil) the top seeds.

Argentina topped group A in the first round, comfortably beating both Bulgaria and the Republic of Korea, who were both eliminated, and playing a dour 0–0 draw against Italy, the defending champions, who qualified automatically in second behind Argentina. The hosts, Mexico, impressed in winning group B, beating a strong Belgium team and a weak Iraq team, who finished bottom of the group, and tying Paraguay, who finished in second place. The Soviet Union won group C, finishing ahead of France on goal differential, with weak sides from Hungary and Canada (the latter making their first World Cup appearance) going out of the competition. Brazil played some beautiful soccer as they won all three games to top group D, Spain finishing second, with neither Northern Ireland nor Algeria managing to win a game. Group E was dominated by Denmark, who won all three games, West Germany scraping through in second position with a win, a draw and a loss and Uruguay finishing above Scotland in third place. Group F was surprisingly won by Morocco, with England finishing in second place, Poland in third and Portugal in fourth. Along with the top two teams in those six groups, Belgium, Bulgaria, Poland and Uruguay also qualified for the next round as the best-placed third-place finishers from the six groups.

The second round of knockout games began with Mexico comfortably disposing of Bulgaria 2–0 on 15 June. The second game that day was the highlight of the round, with Belgium defeating the Soviet Union 4–3 after extra time. A talented Brazil side impressed with a 4–0 dismantling of Poland, while Argentina had one of their less impressive games of the tournament in a 1–0 win over Uruguay. Defending champions Italy fell to France 2–0, the brilliant Michel Platini at the heart of a stylish French team that had won the 1984 UEFA European Football Championship. Morocco, the first African team to advance beyond the first round of the World Cup, gave West Germany a considerable scare in their second-round game, the Europeans only going through by a single goal scored by Lothar Matthäus just three minutes from the end of the game. England comfortably beat Paraguay 3–0, Gary Lineker scoring twice on the way to becoming the winner of the Golden Shoe as the tournament's top scorer, ending with six goals to his credit. A strong Denmark team was beaten surprisingly easily by Spain 5–1, Spanish forward Emilio Butragueño scoring a hat trick of goals.

The quarterfinal stage featured some of the most exciting and dramatic games in World Cup history. It began with a classic encounter between two of the tournament favorites, Brazil and France. Careca put Brazil ahead in the 17th minute, but France equalized through Michel Platini in the 40th minute. Brazil's star player Zico missed a chance to score from the penalty spot in normal time, and the game ended in a penalty shoot-out won by France 4–3, their goalkeeper Joel Bats saving two Brazil kicks. Penalty kicks decided a game again following a dull 0–0 draw between West Germany and hosts Mexico, who exited in painful fashion, losing 4–1 in the penalty shoot-out. A memorable game then took place between Argentina and England, with the best and worst of Argentinean captain Diego Maradona on display: his first goal, opening the scoring in the game in the 51st minute, came from a clear and deliberate handball by Maradona lifting the ball over England goalkeeper Peter Shilton, an infringement remarkably missed by the match officials. But Maradona followed this with his second goal just three minutes later, brilliantly dribbling the ball almost the length of the field and slaloming past several hapless England defenders before stroking the ball past Shilton to make it 2–0 to Argentina. England pulled a goal back from another Gary Lineker strike, but despite further chances, was unable to tie the game. A third penalty shoot-out decided the final quarterfinal game, with a 1–1 tie between Spain and Belgium decided by a penalty shoot-out in the Belgians favor.

In the first semifinal, West Germany managed to nullify the electric talents of France's Platini, Jean Tigana and Alain Giresse, with an early goal by Andreas Brehme followed by a late strike from Rudi Völler, giving the West Germans a 2–0 win. Diego Maradona continued to stamp his genius on the tournament in the second semifinal, scoring twice in the second half to overwhelm Belgium in a game that ended with a 2–0 win for Argentina. France claimed third place following a play-off game with Belgium that ended in a penalty shoot-out won by the French. In the final, with 114,600 officially in attendance at the Estadio Azteca in Mexico City, West Germany's Lothar Matthäus managed to keep a tighter leash on Maradona than any other defender had managed in the tournament. Argentina, though, still managed to go 2–0 up in the first half, with goals from Jose Brown in the 23rd minute and Jorge Valdano in the 55th minute. West Germany staged a spirited comeback in the second half, as

Karl-Heinz Rummenigge scored in the 74th minute and Völler equalized for the West Germans in the 80th minute. But as if on cue, Maradona awoke from a quiet game by playing a perfect pass through on goal for his teammate Jorge Burruchaga to score the goal that gave Argentina a 3–2 win and their second World Cup title. Fittingly, Diego Maradona was awarded the Golden Ball as the tournament's best player.

FIRST ROUND

Group A

31 May		Bulgaria	1–1	Italy			
2 June		Argentina	3–1	South Korea			
5 June		Italy	1–1	Argentina			
5 June		South Korea	1–1	Bulgaria			
10 June		Italy	3–2	South Korea			
10 June		Argentina	2–0	Bulgaria			
Team	P	PTS	W	D	L	GF	GA
Argentina	3	5	2	1	0	6	2
Italy	3	4	1	2	0	5	4
Bulgaria	3	2	0	2	1	2	4
South Korea	3	1	0	1	2	4	7

Group B

3 June		Mexico	2–1	Belgium			
4 June		Paraguay	1–0	Iraq			
7 June		Mexico	1–1	Paraguay			
8 June		Belgium	2–1	Iraq			
11 June		Mexico	1–0	Iraq			
11 June		Paraguay	2–2	Belgium			
Team	P	PTS	W	D	L	GF	GA
Mexico	3	5	2	1	0	4	2
Paraguay	3	4	1	2	0	4	3
Belgium	3	3	1	1	1	5	5
Iraq	3	0	0	0	3	1	4

Group C

1 June		France	1–0	Canada
2 June		Soviet Union	6–0	Hungary
5 June		France	1–1	Soviet Union
6 June		Hungary	2–0	Canada
9 June		France	3–0	Hungary
9 June		Soviet Union	2–0	Canada

Team	P	PTS	W	D	L	GF	GA
Soviet Union	3	5	2	1	0	9	1
France	3	5	2	1	0	5	1
Hungary	3	2	1	0	2	2	9
Canada	3	0	0	0	3	0	5

Group D

1 June		Brazil	1–0	Spain	
3 June		Algeria	1–1	Northern Ireland	
6 June		Brazil	1–0	Algeria	
7 June		Spain	2–1	Northern Ireland	
12 June		Brazil	3–0	Northern Ireland	
12 June		Spain	3–0	Algeria	

Team	P	PTS	W	D	L	GF	GA
Brazil	3	6	3	0	0	5	0
Spain	3	4	2	0	1	5	2
Northern Ireland	3	1	0	1	2	2	6
Algeria	3	1	0	1	2	1	5

Group E

4 June		Uruguay	1–1	West Germany	
4 June		Denmark	1–0	Scotland	
8 June		West Germany	2–1	Scotland	
8 June		Denmark	6–1	Uruguay	
13 June		Denmark	2–0	West Germany	
13 June		Scotland	0–0	Uruguay	

Team	P	PTS	W	D	L	GF	GA
Denmark	3	6	3	0	0	9	1
West Germany	3	3	1	1	1	3	4
Uruguay	3	2	0	2	1	2	7
Scotland	3	1	0	1	2	1	3

Group F

2 June		Morocco	0–0	Poland	
3 June		Portugal	1–0	England	
6 June		England	0–0	Morocco	
7 June		Poland	1–0	Portugal	
11 June		Morocco	3–1	Portugal	
11 June		England	3–0	Poland	

Team	P	PTS	W	D	L	GF	GA
Morocco	3	4	1	2	0	3	1
England	3	3	1	1	1	3	1
Poland	3	3	1	1	1	1	3
Portugal	3	2	1	0	2	2	4

ROUND OF 16

15 June	Mexico	2–0	Bulgaria
15 June	Belgium	4–3 AET	Soviet Union
16 June	Argentina	1–0	Uruguay
16 June	Brazil	4–0	Poland
17 June	France	2–0	Italy
17 June	West Germany	1–0	Morocco
18 June	England	3–0	Paraguay
18 June	Spain	5–1	Denmark

QUARTERFINALS

21 June	France	1–1 AET 4–3 PSO	Brazil
21 June	West Germany	0–0 AET 4–1 PSO	Mexico
22 June	Belgium	1–1 AET 5–4 PSO	Spain
22 June	Argentina	2–1	England

SEMIFINALS

25 June	Argentina	2–0	Belgium
25 June	West Germany	2–0	France

THIRD-PLACE GAME

28 June	France	4–2 AET	Belgium

FINAL

29 June	Argentina	3–2	West Germany

1990 WORLD CUP

Host Nation: Italy
Dates: 8 June to 8 July 1990
Teams: 24
Matches: 52
Winner: West Germany
Runner-Up: Argentina
Third Place: Italy
Fourth Place: England
Golden Shoe: Salvatore Schillaci (Italy), 6 goals

The 14th edition of the World Cup was held in Italy for the second time, 56 years after it had first hosted the tournament in 1934, with the tournament's 52 games kicking off on 8 June 1990. West Germany lifted the World Cup Trophy for the third time a month later on 8 July, beating defending World Cup champions Argentina in the final 1–0. Italy had invested considerably in infrastructure for the tournament, with 10 stadiums receiving massive renovations and 2 entirely new arenas built for the World Cup games in Turin and Bari. The soccer itself at the World Cup was often defensive and dull, with a record low 2.2 goals scored per game, though the romance surrounding the staging of the games in the Italian peninsula won over a global audience with plenty of drama throughout the tournament.

The format of the competition was unchanged from the 1986 World Cup, with 24 teams taking part, separated into six groups of four for the first round. The top two teams in each group qualified for the next round, along with the four best third-placed teams. The 16 remaining teams then played a straight knockout format until the final. The opening game of the first round in group B produced a considerable surprise: defending champions, Argentina, were beaten 1–0 by Cameroon, despite the African team having two players sent off. Cameroon followed that result by also beating Romania, topping the group. Romania finished second and Argentina third, the latter only qualifying for the next round as one of the best third-placed finishers, with the Soviet Union finishing in fourth place. In group A, Italy began in imperious form by winning all three games, with unfancied striker Salvatore Schillaci scoring twice in the first round on his way to winning the Golden Shoe as the top scorer in the tournament, ending up with six goals. Czechoslovakia finished in second place behind Italy, with Austria in third and the United States last, the Americans losing all three games. Brazil began in fantastic form in group C, winning all three of their games, Costa Rica surprisingly taking second place ahead of Scotland in third and Sweden in fourth. West Germany piled on the goals in winning group D, beating Yugoslavia, who finished second, and the United Arab Emirates, who ended up last, along with a draw against Colombia, who qualified in second place. Group E saw Spain and Belgium progress automatically in first and second, with Uruguay in third and the Republic of Korea heading home after losing all three games. England only won one game in the first round but still topped group F ahead of the Republic of Ireland in second place, the Netherlands tying all three games and finishing third, with Egypt coming last. Along with Argentina, the other best third-placed teams to qualify for the second round were Colombia, Uruguay and the Netherlands.

The second round started on 23 June with Cameroon beating Colombia 2–1 after extra time and thus becoming the first African team to qualify for the quarterfinals of the World Cup. Veteran Roger Milla, who came on as a substitute, scored both of Cameroon's goals, the second after a howling error by eccentric Colombian goal-keeper René Higuita. Czechoslovakia easily beat Costa Rica 4–1, and then Brazil made a disappointingly early exit, losing to Argentina 1–0 despite having the better of the play. A bitter game between West Germany and the Netherlands ended with the West Germans going through 2–1, with Frank Rijkaard from the Dutch side and Rudi Völler from West Germany both disgracefully sent off for spitting at each other. There was heartbreak for Romania, losing in a penalty shoot-out to the Republic of Ireland after a 0–0 tie, while hosts Italy cruised through 2–0 over Uruguay. Spain left a World Cup competition earlier than expected once again, losing 2–1 to an excellent Yugoslavia side after extra time, and England scraped past Belgium, the winning goal in a 1–0 game coming from David Platt in the 119th minute in extra time.

The quarterfinals kicked off on 30 June with a dull game between Yugoslavia and Argentina, the latter going through thanks to a victory in the penalty shoot-out after a 0–0 tie. Hosts Italy edged past the Republic of Ireland 1–0 later that evening, while the same scoreline saw West Germany advance past Czechoslovakia the next day. The final quarterfinal was the most dramatic, as England rather fortunately beat Cameroon 3–2 despite being 2–1 down until Gary Lineker's 83rd-minute penalty tied it up. A second penalty from Lineker in extra time saw England go through. The semifinals both ended in 1–1 ties decided by penalty shoot-outs. Hosts Italy experienced heart-break first, in front of almost 60,000 in Naples, with a Salvatore Schillaci first-half goal canceled out by a Claudio Caniggia strike for Argentina in the 67th minute and then a penalty shoot-out where the hero was Argentina's goalkeeper Sergio Goyco-chea, who saved two penalties, as he had also done in the previous round. West Germany and England then played to a 1–1 tie, Paul Gascoigne starring for the English and the West Germans inspired by Lothar Matthäus. Misses by both Chris Waddle and Stuart Pearce saw England exit, eventually finishing in fourth place after losing the third-place play-off to Italy. The final was one of the worst in World Cup history, with Argentina's Diego Maradona unable to demonstrate the form that had led his country to victory in 1986 and his teammate Pedro Monzón earning an undesirable historical distinction as the first player to be sent off in a World Cup final. The sole goal in the game came from Andreas Brehme for West Germany from the penalty spot, after a foul by Argentina's Gustavo Dezotti, who was also sent off for his second yellow-card offense. West Germany's 1–0 win meant they had become the third team after Brazil and Italy to win three World Cup titles.

FIRST ROUND

Group A

9 June		Italy	1–0	Austria			
10 June		Czechoslovakia	5–1	United States			
14 June		Italy	1–0	United States			
15 June		Czechoslovakia	1–0	Austria			
19 June		Italy	2–0	Czechoslovakia			
19 June		Austria	2–1	United States			
Team	**P**	**PTS**	**W**	**D**	**L**	**GF**	**GA**
Italy	3	6	3	0	0	4	0
Czechoslovakia	3	4	2	0	1	6	3
Austria	3	2	1	0	2	2	3
United States	3	0	0	0	3	2	8

Group B

8 June		Cameroon	1–0	Argentina			
9 June		Romania	2–0	Soviet Union			
13 June		Argentina	2–0	Soviet Union			
14 June		Cameroon	2–1	Romania			
18 June		Argentina	1–1	Romania			
18 June		Soviet Union	4–0	Cameroon			
Team	**P**	**PTS**	**W**	**D**	**L**	**GF**	**GA**
Cameroon	3	4	2	0	1	3	5
Romania	3	3	1	1	1	4	3
Argentina	3	3	1	1	1	3	2
Soviet Union	3	2	1	0	2	4	4

Group C

10 June		Brazil	2–1	Sweden			
11 June		Costa Rica	1–0	Scotland			
16 June		Brazil	1–0	Costa Rica			
16 June		Scotland	2–1	Sweden			
20 June		Brazil	1–0	Scotland			
20 June		Costa Rica	2–1	Sweden			
Team	**P**	**PTS**	**W**	**D**	**L**	**GF**	**GA**
Brazil	3	6	3	0	0	4	1
Costa Rica	3	4	2	0	1	3	2
Scotland	3	2	1	0	2	2	3
Sweden	3	0	0	0	3	3	6

Group D							
9 June		Colombia	2–0	United Arab Emirates			
10 June		West Germany	4–1	Yugoslavia			
14 June		Yugoslavia	1–0	Colombia			
15 June		West Germany	5–1	United Arab Emirates			
19 June		West Germany	1–1	Colombia			
19 June		Yugoslavia	4–1	United Arab Emirates			
Team	P	PTS	W	D	L	GF	GA
West Germany	3	5	2	1	0	10	3
Yugoslavia	3	4	2	0	1	6	5
Colombia	3	3	1	1	1	3	2
United Arab Emirates	3	0	0	0	3	2	11
Group E							
12 June		Belgium	2–0	Korea Republic			
13 June		Uruguay	0–0	Spain			
17 June		Belgium	3–1	Uruguay			
17 June		Spain	3–1	South Korea			
21 June		Spain	2–1	Belgium			
21 June		Uruguay	1–0	South Korea			
Team	P	PTS	W	D	L	GF	GA
Spain	3	5	2	1	0	5	2
Belgium	3	4	2	0	1	6	3
Uruguay	3	3	1	1	1	2	3
South Korea	3	0	0	0	3	1	6
Group F							
11 June		England	1–1	Republic of Ireland			
12 June		Netherlands	1–1	Egypt			
16 June		England	0–0	Netherlands			
17 June		Republic of Ireland	0–0	Egypt			
21 June		England	1–0	Egypt			
21 June		Republic of Ireland	1–1	Netherlands			
Team	P	PTS	W	D	L	GF	GA
England	3	4	1	2	0	2	1
Republic of Ireland	3	3	0	3	0	2	2
Netherlands	3	3	0	3	0	2	2
Egypt	3	2	0	2	1	1	2

ROUND OF 16			
23 June	Cameroon	2–1 AET	Colombia
23 June	Czechoslovakia	4–1	Costa Rica
24 June	Argentina	1–0	Brazil
24 June	West Germany	2–1	Netherlands
25 June	Republic of Ireland	0–0 AET 5–4 PSO	Romania
25 June	Italy	2–0	Uruguay
26 June	Yugoslavia	2–1 AET	Spain
26 June	England	1–0 AET	Belgium
QUARTERFINALS			
30 June	Argentina	0–0 AET 3–2 PSO	Yugoslavia
30 June	Italy	1–0	Republic of Ireland
1 July	West Germany	1–0	Czechoslovakia
1 July	England	3–2 AET	Cameroon
SEMIFINALS			
3 July	Argentina	1–1 AET 4–3 PSO	Italy
4 July	West Germany	1–1 AET 4–3 PSO	England
THIRD-PLACE GAME			
7 July	Italy	2–1	England
FINAL			
8 July	West Germany	1–0	Argentina

1994 WORLD CUP

Host Nation: United States
Dates: 17 June to 17 July 1994
Teams: 24
Matches: 52
Winner: Brazil
Runner-Up: Italy
Third Place: Sweden
Fourth Place: Bulgaria
Golden Shoe: Tie—Oleg Salenko (Russia), Hristo Stoichkov (Bulgaria), 6 goals each

The 1994 World Cup was held in the United States from 17 June to 17 July 1994, with 24 teams taking part and playing a total of 52 games. A record aggregate 3,587,538 fans attended the games, at a record average attendance of 68,991 per match. Both records still stand today and justified the decision of FIFA to award the tournament to a country where soccer lagged well behind baseball, American football, basketball and ice hockey as a major spectator sport domestically. The United States did not have a professional, outdoor, first-division soccer league at the time, though the World Cup staged there proved to be a spur toward the launch of Major League Soccer in 1996. The tournament itself proved to be exciting, with more goals scored than the previous World Cup held in Italy four years earlier, at an average of 2.7 goals per game compared to 2.2 in 1990. This came after FIFA introduced three points for a win in group play for the first time, up from two points previously, in order to encourage more attacking play. Brazil ended the competition as champions for the fourth time, beating Italy in the final through a penalty shoot-out.

The qualifying competition for the final tournament had seen a record 147 countries take part, with England, France and reigning UEFA European Football Championship winners Denmark the most surprising teams to fail to qualify. Hosts the United States qualified automatically, taking their place in group A for the first round, which divided up the 24 teams into six groups of four teams, with the top two in each qualifying for the next round. Four best third-place finishers also went on to the second round to make up a field of 16 that then played single-match knockout rounds leading up to the final. Also in group A were Romania, Switzerland and Colombia, the latter finishing last and facing tragedy when defender Andres Escobar was shot dead on his return home after scoring a crucial own goal against the United States. Romania won the group ahead of Switzerland in second, the United States finishing third but still moving on to the next round as one of the best third-placed teams. The United States' game against Switzerland also saw a game played indoors for the first time, at the Pontiac Silverdome in Pontiac, a suburb of Detroit. Group B was comfortably won by Brazil, Sweden taking second place, with Russia and Cameroon going out of the tournament. Amazingly, Russia's Oleg Salenko ended up as the tournament's joint top scorer due to his six goals in the first round, including a record five in one game as Russia beat Cameroon 6–1. Germany topped group C, Spain in second place with the Republic of Korea and Bolivia exiting. Group D saw controversy, as Argentinean star Diego Maradona failed a drug test after Argentina's first game and withdrew from the tournament. Argentina struggled through to the second round as one of the best third-place teams, finishing behind Bulgaria and an exciting Nigeria team who won the group. In group E, all four teams ended up on four points with goals scored separating the teams as the tiebreaker, leaving Mexico in first, Italy in second, the Republic of Ireland also qualifying as one of the best third-placed teams and Norway bowing out. Group F was won by the Netherlands, Saudi Arabia coming second and Belgium another third-placed qualifier, with Morocco losing all three games and finishing last.

The second round began on 2 July with a tight 3–2 win for Germany over Belgium, followed by Spain easily beating Switzerland 3–0. Saudi Arabia lost to Sweden 3–2 on 3 July, before the game of the round between Romania and Argentina, the former winning 3–2 thanks to a winning goal by their creative midfield force Gheorghe Hagi. On American Independence Day, the fourth of July, the United States lost 1–0 to Brazil but put in a strong performance against the eventual champions, their best display of the tournament. The other match that day saw the Netherlands beat the Republic of Ireland 2–0. The final second-round games took place on 5 July, Nigeria losing a heartbreaking game to Italy after taking an early lead, with Italy's star Roberto Baggio scoring twice, including a winning penalty kick in the 100th minute.

The quarterfinals took place on 9 and 10 July, beginning with a victory for Italy over Spain by two goals to one, Italy's illustrious Baggio scoring the winner in the 87th minute and sending Spain back home from a World Cup empty-handed once again. The game of the round was between the Netherlands and Brazil in Dallas, with the Dutch fighting back to tie the game 2–2 after going 2–0 down in the first half, only to concede a winning goal by Brazil's Branco in the 81st minute. The surprise of the tournament came when reigning champions Germany were beaten 2–1 by Bulgaria in the third quarterfinal, despite the Germans taking the lead in the 47th minute. A tying goal by the electric Hristo Stoichkov, on his way to tying Oleg Salenko for the Golden Shoe as the tournament's top scorer, was followed by a winner from Yordan Letchkov to put Bulgaria through. They were joined in the semifinals by Sweden, who went through after a penalty shoot-out victory over Romania following a thrilling 2–2 tie.

The semifinals on 12 July were disappointing games. Bulgaria was beaten 2–1 by Italy in front of 74,110 at Giants Stadium in New Jersey, Roberto Baggio scoring twice and confirming himself as one of the tournament's outstanding players. Brazil beat Sweden 1–0 at the Rose Bowl in Pasadena, California, 91,856 in attendance, a goal by their supreme goal poacher Romário settling the game in the 80th minute. Romário would go on to win the Golden Ball award as the tournament's best player. In the third-place play-off that followed on 16 July, Sweden easily beat Bulgaria 4–0. The final took place on 17 July at the Rose Bowl, 94,194 officially attending the game. Italy and Brazil both played in a subdued style, Brazilian flair tempered by their pragmatic holding defensive midfielders Dunga and Zinho, while Italy was superbly marshaled from the back by the peerless Franco Baresi. No goals were scored, and the final became the first in World Cup history to be settled by a penalty shoot-out. There were four misses in the shoot-out, but the deciding error came from a tired Roberto

Baggio, carrying an injury, as with Italy's fifth kick he launched it over the crossbar, giving Brazil their fourth World Cup title.

FIRST ROUND							
Group A							
18 June		United States	1–1	Switzerland			
18 June		Romania	3–1	Colombia			
22 June		Switzerland	4–1	Romania			
22 June		United States	2–1	Colombia			
26 June		Romania	1–0	United States			
26 June		Colombia	2–0	Switzerland			
Team	*P*	*PTS*	*W*	*D*	*L*	*GF*	*GA*
Romania	3	6	2	0	1	5	5
Switzerland	3	4	1	1	1	5	4
United States	3	4	1	1	1	3	3
Colombia	3	3	1	0	2	4	5
Group B							
19 June		Cameroon	2–2	Sweden			
20 June		Brazil	2–0	Russia			
24 June		Brazil	3–0	Cameroon			
24 June		Sweden	3–1	Russia			
28 June		Russia	6–1	Cameroon			
28 June		Brazil	1–1	Sweden			
Team	*P*	*PTS*	*W*	*D*	*L*	*GF*	*GA*
Brazil	3	7	2	1	0	6	1
Sweden	3	5	1	2	0	6	4
Russia	3	3	1	0	2	7	6
Cameroon	3	1	0	1	2	3	11
Group C							
17 June		Germany	1–0	Bolivia			
17 June		Spain	2–2	South Korea			
21 June		Germany	1–1	Spain			
23 June		South Korea	0–0	Bolivia			
27 June		Spain	3–1	Bolivia			
27 June		Germany	3–2	South Korea			

Team	P	PTS	W	D	L	GF	GA
Germany	3	7	2	1	0	5	3
Spain	3	5	1	2	0	6	4
South Korea	3	2	0	2	1	4	5
Bolivia	3	1	0	1	2	1	4

Group D

21 June	Argentina	4–0	Greece
21 June	Nigeria	3–0	Bulgaria
25 June	Argentina	2–1	Nigeria
26 June	Bulgaria	4–0	Greece
30 June	Nigeria	2–0	Greece
30 June	Bulgaria	2–0	Argentina

Team	P	PTS	W	D	L	GF	GA
Nigeria	3	6	2	0	1	6	2
Bulgaria	3	6	2	0	1	6	3
Argentina	3	6	2	0	1	6	3
Greece	3	0	0	0	3	0	10

Group E

18 June	Republic of Ireland	1–0	Italy
19 June	Norway	1–0	Mexico
23 June	Italy	1–0	Norway
24 June	Mexico	2–1	Republic of Ireland
28 June	Republic of Ireland	0–0	Norway
28 June	Italy	1–1	Mexico

Team	P	PTS	W	D	L	GF	GA
Mexico	3	4	1	1	1	3	3
Republic of Ireland	3	4	1	1	1	2	2
Italy	3	4	1	1	1	2	2
Norway	3	4	1	1	1	1	1

Group F

19 June	Belgium	1–0	Morocco
20 June	Netherlands	2–1	Saudi Arabia
25 June	Belgium	1–0	Netherlands
25 June	Saudi Arabia	2–1	Morocco
29 June	Netherlands	2–1	Morocco
29 June	Saudi Arabia	1–0	Belgium

Team	P	PTS	W	D	L	GF	GA
Netherlands	3	6	2	0	1	4	3
Saudi Arabia	3	6	2	0	1	4	3
Belgium	3	6	2	0	1	2	1
Morocco	3	0	0	0	3	2	5

ROUND OF 16

2 July	Germany	3–2	Belgium
2 July	Spain	3–0	Switzerland
3 July	Sweden	3–1	Saudi Arabia
3 July	Romania	3–2	Argentina
4 July	Netherlands	2–0	Republic of Ireland
4 July	Brazil	1–0	United States
5 July	Italy	2–1 AET	Nigeria
5 July	Bulgaria	1–1 AET 3–1 PSO	Mexico

QUARTERFINALS

9 July	Italy	2–1	Spain
9 July	Brazil	3–2	Netherlands
10 July	Bulgaria	2–1	Germany
10 July	Sweden	2–2 AET 5–4 PSO	Romania

SEMIFINALS

13 July	Italy	2–1	Bulgaria
13 July	Brazil	1–0	Sweden

THIRD-PLACE GAME

16 July	Sweden	4–0	Bulgaria

FINAL

17 July	Brazil	0–0 AET 3–2 PSO	Italy

1998 WORLD CUP

Host Nation: France
Dates: 10 June to 12 July 1998
Teams: 32
Matches: 64
Winner: France
Runner-Up: Brazil
Third Place: Croatia
Fourth Place: Netherlands
Golden Shoe: Davor Šuker (Croatia), 6 goals

The 16th staging of the World Cup was held in France from 10 June to 12 July 1998, attended by 2,785,100 spectators at an average of 43,517 fans at each of the 64 games played in 10 different French stadiums. It was won by France, taking their first World Cup title, after defeating Brazil in the final. A total of 32 teams took part, the largest-ever number for the World Cup, as the field was expanded from the 24 that took part at the previous tournament in 1994. The qualifying competition to determine the final 32 teams featured a record 174 countries entering, 168 actually playing, and took place over 643 games in front of over 15 million fans at games around the world. In the tournament itself in France, 171 goals were scored, at an average of 2.7 a game, the same as in 1994. A new innovation in the rules meant that a goal scored in extra time during the knockout rounds was more valuable than ever before: it would now be known as the Golden Goal, and the game would end immediately with the scoring team victorious.

Due to the expansion of the tournament, the format of the first round was changed from the setup in 1994, with the 32 teams broken down into eight groups of four teams who played each other once and the top two teams from each group advancing to the first of four single-elimination rounds that led to the final on 12 July. The first round began on 10 June, with defending World Cup champions Brazil opening group A with a 2–1 victory over Scotland. Brazil went on to qualify top of the group at the end of the first round despite their first World Cup group stage defeat since 1966 to Norway, the Scandinavians coming in second place, while Morocco and Scotland exited the tournament. Group B was topped by Italy, Chile in second, with Austria and Cameroon going out. France won all three games to win group C, though suffered a blow with playmaker Zinedine Zidane sent off against Saudi Arabia. Fellow Europeans Denmark qualified in second place, with South Africa and Saudi Arabia both leaving the competition without winning a game. In group D, Nigeria beat Spain 3–2 in their opening match, the African country topping the group and the Spaniards exiting in third place. Paraguay qualified in second place behind Nigeria, and Bulgaria finished last. The Netherlands won group E, Mexico finished second, while both Belgium and the Republic of Korea failed to win a game. Group F was won by Germany ahead of the Netherlands in second place. Iran went out after finishing third but beat the United States 2–1 in an encounter hyped up for the historical overtones to it politically, with the Americans failing to win a game in France during the tournament. Romania topped group D ahead of England in second place, Colombia and Tunisia heading home, determining the last of the 16 qualifiers for the second round.

The knockout rounds began on 27 June in Paris with Brazil comfortably beating Chile 4–1. Italy beat Norway 1–0, and then Denmark surprisingly beat Nigeria by a comfortable score of four goals to one. Without the suspended Zinedine Zidane, serving a ban for his red card during the first round, France struggled to move past Paraguay, until French defender Laurent Blanc scored the first Golden Goal in World Cup history to send the hosts to the next game. Germany edged past Mexico 2–1 with two late goals after being 1–0 down, while the Netherlands beat Yugoslavia by the same scoreline. The most exciting game of the second round came in Saint-Étienne, where old rivals England and Argentina played a riveting game that ended 2–2, with the incidents including a red card for David Beckham, a fantastic goal by young forward Michael Owen and then a penalty-shoot-out victory for Argentina, after both Paul Ince and David Batty missed penalties for England. In the final second-round game, Croatia beat Romania thanks to a goal by striker Davor Šuker.

The quarterfinals began on 3 July, with France again failing to impress but also again advancing. They played to a 0–0 tie with Italy, before winning a penalty shoot-out 4–3, the Italians exiting the World Cup for the third consecutive time on penalty kicks. The second game that day offered up many more goals, with Brazil beating Denmark 3–2, thanks to a pair of strikes by Rivaldo. A sparkling Croatia side dismantled Germany, winning 3–0 in the third quarterfinal in Lyon. The final game of the round was a classic encounter between two high-quality teams, as the Netherlands beat Argentina 2–1, Dennis Bergkamp scoring a memorable winning goal in the 89th minute, deftly controlling a long pass and lashing it into the goal from a tight angle. In their semifinal against Brazil in Marseilles on 7 July, the Netherlands again scored a crucial late goal, this time from Patrick Kluivert in the 87th minute to tie the game 1–1, Brazil having taken the lead through their prolific striker Ronaldo in the 46th minute. With both teams afraid of conceding a Golden Goal, extra time was filled with cautious play, and the game was decided by a penalty shoot-out, won by Brazil after misses for the Dutch by Phillip Cocu and Ronald de Boer. In the second semifinal, on 8 July in Stade de France in the northern suburbs of Paris, the hosts France finally played up to their potential with a 2–1 win over Croatia, with defender Lilian Thuram the unlikely scorer of France's two goals. Croatia's goal came from Šuker, who would score again in the Croatian victory over the Netherlands in the third-place play-off and end up as the tournament's top scorer with six goals.

The 1998 World Cup final took place on 12 July at the Stade de France, with 80,000 in attendance, but controversy dogged the game before kickoff even took place: Brazil had sensationally dropped their star player, Ronaldo, from the initial lineups given to FIFA, a completely unexpected decision that immediately set off conspiracy theories and raised questions still unanswered today. But before the game began, Ronaldo was restored to the lineup, with rumors spreading that key Brazil- and Ronaldo-sponsor Nike had demanded his inclusion. Whatever the truth, Ronaldo, usually an electric force, was strangely subdued throughout the game, with France quickly taking charge in the first half thanks to two goals from Zinedine Zidane in the 27th and 46th minutes.

Brazil had no answer for a French team that had found its stride after a slow start to the tournament, with Emmanuel Petit adding another goal in the 90th minute to end the game with a 3–0 win for the hosts. France had won their first World Cup.

FIRST ROUND							
Group A							
10 June			Brazil	2–1	Scotland		
10 June			Morocco	2–2	Norway		
16 June			Scotland	1–1	Norway		
16 June			Brazil	3–0	Morocco		
23 June			Morocco	3–0	Scotland		
23 June			Norway	2–1	Brazil		
Team	*P*	*PTS*	*W*	*D*	*L*	*GF*	*GA*
Brazil	3	6	2	0	1	6	3
Norway	3	5	1	2	0	5	4
Morocco	3	4	1	1	1	5	5
Scotland	3	1	0	1	2	2	6
Group B							
11 June			Cameroon	1–1	Austria		
11 June			Italy	2–2	Chile		
17 June			Chile	1–1	Austria		
17 June			Italy	3–0	Cameroon		
23 June			Italy	2–1	Austria		
23 June			Chile	1–1	Cameroon		
Team	*P*	*PTS*	*W*	*D*	*L*	*GF*	*GA*
Italy	3	7	2	1	0	7	3
Chile	3	3	0	3	0	4	4
Austria	3	2	0	2	1	3	4
Cameroon	3	2	0	2	1	2	5
Group C							
12 June			Denmark	1–0	Saudi Arabia		
12 June			France	3–0	South Africa		
18 June			France	4–0	Saudi Arabia		
18 June			South Africa	1–1	Denmark		
24 June			France	2–1	Denmark		
24 June			South Africa	2–2	Saudi Arabia		

Team	P	PTS	W	D	L	GF	GA
France	3	9	3	0	0	9	1
Denmark	3	4	1	1	1	3	3
South Africa	3	2	0	2	1	3	6
Saudi Arabia	3	1	0	1	2	2	7

Group D

12 June	Paraguay	0–0	Bulgaria
13 June	Nigeria	3–2	Spain
19 June	Nigeria	1–0	Bulgaria
19 June	Spain	0–0	Paraguay
24 June	Spain	6–1	Bulgaria
24 June	Paraguay	3–1	Nigeria

Team	P	PTS	W	D	L	GF	GA
Nigeria	3	6	2	0	1	5	5
Paraguay	3	5	1	2	0	3	1
Spain	3	4	1	1	1	8	4
Bulgaria	3	1	0	1	2	1	7

Group E

13 June	Netherlands	0–0	Belgium
13 June	Mexico	3–1	South Korea
20 June	Netherlands	5–0	South Korea
20 June	Belgium	2–2	Mexico
25 June	Belgium	1–1	South Korea
25 June	Netherlands	2–2	Mexico

Team	P	PTS	W	D	L	GF	GA
Netherlands	3	5	1	2	0	7	2
Mexico	3	5	1	2	0	7	5
Belgium	3	3	0	3	0	3	3
South Korea	3	1	0	1	2	2	9

Group F

14 June	Yugoslavia	1–0	Iran
15 June	Germany	2–0	United States
21 June	Germany	2–2	Yugoslavia
21 June	Iran	2–1	United States
25 June	Germany	2–0	Iran
25 June	Yugoslavia	1–0	United States

Team	P	PTS	W	D	L	GF	GA
Germany	3	7	2	1	0	6	2
Yugoslavia	3	7	2	1	0	4	2
Iran	3	3	1	0	2	2	4
United States	3	0	0	0	3	1	5

Group G

15 June		Romania	1–0	Colombia
15 June		England	2–0	Tunisia
22 June		Colombia	1–0	Tunisia
22 June		Romania	2–1	England
26 June		Romania	1–1	Tunisia
26 June		England	2–0	Colombia

Team	P	PTS	W	D	L	GF	GA
Romania	3	7	2	1	0	4	2
England	3	6	2	0	1	5	2
Colombia	3	3	1	0	2	1	3
Tunisia	3	1	0	1	2	1	4

Group H

14 June		Croatia	3–1	Jamaica
14 June		Argentina	1–0	Japan
20 June		Croatia	1–0	Japan
21 June		Argentina	5–0	Jamaica
26 June		Jamaica	2–1	Japan
26 June		Argentina	1–0	Croatia

Team	P	PTS	W	D	L	GF	GA
Argentina	3	9	3	0	0	7	0
Croatia	3	6	2	0	1	4	2
Jamaica	3	3	1	0	2	3	9
Japan	3	0	0	0	3	1	4

ROUND OF 16

27 June		Brazil	4–1	Chile
27 June		Italy	1–0	Norway
28 June		Denmark	4–1	Nigeria
28 June		France	1–0 AET	Paraguay
29 June		Germany	2–1	Mexico

29 June	Netherlands	2–1	Yugoslavia
30 June	Argentina	2–2 AET 4–3 PSO	England
30 June	Croatia	1–0	Romania
QUARTERFINALS			
3 July	France	0–0 AET 4–3 PSO	Italy
3 July	Brazil	3–2	Denmark
4 July	Croatia	3–0	Germany
4 July	Netherlands	2–1	Argentina
SEMIFINALS			
7 July	Brazil	1–1 AET 4–2 PSO	Netherlands
8 July	France	2–1	Croatia
THIRD-PLACE GAME			
11 July	Croatia	2–1	Netherlands
FINAL			
12 July	France	3–0	Brazil

2002 WORLD CUP

Host Nation: Republic of Korea / Japan
Dates: 31 May to 30 June 2002
Teams: 32
Matches: 64
Winner: Brazil
Runner-Up: Germany
Third Place: Turkey
Fourth Place: Republic of Korea
Golden Shoe: Ronaldo (Brazil), 8 goals

The 2002 World Cup was the first to be hosted by two nations, taking place in the Republic of Korea and Japan from 31 May to 30 June 2002, and was also the first to be hosted in Asia. A total of 2,705,197 fans attended the 64 games featuring 32 teams, at an average crowd of 42,268 per match. An entertaining tournament was won by Brazil, claiming their record fifth World Cup title, defeating Germany in the final. The tournament saw 161 goals scored, at an average of 2.5 per match, slightly down from the rate at the previous 1998 World Cup. Qualification for the tournament had begun with 199 registered teams entering the competition, though only 193 actually took part in the record 777 games contested across the world to determine the 29 qualifiers who would join the automatic qualifiers at the World Cup, defending World Cup champions France and the two hosts, the Republic of Korea and Japan.

The first round of the tournament divided the 32 teams up into eight groups of four, playing against each other once, with the top two in each group going on to the knockout stage. From there, single-elimination rounds would lead from the round of 16 to the final. In the first round, group A began play with a big upset, defending World Cup champions France losing to Senegal, appearing at the World Cup for the first time. France, a shadow of their 1998 selves, could not recover from that defeat, tying with Uruguay and then losing to Denmark to exit the competition in ignominy. Denmark won the group with Senegal in second. Spain impressed by winning all three of their games to top group B, Paraguay finishing in second place with South Africa and Slovenia exiting. Brazil dominated group C, victorious in their three games, with forward Ronaldo in outstanding form. Turkey squeezed through in second place ahead of Costa Rica and China. Group D was full of upsets, as hosts the Republic of Korea won the group, with the United States surprisingly beating Portugal 3–2 and finishing in second place, Portugal and Poland eliminated. In group E, Germany and the Republic of Ireland qualified in first and second place at the expenses of Cameroon and Saudi Arabia. Sweden won group F, while Argentina was eliminated due to their loss to England, who went through in second, with Nigeria coming last. Mexico in first place and Italy in second qualified from group G, Croatia and Ecuador going out. Hosts Japan topped group H, Belgium in second place, with Russia and Tunisia eliminated.

The round of 16 began on 15 June with Germany defeating Paraguay 1–0 and England coasting past Denmark 3–0. Sweden and Senegal then put on an exciting game, the latter becoming the second African team to reach the quarterfinals stage of any World Cup after winning the game 2–1 after extra time. A penalty shoot-out then decided a 1–1 tie between Spain and the Republic of Ireland in Spanish favor, while the United States defeated their southern neighbors Mexico 2–0. Brazil beat Belgium by the same scoreline, Ronaldo scoring two more goals. Japan became the first of the hosts to go out, losing 1–0 in Miyagi to Turkey. The other host nation, the Republic of Korea, impressively defeated Italy 2–1 after extra time, thanks to a winning goal from a header by Ahn Jung-Hwan. Ahn happened to play for Italian club Perugia at the time, who pettily fired the Korean forward after the World Cup in retaliation for his goal against Italy.

The Republic of Korea, with a wave of national enthusiasm sweeping the host nation, then faced Spain in the quarterfinals, in a controversial game that saw two apparent Spanish goals disallowed by the referee for questionable infringements. There was no score in the game, which was decided by a penalty shoot-out, and a miss by Spain's Joaquin gave the Koreans victory. Germany won a tight game with the United States 1–0, and Turkey similarly beat Senegal by the same scoreline. England led Brazil 1–0 early on in Shizuoka, but Brazil fought back to win 2–1 thanks to goals from Rivaldo and Ronaldinho, despite the latter's red card in the 57th minute. The semifinals proved to be tightly fought games. First, in Seoul, Germany finally quelled the surprising

Koreans' run in the competition, a lone goal by German midfielder Michael Ballack separating the two teams, though Ballack also received a suspension for the final for an accumulation of yellow cards. Brazil, thanks to yet another goal from the powerful play of Ronaldo, beat Turkey 1–0 in Saitama.

The 2002 World Cup final took place on 30 June in Yokohama, 69,029 in attendance at International Stadium Yokohama. Missing Ballack and facing a Brazil side inspired by their trio of talented attackers Rivaldo, Ronaldinho and Ronaldo, Germany went down 2–0, with Ronaldo scoring two more to take his tally for the tournament to eight goals and take the Golden Shoe as the top scorer in the competition. Both goals went past German goalkeeper Oliver Kahn, who had enjoyed an outstanding tournament up to that point, and Kahn was still awarded the Golden Ball as the tournament's best player. Turkey beat South Korea in the consolation play-off for third place, and Brazil lifted the World Cup Trophy for a record fifth time.

FIRST ROUND							
Group A							
31 May		Senegal	1–0	France			
1 June		Denmark	2–1	Uruguay			
6 June		France	0–0	Uruguay			
6 June		Denmark	1–1	Senegal			
11 June		Denmark	2–0	France			
11 June		Senegal	3–3	Uruguay			
Team	*P*	*PTS*	*W*	*D*	*L*	*GF*	*GA*
Denmark	3	7	2	1	0	5	2
Senegal	3	5	1	2	0	5	4
Uruguay	3	2	0	2	1	4	5
France	3	1	0	1	2	0	3
Group B							
2 June		Paraguay	2–2	South Africa			
2 June		Spain	3–1	Slovenia			
7 June		Spain	3–1	Paraguay			
8 June		South Africa	1–0	Slovenia			
12 June		Spain	3–2	South Africa			
12 June		Paraguay	3–1	Slovenia			
Team	*P*	*PTS*	*W*	*D*	*L*	*GF*	*GA*
Spain	3	9	3	0	0	9	4
Paraguay	3	4	1	1	1	6	6
South Africa	3	4	1	1	1	5	5
Slovenia	3	0	0	0	3	2	7

Group C

3 June		Brazil	2–1	Turkey		
4 June		Costa Rica	2–0	China		
8 June		Brazil	4–0	China		
9 June		Costa Rica	1–1	Turkey		
13 June		Brazil	5–2	Costa Rica		
13 June		Turkey	3–0	China		

Team	P	PTS	W	D	L	GF	GA
Brazil	3	9	3	0	0	11	3
Turkey	3	4	1	1	1	5	3
Costa Rica	3	4	1	1	1	5	6
China	3	0	0	0	3	0	9

Group D

4 June		South Korea	2–0	Poland		
5 June		United States	3–2	Portugal		
10 June		South Korea	1–1	United States		
10 June		Portugal	4–0	Poland		
14 June		South Korea	1–0	Portugal		
14 June		Poland	3–1	United States		

Team	P	PTS	W	D	L	GF	GA
South Korea	3	7	2	1	0	4	1
United States	3	4	1	1	1	5	6
Portugal	3	3	1	0	2	6	4
Poland	3	3	1	0	2	3	7

Group E

1 June	Republic of Ireland	1–1	Cameroon		
1 June	Germany	8–0	Saudi Arabia		
5 June	Germany	1–1	Republic of Ireland		
6 June	Cameroon	1–0	Saudi Arabia		
11 June	Germany	2–0	Cameroon		
11 June	Republic of Ireland	3–0	Saudi Arabia		

Team	P	PTS	W	D	L	GF	GA
Germany	3	7	2	1	0	11	1
Republic of Ireland	3	5	1	2	0	5	2
Cameroon	3	4	1	1	1	2	3
Saudi Arabia	3	0	0	0	3	0	12

Group F

2 June		England	1–1	Sweden
2 June		Argentina	1–0	Nigeria
7 June		Sweden	2–1	Nigeria
7 June		England	1–0	Argentina
12 June		Sweden	1–1	Argentina
12 June		Nigeria	0–0	England

Team	P	PTS	W	D	L	GF	GA
Sweden	3	5	1	2	0	4	3
England	3	5	1	2	0	2	1
Argentina	3	4	1	1	1	2	2
Nigeria	3	1	0	1	2	1	3

Group G

3 June		Mexico	1–0	Croatia
3 June		Italy	2–0	Ecuador
8 June		Croatia	2–1	Italy
9 June		Mexico	2–1	Ecuador
13 June		Mexico	1–1	Italy
13 June		Ecuador	1–0	Croatia

Team	P	PTS	W	D	L	GF	GA
Mexico	3	7	2	1	0	4	2
Italy	3	4	1	1	1	4	3
Croatia	3	3	1	0	2	2	3
Ecuador	3	3	1	0	2	2	4

Group H

4 June		Japan	2–2	Belgium
5 June		Russia	2–0	Tunisia
9 June		Japan	1–0	Russia
10 June		Tunisia	1–1	Belgium
14 June		Japan	2–0	Tunisia
14 June		Belgium	3–2	Russia

Team	P	PTS	W	D	L	GF	GA
Japan	3	7	2	1	0	5	2
Belgium	3	5	1	2	0	6	5
Russia	3	3	1	0	2	4	4
Tunisia	3	1	0	1	2	1	5

ROUND OF 16			
15 June	Germany	1–0	Paraguay
15 June	England	3–0	Denmark
16 June	Senegal	2–1 AET	Sweden
16 June	Spain	1–1 AET 3–2 PSO	Republic of Ireland
17 June	United States	2–0	Mexico
18 June	Turkey	1–0	Japan
18 June	South Korea	2–1 AET	Italy
QUARTERFINALS			
21 June	Brazil	2–1	England
21 June	Germany	1–0	United States
22 June	South Korea	0–0 AET 5–3 PSO	Spain
22 June	Turkey	1–0 AET	Senegal
SEMIFINALS			
25 June	Germany	1–0	South Korea
25 June	Brazil	1–0	Turkey
THIRD-PLACE GAME			
29 June	Turkey	3–2	South Korea
FINAL			
29 June	Brazil	2–0	Germany

2006 WORLD CUP

Host Nation: Germany
Dates: 9 June to 9 July 2006
Teams: 32
Matches: 64
Winner: Italy
Runner-Up: France
Third Place: Germany
Fourth Place: Portugal
Golden Shoe: Miroslav Klose (Germany), 5 goals

The 18th staging of the World Cup was held in Germany from 9 June to 9 July 2006. Thirty-two teams took part, with the hosts having qualified automatically and the other 31 progressing out of a qualifying tournament that saw 198 countries initially enter. At the finals tournament in Germany, 64 games were played, attended by 3,359,439 spectators, at an average of 52,491 per game played at 12 different stadiums. In those 64 games, 147 goals were scored at an average of 2.3 per game, a lower goal-scoring ratio than in the previous World Cup in 2002. Italy won the tournament, claiming their fourth World Cup title, beating France in the final on 9 July, a game made particularly notable by Zinedine Zidane's sending off for head-butting Italian Marco Materazzi.

The 32 teams in the finals tournament were divided into eight groups of four teams, with the top two teams in each group qualifying for the round of 16, from which single-game elimination rounds would lead up to the final. Group A began play on 9 June with the hosts Germany winning 4–2 over Costa Rica, going on to win the group with further victories over Poland and then Ecuador, who qualified in second place. Group B was won by England, Sweden finishing as runners-up with Trinidad and Tobago along with Paraguay going out. Argentina won group C, packed with quality teams and given the proverbial "Group of Death" moniker by the media, with the Netherlands coming second, Côte d'Ivoire third and Serbia and Montenegro fourth. Argentina was magnificent in a 6–0 demolition of the latter in Gelsenkirchen. Portugal strolled through group D, winning all three games over Mexico (who came second), Angola and Iran (who were both eliminated). Group E was won by Italy, advancing with Ghana at the expense of the United States and the Czech Republic. Brazil beat Croatia, Japan and Australia in group F, the latter also qualifying for the next round in second place. In group G, Switzerland's tight defense saw them win the group with no goals conceded in three games, finishing ahead of France in second place, the Republic of Korea and Togo going out.

The round of 16 kicked off on 24 June, with hosts Germany beating Sweden 2–0 in Munich. Argentina defeated Mexico 2–1 after extra time, thanks to a winning goal by Maxi Rodriguez. A trio of 1–0 scorelines then followed, as England beat Ecuador, Portugal beat the Netherlands, in an ill-tempered affair that saw four players sent off by referee Valentin Ivanov, and Italy defeated Australia 1–0 through a penalty in the fifth minute of added time at the end of 90 minutes. A dull game between Switzerland and Ukraine petered out in a 0–0 tie, with the Ukrainians winning on a penalty shoot-out, as Switzerland went out of the competition without conceding a goal. Brazil beat Ghana 3–0 in Dortmund, while Spain exited earlier than expected from the World Cup once again, despite taking a lead in the first half against France, with goals from Franck Ribéry, Patrick Vieira and Zinedine Zidane sending the French through with a 3–1 win.

The first quarterfinal took place in Berlin on 30 June at the Olympic Stadium, 72,000 in attendance to see Germany tie with Argentina in normal time and the host nation go through on a penalty shoot-out after misses by Argentines Roberto Ayala and Esteban Cambiasso. Later that day, Italy easily beat Ukraine 3–0, with one goal from Gianluca Zambrotta and two from Luca Toni. England exited at the quarterfinal stage for the second straight tournament, losing on penalty kicks to Portugal after a

0–0 tie, with Wayne Rooney sent off in the second half. Misses by Frank Lampard, Steven Gerrard and Jamie Carragher in the penalty shoot-out doomed England. Brazil then lost 1–0 to France, inspired by Zidane, who set up the goal for Thierry Henry in the 57th minute that proved decisive.

The first semifinal took place in Dortmund on 4 July, with the host nation Germany taking on Italy. No goals were scored in normal time, and with the end of extra time approaching, it appeared the game would be decided by a penalty shoot-out, until Italy scored in the 119th minute through the unlikely source of defender Fabio Grosso, followed by a second for the Italians shortly after with a goal by Alessandro Del Piero. The following day, at the Allianz Arena in Munich, 66,000 saw France advance past Portugal 1–0, via a penalty from Zinedine Zidane following a foul on Thierry Henry by Ricardo Carvalho. Zidane was in inspired form and would later be awarded the Golden Ball as the tournament's best player. Germany went on to win the consolation game for third place with Portugal 3–1 and could also console themselves with the Golden Shoe award given to their forward Miroslav Klose as the tournament's top scorer.

The final took place on 9 July, a tense, tight and controversial game. Zinedine Zidane scored another penalty in the seventh minute following a foul on Florent Malouda by Marco Materazzi. But Italy equalized in the 19th minute through a powerful header by Materazzi from a corner kick, and their tight defense, led by their captain Fabio Cannavaro, kept Zidane in check for the remainder of normal time. Zidane finally exploded in the 110th minute but in an unseemly and unexpected manner caught on television: an altercation off the ball with Materazzi incited the Frenchman to headbutt the Italian in the chest, sending him sprawling to the ground. The fourth official, perhaps influenced by a television replay, informed the referee of the offense, and Zidane was sent off, an ignominious end to a magnificent international career for the Frenchman. The game ended in a 1–1 tie, and the winner was determined by a penalty shoot-out: a miss for France by David Trezeguet, hitting the crossbar, resulting in victory for Italy, who claimed their fourth World Cup title.

FIRST ROUND							
Group A							
9 June		Germany		4–2	Costa Rica		
9 June		Ecuador		2–0	Poland		
14 June		Germany		1–0	Poland		
15 June		Ecuador		3–0	Costa Rica		
20 June		Germany		3–0	Ecuador		
20 June		Poland		2–1	Costa Rica		
Team	*P*	*PTS*	*W*	*D*	*L*	*GF*	*GA*
Germany	3	9	3	0	0	8	2
Ecuador	3	6	2	0	1	5	3
Poland	3	3	1	0	2	2	4
Costa Rica	3	0	0	0	3	3	9

Group B

10 June		England	1–0	Paraguay		
10 June		Trinidad and Tobago	0–0	Sweden		
15 June		England	2–0	Trinidad and Tobago		
15 June		Sweden	1–0	Paraguay		
20 June		Sweden	2–2	England		
20 June		Paraguay	2–0	Trinidad and Tobago		

Team	P	PTS	W	D	L	GF	GA
England	3	7	2	1	0	5	2
Sweden	3	5	1	2	0	3	2
Paraguay	3	3	1	0	2	2	2
Trinidad and Tobago	3	1	0	1	2	0	4

Group C

10 June		Argentina	2–1	Côte d'Ivoire		
11 June		Netherlands	1–0	Serbia and Montenegro		
16 June		Argentina	6–0	Serbia and Montenegro		
16 June		Netherlands	2–1	Côte d'Ivoire		
21 June		Netherlands	0–0	Argentina		
21 June		Côte d'Ivoire	3–2	Serbia and Montenegro		

Team	P	PTS	W	D	L	GF	GA
Argentina	3	7	2	1	0	8	1
Netherlands	3	7	2	1	0	3	1
Côte d'Ivoire	3	3	1	0	2	5	6
Serbia and Montenegro	3	0	0	0	3	2	10

Group D

11 June		Mexico	3–1	Iran		
11 June		Portugal	1–0	Angola		
16 June		Mexico	0–0	Angola		
17 June		Portugal	2–0	Iran		
21 June		Portugal	2–1	Mexico		
21 June		Iran	1–1	Angola		

Team	P	PTS	W	D	L	GF	GA
Portugal	3	9	3	0	0	5	1
Mexico	3	4	1	1	1	4	3
Angola	3	2	0	2	1	1	2
Iran	3	1	0	1	2	2	6

Group E

12 June		Italy	2–0	Ghana		
12 June		Czech Republic	3–0	United States		
17 June		Italy	1–1	United States		
17 June		Ghana	2–0	Czech Republic		
22 June		Italy	2–0	Czech Republic		
22 June		Ghana	2–1	United States		

Team	P	PTS	W	D	L	GF	GA
Italy	3	7	2	1	0	5	1
Ghana	3	6	2	0	1	4	3
Czech Republic	3	3	1	0	2	3	4
United States	3	1	0	1	2	2	6

Group F

12 June		Australia	3–1	Japan		
13 June		Brazil	1–0	Croatia		
18 June		Brazil	2–0	Australia		
18 June		Japan	0–0	Croatia		
22 June		Brazil	4–1	Japan		
22 June		Croatia	2–2	Australia		

Team	P	PTS	W	D	L	GF	GA
Brazil	3	9	3	0	0	7	1
Australia	3	4	1	1	1	5	5
Croatia	3	2	0	2	1	2	3
Japan	3	1	0	1	2	2	7

Group G

13 June		France	0–0	Switzerland		
13 June		South Korea	2–1	Togo		
18 June		France	1–1	South Korea		
19 June		Switzerland	2–0	Togo		
23 June		France	2–0	Togo		
23 June		Switzerland	2–0	South Korea		

Team	P	PTS	W	D	L	GF	GA
Switzerland	3	7	2	1	0	4	0
France	3	5	1	3	0	3	1
South Korea	3	4	1	1	1	3	4
Togo	3	0	0	0	3	1	6

Group H							
14 June			Spain	4–0	Ukraine		
14 June			Tunisia	2–2	Saudi Arabia		
19 June			Spain	3–1	Tunisia		
19 June			Ukraine	4–0	Saudi Arabia		
23 June			Spain	1–0	Saudi Arabia		
23 June			Ukraine	1–0	Tunisia		
Team	*P*	*PTS*	*W*	*D*	*L*	*GF*	*GA*
Spain	3	9	3	0	0	8	1
Ukraine	3	6	2	0	1	5	4
Tunisia	3	1	0	1	2	3	6
Saudi Arabia	3	1	0	1	2	2	7
ROUND OF 16							
24 June			Germany	2–0	Sweden		
24 June			Argentina	2–1 AET	Mexico		
25 June			England	1–0	Ecuador		
25 June			Portugal	1–0	Netherlands		
26 June			Italy	1–0	Australia		
26 June			Ukraine	0–0 AET 3–0 PSO	Switzerland		
27 June			Brazil	3–0	Ghana		
27 June			France	3–1	Spain		
QUARTERFINALS							
30 June			Germany	1–1 AET 4–2 PSO	Argentina		
30 June			Italy	3–0	Ukraine		
1 July			Portugal	0–0 AET 3–1 PSO	England		
1 July			France	1–0	Brazil		
SEMIFINALS							
4 July			Italy	2–0 AET	Germany		
5 July			France	1–0	Portugal		

THIRD-PLACE GAME			
8 July	Germany	3–1	Portugal
FINAL			
9 July	Italy	1–1 AET 5–3 PSO	France

2010 WORLD CUP

Host Nation: South Africa
Dates: 11 June to 11 July 2010
Teams: 32
Matches: 64
Winner: Spain
Runner-Up: Netherlands
Third Place: Germany
Fourth Place: Uruguay
Golden Boot: Thomas Müller (Germany), 5 goals

The World Cup headed to the African continent for the first time, in 2010, with the 19th World Cup hosted by South Africa in June and July. It was won by Spain, claiming their first World Cup title, defeating the Netherlands in the final. Qualification for the 2010 World Cup began in August 2007, with a record total of 205 countries attempting to qualify for 31 places at the finals and South Africa qualifying automatically as hosts to make up the field of 32. The qualification campaign concluded in November 2009 with one of the most controversial moments in the history of World Cup qualification when France forward Thierry Henry deliberately handled the ball (unnoticed by the referee) while setting up William Gallas for the decisive goal that gave France the win in their play-off game against the Republic of Ireland to qualify for the World Cup at Irish expense in controversial fashion. The games in South Africa at the World Cup were played at 10 stadiums in 9 different cities, each noisily accompanied by the buzzing sound of plastic *vuvuzela* horns blown by thousands of fans at every game. The 64 matches attracted a total of 3.18 million spectators at the 64 games, the third-highest total in World Cup history.

As in the previous three World Cup tournaments, eight groups of four teams each played in the first round, with the top two in each group qualifying for the second stage. In group A, France, who had reached the final in the 2006 World Cup, was eliminated after failing to win a game, with the team in open revolt against their coach, Raymond Domenach. Hosts South Africa defeated France but were unable to win either of their other games against Uruguay and Mexico, the latter two qualifying with Uruguay winning the group. Group B was won by a free-scoring Argentina team coached by their former star player Diego Maradona, the Republic of Korea qualifying in second place, with Greece and Nigeria eliminated. The United States won group C, the first time they had won a group in the first round of a World Cup, finishing ahead of England in second place, Algeria and Slovenia going home. In group D, Germany qualified at the top of the group ahead of Ghana in second, the lone African team to qualify for the second stage. Australia and Serbia were eliminated. The Netherlands won group E, Japan coming second, Denmark and Cameroon going out. Paraguay and Slovakia qualified from group F in first and second place respectively, New Zealand finishing third after tying all three games, and in the biggest surprise of the opening stage, defending champions Italy came in fourth place and failed to win a game. Brazil won group G, Portugal coming in second place, with Côte d'Ivoire and North Korea (appearing at their first World Cup since 1966) eliminated. Spain topped group H, Chile in second, with Switzerland and Honduras heading home.

In the round of 16, Uruguay began play on 26 June by beating the Republic of Korea 2–1. The United States then lost to Ghana after extra time, a winning blast by Asamoah Gyan giving the Ghanaians a 2–1 win. The next day, Germany defeated England 4–1, the game marked by a wrongly disallowed goal for England's Frank Lampard, prompting FIFA to promise greater help for referees at future tournaments on goal-line calls. Argentina beat Mexico 3–1 with another refereeing controversy regarding a missed offside call on Carlos Tévez for Argentina's first goal. On 28 June, the Netherlands beat Slovakia 2–1, and Brazil beat Chile 3–0. Japan against Paraguay on 29 June ended scoreless, the game decided by penalty kicks, with the South Americans advancing at the expense of the Japanese.

The quarterfinals began on 2 July, with the Netherlands facing Brazil in the first game at Nelson Mandela Bay Stadium in Port Elizabeth. Despite going down a goal in the first half, the Dutch prevailed 2–1, thanks to two goals by Wesley Sneijder. Later that day, at Soccer City stadium in Johannesburg, Uruguay and Ghana tied 1–1, with Uruguay proceeding to the semifinals after winning on a penalty shoot-out. The game was marred by a controversial moment in the last minute of extra time, as Uruguayan forward Luis Suárez deliberately handled a ball on the goal line to stop a goal-bound shot. The referee called a penalty, but it was missed by Ghana's Asamoah Gyan. In the final two quarterfinal games on 3 July, Germany easily defeated a disorganized Argentina 4–0 in Cape Town, and Spain beat Paraguay 1–0 at Ellis Park Stadium, Johannesburg.

The first 2010 World Cup semifinal took place in Cape Town Stadium and was won 3–2 by the Netherlands over Uruguay, the Europeans resisting a late comeback by the South Americans. The next day, at Moses Mabhida Stadium in Durban, Spain controlled play against Germany and went through to the final with a 1–0 win, Carles Puyol providing the lone goal with a thumping header. Uruguay then lost the third-place play-off to Germany on 10 July, but there was some consolation for them as their impressive forward Diego Forlán was awarded the Golden Ball by FIFA as the best player of the tournament.

Soccer City in Johannesburg played host to the final on 11 July, with 84,490 in attendance for the Netherlands against Spain. But, with the Dutch incessantly fouling the Spanish to try and break up their usual passing rhythm, it was referee Howard Webb who took center stage, giving out a record 14 yellow card cautions and 1 red card, in extra time, to Dutchman John Heitinga. By all accounts, Spain deserved the win in the face of a negative and cynical Dutch performance, which the Spaniards achieved thanks to a neatly played goal deep into extra time by Andrés Iniesta in the 116th minute, to win Spain the World Cup for the first time.

FIRST ROUND							
Group A							
11 June		South Africa	1–1	Mexico			
11 June		Uruguay	0–0	France			
16 June		Uruguay	3–0	South Africa			
17 June		Mexico	2–0	France			
22 June		Uruguay	1–0	Mexico			
22 June		South Africa	2–1	France			
Team	*P*	*PTS*	*W*	*D*	*L*	*GF*	*GA*
Uruguay	3	7	2	1	0	4	0
Mexico	3	4	1	1	1	3	2
South Africa	3	4	1	1	1	3	5
France	3	1	0	2	2	1	4
Group B							
12 June		South Korea	2–0	Greece			
12 June		Argentina	1–0	Nigeria			
17 June		Argentina	4–1	South Korea			
17 June		Greece	2–1	Nigeria			
22 June		Nigeria	2–2	South Korea			
22 June		Argentina	2–0	Greece			
Team	*P*	*PTS*	*W*	*D*	*L*	*GF*	*GA*
Argentina	3	9	3	0	0	7	1
South Korea	3	4	1	1	1	5	6
Greece	3	3	1	0	2	2	5
Nigeria	3	1	0	1	2	3	5
Group C							
12 June		England	1–1	United States			
13 June		Slovenia	1–0	Algeria			
18 June		Slovenia	2–2	United States			
18 June		England	0–0	Algeria			
23 June		England	1–0	Slovenia			
23 June		United States	1–0	Algeria			

Team	P	PTS	W	D	L	GF	GA
United States	3	5	1	2	0	4	3
England	3	5	1	2	0	2	1
Slovenia	3	4	1	1	1	3	3
Algeria	3	1	0	1	2	0	2

Group D

13 June	Ghana	1–0	Serbia
13 June	Germany	4–0	Australia
18 June	Serbia	1–0	Germany
19 June	Ghana	1–1	Australia
23 June	Germany	1–0	Ghana
23 June	Australia	2–1	Serbia

Team	P	PTS	W	D	L	GF	GA
Germany	3	6	2	0	1	5	1
Ghana	3	4	1	1	1	2	2
Australia	3	4	1	1	1	3	6
Serbia	3	3	1	0	2	2	3

Group E

14 June	Netherlands	2–0	Denmark
14 June	Japan	1–0	Cameroon
19 June	Netherlands	1–0	Japan
19 June	Denmark	2–1	Cameroon
24 June	Japan	3–1	Denmark
24 June	Netherlands	2–1	Cameroon

Team	P	PTS	W	D	L	GF	GA
Netherlands	3	9	3	0	0	5	1
Japan	3	6	2	0	1	4	2
Denmark	3	3	1	0	2	3	6
Cameroon	3	0	0	0	3	2	5

Group F

14 June	Italy	1–1	Paraguay
15 June	New Zealand	1–1	Slovakia
20 June	Paraguay	2–0	Slovakia
20 June	Italy	1–1	New Zealand
24 June	Slovakia	3–2	Italy
24 June	Paraguay	0–0	New Zealand

Team	P	PTS	W	D	L	GF	GA
Paraguay	3	5	1	2	0	3	1
Slovakia	3	4	1	1	1	4	5
New Zealand	3	3	0	3	0	2	2
Italy	3	2	0	2	1	4	5

Group G

15 June	Côte d'Ivoire	0–0	Portugal
15 June	Brazil	2–1	North Korea
20 June	Brazil	3–1	Côte d'Ivoire
21 June	Portugal	7–0	North Korea
25 June	Portugal	0–0	Brazil
25 June	Côte d'Ivoire	3–0	North Korea

Team	P	PTS	W	D	L	GF	GA
Brazil	3	7	2	1	0	5	2
Portugal	3	5	1	2	0	7	0
Côte d'Ivoire	3	4	1	1	1	4	3
North Korea	3	0	0	0	3	1	12

Group H

16 June	Chile	1–0	Honduras
16 June	Switzerland	1–0	Spain
21 June	Chile	1–0	Switzerland
21 June	Spain	2–0	Honduras
25 June	Spain	2–1	Chile
25 June	Switzerland	0–0	Honduras

Team	P	PTS	W	D	L	GF	GA
Spain	3	6	2	0	1	4	2
Chile	3	6	2	0	1	3	2
Switzerland	3	4	1	1	1	1	1
Honduras	3	1	0	1	2	0	3

ROUND OF 16

26 June	Uruguay	2–1	South Korea
26 June	Ghana	2–1 AET	United States
27 June	Argentina	3–1	Mexico
27 June	Germany	4–1	England
28 June	Netherlands	2–1	Slovakia

28 June		Brazil	3–0	Chile
29 June		Paraguay	0–0 AET 5–3 PSO	Japan
29 June		Spain	1–0	Portugal
QUARTERFINALS				
2 July		Uruguay	1–1 AET 4–2 PSO	Ghana
2 July		Netherlands	2–1	Brazil
3 July		Germany	4–0	Argentina
3 July		Spain	1–0	Paraguay
SEMIFINALS				
6 July		Netherlands	3–2	Uruguay
7 July		Spain	1–0	Germany
THIRD-PLACE GAME				
10 July		Germany	3–2	Uruguay
FINAL				
11 July		Spain	1–0 AET	Netherlands

2014 WORLD CUP

Host Nation: Brazil
Dates: 12 June to 13 July 2014
Teams: 32
Matches: 64
Winner: Germany
Runner-Up: Argentina
Third Place: Netherlands
Fourth Place: Brazil
Golden Boot: James Rodríguez (Colombia), 6 goals, 2 assists

The World Cup headed to South America for the fifth time, with Brazil hosting the 20th World Cup in June and July. It was won by Germany, giving the nation its fourth World Cup title, when they beat Argentina 1–0 in extra time in the final. Qualification for the 2014 World Cup began in June 2011 with a match pitting Montserrat against Belize and ended in November of 2013 when Uruguay eliminated Jordan to become the final qualifier. A total of 207 countries (a new record) attempted to qualify for

31 places at the finals along with Brazil, who automatically qualified as hosts. The games in Brazil were played at 12 stadiums in 12 different cities, each stadium a testament to the uniqueness of the host city's people and the diversity of Brazilian culture. Though a marvel of engineering, the excess of each building did not go unnoticed as Brazil was steeped in charges of corruption when much of the estimated $11.7 billion (making it the most expensive World Cup ever) was unaccounted for, feared lost amid charges of fraud and suspicious ties between politicians and contractors. The 64 matches attracted a total of 3,429,873 million spectators at the 64 games (an average of 53,592 per match), making it second only to the 1994 World Cup in the United States in terms of the third-highest attendance in World Cup history.

With the 32 teams again separated into eight groups of four, the World Cup began with a group-A game pitting host Brazil against Croatia. Though Croatia went up early, a controversial penalty and two Neymar goals saw a Brazil win and an exciting start to what would become a record-tying tournament in terms of goals. Tied on seven points with Mexico, Brazil won group A on superior goal differential while a lone Croatia win over Cameroon secured them third place. Group B was won by defending runners-up Netherlands, winners of all three games, including a 2–0 win over a surprise second-place Chile. Defending champions Spain, after losing 5–1 to the Dutch in the opening game, never recovered and could only manage a win over winless Australia in their final group game to take third. Led by Golden Boot winner James Rodríguez, Colombia won a wide-open group C; second place was taken by Greece in controversial fashion when Georgios Samaras converted a phantom Côte d'Ivoire penalty late in stoppage time. Japan could only manage a tie to round out the group. In group D, perennial powerhouses Italy and England were both sent home after scoring a combined four points. Uruguay backed up their fourth-place finish from four years ago by finishing second in the group, a point behind a defensively minded Costa Rican team that allowed only one goal. In the most controversial moment of the 2014 World Cup, Uruguay lost star forward Luis Suárez for the remainder of the tournament when he was banned for biting Italian defender Giorgio Chiellini in their final game. France and Switzerland finished 1–2 in a relatively weak group E, both ahead of Ecuadorian and Honduran sides still struggling to catch up in terms of talent. Behind the four goals of Lionel Messi, Argentina won all three games in group F to finish first while Nigeria's 1–0 win over first-time participant Bosnia and Herzegovina proved decisive in locking up second place. Unfortunately for Iran, a last-minute goal by Argentina meant a fourth-place finish. In what many called the "Group of Death," the United States finished second in group G behind Germany after beating Ghana for the first time in three tournaments. Though the round of 16 was seemingly locked up for the Americans late in the game, ahead 2–1 over Portugal, a last-second stoppage-time goal off a Ronaldo cross meant that all spots were up for grabs going into the final game. A 1–0 American loss to Germany and a 2–1 Portugal win over Ghana meant a Portuguese and Ghanaian exit. In group H, Belgium decisively won the group with nine points and Algeria snuck into the round of 16 after Russia and South Korea both failed to win a game.

In the round of 16, Brazil nervously edged Chile on penalties, and Colombia beat a Suárez-less Uruguay 2–0 to kick off the elimination rounds. Day two saw a newly unified French team dispatch Nigeria 2–0, while Germany needed added extra time against an Algerian side that gave them fits before winning 2–1. In a game where Mexico often looked to be the better side, day three saw the Netherlands again prove why they are one of the world's elite when they scored a late equalizer in the 88th minute and the eventual winner in the 90th minute on a clumsy penalty by Mexican defender Rafael Márquez. Day three also saw Greece again get a last-minute goal, this time to force added extra time, but Costa Rica proved decisive from the spot when they finished all five of their penalties. In the final round of 16 games, a late extra-time goal by Ángel Di María, off a Messi assist, proved to be the winner over Switzerland. Belgium survived a late Chris Wondolowski howler in regulation against the United States and beat American goalkeeper Tim Howard twice in added extra time in an exciting 2–1 game.

On 4 July, the quarterfinals began with nervous host Brazil facing a confident Colombian side, and though an early Thiago Silva goal was followed up by a spectacular David Luiz free kick, Brazil, and Brazilian fans, never seemed to fully relax, especially after an 80th-minute penalty by James Rodríguez. The final whistle set off intense celebrations in Fortaleza and throughout Brazil, but an in-game booking of Silva and a broken Neymar vertebrae meant Brazil would be without both for their semifinal game. Game two saw German Mats Hummels's header prove to be the winner against France. The following day, the Netherlands and Costa Rica game was scoreless until penalties. It was a late goalkeeper change, with Tim Krul getting the call, that proved decisive after he stopped two Costa Rican kicks to advance the Netherlands back to the semifinals. In a second-game matchup of Argentina and Belgium, an early Gonzalo Higuaín goal and Messi's dominance throughout, coupled with a lack of creativity out of the Belgians, meant a 1–0 final score and a set field for the semifinals.

The first semifinal took place in Belo Horizonte at the Estádio Mineirão and saw another record fall, this time for the worst semifinal defeat in World Cup history (or best win, depending on your perspective) when host Brazil was blown out by Germany, 7–1. Without star Neymar or captain Silva, Brazil lacked confidence and never looked comfortable and quickly found themselves down 5–0 after only 29 minutes. Only a 90th-minute goal by Oscar could save any face, but the Brazilian fans said it all when they gave a standing ovation to the Germans after their seventh goal. The next day's semifinal, between Argentina and the Netherlands at the Arena Corinthians in São Paulo, proved to be a far-less-entertaining match as both teams lacked creativity. A scoreless 120 minutes went by before Argentinian goalkeeper Sergio Romero took the spotlight with his two saves in penalties to send Argentina through to the final against Germany. Relegated to the third-place game, the Netherlands took their frustration out on a reeling Brazilian side at the Estádio Nacional de Brasília with early goals by Robin van Persie and Daley Blind and a late goal by Georginio Wijnaldum for a 3–0 final. With an embarrassing 10 goals allowed in two games for Brazil, Luiz Felipe Scolari saw his second stint as the head coach of Brazil end abruptly as he and Brazil parted ways immediately following the tournament.

The close of the 2014 World Cup in Brazil was a matchup of German and Argentinian sides that were meeting at the World Cup for the seventh time and a record third time in the final. Played at Estádio do Maracanã in Rio de Janeiro in front of 74,738 spectators, this meeting of powerhouses matched up the organization and discipline of Germany versus the skill of Lionel Messi. A German win would mean a fourth World Cup title (tying them with Italy all-time), and it also would mean the first European title on South American soil. Still missing their star striker, Di María, Argentina was held to zero shots on target. Germany also could not find the target until the 113th minute, when German substitute Mario Götze lived up to his Super Mario nickname by scoring a spectacular goal off a chest trap and clinical finish. When it was all over, Germany had scored an astonishing 18 goals to go along with only 4 conceded, and German fans finally had another title after 24 years of waiting.

FIRST ROUND							
Group A							
12 June		Brazil	3–1	Croatia			
13 June		Mexico	1–0	Cameroon			
17 June		Brazil	0–0	Mexico			
18 June		Croatia	4–0	Cameroon			
23 June		Brazil	4–1	Cameroon			
23 June		Mexico	3–1	Croatia			
Team	*P*	*PTS*	*W*	*D*	*L*	*GF*	*GA*
Brazil	3	7	2	1	0	7	2
Mexico	3	7	2	1	0	4	1
Croatia	3	3	1	0	2	6	6
Cameroon	3	0	0	0	3	1	9
Group B							
13 June		Netherlands	5–1	Spain			
13 June		Chile	3–1	Australia			
18 June		Netherlands	3–2	Australia			
18 June		Chile	2–0	Spain			
23 June		Netherlands	2–0	Chile			
23 June		Spain	3–0	Australia			
Team	*P*	*PTS*	*W*	*D*	*L*	*GF*	*GA*
Netherlands	3	9	3	0	0	10	3
Chile	3	6	2	0	1	5	3
Spain	3	3	1	0	2	4	7
Australia	3	0	0	0	3	3	9
Group C							
14 June		Colombia	3–0	Greece			
14 June		Côte d'Ivoire	2–1	Japan			

19 June		Colombia	2–1	Côte d'Ivoire		
18 June		Japan	0–0	Greece		
24 June		Greece	2–1	Côte d'Ivoire		
24 June		Colombia	4–1	Japan		

Team	P	PTS	W	D	L	GF	GA
Colombia	3	9	3	0	0	9	2
Greece	3	4	1	1	1	2	4
Côte d'Ivoire	3	3	1	0	2	4	5
Japan	3	1	0	1	2	2	6

Group D

14 June		Costa Rica	3–1	Uruguay		
14 June		Italy	2–1	England		
19 June		Uruguay	2–1	England		
20 June		Costa Rica	1–0	Italy		
24 June		Costa Rica	0–0	England		
24 June		Uruguay	1–0	Italy		

Team	P	PTS	W	D	L	GF	GA
Costa Rica	3	7	2	1	0	4	1
Uruguay	3	6	2	0	1	4	4
Italy	3	3	1	0	2	2	3
England	3	1	0	1	2	2	4

Group E

15 June		Switzerland	2–1	Ecuador		
15 June		France	3–0	Honduras		
20 June		France	5–2	Switzerland		
20 June		Ecuador	2–1	Honduras		
25 June		Switzerland	3–0	Honduras		
25 June		France	0–0	Ecuador		

Team	P	PTS	W	D	L	GF	GA
France	3	7	2	1	0	8	2
Switzerland	3	6	2	0	1	7	6
Ecuador	3	4	1	1	1	3	3
Honduras	3	0	0	0	3	1	8

Group F

| 15 June | | Argentina | 2–1 | Bosnia and Herzegovina | | |
| 16 June | | Iran | 0–0 | Nigeria | | |

21 June	Argentina	1–0	Iran			
21 June	Nigeria	1–0	Bosnia and Herzegovina			
25 June	Argentina	3–2	Nigeria			
25 June	Bosnia and Herzegovina	3–1	Iran			

Team	P	PTS	W	D	L	GF	GA
Argentina	3	9	3	0	0	6	3
Nigeria	3	4	1	1	1	3	3
Bosnia and Herzegovina	3	3	1	0	2	4	4
Iran	3	1	0	1	2	1	4

Group G

16 June	Germany	4–0	Portugal			
16 June	United States	2–1	Ghana			
21 June	Germany	2–2	Ghana			
22 June	United States	2–2	Portugal			
26 June	Germany	1–0	United States			
26 June	Portugal	2–1	Ghana			

Team	P	PTS	W	D	L	GF	GA
Germany	3	7	2	1	0	7	2
United States	3	4	1	1	1	4	4
Portugal	3	4	1	1	1	4	7
Ghana	3	1	0	1	2	4	6

Group H

17 June	Belgium	2–1	Algeria			
17 June	Russia	1–1	Korea Republic			
22 June	Belgium	1–0	Russia			
22 June	Algeria	4–2	Korea Republic			
26 June	Algeria	1–1	Russia			
26 June	Belgium	1–0	Korea Republic			

Team	P	PTS	W	D	L	GF	GA
Belgium	3	9	3	0	0	4	1
Algeria	3	4	1	1	1	6	5
Russia	3	2	0	2	1	2	3
Korea Republic	3	1	0	1	2	3	6

ROUND OF 16			
28 June	Brazil	1–1 AET 3–2 PSO	Chile
28 June	Colombia	2–0	Uruguay
29 June	Netherlands	2–1	Mexico
29 June	Costa Rica	1–1 AET 5–3 PSO	Greece
30 June	France	2–0	Nigeria
30 June	Germany	2–1 AET	Algeria
1 July	Argentina	1–0 AET	Switzerland
1 July	Belgium	2–1 AET	United States
QUARTERFINALS			
4 July	Brazil	2–1	Colombia
4 July	Germany	1–0	France
5 July	Argentina	1–0	Belgium
5 July	Netherlands	0–0 AET 4–3 PSO	Costa Rica
SEMIFINALS			
8 July	Germany	7–1	Brazil
9 July	Argentina	0–0 AET 4–2 PSO	Netherlands
THIRD-PLACE GAME			
12 July	Netherlands	3–0	Brazil
FINAL			
13 July	Germany	1–0 AET	Argentina

A

ACEROS, GERMÁN. B. 30 September 1938, Bucaramanga, Colombia. Colombia's first appearance in the World Cup finals came in 1962, at the seventh World Cup hosted in fellow South American nation Chile. Germán Aceros was the fulcrum of the Colombian team that surprised many observers with their performances, despite a first-round elimination. Their qualification ahead of Peru for the competition itself came as a surprise, and Aceros played a critical role in a two-legged contest. Colombia secured a 1–0 win in the home leg on 30 April 1961 and then traveled to Lima, Peru, going 1–0 down early in the game. Aceros, though, scored an equalizing goal that sent Colombia to Chile. Aceros played in all three games in Chile, with his country placed in group two alongside the Soviet Union, Yugoslavia and Uruguay. Colombia began with a 2–1 defeat to two-time World Cup winners Uruguay, having led at halftime in a surprisingly strong showing in Arica on 30 May. Four days later, Aceros took part in one of the most memorable games in World Cup history, as Colombia faced reigning European champions the Soviet Union in Arica. The Soviets raced to a 3–0 lead after only 11 minutes, but 10 minutes later, Aceros kept Colombia in the game by starting and finishing a fine passing move, Rolando Serrano seeing him up and Aceros floating the ball over legendary Soviet goalkeeper Lev Yashin into the back of the net to keep the score to 3–1. In the second half, the Soviets extended their lead to 4–1, before one of the most remarkable comebacks in World Cup history took place, Aceros playing a central role as Colombia came back to tie the game 4–4 and earn their first World Cup point. Aceros's final game at any World Cup was underwhelming, however, when, four days later, Yugoslavia crushed Colombia 5–0. Aceros would not take part in another World Cup, as Colombia did not qualify again until 1990.

ADEMIR. B. 8 November 1922, Rio de Janeiro, Brazil. D. 11 May 1996. Ademir, as he was commonly known, was born as Ademir Marques de Menezes and was an outstanding forward for Brazil from 1945 to 1953. During that period, Ademir scored 32 goals in just 39 games for his country and was the top scorer at the 1950 FIFA World Cup, scoring nine goals in just six games. He failed to score in the crucial last game of the competition, however, as Brazil lost to Uruguay 2–1, a result that made the Uruguayans World Cup winners for the second time and denied the Brazilians the title on home soil.

ALBERT, FLÓRIÁN. B. 15 September 1941, Hercegezante, Hungary. D. 31 October 2011. Flórián Albert was a graceful, prolific goal-scoring forward for his native Hungary and Hungarian club team Ferencváros, winner of the European Footballer of the Year award in 1967. Albert scored 31 goals in 75 games for Hungary between 1959 and 1974. He appeared in the FIFA World Cup finals tournament on two occasions, in 1962 and 1966, scoring a total of four goals in seven games in the two competitions combined, as Hungary reached the quarterfinals stage on both occasions. He was the joint top scorer in the 1962 World Cup. Albert also won a bronze medal at the 1960 Olympic Games Football Tournament for his part in Hungary's third-place finish, scoring five goals in five games in the competition. With his club team, Ferencváros, Albert won numerous Hungarian-league championship winners' medals and reached European glory with victory in the 1965 Inter-Cities Fairs Cup, the forerunner to the UEFA Cup. Albert retired in 1974, five years after a serious right-leg injury limited his abilities on the field. In 2007, Ferencváros renamed their home stadium in Albert's honor, naming it the Stadion Albert Flórián (Flórián Albert Stadium).

ALGERIA. Commonly known as Les Fennecs (The Desert Foxes). Algeria has appeared in four FIFA World Cup finals tournaments (1982, 1986, 2010 and 2014). Soccer was first played in Algeria in the late 19th century, its first club—FC Musulman de Mascara—founded in 1913. Algerian soccer's governing body, Fédération Algérienne de Football, was established in 1962 just weeks after Algeria gained independence from France, 130 years after its colonization. In the decades leading up to independence, soccer was seen as a key expression of Algeria's liberation movement, as one Algerian liberation leader put it in the late 1950s: "On a man to man basis, on the field of football, we can show them who is really superior." This became a source of controversy in the run-up to the 1958 World Cup. Mustapha Zitouni, a 29-year-old Algerian who played in France and had recently represented France at the international level, including a superb performance against Spain that had attracted the interest of Real Madrid, was selected to play for Algeria's colonial overlords in Chile. Zitouni was then approached by the Front de Libération Nationale, Algeria's revolutionary independence movement, to be part of an Algerian team that would tour the world. The timing was deliberately made to disrupt France's World Cup plans and make a powerful statement for Algerian independence. Zitouni agreed, turning down the chance to appear at the World Cup, and was joined in his rebellion against colonialism by eight other Algerian professionals playing in France, including, most notably, Rachid Mekhloufi, a brilliant forward for AS Saint-Étienne in France also on the 1958 World Cup roster. The FLN-recruited team played in 14 countries between 1958 and 1962, though FIFA refused an application for membership by the government in exile, joining the federation in 1962 after Algeria's independence.

The northwestern African country's first appearance at the World Cup finals came in 1982 in Spain, the first time Africa had been awarded two automatic qualification places at the World Cup, with Algeria failing to claim Africa's lone automatic spot in previous competitions. Their FIFA World Cup debut in Spain was one of the most remarkable games in the history of the competition: facing West Germany in the opening match of group two at El Molinón stadium in Gijón on 16 June, cheered on by a vociferous Algerian contingent among the 45,000 in attendance, the North Africans shocked the two-time World Cup champion Europeans with a 2–1 victory. The scoring was opened on a scorching hot day in the 54th minute by Rabah Madjer, following a fine pass by Djamel Zidane to Faouzi Mansouri that led to a deflected shot falling to Madjer six yards out, the 23-year-old Algerian forward driving the ball home with aplomb. Algeria continued to create chances with precise creative passing and speedy counterattacks orchestrated by Zidane, though West Germany provided plenty of pressure on the Algerian goal and equalized through their captain Karl Heinz Rummenigge in the 67th minute with a close-range finish following a cross by Felix Magath. Parity would last for less than a minute, as Algeria broke forward again straight from the restart to score a mirror image of Rummenigge's goal. African Footballer of the Year Lakhdar Belloumi swept the ball in from inside the six-yard box after a precise left-footed cross by Salah Assad. It was not, though, the first time Algeria had beaten West Germany: on 1 January 1964, the Africans had earned a remarkable 2–0 victory over the Europeans in Algeria's capital, Algiers.

Algeria's second group game five days later proved to be a severe disappointment, Austria taking a 2–0 win with two second-half goals by Walter Schachner and Hans Krankl. Algeria's was far too lax during the second period, with an aggressive Austrian side taking advantage. Heading into their final game of the group stage just three days later on 24 June, Algeria knew they needed to defeat Chile (who had lost their two previous games) to have a chance of progression to the next round. Playing at Estadio Carlos Tartiere in Oviedo in front of a crowd of just 16,000 fans, Algeria raced to a 3–0 lead by the 35th minute with a stunning display of attacking soccer. Assad began the scoring in the 7th minute after a fine move involving Tedj Bensaoula and Rabah Madjer, sweeping the ball home from eight yards out. Assad scored again in the 31st minute, the ball deflected into the goal off Chilean captain and three-time South American player of the year Elias Figueroa. Four minutes later, Chile's defense allowed Algeria to waltz unchallenged to the edge of their penalty area, Tedj Bensaoula making the South Americans pay with a low drive from 20 yards into the bottom left corner of the goal. The second half saw Chile give the Algerians a scare, scoring through a penalty by Miguel Neira in the 59th minute and then pulling to within a goal of Algeria with a fine 73rd-minute individual goal by Juan Letelier. Algeria held on for a 3–2 win, but their hopes of qualification for the next round were dashed the next day in highly controversial circumstances: Austria and West Germany played their final game of the competition in Gijón with the advantage of knowing that a win by one or two goals for the Germans would advance both teams at Algeria's expense. Germany took an early lead in the 10th minute from a goal by Horst Hrubesch, and from there, both teams were entirely content to sit back and qualify together with this scoreline, to the infuriation of the Algerians and the neutrals present. This apparent collusion led to a rule change by FIFA for the next World Cup, with all final group games to be played at the same time. It was of no consolation to Algeria.

Algeria did, though, qualify for that next World Cup in Mexico in 1986. They had the misfortune to be placed in group D alongside Brazil, Spain and Northern Ireland. Their campaign began against the latter on 3 June at Tres de Marzo stadium in Guadalajara, with six survivors appearing in the Algerian team from the corresponding 1982 World Cup opener for the North Africans, including Assad, Madjer, Mansouri and Zidane. The game, sloppy and slow paced in general, began poorly for Algeria, with Manchester United's Norman Whiteside scoring with a deflected shot after just six minutes from a free kick 20 yards out. Algeria pressed hard in a game that became increasingly physical and unpleasant, four yellow cards issued by Russian referee Valeri Butenko, and equalized in the 59th minute from a free kick 25 yards from goal, a direct shot powered low into the right-hand corner by Zidane to earn Algeria one point in a 1–1 tie. That was to be Algeria's only goal of the competition: three days later, again in Guadalajara, an outstanding Brazil team was held by Algeria to a goal-less first half, but a goal by Careca in the 66th minute proved to be the difference in a 1–0 win for the South Americans following poor defending by the Algerians. A victory against Spain in the final round of group games on 12 June would have been enough for Algeria to qualify into the knockout stage, but it was not to be at the game in Monterrey, the Spaniards taking a 15th-minute lead and eventually winning 3–0 with two further goals in the second half. Algeria was eliminated, and a golden generation of Algerian players soon retired.

Algeria's success in the 1980s was built off the back of infrastructure improvements in Algerian soccer made in the 1970s, as under President Houari Boumedienne all its leading clubs received funding from state-owned companies, with staff, equipment and facilities rapidly improved. The country's instability in the 1990s, with a deadly civil war devastating the country, undid much of the progress made and severely impacted on Algeria's national sporting infrastructure and priorities. The nadir was reached for Algeria in the qualifying competition for the 2006 World Cup, as Algeria won only one of ten qualifying games and scored only eight goals. The Fédération Algérienne de Football has attempted to kick-start investment into domestic soccer in recent years with professionalization of its domestic league, and Algeria qualified for the World Cup for the first time in 24 years in 2010—though most of its best players have migrated to European leagues.

Qualification for the World Cup came via a tempestuous and high-profile play-off victory over Egypt in November 2009, after the two countries had finished tied in the qualifying competition, neutral Sudan hosting a 1–0 win for Algeria over the reigning Africa Cup of Nations champions to claim the 32nd and final spot at the 2010 World Cup. In South Africa, an Algerian team coached by Rabah Saâdane—who had been part of Algeria's coaching staff at the 1982 World Cup and head coach at the 1986 World Cup—failed to win a game but by no means embarrassed themselves. The bulk of Algeria's squad for the 2010 World Cup plied their trade in the leading European leagues, led by experienced captain Yazid Mansouri. Placed in group C with Slovenia, England and the United States, Algeria kicked off their campaign on 13 June in Polokwane against the Slovenians, going down to a cruel 1–0 defeat. Algeria failed to capitalize on their early opportunities against Slovenia and then lost forward Abdelkader Ghezzal to a red card, his second yellow coming for a deliberate handball in the Slovenian penalty area in the 73rd minute, just 15 minutes after the Algerian had entered the game as a substitute. A tight game ended disastrously for Algeria when, in the 79th minute, Slovenian midfielder Robert Koren cut in from a left and fired a shot from outside the penalty area that slipped through the grasp of the flailing and inexperienced hands of Algerian goalkeeper Faouzi Chaouchi. Chaouchi, who had performed heroically to get Algeria to the World Cup with his play-off performance against Egypt, had been made first choice by Saâdane in goal despite questions over his temperament following his headbutt on an opponent in an Africa Cup of Nations semifinal against Egypt just months before the start of the World Cup.

For Algeria's second group game against England six days later in Cape Town, Raïs M'Bolhi started in goal instead of Chaouchi only weeks after making his debut for the country on 28 May against the Republic of Ireland. M'Bolhi proved to be an inspired selection, however, keeping a clean sheet against England in a 0–0 tie despite 15 shots from the English. Algeria had plenty of their own opportunities, edging possession though rarely threatening David James in England's goal. That left Algeria with a chance to qualify for the next round, facing the United States in a decisive game on 23 June in Pretoria. Algeria, needing a win to qualify, had three players booked and one sent off (captain Antar Yahia for receiving two yellow cards in the 93rd minute) in a thrilling game won by the United States in the 91st minute thanks to a tremendous goal by Landon Donovan as Algeria's legs tired rapidly in the closing minutes.

Failure to score a goal in the previous tournament led to a refocusing of energy in Algerian football, and as a testament to the work, qualification for the 2014 World Cup in Brazil saw Algeria easily top their group with five wins in six games in the second round of the Confederation of African Football (CAF). A third-round home-and-home play-off against Burkina Faso for one of Africa's five World Cup slots saw a controversial away 3–2 Algerian loss, the controversy stemming from a penalty awarded for a phantom handball in the 86th minute. Needing only a 1–0 home win to even up the aggregate and go through on away goals, Algeria and the surprising Burkina side played a physical match. Poor Burkina defending that allowed Algeria's Madjid Bougherra to finish his own deflection and some unfortunate placement of woodwork in stoppage time meant Algeria advanced as Northern Africa's only entrant.

In Brazil, Algeria was placed in group H along with Belgium, Korea Republic and Russia. Algeria's first group game was played at Belo Horizonte's Estádio Mineirão against a heavily favored Belgian side. Though underdogs, the Desert Foxes proved to be the brighter side in the first half. Following possession and free kicks deep in the Belgian end, Algeria was finally rewarded in the 25th minute with their first World Cup goal since 1986—a run of 506 scoreless minutes—when Sofiane Feghouli was dragged down from behind and calmly finished the awarded penalty. It was not until Belgium shook up its roster in the second half that the favorites were able to find the back of the net with Marouane Fellaini scoring in the 70th minute and Dries Mertens in the 80th for a 2–1 Algerian loss.

Playing their second group game against the Korea Republic, Algeria finally put together a dominant performance in a 4–2 dismantling of the Taeguk Warriors. Three first-half goals meant a comfortable lead, and though the Warriors gave the Desert Foxes a little scare, scoring a goal five minutes after kickoff, a goal by Yacine Brahimi in the 62nd minute restored the three-goal lead. Though the Koreans scored again in the 72nd minute, it was too little, too late, and the Algerian side had become not only the first African team to score four goals in a World Cup match, but also they had their first World Cup win since 1982.

Going into the final group game, Algeria needed to beat the slightly favored Russian side to guarantee advancement but found themselves down just six minutes in when Aleksandr Kokorin headed home a Dmitri Kombarov cross. Algeria battled back and leveled the game in the 60th minute when Islam Slimani headed home a Abdelmoumene Djabou free kick; the goal was not without controversy as video evidence clearly shows a green laser light shining on the Russian goalkeeper just before the kick. The win meant history as Algeria had finally advanced out of the group stage.

In the round-of-16 game played in Porto Alegre, Algeria found itself with the opportunity to make up for the "Disgrace of Gijón" 32 years earlier when they faced Germany. For the 90-plus minutes of regulation time, Algerian goalkeeper M'Bolhi kept Germany scoreless, and an upset seemed possible. In added extra time, however, Algerian momentum was short-lived as German substitute André Schürrle scored a clever full-speed back-heel flick in the 92nd minute to put Germany up 1–0. The game looked over in the 120th minute when Mesut Özil hammered home a blocked Schürrle shot for a seemingly insurmountable two-goal lead, but Algeria again showed their resolve when, in the 121st minute, Djabou rocketed home a Feghouli cross. Algeria managed one more chance, a weak header hit right to the German keeper, and the Desert Foxes' World Cup was over. They went home in 14th place with seven goals for and seven against.

ALLEMANDI, LUIGI. B. 8 November 1903, San Damiano Macra, Italy. D. 25 September 1978. One of the most experienced players on Italy's 1934 World Cup–winning team on home soil was Luigi Allemandi, who had made his debut for his country almost a decade earlier in November 1925 in a 2–1 win for Italy over Yugoslavia. Allemandi became a bedrock of Italy's watertight defense and was called on to captain his country in Italy's critical World Cup qualifier against Greece in March 1934, a game the Italians won 4–0. At the 1934 World Cup, Allemandi was one of five Italians to play in all five games, including the final, a 2–1 win after extra time over Czechoslovakia in Rome. Allemandi made a further 10 appearances for Italy in the 1930s, playing in Italy's famous loss to England in London in the autumn of 1934, then taking over as captain for his final eight international games, his last coming in December 1936. At club level, Allemandi starred for Juventus, Internazionale, Roma and Venezia, playing briefly for Lazio in 1939 before his retirement.

AMOROS, MANUEL. B. 1 February 1962, Nîmes, France. Manuel Amoros, a diminutive attacking fullback of Spanish descent, represented France at the World Cup finals in 1982 and 1986, as well as playing in 14 World Cup qualifying matches. Amoros made his World Cup debut on 21 June 1982 at the age of 20 in a 4–1 win for France over Kuwait, receiving a caution in the 68th minute. His aggressive play earned him a yellow card in France's subsequent game, a 1–1 draw with Czechoslovakia three days later in Valladolid, and Amoros was thus suspended for France's final group game. Amoros returned to the French side for their second game in the second-round group stage against Northern Ireland, a 4–1 win that saw France qualify for the semifinal stage. There, France faced West Germany in what became an infamous game decided on penalty kicks, though Amoros himself almost won it for France in the 89th minute with a wondrous dipping drive from 35 yards out that struck the West German crossbar. After four goals in a remarkable extra-time period left the game tied at 3–3, Amoros converted his penalty in the shoot-out, but France was eliminated from the World Cup after misses by Didier Six and Maxime Bossis. Amoros appeared in the third-place consolation game, won by France 3–2 over Poland.

Amoros then represented France as they won the 1984 UEFA European Championship, though his best-remembered contribution from that tournament was a headbutt on Danish midfielder Jesper Olsen that earned the Frenchman a red card. Amoros was a first-choice selection for France at the 1986 World Cup in Mexico, playing the entirety of all three group stage games as France qualified for the knockout stage with two wins and a draw, Amoros booked in a 1–1 tie with the Soviet Union. Amoros then played a critical role in France's pulsating quarterfinal with Brazil: with France down 1–0 toward the end of the first half, Amoros initiated an attacking move that led to Michel Platini's equalizer for the French. The scoreline remained 1–1 at full-time, and Amoros would again take the second penalty in a World Cup shoot-out and again made no mistake, calmly placing it perfectly past Carlos into the corner of the Brazilian goal. France went on to win the shoot-out 4–3. Amoros and France then once more faced West Germany in the World Cup semifinal and once more the French went out of the competition to their neighbors, defeated 2–0, Amoros playing the entire game, not his best of a distinguished World Cup career. A foul by Amoros on the edge of France's penalty area led to Germany's first goal, a free kick from Andreas Brehme driven through the hands of French goalkeeper Joel Bats. Amoros was arguably then at fault for West Germany's second goal, with France exposed on the break for a fine counterattack goal by Rudi Völler in the 90th minute as the French pushed for an equalizer. Amoros played in the third-place play-off against Belgium three days later, scoring a penalty in extra time as France won 4–2 to earn him a second third-place medal and his only goal for France.

In 1987, Amoros took over France's captaincy and played in seven qualifying games for the 1990 World Cup, though France failed to qualify for the finals for the fourth time in its history. Amoros, who played his club soccer primarily for Olympique de Marseille and Monaco, retired from international play in 1992, ending his career with 82 appearances and 1 goal for France.

ANDERSSON, KENNET. B. 6 October 1967, Eskilstuna, Sweden. Kennet Andersson starred at the 1994 World Cup in the United States for Sweden, scoring five goals in seven games as his country finished in third place. Strikingly tall at six feet, four inches, Andersson used his height to his advantage in Sweden's direct, tidy system of play. He made his World Cup finals debut on 19 June 1994, entering Sweden's game against Cameroon as a second-half substitute, replacing Klas Ingesson as Sweden came back to earn a 2–2 draw. Andersson started Sweden's next game against Russia in place of Jesper Blomqvist, his physical presence helping to create space for the quicksilver Martin Dahlin, who scored his second of the game with a diving header from Andersson's cross in the 81st minute to give Sweden a 3–1 victory. Sweden's final group game came against Brazil, with Andersson scoring his first goal and giving Sweden the lead in the 21st minute. Andersson chested down a through ball from Tomas Brolin on the edge of the area and then unleashed a magnificent lofted finish with the outside of his right foot. Brazil tied the game in the second half through Romário, the 1–1 result meaning Sweden qualified for the knockout stage by finishing in second place in their group behind the Brazilians.

Sweden's second-round game, a 3–1 win over Saudi Arabia, saw Andersson net two goals and assist on one. The first Swedish goal came in the sixth minute, Andersson taking the ball from a throw-in on the left byline and turning to swing in a cross that again found the head of Dahlin to give Sweden a 1–0 lead. In the 51st minute, Andersson scored with an accurate low left-footed strike from 20 yards out, doubling his tally in the 88th minute with a fine right-footed strike that rebounded into the net off the inside of the post from 12 yards out after neat buildup play by Brolin and Dahlin. Andersson had made himself a fixture in this Swedish team alongside his slighter attackers and would play a crucial role in their quarterfinal at Stanford Stadium against Romania: trailing 2–1 with just five minutes remaining in extra time, Sweden equalized when Andersson rose above Romanian goalkeeper Florin Prunea on a pass from Swedish captain Roland Nilsson, leveraging his height to take the game into penalty kicks. Andersson became the first Swede to score in the shoot-out following a miss on the first kick by Håkan Mild, Sweden going on to claim victory after misses by Dan Petrescu and Miodrag Belodedici for Romania. Andersson started the semifinal in a rematch against Brazil on 13 July at the Rose Bowl in Los Angeles, but Sweden could not find a way to break down the Brazilians, eliminated with a 1–0 defeat. There remained the third-place play-off against Bulgaria for Andersson to claim his fifth goal of the World Cup in a 4–0 win for Sweden, as he finished tied in third place in the scoring charts for the competition, behind Oleg Salenko and Jürgen Klinsmann with six goals each. Andersson continued to play for Sweden throughout the 1990s, playing in 10 World Cup qualifying games and scoring 7 goals but not again appearing at a World Cup finals tournament as Sweden failed to qualify in 1998, while the 2002 competition came after Andersson's retirement.

ANDRADE, JOSÉ. B. 22 November 1901, Salto, Uruguay. D. 5 October 1957. Uruguay's 1930 World Cup–winning team owed much to its right-half, José Andrade, who played in all four of his country's games at the competition, including the 4–2 victory over Argentina in the final. Andrade, unlike most of his teammates, did not hail from Uruguay's capital city, Montevideo, born in Salto in Uruguay's northwest, the second-largest city in the country. Andrade moved to Montevideo at the start of the 1920s, quickly becoming a fixture in Uruguay's national team, with whom he won three Copa América championships in 1923, 1924 and 1926, as well as two gold medals at the Olympic Games Football Tournament in 1924 and 1928. Andrade, of African origin, became known as the "Black Marvel" to the French press at the 1924 Olympics in Paris. He was the subject of abuse from Argentinean fans in a 1925 game that was abandoned when Uruguay refused to return to the field after a riot broke out. Like his teammates, Andrade was an amateur player who earned a living in various occupations, including as a carnival musician and as a shoe shiner. Following the 1924 Olympics, Andrade earned celebrity status in Paris, remaining there for some time after the tournament, and was later called the "first international soccer idol" by writer Eduardo Galeano. At club level, Andrade starred for Nacional in the 1920s and Peñarol in the 1930s, Montevideo's two leading teams. He retired from international play in 1930 after 34 appearances for Uruguay, dying in poverty in 1957 after contracting tuberculosis.

ANDREOLO, MICHELE. B. 6 September 1912, Montevideo, Uruguay. D. 14 May 1981. One of several internationals on Italy's 1938 World Cup–winning squad who had not been born in Italy, Michele Andreolo played in the World Cup final against Hungary in Paris on 19 June 1938 and was known as powerful center-half who held Italy's midfield together. Andreolo was born in Uruguay and began his club career with Nacional of Montevideo, but like many South Americans of his era, he moved to Italy in the 1930s to earn a better living as a player. He joined Bologna in 1935 and, with Italian ancestry, began playing for Italy's national team the next year. Such selections were controversial, though Andreolo's parents had both emigrated from the Cilento region in Southern Italy to Uruguay not long before his birth. Regardless, Andreolo made his debut against Austria in a 2–2 draw. Andreolo cemented a regular place in Italy's talented side immediately and was selected for the 1938 World Cup team, as Italy looked to defend their title won in 1934 on home soil, by coach Vittorio Pozzo. Andreolo was one of eight players on the 1938 World Cup team to play in all four games in the Italian triumph, as they became the first country to win two World Cup trophies. He continued playing internationally until 1942, collecting 26 caps, also serving in wartime for Italy and eventually retiring from club play in 1950, having won three Italian league titles with Bologna.

ANGOLA. Commonly known as the Palancas Negras (Black Antelopes). The Southern African nation Angola has appeared at one FIFA World Cup finals tournament, the 2006 competition held in Germany. That appearance came 21 years after Angola's independence from Portugal, with Angola's first official international game taking place in 1977 against Cuba—whose troops had participated in the Angolan civil war—a 1–0 win for the Africans. Soccer had long been popular in Angola, the country's national sport, and is governed by the Federação Angolana de Futebol. Angola's debut in World Cup qualifying was for the 1986 competition in Mexico. Angola recorded a win in its first game against Senegal but failed to win its three remaining games and was eliminated following a 3–2 defeat to Algeria. Angola advanced to the second-round group stage of qualifying for the 1990 World Cup but won only one game in its group, against Gabon, outclassed by group winners Cameroon and second-place Nigeria. For the 1994 World Cup in the United States, Angola fell at the first round of African qualifying, registering just one win in six games played. Four years later, Angola's performance in qualifying improved, though Angola still failed to reach the final tournament in France. On this occasion, Angola finished second in their qualifying group to Cameroon, ahead of both Zimbabwe and Togo, recording two wins. Angola's upward trend continued for the 2002 World Cup—though again finishing second in their qualifying group and failing to earn a berth at the finals in Japan and South Korea, they won three games for the first time.

With Angola's 15-year civil war having ended in 2002, its sporting prospects improved, and Angola earned their breakthrough in world soccer and a passage to Germany for the 2006 World Cup by topping their group in the second round of the

African qualifying competition, finishing ahead of Nigeria in group four by recording six wins, three draws and only one loss, conceding only six goals in ten games. Angola tied with Nigeria on points but finished ahead of one of the continent's leading soccer nations based on a better head-to-head record against the Nigerians. Angola richly deserved qualification, sealed by a 1–0 win over Rwanda, having beaten Nigeria 1–0 at home along with a 1–1 tie in Nigeria. This came despite Angola having almost failed to qualify for the second-round group stage in the first place—their two-legged first-round tie against African minnows Chad in the fall of 2003 saw them lose 3–1 in the first leg, but after bringing in coach Luis Gonçalves to replace Brazilian Ismael Kurtz following that defeat, Angola turned around their fortunes with a 2–0 win to advance at Chad's expense on the away-goals rule.

In Germany, Angola was fittingly drawn in a group with former colonial rulers Portugal, along with Mexico and Iran. Gonçalves, a youthful Angolan native who had led Angola to victory at the 2003 African Youth Championship, led Angola on to the world stage with little known and little expected of a team lacking in stars known worldwide, many of Angola's players part-time professionals in the domestic Angolan league. They were captained by the experienced Akwá, a forward with a prolific goal-scoring record internationally. Akwá would ideally have been paired in attack with Benfica striker Mantorras, though the latter's constant injury problems hampered him again in Germany, and he started Angola's opening game against Portugal on the bench. In that game, on 11 June in Cologne, Angola acquitted themselves well in a 1–0 defeat against one of the favorites for the competition, despite conceding a goal to Portuguese striker Pauleta, set up by a dashing run from Luís Figo, in only the fourth minute. Five days later, in Hanover, Angola held Mexico—who had won their first game of the group 3–1 over Iran—to a 0–0 tie to earn their first point in the World Cup finals, with stout defense holding the North Americans scoreless despite losing their defensive stalwart André Macanga to a red card in the 79th minute, experienced Angolan goalkeeper João Ricardo making a number of key saves.

The result against Mexico meant that Angola still stood a chance to qualify for the next round with victory in their final group game on 21 June in Leipzig if other results also went their way. That possibility seemed as if it could become a reality when, in the 60th minute, Aboutrika—who had entered the game as a substitute forward replacing Akwá just nine minutes earlier—was left unmarked at the back post and headed in a cross from right-winger Zé Kalanga. Angola's lead would only last for 15 minutes, however, as an Iranian corner kick delivered by Mehdi Mahdavikia was headed in for the equalizer by Sohrab Bakhtiarizadeh, loosely marked by the substitute forward Love. The result was a fair one, with Iran edging the game in terms of possession but Angola still creating as many good scoring chances as their Asian opponent. Their second tie eliminated Angola from the competition in Germany, but the country's respectable showing at their first World Cup earned the team a presidential welcome back home following the tournament. Angola's hopes of qualifying for the 2010 World Cup were hampered by Gonçalves's resignation as manager just days before the competition began, and Angola disappointingly finished behind Benin in the second-round group stage, thus eliminated from contention for World Cup qualification in South Africa. In 2014, Angola only lost one match during qualifying, but their inability to do anything other than draw (save for a forfeit 3–0 win over Liberia) meant a third-place group finish in qualifying and again missing out on the World Cup finals.

ARDILES, OSVALDO. B. 3 August 1952, Bell Ville, Argentina. Participating in 11 games across 2 World Cup finals tournaments in 1978 and 1982 for Argentina, Osvaldo "Ossie" Ardiles was a slightly built midfielder, tenacious in his tackling yet critical as a creative playmaker. Ardiles, then playing for Huracán in his native Argentina, made his international debut in 1973 but was not selected for the 1974 World Cup team that traveled to West Germany. By 1978, Ardiles was an Argentinean regular and was selected for the 1978 squad as Argentina aimed to win the World Cup as hosts. Ardiles played in all three first-round group games, his industrious hard-working play and neat passing a key feature of Argentina's success, as they won their first two games before a loss to Italy with qualification for the next round already secured. Ardiles played in Argentina's hard-working 2–0 win over Poland in the first game of the second-round group stage but picked up an injury in the first half of Argentina's second game against Brazil, substituted and replaced by Ricardo Villa. The injury kept Ardiles out of Argentina's third, crucial 6–0 win over Peru that secured the hosts a place in the World Cup final against the Netherlands. Argentina's coach, César Luis Menotti, faced a difficult decision as Ardiles attempted to recover in time for the final in Buenos Aires on 25 June, a semi-fit Ardiles ultimately selected for the game, seen as crucial to countering the quality of the Dutch midfield. The decision seemed to be vindicated in the first half as Ardiles ran the midfield with his typical industry, playing a critical role connecting defense with attack, Mario Kempes giving Argentina a 1–0 lead with a 38th-minute goal. Ardiles, though, was visibly hampered by injury and fatigue early in the second half and was substituted in the 65th minute. Argentina conceded an equalizer to the Dutch 17 minutes later but ultimately triumphed 3–1 after extra time, giving Ardiles a World Cup winners' medal.

Ardiles's performances earned him a high-profile transfer to Tottenham Hotspur in England, contributing greatly to the club's success in the FA Cup in 1981 and 1982, though he left before the 1982 final to join Argentina for preparations for the 1982 World Cup in Spain. An experienced Argentina team with the addition of the world's most expensive player, Diego Maradona, was favored by many to defend their title, but the competition ended in disappointment as Argentina was eliminated in the second-round group stage following defeats to Italy and Brazil. Ardiles's performances had been strong, scoring his one and only World Cup finals goal in a 4–1 win over Hungary in Alicante, scoring a poacher's goal from close range after a defensive mistake. Ardiles retired from international play in 1982 and from club play in 1991 and has become a well-traveled coach in the years since.

ARGENTINA. Commonly known as La Albiceleste (The White and Sky Blue). Two-time winners of the FIFA World Cup in 1978 and 1986, Argentina also hosted the competition for their first victory in 1978 and finished as runners-up on two other occasions (1930, 1990). Soccer in Argentina was introduced by British emigrants in the late 19th century, and the South American country played its first international game in 1902 against Uruguay in the Uruguayan capital, Montevideo, the start of a fierce rivalry with their neighbors across the Río de la Plata. Prior to the establishment of the World Cup, Argentina finished as runners-up in the 1928 Olympic Games Football Tournament and won South America's regional championship, the Copa América, four times in the 1920s. This success meant they entered the inaugural World Cup in 1930 as favorites for the competition alongside hosts and reigning Olympic champions Uruguay. Argentina, coached jointly by Juan Tramutola and Francisco Olazar, was placed in group one of the 1930 World Cup's first-round stage, featuring 13 nations, along with Chile, France and Mexico. Argentina began their campaign on 15 July with a 1–0 win over France, Luis Monti scoring the winning goal direct from a free kick 20 yards from goal, a fortunate victory in a tightly fought game.

Argentina's mediocre performance in its opening game prompted Olazar and Tramutola to make drastic changes to their lineup for their second game three days later against Mexico. Seven players were dropped from Argentina's starting lineup, including their previous game's lone goal scorer Monti and captain Manuel Ferreira—though the latter's absence was excused because he had to take a university exam. Goalkeeper Ángel Bossio was made captain for the Mexico game, and in came Guillermo Stábile for his debut. Stábile proved to be an instant success, scoring in the eighth minute for the first of his three goals in the game in what turned into a high-scoring 6–3 win for Argentina. Along with Stábile's hat trick, Francisco Varallo scored once and Adolfo Zumelzú twice for Argentina. Stábile's scoring streak continued in Argentina's final group game against Chile on 22 July at the Estadio de Centenario, scoring in the 12th and 13th minutes, Evaristo adding a third in the 51st minute for a 3–1 win that sealed Argentina's passage to the next round. Ferreira had returned to the lineup as captain, along with Luis Monti, the latter sparking a brawl between the teams following a trademark kick by Monti on Chile's Arturo Torres that required police assistance to break up. Argentina thus had considerable momentum as they prepared for the semifinal against the United States on 26 July, the Americans having surprisingly qualified from their group ahead of Romania and Peru. With a crowd of 72,886 in attendance at Estadio de Centenario, a 6–1 final scoreline was flattering to Argentina, as they only led 1–0 at halftime through a goal by Luis Monti. But with American goalkeeper Jimmy Douglas hobbled by a twisted ankle, a deluge of second-half goals came for Argentina from Alejandro Scopelli in the 56th minute, Stábile in the 69th and 87th minutes and Carlos Peucelle in the 80th and 85th minutes.

A packed Estadio de Centenario, including thousands of Argentineans who had made the short hop across the Río de la Plata for the first World Cup final, was in a frenzied state by the time of kickoff at 3:30 p.m. on 30 July 1930, as hosts Uruguay faced Argentina. The days before the final had been tumultuous for the Argentinean team, with their own fans sending death threats to Luis Monti, demanding victory or promising death instead. The game itself, once underway as the firecrackers died down, did not disappoint: Uruguay took an early lead through Pablo Dorado in the 12th minute, but Argentina equalized just 8 minutes later and held the lead at halftime thanks to Stábile's eighth goal of the tournament in the 37th minute with a marvelous goal, receiving the ball 12 yards out, turning to beat two defenders and strike the ball into the far corner from a difficult angle. Uruguay, though, came storming back in the second half, leveling the score through Pedro Cea in the 57th minute, taking the lead

3–1 in the 68th minute and confirming their victory with a fourth in the 89th minute to make it 4–1. Bitter mobs in Buenos Aires rioted in the streets in response to defeat, damaging the Uruguayan consulate in the Argentinean capital. One consolation was the Golden Shoe awarded to Stábile as the top goal scorer in the competition.

It would be 48 years until Argentina reached the final of the World Cup again. In 1934, at the World Cup in Italy, Argentina traveled by sea to Europe in order to play just one game, a 3–2 defeat to Sweden that saw them eliminated in the first round. The team coached by Felipe Pascucci was without any of their players from 1930, instead featuring an amateur team—though one Argentinean professional, Luis Monti, was now playing for Italy, which went on to win the competition at home. Argentina did not enter the next World Cup in 1938, in part to express its disappointment at awarding the 1938 World Cup hosting rights to France rather than returning to South America in Argentina. Nor did Argentina enter the next two World Cups following World War II in 1950 and 1954. In 1950, a dispute with the host Brazilian federation preceded Argentina's withdrawal. In 1954, with the World Cup in Switzerland, Argentina preferred isolation and avoided the risk of defeat under the Peronist nationalist government. Without their own country represented, many of Argentina's best players instead turned out for Italy at the 1938 World Cup, having gained citizenship while playing in Europe. Two generations of Argentina's best players thus missed the chance to show their worth on the world stage, instead showing their quality at the Copa América, won six times by Argentina out of the nine times they contested it in their 24-year absence from the World Cup between 1934 and 1958.

Argentina's return to the World Cup in 1958 took place in Sweden but did not feature the best Argentinean players from their victory at the 1957 Copa América: the nation's brilliant attacking trio of Humberto Maschio, Antonio Angelillo and Omar Sívori were all recruited by Italian clubs, and none would play again for Argentina, acquiring Italian citizenship and representing Italy at the next World Cup in 1962. The Argentina side that did go to Switzerland was coached by 1930 World Cup hero Guillermo Stábile, who had led his country to six Copa América titles but could do little with a weakened group of players ill-matched for the competition in Europe. Despite taking the lead in the second minute of their first game against West Germany in the group stage on 8 June through superb right-winger Omar Oreste Corbatta, Argentina succumbed to a 3–1 defeat. Three days later, Argentina gave themselves a chance of qualification to the next round with a 3–1 victory over Northern Ireland with Corbatta from the penalty spot, Norberto Menendez and Ludovico Avio striking the goals. That, though, was only a prelude to perhaps the most humiliating scoreline in Argentina's World Cup history: needing a win to qualify for the next round, Argentina was comprehensively trounced 6–1 by Czechoslovakia on 15 June in Helsingborg, leaden footed and outclassed by the Europeans. Corbatta scored his third goal of the competition, but it was of little consolation, and the team returned home to vituperative press attention and public criticism that even damaged the reputation of the Peronist government, soon (albeit briefly) ousted from power.

At the 1962 World Cup in Chile, Argentina was coached by Juan Carlos Lorenzo early in what would be a long and illustrious career for the former Boca Juniors and Sampdoria forward, picked for his experience in Italy as a player and in Spain as a coach, as Argentina looked to modernize their approach following their 1958 humiliation. A physical, athletic approach to play was now grafted onto Argentina's tradition of technically gifted individuals who focused on dribbling and short passing, with fitness, discipline and running at speed emphasized by Lorenzo. The approach seemed promising in Argentina's first group game on 30 May in Rancagua, as they defeated Bulgaria 1–0, thanks to a goal from San Lorenzo star Héctor Facundo. Argentina's next game, against England, showed how far Lorenzo's team still had to go to compete with the leading European teams: the English dominated a game they won 3–1, with the only consolation for Argentina a late goal by José Sanfilippo. Argentina still had a chance at qualification heading into their final group game, on 6 June against the much-fancied Hungarians in Rancagua, but grinding out a 0–0 draw was not enough when England earned the point they needed the next day against Bulgaria, Argentina eliminated in third place in the group. Argentina headed back from their first World Cup in 24 years bitterly disappointed.

Domestically, the modernization of Argentinean soccer along the lines of a focus on defense and physical fitness continued apace, bringing Argentinean club teams great success internationally. But this did not translate into success at World Cup level for the national team, as 1962 was followed by controversial elimination at the 1966 World Cup in England at the quarterfinal stage. Argentina headed into the 1966 World Cup still managed by Juan Carlos Lorenzo, who had led them to a somewhat disappointing third place at the 1963 Copa América since the 1962 World Cup. They had, though, enjoyed success otherwise: at the 1964 Nations' Cup held to celebrate the 50th anniversary of Brazil's soccer confederation, Argentina dispatched Portugal 2–0, Brazil 3–0 and England 1–0, earning some revenge for their 1962 defeat. In World Cup qualifying the following year, Argentina cruised through unbeaten. Their last World Cup warm-up game, though, did offer a warning, as Argentina lost 3–0 to Italy in Turin. Lorenzo's squad for the 1966 World Cup included only five survivors from the 1962 competition.

For Argentina's opening group game against Spain, Lorenzo selected one survivor from 1962, Antonio Rattín, as his captain. Rattín was a tall and elegant halfback who had led Boca Juniors to three successive Argentinean championships heading into the competition. In a physical contest at Villa Park in Birmingham on 13 July, Argentina opened the scoring through the prolific River Plate striker Luis Artime in the 65th minute, Pirri equalizing for Spain six minutes later, with Artime then grabbing a winner for Argentina in the 79th minute. Argentina's creative force was Erminio Onega, his incisive passing carving apart Spain throughout the game. Three days later, on 16 July, Argentina faced West Germany at Villa Park, with Onega drawing considerable attention in a goal-less draw, while a cynical streak to Argentina's play was manifested most brutally in the 65th minute, Rafael Albrecht sent off by Yugoslavian referee Konstantin Zecevic for the second of two blatant and aggressive fouls after kneeing Wolfgang Weber. Albrecht's dismissal drew vehement protests from his teammates, and following the game, both Albrecht and Argentina were warned that any repetition of the incident would result in further action. Argentina's final group game passed without major incident, a 2–0 over Switzerland at Hillsborough Stadium in Sheffield, the goals coming from Artime in the 53rd minute and Onega in the 81st minute.

In the quarterfinals, Argentina was drawn to face hosts England at Wembley Stadium, in a game still vividly remembered in both countries decades on and that would immediately disrupt South American and European relations in world soccer. The match began sloppily in front of a partisan home crowd numbering 90,584, with aggressive play from both teams, neither team establishing any rhythm with midfielders and defenders pressing and closing down at an intense, uncompromising pace. In the 35th minute, the game erupted, with Argentinean captain Antonio Rattín sent off by West German referee Rudolf Kreitlein. The German referee had infuriated Argentina up to that point, with a series of questionable decisions awarded to England and Jorge Solari booked for dissent by the referee before Rattín's dismissal. Rattín, who had already been cautioned for a foul on Charlton, was sent off for apparent dissent against Kreitlein, though the German admitted the next day that he did not speak Spanish (and nor did Rattín speak German). Argentina's furious reaction delayed the game for seven minutes, with several players accosting the referee and the training staff entering the field of play. Despite being reduced to 10 men, Argentina was not overrun by the English, with the incisive Onega continuing to pull strings that England could barely contain in midfield. The first and final goal of the game finally came in the 78th minute, when Argentina allowed space wide on the left for Martin Peters to drift in a left-footed cross to the near post, English forward Geoff Hurst losing his defender and flicking the ball over Argentina's Antonio Roma into the far corner of the net. Argentina created little after that, losing 1–0 in acrimonious circumstances, with the referee again surrounded by Argentinean players and staff following the final whistle.

South American pride had already been dented and suspicions of European bias in the World Cup's refereeing raised by Brazil's early exit, and the manner of Argentina's departure stoked further accusations. In contrast, England's coach Alf Ramsey branded Argentina "animals" in a television interview after the game. Argentina, though defeated, returned to a presidential welcome. Politics played a role in the heightened tension surrounding the game, with Britain's victory in the Malvinas War still bitterly fresh, and one Buenos Aires newspaper reported the result with the comment that "First they stole the Malvinas from us, and now the World Cup." FIFA, though, led by their English president Sir Stanley Rous, saw the incident very differently: the Argentinean Football Association was fined the maximum amount allowed in its statutes, 1,000 Swiss francs; Rattín was suspended for the next four international games; Roberto Ferreira was suspended for his next three international games; Erminio Onega, accused of having spat in the face of a FIFA official, was also suspended for his next three international games; and Argentina's entry into the 1970 World Cup would only be allowed if "certain assurances are given as to the conduct of the team officials and players."

Despite the controversy, Argentina was allowed to enter the 1970 World Cup qualifying competition. It was, however, a disastrous effort, resulting in Argentina's first, and to date only, failure to qualify for the World Cup (having previously withdrawn from the 1938, 1950 and 1954 World Cups). Since the 1966 World Cup, Argentina had finished a respectable second at the 1967 Copa América, losing to Uruguay 1–0 in the final, but had then struggled in a series of friendlies and exhibition trophy games, winning only 4 of 16 games from the beginning of 1968 until the start of World Cup qualifying in July 1969. That led to a change in coach for the qualifiers, with the legendary former Argentinean star player Adolfo Pedernera taking over from Humberto Maschio. It was to no avail: Argentina slumped to defeats in its first two games, away against Bolivia in La Paz and away against Peru in Lima. A 1–0 win in Buenos Aires on 24 August revived Argentina's hopes, but failure to beat Peru with a 1–1 tie in Buenos Aires a week later resulted in Argentina's elimination from contention to qualify for the World Cup in Mexico.

Results had improved for Argentina by the time of qualification for the 1974 World Cup, to be held in West Germany, began in September 1973. Coached by former River Plate and Juventus star Omar Sívori, Argentina began their qualifying campaign with a 4–0 win at home to Bolivia in Buenos Aires, followed by a tie away in Asunción against Paraguay. Qualification for the 1974 World Cup was secured with further wins over Bolivia in La Paz and over Paraguay in Buenos Aires. The Paraguay game would, though, be Sívori's last in charge of Argentina, as a dispute with the Argentinean Football Federation led to his departure only weeks later. In his place, Vladislao Cap, an Argentinean of Polish and Hungarian extraction who had starred for Racing Club and River Plate in the 1960s, was appointed alongside José Varacka. Warm-up games in May 1974 saw Argentina defeat Romania and France, draw with England and lose to the Netherlands, who would prove to be the outstanding force of the World Cup. Argentina was drawn into group four, along with 1970 World Cup finalists Italy, a talented Polish team and little known Haiti. Argentina's squad for the tournament featured only one player who had previously appeared at a World Cup finals tournament, veteran 31-year-old defender Roberto Perfumo, selected as captain. There was, though, young talent in the 19-year-old forward Mario Kempes, with a remarkable goal-scoring record in the Argentinean league, and the promising 24-year-old goalkeeper Ubaldo Fillol.

Argentina's first group game was in Stuttgart on 15 June against Poland, beginning in disastrous fashion when Argentinean goalkeeper Daniel Carnevali dropped a corner kick to the feet of brilliant Polish striker Grzegorz Lato, who swept the ball into the empty net in just the seventh minute. Argentina was unable to contain a speedy Polish attack only one minute later, Andrzej Szarmach doubling the Polish lead by racing into a hole at the Argentinean defense and finishing with aplomb. Argentina fought their way back into the game in the 60th minute, Kempes setting up Ramón Heredia who finished with a sublime curling shot over Jan Tomaszewski in the Polish goal. But only two minutes later, comically poor distribution by Carnevali gave Lato an easy chance to finish and make it 3–1, the Polish striker making no mistake for his second goal of the game. Carlos Babington pulled one back for Argentina four minutes later, but there would be no equalizer and a 3–2 defeat for Argentina to open their campaign.

Argentina's second game came on 19 June against an experienced but aging Italian side. A tight back-and-forth game was illuminated in the 19th minute by a fantastic goal from René Houseman, the 21-year-old Huracán winger striking a left-footed shot into the top corner past Dino Zoff. Italy ratcheted up the pressure and, in the 35th minute, scored a fortunate equalizer when Italian midfielder Romeo Benetti chested a ball toward the Argentinean goal that was deflected into the net by Perfumo for an own goal. Zoff's acrobatics kept the score level in the second half, saving a superb drive from outside the area by Ruben Ayala, Argentina's outstanding player alongside Carlos Babington. Italy, after introducing substitute Franco Causio in the 66th minute, had the better of the chances, but the game ended 1–1. This meant that heading into the final group game, Argentina knew they would need Poland to defeat Italy and that they'd need to improve their goal differential by enough to qualify ahead of Italy on that tiebreaker, both games kicking off at the same time. Argentina faced Haiti, already eliminated, having lost both games and having conceded ten goals while scoring only one in the process. It did not take Argentina long to take command of the game, Héctor Yazalde scoring in the 15th minute, René Houseman finishing in the 18th minute and Ruben Ayala making it 3–0 10 minutes after halftime. Emmanuel Sanon pulled one back for Haiti in the 63rd minute, but Yazalde scored his second of the game five minutes later to wrap up a 4–1 win. It proved to be enough for Argentina to qualify for the next round and eliminate Italy, who fell 2–1 to group winners Poland.

The second round divided the eight remaining teams into two groups of four teams. Argentina was drawn with defending World Cup champions Brazil, hosts West Germany and a supremely talented Dutch team. Argentina faced the Netherlands first, on 26 June in Gelsenkirchen. From kickoff, it became clear Argentina was no match for the Dutch in midfield, allowing Johan Cruyff far too much time and space to orchestrate play: it was just 10 minutes until Cruyff ran onto a through ball, dinked the ball around Carnevali in the Argentinean goal and knocked it into the empty net. So one-sided was the contest that it was a surprise it took the Netherlands another 15 minutes to score, the ball constantly brought with menace to the edge of the Argentinean penalty area. Ruud Krol scored the second, slamming the ball in from 20 yards out after a goalmouth scramble following a corner. The third Dutch goal came from a back-post header by Johnny Rep in the 73rd minute, and Cruyff rubbed salt into Argentina's wounds with a fourth unanswered goal in the last minute, a right-footed volley driven low past Carnevali. A humiliating result for Argentina showed how far they still had to go to match the best in the world.

Four days later, Argentina faced Brazil, who, while no longer the force they had been as World Cup winners in 1970, still featured the likes of Jairzinho and Rivelino. Brazil took the lead in the 32nd minute, a 25-yard strike from Rivelino that Carnevali could only get his fingertip on as it drove into the bottom corner of his goal. Argentina equalized only three minutes later, though, a 25-yard free kick from Miguel Brindisi— captain in the absence of Perfumo—striking the underside of the crossbar into the goal. A Brazilian winner came in the 49th minute, lax Argentinean defending allowing an unmarked Jairzinho to head home yards from goal. The result eliminated Argentina from contention, rendering their final game, a 1–1 tie with East Germany with a third goal of the competition scored by René Houseman, meaningless.

Argentina was awarded the right to host the 1978 World Cup by FIFA back in 1964, and it was to be the first time the competition was held in South America since Chile in 1962. Political conditions in Argentina—ruled by a military junta accused of gross human-rights violations—meant that controversy swirled around the world ahead of the competition, with both ethical concerns and questions about the safety of teams traveling to the tournament raised. Infrastructure delays and ballooning costs only exacerbated calls in Western Europe for the tournament to be moved with threats of a boycott raised, vehemently resisted in South America. The World Cup, though, went ahead in Argentina, the junta investing a huge amount of effort in an attempt to complete the necessary infrastructure and purchase international credibility with the competition.

On the field, Argentina's coach César Luis Menotti had spent four years trying to build a team capable of challenging for the World Cup, following the glaring deficiencies in Argentina's abilities illustrated all too vividly at the 1974 tournament. Positive results did not come immediately: an early Copa América exit in 1975 followed with two defeats to Brazil, with mixed friendly results following. Results began to turn in Menotti's favor in the year ahead of the World Cup, with automatic qualification meaning friendly games would be the country's only preparation, securing 9 wins in their final 11 games from May 1977 onward. Menotti had built a team vastly different from the core that had played in 1974, with the only holdovers Ubaldo Fillol, Rubén Galván, René Houseman and Mario Kempes. All of Menotti's selections, bar Kempes (now starring as a prolific goal scorer for Valencia in Spain), were based domestically in Argentina, with a long training camp and series of friendlies familiarizing themselves. Selected as captain was the imperious Daniel Passarella, a central defender with a goal-scoring knack roaming forward in aggressive fashion, a star at River Plate. Many who would later ply their trade in Europe, such as Osvaldo Ardiles, Ricardo Villa and Alberto Tarantini, made up a youthful, gifted core of the team. One gifted young player who wasn't included, however, was Diego Maradona, who would have to wait four years to make his World Cup debut.

Argentina was drawn in group one with three European heavyweights: Italy, France and Hungary. Their first game was against Hungary, not the force they had been in the 1950s but a dangerous opponent nonetheless. At El Monumental stadium in Buenos Aires, a partisan crowd of over 70,000 in attendance waved thousands of flags and showered the stadium with confetti and streamers ahead of kickoff, roaring their approval as the team acknowledged them. Yet Hungary shocked the home team by taking an early lead, Károly Csapó scoring after just 10 minutes, following a series of rough tackles early on that had thrown Argentina from establishing any rhythm. Zombori's driven shot, Hungary's first of the game, was only parried by Argentina's goalkeeper Ubaldo Fillol into the path of the onrushing Csapó, who hit it first time into the roof of Argentina's net. It only took five minutes for Argentina to level the score, after a goalkeeping error by Hungary's Sándor Gujdár, who spilled a free kick driven straight at him from Kempes right at Leopoldo Luque's feet, the Argentinean making no mistake from a few yards out. Argentina dominated possession, attacking patiently and relentlessly, while Hungary looked to steal a goal on the break, continuing to be aggressive in their challenges with Tibor Nyilasi and András Törőcsik both cautioned by the referee. It took until the 83rd minute, though, for Argentina to break through the Hungarian defense, Gallego sending a hopeful ball upfield that bounced to the substitute Daniel Bertoni, who poked it in for the winning goal and a final score of

Argentina 2–1 Hungary. That was not the end of the action, however, as the Hungarians flew in with increasingly violent tackles, Törőcsik sent off in the 88th minute and Nyilasi one minute later for receiving second cautions.

Argentina faced France next on 6 June, the Europeans having opened their campaign with a 2–1 defeat to Italy, the home nation again playing at El Monumental. A talented French team led by a young Michel Platini came out with far more attacking intent than the Hungarians in the previous game, and it took 45 minutes for Argentina to break the deadlock (Kempes had struck the post with a fierce drive three minutes earlier) and at that in controversial circumstances: a driving run into the penalty area by Kempes saw his shot strike the hand of French defender and captain Marius Trésor, a seemingly unintentional handball that referee Jean Dubach of Switzerland deemed worthy of a penalty awarded to Argentina to considerable French protest. Daniel Passarella buried the penalty to give Argentina a lead at halftime. The French came back strong in the second half and made it 1–1 in the 60th minute, Bernard Lacombe lofting a shot over Fillol onto the crossbar, the rebound falling neatly to Platini, who easily steered it in. The winning goal for Argentina came in the 73rd minute, a move starting in Argentina's half, ending with a magnificent individual strike by Luque from 25 yards, who flicked the ball up to himself and then struck it sweetly in, no Frenchman having challenged Argentina during the entire attack. Further French chances ensued, but Argentina held on to qualify to the next round and eliminate the French. The final game between Italy and Argentina would only determine who topped the group, both teams having already qualified, Italy winning 1–0 by a 67th-minute goal from Roberto Bettega.

The second-round group stage paired the eight remaining teams into two groups of four. In group A, Argentina was joined by 1970 World Cup winners Brazil along with Poland and Peru. Poland was the first opponent for Argentina on 14 June in Rosario, in a smaller and far more compact venue than El Monumental in Buenos Aires, the raucous home crowd practically breathing onto the pitch. It was in this game Kempes truly found his stride, heading in his first goal of the competition in the 12th minute from a deep cross by Bertoni. He struck again in the 71st minute, poaching in the penalty area with style after a superb run from Ardiles half the length of the pitch had carved open the Polish defense. Argentina next faced Brazil, who had defeated Peru 3–0 in their opening game, leaving the two the favorites to claim the winning spot in the group and a place in the World Cup final. Stalemate ensued with a 0–0 tie. In the final group game, Argentina had the advantage of playing Peru—who had lost to Poland in their second game—later in the day on 21 June than Brazil's game against Poland, thus knowing exactly what they'd need to do to qualify. Brazil defeated Poland 3–1, which meant Argentina would have to defeat Peru by a margin of at least four goals. This they did, Peru putting up little fight in a crushing 6–0 Argentinean win, Kempes and Luque both netting two goals each with Tarantini and Houseman scoring the others.

On 25 June, Argentina played in their second World Cup final, this time with a considerable home-field advantage, in front of a vibrant and baying crowd of over 70,000 at El Monumental in Buenos Aires. Their opponents, the Netherlands, were playing in their second consecutive World Cup final, and Argentina vividly recalled that the Dutch had put them to the sword four years earlier in the preliminary rounds, though they would not this time face the maestro of that defeat, Johan Cruyff, who had not traveled to Argentina. Ardiles, who had missed the previous game against Peru, returned to the lineup, a mercurial addition that the Dutch would have trouble containing. The start of the game was controversial and almost farcical, Argentina making the Netherlands wait minutes before taking the field, and the game then a subject of further gamesmanship as the Dutch complained about the choice of ball and then a further delay over an Argentinean complaint about a bandage worn by René van de Kerkhof. Once underway, the pettiness seemed to continue with a game pockmarked by fouls, though Johnny Rep almost broke the deadlock for the Dutch with a fierce header just wide within 10 minutes. Ardiles and Bertoni continued to combine well, the Dutch captain Ruud Krol booked for a crude challenge on the latter after a driving run forward in the 15th minute. The game began to open up, Passarella missing a fine chance with a blast over the bar for Argentina and Fillol making a superb save for Argentina from Rep to keep the scores level. In the 35th minute, the breakthrough for Argentina came as Ardiles broke forward and fed Luque on the edge of the Dutch penalty area, the ball poked over to Kempes who surged past two Dutch defenders and slid the ball underneath Jan Jongbloed for his fifth of the World Cup. Passarella nearly doubled Argentina's advantage before halftime, a header from a free kick directed into Jongbloed's arms, but the Dutch came straight back, Rensenbrink denied at close range by a sliding kick save from Fillol. The Dutch began the second half with urgency, Ardiles in the midfield tiring, giving the ball away repeatedly and replaced in the 65th minute by Omar Larrosa. Houseman then replaced Ortiz in the 74th minute. Argentina was steadied by Passarella's leadership from the back, Luque nearly doubling Argentina's lead on a breakaway, but the Dutch continued to press hard, quieting the home crowd, and found an equalizer in the 82nd minute: a dreadful clearance from Tarantino from the left-back position set up a Dutch attack, René van de Kerkhof picking out substitute Dick Nanninga for a free header at the back post buried into the Argentinean goal. That took the game to extra time, Argentina becoming increasingly ragged at the back. The final whistle and the start of extra time allowed Argentina to reorganize, play tightening up as both teams tired. Argentina took the lead deep into the first period of extra time, Bertoni feeding Kempes, who bullishly drove his way into the Dutch penalty area past two defenders and the goalkeeper, who could only deflect the ball back into Kempes's path, finishing from yards out. Argentina now overran a Dutch team pushing forward, Luque missing a one-on-one with goalkeeper with eight minutes left. Just three minutes later, Argentina sealed their victory as Bertoni and Kempes again combined, the latter's bursting run ending with the ball bobbling to Bertoni, who slid the ball into the net. Argentina's 3–1 victory made the South Americans world champions for the first time.

In the run-up to the 1982 World Cup, Menotti faced both the challenge and the opportunity of integrating the great young Diego Maradona into his World Cup–winning team, a process that began disappointingly for the senior team with a first-round exit at the 1979 Copa América but success at the FIFA World Youth Championship, a Maradona-led team coached by Menotti taking the title. As world champions, Argentina did not have to qualify for the 1986 World Cup to be held in Mexico, instead playing a series of friendly results that suggested Menotti had not found a winning formula despite the inclusion of Maradona, as Argentina won just two of its last seven friendlies heading into the World Cup. Half of Menotti's final 22 to travel to Mexico had been part of the 1978 squad, most notably the core of the side in Kempes, Passarella, Bertoni and Ardiles retained, though Kempes's striking foil, Luque, was not included. The 21-year-old Maradona, his tremendous dribbling, passing and finishing increasingly evident, was naturally selected to make his World Cup debut. Argentina was placed into group three, a seemingly weak group, containing a young Belgian team, Hungary and El Salvador.

In Barcelona on 13 June, Argentina faced Belgium in Barcelona, the opening game of the World Cup. The deep-lying Belgians contained the South Americans with surprising ease, Argentina lacking the spark and Maradona surprisingly unable to provide it, apart from a free kick that struck the crossbar. Belgium, in fact, created more chances in the first half. The lone goal of the game instead came, to the shock of the defending world champions, for Belgium, a 62nd-minute strike by Erwin Vandenbergh, left completely alone by the Argentinean defense on a counterattack. Criticism in the Argentinean press following the defeat was intense: questions were raised about Maradona's deep role and even whether defeat in the recent Malvinas War had weighed on the team's morale. In Alicante five days later, Argentina's World Cup campaign got back on track with a 4–1 defeat of Hungary, who themselves had defeated El Salvador 10–1 in their opening game. The scoring began with Bertoni sweeping in a cross from close range at the back post, but this game was truly the Maradona show: he scored his first World Cup goal in the 28th minute, heading in from close range after a deflected shot, and doubled his tally in the 58th minute, a fantastic left-footed drive finding a gap at the near post from 15 yards out. Just three minutes later, Ardiles added a fourth, with Hungary scoring a consolation goal in the 76th minute. On 23 June, in Alicante, Argentina knew that a victory over an extremely weak El Salvador team would secure their passage into the next round, and they took the lead 22 minutes in when Gabriel Calderon was dragged down in the El Salvadorian penalty area, Passarella driving home the penalty down the middle of the goal. Argentina's victory was confirmed in the 54th minute with a delightful individual goal from Daniel Bertoni, drifting in from the right touchline past three defenders before curling the ball in from 20 yards out with his left foot.

The second-round group stage paired Argentina with World Cup heavyweights Italy and Brazil. The first game saw Argentina take on Italy in Barcelona on 29 June. The Italian game plan was cynical and clear: Claudio Gentile would kick, push and shove Maradona out of the game, the Italian repeatedly pulling and tripping the young Argentinean on almost every dribble, illegally hounding him even off the ball. The Romanian referee, Nicolae Rainea, disgracefully only cautioned Gentile once. Argentina's defensive frailties were more fairly exposed by the Italians in the second half, a sweeping Italian move seeing Giancarlo Antognoni slip the ball to Marco Tardelli, who beat Fillol in the Argentina goal from a tight angle 15 yards out in the 57th minute. Italian goalkeeper Dino Zoff denied Passarella an equalizer with a header a few minutes later, but Italy then exposed Argentina on the counterattack with 67 minutes gone, a miss by Paolo Rossi resulting in Antonio Cabrini finding space to give Italy a

2–0 lead. Passarella did pull one back for Argentina in the 83rd minute, striking a free kick from 25 yards into the goal before Italy had readied their defense, Rainea controversially allowing the goal to stand. But it was not enough for Argentina, with a 2–1 defeat meaning their final second-round group game against Brazil in Barcelona on 2 July was a must-win. Brazil took an early lead through their midfield maestro Zico after only 11 minutes had elapsed, but the game remained even throughout the first half, both teams cagily trying to carve out chances without risking too much. Argentina's pressing in the second half did not result in a goal, forward Ramon Diaz—who had come on as a substitute for a tired-looking Kempes—unable to finish half-chances. Brazil hammered the nails into Argentina's coffin in the 66th and 75th minute, with goals from Serginho and Júnior respectively, a late goal from Diaz not enough for the beaten and eliminated defending world champions. A frustrated Maradona was sent off in the 85th minute for a petulant kick, and Argentina went home in disgrace.

Argentina's defeat demanded an overhaul of the team in time for the 1986 World Cup in Mexico: the 1978 veterans were phased out and a younger team built around Maradona, going from strength to strength as a star in Europe for Barcelona and Napoli between World Cups. Menotti also departed as coach, replaced by Carlos Bilardo, who was successfully coaching Estudiantes in the Argentinean league, the team he had starred for in the 1960s. Bilardo was known for his willingness to embrace a certain cynicism in his approach as both a player and a coach, a departure for the elegance preferred by Menotti. Following his appointment in 1983, Bilardo flew to Spain and offered Maradona the national-team captaincy, ensconcing Maradona as the fulcrum of the team. Maradona was given a separate training regimen, and Bilardo was able to convince the rest of the team to build their play to support the world's best player and embrace his special status. Bilardo would work to ensure that Maradona was protected on the field so that a repetition of Gentile's treatment of the Argentinean at the 1982 World Cup would not be repeated. Qualification for the 1986 World Cup took place in 1985, and Bilardo's team took care of business in straightforward fashion, winning their first four qualifying games and advancing to the finals in Mexico with ease.

Bilardo's 22-man squad for the 1986 World Cup finals included only 5 veterans from the 1982 team and only 5 players—including Passarella, appearing at his third World Cup—over the age of 30. Argentina was paired in the first-round group stage with defending World Cup champions Italy along with Bulgaria and South Korea. The Koreans were Argentina's first opponents in Mexico City at Estadio Olímpico Universitario, Maradona captaining the side and Nery Pumpido in goal for his first World Cup start. Passarella, though, missed the game with a late withdrawal due to a stomach virus. Argentina took little time to put the Koreans to the sword, Maradona immediately taking the charge with mazy, direct dribbling, winning a free kick that he took and resulted in an opening goal after only six minutes for Valdano. Burruchaga then struck the post from long range before Oscar Ruggeri made it two for Argentina, heading in from another free kick by Maradona. Valdano tapped in a third for Argentina a minute after halftime as Argentina coasted to victory, despite the Koreans pulling one back late on. Argentina now faced a tough test against Italy in Puebla. This time, Italy did not have Gentile to harass Maradona, Bagni instead assigned to try to restrict the world's best player. Italy took the lead early in the game in odd circumstances, Oscar

Garré curiously handling an innocuously bouncing ball just inside Argentina's penalty area, Altobelli scoring from the spot. Bagni could not contain Maradona, however, repeatedly bursting through the Italian defense and finding his reward in the 34th minute, flicking the ball with his left foot from an awkward angle past Galli in the Italian goal. The game ended 1–1, meaning Argentina knew that victory against Bulgaria in their final group game would win them the group, poor Bulgarian defending making this a straightforward task: Valdano scored the first after just three minutes, and Maradona set up the second with a run down the left byline that left a Bulgarian in his wake, picking out Burruchaga's head with a pinpoint cross to seal a 2–0 win for Argentina.

In the second round, for this World Cup a knockout stage, Argentina faced their rivals from across the Río de la Plata, Uruguay, in front of a compact crowd of 26,000 in Puebla. Maradona was in irresistible form, Uruguay entirely unable to contain his distribution or his dribbling, tight spaces turned into wide-open vistas for the Argentinean. Maradona set up Valdano for a diving header in the first half that the forward somehow sent wide, later striking the crossbar with a dipping 30-yard free kick, before the breakthrough finally came 42 minutes into the game, Maradona starting a move in midfield that saw the ball break to forward Pedro Pasculli eight yards out for an easy finish, the only goal of the game.

The result moved Argentina on for what immediately became a hotly anticipated clash with England, political overtones—just four years after the Malvinas War— seeping into the buildup to the game. In front of over 115,000 fans at the Azteca in Mexico City, the stage and the headlines were stolen by Maradona once more. The Argentinean maestro scored both goals, studies in contrast. The first came drenched in controversy: Maradona dribbled the ball past three English defenders on a driving run from the left flank, then played a pass to Jorge Valdano that was deflected backward by England's Steve Hodge and left him one-on-one with English goalkeeper Peter Shilton. The ball looping in the air, Maradona challenged Shilton for the ball and reached it first—with his fist. The offense went unnoticed by referee Ali Bennaceur, and Argentina took the lead thanks to what Maradona would later famously call the "hand of God." Maradona's second goal, just four minutes later, was wildly brilliant. Receiving the ball inside his own half, Maradona surged past almost every member of the England team with a mix of strength, pace and jinks before sliding the ball past Shilton for a goal considered one of the greatest of all time. Though England pulled one goal back, Maradona's superb and controversial display propelled Argentina to the semifinal stage.

In the last four, Argentina faced another European team, a talented Belgian 11. Once again, Maradona scored twice, and the Belgians had no reply. His first came after 51 minutes, finishing first time from a deft through ball by Jorge Burruchaga, and his second coming after another bewildering solo run, driving past four Belgian defenders before firing into the corner past Jean-Marie Pfaff. The 2–0 win pushed Argentina on to the World Cup final for the second time in eight years, there facing European opposition for the third straight game in the form of West Germany. Having seen Maradona tear apart England and Belgium, the West Germans set out to nullify Maradona by shadowing his every move, a strategic ploy that succeeded in keeping Maradona largely quiet early in the game—but opened up space for the rest of his team. With only 23 minutes gone, defender José Luis Brown gave Argentina the lead from a set piece, heading in Burruchaga's curling free kick into the top corner. The South Americans doubled their lead in the 56th minute, Hector Enrique slipping the ball through to Jorge Valdano, who found himself clean through on goal and calmly rolled the ball past Harald Schumacher in the German goal. With only 15 minutes remaining, however, the West Germans clawed themselves back into the game, Karl-Heinz Rummenigge finishing scrappily, and then tied the score from a corner in the 81st minute, thanks to a Rudi Völler header. Just as it appeared the momentum was with the Europeans, three minutes later, Maradona—fittingly enough—found a way to break the tie: surrounded in midfield, he flashed a pass through to Burruchaga, who slid the ball beyond Schumacher to make the score 3–2. Argentina had claimed a second World Cup title, thanks largely to Diego Maradona.

Four years later, at the 1990 World Cup in Italy, Argentina—once more led by Diego Maradona on the field and by Carlos Bilardo on the bench—reached the final again. But there was much less of the virtuous Maradona in this tournament. In the first round, Argentina's opponents in group B were comprised of Cameroon, Romania and the Soviet Union, a seemingly straightforward set of games. Opening the competition as defending champions on 8 June in Milan, in front of a crowd of over 70,000 at the San Siro, Argentina began with a surprising and disappointing 1–0 defeat to Cameroon. Most remarkable of all was that Argentina lost despite ending the game with 11 men on the field to Cameroon's 9: the African team hammered at Argentina with force and at times too much venom, resulting in the expulsions of both André Kana-Biyik in the 61st minute and Benjamin Massing 2 minutes from full-time. Cameroon's tough play largely nullified Maradona, isolated up front in the first half and only starting to come alive with the introduction of a talented newcomer to the team, gifted forward Claudio Caniggia, at halftime. Even with only 10 men to 11 in the 67th minute, though, Cameroon managed to break down a malfunctioning Argentina defense: a free kick floated into the penalty area was defended in cumbersome fashion, with a calamitous piece of goalkeeping by Nery Pumpido allowing François Omam-Biyik's seemingly innocuous header to sneak in. The disastrous result was soon ameliorated by a 2–0 win in Naples for Argentina over the Soviet Union, Maradona turning on the style in the city he had become a legend in for local club Napoli. It was not a performance without controversy, though: once again, Maradona was not spotted for handling the ball, this time on his own goal line, saving clearly with his arm from Oleg Kuznetsov's header. Argentina scored once in each half, through Pedro Troglio and Jorge Burruchaga, but it would be remembered for a terrible injury to Pumpido, who broke his leg and was replaced in goal by Sergio Goycochea—who would go on to become one of the stars of the tournament. Qualification to the next round was secured by Argentina against Romania, in Naples again, Pedro Monzón scoring in the 62nd minute for the South Americans, only for the Europeans to equalize 6 minutes later.

Argentina's failure to win had seemingly critical consequences: it meant a second-placed finish in the group behind Cameroon, thus setting up a tough tie against historic rivals Brazil in Turin. Early in the game, it seemed the Brazilians would be too strong for Argentina, forcing a string of fine saves from Goycochea, while Maradona hobbled from the hacks he had received in the tournament and fouled repeatedly again in this game. But Brazil came to regret profligacy in front of goal, and it was Maradona who provided the dagger: with only eight minutes and the score tied, he received the ball in the center circle, surrounded by yellow Brazilian jerseys. With a searing run that used all of his ability to stay low to the ground and twist past opponents, Maradona evaded the attempts of five Brazilians to challenge him, drawing enough attention to free Caniggia, to whom he slipped the ball: one-on-one with the goalkeeper, the blond, shaggy-haired forward pushed past Taffarel and finished in style to seal a remarkable win for Argentina.

Argentina's positive result over rivals Brazil moved Maradona's team on to play Yugoslavia in the next round, a country on the verge of cracking up politically but with a remarkable set of creative players on its team. Neither team, though, could find a breakthrough during the game in Florence, even though Argentina played with a man-up advantage for an hour, after the expulsion of Refik Šabanadžović after only 31 minutes for his second yellow card. Extra time could not break the deadlock, and the game went to a penalty shoot-out. Dragan Stojković struck the crossbar with Yugoslavia's first kick, while Argentina converted their first two through José Serrizuela and Jorge Burruchaga. There was shock when Maradona, of all people, missed Argentina's third kick, but the error was soon forgotten when Goycochea saved penalties from both Dragoljub Brnović and Faruk Hadžibegić to seal the tiebreaker.

Naples was again the location for Argentina's next game, against host nation Italy. Maradona, hero of Naples, tried to win support for his country over the Italians by appealing to civic over national pride, with mixed results. After 20 minutes, Argentina fell behind, a save from Goycochea falling to the feet of Salvatore Schillaci, who made no mistake from six yards out. As the game wore on, Argentina's pressure paid off, Italian nerves visible; in the 67th minute, Maradona drifted the ball wide to Julio Olarticoechea, who sent in a looping cross headed in by Caniggia, beating goalkeeper Walter Zenga to the ball. The scored tied after 90 minutes, Argentina headed to extra time again. The South Americans only stayed in the game thanks to a fantastic save by Goycochea, a stretching dive tipping over a brilliant 25-yard free kick by Roberto Baggio. It got little easier for Argentina with a red card shown to Ricardo Custi only 13 minutes into the added period, for his second caution. But despite several driving Italian attacks, Argentina's defense held firm. The first six penalties, three from each team, were converted successfully. Goycochea became the hero again, saving from both Roberto Donadoni and Aldo Serena's spot kicks, while Maradona this time scored, giving Argentina passage to a second successive World Cup final and leaving the Italian nation heartbroken.

Argentina's opponents in Rome had also reached their second successive World Cup final, with a rematch against West Germany watched by 74,000 fans at the grand Olympic Stadium. Critically, though, Argentina had to line up without arguably their best player of the tournament—not Maradona, this time, but forward Claudio Caniggia, one of four Argentineans suspended for yellow card accumulation earlier in the competition. Meanwhile, Maradona remained hobbled by injury, and Argentina's threadbare team resorted to base tactics in the absence of creative alternatives: a series of fouls, at times brutal, meant expulsions for both Pedro Monzón and Gustavo Dezotti, who became the first two men to receive red cards in any World Cup final, the former in the 65th minute and the latter in the 87th. It had only been two minutes before Dezotti's removal that West Germany finally took the lead and scored what proved to be the only goal of the game. It came predictably enough from a foul in the penalty area when Roberto Sensini took Rudi Völler down, though Argentina objected vociferously to the penalty call made by referee Edgardo Codesal Méndez of Mexico. Regardless, Andrea Brehme converted the kick, and there was little sympathy for Argentina after a defeat in a game in which they had contributed almost nothing creatively, a stricken Maradona notable this time only for his absence of involvement in the play.

Argentina's path to the next World Cup in the United States, under head coach Alfio Basile, proved to be lengthy. A very disappointing South American qualifying campaign saw Argentina finish second in their group, only winning three out of six games that included a pair of defeats to group victors Colombia—who thumped the Argentineans 5–0 in the final game of qualifying. That meant Argentina faced a play-off against Australia to secure a spot in the U.S., squeaking through after a 1–1 tie in Sydney was followed by a 1–0 win in Buenos Aires. An inauspicious route to the World Cup finals was marked by more controversy involving Diego Maradona, who had left Italy after a drug scandal involving cocaine, with his appearances for the national team labored when he returned for the play-off series against Australia. Despite this, a roster featuring Maradona, Caniggia—also returning after a drug scandal—midfield general Fernando Redondo and the dynamic young forward Gabriel Batistuta promised to be highly competitive, on paper at least.

Argentina began with an unexpected flying start, Maradona suddenly in fine physical condition. Near Boston, at Foxboro Stadium, Argentina dismantled Greece with imperious ease, Batistuta notching a hat trick and Maradona the other goal in a 4–0 win. Again at Foxboro, Argentina started poorly four days later against a powerful Nigerian team, conceding early to a goal from Samson Siasia, beating Argentina's goalkeeper, Luis Islas, who had strayed far from his line. But Caniggia soon equalized in the 21st minute, crashing in the rebound from a 30-yard free kick by Batistuta saved by Nigerian goalkeeper Peter Rufai. The last goal of the game, and the winner, came only seven minutes later after another Nigerian foul in midfield; Maradona cheekily played a quick through ball to Caniggia, who speared in toward the goal and curled his shot into the far post past Rufai.

Argentina appeared to be on a roll, but the tournament suddenly turned into a disaster when, before the South Americans' next game against Bulgaria, Maradona was announced to have failed a drug test, found positive for use of ephedrine, a banned substance. The news destroyed morale in the Argentinean team, who—without Maradona—crashed to a 2–0 defeat to the Bulgarians in Dallas at the Cotton Bowl. Only hours after the loss, Maradona's tournament was over, banished by FIFA. Argentina's two wins still saw them progress to the next round as one of the best third-place losers in the first-round stage, drawn to face Romania at the Rose Bowl in Los Angeles that—even without the presence of Maradona, who had played his last World Cup game—would prove to be one of the games of the tournament. A rollercoaster matchup saw Ilie Dumitrescu give Romania the lead after 11 minutes, only for Caniggia to tie the scores 5 minutes later from the penalty spot. A mere 2 minutes passed before Dumitrescu restored Romania's lead, and they found a two-goal cushion in the 58th minute through Gheorghe Hagi. Abel Balbo threatened an Argentinean resurgence, scoring in the 75th minute, but without Maradona, there was to be no more magic for Argentina, and their tournament—and an era under Diego's inspiration that stretched back over a decade—was over.

Without Maradona, Argentina's qualification campaign for the 1998 World Cup in France was built around his heir apparent, the team's new midfield maestro, Ariel Ortega. Wearing Diego's number 10 jersey, he began qualifying by scoring twice in a 3–1 win over Bolivia and helped lead Argentina to top South American qualifying, with only 2 losses in 16 games, fired also by goals from lethal strike pair Gabriel Batistuta and Hernán Crespo. The former had initially been left out in qualifying by Argentina's new coach, 1978 World Cup–winning captain Daniel Passarella, but found a rich vein of form upon his return, helping the South Americans steady the ship after a nervous pair of games against Ecuador (a 2–0 defeat) and Peru (a 0–0 tie). In France, Argentina faced Japan, Croatia and Jamaica in group H, in what looked like a good opportunity for Passarella's men to top the pool during the first-round stage.

Argentina began with a 1–0 win over the Japanese in Toulouse, but it was a far-from-sprightly display, the winner coming following a fortuitous deflection falling to Batistuta, who finished with aplomb. "Bati-goal," as the forward was known, later hit the post twice—once wrongly called for offside—though Japan unsettled Argentina's defense as much as the South Americans attacked the Asian team's defense. A week later in Paris, at the Parc des Princes, Argentina hit form in fantastic style against an experienced Jamaican team: Ortega scored twice, while Batistuta completed a hat trick in only 10 minutes between the 73rd and 83rd minutes, with Jamaica having been reduced to 10 men for half the game following the dismissal of Darryl Powell. Batistuta completed his hat trick after Ortega had been fouled in the box, Jamaica unable to find any way to contain the creative fulcrum of Argentina's team.

A third consecutive win, and passage to the next round, was obtained by Passarella's men with a win over Croatia in Bordeaux on 26 June. Argentina found the only breakthrough of the game thanks to a chipped pass by Ortega that received a slight deflection before landing at the feet of Mauricio Pineda, with the fullback rewarded for a surging run as he slammed the ball home. The 1–0 win saw Argentina advance to the second round as group winners, earning a matchup with old foes England in Saint-Étienne on 30 June, with the ghosts of the infamous games between the two nations in 1966 and 1986 helping build up the buzz before kickoff. Immediately after the game started, it was clear this would also be a memorable game: only five minutes in, England goalkeeper David Seaman brought down Argentina's captain Diego Simeone in the penalty area, Gabriel Batistuta converting the resulting penalty kick. Not even four minutes had passed before referee Kim Milton Nielson had awarded England a penalty as well, Michael Owen tumbling easily under contact from Roberto Ayala. England captain Alan Shearer scored past Carlos Roa to tie the scores. The momentum swung to England sharply when David Beckham fed Michael Owen through an Argentina defense suddenly revealed as plodding, the England forward streaking away to score.

Yet Argentina scored again, critically, just before halftime. From a free kick 25 yards out, midfield playmaker Juan Sebastián Verón cleverly fed a short, deceptive through ball to Javier Zanetti, who punched his left-footed shot past Seaman from 10 yards out. Argentina seemed to have the game sealed shortly after halftime, when David Beckham was given a red card following provocation by Diego Simeone, but Ortega had suddenly disappeared in contrast to his performances earlier in the competition, and England's stout defense kept Argentina at bay. Indeed, England might have stolen but for Sol Campbell's injury-time header being ruled out for an infringement by Shearer. Batistuta came closest for Argentina, yet neither team could find the net during the rest of normal or extra time, and penalties would decide the winning team. That winner would be Argentina: though Crespo had his shot saved by Seaman, Sergio Berti, Verón, Marcelo Gallardo and Roberto Ayala all converted their penalties, while Paul Ince and David Batty both had their shots saved by Carlos Roa.

Advancing once again to the last eight in the World Cup finals, Argentina next faced the Netherlands in Marseille on 4 July in what would prove to be a pulsating affair, a rematch of the 1978 World Cup final. Twelve minutes had passed when Argentina's midfield lackadaisically allowed Ronald de Boer to coast through and, via a neat header from Denis Bergkamp, set up Patrick Kluivert to give the Dutch the lead. Verón, though, quickly conjured up an equalizer for Argentina within five minutes, slicing a low through ball to forward Claudio Lopez, who composed himself for what seemed an age before sliding his strike underneath the goalkeeper. A game of considerable skill was also marked by plenty of foul play, with eight cards issued, including reds for the Netherlands' Arthur Numan in the 76th minute and Ortega in the 87th minute—the Argentinean had been booked for diving in the penalty area and reacted by headbutting Dutch goalkeeper Edwin van der Sar, earning an immediate second yellow and an expulsion. Ortega's sending off marked Argentina's failure to take advantage of an extra man for 11 minutes, and it would cost the South Americans dearly: only 2 minutes later, and on the cusp of full-time, Bergkamp carved a winner out of a half-chance by brilliantly controlling a long pass, wrong-footing Ayala with a sharp turn and rifling past Roa, all in one sumptuous motion. There was no time for Argentina to reply. Elimination led to the resignation of head coach Daniel Passarella the next day.

For the second consecutive cycle, Argentina topped South American qualifying for the 2002 World Cup—and by some distance. Argentina won 13 of 18 games played, only losing 1, finishing 12 points ahead of Ecuador in second place and 13 ahead of Brazil in third. Passarella's replacement, Marcelo Bielsa, instituted a fluid, attacking style of play down the flanks with Verón, Batistuta and Crespo in devastating form throughout the qualifying campaign. Hopes were thus high for Argentina heading into the World Cup finals held in South Korea and Japan, with Argentina placed in group F alongside Sweden, England and Nigeria—a pool quickly termed the "Group of Death."

In Kashima, Argentina began with a 1–0 win over Nigeria. Dominating possession, with Verón both captaining the team and pulling the strings from midfield, Argentina could have scored multiple goals but settled for the win thanks to a far-post header by Batistuta from a Verón corner. Argentina seemed well placed to mount a strong campaign, but against England in Sapporo, Bielsa's men surrendered the initiative, appearing tired and unable to control the ball. England threatened early, with Michael Owen hitting the post, and the only goal of the game came when Owen was taken down in the penalty area by Mauricio Pochettino, David Beckham scoring the penalty. Argentina's pressure in the second half drew few dividends, with England continuing to enjoy the clearer chances, Bielsa surprisingly having substituted Verón at halftime. The result left Argentina knowing a win over Sweden in the concluding game in Miyagi, Japan, would almost certainly be a necessity. Argentina came out flying, piling enormous pressure on a defensive Sweden team—but by halftime, the scores remained level, despite several good chances created for Batistuta in the air. As Argentina became increasingly nervous in the second half, needing a goal, the Swedes struck through Anders Svensson, curling in a 30-yard free kick. An equalizer came far too late for Bielsa's team, Ortega fouled for a penalty kick: though the penalty was missed, Crespo drove in the rebound. It was too little, too late, though, and Argentina could only think about what might have been given the enormous promise coming into the tournament. Bielsa's men had only scored two goals in three games, despite a surfeit of attacking intent and talent.

Bielsa remained as Argentina's coach until 2004, winning a gold medal that year at the Olympic Games in Athens, but was replaced by José Pékerman during the 2006 World Cup qualification cycle. Pékerman had successfully coached Argentina at the U-20 level and was thus very familiar with many of the players on the senior team. Though results in qualifying were mixed for Argentina, passage to Germany for the 2006 World Cup was achieved in spectacular style with a 3–1 win over Brazil in Buenos Aires, the strings pulled brilliantly by the immensely talented midfielder Juan Román Riquelme, who scored one, Crespo also scoring twice. Crespo had struck up a fine forward partnership with Javier Saviola, and with Riquelme at playmaker, Argentina's precise passing promised much once again heading into the competition in Germany. Young stars such as Lionel Messi, Carlos Tévez and Javier Mascherano offered talent and bite in-depth.

Pékerman's team was drawn alongside the Netherlands, Côte d'Ivoire and Serbia and Montenegro in group C. Opening up against Côte d'Ivoire on 10 June in Hamburg, Argentina initially struggled to contain the African team, until Riquelme asserted control in the center of the field. Roberto Ayala struck the post with a header from a corner before Crespo gave Argentina the lead 24 minutes in, pouncing on a loose ball in predatory fashion from six yards out. Argentina scored again 14 minutes later, Riquelme slipping through an exquisite through ball for Saviola, who tucked it underneath the onrushing Ivorian goalkeeper, Jean-Jacques Tizié, into the net. That was enough for the win, though Argentina had to fend off fierce pressure from Côte d'Ivoire, who scored through Didier Drogba in the 82nd minute. Six days later, Argentina, against Serbia and Montenegro, put on a show rarely matched in the history of the World Cup. Maxi Rodriguez began the scoring after only six minutes, but it was Argentina's second goal, scored by Esteban Cambiasso, which would be endlessly replayed around the world: a flourishing, fantastic 24-pass combination ended with Cambiasso's finish. Argentina proved far from done, scoring four more—Rodriguez again, then Crespo, Tévez and Messi—for a 6–0 final score, a devastating illustration of what that combination of players could produce.

With both teams already through to the next round, Pékerman rested some of his key players for Argentina's final group game against the Netherlands. A 0–0 tie—Riquelme came closest to scoring, his free kick deflected onto the post—was good enough for Argentina to win the group and advance to face Mexico in the second round. That game took place in Leipzig on 24 June, 43,000 fans in attendance at Red Bull Arena for a pulsating affair. Only five minutes had passed when Mexico took the lead—Mario Mendez's free kick found the feet of a sliding Rafa Márquez, putting the ball past Roberto Abbondanzieri in the Argentinean goal. Argentina replied from a set piece a mere five minutes later; Riquelme swung in a corner attacked by Crespo, who just got his cleat to it and forced it into the goal. Crespo should have given Argentina the lead in the 23rd minute, but his flick over Mexican goalkeeper Oswaldo Sánchez drifted wide. Neither team could break the deadlock until extra time. The winner, when it came, was simply sublime: Argentina's Maxi Rodriguez struck a first-time volley from the far edge of the penalty area, sending the ball dipping and swirling into the top corner. It was a fine way for Argentina to seal a spot in the quarterfinals.

Argentina now faced the host nation, Germany, in the capital Berlin, 72,000 at the Olympic Stadium providing a partisan atmosphere. Much was expected of a matchup between the two most adventurous teams in the tournament to date, but in the end, it was a largely cagey affair. Argentina found a breakthrough in the 50th minute, Ayala powering home a towering header from a Riquelme corner. But only 10 minutes from full-time, the host nation leveled the score; Michael Ballack's cross was flicked onto the head of predatory forward Miroslav Klose, who nodded the ball in. Neither team came close to scoring again, and the winner was decided by a penalty shoot-out. Germany's finishing was far more clinical, scoring four out of four to claim the victory, Ayala and Cambiasso both having poor spot kicks saved by German goalkeeper Jens Lehmann. A hugely promising World Cup venture led by Pékerman petered out in frustrating fashion for Argentina.

Argentina began the South American qualification cycle for the 2010 World Cup led by head coach Alfio Basile, who had replaced Pékerman, but by the fall of 2008, Basile himself would be gone and replaced by Diego Maradona, who had little previous coaching experience. The change came after a series of disappointing results— Argentina won the first three games in the lengthy qualification process but then only claimed one victory in the next seven games, leading to Basile's dismissal. Maradona would rely on his authority as a national legend in lieu of actual coaching expertise, but he had plenty of talent at his disposal with the world's best player, Lionel Messi, alongside the elite world-class quality of forwards Gonzalo Higuaín, Carlos Tévez and Sergio Agüero (the latter actually married to Maradona's daughter). The ups and downs of Maradona's management were made apparent immediately; his first qualifier in charge was a 4–0 win over Venezuela, but his second was a disastrous 6–1 defeat to Bolivia, albeit the latter played in the altitude of La Paz. Argentina's shaky form continued, with defeats to Ecuador, Brazil and Paraguay coming to leave Argentina with a must-win game away against Uruguay in order to claim the fourth automatic South American qualifying spot. In Montevideo, Maradona's men were up to the task, a late goal from Mario Bolatti giving Argentina the victory and passage to South Africa.

In South Africa, Maradona looked to have a settled, talented lineup in place, with Javier Mascherano controlling Argentina defensively and Juan Sebastián Verón as the orchestrator from midfield. If Messi could find the form for Argentina he had for

Barcelona at club level, Maradona's supporters argued, the South Americans would be a contender for the World Cup. Argentina seemed to be helped by a favorable draw, placed in group B with Nigeria, Greece and South Korea. At Ellis Park in Johannesburg, Argentina began with what was almost a bang against Nigeria but ended as a 1–0 win that could have seen Maradona's selection score multiple times. In the event, Gabriel Heinze's diving header from a corner kick just six minutes into the game was the only score, Nigerian goalkeeper Vincent Enyeama making numerous smart stops to keep it to 1–0. Against South Korea, again in Johannesburg, though this time at the expansive Soccer City Stadium, the floodgates did open for Argentina, a 4–1 win fired by a hat trick for Gonzalo Higuaín, the first hat trick of the 2010 World Cup. The scoring was opened for Argentina by an own goal from Park Chu-Young, inadvertently slicing an attempted clearance from a free kick into his own net. Higuaín then notched up his hat trick with a downward header, a tap-in from two yards after Messi's shot had rebounded off the post and another close-range finish with his head. South Korea's only goal came from a worrying lapse in concentration, though, Martín Demichelis dwelling on the ball and allowing Lee Chung-Young to steal it away on the edge of the area. Already through to the next round, Maradona made multiple changes for Argentina's next game against Greece, resting multiple key starters. The South Americans still claimed a 2–0 win, though, Martín Demichelis and Martin Palermo both scoring late on, in the 77th and 89th minutes respectively.

Argentina's captain, Messi, was in fine creative form against Greece, a trend that Argentina would need to continue in the knockout stage, with Mexico the opponents in the last 16. Playing again at Soccer City Stadium, the Mexicans threatened first, Carlos Salcido's long-range drive striking the crossbar. Messi proved to be instrumental in Argentina's first goal, helping set up Tévez for a close-range finish. Argentina doubled the lead thanks to a terrible mistake by a Mexican defender, who inadvertently passed the ball to Higuaín right on the edge of the penalty area; the Argentinean forward found his fourth goal of the competition by rounding the goalkeeping and slotting home. A third goal came from Tévez, who unleashed an unstoppable 25-yard drive. Mexican pressure yielded one consolation goal, fired home by Chicharito, but Argentina progressed comfortably with a 3–1 win.

After four successive wins, Maradona appeared to have inspired Argentina to become serious contenders for the World Cup, but his lack of experience—and Argentina's defensive deficiencies—were to be cruelly exposed against Germany at the quarterfinal stage in Cape Town at Green Point Stadium. Four years ago, the Germans had eliminated Argentina at the same stage, and only three minutes in, the Europeans took charge once again when Thomas Müller flicked in a header. Argentina created little in response, Messi subdued, and as Maradona threw men forward in the second half, the Germans rapidly took advantage: Miroslav Klose tapped in a second 68 minutes in, Arne Friedrich scoring a third in the 89th minute, with Klose confirming the rout with a fourth goal, Argentina unable to reply. The result left Maradona devastated, and he was soon replaced as head coach by Sergio Batista. In 2011, Alejandro Sabella was appointed in place of Batista during the qualification cycle for the 2014 World Cup in Brazil, as Argentina looked to find an elusive third world crown almost three decades since the nation's last triumph in 1986.

Qualifying for the 2014 World Cup in Brazil saw Argentina matching the expectations of the pundits who predicted La Albiceleste would challenge for the trophy. Though things started off rather slow (one win, a draw and a loss in their first three games), Argentina didn't lose another match—competitive or friendly—until a 3–2 away defeat to Uruguay on the last day of qualifying. When the qualification process was over, Argentina showed just how dominant they could be on both sides of the ball, finishing with the second-best defensive record (their 15 allowed goals was second only to Colombia) to go along with the best attack (35 goals in 16 matches).

Placed into group F with Iran, Nigeria and Bosnia and Herzegovina, Argentina's campaign got off to a great start at the Estádio do Maracanã in Rio de Janeiro against Bosnia and Herzegovina when, in the third minute, Sead Kolašinac misplayed an Argentinean free kick into the back of his own net. Though the early goal set the Dragons back on their heels, the game wasn't decided until Messi delivered a clinical left-footed finish off the left post following a crafty give-and-go with Gonzalo Higuaín in the 65th minute. A goal in the 85th minute by Vedad Ibišević (Bosnia and Herzegovina's first-ever World Cup goal) made the final score 2–1. The second group game, played at Estádio Mineirão in Belo Horizonte, almost saw heartbreak for the Argentinean fans as Iran put together one of the better defensive matches of the tournament and almost won outright when they came out of their defensive shell in the second half and attacked the flanks of the Argentinean defense. Had it not been for the fingers of Sergio Romero and a controversial non-call in the Argentinean box, Iran may have pulled off one of the biggest World Cup upsets. Instead, Messi proved again why he is one of the world's greatest players when, in the 91st minute, he turned a simple return pass at the top right corner of the Iranian box into one of the more memorable goals of the tournament: a beautifully curled left-footed shot into the side netting for the win. Already through to the round of 16, Argentina needed only a tie against Nigeria to win their group, and three minutes in, after Messi blasted home a rebounded Ángel Di María shot from nine yards out, it looked like a guarantee. Sitting on four points and needing at least a tie to advance, Nigeria proved their mettle a minute later by pushing the pace and scoring a brilliantly struck screamer from the left corner of the penalty box. Tied at 1–1, the game remained wide open until just before the halftime whistle when Messi curled a beautifully struck free kick into the top-right corner from 25 yards out. A Nigerian equalizer immediately after half was countered minutes later when Marcos Rojo took advantage of poor defending and an opportune knee placement to knock home a beautifully placed Ezequiel Lavezzi corner in the 50th minute to finalize the scoring and march La Albiceleste into the round of 16.

Having secured the full nine points to advance first out of their group, Argentina was matched with a Switzerland side that finished second in group E behind France. At the Arena Corinthians in São Paulo, and perhaps taking a page out of Iran's playbook, the Swiss side sat back on defense and forced the Argentineans to attempt to break through a host of red shirts while patiently looking to counter. It almost worked too when, in the 45th minute, Sergio Romero had to parry wide a Granit Xhaka blast. With neither team able to break through in full time, it looked as though the Swiss were content to play for penalties; Argentina had other ideas though, and after winning the ball at midfield, Messi quickly found the ball at his feet in the middle of the field and tore toward the goal. Seeing the last defender commit, Messi calmly laid the ball square to a wide-open Di María, who clinically finished past a diving Diego Benaglio to send the stadium erupting in a frenzy of sky blue and white celebrations and push Argentina into a quarterfinal matchup with Belgium at the Estádio Nacional de Brasília in Brasília.

On this day, Lionel Messi was awarded his 91st cap, tying him with the Argentinean great Diego Maradona, and he used the moment to put on a show. Though he did not get the winner (that distinction went to Gonzalo Higuaín, who, in the eighth minute, turned and rifled a volley off a deflection into the side netting past a stunned Thibaut Courtois), it was Messi's play that kept the Belgian defenders on their heels most of the day. Belgium was not without their chances though, especially late, as Daniel Van Buyten and substitute Romelu Lukaku battered a weary Argentine back line, but they could not break through. As the final whistle blew, Argentina was through to the semifinals for the first time in 24 years.

Back again at the Arena Corinthians in São Paulo, Argentina was faced with the daunting task of playing a high-powered Netherlands team without their star striker Di María, who was injured in the first half of Argentina's win over Belgium. Though both teams are known more for their scoring prowess, it became evident early on that neither coach was willing to take too many risks offensively; the result was 120 goalless minutes that saw only 15 shots, 7 of which missed the target. In the ensuing penalty shoot-out, Argentina's first four shooters (Messi, Ezequiel Garay, Sergio Agüero and Maxi Rodríguez) all made their shots, but it was Argentina's goalkeeper Sergio Romero who was the hero of the match, making two splendid saves to send Argentina through to a rematch of their last World Cup Final, a 1990 1–0 loss to West Germany.

Playing at Estádio do Maracanã in Rio de Janeiro in front of 74,738 spectators, Argentina had high hopes of avenging not only the 1990 loss but also the 4–0 quarterfinal debacle against Germany in the 2010 World Cup in Cape Town. Coming into the game still missing their star striker Di María, La Albiceleste looked like a side that would struggle against the high-powered Germans. Sticking to their game plan of a strong defense and quick counters, Argentina created two great chances, but neither Gonzalo Higuaín in the first half nor Messi in the second could find the back of the net. Had it not been for a spectacular goal in the 113rd minute by German sub Mario Götze, Argentina's superb penalty form may have led them to victory. Argentina finished the tournament as runners-up for the third time, with eight goals for and four against.

ATTENDANCE. Attendance at the World Cup final tournament has risen dramatically since the first competition in 1930, on both an aggregate basis and per game, according to official FIFA figures. The 1930 World Cup in Uruguay attracted a total of 590,549 fans, at an average of 32,808 per game. Attendance was hampered early in the tournament because the stadium's intended sole host stadium in the Uruguayan capital, Montevideo, Estadio de Centenario, was not completed in time for the opening of the competition: the first five games at the competition were instead held at the smaller Montevideo venues Estadio Pocitos and Estadio Parque Central. The historic first-ever World Cup game, on 13 July at Estadio Pocitos, in fact attracted only a little over 4,000 fans. The final, however, at Estadio de Centenario attracted an official capacity crowd of 68,346, though it is believed many more fans attended uncounted. The next World Cup, held in eight different venues across Italy, had lower attendance than the inaugural World Cup, though did attract large numbers of traveling fans from neighboring European countries. The total attendance was 363,000, at an average of 21,352. Games involving the host nation in fact drew smaller than expected crowds, only 25,000 in Rome for Italy's first game against the United States on 27 May. By the final on 10 June, interest and excitement had grown, and around 55,000 fans attended Italy's victory over Czechoslovakia at a sold-out Stadio Nazionale PNF in Rome.

For the first time, the 1950 World Cup—the first held since 1938—attracted over one million fans at the tournament held in Brazil, its first return to South America for 20 years. A total of 1,045,246 fans attended 22 games played, at an average of 47,511. Attendance was greatly boosted by the record numbers for games held at the Maracanã stadium in Rio de Janeiro, purpose-built for the World Cup and holding almost 200,000 fans. The official attendance for the last game of the 1950 World Cup, between Brazil and Uruguay, was a record 172,772 paying spectators with a total count of 199,854 present in the stadium officially—and possibly many more in actual fact. Attendances at the Maracanã were far higher for games featuring Brazil than those between other countries: only 19,970 spectators watched Spain's 2–0 win over Chile on 29 June. Attendances at Brazil's other host stadia were also much smaller than at the Maracanã, with a crowd as small as 7,336 viewing Yugoslavia versus Switzerland at Estádio Independência in Belo Horizonte. The United States' famous 1–0 victory over England at the same venue was only seen by 10,151 spectators on 29 June.

Back in Europe, in Switzerland, the 1954 World Cup saw more matches played than in 1950—26 rather than 22—but less total fans actually attending, 768,807 total fans at an average of 29,561 per game. Six Swiss venues were used, with the final held at Wankdorf Stadium, Bern, in front of 62,500 fans. Aside from the final, the largest attendances were at St. Jakob Stadium in Basel, with six games held there, and over 50,000 filling the stadium for Hungary's 8–3 win over West Germany in the first round and the semifinal victory for the West Germans against Austria, large numbers of traveling fans present. The World Cup remained in Europe for the 1958 tournament, moving to Sweden. The competition continued its expansion, 10 more games played than in 1934, as 819,810 attended the 36 games. While the aggregate attendance grew due to the number of games played, the number of fans per game dropped to only 23,423, the lowest number since 1934. Only one game at the first-round stage attracted over 30,000 spectators, the tournament's opening game between defending champions West Germany and Argentina, 31,156 at Malmö Stadion. Sweden's games attracted the largest crowds in the knockout stage, the largest crowd of the competition in the final for Sweden's 5–2 defeat to Brazil, with 49,737 at Råsunda Stadium in Sweden.

Following the pattern of the World Cup to date, when the competition returned to South America in 1962, attendance once again outstripped that seen on European shores. Chile hosted the 1962 World Cup at four venues, with 893,172 fans attending—a slightly lower number than in 1958—but with four fewer games played this time than four years earlier, average attendance rose to 27,911. This was despite the fact three of Chile's World Cup stadia had capacities of less than 20,000; the largest, showpiece venue was Estadio Nacional in Santiago, with a capacity of 67,000. This led to a massive disparity in the crowds attending the first-round games. Group-one games, played at Estadio Carlos Dittborn in the small port city of Arica, barely attracted crowds in the four figures. Group-two games, taking place at Estadio Nacional in Santiago, all attracted huge crowds exceeding 60,000 per game. Group three, in Viña del Mar at Estadio Sausalito, attracted middling crowds ranging between 10,000 and 20,000. Group-four games, in the small central Chilean city of Rancagua at Estadio El Teniente, did not reach four figures in attendance for any games. This disparity continued into the knockout stage; only one quarterfinal was played at Estadio Nacional, Yugoslavia's 1–0 win over West Germany, 63,324 attending. Hosts Chile's exciting 2–1 win over the Soviet Union was only seen by 17,268 fans at the small Estadio Carlos Dittborn in Arica, while the other games in Rancagua and Viña del Mar only attracted 11,690 and 17,736 fans each respectively. The semifinals proved to be even more of a contrast in attendance. A mere 5,890 fans paid to watch Czechoslovakia defeat Yugoslavia at the Estadio Sausalito in Viña del Mar, an all-European affair of little interest to the South American public. On the same day in Santiago, the other semifinal was contested between Brazil and Chile and seen by the tournament's largest crowd of 76,594 fans, the Brazilians winning 4–2 on the way to their second successive World Cup title. The final, which saw Brazil defeat Czechoslovakia 3–1, attracted 68,670 spectators, and only slightly fewer—66,697—watched Chile's third-place play-off victory over Yugoslavia, both at Estadio Nacional.

In 1966, England hosted the World Cup for the first time, and massive interest in the tournament combined with eight host venues that all exceeded 40,000 in capacity meant World Cup attendance records were smashed. At an average of 48,847 for the 32 matches played, a total of 1,563,135 spectators attended the World Cup. The venue for all of England's games and the final was Wembley Stadium in London, with its near 100,000 capacity. Wembley hosted all of the games in group one. Group-two games were split between Hillsborough in Sheffield and Villa Park in Birmingham, with the latter attracting crowds averaging around 50,000 for the first-round games. Group three saw games at Goodison Park in Liverpool and Old Trafford in Manchester: the largest crowd to attend a game in this group saw a marquee matchup between Eusébio's Portugal and Pelé's Brazil, 58,479. Attendances were weakest in group four, with two northeast stadiums, Ayresome Park in Middlesbrough and Roker Park in Sunderland, unable to attract any crowds over 30,000 for the six games played. At the quarterfinal stage, over 40,000 saw Portugal defeat North Korea at Goodison Park, 27,000 at Roker Park for the Soviet Union's 1–0 win over Hungary, 40,007 at Hillsborough for West Germany's thrashing of Uruguay 4–0 and hosts England watched by 90,584 for their controversial 1–0 win against Argentina at Wembley. England again attracted a massive crowd in their semifinal, again at Wembley, 94,943 watching them defeat Portugal. A much smaller crowd in Liverpool watched the other semifinal at Goodison Park, only 38,273 there to see West Germany defeat the Soviet Union. In the third-place play-off, Portugal continued to be a strong draw, 87,696 at Wembley for their 2–1 win versus the Soviet Union on 28 July. The final, also at Wembley two days later, unsurprisingly attracted a packed-in capacity crowd of 96,924 for England's win against the West Germans.

For the first time, in 1970, North America hosted the World Cup, as the tournament took place in the hot summer sun of Mexico. Attendance records were broken once more, on both an aggregate and average basis: a total of 1,603,975 fans attended the 32 games played, averaging 50,124 each. Five Mexican cities played host: Guadalajara, León, Mexico City, Puebla and Toluca. The largest stadium used was the Estadio Azteca in Mexico City, with a capacity exceeding 100,000. Indeed, a record crowd of 107,160 attended the World Cup opening game on 31 May at the Estadio Azteca for Mexico's 0–0 draw with the Soviet Union. All group-one games were held in Mexico City, with attendances exceeding 90,000 for all but one game—and that, between the Soviet Union and El Salvador, had a crowd of 89,979. Crowds were smaller in the three other first-round groups, with only the group-three games held in Guadalajara attracting crowds of over 30,000, a high of 66,834 on 7 June, watching Brazil's classic defeat of England at Estadio Jalisco. Attendance at the quarterfinal stage was disappointing, with only one game—Brazil's 4–2 defeat of Peru—attracting a crowd over 50,000 at Estadio Jalisco in Guadalajara. Mexico played at the smaller Estadio Luis Dosal in Toluca in front of 26,851 rather than in Mexico City, where at the Azteca, only 26,085 watched Uruguay beat the Soviet Union 1–0 after extra time. Despite the all-European matchup, the Azteca was far fuller for the semifinal between West Germany and Italy held there, the Italians triumphing in front of 102,444 fans. Brazil, meanwhile, comfortably beat Uruguay in Guadalajara, 51,261 in attendance. The third-place play-off brought over 100,000 fans to the Azteca once more, 104,403 in the stadium on 20 June for West Germany's 1–0 win against Uruguay. The final, broadcast in Technicolor around the world, attracted an official paying crowd of 107,412, a record for the final as Brazil defeated Italy 4–1.

In 1974, the World Cup returned to Europe in West Germany. Though aggregate attendance grew to 1,865,753, a rise from 1970, that was attributable to an additional four games played. The average attendance actually declined slightly, to 49,098. A record nine stadia were used in Dortmund, Düsseldorf, Frankfurt, Gelsenkirchen, Hamburg, Hanover, Munich, Stuttgart and West Berlin. Each stadium had a capacity exceeding 40,000. The World Cup kicked off in front of a crowd of 81,100 in the West German capital Berlin, as the hosts defeated Chile 1–0 in the Olympiastadion. The smallest crowd of the first was, perhaps unsurprisingly given the political situation, present for East Germany's first game against Australia at the Volksparkstadion in Hamburg, only around 17,000 fans present. When the two Germanys met to close group one, though, over 60,200 were at the Volksparkstadion. The largest attendances elsewhere in the first round came for Italy's games, the largest a reported 70,100 for their game against Poland at the Neckarstadion in Stuttgart. The second-round group stage attracted at least 40,000 fans to 11 of the 12 games, the lowest attendance 39,400 for Argentina versus Brazil in Hanover at Niedersachsenstadion. The largest crowd of the round saw 68,348 fans attend East Germany's 2–0 defeat to the favorites the Netherlands in Gelsenkirchen at Parkstadion. The Netherlands progressed to the final along with West Germany. The third-place play-off came first, Brazil losing 1–0 to Poland in front of 77,100 fans at Olympiastadion in Munich on 6 July. The next day, a slightly larger crowd—though not the largest of the competition—met at the same stadium, 78,200 watching the hosts beat the Dutch 2–1.

The World Cup returned to South America for the first time in 16 years in 1978, heading to Argentina. The number of games played rose once more, to 48, but both aggregate and average attendance fell from the 1974 marks, down to 1,545,791 and 40,678 respectively. Only six venues were utilized in Argentina. The smallest was Estadio Ciudad de Mendoza in Mendoza, with roughly 40,000-capacity stadia in Rosario, Mar del Plata and Córdoba. The two largest stadia were both in the capital Buenos Aires, the 50,000-capacity Estadio José Amalfitani and the venue for the final and the opening game, Estadio Monumental. The games began at the Monumental on 1 June with defending champions West Germany drawing 0–0 with Poland in front of 67,579 spectators. The largest crowds of the first round were registered for Argentina's three group-round games, each at Estadio Monumental: 71,615 for their game against Hungary, 71,666 versus France and 71,712 as Argentina lost to Italy. The smallest crowds of the round were at the Estadio Gigante de Arroyito in Rosario, Poland against Tunisia only drawing 9,624 fans. In the second round, attendances were lower than they might have been as Argentina's loss to Italy in the last game of the first round meant they played their second-round group games at the smaller Estadio Gigante de Arroyito in Rosario rather than at the Monumental in Buenos Aires. The largest crowd of the round still came at the Monumental, for Italy's 0–0 tie with West Germany, attended by 67,547 spectators. Both the third-place play-off and the final were then hosted at the Monumental, on 24 June and 25 June respectively. Brazil clinched third place in front of 69,569 fans, while Argentina became world champions for the first time, 71,483 present as they defeated the Netherlands 3–1.

With the World Cup expanding from 16 teams to 24 for the 1982 World Cup in Spain, the number of matches also grew to 52, 14 more than in 1978. This led to the aggregate attendance for the tournament passing the two-million mark for the first time, at 2,109,723. The average attendance was 40,517, with a record 17 stadia used across 14 different cities. Each stadium was above 30,000 in capacity, the two largest the Santiago Bernabéu stadium in Madrid and Camp Nou in Barcelona, both able to accommodate over 90,000 spectators. Some of the smaller stadia used, though, had trouble attracting large crowds: only around 11,000 fans attended the first-round game between Peru and Cameroon at Estadio de Riazor in La Coruña, for example. The largest crowd of the first round attended the only game held in that round at Camp Nou, 95,000 spectators watching the defending champions Argentina fall 1–0 to Belgium. Attendance in the second stage rose considerably with the Bernabéu and Camp Nou hosting 6 of the 12 games played. The largest crowd was seen for Spain's 2–1 defeat to West Germany at the Bernabéu on 2 July, 90,089 present. With Spain eliminated at the second-round stage, attendance for the semifinals and third-place play-off proved a disappointment. Camp Nou was less than half full, with around 50,000 there for Italy's 2–0 win over Poland on 8 July. The legendary semifinal between West Germany and France on the same day, won on penalties by the former, drew around 70,000 in Seville at Estadio Ramón Sánchez Pizjuán. The third-place game between Poland and France, on 10 July, drew even fewer fans, a count of 28,000 in Alicante at Estadio José Rico Pérez. The final, at least, did sell out at the Bernabéu, with an announced attendance of 90,000 present.

In 1986, Mexico became the first country to host the World Cup twice, only 16 years after the 1970 World Cup was held there. Compared to 1970, more fans in total attended the 1986 World Cup: 2,394,031 in the later tournament compared to 1,603,975 in 1970, though there were 20 more games played in 1986 than in 1970. Average attendance was 46,039 in 1986, compared to 50,124. The 1986 World Cup utilized 12 venues, the largest once again Estadio Azteca. The 1982 World Cup champions, Italy, began the competition at the Azteca in Mexico City, 96,000 fans in attendance. Huge crowds filled the Azteca for all of Mexico's games, each first-round group game attracting over 100,000 spectators, including a high of 114,600 for Mexico versus Paraguay on 7 June. The second round continued with Mexico attracting the largest crowd, 114,580 at the Azteca for their 2–0 win over Bulgaria, with almost 100,000 also at the Azteca for England's 3–0 defeat of Paraguay. The smallest crowd in the second round came in Monterrey, only 19,800 present for a 1–0 West German win over Morocco. The four quarterfinal games, one each in Guadalajara, Monterrey, Puebla and Mexico City, all attracted crowds exceeding 40,000. The largest, again, was in Mexico City as Diego Maradona's Argentina beat England 2–1, an enthralled official-capacity crowd of 114,580 spectators present. Meanwhile, the hosts lost on penalty kicks to West Germany in Monterrey in front of a capacity 41,700 crowd. The first semifinal was held in Guadalajara at Estadio Jalisco, with 45,000 spectators watching France's 2–0 exit to West Germany. The Azteca was once again sold out for the second semifinal, Maradona scoring twice as Argentina defeated Belgium 2–0. The third-place play-off took place on 28 June, a small crowd of 21,000 watching France beat Belgium 4–2 after extra time. A capacity crowd officially registered at 114,600 packed the Azteca for Argentina's 3–2 win over West Germany on 29 June.

In 1990, 24 teams again participated in the next World Cup, with 52 games played once again. Attendance at the tournament held in Italy rose slightly, with 2,516,215 spectators in total, at an average of 48,388 per game. Across Italy, 12 venues were utilized, ranging from the smallest, Stadio Luigi Ferraris in Genoa with a capacity of 36,000, to the largest, the 86,000-capacity San Siro in Milan. The competition began at the latter stadium on 8 June, 73,780 fans attending for Argentina's surprising 1–0 loss to Cameroon. Italy consistently drew crowds of around 73,000 for their first-round games held at the Olympic Stadium in Rome, but the largest crowd of the first round came at the San Siro for West Germany's 4–1 win over Yugoslavia, watched by 74,765 fans. The largest crowd of the second round again featured West Germany, playing the only game held at the San Siro that round, 74,559 spectators there for the West German win over the Netherlands, 2–1. Slightly fewer packed into Rome's Olympic Stadium for the hosts Italy's 2–0 defeat of Uruguay, 73,303 present. The smallest crowd of the round was 31,818, at the Stadio Luigi Ferraris in Genoa for the Republic of Ireland's penalty shoot-out triumph over Romania. In the quarterfinal stage, the attendances were 38,971 for Argentina's penalty shoot-out over Yugoslavia; 73,303 at Rome's Olympic Stadium, as Italy defeated the Republic of Ireland; the largest crowd of the round, 73,347, for West Germany's 1–0 win over Czechoslovakia at the San Siro and 55,205 at Stadio San Paolo in Naples, watching England beat Cameroon 3–2. Neither semifinal was held at the two largest venues of the competition. Instead, Stadio San Paolo welcomed 59,978 for Argentina's penalty shoot-out win over Italy and Stadio delle Alpi in Turin for another game decided by a penalty shoot-out, West Germany beating England. The third-place game was held in Bari at Stadio San Nicola on 7 July, 51,426 watching the hosts claim third place ahead of England. The next day, the final was held at a sold-out Olympic Stadium in Rome, 73,606 the official spectator count.

The World Cup's first visit to the United States, not a traditional soccer power-house, smashed attendance records and set marks that still stand today. Nine venues, none built for soccer but each adapted for the World Cup, that traditionally hosted American football were used, and their massive size and the interest in the competition across the country led to the great numbers of spectators attending. Each stadium used was above 50,000 in capacity, the largest the Rose Bowl in California, able to hold almost 100,000 fans. The World Cup began at Soldier Field in Chicago, a sold-out crowd of 63,117 watching defending champions West Germany beat Bolivia 1–0. Only one attendance in the entire first round dipped below 50,000: Nigeria versus Bulgaria only drew 44,132 fans at the Cotton Bowl in Dallas on 21 June. The largest first-round crowds were registered at the Rose Bowl, over 93,000 fans at each of its three group-A games featuring the United States. The average attendance for the second round was a remarkable 66,877, the largest crowd again at the Rose Bowl for Romania's dramatic 3–2 defeat of Argentina. Attendances at the quarterfinal stage, which did not include a game at the Rose Bowl, ranged from 53,400 in Foxborough at Foxboro Stadium to 83,500 at Stanford Stadium in northern California. The first semifinal, between Italy and Bulgaria, drew 74,110 fans at Giants Stadium in New Jersey, while the second semifinal at the Rose Bowl saw 91,500 in attendance for Brazil's 1–0 win over Sweden. The final was also at the Rose Bowl, Brazil's penalty shoot-out win over Italy seen by 94,194 spectators. That gave the 1994 World Cup a cumulative attendance of 3,587,538, at an average of 68,991 for the 52 games played. Even though the World Cup has since expanded to 64 games, that aggregate record of spectators has yet to be broken.

The World Cup returned to Europe in 1998, with the tournament hosted by France for the second time, 60 years on from its 1938 staging. Staged in far-smaller stadia than the 1994 World Cup, the 1998 edition was attended by 2,785,100 fans, the 64 matches—12 more than in 1994—averaging 43,517 fans each. Only two of the ten venues used exceeded a 50,000 capacity, Stade Vélodrome in Marseille and Stade de France on the outskirts of Paris. A capacity crowd numbering 80,000 watched the opening game on 10 June at the Stade de France between Brazil and France. Much smaller crowds were recorded elsewhere in the first round—only 29,800, a near-capacity crowd at Stade de la Mosson in Montpelier for the next game held, Morocco versus Norway. A high of 77,000 fans in the second round was recorded at the Stade de France for the host's game against Paraguay. The same high of 77,000 was recorded at the quarterfinal stage at the same venue, France beating Italy on a penalty shoot-out. An average crowd of 51,650 was recorded across the four games. At the semifinal stage, 54,000 spectators attended Brazil versus Netherlands at the Stade Vélodrome in Marseille. Another capacity crowd, officially registered at 76,000, watched the second semifinal at the Stade de France, France beating Croatia 2–1. The third-place play-off, Netherlands taking on Croatia, attracted 45,500 fans at the Parc des Princes in Paris. The final, on 12 July, again sold out the Stade de France, 80,000 the officially registered crowd for France's 3–0 win over Brazil.

The 2002 World Cup was the first to be staged in Asia as well as the first to be held across two countries, in Japan and South Korea. A record 20 venues were used, 10 in each country. The largest in Japan was the International Stadium Yokohama, holding almost 73,000, and the largest in South Korea was Seoul World Cup Stadium, with a capacity of 67,000. Defending World Cup champions France kicked the World Cup off in Seoul, a reported crowd of 62,561 present. The largest two attendances in the first round not surprisingly involved the hosts' games: 60,778 at Daegu World Cup Stadium on 10 June for South Korea against the United States, while Yokohama welcomed 66,108 fans for Japan's second group game against Russia. Attendances in the round of 16 ranged from only 25,176 for Germany's 1–0 win over Paraguay at Jeju World Cup Stadium in South Korea to 45,666 for host Japan's loss to Turkey at Miyagi Stadium. With neither of the tournament's largest two venues used at the quarterfinal stage, attendance averaged at 42,780 for the round's four games, the largest at Shizuoka Stadium in Japan for Brazil's 2–1 victory over England, 47,436 present. Seoul's World Cup Stadium was the location for the first semifinal, hosts South Korea's 1–0 loss to Germany watched by 65,256 spectators. The second semifinal, at Saitama Stadium, was at capacity with 61,058 watching Brazil defeat Turkey. The third-place game in Daegu drew 63,483 fans for South Korea's 3–2 defeat to Turkey. The final, on 30 June, was held at the tournament's largest stadium in Yokohama, Japan, a crowd of 69,029 fans there for Brazil's 2–1 win against Germany. That gave the 2002 World Cup a grand total of 2,705,197 fans, averaging 42,268 over the 64 games played.

Africa hosted the World Cup for the first time in 2010. The 64 matches in South Africa were attended by a total of 3,178,856 spectators, or 49,670 per game. This fell short of the totals set in 1994 in the United States. A total of 10 venues were used, several custom-built for the competition, including the largest stadium used, Soccer City in Johannesburg. Soccer City was the venue for the opening game of the competition, featuring South Africa against Mexico, a crowd of 84,490 in attendance. Soccer City then featured the largest crowd in the second round, 84,377 for Argentina's 3–1 win over Mexico. Attendances in the second round ranged considerably, with the smallest crowd 30,597 for Uruguay against South Korea at the 42,000-capacity Nelson Mandela Bay Stadium in Port Elizabeth. The second-largest crowd was in Durban, 61,961 at Moses Mabhida Stadium for the Netherlands versus Slovakia. The average crowd for the quarterfinal stage's four games was 60,915. Soccer City Stadium once again led the way, 84,017 there for Uruguay against Ghana. Cape Town Stadium hosted Argentina against Germany, 64,100 in attendance, slightly larger than the crowd at Ellis Park Stadium in Johannesburg for Paraguay versus Spain. The smallest crowd was again in Port Elizabeth, though Nelson Mandela Bay Stadium was this time close to capacity with the Netherlands 2–1 win over Brazil seen by 40,186 spectators. Soccer City was not a semifinal venue, so the largest crowd came in Cape Town, 62,479 present for the Netherlands win over Uruguay. A slightly smaller crowd, 60,960, watched Spain defeat Germany at Moses Mabhida Stadium in Durban. Two games remained, with 36,254 at Nelson Mandela Bay Stadium for the third-place game between Uruguay and Germany. Soccer City was sold out for the final, Spain winning 1–0 against the Netherlands, their first World Cup victory watched by 84,490 fans.

In 2014, the World Cup headed to South America for the fifth time with Brazil hosting the 20th edition in June and July. The 64 matches attracted a total of 3,429,873 spectators at the 64 games (average of 53,592 per match), making it second only to the 1994 World Cup in the United States in terms of the highest attendance in World Cup history. The games in Brazil were played at 12 stadiums in 12 different cities. The opening game between Brazil and Croatia was played at the Arena Corinthians (Arena de São Paulo) in front of 62,103 fans. The final game, a 1–0 German win over Argentina, was played at the largest stadium in this World Cup, the Maracanã in Rio de Janeiro, with 74,738 spectators in attendance. Amid a more than $3 billion price tag, seven of the stadiums were new: Estádio Nacional de Brasília (65,702 seats), Arena de São Paulo (Arena Corinthians, 59,955 seats), Arena Pernambuco in Recife (40,604 seats), Arena Pantanal in Cuiabá (39,553 seats), Arena da Amazônia in Manaus (39,573 seats), Arena das Dunas in Natal (39,304 seats) and Arena da Baixada in Curitiba (37,634 seats). Five of the stadiums were renovated: the Maracanã in Rio de Janeiro (74,738), Arena Castelão in Fortaleza (57,747 seats), Mineirão in Belo Horizonte (56,091 seats), Estádio Beira-Rio in Porto Alegre (42,153 seats) and Arena Pantanal in Cuiabá (39,553 seats). With more than 3.4 million spectators, stadiums were filled to 98.3 percent capacity, according to FIFA.

AUSTRALIA. Commonly known as the Socceroos. Like many other former British colonies, Australia has not embraced soccer—and hence the World Cup—as a premier sport, instead preferring cricket, rugby and its own football code, Australian Rules Football. Australia's national soccer team has made considerable strides in recent decades, qualifying for the last three World Cup finals for the first time in their history. The Australian national team played its first international in 1922 against New Zealand, but over four decades would pass before the Socceroos would attempt to qualify for the World Cup. Australia's first World Cup qualification game came in 1965, on 21 November in Phnom Penh against North Korea. The winner of a two-game series would go through to the 1966 World Cup in England, but the North Koreans found little difficulty in brushing aside a massively inexperienced Australian team, winning 6–1 at home and 3–1 in Australia. Les Scheinflug scored Australia's first World Cup qualifying goal with his 70th-minute penalty kick in the first game. Australia's attempt to qualify for the 1970 World Cup in Mexico saw the country achieve its first qualifying victories, beating both Japan and South Korea in the first round of the Asian pool. In the second round, Australia advanced past Rhodesia following a three-game series decided by the Socceroos' 3–1 win in Mozambique on 29 November 1969. However, Australia fell at the final qualifying hurdle, losing 1–0 away at Israel and only securing a 1–1 tie at home in the second game of the series.

With Ralé Rašić, a Yugoslavian immigrant to Australia and a former professional player in his native country, in charge as national team coach, the Socceroos took considerable strides forward in a successful qualifying campaign for the 1974 World Cup in West Germany. Australia breezed through the first round of qualifying, topping a group containing Iraq, Indonesia and New Zealand without losing a game. In the final round, Australia twice tied South Korea before a one-off game settled who would advance to the World Cup finals: Rašić's men secured a historic win on 13 November, defeating South Korea 1–0 through a goal by Jimmy Mackay. In West Germany, Australia faced a difficult first-round group, drawn with the host nation, neighboring East Germany and Chile, who had come through a tough South American qualifying campaign. Rašić's roster for the competition drew largely on immigrants to Australia, around a dozen players hailing from Great Britain originally, alongside a smattering of native-born players and a handful from what was then Yugoslavia. It was a hodgepodge team but one whose experience would make them a surprisingly tough nut to crack in West Germany. Australia began against the East Germans, who were held scoreless for almost the first hour of play, until Jürgen Sparwasser broke clear onto the Australian goal and his goal-bound shot was cleared into the net following a desperate lunge by Australian defender Colin Curran. The East German lead was doubled and Australia's defeat assured 14 minutes later, Joachim Streich finishing from a breakaway down the flanks the Socceroos were unable to contain. In Australia's next game, West Germany found it easier to break down the Australians, with goals in the 12th, 34th and 53rd minutes by the eventual champions condemning Australia to a second successive defeat—though it was not as one sided as the eventual scoreline suggested, the Socceroos creating multiple good chances of their own. That result left Rašić's team with only pride to play for in the final game of their first World Cup finals appearance, but they did achieve a creditable 0–0 draw with Chile in Berlin at the Olympic Stadium to secure a first World Cup point.

After a 32-year absence, the Socceroos found themselves back in the World Cup in 2006 after a play-off victory over Uruguay was decided in penalties. Led by Guus Hiddink, Australia was placed into group F with Japan, Croatia and defending champions Brazil. In their opening game, Tim Cahill led the way with two goals and John Aloisi added another to secure not only a 3–1 win but also the first goals ever in a World Cup finals for the Socceroos. The three goals, all coming in the last seven minutes, also set a record for latest three goals ever scored. After a 2–0 loss to Brazil, the Socceroos tied Croatia 2–2 to send themselves through to the knockout stage where they were subsequently eliminated by eventual champions Italy, 1–0.

Qualification for South Africa in 2010 was considerably easier, as Australia found themselves winning their final qualification group by a full five points. Drawn into group D with Germany, Ghana and Serbia, coach Pim Verbeek's decision to face Germany without a true striker in their opening game meant a 4–0 loss and heavy criticism. Though they tied Ghana 1–1 and beat Serbia 2–1, it was the heavy first-game loss that ultimately led to their elimination from the tournament.

After easy qualification for 2010, qualifying for their third-straight World Cup, this time in Brazil, proved a bit more difficult. What should have been an easy opening phase of the Asian Football Confederation (AFC) instead saw a narrow comeback-win over Thailand and a loss to Oman before the Socceroos ultimately won their group. The second phase started off just as slow, with two draws and a loss to Jordan before their first win, and the Australians needed a win against Iraq in their final qualification game to advance. In October of 2013, after back-to-back 6–0 defeats at the hands of Brazil and France, head coach Holger Osieck was replaced by a local hero, former

Brisbane Roar, Melbourne Victory and National Youth Teams coach Ange Postecoglou. With little international coaching experience, this choice was viewed skeptically by many, but Ange's coaching style immediately made the Aussie side more competitive and fun to watch.

Placed into group B with defending champions Spain, defending runners-up Netherlands and a tough Chilean side, expectations were not high. At the Arena Pantanal, in Cuiabá, Australia opened play against a Chilean side that was, on paper, their easiest opponent but found themselves on their back heels just 12 minutes into the match when Alexis Sánchez finished a flicked header from four yards out. Two minutes later, Jorge Valdivia roofed a Sánchez pass from 17 yards out, and the game started to feel out of reach until Aussie captain Tim Cahill leapt up between two Chilean defenders to head home an Ivan Franjic cross to pull the Socceroos within one. Though they battled, Australia was unable to find the net in the second half, and a stoppage-time Chilean goal made the final 3–1.

The second group game, played at Estádio Beira-Rio in Porto Alegre, saw the Socceroos again go down early, this time in the 20th minute to a supremely confident Dutch side coming off a 5–1 revenge-fueled thrashing of Spain. A minute later, Cahill scored what was surely the goal of the match (if not the tournament) when he volleyed home a rocket from eight yards out to pull them level. With the Dutch back on their heels, Australia took the lead in the 54th minute on a Mile Jedinak penalty following a Dutch handball in the box, but Australia's elation was short-lived as Robin van Persie knotted the game back up in the 58th minute following some shoddy Aussie defending. To add insult to injury, Memphis Depay put the game out of reach in the 68th minute when Australian goalkeeper Matt Ryan failed to stop his poorly struck 30-yard shot.

In the final group game, played at Arena da Baixada, in Curitiba, the Australians faced a Spanish side that was surprisingly sitting even with them in the standings at zero points. Unfortunately for the Australians, with their hero Tim Cahill having to sit this one out due to an accumulation of yellow cards, the Spanish side everyone expected to see finally came to play. In the 36th minute, a poorly marked David Villa cheekily back flicked the ball past Ryan to make the score 1–0. Though Australia battled, the Spanish possession and ensuing pressure was too much, and the game was put out of reach with goals in the 69th and 82nd minutes. Australia finished 30th out of 32 teams with zero points and a goal differential of –6.

AUSTRIA. Commonly known as Das Team. The golden age of Austria's best-ever team, the "Wunderteam" of the 1930s, coincided with the first decade of World Cup play. Austria's national team had begun play in the early 1900s and, under legendary coach Hugo Meisl in the 1920s, adopted radical tactics—emphasizing passing on the ground over earlier play—that quickly propelled Austria into the elite ranks of international soccer. Austria, though, would not have a chance to prove their quality at the inaugural 1930 World Cup, refusing to travel to Uruguay for the competition. But in 1931 and 1932, the Austrians' unbeaten streak of 14 games marked them out as key contenders for the 1934 World Cup in Italy—a 4–2 win over the fancied host nation in the buildup to the competition only heightened expectations, with the brilliant Matthias Sindelar guiding the team from the center-forward position. With the competition a straight knockout format in 1934, Austria began by eliminating France in unimpressive fashion, only finding a winner deep into extra time for a 3–2 victory. Against Hungary at the quarterfinal stage, a rough battle was won by Austria in far-more-impressive style, a 2–1 win thanks to goals from captain Johann Horvath in the first half and from Karl Zischek in the second half. Without Horvath due to injury, Austria went into the semifinal against Italy in Milan weakened, the situation worsened by heavy rain not conducive to Meisl's men's style of play. The Italians proved far more dynamic than the Austrians in the first half, scoring through Enrique Guaita. Austrian pressure in the second half resulted in good chances, no better than for Zischek at the game's death, his run leaving him a fine chance to equalize—his shot, though, went wide, and Austria went out of the competition. Demoralized, Austria lost again to Germany in the third-place game, 3–2.

By the time of the 1938 World Cup in France, Meisl was dead, and the dark politics of 1930s Europe meant that Austria no longer existed, annexed by Germany in March 1938. That meant even though Austria qualified for the World Cup, their players were only able to compete—with great reluctance—as part of a united German–Austrian team. Austria did not attempt to compete in the first World Cup held after World War II in 1950 but returned in 1954 with another strong team coached by one of the Wunderteam members, Walter Nausch. The team's play revolved around Ernst Ocwirk, a star at Austria Wien who would go on to fame and fortune in Italy playing for Sampdoria, a center-half with deep-lying playmaking abilities. Austria's campaign began with a hard-fought win over Scotland in Zurich, a 1–0 result secured by Erich Probst's 33rd-minute strike, the Austrians fighting off numerous dangerous Scottish attacks throughout the game. Again in Zurich, Austria's second and last group game brought back memories of the Wunderteam with a 5–0 demolition of Czechoslovakia, four up by halftime. Ernst Stojaspal claimed two for Austria while Probst added to his tournament tally with a hat trick.

There would be even more goals in Austria's next game against host nation Switzerland in Lausanne: 12 in total, to date still a record for aggregate scoring in a World Cup finals game. Played in considerable heat, the Swiss stormed to a 3–0 lead in just 19 minutes, leaving Austrian hopes seemingly in tatters. But goals from Theodor Wagner, Alfred Koerner and Wagner again between the 25th and 27th minutes—three goals in three minutes—tied the game. By halftime, the Austrians led 5–4 despite missing a penalty, with further goals that half from Ocwirk and Koerner. The scoring pass sagged in the second half, but three more goals still came, two to the Austrians through Wagener and Probst.

Austria's remarkable 7–5 win earned a semifinal fixture in Basel against West Germany in front of a crowd of 58,000. It would be another high-scoring affair, but this time the Austrians were on the receiving end of most of the goals, falling apart in miserable fashion despite being heavy favorites to win. Nausch surprisingly replaced Kurt Schmied in goal with Walter Zeman, who had recently acquired an error-prone reputation that would not be helped in Basel. By halftime, the West Germans were up by two goals, and though Probst pulled one back with his fifth goal of the competition in the 51st minute, West German superiority was quickly restored first by a Fritz Walter penalty and then three further goals for a final score of Austria 1, West Germany 6. It was a bitter pill that revealed the Austrians had passed their best of recent seasons, and even a win over Uruguay in the third-place game—giving Austria their best-ever World Cup finish to date—was of little consolation.

Austria would never again hit the heights of the nation's first two World Cup experiences in 1934 and 1954, a relatively small fish in increasingly competitive European waters. Austria did qualify with ease for the 1958 World Cup in Sweden, winning its qualifying group containing the Netherlands and Luxembourg unbeaten in four games. Coached by Josef Argauer, four survivors from Austria's debacle against West Germany in 1954 survived for the nation's opening game at the 1958 World Cup—Ernst Happel, Karl Koller, Alfred Koerner and Walter Schleger. Once again, the Austrians proved no match for the opposition, the Brazilians—en route to winning their first World Cup title—comfortably dismissing an Austrian team lacking in energy with three unanswered goals in Uddevalla. Matters failed to improve for Austria against the Soviet Union in Boras despite tinkering to the lineup—Happel and Schleger dropped to the bench—succumbing to a 2–0 defeat. Against England, Austria finally got on the score sheet and twice led thanks to long-range strikes from Koller and Koerner—but were twice pegged back, ending with a 2–2 tie and an early exit from the World Cup.

Limited by financial constraints, Austria—unable to countenance the cost of travel to South America—withdrew from qualifying for the 1962 World Cup in Chile. By the time Austria returned to qualifying for the 1966 World Cup, the team's fall from grace became all too apparent, failing to win a game in a qualifying group containing Hungary and East Germany under head coach Eduard Frühwirth. With Slovak Leopold Šťastný taking over from Frühwirth as coach, Austria enjoyed a slightly better showing in its unsuccessful attempt to qualify for the 1970 World Cup, winning three of six group games, but still finished behind both Scotland and West Germany, a critical pair of defeats to the latter showing the Austrians lacked world-class quality. But, with the consistency of continuing under the stewardship of Šťastný, Austria's results in qualifying for the 1974 World Cup markedly improved. Austria won three of their first four games, including an impressive 2–0 defeat of Sweden thanks to goals from Thomas Parits and Peter Pumm, and ultimately finished tied with the Swedes at the top of the group both on points and goal difference. This forced a play-off game between the two teams to determine which would travel to West Germany for the World Cup. The matchup took place on neutral ground in Gelsenkirchen, West Germany, and was won 2–1 by the Swedes, ending a promising campaign by Austria.

By 1978, with former Austrian international Helmut Senekowitsch now at the coaching helm, Austria's growing experience saw them advance through qualifying for the first time in two decades. Austria topped a qualifying group with East Germany, Turkey and Malta in it, unbeaten with four wins and two draws. Austria twice tied East Germany and won a critical away fixture in Izmir, Turkey, a 1–0 win thanks to a goal from Herbert Prohaska. In Argentina at the 1978 World Cup finals, Austria found themselves placed in a seemingly tricky group, alongside three-time world champions Brazil, perennial dark horses Spain and a tidy Swedish team. But with Hans Krankl—who would go on to score prolifically for Barcelona—at forward, the

Austrians proved more than competitive in the group: in fact, they won the group after only two games. Austria began their opening game in blistering style: against Spain in Buenos Aires, forward Walter Schachner showed his flair and pace with a vibrant run through the Spanish defending and a finish that flashed in past Miguel Angel at the near post in the ninth minute. Twelve minutes later, Spain equalized with some fortune, a strike from Dani deflecting off Austrian defender Erich Obermayer into the net past Friedl Koncilia. Spain's pressure gave them several opportunities to take the lead, with an apparent goal disallowed for a foul on Koncilia and a shot cleared off the Austrian line by captain Robert Sara. Austria developed chances too, though, and found a winner when Kurt Jara's shot was blocked and fell to the feet of Krankl eight yards out, who calmly stroked it into the net, giving the Austrians a 2–1 win. Qualification for the next round was secured by Austria with a 1–0 win over Sweden, again in Buenos Aires, after Herbert Prohaska was tripped in the penalty area, Krankl converting the resulting spot kick. In Mar del Plata, Brazil defeated Austria 1–0 in the last group game, but the result still left Austria topping the group.

The second-round stage, another group format, saw Austria placed with West Germany, the Netherlands and Italy, all of whom had reached the World Cup final earlier in the 1970s. The Dutch gave Austria a lesson in how to control play by almost scoring at will in Cordoba, a 5–1 win exhibiting the best of the Netherlands' "Total Football" and a surprisingly poor showing from the Austrians. A much-better performance followed back in Buenos Aires against Italy, but Paolo Rossi still found the only goal of the game for the Italians, the Austrians denied a clear call for a penalty late on. The result eliminated Austria, but a game against West Germany still had tremendous meaning for the nation, and in Cordoba, a result still recalled and celebrated today by Austrians was achieved. A 3–2 win was secured thanks to an own goal by West Germany's Berti Vogts, a penalty from Krankl and a winner from Krankl again with only three minutes remaining, a bewitching run ended with a low finish under West German keeper Sepp Maier. Austria left Argentina with heads held high.

Ironically, Austria and West Germany were then paired together in qualifying for the 1982 World Cup, to be held in Spain. West Germany proved too strong for Austria in the two qualifiers between the two nations, but those proved to be Austria's only defeats of the campaign, finishing second in a group also containing Bulgaria, Albania and Finland. That advanced Austria to the World Cup finals for the second consecutive tournament. Now coached by Georg Schmidt, Austria retained a core of experience from the 1978 competition for its 1982 World Cup roster, including goalkeeper Friedl Koncilia, captain Erich Obermayer and the dynamic attackers Hans Krankl and Walter Schachner. Austria's group at the World Cup also included West Germany (once again), Algeria and Chile. It was against the latter that Austria began their campaign on 17 June in Oviedo. Chile almost took an early lead with Carlos Caszely seemingly clean through on goal, but a fantastic last-ditch tackle by Bruno Pezzey averted the danger. Austria began to press hard down the wings, and this approach brought fruit when Schachner flicked a cross with his head into the bottom corner. Disaster appeared to have struck for Austria when Bernd Krauss's clumsy challenge on Caszely resulted in a penalty, but Caszely himself dragged the spot kick wide. Tremendous goalkeeping at both ends kept the scores tied from there, Krankl's header denied by a brilliant tip from Chilean goalkeeper Mario Osbén, who also deflected a drive from Schachner onto the post.

The 1–0 win over Chile would prove critical for Austria, next facing Algeria again in Oviedo, after the African team's shocking win over West Germany. The Algerians, though, found it difficult to contain Krankl and Schachner, even though Koncilia in the Austrian goal had to make multiple smart saves early on. Schachner scored Austria's first at 55 minutes, after a flowing move gave him a chance to finish from 10 yards out. Another Austrian break was rewarded 12 minutes later, Krankl cracking in the ball with a piercing left-foot drive from 20 yards out. The Algerians had no reply. The result meant that by the time Austria faced West Germany in Gijón on 25 June, both teams knew that a win by one or two goals for the West Germans would mean both teams advancing to the next round at the expense of Algeria, who had played their last group game the day before against Chile. To the dismay of a watching world, it quickly appeared both teams had agreed to a 1–0 win for West Germany, who scored after 10 minutes with both teams then seemingly content to sit back for the remainder of the game, no further goals coming. That game helped prompt FIFA to ensure future final rounds of games in the group stage would take place at the same time as each other. It was a far cry for Austria from the joy of their game against West Germany in the World Cup four years previously.

Regardless, Austria moved on to the second-round group stage, meeting there France and Northern Ireland. In Madrid, the Austrians first took on France, boasting the likes of Jean Tigana and Alain Giresse. The game was decided by one strike, a splendid left-footed free kick by Bernard Genghini that dipped mercurially into the top left-hand corner of Friedl Koncilia's net. The result made Austria's next game against the Northern Irish a must-win. Played again in Madrid's searing heat, the game nevertheless fizzed and popped, with four goals scored. The Northern Irish took the lead with a close-range header from Billy Hamilton, the only goal before the half. Schmidt made two key changes at the break that would enliven a seemingly dulled Austrian attack, with Reinhold Hintermaier replacing Max Hagmayr and Kurt Welzl coming on for Johann Pregesbauer. The moves paid dividends only five minutes into the second half, slightly fortuitously as Bruno Pezzey deflected in long-range drive headed wide. But Austria had the initiative and took the lead when, from a set piece 25 yards out, Hintermaier lashed the ball in. Northern Ireland, though, found an equalizer that dashed Austria's chances of progression, Koncilia foolishly leaving his line and Hamilton scoring his second with a dramatic header. The 2–2 draw meant that with France's 4–1 win over Northern Ireland in the last game of the group, the Austrians headed home.

Yugoslavian Branko Elsner was installed as coach for the 1986 World Cup qualifying campaign, his second stint in charge of Austria after a caretaker role in 1975. It proved to be a disappointing reign, with Austria only winning 5 of the 18 games he managed. That included an unsuccessful qualifying effort, Austria finishing third in a four-team group behind Hungary and the Netherlands.

Austria turned to a member of the 1978 World Cup team, Josef Hickersberger, to coach the team for the 1990 qualifying campaign. Despite defeats to Turkey and the Soviet Union, Austria qualified in second place of a group also containing East Germany and Iceland, winning three out of eight games. At the 1990 World Cup in Italy, Hickersberger's team was placed in group A with host nation Italy, Czechoslovakia and the United States. Starting out against Italy in Rome at the Olympic Stadium, Austria unambitiously set out a defensive stall and frustrated the Italians for 78 minutes, until Salvatore Schillaci—on as a substitute—found space and headed home a cross from Gianluca Vialli. All Austrians defending and fine goalkeeping from Klaus Lindenberger proved to be for naught. Austria offered little more as an offensive force against Czechoslovakia in Florence, losing to a penalty from Michal Bílek. Austria then faced the United States, who had also lost both games up until then, once again in Florence. The Austrians finally made a mark on the score sheet when Andreas Ogris scored a solo goal that seemed to come out of nowhere 49 minutes in, picking up a ball inside his own half and outstripping the American defense before finishing past Tony Meola in the United States' goal. A second goal came 14 minutes later for the Austrians, Michael Streiter penetrating down the American flank and providing a good chance for Gerhard Rodax, who tucked a shot away from 13 yards out. Austria, though, finished the competition on a downbeat note by conceding to the Americans when Tab Ramos broke through the defense and set up Bruce Murray, whose shot squirmed embarrassingly through the legs of Lindenberger. Austria headed home, and after a disappointing start to the 1992 European Championship qualifying campaign, Hickersberger resigned.

Placed in a difficult six-team group in qualifying for the 1994 World Cup in the United States, Austria—coached at various points by Ernst Happel, Dietmar Constantini and Herbert Prohaska—won only three of ten games, finishing fourth and well out of contention to advance on to the finals. Prohaska, though, improved results and stayed on as coach for the 1998 World Cup cycle, leading the Austrians back to the World Cup in France at the top of a group with Scotland, Sweden, Latvia, Estonia and Belarus in it. Austria qualified in spectacular style, winning eight of ten games, including impressive wins home and away against Sweden, fired by forward Toni Polster, who would go on to become the top scorer in Austrian international history. Group B, with Chile, Cameroon and Italy, provided the opposition for Austria in France.

Austria's opening game against Cameroon in Toulouse proved to be a disappointment, with neither team able to carve out many opportunities for much of the game, Heimo Pfeifenberger coming closest to breaking the deadlock with a 30-yard drive saved well by Jacques Songo'o in the Cameroon goal. Cameroon took the lead 77 minutes in, Pierre Njanka skipping past Wolfgang Feiersinger and Peter Schöttel before finishing from 10 yards out. Austria found an equalizer in injury time after 90 minutes had passed, a corner sloppily defended by Cameroon allowing the ball to drop to Polster, who drove it home high into the roof of the net. Austria's next game against Chile in Saint-Étienne followed a remarkably similar pattern. Michael Konsel's superb goalkeeping in the Austrian net kept the South Americans at bay for 70 minutes, until Marcelo Salas forced the ball in from close range. But Austria again found an equalizer in injury time, this time thanks to Ivica Vastić, who curled in a stunning shot from 20 yards out to tie the scores. Facing Italy in the suburbs of Paris at the Stade de France, Austria needed a win against Italy to move on to the next round but, after a scoreless first half, fell behind for the third straight game when Christian

Vieri beat Konsel to a cross and headed home. Austria could create little, and Italy sealed victory after 90 minutes when substitute Roberto Baggio tapped in from five yards out. Though Austria again found a third straight injury-time goal, a penalty kick by Andreas Herzog after Hannes Reinmayr was fouled by Alessandro Costacurta, it was too little, too late on this occasion, and Austria departed from the competition.

The year 1998 marks the last occasion Austria appeared at the World Cup finals. Coached by Otto Barić, Austria finished second in its qualifying group for the 2002 World Cup behind Spain, only one defeat in eight games meaning they moved on to the play-offs for a place at the World Cup—but they were crushed by Spain 6–0 on aggregate, 1–0 at home and 5–0 away. Austria's legendary star Hans Krankl took charge for the 2006 qualifying effort, but despite starting with a creditable 2–2 draw against England, Austria won only one of the country's next seven games, with Krankl removed as coach by the fall of 2005 and a third-place finish in the group meaning the Austrians missed out on the World Cup again. Austria improved little in qualifying for the 2010 World Cup, under the coaching of first Karel Brückner and then Dietmar Constantini, finishing third and failing to move on to South Africa, winning only four of ten games behind Serbia and France. Switzerland's Marcel Koller took over head-coaching duties in 2011 as Austria prepared for the 2014 World Cup qualifying cycle. With 17 points in the group stage, Austria finished in third, three points behind Sweden for the play-off spot and out of the World Cup finals in Brazil.

B

BAGGIO, ROBERTO. B. 18 February 1967, Caldogno, Italy. Roberto Baggio is one of the greatest Italian players of all time and was the winner of both the FIFA World Player of the Year award and the European Footballer of the Year award in 1993 at the peak of his career. The next year, Baggio led Italy to the final of the 1994 FIFA World Cup, generally regarded as their best performing player in the tournament, though Italy lost the final game to Brazil on a penalty shoot-out, with Baggio famously missing the decisive penalty kick. Baggio played a total of 56 games for Italy, usually operating as a creative forward, scoring 27 goals for his country. He also played for Italy at the 1990 FIFA World Cup, where they finished in third place. Baggio played his club career for several Italian teams, his best period coming with Juventus, with whom he won the UEFA Cup in 1993 and the Italian league championship in 1994, before he was transferred to AC Milan, where he again won the Italian league championship in 1996. He also played for Internazionale, Bologna and Brescia before his retirement from playing in 2004. Baggio was nicknamed the "Divine Ponytail," in a nod to his hairstyle and his Buddhist beliefs, and was known on the field for his stylish, skillful play.

BALLESTRERO, ENRIQUE. B. 18 January 1905, Colonia del Sacramento, Uruguay. D. 11 October 1964. The winning goalkeeper in the inaugural World Cup final in 1930 was Uruguayan Enrique Ballestrero, keeping goal for the hosts Uruguay at the age of 25. Ballestrero played in all four of Uruguay's games at the competition, keeping clean sheets in Uruguay's group-stage matchups against Peru and Romania and conceding one goal in the semifinal against Yugoslavia. Ballestrero conceded two goals in the final, a 4–2 win over Argentina. Ballestrero continued playing internationally for Uruguay throughout the 1930s, starting in goal during their 1935 Copa América victory. The six-foot-tall goalkeeper played domestically in Uruguay until his retirement in 1937.

BARTHEZ, FABIEN. B. 28 June 1971, Lavelanet, France. Six feet tall, Fabien Barthez shares the record for the most clean sheets (no goals conceded in a game) at the World Cup for a goalkeeper along with Peter Shilton, with 10 in his 17 World Cup games. Barthez played for France at three straight World Cup final tournaments, in 1998, 2002 and 2006. Barthez's 17 World Cup games included 2 finals: a 3–0 win over Brazil in France on 12 July 1998 and a 1–1 draw—with defeat on penalty kicks—to Italy in Berlin, Germany, on 5 July 2006. Behind a remarkably strong back line, including Laurent Blanc and Marcel Desailly, Barthez only conceded two goals in France's seven games in the 1998 World Cup. The 2002 World Cup was a disappointment, Barthez taking part in all three games as France was eliminated during the group stage, conceding three goals in three games, including defeats to both Senegal and Denmark. In 2006, France returned to form, and Barthez only let in three goals in seven games during the tournament. Remarkably, Barthez only once conceded more than one goal in Barthez's 17 World Cup games, in the 2–0 defeat to Denmark in 2002. Barthez, who made his debut for France in 1994, made a total of 87 appearances for his country. He also won the 2000 UEFA European Championship as France's starting goalkeeper. With his club sides, Barthez won a number of honors, including the UEFA Champions League title with Marseille in 1993 and two Premier League championships with Manchester United in 2001 and 2003.

BASORA, ESTANISLAU. B. 18 November 1926, Barcelona, Spain. D. 16 March 2012. At the 1950 World Cup held in Brazil, Estanislau Basora played in six games for Spain, scoring four goals to finish as joint third top scorer in the competition. Basora was at the time starring for his hometown team Barcelona, an attacking winger or forward with an impressive goal-scoring record. He made his mark for Spain in 1949 with a terrific hat trick in a 5–1 win over France in Colombes on 19 June. Basora then scored against Portugal in April 1950, in a World Cup qualifying game. Once the World Cup got underway in Brazil two months later, Basora scored his first World Cup goal in his first game as Spain defeated the United States 3–1 on 25 June 1950 to open their first-round group-stage campaign and followed that up with a goal in Spain's second group game against Chile, a 2–0 win. Basora did not score in Spain's next game against England, but he did set up the winning goal for Zarra to give Spain another victory, this time 1–0. Basora then played a critical role in Spain's opening game in the final-round group stage, scoring twice against Uruguay in a 2–2 tie. Basora's first goal against the Uruguayans squared the game at 1–1 in the 37th minute, a dramatic diving header burying the ball low into the net. Just two minutes later, Basora was freed 15 yards from goal and finished past Roque Máspoli in the Uruguayan goal. Spain's efforts, though, had exhausted them, and that was to be Basora's last goal of the competition, as the Spaniards crumbled 6–1 to Uruguay and 3–1 to Sweden in their final two games, resulting in a fourth-place finish for the Spanish. Spain did not qualify for either the 1954 or 1958 World Cup, though Basora played in one qualifier for the 1958 World Cup in Sweden in 1957—scoring twice in a game against Scotland—he ended his international career that year with a total of 13 goals in 22 games.

BATISTUTA, GABRIEL. B. 1 February 1969, Reconquista, Argentina. Gabriel Batistuta is the all-time leading scorer for Argentina's national team, having tallied 56 goals in just 78 games for his country between 1991 and 2002. He was a fast, powerful forward with a blistering and accurate shot. Batistuta appeared at three FIFA World Cup finals tournaments, though Argentina did not progress further than the quarter-finals with Batistuta on any of those occasions. His greatest international success came in 1993, with Batistuta playing a major role in Argentina's victory in the Copa América that year. He scored twice in the final as Argentina defeated Mexico 2–1. At club level, the longest spell of Batistuta's career came playing for Fiorentina in Italy from 1991 to 2000, though his greatest honor came after he moved to AS Roma in 2000, winning the Italian league championship in 2001. He retired in 2005.

BATTLE OF BORDEAUX. The 1938 World Cup in France featured one of the most brutal games in World Cup history on 12 June 1938 at Stade du Parc Lescure in Bordeaux. A quarterfinal game between Brazil and Czechoslovakia, two of the favorites to win the competition, degenerated into an extremely physical and violent contest the Hungarian referee Pal von Hertzka found extremely difficult to contain. The injuries sustained included a broken leg for the gifted Czech forward Oldřich Nejedlý and a broken right arm for his compatriot František Plánička, Czechoslovakia's goalkeeper, who bravely soldiered on to the end of the game. No fewer than three players were sent off: Brazil's Zezé Procópio and Machado, along with Jan Říha of Czechoslovakia. Zezé was sent off for kicking Nejedlý in the 19th minute, starting much of the trouble, while Machado and Říha were dismissed for fighting just before halftime. The game ended 1–1, necessitating a replay, which was noted for its fair conduct, refereed by Georges Capdeville.

BEARZOT, ENZO. B. 26 September 1927, Aiello del Friuli, Italy. D. 21 December 2010. Italy won their third World Cup title in 1982 in Spain under the coaching of Enzo Bearzot, who also coached Italy at the 1986 World Cup in Mexico. Bearzot began his coaching career in 1966 after a playing career that saw him play over 250 games in Serie A and represent Italy on one occasion at the international level. After a brief period as an assistant coach at Torino in 1967 and 1968, for whom Bearzot had played on over 150 occasions, and then as a head coach at lower-division-side Prato for one year, Bearzot was appointed to run Italy's U-23 national team in 1969. Bearzot assisted Italy's senior national team alongside Fulvio Bernardini at both the 1970 and 1974 World Cups: Italy was a finalist in the former competition and was eliminated in the first round in the latter. Following Italy's World Cup failure in 1974, Bearzot was appointed as coach in 1975, his first game in charge a 0–0 tie with Finland in September of that year. Bearzot's early years in charge were not a success, as Italy failed to qualify for the 1976 European Championships, but Bearzot then led them to qualify for the 1978 World Cup in Argentina.

The 22-man squad selected by Bearzot for the 1978 World Cup illustrated the scale of his overhaul of Italy's aging 1974 World Cup team, with only three players from the previous competition selected in 1978. Bearzot had invested in growing a young team over the long term, with only two players over the age of 30 selected, veteran goalkeeper and captain Dino Zoff and midfielder Claudio Sala. The youthful talent included 21-year-old striker Paolo Rossi, who scored one as Italy opened their World Cup campaign with a 2–1 win over France on 2 June, Renato Zaccarelli scoring the other. A 3–1 win over Hungary and a 1–0 win over Italy saw Bearzot's men win the group and qualify for the second-round group stage. There, Italy was placed with the Netherlands, West Germany and Austria, the group winner to advance to the final. Italy opened with a tight 0–0 draw with West Germany on 14 June and then defeated Austria 1–0 four days later thanks to a Rossi goal. That meant Italy's game with the

Netherlands on 21 June would determine which of the two teams would advance to the World Cup final. Italy led at halftime thanks to a Dutch own goal, but the Netherlands' pressure told in the second half, scoring twice for a 2–1 win that eliminated Italy from the tournament.

It had, however, been a promising competition for the Italians, and Bearzot was retained as coach as Italy hosted the 1980 European Championship. The tournament was a disappointment on home turf; though unbeaten at the group stage, Italy did not qualify for the final and finished in fourth place. Bearzot kept faith with his young squad, qualifying for the 1982 World Cup in Spain with an unbeaten campaign. The final 22 Bearzot selected to travel to Spain included a core built around the 1978 team, including Rossi, Antonio Cabrini, Dino Zoff and Francesco Graziani, along with talented young defenders Franco Baresi and Giuseppe Bergomi. Bearzot applied a light tactical hand to his teams, preferring his players to express themselves creatively, with Scirea operating as a libero and the wide players given freedom to roam forward. A front three pairing of Conti, Rossi and Graziani was Bearzot's preferred combination in attack.

For Italy's opening game on 14 June 1982 against Poland, 7 of Italy's starting 11 had played in Italy's last game of the 1978 World Cup against the Netherlands. Italy, though, began the competition in poor form, drawing 0–0 with Poland, 1–1 with Peru and 1–1 with Cameroon in the first-round group stage. It was still enough for Italy to qualify for the second-round group stage, however, and Bearzot kept faith with his lineup, including Rossi, who had yet to score and was controversially recalled by the coach after a long ban for a betting scandal. In the second round, Bearzot's confidence was vindicated, as Italy hit their stride with a 2–1 win over Argentina, and Rossi then suddenly finding his form with a hat trick for the Italians in a 3–2 win over Brazil that sent Italy to the semifinal stage. Italy faced Poland in the semifinal, with Bearzot making only one change from the semifinal, Bergomi replacing Fulvio Collovati, who had left the Brazil game with injury. Rossi, in superb form, scored twice as Italy won 2–0 to advance to the World Cup final. Italy's opponent was West Germany. Bearzot made one change in his lineup from the semifinal, Claudio Gentile replacing Giancarlo Antognoni. It was a game dominated by Italy, which won 3–1 with goals from Rossi, Marco Tardelli and Alessandro Altobelli, Bearzot becoming Italy's first World Cup–winning coach since 1938.

Bearzot's world champions then suffered a shockingly poor qualifying campaign for the 1984 European Championships, winning only one out of eight qualifying games. Italy qualified automatically for the 1986 World Cup, but Bearzot failed to meld new blood with many of the veterans from 1982 that he retained faith in. Italy unconvincingly qualified for the second round with only one win in three group games, that against unfancied South Korea, and tumbled out in the second round, outclassed by reigning European champions France 2–0. It was to be Bearzot's last game in charge of Italy. He ended his reign as a World Cup–winning coach, with his total record as coach of Italy weighing in at 51 wins, 28 draws and 25 defeats in 104 games.

BECKENBAUER, FRANZ. B. 11 September 1945, Munich, Germany. Franz Beckenbauer is the only man to have both captained and coached a FIFA World

Cup–winning team, doing so with West Germany in 1974 and 1990 respectively. He is regarded as the greatest German player of all time, having established an innovative presence in the game by playing a consistently creative role from initially defensive positions on the field. Beckenbauer began his professional career with Bayern Munich in 1964, leading the club to the top tier of German soccer, the Bundesliga. He made his debut for West Germany the next year and played in the World Cup in 1966, taking home a runners-up medal after a 4–2 defeat in the final to England. Bayern Munich went on to achieve ever-greater success in the late 1960s with Beckenbauer anchoring the team, winning the West German Cup in 1966, 1967 and 1969, the UEFA Cup Winners' Cup in 1967 and, after Beckenbauer took over the team captaincy in 1968, the Bundesliga championship in 1969.

The 1970s would prove to be Beckenbauer's most glorious years as a player; he began to play a new role as a libero, organizing the team in defense but also bringing the ball forward to launch attack after attack. The German media saluted his overall dominance of the game by nicknaming him Der Kaiser (the Emperor). The 1970 World Cup saw West Germany fall 4–3 to Italy in the semifinal, but in 1974 on home soil, Beckenbauer captained his country to their second World Cup championship as they defeated the Netherlands 2–1 in the final. Beckenbauer and his teammates followed this up with victory in the UEFA European Football Championship in 1972. In club soccer, Bayern Munich reached new heights with Beckenbauer playing a starring role, winning the Bundesliga three successive times from 1972 to 1974 and dominating the continent with European Cup titles in 1974, 1975 and 1976, followed by victory in the Intercontinental Cup that same year. Beckenbauer won the European Footballer of the Year award in both 1972 and 1976. In 1977, Beckenbauer moved to the riches of the North American Soccer League in the United States, winning the Most Valuable Player award in his first season with the New York Cosmos, going on to win the Soccer Bowl three times with the Cosmos. Beckenbauer returned to the Bundesliga for two seasons with Hamburg from 1981 to 1982 and then spent one last season back with the Cosmos preceding his retirement in 1983.

Just a year later, Beckenbauer was named head coach of the West German national team, replacing Jupp Derwall, whose side had failed at the 1984 UEFA European Football Championship. Beckenbauer led West Germany to the final of the 1986 World Cup in Mexico, where they lost to a Diego Maradona–inspired Argentina team, but they would win the World Cup for the third time four years later under Der Kaiser, beating England on penalties in the semifinal and taking revenge on Argentina in the final, winning 1–0. This made Beckenbauer the first man to both captain and head coach World Cup–winning teams. Beckenbauer then moved into club management in the early 1990s, before becoming an administrator, leading the hosting of the 2006 World Cup staged in Germany and joining the FIFA Executive Committee in 2007.

BELGIUM. Commonly known as Rode Duivels or Les Diables Rouges (The Red Devils). Out of the 20 World Cup competitions contested to date, Belgium—for a relatively small country—has an impressive record of having appeared in 12 of them, though the nation's first win at a finals tournament did not take place until 1970 and its best appearance was at the 1986 World Cup, finishing in fourth place.

Belgium appeared at the inaugural World Cup in 1930, one of only four European teams to accept an invitation to participate and make the long journey by boat to Uruguay. Belgium had by then almost three decades of international experience as a pioneering member of FIFA and as coach employed Hector Goetinck, who had played for the country between 1906 and 1923. But in Uruguay, Belgium performed dismally, deservedly losing 3–0 to a fit and strong United States in a game played in poor conditions at Parque Central stadium in Montevideo. Belgium lost again a week later, this time at Estadio Centenario in front of a small crowd of 12,000 in a stadium that could hold almost 10 times that. This time, the Belgians lost by a single goal, a 40th-minute strike by Luis Vargas Pena. Belgium departed from Uruguay with two defeats and no goals to their name.

Still under the coaching of Hector Goetinck, Belgium made the shorter trip to Italy for the 1934 World Cup, but only lasted for one game in the competition's straight-elimination format. Belgium's defeat came at the hands of Germany in Florence on 27 May, a small crowd of 8,000 on hand. Though Germany scored first in the 25th minute, two strikes by Bernard Voorhoof in the 29th and 43rd minutes meant Belgium held the lead at the break. Belgium, though, could not hold firm, conceding an equalizer in the 49th minute, and were then torn to shreds as Edmund Conen scored three more for Germany between the 66th and 87th minutes for a final scoreline of 5–2 to the Germans. Belgium qualified for the 1938 World Cup under English coach Jack Butler, who had made his name locally in charge of Royal Daring in Brussels, finishing second in a group also containing the Netherlands and Luxembourg. Again a single-elimination competition, Belgium once more only lasted for 90 minutes at a World Cup, losing in the first round 3–1 to host nation France in Paris. The French scored as early as the first minute and led by two after 16 minutes. Henri Isemborghs pulled one back for the Belgians shortly before halftime, but the French added a third in the 69th minute to confirm a victory that eliminated Belgium.

The World Cup resumed play after a break for World War II in 1950, but Belgium was not yet able to allocate the resources to take part, withdrawing from the qualifying competition. By 1953, though, Belgium was ready to resume World Cup play, taking part in the European qualifiers for the 1954 World Cup in Switzerland. Belgium was guided by head coach Dugald Livingstone, a former Celtic and Everton star who had made his coaching name with Sparta Rotterdam and the Republic of Ireland. He brought immediate success, with Belgium winning three of its four games and tying the other to top a qualifying group ahead of Sweden and Finland. The team's star was Beerschot of Antwerp's star forward Henri "Rik" Coppens, who had finished as top scorer in the Belgian league during the previous two seasons, who despite his short stature could hold up the ball impressively, as well as break through defenses seemingly at will with his dribbling skill.

Belgium's first game in Switzerland was in Basel against England, who along with hosts Switzerland and Italy made up their opposition in group four of the first-round stage. Belgium's matchup with England proved to be a goal-fest, with Coppens in fine form. But though the Belgians struck first, Léopold Anoul scoring in the fifth minute, they found themselves 3–1 down by midway through the second half, the English running the Belgian defense ragged. But Coppens pulled one back with a smart finish in the 67th minute, and Belgium then took the lead four minutes later, Anoul scoring his second. With FIFA ruling games tied at 90 minutes would go into extra time at this World Cup, 30 minutes more would be played: England scored right away through Nat Lofthouse, but an own goal from Englishman Jimmy Dickinson tied the score at 4–4. No further breakthrough came, but Belgium had earned an extraordinary point. However, while the game showed Livingstone's men could score, the four goals conceded pointed to a porous defense exploited by Italy against Belgium in Lugano three days later. The Belgians, clearly tired after the exertion against the English, crumbled to a 4–1 defeat, only pulling back a consolation late on. The result eliminated Belgium, finishing bottom of the group.

Having passed through every World Cup qualifying campaign it had competed in until this point, Belgium would now enter a barren period, failing to qualify for the 1958, 1962 and 1966 World Cup finals, with Constant Vanden Stock's decade in charge as coach (1958–1968) proving signally unsuccessful in this regard. His successor, Raymond Goethals, led Belgium back to the World Cup finals in 1970. The Belgians qualified for the competition in Mexico with an impressive set of results, topping a difficult group that included Spain, Yugoslavia and Finland, including a crucial 2–1 win over Spain in November 1969. The team's star player was Anderlecht's Paul van Himst, a prolific scorer for club and country and the captain for the 1970 World Cup. He was one among an array of stars drawn from Belgium's increasingly strong domestic scene, alongside Standard Liège's gifted midfielder Wilfried Van Moer and Raoul Lambert, a prolific forward for Club Brugge.

In Mexico, Belgium faced the Soviet Union, El Salvador and Mexico in group one. They began by brushing aside an outmatched El Salvador 3–0, the first and second goals coming from Van Moer and then a third from the penalty spot by Raoul Lambert. The result gave Belgium the country's first win in the World Cup finals. A promising start for Belgium came to a stunning halt in Mexico City at the Azteca, almost 100,000 in attendance as the Soviet Union surprisingly put Belgium to the sword: four goals to the Soviets and only one for Belgium, Lambert scoring a consolation in the 86th minute, the game long since lost. A dispirited Belgium, reportedly riven by internal conflicts, returned to the Azteca to face the host nation Mexico four days later, 110,000 extremely partisan fans filling the giant arena. To the Belgians, it also appeared the referee may have been partisan: the lone goal of the game came in a controversial manner after 15 minutes from the penalty spot, a decision by the referee seen as extremely dubious by neutral observers. Belgium could not break through a packed Mexican defense for the remainder of the game, exiting after highly disappointing finish to the competition.

Raymond Goethals remained in charge of Belgium for the 1974 qualifying cycle, after a successful 1972 European Championship campaign, with the Belgians finishing in third place. Placed in a four-team qualifying group out of which only one nation would progress, Belgium finished second behind the Netherlands and ahead of Norway and Iceland. Belgium won as many points as the Netherlands (who would go on to reach the 1974 World Cup final), ten, with four wins in six games, but the Dutch team's superior goal difference saw them advance at the Belgians' expense. Amazingly, Belgium did not concede a goal in qualifying, but only scored 12, while the

Netherlands conceded 2 but scored 24. It was a strong effort by Belgium that included twice tying the Dutch, a 0–0 tie in the last game of the group stage proving critical—and controversial. In the 89th minute of the game in Amsterdam, a free kick by Paul van Himst found Jan Verheyen, who scored what would surely have been a winning goal had it not been wrongly disallowed for offside. The brutal decision eliminated Belgium, and the Dutch went on to strut on the world stage in West Germany at the 1974 World Cup.

Four years later, Belgium again faced the Netherlands in World Cup qualifying, again also joined by Iceland along with one different face, Northern Ireland, in group four. This time, the Netherlands clearly had the upper hand, defeating Belgium both home and away. The Belgians only secured three wins out of six games, under new coach Guy Thys, who had most recently led Royal Antwerp to domestic success. Thys stayed in charge following the failure to qualify for the 1978 World Cup, and with a talented crop of young players developing, the Belgians finished a surprising second at the 1980 European Championship, with the emergence of midfielder Jan Ceulemans. Belgium topped qualifying for the competition in Spain, finishing ahead of France, the Republic of Ireland, the Netherlands and Cyprus, an impressive performance in a difficult group, only conceding 9 goals in 11 games.

Placed in group three in Spain at the World Cup finals, Belgium's opponents in the first round would be Argentina, Hungary and El Salvador. Belgium and Argentina kicked off the competition, with the Europeans taking on the defending World Cup champions, who had the addition of the brilliant young talent Diego Maradona. But a highly disciplined Belgian performance kept Maradona in check in Barcelona, Pfaff making a series of world-class saves. Belgium carved out a number of good chances in the first half, with 22-year-old forward Alex Czerniatynski missing the best one, somehow planting a header wide in front of an open goal from less than six yards out. Midway through the second half, Anderlecht star Franky Vercauteren found space on the left wing and curled in a delightful cross into the path of Erwin Vandenbergh, who finished coolly from 10 yards out. The goal gave Belgium a 1–0 win and marked them out as dark-horse contenders for the competition. Belgium continued to demonstrate a miserly defense in Elche against El Salvador, keeping a second clean sheet and winning 1–0 once more with a goal from Ludo Coeck—the South Americans, who had conceded 10 in their previous game to Hungary, packed a defense that Belgium found hard to break down. Coeck's strike came in the 19th minute, a long-range strike from over 30 yards out and dipped and bounced past a bemused Luis Guevara Mora in the El Salvador goal. Belgium secured qualification to the second round against Hungary, again in Elche, by earning a point in a 1–1 draw. József Varga had given the Hungarians the lead in the 27th minute, with the goal coming as no surprise in a game wide open early on, bursting through an unusually confused Belgian defense and lashing home high into the roof of the net. But Belgium found the equalizer with less than 15 minutes remaining in the game, Czerniatynski side-footing home from an unmarked position just above the penalty spot.

In the second round, also a group stage, Belgium joined Poland and the Soviet Union for round-robin games held in Barcelona. It was to prove to be immensely disappointing for the Belgians. Against Poland, Belgium came out lackluster, Van der Moer a shadow of his earlier self and substituted at halftime. By then, two goals from Zbigniew Boniek had given Poland what proved to be an unassailable lead, and he secured his hat trick in the second half, with Belgium unable to offer any goals in return. Thys made a number of changes for Belgium's second game against the Soviet Union, with van Moer, Gerard Plessers and Czerniatynski all benched, Guy Vandersmissen and Rene Verheyen coming in as a change of pace for Belgium offensively. The changes seemed as if they would reap rewards for Belgium, who started stronger than the Soviets, but early in the second half, a smart Soviet move found space for Khoren Oganesian, who struck a neat volley past Jacques Munaron from 15 yards out. Belgian pressure could not yield a tying goal, and Belgium's defeat left them eliminated and bottom of the group.

Belgium's tough defense was again at the heart of a successful qualifying campaign for the 1986 World Cup, remaining under the stewardship of Guy Thys. The Belgians conceded only three goals in six games in a qualifying group featuring Poland, Albania and Greece, but a lack of goals—Belgium only scoring seven—meant only half of those games were won, and Belgium finished second behind Poland. This was enough to advance Belgium to a play-off with the Netherlands for a spot at the 1986 World Cup finals in Mexico. In a two-game series, Belgium went through on aggregate due to away goals scored, winning 1–0 at home (thanks to a goal by Franky Vercauteren) and losing 2–1 away, Georges Grün scoring the critical goal for the Belgians with only five minutes in the game remaining. The qualifying campaign saw Enzo Scifo, only 18 years old, emerge as the fulcrum of the team, a brilliant midfield talent who scored his first international goal during qualifying against Albania.

The host nation Mexico, Paraguay and Iraq comprised the group Belgium entered in the first round at the 1986 World Cup finals, a comparatively easy set of opposition for Thys's men. But playing the host nation in their first game meant kicking off at Mexico City's enormous and intimidating Azteca stadium, over 110,000 partisan fans in attendance. Whether it was the setting or not, Belgium began with an uncharacteristically poor defensive effort on set pieces: conceding a first goal in the 23rd minute due to sloppy marking from a free kick and a second from a corner just before halftime. Belgium pulled one back from a set piece as well, Erwin Vandenbergh heading in from a long throw, but could not find an equalizer, losing 2–1. Thys's team improved in Toluca against Iraq, securing a much-needed 2–1 win: Scifo began the scoring only 16 minutes in with a low drive that bounced underneath Iraq's goalkeeper Raad Hammoudi, and five minutes later, it was 2–0 after Frank Vercauteren was fouled in the penalty area, Nico Claesen converting the spot kick. Iraq went down to 10 men after 52 minutes, Basil Gorgis sent off for two cautions, but Belgium could not press home the advantage and instead complacently conceded a goal to the Iraqis 7 minutes later, Belgian goalkeeper Jean Marie Pfaff unable to stop a hard drive from Ahmed Radhi.

Belgium showed few signs of major improvement when taking on the Paraguayans, again in Toluca, on 11 June. Paraguay had already confirmed a place in the next round, while the Belgians needed to avoid defeat to progress. Frank Vercauteren opened the scoring for Belgium after half an hour with a seemingly fortunate left-footed, looping strike. Five minutes after the break, Roberto Cabanas beat Belgium's offside trap to level the scores, but the Europeans reclaimed the lead within 10 minutes, Daniel Veyt finishing neatly over the onrushing Paraguayan goalkeeper. Not long after, Belgium believed they had taken a definitive 3–1 lead when Scifo curled in a sumptuous free kick, but the strike was disallowed by the referee, who had indicated the kick was to be indirect. Cabanas, though, again found space in the Belgian penalty area and scored past Pfaff to make the score 2–2. The result meant Belgium did move on to the second round as a best-placed third-place finisher, but they had not advanced in anything like convincing style.

The style, it would turn out, would be turned on by Belgium in the knockout stage. The rollercoaster began with a matchup against the Soviet Union in León, seven goals flying in. Thys made changes, Claesen and Patrick Vervoort paired upfront, an effective move that made up for a leaky defensive effort. There was nothing Pfaff could do to prevent the Soviets taking the lead 27 minutes in, a rocket from Igor Belanov 20 yards out. Scifo tied the scores 56 minutes in, ghosting in at the far piece to deftly knock in a cross, but 14 minutes later, Belanov dinked in over Pfaff to put the Soviet Union 2–1 up. Jan Ceulemans ensured the game would go to extra time, his 77th-minute strike coming from a long, hopeful pass. In the added period, Belgium grabbed control of the game with goals in the 102nd and 110th minutes from Stéphane Demol and Nico Claesen. Though the Soviets found a third goal, Belgium's offensive surge saw them into the quarterfinal stage.

In Puebla, Belgium's opposition in the last eight would be Spain, and this time Belgium's defense would be firmer, Pfaff showing his outstanding skills in goal. The Belgians would rely on the break to unravel the Spanish, Frank Vercauteren whipping in a left-footed cross, Ceulemans burying a header. Thys's team frustrated the Spanish until five minutes from the end, Juan Antonio Senor flashing in a first-time drive from 25 yards out. The two teams could not be separated in extra time, and penalty kicks had to be used to decide a winner. Belgium coolly converted all five of their kicks, while Pfaff—playing up his personality in goal—seemed to distract Spain's second penalty taker, Eloy, making him wait before a scrambling dive to his right stopped the weak shot. It was enough to take Belgium through 5–4 in the shoot-out.

For the first time, Belgium reached the last four of the World Cup. Back at the Azteca, Thys's team faced the daunting challenge of Diego Maradona's Argentina, the world's best player in unstoppable form. Thys's tactic was for Belgium to mass in defense and try to deny Maradona space to operate, while the Belgian captain Ceulemans was the offensive outlet. The strategy worked in the first half, 0–0 at the break, but Maradona at his best could not be denied: in the 51st minute, he cut into the penalty area and needed only one flick of his left foot to give Argentina the lead. He scored again, 12 minutes later, this time bursting aside a phalanx of Belgian defenders before cutting a shot back across Pfaff and into the net. There was little Thys and Belgium could do, unable to conjure up a goal and exiting at the hands of the tournament's dominant force. Belgium still had third place to play for against France and again found themselves in a goal-fest: the two teams alternated four goals in the first half, Ceulemans and Claesen scoring for Belgium, but the French found the upper hand in the extra time, scoring twice. Belgium departed with fourth place, to date the country's best result in the World Cup, a remarkable achievement by Pfaff with a team few had expected to go so far, with Ceulemans undoubtedly Belgium's star of the competition.

Belgium's strong run of form continued into the 1990 World Cup in Italy. This time, Enzo Scifo was the star of the show. Belgium qualified for the competition unbeaten in eight games; Thys had stepped down from his role as coach in June 1989 but returned to the role eight months later and led Belgium at the World Cup, with the team still captained by Ceulemans and with the talented Michel Preud'homme in goal. In Italy, Belgium's first-round group contained Spain, Uruguay and South Korea. Thys's team began with a straightforward 2–0 win over a limited South Korean team in Verona, with second-half goals from Marc de Grijse and Michel de Wolf. Belgium continued in fine form against Uruguay, again in Verona, 2–0 up by halftime through strikes by Leo Clijsters and Enzo Scifo. By halftime, though, Belgium had been reduced to 10 men, defender Eric Gerets dismissed for two cautionable offenses. It made little difference in the second half: Ceulemans scored on a counterattack to give Belgium a 3–0 lead, a consolation goal for Uruguay making little difference.

A defeat to Spain in Belgium's final group game, 2–1, meant a second-place finish, Patrick Vervoort scoring the Belgians' only goal. The result meant that Belgium faced England in the second round in Bologna. The Belgians lost 1–0 in dramatic, cruel fashion: with no goals scored in the regulation 90 minutes, the game had gone to extra time and the winner from David Platt as late as the 119th minute. Belgium had arguably had the better of the play, Ceulemans hitting the post in the first half and Scifo doing the same in the second, but with one swing of the foot by Platt, Thys's team was eliminated.

Paul van Himst, a star for Anderlecht and the Belgium national team in the 1960s and 1970s, took over as coach from Thys for the 1994 World Cup qualifying campaign. Belgium qualified alongside Romania from UEFA qualifying group four, finishing ahead of the Czech Republic, Wales, Cyprus and the Faroe Islands to advance to the competition in the United States. Belgium was drawn in group F with Morocco, Saudi Arabia and bitter rivals the Netherlands. With Ceulemans now retired, Georges Grün was Belgium's captain at the World Cup, though the team rotated around Scifo's play in midfield more than ever. In Orlando, at the Citrus Bowl, Belgium began with a tight game against Morocco. The only goal came in the 11th minute, scored for Belgium by Marc de Grijse. Then came the critical matchup with the Dutch, again at the Citrus Bowl. Belgium's forwards clearly unsettled a disorganized Dutch defense, and the sole goal of the game came when Belgian defender Philippe Albert forced the ball home from a corner. Facing Saudi Arabia in the last game of the group, van Himst's team had a fine opportunity to clinch victory in the group with a win. Belgium, though, lost 1–0, dropping to third and only advancing as one of the best third-placed teams, conceding a goal from a wondrous dribble by Saeed Al-Owairan. That forced Belgium to face the defending world champions Germany in the round of 16. At Soldier Field in Chicago, the Germans—with the dangerous forward pair of Jürgen Klinsmann and Rudolf Völler —peppered Preud'homme with shots, and between them, they had scored three goals by halftime. Belgium, though, scored one through Grün, and a late goal by Philippe Albert resulted in a deceptive 3–2 scoreline, with the Belgians even feeling robbed of a penalty not given by Swiss referee Kurt Roethlisberger.

In 1998, Belgium qualified for a fifth straight World Cup, this time under the charge of former Standard Liège star Wilfried Van Moer. The Belgians had finished second in their qualifying group, behind perennial rivals the Netherlands, but qualified for the competition in France by beating the Republic of Ireland in a play-off. It proved to be an enormously frustrating tournament for Belgium, who tied all three games. Belgium was once again paired with the Netherlands, opening the competition against the fancied Dutch. Scifo, now 32, began the game on the bench, and Belgium's plodding defensive style kept the score to a 0–0 stalemate, the Dutch reduced to 10 men with the expulsion of Patrick Kluivert eight minutes before full-time. Belgium's next opponents, Mexico, also failed to finish the game with 10 men, Pável Pardo sent off with only 28 minutes gone, given a straight red card following a tackle from behind on Vital Borkelmans. That gave Belgium the initiative, quickly capitalizing with a pair of goals by Marc Wilmots. The first came with Wilmots finishing from a corner, the second a fine goal from a Scifo pass, Wilmots beating three Mexican defenders before finishing from the edge of the penalty area. Disaster struck for Belgium in the 55th minute: Gert Verheyen was dismissed for a foul in the penalty area, Mexico pulling one back from a spot kick and finding an equalizer via a spectacular finish from Cuauhtémoc Blanco. A third tie against South Korea meant that for the first time in Belgium's World Cup finals appearances since 1970, the country would not advance past the first round. Needing to win, Belgium took the lead early with a Luc Nilis goal from 12 yards out after a scramble in the penalty area but conceded a tying goal with less than 20 minutes remaining. Belgium's desperate attempts to score a winner came to naught.

Belgium reached a sixth straight World Cup in 2002, qualifying for the tournament in Japan and South Korea, again qualifying via the play-offs after finishing behind Croatia, defeating the Czech Republic with a pair of 1–0 wins. Coached by Robert Waseige, Belgium faced Japan, Russia and Tunisia in the first round. The Belgians faced host nation Japan first, with team captain Marc Wilmots giving the Europeans the lead in the 57th minute with an overhead kick, outplaying the Asian team to that point. But Japan equalized only two minutes later, a lapse by Jacky Peeters allowing in Takayuki Suzuki to score, and 10 minutes later, Japan scored again to take a 2–1 lead. Belgium fought back and earned a point thanks to Peter Van Der Heyden roving forward and chipping in with 75 minutes gone. Belgium's pattern of draws continued against Tunisia, settling for a fifth-successive tie in the World Cup finals stretching back to 1998 after Raouf Bouzaiene's strike canceled out the lead given to Belgium by Marc Wilmots early on. Belgium thus needed to defeat Russia to qualify for the second round, and this was achieved with a 3–2 win. Belgium's thrilling win came thanks to goals from Johan Walem, Wesley Sonck and Marc Wilmots, the latter scoring his fifth World Cup finals goal in seven appearances to date in the 1998 and 2002 tournaments. The impressive win secured Belgium second place in the group and a matchup with Brazil in the second round. Though the eventual champions defeated Belgium 2–0, the European team created multiple good chances and had a goal by Wilmots harshly disallowed for an apparent push on the goalkeeper. The South Americans did not put the game to bed until late in the second half, Rivaldo scoring in the 67th minute and Ronaldo securing the win in the 87th to eliminate Belgium.

After qualifying for six straight World Cup finals, Belgium then failed to qualify for two successive competitions, not reaching Germany in 2006 or South Africa in

2010. Belgium's 2006 qualifying effort was distinctly dismal, finishing fourth in a six-team group behind Serbia and Montenegro, Spain and Bosnia and Herzegovina. Belgium performed no better in 2010 World Cup qualifying, again finishing in fourth in their group and again with both Spain and Serbia and Montenegro ahead of them—though this time, with Turkey rather than Bosnia and Herzegovina also finishing above the Belgians.

Led by 2002 captain Marc Wilmots, qualifying for 2014 was a completely different story. The Belgians finished first in UEFA's group A, a full nine points ahead of second-place Croatia, easily guaranteeing them a spot. For years Les Diables Rouges had been building toward something special, and many people believed that, especially after this performance, Belgium was a dark horse to win the whole thing. In 10 qualifying games, the only setbacks were draws home and away to a pesky Croatian side that also qualified.

Placed into group H with Algeria, Korea Republic and Russia, Belgium looked like a supremely confident side and finished the group stage with a full nine points. In game one, played at Estádio Mineirão in Belo Horizonte, the Belgians faced an Algerian side looking to advance out of the group stage for the first time in their history. Though they controlled much of the ball in the first half, the Red Devils were unable to create many meaningful chances and instead found themselves on the wrong end of a breakaway in the 25th minute when Jan Vertonghen bungled a tackle that led to a Sofiane Feghouli penalty conversion. At halftime, Wilmots inserted Dries Mertens and Marouane Fellaini and was rewarded with a goal by both for the 2–1 win.

Game two saw a chess match between Wilmots and his Russian counterpart, Fabio Capello, which resulted in a boring game (as evidenced by cameras catching fans asleep in the stands) until the 88th minute when 19-year-old substitute Divock Origi, making only his fourth appearance (and second in two games), played the ball to Eden Hazard. Hazard craftily dribbled around and through the defense before finding Origi wide open nine yards out for the game winner. Now wholly in control of their group, Belgium needed just a point out of their final group match against Korea Republic to finish on top of their group. They played like a team that had already moved on, and the game itself was unremarkable until the 45th minute when Steven Defour was issued a straight red for stepping on Korean forward Kim Shin-wook after a late challenge. Even playing down a man, Belgium still looked like the better side against a Korean team struggling to find an identity in the tournament. A follow-up of an Origi blast by Jan Vertonghen in the 77th minute sealed Belgium's advancement to the round of 16 and a date with the United States.

Against the Americans, a Belgium side full of stars asserted their dominance immediately when, a minute in, Origi found himself one versus one with U.S. goalkeeper Tim Howard. Howard's play in goal set the tone with tremendous save after save, keeping the score locked at 0–0. Ironically though, the United States had a clear chance to win it in the 91st minute when a flicked header by Jermaine Jones saw Chris Wondolowski alone at the six with a tap in. Inexplicably, Wondolowski sent the ball high and wide over the bar. Given life, Belgium dominated from the start of extra time, and Kevin De Bruyne clinically settled a deflected Romelu Lukaku cross, beat two defenders and blasted a right-footed shot past a diving Howard into the far-post side netting. From there, Belgium dominated and, in the 105th minute, the game seemed to be over as De Bruyne found a streaking Lukaku, who blasted a first-time rocket near post. With a seemingly insurmountable two-goal lead with one 15-minute period to play, the Americans proved their mettle when substitute Julian Green volleyed a brilliant Michael Bradley through ball on his first touch of the game past a stunned Courtois. Back on their heels, Belgium weathered a close miss by Jones and a brilliant free kick in the final 15 to advance to the quarterfinals against Argentina.

A rematch of a 1982 1–0 group win and a 1986 semifinal that resulted in a 2–0 loss, the game at Estádio Nacional de Brasília in Brasília shaped up to be a showcase of powerhouses. Unfortunately for the Belgians, the first 20 minutes were all Argentina. In the eighth minute, Gonzalo Higuaín spun and volleyed a first-time shot past Courtois, and it looked, for all intents and purposes, like the game would turn into a rout. Had it not been for an Ángel Di María injury in the 29th minute, Belgium may very well have seen their tournament chances over; however, after weathering some heavy pressure, second-half subs Mertens and Lukaku breathed life into the Belgian side. Though they never really troubled goalkeeper Sergio Romero, the last 10 minutes saw the Red Devils look to bulldoze their way straight to goal as Fellaini and Lukaku used their size and strength to create chances. Sadly for the Belgian supporters, neither was able to finish, and Belgium saw its 2014 tournament finish in sixth place with a goal differential of +3.

BELQOLA, SAID. B. 30 August 1956, Tifelt, Morocco. D. 15 June 2002. At the 1998 World Cup in France, Said Belqola became the first African to referee a World Cup final, overseeing France's 3–0 win over Brazil at the Stade de France on 12 July 1998. The Moroccan, 41 years old at the time, became the second referee in World Cup history to send off a player in the final, dismissing Marcel Desailly of France for two yellow-card offenses eight years after the first red card in a final had been issued by Mexican referee Edgardo Codesal in 1990. Belqola had earned a reputation as a high-quality international referee in the 1990s at the Africa Cup of Nations in 1996 and 1998 and the warm-up competition for the 1998 World Cup, the 1997 Tournoi de France. At the 1998 World Cup, Belqola refereed two games in the first round: United States versus Germany in the first round on 15 June, issuing five cautions, and Argentina versus Croatia on 26 June, handing out seven yellow cards in a foul-ridden game. Curiously, Belqola was not selected to referee any of the knockout-stage games until the final, where he was assisted by Englishman Mark Warren and Saudi Arabian Achmat Salie. As well as the red card to Desailly, Belqola also booked Júnior Baiano of Brazil along with French captain Didier Deschamps and Christian Karembeu during the game. Belqola was not a full-time referee, also working as a customs officer in his native Morocco, fluent in English and French as well as Arabic. He passed away in 2002 after a long battle with cancer.

BENE, FERENC. B. 17 December 1944, Balatonújlak, Hungary. D. 27 February 2006. At the 1966 World Cup in England, Ferenc Bene scored four goals for Hungary, finishing as the joint third top scorer in the competition. Bene made his debut for Hungary in 1962 and played a key role as Hungary finished in third place at the

1964 UEFA European Championship, scoring twice in two games in the finals. Bene starred at the 1964 Olympic Games Football Tournament, contributing a remarkable ten goals in five games as Hungary won the gold medal. At the 1966 World Cup, Hungary was placed into group three along with reigning World Cup champions Brazil, a Portuguese team based around the brilliant Eusébio and Bulgaria. Hungary's team, though not as strong as in the early 1950s, included one of the world's best players, who played a key role in generating chances for Bene, center-forward Flórián Albert. To use his speed and shifty skills, Hungarian coach Lajos Baróti lined Bene up on the right wing. Hungary found little reward for their technically excellent performance in their opening game against Portugal in Manchester, though Bene did score in the 60th minute after Portuguese goalkeeper Carvalho, under pressure from Albert, spilled the ball at his feet for an easy finish. Hungary found far more success with a stunning 3–1 victory over Brazil on 15 July at Goodison Park in Liverpool, Albert magnificent and Bene opening the scoring in only the second minute: Bene received the ball just outside the Brazilian penalty area, swerving first left and then right with characteristic poise, leaving his defender on the floor and then beating another defender with a turn inside and slotting the ball past Gilmar in the Brazilian goal with the inside of his left foot. Tostão equalized for Brazil, but János Farkas made it 2–1 to Hungary with 64 minutes gone, Bene providing a pinpoint cross from the right that Farkas hammered home on the volley. Bene then won the penalty that sealed a famous 3–1 for Hungary, twisting and turning past two defenders to draw a foul, Kálmán Mészöly scoring the resulting penalty. Hungary had handed Brazil their first World Cup defeat since 1954. Hungary qualified for the knockout with a further victory over Bulgaria, Bene scoring the third goal with a thumping running header from a corner. In the quarterfinal, at Roker Park in Sunderland on 23 July, Hungary faced the Soviets, by whom they were overpowered, 2–0 down at halftime. Bene scored his fourth and final goal of the competition with 57 minutes gone, finishing from a tight angle six yards out, but it was to no avail, Hungary losing 2–1. Bene continued playing internationally for Hungary until the late 1970s, notching 36 goals in 72 total games for his country, but Hungary did not qualify for either the 1970 or 1974 World Cup finals, even though Bene recorded several more goals to end his international career with 10 goals in 15 World Cup qualifying games. Bene retired in 1978, having played his entire club career for Hungarian team Újpesti Dózsa, scoring over 300 goals for the club.

BERTOLINI, LUIGI. B. 13 September 1904, Busalla, Italy. D. 11 February 1977. Luigi Bertolini was part of Italy's tremendous midfield at the 1934 World Cup, playing in four of Italy's five games as they won the World Cup (missing the quarterfinal victory over Spain), clinching the trophy on home soil with a 2–1 win over Czechoslovakia in the final in Rome. Bertolini was one of the most experienced players on the team, 30 years old and having made his debut almost six years earlier in December 1929. Following the 1934 World Cup, Bertolini played only three more games for his country before his international retirement in 1935, including in the brave Italian defeat to England at Highbury in November 1934. At club level, Bertolini's most successful period of play came from 1931 to 1937 with Juventus, winning four Serie A titles during that time.

BERTONI, DANIEL. B. 14 March 1955, Bahía Blanca, Argentina. A tenacious and creative midfielder, Daniel Bertoni played for Argentina at two World Cup finals, playing a crucial role in Argentina's first world-championship victory in 1978 and appearing again at the 1982 competition. Bertoni made his debut for Argentina in 1974 at just 19 years old, but though he was in the preliminary squad for the 1974 World Cup in West Germany, he was not selected in the final 22 to travel there. Bertoni made a strong impact at club level ahead of the 1978 World Cup, winning the Copa Libertadores three times with Argentinean team Independiente. Bertoni picked up an injury ahead of the start of the 1978 World Cup held in his native Argentina, forcing him to the bench for Argentina's opening game against Hungary, but he entered the game in the 67th minute and made a crucial contribution by scoring the winning goal in the 83rd minute, the ball deflecting to Bertoni 10 yards out for a simple finish. Despite this contribution, Argentina's coach César Luis Menotti left Bertoni on the bench for the entirety of their next game against France, a 2–1 win. Bertoni returned to the starting lineup for Argentina's final first-round group game against Italy, both teams already having qualified for the next round, and kept his place for the next game against Poland in Rosario, the first of the second-round group stage. Bertoni created the first goal for Argentina in a 2–0 win, delivering a deep cross for Mario Kempes to head home. Bertoni then played 90 minutes against Brazil, a 0–0 tie, and 64 minutes in a 6–0 win over Peru in Argentina's final second-round group game that sealed the country's place in the World Cup final against the Netherlands. Bertoni would play a key role in Argentina's 3–1 victory after extra time, constantly causing the Dutch problems as he linked up superbly with Kempes. This led to a goal in the 15th minute of extra time, as Bertoni slipped the ball to Kempes, the Argentinean forward then rampaging through the Dutch defense to give Argentina the 2–1 lead. Bertoni then capped the game and sealed the World Cup for Argentina with five minutes remaining of extra time, combining again with Kempes to find himself with a good chance from 12 yards out that he struck accurately into the net.

Bertoni was again selected by Menotti to represent Argentina at the 1982 World Cup in Spain, now a veteran of the team, but the tournament ended in disappointment for Bertoni with elimination at the second-round stage. Bertoni played in all five games, scoring the first goal in Argentina's first-round victory over Hungary, finding himself open at the edge of the six-yard box to poach a goal from a free kick, as Argentina won 4–1 thanks largely to a virtuoso performance by a young Diego Maradona. Bertoni found the net again in Argentina's next game, a 2–0 win over an overmatched El Salvador in their final first-round group game. Bertoni's goal, the second of the game, was a marvelous individual effort: picking the ball up by the right touchline, Bertoni cut inside with the ball, dribbling past three El Salvadorian defenders before curling the ball sweetly into the bottom corner of the net from 20 yards out with his left foot. The second-round group stage, though, went disastrously for Bertoni and Argentina, as they lost 2–1 to Italy in Barcelona and then 3–1 to Brazil also in Barcelona, Maradona sent off in a dismal defeat that eliminated Argentina, an unfitting end to Bertoni's World Cup finals career. Bertoni was selected for the preliminary squad in 1986, a World Cup Argentina would go on to win, but coach Carlos Bilardo preferred Jorge Valdano to him for the final 22.

Bertoni ended his club career, which had seen him play successfully in Spain and Italy since the 1978 World Cup, the following year.

BILARDO, CARLOS. B. 16 March 1939, Buenos Aires, Argentina. With Diego Maradona the star of the tournament, Carlos Bilardo coached Argentina to a second World Cup title in 1986, winning the competition in Mexico. Renowned as a former star player for Estudiantes in Argentina during the 1960s, he had struggled managing Colombia from 1979 to 1982, failing to qualify for the World Cup; he won the league title with Estudiantes on his return there as coach in 1982 and was quickly picked to take charge of the national team. His central challenge and opportunity with Argentina was working out how to build the team around the genius of Diego Maradona, whose only World Cup appearance so far had been a disaster in Spain in 1982. Bilardo had been known as a hard man as a player, and his approach as a coach was similarly driven by a desire for results rather than any interest in romantic notions of how the game should be played.

Bilardo brought in a youthful team to support Maradona, given free rein in an innovative 3-5-2 formation that featured seven players holding the game defensively but allowing the front three to operate with freedom to roam. At the 1986 World Cup, after Bilardo had led Argentina through qualifying with four wins in six games, Bilardo's tactics worked to perfection with the brilliance of Maradona meaning that, despite fielding a largely defensive team, Argentina could unlock any opposition. Argentina topped group A in the first round, winning by two goals against both South Korea and Bulgaria, while also holding defending world champions Italy to a 1–1 draw. In the second round, Bilardo's team beat neighbors Uruguay 1–0, Pedro Pasculli scoring the only goal of the game. The quarterfinal game against England was billed as a grudge match—the two countries had been at war only four years previously—but it was the full spectrum of Maradona's abilities that was on display. He scored twice, one a controversial handball missed by the referee and the other a virtuoso solo effort, in a 3–1 win for Argentina. In the semifinal, it was Maradona who again unpicked the opposition, Belgium, despite being stymied in the first half, scoring twice in the second period. The final proved to be a comprehensive win for Argentina and a confirmation of the success of Bilardo's tactical framework, as his team won 3–1 in front of 115,000 fans at the Azteca in Mexico City.

Four years later, Bilardo led Argentina to the World Cup finals again, this time in Italy. Despite the 1986 title, Bilardo's tactics were a focus for media criticism in Argentina. In Italy, he had at his disposal not just the brilliance of Maradona but also one of the world's leading up-and-coming strikers, Claudio Caniggia. Curiously, though, Bilardo did not start Caniggia in Argentina's first game at the World Cup against Cameroon, and with Maradona stifled, Argentina stumbled to a shocking 1–0 defeat, even though their opponents ended up with only 10 men on the field due to a pair of red cards. With Caniggia inserted into the starting lineup for the remaining two group games, Argentina squeezed through to the second round with a win over the Soviet Union and a draw against Romania but only advanced as one of the best third-placed group-stage teams. Injuries slowed Argentina—the rough treatment dished out to Maradona meant he was a shadow of the player who had dominated the 1986 competition—and Bilardo's team increasingly turned to the coach's trademark hard-nosed tactics to get under the skin of the opposition. In Turin, Argentina then pulled of a surprising 1–0 victory over Brazil, outplayed in possession but taking advantage of a rare opportunity with Caniggia finding the net late on. Argentina, playing disruptive, defensive soccer, then squeezed past both Yugoslavia at the quarterfinal and Italy at the semifinal stages via penalty shoot-outs. Argentina had only scored two goals in the elimination rounds, but Bilardo's tough, pragmatic tactics had pulled them to a second successive final. Here, with Caniggia missing suspended, Argentina unraveled in a rematch from the 1986 final with West Germany. Both Pedro Monzón and Gustavo Dezotti were sent off, and Argentina lost to a penalty kick from Andreas Brehme. Bilardo left his post after the 1990 World Cup. Two decades later, he served his country again at the World Cup at the age of 71, this time behind the scenes as a general manager for the national team at the 2010 World Cup, with his former star pupil Diego Maradona now at the helm. The setup was not a great success, with a talented Argentina struggling to qualify and then departing at the quarterfinal stage with a one-sided 4–0 defeat to Germany.

BÍRÓ, SÁNDOR. B. 19 August 1911, Hungary. D. 7 October 1988. Among Sándor Bíró's 54 appearances for Hungary between 1932 and 1946, 4 came at the 1938 World Cup in France, as Bíró played in every game for Hungary at the competition. After participating in wins over the Dutch East Indies, Switzerland and Sweden, Bíró was part of the Hungarian team that went down 4–2 to Italy in the third World Cup final. A defensive stalwart for his country and several leading Hungarian club teams in a long career, Bíró was also part of Hungary's 22-man team that traveled to the 1934 World Cup in France, though he did not appear in either of Hungary's two games at the competition. His 54th and final outing for Hungary came in October 1946, as Hungary defeated Austria 2–0.

BOLIVIA. Commonly known as La Verde (The Green). The South American nation Bolivia appeared at two of the first four World Cup finals held—in 1930 and 1950—but has only reached that same stage on one occasion since then, in 1994. Bolivia has traditionally struggled to compete with the powerhouse nations of South American World Cup qualifying, such as Brazil, Argentina and Uruguay. The Bolivians did not need to qualify for the first World Cup in 1930, an invitational tournament in Uruguay. Bolivian soccer had only recently begun to develop, the nation taking part in Copa América tournaments in 1926 and 1927, though losing all seven games across the two competitions. Bolivia fared no better in Uruguay for the World Cup. Paired with Yugoslavia and Brazil in group two in the first round, Bolivia lost to both teams by the resounding scores of 4–0, against the Europeans on 17 July and against their fellow South Americans three days later. That left Bolivia bottom of the group and eliminated. With Bolivia's national-team funds extremely limited, the country did not enter qualifying for either the 1934 or 1938 World Cup competitions in Italy and France, with projected travel costs likely precluding participation. The World Cup returned to South America in 1950, and after Argentina withdrew from Bolivia's qualifying group, Bolivia advanced to the competition in Brazil. Bolivia, coached by

Italian Mario Pretto, a former star for Napoli, played one game in the competition, and it was a disaster. With an awkward first-round setup due to late withdrawals by several nations, Bolivia's group consisted of only one other team—Uruguay, who would go on to win the competition. The Uruguayans had little trouble putting an inexperienced Bolivian team to the sword, scoring four goals in either half without reply.

Fully 44 years would pass until Bolivia again appeared at the World Cup. The Bolivians advanced to the 1994 World Cup after finishing in the second qualifying spot from a group won by Brazil and also containing Uruguay, Ecuador and Venezuela. It was Bolivia's first successful qualifying campaign and included a memorable 2–0 win over Brazil on 25 July 1993 at Estadio Hernando Siles, La Paz, Bolivia. That result inflicted Brazil's first-ever defeat in a South American World Cup qualifier, orchestrated by an outstanding midfield of Marco Etcheverry, Milton Melgar, Julio César Baldivieso and Erwin Sánchez. Etcheverry, known as El Diablo and arguably Bolivia's greatest-ever talent, scored the first in the 88th minute and Alvaro Pena the second only one minute later. The fortunes of Brazil and Bolivia would diverge at the World Cup finals in the United States, however. While Brazil went on to win the World Cup, Bolivia scored only one goal and failed to win a game, eliminated at the first-round stage. The South Americans lost to Germany 1–0 in the opening game of the competition at Chicago's Soldier Field, tied 0–0 with South Korea near Boston at Foxboro Stadium and lost 3–1 back at Soldier Field to Spain, Bolivia's only goal of the competition coming in that game from Erwin Sánchez. Since 1994, Bolivia has failed to advance from South American qualifying for the World Cup.

BOSNIA AND HERZEGOVINA. Commonly known as Zmajevi (The Dragons) or Zlatni Ljiljani (The Golden Lilies). The game of football reached Bosnia and Herzegovina early in the 20th century, and under Austro-Hungarian rule, official competition began in 1908. Following the creation of the Republic of Yugoslavia in 1918, there was an increase in the number of leagues, and in 1920, the Sarajevo football sub-association was founded.

The Sarajevo sub-association became the Football Federation of Bosnia and Herzegovina after the Second World War, and Bosnia and Herzegovina's best sides played in the Yugoslavian first, second and third divisions with moderate success, while its best players were chosen to represent SFR Yugoslavia national football team.

Bosnia and Herzegovina declared independence on 3 March 1992 and received international recognition the following month on 6 April 1992. On the same date, the Serbs responded by declaring the independence of the Republika Srpska and laying siege to Sarajevo, marking the start of the Bosnian War. Bosnia and Herzegovina (using mainly players from the FK Sarajevo) played their first international match against Iran in Tehran a few months later, but the game was never recognized due to Bosnia and Herzegovina not yet being a member of FIFA. The team's first FIFA-recognized match, played on the 30th of November 1995 in Tirana against Albania, came just nine days after the Dayton Agreement brought an end to the Bosnian War.

Since the country was not recognized by FIFA until July of 1996, the Dragons didn't have a chance to qualify for the 1994 World Cup finals in the United States. Bosnia and Herzegovina is the only nation in modern times to become a member of

FIFA before they were a part of their continental organization, joining UEFA in 1998. The Dragons' first international victory came against the 1994 World Cup runners-up, Italy, on 6 November 1996.

By the time Bosnia and Herzegovina became eligible for qualification, the toll of countrywide unrest and strife saw a drop-off in play, and in their first major tournament-qualification attempt (for the 1998 World Cup in France), Bosnia and Herzegovina started off poorly with a 3–0 loss to Greece and finished fourth in their group and out of qualification. The 2002 World Cup qualification was no better, and the poor form continued, ultimately ending up with another fourth-place finish.

By the time qualification for 2006 came around, things had begun to change, and the Dragons just missed qualifying after tying a very beatable Lithuanian team at home and giving up an equalizer to second-place Spain in the 96th minute while playing down two men. In 2010, Miroslav Blažević was hired as the manager, and a subsequent second-place group finish placed them in a UEFA play-off with Portugal. Two 1–0 losses kept them from their first World Cup.

With new coach Safet Sušić leading the 2014 qualifying, Bosnia and Herzegovina had an outstanding campaign, winning eight of their ten matches (one draw and one loss). Bolstered by 30 goals in 10 games (the fourth-highest tally in European-zone qualifying) and a stalwart defense that gave up only six goals, Bosnia and Herzegovina's goal difference proved crucial as it edged them past a Greece side that finished level on points. Finishing first in their group meant an automatic berth, and the Dragons were finally on their way to their first appearance at a FIFA World Cup, in Brazil, 2014.

Drawn into group F with Argentina, Iran and Nigeria, expectations for advancement were high. Their opening game against Argentina got off to an auspicious beginning when Sead Kolašinac misplayed an Argentinean free kick into the back of his own net two minutes and nine seconds into the game for the fastest own goal in the history of the FIFA World Cup. Though the early goal set the Dragons back on their heels, the game wasn't decided until Messi delivered a clinical left-footed finish off the left post following a crafty give-and-go with Gonzalo Higuaín in the 65th minute. A brilliant one-versus-one goal in the 85th minute by Vedad Ibišević did give Bosnia and Herzegovina their first ever World Cup goal, but the final remained 2–1.

Against Nigeria, at the Arena Pantanal, in Cuiabá, Bosnia and Herzegovina again saw heartbreak when a tightly contested match was unjustly affected by a poorly called offsides against Edin Džeko just as the Dragons were gaining momentum. Moments later, Džeko broke through to goal again, but Nigerian goalkeeper Vincent Enyeama was up to the task. In the 29th minute, Nigeria was the beneficiary of another controversial call, this time by the opposite line judge, when Emmanuel Emenike tossed Bosnia defender Emir Spahić down and found an unmarked Peter Odemwingie for a tap in from six yards out. The Dragons were unable to create much in the second half, and the final was a 1–0 loss that knocked them out of the tournament. Too little, too late, the Dragons' third group game, against Iran, was the result Bosnia and Herzegovinian supporters were hoping to see from the start. In the rain, Džeko finally found his form when he rifled a low screamer from the 18 off the post in the 23rd minute. After the break, the Dragons struck again, this time taking advantage of a rare Iranian defensive error and some superb playmaking to find Miralem Pjanić in the 60th minute. Iran's Reza Ghoochannejhad's goal in the 82nd minute gave Iran life, but a quick counter by Avdija Vršajević a minute later sealed the first-ever World Cup points and win for the Dragons. Bosnia and Herzegovina finished their first-ever World Cup in 20th place, with a goal differential of 0.

BOTASSO, JUAN. B. 23 October 1908, Buenos Aires, Argentina. D. 5 October 1950. Argentina's goalkeeper in the inaugural World Cup final in 1930 was Juan Botasso, who conceded four goals in a 4–2 defeat to hosts and bitter rivals Uruguay. It was only Botasso's second game of the competition, his first coming in the semifinal, as Argentina defeated the United States 1–0. He had replaced the unreliable Ángel Bossio in goal but did not prove to be a great replacement, conceding five goals in his two games. It was Botasso's only appearance at a World Cup, playing in a total of nine games for his country, passing away in 1950, aged just 42.

BRAZIL. Commonly known as A Seleção (The Selection) and Verde-Amarela (The Green and Yellow). No country has been more successful in World Cup competition than Brazil. The South American nation has appeared in every single tournament, never failing to qualify. Brazil has taken home the championship five times, a record, winning the competition on four different continents—Europe (1958, Sweden), South America (1962, Chile), North America (1970, Mexico and 1994, United States) and Asia (2002, South Korea and Japan). No country's people take more pride in its World Cup record than Brazil, and as a result, nowhere is the pressure greater for the country to succeed.

It took 28 years of World Cup competition for Brazil to win a title for the first time. The South American country began playing international soccer in 1914 but in the 1920s was no match for its continental rivals Uruguay and Argentina. Brazil had advanced little by the 1930 and 1934 World Cup competitions, but in 1938, led by the competition's top scorer Leônidas (nicknamed the "Black Diamond") with seven goals, Brazil reached the semifinal stage, losing there to eventual champions Italy. Brazil was now marked as contenders, and the country was chosen as the host for the 1950 World Cup when the competition resumed following World War II. Brazil put on an enormous effort to host the tournament, including the construction of the enormous centerpiece of the World Cup, the 200,000-capacity Maracanã in Rio de Janeiro, even though it was yet to be entirely completed when the first game kicked off in June 1950. Brazil's preparation was intense, with the team sequestered in a four-month training camp ahead of the tournament, while public interest reached intense levels in a soccer-mad nation. Brazil began with a comfortable 4–0 win over Mexico in the opening game of the first-round group stage at the Maracanã on 24 June, with two goals from Ademir and one a piece from Jair and Baltazar. Yet four days later, in São Paulo, Brazil's defense let them down as the South Americans slipped to a surprising 2–2 draw with Switzerland, despite twice leading. Brazilian coach Flávio Costa had made multiple changes from the opening game, switching the back line seemingly to please the crowd in São Paulo by featuring products from the region. Brazil played much better in a win over Yugoslavia in the final group game to advance to the second round, two goals with no reply coming from Ademir and Zizinho, one in either half.

The 1950 World Cup featured an unusual setup, with no elimination stage following the first round but instead a second-round pool featuring the winners of each group, each playing the other once with the team accruing the most points becoming world champions. Now Brazil turned on the style. Brilliant individual skill merged with hypnotic teamwork as the Brazilians tore apart Sweden in their first matchup, Ademir netting four times, Chico twice and Maneca once in an emphatic 7–1 win at the Maracanã. The Brazilians did not let up against Spain, a 6–1 win again at the Maracanã featuring two goals for Chico, one each from Ademir, Zizinho, Jair and a Spanish own goal by Jose Parra. Heading into the final game of the competition, all Brazil needed to do was tie with Uruguay to seal a World Cup title for the first time. After emphatic victories over Spain and Sweden, anticipation was at fever pitch, with an entire nation expecting glory and over 200,000 fans packing into the Maracanã by any means possible. Even though Brazilian coach Flávio Costa warned against complacency ahead of kickoff, victory was the only word on the lips of almost every Brazilian on 16 July 1950, in what was effectively a World Cup final. Uruguay held firm in the face of a first-half Brazilian onslaught, 0–0 at halftime. But early in the second period, Brazil broke through, Ademir and Zizinho combining to open up Uruguay's defense and freeing up the space for Friaça to score. Victory now seemed inevitable, but the floodgates did not open, and 20 minutes later, Juan Schiaffino stole into space and equalized from Alcides Ghiggia's cross. The Brazilians were rattled, and in the 79th minute, Uruguay dealt what turned out to be a deadly blow: this time it was Ghiggia himself who finished. Rio was shocked, but Uruguay had claimed a second World Cup title, while the host nation still awaited a first.

Four years later, Brazil attempted to recover from the shellshock of 1950 in Switzerland at the 1954 World Cup, with Zezé Moreira installed as coach but without the star duo from the previous tournament, Ademir and Zizinho. Brazil joined Yugoslavia, Mexico and France in group one of the first-round stage, though the team only played against the first two nations. Brazil began in spectacular manner, thrashing Mexico 5–0 with two goals from Pinga and one each from Didi, Julinho and Baltazar. In Lausanne, Brazil and Yugoslavia then played out a tight, high-quality game, ending 1–1 after extra time (tournament rules meant any game tied at 90 minutes required an extra period), Brazil's goal coming from Didi. That result advanced Brazil to the quarterfinal stage and a matchup with tournament favorites Hungary in what became one of the most infamous games in World Cup history, the so-called Battle of Bern. A much-anticipated matchup between two of the tournament's most attacking teams descended into open fighting on the field between the players after being pockmarked by violent fouls, with the violent exchanges continuing in the locker room after the game. In the 71st minute, Hungary's József Bozsik and Brazil's Nílton Santos exchanged punches and were sent off by English referee Arthur Ellis, who then expelled Humberto as well eight minutes later following a kick on Gyula Lóránt. The scoring was almost lost in the melees, but in the event, Hungary won 4–2, and Brazil departed with a considerable cloud hanging over the actions of multiple players, though FIFA did not take any further disciplinary action.

Brazil won its first World Cup at the 1958 competition in Sweden, but the South Americans almost did not make it to the tournament: in a two-legged qualifier with

Peru, Brazil only squeaked through 2–1 on aggregate, thanks to a 1–0 win at home in Rio on 21 April 1957 due to a goal by Didi. By the time the competition in Sweden rolled around the next year, Brazil were the hot favorites, even though no country had ever won a World Cup outside of its own continent to that date. Brazil itself was transforming that year, a new capital—Brasília—under construction, and all the momentum seemed to feed into a team featuring a newcomer to the international scene, a 17-year-old known as Pelé. The other great talent on the team was the nimble winger Garrincha, though neither was selected in Brazil's opening first-round group game against Austria by head coach Vicente Feola, who had made his name coaching São Paulo FC. Feola opted for safer choices than the unproven talent of Garrincha and Pelé, and Brazil beat the Austrians handily without either, with two goals from José Altafini and one by Nílton Santos. In Brazil's second group game against England, however, the Brazilian attack was lackluster, and a 0–0 tie was ground out. That prompted Feola to introduce Garrincha and Pelé for their World Cup debuts in the final group game versus the Soviet Union: within five minutes of kickoff, both had hit the post, and the Brazilians bamboozled their opponents with insouciant ease. The two goals in a 2–0 win came from Vava, but it was the two newcomers who dominated, teasing and tormenting the Soviet defense seemingly at will.

In Gothenburg, Brazil's march to the World Cup continued with a 1–0 win over a strong Wales team, Pelé scoring his first World Cup goal in the 66th minute, chesting the ball down and turning suddenly past Welsh defender Mel Charles with a backward flick, before poking the ball home. The French were the next victims, this time at Råsunda Stadium just outside Stockholm, crashing 5–2 to the Brazilians. Vava and Didi scored in the first half, and then Pelé let loose after the half, claiming a magical hat trick, Brazil winning 5–2. The same score in favor of Brazil was registered in the final, again at the Råsunda Stadium, with the host nation Sweden falling to two goals each from Vava and Pelé and one by Mário Zagallo. Brazil, finally, could take the world championship home.

As holders of the title, Brazil qualified automatically for the 1962 World Cup in Chile, with Aymoré Moreira taking charge of coaching duties, in place of Vicente Feola. Moreira, a native of Rio, had played for Brazil in the 1930s and briefly coached his country previously in 1953. Moreira was able to call on nine veterans from the 1958 team, including Pelé and Garrincha. In Brazil's opening game against Mexico in the first-round group stage, it appeared a beat had not been skipped, Pelé scoring one and Mário Zagallo the other in a 2–0 win in Sausalito. Pelé's goal, though, was to be his last contribution of the tournament: early in Brazil's second game versus Czechoslovakia, a 0–0 draw, he aggravated an existing groin injury and did not play again in the tournament. His replacement in the lineup, Amarildo, scored twice in Brazil's next game, a 2–1 win over Spain that earned the South Americans passage to the next round. In the elimination stage that followed, Garrincha took over and mitigated the loss of Pelé in the way only the magical winger could. He scored twice as Brazil dismissed England 3–1 in the quarterfinal, then twice more at the semifinal stage in a 4–2 win against host nation Chile. In the final, Brazil faced Czechoslovakia again. Brazil fell behind early on after only 16 minutes, Josef Masopust cutting through the Brazilian back line and finishing low past Gilmar in goal. Brazil struck back immediately, however, when a minute later, Amarildo sliced past two Czech defenders on the left edge of the penalty area and fired into the net inside an unguarded near post. The game remained tight, but late in the second half, Brazil found security, Zito scoring in the 69th minute and Vava confirming a second world title with a 78th-minute goal, for a 4–1 final scoreline.

Only Italy had ever won successive World Cups previously (in 1934 and 1938), so in 1966, Brazil attempted to do the unprecedented and win a third straight title in England. Vicente Feola, coach of the 1958 winning team, returned in charge for the competition, with much of the 1962 team retained—including a healthy Pelé and a less fit Garrincha. Brazil began confidently in group-round play with a 2–0 win over Bulgaria at Goodison Park in Liverpool, the site for all three of Feola's team's games. Pelé and Garrincha scored the goals, both direct from free kicks. Brazil's World Cup then went off the rails against Hungary in a splendid game, playing without Pelé, who had been the victim of aggressive Bulgarian tackling in the previous game. Ferenc Bene scored for the Hungarians after only two minutes, but thanks to a Tostão equalizer, scores were tied at halftime. With Flórián Albert pulling the strings, Hungary's quality prevailed in the second half, twice scoring to give Brazilian a first defeat in the World Cup since 1954. Pelé returned to the lineup for a critical final group game versus a talented Portuguese team. It was one of seven changes made by Feola, Garrincha dropped and Pelé himself hardly fit to return to the field. The Brazilian star was soon again kicked out of the game, with English official George McCabe doing little to protect him. Portugal, though, won by virtue of the quality of teamwork on display, a 3–1 win generated by Eusébio, who scored twice. Brazil departed, losing the world championship crown.

In 1970, Brazil would regain the World Cup with a series of performances in Mexico still ranked by most as the greatest in the competition's history. This came despite the fact that the team's coach, Mário Zagallo—who had played for Brazil at the 1958 and 1962 World Cups—only took over in March 1970, three months before the competition began, replacing João Saldanha. Saldanha had led the Brazilians comfortably through qualifying, but his increasingly erratic behavior saw him dismissed on the eve of the World Cup. Captained by Carlos Alberto Torres, Brazil featured a phalanx of attacking talent: alongside Pelé on the forward line were Tostão, who recovered just in time after suffering a detached retina in 1969, left-winger Rivelino, the intelligent playmaker Gérson and the outstanding Jairzinho, who scored in every game of the competition, notching seven goals.

In the first-round group stage, Brazil's opponents all hailed from Northern or Eastern Europe (Czechoslovakia, England, Romania), an advantage for the South Americans with games played in the heat of the Mexican sun. Though Brazil began by going a goal down to Czechoslovakia against the Europeans in Guadalajara, Rivelino, Pelé and Jairzinho (twice) found the net for a comfortable opening 4–1 win. That was followed by one of the most famous matchups of all time, as Brazil took on defending world champions England, again in Guadalajara. Without Gérson, who had suffered a leg injury, Brazil found England extremely tough to beat: in no small part due to Gordon Banks, who made a miraculous twisting save from Pelé in only the 10th minute. Brazil's goal, the only one of the game, came in the second half after Pelé set Jairzinho up for a neat finish past Banks. It had been a clash of the titans, but Brazil bested the world champions. Remaining in Guadalajara, Brazil claimed a third successive victory in the group stage with a 3–2 win against Romania, thanks to two goals from Pelé and one from Jairzinho.

In the next round, the quarterfinal stage, Brazil faced Peru, who had finished as runners-up to West Germany in the group-round stage but had impressed with displays of attacking verve. Little changed in this matchup, as both teams played open, flowing soccer. This ultimately favored the quality of Brazil, though it made for a compelling game. Gérson returned to the Brazilian lineup and imposed himself with his playmaking ability. Six goals were spread throughout the game, four to Brazil, scored by Rivelino, Tostão (2) and Jairzinho. In the semifinal, Brazil faced a South American team again, this time long-time rivals Uruguay in Guadalajara. Brazil fell behind for the second time in the tournament to a goal from Luis Cubilla but struck back with three unanswered goals from Clodaoldo, Jairzinho and Rivelino. Despite the Uruguayans' physical play, Brazil's style was unstoppable, and Pelé almost put a remarkable cherry on top near the end, beguiling Uruguayan goalkeeper Ladislao Mazurkiewicz with a feint that allowed the ball to run past him before finishing just wide.

Brazil met Italy in the final, both two-time World Cup winners, with eternal glory on the line in Mexico City at the Azteca stadium—FIFA had announced that the first three-time winner would be able to keep the Jules Rimet Trophy forever. Italy came out to stifle the Brazilians with a defensive display, but it was one that never looked like working, such was the sophistication and sheer cutting edge from the South Americans. Pelé opened the scoring, leaping to head in a Rivelino cross after 18 minutes, though the score was level at halftime, Roberto Boninsegna equalizing with 37 minutes gone. Gérson restored the Brazilian lead 66 minutes in, striking from long range, and Jairzinho made it 3–1 five minutes later, bursting into the box and finishing from a Pelé pass. In the 86th minute, Carlos Alberto scored a goal that epitomized Brazil's brilliant play throughout the tournament. The ball was passed from Brazilian to Brazilian with simple but bewitching grace in a move that started deep in Brazil's own half and ended when Pelé casually laid the ball off to his right into the penalty area, Carlos Alberto striking the ball first time hard into the bottom corner: 4–1 to Brazil and a third world championship was claimed by the South Americans.

After winning three World Cup titles out of four tournaments played between 1958 and 1970, Brazil would not win another title until 1994, a barren spell for a country with enormous expectations that would ultimately change how the team played the game, eventually moving away from the flamboyance of 1970. At the 1974 World Cup in West Germany, much of the color of Brazil's performances four years previously was gone. So, too, was Pelé, along with Tostão and Gérson, though Zagallo was still in charge of the team. In the first round, Brazil's group contained Scotland, Yugoslavia and Zaire. Brazil scraped through to the second round in unimpressive style, tying 0–0 with both Yugoslavia and Scotland to start the tournament and only sealing passage to the next stage with a 3–0 win over Zaire, who had been crushed 9–0 by Yugoslavia in the Africans' previous game. The format of the 1974 World Cup meant that the second stage was another group round, Brazil placed with the Netherlands, East Germany and Argentina. In Hanover, a goal from a Rivelino free kick gave Brazil a win in the opener against East Germany and followed that up in the same city with a 2–1 win over Argentina, thanks to goals by Rivelino and Jairzinho, in the first meeting of the two South American giants at a World Cup finals tournament. With the Dutch also having won both games, the match between the Netherlands and Brazil in Dortmund would decide who advanced to the final. The Dutch prevailed, a 2–0 win confirming Brazil no longer had the magic of 1970. This was further hammered home as Brazil succumbed to a disappointing 1–0 defeat to Poland in the third-place consolation game in Munich.

Brazil qualified for the 1978 World Cup in Argentina in impressive style, going unbeaten in six qualifying games. Cláudio Coutinho coached the team, with an emphasis on fitness and endurance rather than the fluid passing and movement of earlier glory years. Melding old and new was the challenge facing Coutinho, with the old star Rivelino joined with the player considered to be Brazil's future, the sparkling creative talent Zico. In the first round, Brazil faced all-European opposition in Sweden, Spain and Austria. The South Americans only managed to win one of three games, a 1–0 win over Austria coming after a 1–1 draw with Sweden and a 0–0 tie with Spain. That was still enough to eke Brazil through to the second-round group stage, now facing Peru, Poland and Argentina. Brazil began with a comfortable 3–0 win versus Peru, the goals coming from Dirceu (2) and Zico, but Brazil then stumbled against Argentina as the South Americans met for a second successive World Cup, a 0–0 tie against the host nation. A 3–1 win over Poland was not enough to see Brazil through to the final, finishing behind Argentina on goal difference after the hosts racked up six unanswered goals against Peru. Argentina had the advantage of playing after Brazil had finished, thus knowing they needed to win by at least four goals, while allegations about the Peruvians' lack of effort soon filled the Brazilian media. Again, Brazil played a third-place play-off, winning this time, defeating Italy 2–1.

Heading into the 1982 World Cup in Spain, with Zico now at his peak and partnered with the gifted Socrates in midfield, expectations for the Brazilians under head coach Telê Santana were as high as they had been since 1970. Brazil breezed through qualifying with a free-flowing style of play not seen in over a decade, winning four games out of four. In Spain, Brazil's first-round opponents were to be Scotland, the Soviet Union and New Zealand, a relatively straightforward draw. The Brazilians had little trouble qualifying from the group, winning all three games and scoring 10 goals while only conceding twice. That moved Brazil on to the second group stage, joined in group three by defending champions Argentina and two-time winners Italy. Brazil began by defeating Argentina as the two countries met in the final stages for the third successive World Cup, a 3–1 win through goals scored by Zico, Serginho and Júnior in Barcelona. Zico was the orchestrator, helping set up two goals along with scoring his own. Brazil, then, needed to defeat Italy to top the mini-group and head to the semifinal stage. But in Barcelona again, the wheels came off Brazil's express. Paolo Rossi scored for Italy after five minutes, and though the game rolled back and forth, with Socrates and Falcão both scoring, Brazil never led and went down 3–2 with Rossi claiming a hat trick. For all Brazil's skill and style going forward, defensive frailty ultimately meant that Brazil departed, Italy the eventual champions, matching Brazil's record of three World Cup titles won.

Expectations remained high for Brazil at the 1986 World Cup in Mexico. Brazil remained under the attack-minded coaching of Telê Santana, though he had only returned to the team in 1985, after resigning following the 1982 tournament. Brazil qualified for Mexico comfortably, unbeaten, and for the finals, the talented Careca, a star forward for São Paulo, was added to the veteran mix of Zico, Socrates and Falcão. In the first round, Brazil won all three group-stage games, with wins over Spain, Algeria and Northern Ireland, Careca in particularly fine form with a goal against the Spanish and two against the Northern Irish. Brazil then crushed Poland 4–0 in Guadalajara in the second round, goals from Socrates, Josimar, Edinho and Careca setting Brazil up as one of the favorites for the title. In the quarterfinals, Brazil faced France, the reigning European champions, inspired by Michel Platini. The game turned out to be a classic. Careca gave Brazil the lead 17 minutes in, finishing off a fluid passing move with a blistering strike into the roof of the net. Brazil's lead did not last until halftime, Platini poaching a goal at the far post. In the second half, Zico had the best chance of providing a winner, but his penalty was saved by French goalkeeper Joel Bats. With no further score, the game was decided on penalty kicks; Zico made his in the shoot-out, but both Socrates and Julio Cesar missed their kicks, resulting in Brazil's elimination.

Brazil qualified for the 1990 World Cup in Italy, topping a group containing Chile and Venezuela. Sebastião Lazaroni's roster was perhaps the least star-studded Brazil had fielded since the 1950s, even though it featured talents including Careca and Vasco de Gama's Bebeto. Brazil progressed through the first round with a trio of one-goal victories, dispatching Sweden, Costa Rica and Scotland. Careca and Müller each tallied two goals, though Brazil did not offer the same flair they had shown under Santana in the 1982 or 1986 tournaments. In the second round, Brazil faced perennial rivals Argentina in Turin. Claudio Caniggia scored the only goal of the game after a mazy run by Diego Maradona. The game was not without controversy: Brazil's left-back Branco claimed after the game that he had been passed a water bottle spiked with a tranquilizer, a piece of foul play Maradona later confirmed.

In 1994, at the World Cup in the United States, Brazil claimed its fourth World Cup title, after a gap of 24 years. That absence of success led Brazil to abandon parts of its traditional attacking strategy on the field, instead integrating more defensive grit in the form of midfielders, such as 1994 midfield destroyer Dunga. Under the stewardship of Carlos Alberto Parreira, Brazil comfortably qualified for the World Cup, winning a five-team group consisting of Bolivia, Uruguay, Ecuador and Venezuela. In the United States, Parreira was able to call on the most lethal strike force in the planet with the diminutive pair of Bebeto and Romário, both supreme goal poachers. Brazil went unbeaten in the first-round group stage, defeating Russia 2–0 (goals from Romário and captain Raí), Cameroon 3–0 (Romário, Márcio Santos and Bebeto) and tying 1–1 with Sweden, Romário scoring for the third successive game. In the second round, Brazil played host nation the United States on 4 July and won a tight game 1–0, thanks to a strike by Bebeto. Brazil's quarterfinal with the Netherlands at the Cotton Bowl in Dallas was a game for the ages, with five goals coming in the second half: Brazil enjoyed the better of it in a 3–2 win, goals coming from Romário, Bebeto and Branco. The semifinal against Sweden was a tense game in contrast to the glut of the previous game; the only goal came finally in the 80th minute, when Romário burst through the

Swedish defense and poked a low strike into the bottom corner. Expectations were heady for Brazil's final against Italy, the two countries boasting six World Cup titles between them. But the game at the Rose Bowl in Pasadena, attended by 94,000 spectators, proved to be a dull affair with neither team generating good chances. For the first time, with no score to break the deadlock after extra time, the World Cup final went to penalty kicks. While Márcio Santos missed the first for Brazil, Romário, Branco and Dunga made no mistake, and when Roberto Baggio ballooned Italy's fifth kick over the bar, Brazil claimed a fourth World Cup title.

In 1998, at the World Cup in France, Brazil reached the World Cup for the fifth time but, for the first time, lost at that stage to the host nation. As defending champions, Brazil did not need to qualify for the tournament and was led by head coach Mário Zagallo—returning 28 years after collecting a winners' medal as coach in 1970 for his country. Brazil's star player was Ronaldo, who had sat on the bench for the entirety of the 1994 tournament, but was, by 1998, a prolific striker in Italy's Serie A for Internazionale. He was accompanied by exciting talents such as Barcelona's pair and two explosive fullbacks, Cafu and Roberto Carlos. Brazil was not overly impressive in the first round, qualifying with a 2–1 win against Scotland, a 3–0 defeat of Morocco, and succumbing to a surprising 2–1 loss to Norway, conceding two late goals. In the knockout stage, Brazil began to score prolifically, first defeating Chile 4–1 in Paris with two goals each from César Sampaio and Ronaldo. In the quarterfinals, Brazil defeated Denmark 3–2 in Nantes, Bebeto and Rivaldo on the score sheet. In the semifinals, Brazil led the Netherlands until three minutes from time thanks to a Ronaldo strike, but a Patrick Kluivert equalizer ultimately forced the game to a penalty shoot-out. Brazil won 4–2, with Ronaldo, Rivaldo, Emerson and Dunga all converting their kicks. Brazil then faced host nation France in the final held at the Stade de France, just outside Paris. The pre-match buildup for Brazil turned into a controversial farce as Ronaldo was at first omitted from the lineup before being restored less than an hour ahead of kickoff, with various theories still unable to fully explain the confusing circumstances. Whatever had happened, Ronaldo was clearly not at full strength on the field, and Brazil sleepwalked to a 3–0 defeat that left a sour taste for the South Americans.

In 2002, Brazil claimed a World Cup title for a record fifth time. Yet Brazil almost did not make it to the competition in Japan and South Korea at all: only scraping through qualification by three points, after Luiz Felipe Scolari took over as coach toward the end of the campaign and steered the Brazilians through. At the World Cup itself, fate also intervened ultimately to Brazil's favor: team captain Emerson was lost to injury just days before the games began, replaced as holding midfielder by Gilberto Silva, who enjoyed a superb tournament. A trio of attackers in a 3-4-2-1 formation perhaps unmatched in the history of the World Cup thrived with a balanced midfield behind them, Rivaldo, Ronaldinho and Ronaldo all enjoying the freedom to devastate opponents. In group C, Brazil first faced Turkey and won a thrilling and controversial game 2–1, thanks to goals from Ronaldo and Rivaldo. The latter strike came after Alpay Özalan fouled Brazilian substitute Luizão outside the penalty area in the 87th minute but saw a penalty awarded to Brazil and converted by Rivaldo. There was more drama just five minutes later, when Hakan Ünsal kicked the ball at

Rivaldo, though the Brazilian simulated a blow from it that resulted in a fine imposed on him by FIFA totaling $7,350. Brazil then had little trouble dispatching China 4–0, with goals from fullback Roberto Carlos and the attacking trio of Rivaldo, Ronaldinho and Ronaldo. Prolific scoring continued to define Scolari's team, with five goals tallied against Costa Rica to finish group play with three wins from three games, though Brazil also conceded twice. Ronaldo scored a pair of goals, along with strikes from Edmílson, Rivaldo and Júnior.

In the second round, Brazil defeated Belgium 2–0 in Kobe, Japan, thanks to second-half goals from Rivaldo and Ronaldo. That result set up Brazil to meet England in the quarterfinal, remaining in Japan for the game in Shizuoka. Brazil fell behind to a goal from Michael Owen, though in added time at the end of the first half, a Rivaldo strike equaled the score. Five minutes into the second half, Ronaldinho lobbed the ball over England goalkeeper David Seaman from more than 40 yards out. That proved to be the winning goal, even though Ronaldinho himself was sent off only seven minutes later for a foul on Danny Mills, leaving Brazil to hold off a lackluster England with 10 men for the rest of the game. Brazil scored only one goal in a game for the first time in the tournament in a rematch with Turkey at the semifinal stage in Saitama, but Ronaldo's strike was enough to separate the two teams and send Brazil to yet another World Cup final. There the Brazilians faced Germany, and Ronaldo scored his seventh and eighth goals of the competition—winning the Golden Boot in the process—to claim the World Cup once more with a 2–0 win.

After winning the title in 2002, the qualification format was changed in 2006, and Brazil found themselves having to qualify instead of being automatically allowed back in as the reigning champion. Thankfully, Brazil qualified on top of their group and found themselves placed into group F with Croatia, Japan and Australia. Brazil finished first in their group with three wins behind seven goals scored and only one allowed. In their round of 16 matchup with Ghana, they continued their dominance behind Ronaldo's third goal of the tournament. A final score of 3–0 meant a quarterfinal game against France, where a Thierry Henry volley off a Zinedine Zidane cross proved to be the game winner that sent Brazil home.

Brazil dominated once again in 2010 qualification as they finished first in the CONMEBOL group. In South Africa, Brazil was placed into group G with Portugal, Côte d'Ivoire and North Korea. With two wins and a tie, Brazil finished atop their group and moved into the round of 16, this time against a Chilean side they easily dispatched 3–0. In the quarterfinal match against the Netherlands, an early goal by Robinho gave Brazil confidence. But two second-half Wesley Sneijder goals ultimately meant a come-from-behind Dutch win and a second consecutive quarterfinal exit for Brazil.

With the World Cup being held in Brazil in 2014, A Seleção was awarded an automatic berth. Fully aware of the high expectations, Brazil set up a gauntlet of high-profile opponents to prepare, and in November of 2012, a managerial change made Luiz Felipe Scolari head coach for the second time in the team's history. Though things looked scary after Brazil went 1-4-1 in their first six games under Scolari (including a 2–1 loss to England in his first game), by the time they reached the 2013 Confederations Cup, Brazil seemed to have found its confidence. After Scolari took over, Brazil lost only 2 of 20 games, and 14 of those games were wins.

Placed into group A with Croatia, Mexico and Cameroon, the chances of advancing seemed high for A Seleção. As the host nation, Brazil kicked off the tournament against Croatia at Arena Corinthians in São Paulo and immediately felt their nation's pressure when an own goal by Marcelo in the 11th minute turned into exactly the start the host nation was hoping to avoid. A brace by Neymar, the first on a weakly struck left-footed shot from 25 yards out in the 29th minute and the second a penalty gift following a phantom foul on Fred in the box in the 70th, gave Brazil life and the lead. A brilliant individual effort by Oscar, in the form of splitting two defenders and toe poking a shot into the low near post in the 91st minute, cemented the win.

In Brazil's second group game, against Mexico, Mexican goalkeeper Guillermo Ochoa had the game of his life, time and time again stopping the Brazilians from point-blank range to secure the 0–0 draw. Sitting atop the table at four points due to goal differential, Brazil needed a win against Cameroon by a greater margin than Mexico or a Mexican draw or loss to win their group; as it turned out, Brazil's 4–1 thrashing of Cameroon left little in doubt. In the 17th minute, Neymar struck when, unmarked at the penalty spot, he first timed a brilliant Luiz Gustavo cross for the lead. Poor defending led to Joël Matip's equalizer nine minutes later, but a quick response by Neymar in the 35th minute and a fortunate non-call on an offsides allowed for a simple header by Fred shortly after half to swing all of the momentum the host team's way. A late goal by Fernandinho following a shoddy Cameroon clear and some brilliant passing sealed the deal for Brazil and advanced them at the top of their table to the round of 16.

Seen by many as a favorable matchup, Brazil had their hands full with a Chilean side brimming with confidence. A Gonzalo Jara own goal (officially credited to David Luiz) in the 18th minute off a Neymar corner got the scoring started, but a poor clearance by Hulk and a clinical Alexis Sanchez finish in the 32nd minute leveled the game. Both teams had their chances in regulation and extra time, but it was a shoot-out win that pushed Brazil through to the quarterfinals for the sixth consecutive time.

Facing Colombia in the quarterfinals, Brazil proved that they could win games of all types. In a physical battle, Brazil's captain Thiago Silva's goal in the 7th minute was offset by his decision in the 64th minute to step in front of Colombia's goalkeeper as he was kicking the ball, resulting in a yellow card and a suspension should Brazil advance. Five minutes later, David Luiz's world-class free kick from 35 yards out gave the Brazilians some breathing room, but Golden Boot–winner James Rodríguez's penalty in the 80th minute made for a tense final 10 minutes before Brazil was finally through to its first World Cup semifinal in 12 years. The suspension of Silva and a hard tackle by Colombian Juan Zúñiga, which resulted in a broken vertebra for Neymar, meant that A Seleção would be facing a powerful German side at anything but full strength.

Whether it was a combination of both, or one on its own, the loss of icon Neymar and the suspension of captain Silva meant that the Brazilian side many expected to win it all looked more like a team that had already given up. An astonishing five goals in the game's first 29 minutes (four coming in a six-minute span) resolutely ended any hopes of a Brazilian comeback. Two second-half goals by André Schürrle meant that Brazil was on its way to the worst semifinal defeat in the history of the World Cup, and only a late goal by Oscar in the 90th minute saved a touch of face for Brazil's third-place matchup against Netherlands.

Sadly for Brazilian fans, the return of Silva could do nothing to reinvigorate the energy of a Brazilian side reeling from the loss of Neymar and the crushing defeat to Germany. An early penalty by Robin van Persie meant the host team again had to play from behind. Fifteen minutes later, a crafty settle-and-finish by Daley Blind made the lead two, and a stoppage-time goal by Georginio Wijnaldum finished the scoring. Scolari was ousted from the Brazilian helm shortly following the World Cup end.

BUFFON, GIANLUIGI. B. 28 January 1978, Carrara, Italy. In 14 appearances in goal for Italy at the 2002, 2006, 2010 and 2014 World Cups, Gianluigi Buffon only conceded nine goals as a stalwart in the net who picked up a winners medal at the 2006 World Cup in Germany. Buffon made his first appearance for Italy in 1997, while a star at club team Parma in Italy's Serie A, and earned a roster spot for the 1998 World Cup in France, where he did not appear in the competition, acting as a backup for starter Gianluca Pagliuca. Four years later, Buffon started every game for Italy during the 2002 World Cup qualifying. In Japan and South Korea, Buffon conceded four goals in Italy's four games, as Italy exited in the round of 16, losing to host nation South Korea 2–1 after extra time. During the round-of-16 match, Buffon saved a penalty after only four minutes against the South Koreans, diving to his right to swat away a spot kick from Ahn Jung-Hwan, but he could do little about either of the later goals. Four years later, Buffon was at his peak, age 28 and a star at club level for Juventus. Conceding only two goals in seven games in Germany, he won the Lev Yashin award as the tournament's best goalkeeper as his performances in the net and the stout defense in front of him became the key to Italy winning a fourth World Cup title. Buffon was again the first choice for Italy at the 2010 World Cup in South Africa but lasted only the first 45 minutes of Italy's first game against Paraguay when, with Italy trailing 1–0 at halftime, Buffon had to be substituted after injuring his back. Diagnosed with a herniated disc in his back, Buffon missed the rest of the competition and Italy was eliminated at the group stage.

While qualifying for the 2014 World Cup in Brazil, Buffon was still in goal for Italy, equaling and surpassing Azzuri legends Paolo Maldini and Fabio Cannavaro for most national team caps. With his fifth World Cup roster spot, Buffon joined Mexican goalkeeper Antonio Carbajal and German footballer Lothar Matthäus as the only players who have participated in five World Cups. As the Italian captain for the first time, Buffon missed the opening game against England due to injury. Returning against Costa Rica and Uruguay, Buffon made several notable saves but lost both games 1–0, meaning an Italian group-stage exit yet again. Buffon has now appeared in 14 World Cup finals games and 26 World Cup qualifiers, with only 25 goals conceded in 40 total appearances.

BULGARIA. Commonly known as Lvovete (The Lions). In 1994, Bulgaria finished in fourth place at the World Cup held in the United States, the country's best finish to date out of the seven times it has appeared in the finals tournament. Bulgaria's first appearance in the World Cup came in 1962, having not entered or failed to qualify for the six previous editions of the competition. At the 1962 World Cup in Chile, Bulgaria lost its first two games, 1–0 to Argentina and 6–1 to Hungary, before bowing out after the first-round group stage following a 0–0 tie with England. Bulgaria qualified for the next World Cup in England in 1966, though it performed even worse than four years previously, losing all three games to Brazil (0–2), Portugal (0–3) and Hungary (1–3). In 1970, Bulgaria appeared in a third straight World Cup, though elimination at the first-round stage followed once again in Mexico. On this occasion, Bulgaria lost 3–2 to Peru, 5–2 to West Germany and only secured a single point once already eliminated in a 1–1 tie with Morocco. Bulgaria's fourth successive World Cup appearance, in 1974, in West Germany, only brought modest improvement: again the Bulgarians exited at the first-round stage, though this time after securing two ties. Those came against Sweden (0–0) and Uruguay (1–1), but in Bulgaria's critical third game against eventual finalists the Netherlands, the Bulgarians came unstuck with a 4–1 loss and exited the competition.

Twenty years passed before Bulgaria returned to the World Cup in 1994, at the tournament held in the United States. That Bulgaria made it across the Atlantic was something of a miracle: Bulgaria trailed France in qualifying by three points with two games remaining but, courtesy of a win over Austria and a surprising French defeat to Israel, finished top of the group after beating France in Paris. That win came courtesy of a winner deep into injury time by Emil Kostadinov, shocking the French. In the U.S., a Bulgarian team coached by Dimitar Penev featured stars such as the talismanic Hristo Stoichkov of Barcelona and playmaker Krasimir Balakov. Yet in Bulgaria's opening game, the country's stretch of games without a win in the World Cup finals moved to 17, following a 3–0 defeat to Nigeria. Bulgaria, though, turned things around against Greece, winning 4–0 thanks to two strikes from Stoichkov and goals from Yordan Letchkov and Daniel Borimirov. Bulgaria then qualified for the elimination stage for the first time thanks to a 2–1 win over an Argentina rattled by Diego Maradona's failed drug test at the competition, the goals coming from Stoichkov and Nasko Sirakov. Bulgaria's second-round game with Mexico descended into farce as Syrian referee Jamal Al Sharif issued 11 cautions and a red card for both teams, who struggled to a 1–1 tie settled on penalty kicks. Bulgaria went through despite a miss by Krasimir Balakov, as one Mexican spot kick sailed wide and two others were saved by Borislav Mihailov. The greatest game in Bulgaria's World Cup history then followed at the quarterfinal stage. Bulgaria defeated the defending world champions, Germany, 2–1, in a thrilling game at Giants Stadium in New Jersey. Though Germany took the league through Lothar Matthäus, Hristo Stoichkov leveled the scores with a magnificent 25-yard free kick, and a winner came with Letchkov heading home 12 minutes from the end. Bulgaria could not repeat the magic against Italy in the semifinal, losing 2–1 in a game not as close as the scoreline suggests, though Stoichkov's strike earned him a share of the tournament's Golden Boot. In the third-place game with Sweden, Bulgaria was easily beaten 4–0, but despite that, it had been a magnificent tournament for Stoichkov and company.

Bulgaria qualified for the 1998 World Cup in France, with a team coached by Hristo Bonev that still revolved around Stoichkov. He was by now 32, though, and the magic of four years earlier could not be replicated. Bulgaria scored only one goal in three games on the way to elimination at the first-round stage. A 0–0 tie with Paraguay was followed by a 1–0 loss to Nigeria and then a dismal 6–1 thrashing by Spain, Emil Kostadinov scoring the only goal of the competition for the Bulgarians. The Eastern European nation has yet to return to the World Cup finals, failing to qualify for the 2002, 2006, 2010 and 2014 World Cups.

C

CABRINI, ANTONIO. B. 8 October 1957, Cremona, Italy. Italian defender Antonio Cabrini won the Best Young Player award at the 1978 World Cup held in Argentina, at the age of 21. Cabrini's marauding runs to support the attack from the left-back position and his tenacity earned him considerable plaudits, even though he was a complete novice at senior international level entering the competition: Cabrini made his debut for Italy in their first game at the 1978 World Cup, a 2–1 win over France. Cabrini played in all seven of Italy's games as they finished in third place. Cabrini's performance cemented his role in the Italian side, and he appeared in seven of Italy's World Cup qualifying campaigns as they advanced to Spain for the 1982 World Cup. There, Cabrini was an important cog in Italy's third World Cup victory, contributing a critical goal in Italy's second-round group-stage victory over Argentina, scoring with a sweetly struck left-footed shot from 15 yards out. In the final against West Germany, Cabrini took the responsibility of taking a penalty that would have given Italy the lead, but dragged his shot wide of the post. Italy, though, went on to win the game 3–1. Cabrini went on to play at the 1986 World Cup in Mexico, his third in succession, making four appearances there to bring his total World Cup games to 18. In 1986, Italy was eliminated at the round-of-16 stage by France, 2–0. Cabrini played his final game for Italy in October 1987, ending his international career after 73 appearances, scoring an impressive nine goals from a defensive position. At club level, Cabrini's greatest success had come playing for Juventus, with whom he won the Italian league title six times as well as the 1985 European Cup, though the latter win was seriously marred by the Heysel Stadium disaster in the final.

ČAMBAL, ŠTEFAN. B. 17 December 1908, Pozsony, Austria-Hungary. D. 18 July 1990. Midfielder Štefan Čambal made his debut for Czechoslovakia in May 1932, a 1–1 draw with Austria, and two years later was among his country's first 11 for the 1934 World Cup final in Italy against the hosts. Czechoslovakia lost the final 2–1, but Čambal played an important role in his country's best-ever finish in a World Cup to date, playing in their victorious qualifying game for the World Cup in October 2010 over Poland, and then in all four of Czechoslovakia's games at the World Cup, the first three victories over Romania, Switzerland and West Germany, respectively. Čambal played his final game for Czechoslovakia in September 1935, a 0–0 tie in a friendly with Yugoslavia, ending his career without having scored for his country in 22 games.

CAMEROON. Commonly known as Les Lions Indomptables (The Indomitable Lions). No African country has qualified for the World Cup more times than Cameroon, who has appeared on seven occasions. That includes the 1990 World Cup when the Indomitable Lions became the first African nation to reach the quarterfinal stage. Cameroon began international play 30 years prior to that in 1960 and qualified for the World Cup for the first time in 1982. The Lions went unbeaten at that competition in Spain, drawing with Peru, Poland and Italy, the latter the only game to feature any goals, a 1–1 draw with Cameroon's goal coming from Grégoire M'Bida. At the 1990 World Cup in Italy, Cameroon, coached by Russian Valeri Nepomnyashchi, began the tournament by providing one of the greatest shocks in its history in the opening game, defeating defending champions Argentina 1–0, thanks to a goal by François Omam-Biyik. That result came even though Cameroon ended the game with nine men, both André Kana-Biyik and Benjamin Massing sent off. Cameroon followed that result by defeating Romania 2–1, both goals coming from substitute Roger Milla, a 38-year-old veteran whose celebratory wiggle at the corner flag earned him global fame. Cameroon's 4–0 defeat to the Soviet Union that ended group-round play was entirely inconsequential, as the African nation won the group regardless.

In the second round, Cameroon faced Colombia in Naples, a game that was scoreless after 90 minutes. Then super-substitute Milla struck again, scoring twice in extra time in what ended up in a 2–1 win for the Lions, a late goal for Colombia of no ultimate consequence. Cameroon progressed to play England, remaining in Naples, in what turned out to be one of the most exciting games of the competition. England led at halftime thanks to a goal from David Platt, but in the second half, Cameroon took charge in the game and scored twice through Emmanuel Kundé in the 61st minute from the penalty spot and Eugène Ekéké only 4 minutes later. Facing elimination, though, England equalized from the penalty spot from a penalty by Gary Lineker in the 83rd minute, the score 2–2 at full-time. Lineker again struck from the spot in extra time after he was fouled in the penalty area. Cameroon's romantic and impressive run was over.

Roger Milla appeared at the 1994 World Cup in the United States, as Cameroon played in a second successive tournament, becoming the oldest man to score in the competition at the age of 42. It was not, though, a successful adventure for the Indomitable Lions. Cameroon began with a creditable 2–2 draw with Sweden, who would finish third in the competition, the Africans' goals coming from David Embe and François Omam-Biyik. At Stanford Stadium against Brazil, though, Cameroon suffered a comprehensive 3–0 defeat, and things got worse when Russia crushed the Lions 6–1 at the same venue, the only saving grace Milla's historic goal. Four years later, in France, Cameroon again exited at the group stage. The Indomitable Lions were coached by Frenchman Claude Le Roy, with most of the country's roster now based in Europe, including Rigobert Song of Lens in France and a young Samuel Eto'o of Barcelona. Cameroon began group play by tying Austria 1–1: the Lions seemed to have had claimed victory with a 77th-minute goal from Pierre Njanka, but a stoppage-time equalizer from Toni Polster denied Le Roy's men the three points. In Montpellier, Italy comfortably beat Cameroon 3–0, meaning that in the Lions' final game they needed to win and for Austria to lose or draw in order to advance to the next round. Austria duly lost to Italy, but Cameroon's hearts were broken when they failed to defeat Chile, tying 1–1. Already down to 10 men by the 51st minute due to

Song's expulsion, Cameroon had an apparent goal disallowed after equalizing in the 56th minute and ended the game and exited the tournament with only 9 men on the field, with Lauren also receiving a red card in the 88th minute.

Cameroon qualified for the 2002 World Cup in South Korea and Japan. Focus on the team came as much from a sleeveless jersey design that had to be altered to meet FIFA's requirements, and with Cameroon having won the previous two editions of the Africa Cup of Nations, hopes were high for the Indomitable Lions. German Winnie Schaeffer was in charge of coaching duties, with Samuel Eto'o now the established star of the team, with a supporting cast including Real Madrid's Geremi. Cameroon began the competition by drawing 1–1 with the Republic of Ireland, the Lions' goal set up by Eto'o and scored by Patrick M'Boma. In Saitama, Eto'o then scored the winning goal in a 1–0 win over Saudi Arabia that meant Cameroon could advance to the next round if the Lions could at least secure one point against Germany, while the Republic of Ireland failed to defeat Saudi Arabia. In a game marked by indiscipline— referee Antonio Lopez Nieto dished out 16 cards, including a red to Cameroon's Patrick Suffo and Germany's Carsten Ramelow—the Lions were outclassed 2–0 and were eliminated at the group stage for the third successive World Cup.

Despite only losing once in qualifying, Cameroon failed to make it to the 2006 World Cup in Germany, coming second in a difficult group topped by Côte d'Ivoire. The Indomitable Lions did advance to the first World Cup held in Africa four years later, with another Frenchman, Paul Le Guen, coaching a team still led by Samuel Eto'o, who scored 9 goals in 11 qualifying games. Cameroon, though, only found the net twice in three games at the World Cup in South Africa, losing all three games. Kicking off with a 1–0 loss to Japan, Cameroon then stumbled to successive 2–1 defeats to Denmark and the Netherlands.

Qualification for the 2014 World Cup in Brazil was no easy task. It took a change in managers midway through qualification and an overturned loss to Togo, due to Togo's fielding of an ineligible player, to get it done. Though they played in what was considered by many to be the most wide-open African group, Cameroon played just well enough to finish ahead of Libya, Congo DR and Togo with 13 points in six matches and advance to the play-off stage against Tunisia. By this time, the Lions had adjusted to new manager Volker Finke's style, drawing 0–0 away and cruising to a 4–1 home win that gave them much-needed confidence heading to Brazil.

Placed into group A with host Brazil, Croatia and Mexico, Cameroon's seventh World Cup appearance was a new African record; the hope this time was that they would advance further than their normal group-stage exit. With world-class players like Schalke's center-back Joël Matip and high-scoring strikers Vincent Aboubakar and Samuel Eto'o, Finke certainly believed that anything was possible.

In their first game, against Mexico in a rain-soaked Estádio das Dunas, in Natal, Cameroon had their chances. It was ultimately the goalkeeping of Mexico's Guillermo Ochoa and the woodwork that kept them from stealing a point, as the game was lost on a 61st-minute strike by Oribe Peralta. Hoping for a better result against Croatia, it seemed that the disarray and divisions felt prior to their arrival—specifically threats by the players to strike over a dispute about bonus pay—followed Cameroon. Though the 4–0 loss was bad enough, this game may be remembered more for the reported match fixing, flagrant red cards and player infighting than anything Croatia achieved. At least for the first half of Cameroon's final game, against host Brazil in Brasília, the Lions seemed to have patched things up. The energy and joy of a Joël Matip equalizer 26 minutes in was short-lived, as Neymar scored his second goal of the game nine minutes later. The Brazilians later added two more goals in the second half for a 4–1 win, and the Lions were sent home. Cameroon finished 31st in the tournament with one goal for and nine against.

CANADA. Commonly known as the Canucks or Les Rouges (The Reds). Canada's lone appearance in the World Cup final tournament came in 1986, with the competition held in Mexico. Canada lost all three games, failing to score a goal and conceding five. Yet their mere qualification for the World Cup was a superb achievement for the country, which they achieved by winning the 1985 CONCACAF Championship that served as the region's World Cup qualifying competition—albeit one missing regional powerhouse Mexico, as the World Cup hosts automatically qualified for the competition. In the final round of the CONCACAF Championship, Canada impressively won the group-stage contest without losing a game, finishing ahead of both Honduras and Costa Rica. The critical qualifier that confirmed Canada's place at the World Cup came on 14 September 1985 with a 2–1 win over Honduras, Czechoslovakian-born Igor Vrablic poking home the winner from a corner after 65 minutes in front of an ecstatic capacity home crowd at King George V Park in St. John's, the capital city of Newfoundland. Many of Canada's players had gained professional experience in the North American Soccer League (NASL), though its collapse at the end of 1984 meant many players now made their living in indoor soccer, hardly ideal preparation for the World Cup. Canada was perhaps unfortunate to be drawn into arguably the toughest group in the first-round stage of the 1986 World Cup, alongside France, Hungary and the Soviet Union. Canada, though, did not look overawed in their opening game against France on 1 June in León, over 65,000 present. Stout Canadian defense delayed the French breakthrough until the 79th minute, Jean-Pierre Papin scoring with a header. Canada lost 1–0 and went on to further defeats by two goals to none against both Hungary on 6 June and the Soviet Union on 9 June. Canada has not qualified for the World Cup since, hampered by the collapse of the NASL with no Canadian team joining Major League Soccer until Toronto FC became a part of the North American league in 2007.

CANNAVARO, FABIO. B. 13 September 1973, Naples, Italy. Fabio Cannavaro was the FIFA World Player of the Year in 2006, recognizing his achievement in captaining Italy to victory at the 2006 FIFA World Cup in Germany, also winning the European Footballer of the Year award that year. Cannavaro is the only defender to have won the FIFA World Player of the Year as of August 2010, known for offering a formidable and composed presence in the center of defense for Italy since 1997 and holding the record number of appearances for his country. He retired from international play in July 2011 following the 2010 World Cup in South Africa, having amassed 136 total appearances for his country. At club level, Cannavaro achieved his greatest success playing for Real Madrid in Spain from 2006 to 2009, twice winning the Spanish league championship. He also won the 1999 UEFA Cup playing for Juventus in his native Italy.

CAPDEVILLE, GEORGE. B. 30 October 1899, France. D. 24 February 1991. The 1938 World Cup final in Paris, France, was refereed by George Capdeville, who officiated over a 4–2 victory for Italy against Hungary. He did not issue any cautions during the game. Capdeville was 39 years old at the time, the third-youngest referee in a World Cup final to date and the only referee to have overseen in a World Cup final in his native country. At the 1938 World Cup, Capdeville also refereed a quarterfinal matchup between Brazil and Czechoslovakia, not issuing any cautions, a replay between the two teams two days after a draw in which referee Pal Von Hertzka had sent off three players. Capdeville also refereed a World Cup qualifier earlier in 1938, a 3–2 win for Belgium over Luxemburg.

CASILLAS, IKER. B. 20 May 1981, Móstoles, Spain. A long-time star goalkeeper for Real Madrid at club level and with more than 140 appearances for Spain at national-team level, Iker Casillas is one of the leading European net-minders of the modern era. He is known not just for his acrobatic goalkeeping but also for his leadership, having captained Spain to victory in the 2008 and 2012 European Championships and most notably the 2010 World Cup title in South Africa. The 2010 competition was Casillas's third appearance at the World Cup, having also taken part in the 2002 tournament in South Korea and Japan and the 2006 edition in Germany. Casillas appeared in five games in South Korea and Japan and conceded only five goals in five games, but he was unable to prevent Spanish elimination on a penalty shoot-out to host nation South Korea in the quarterfinals. In Germany 2006, Casillas conceded four goals in three games, but three of them were against France in Spain's round-of-16 loss. The 2010 World Cup in South Africa saw Spain finally claim the World Cup for the first time, and Casillas was awarded the Golden Glove as the best goalkeeper in the tournament. Casillas had five clean sheets, conceding only two goals in seven games, and he did not let in a single goal during the elimination stage, including Spain's 1–0 win over the Netherlands in the final.

Leading up to Brazil 2014, Casillas racked up individual achievements, becoming Spain's most capped player, holder of the most international clean sheets and the first to reach 100 wins. In Brazil, though, his performances were less than stellar as Spain lost 5–1 to the Netherlands in their opener (a game Casillas called the "worst performance of his career") and 1–0 to Chile in the second game to send the Spaniards home. Casillas has now appeared in 17 World Cup finals games and 31 World Cup qualifiers, with only 29 goals conceded in 48 total appearances.

CASTRO, HÉCTOR. B. 29 November 1904, Montevideo, Uruguay. D. 15 September 1960. Héctor Castro scored Uruguay's first-ever World Cup goal, the winning goal against Peru in their opening group-stage game at the inaugural World Cup held in his home city of Montevideo on 18 July 1930. Castro did not play again at the competition until the final, taking part in Uruguay's 4–2 win over Argentina that made them world champions. He scored Uruguay's fourth goal in that game, hammering the ball home on a counterattack as Argentina searched for the equalizer. Castro had become a mainstay of the Uruguayan national team in the late 1920s, playing in Uruguay's winning teams at both the 1926 Copa América and the 1928 Olympic Games Football Tournament. Following victory in the World Cup, Castro enjoyed further success with his country, playing on the 1935 Copa América winning team. At club level, Castro played most of his career for Montevideo-based Nacional, though he also played briefly for Estudiantes in 1932 and 1933. Castro was known for his disability, having accidentally sawn off his right forearm with an electric saw at the age of 13 while chopping wood. He was known for his fierce play and strength on the field. Castro retired in 1936, having played 25 games for his country, scoring 18 goals. He later briefly coached Uruguay at the international level but did not take a part in any World Cup after 1930 as either a player or a coach, Uruguay not again participating until 1950.

CEA, PEDRO. B. 1 September 1900, Redondela, Spain. D. 18 September 1970. Pedro Cea scored five goals at the 1930 native World Cup held in his native Uruguay to lead his country to victory in the inaugural World Cup, his goal haul only bettered at the tournament by Argentinean Guillermo Stábile. Cea, who played for Nacional in Uruguay at club level, had collected numerous honors at the international level with Uruguay in the 1920s, including gold medals at both the 1924 and 1928 Olympic Games, scoring 5 goals in a total of 10 games. He developed a formidable partnership with fellow Uruguayan and Nacional forward Héctor Scarone, weaving passes together that frequently bedazzled and beat their opponents. Cea, like most of his contemporaries, was an amateur player and sold ice for a living. Cea scored his first World Cup goal during Uruguay's second game at the 1930 World Cup, a 35th-minute strike in a 4–0 Uruguayan win over Romania on 21 July 1930. In Uruguay's semifinal against Yugoslavia, Cea recorded a hat trick in a 6–1 win. His fifth and final World Cup goal was Uruguay's crucial second goal against Argentina in the final, tying the score at 2–2, after a fine individual dribble. Cea retired in 1932, ending his international career with 13 goals in 27 games.

CHILE. Commonly known as La Roja (The Red). One of four South American countries to host the World Cup, enjoying the honor in 1962, Chile has competed in nine World Cup tournaments. Its best finish came, perhaps unsurprisingly, in 1962, when Chile finished in third place as the host nation. Chile had appeared in two earlier World Cup finals competitions. In 1930, at the inaugural World Cup, Chile won its first two games in the first-round group stage. Coached by Hungarian György Orth, Chile defeated Mexico 3–0 and France 1–0. However, with only one team in the four-team group advancing to the next stage, Chile came unstuck with a 3–1 loss to Argentina that eliminated La Roja from the World Cup. Chile did not play again at the World Cup until it returned to South America in 1950, taking part in the tournament in Brazil under head coach Arturo Bucciardi. Chile began with a pair of 2–0 defeats to England and Spain, meaning a 5–2 win over the United States could not prevent elimination at the first stage again.

In 1962, Chile appeared again at the World Cup following a 12-year break—on home soil, as the South American nation hosted the competition. It was remarkable that the competition took place in Chile at all, as, only two years before the competition was due to begin, the nation was struck by a devastating earthquake measuring a record 9.5 on the Richter scale that killed thousands. Chile, though, rallied to host the competition. In the first-round group stage, Chile—coached by former national-team player Fernando Riera—began with a comfortable 3–1 win over Switzerland, thanks to two goals from Leonel Sánchez and one from Jaime Ramirez. Chile's next game turned out to be one of the most controversial in World Cup history. Held in the nation's capital at Nacional stadium, a brutal contest with Italy became known as the "Battle of Santiago." The game came in the wake of disparaging comments about Chile made by two Italian journalists that had inflamed tensions. Referee Ken Aston was faced with the challenge of controlling two sets of players intent on committing violent fouls immediately after kickoff, sending off Italy's Giorgio Ferrini after only 12 minutes—Ferrini requiring a police escort to be convinced to leave the field of play. The violent play continued with Chile's Leonel Sánchez breaking the nose of Humberto Maschio, with physical exchanges continuing throughout the 90 minutes. Chile won 2–0, but the result was almost lost amid the disgraceful scenes. Chile then lost 2–0 to West Germany but qualified for the next round in second place behind the West Germans.

In the elimination stage, Chile defeated a strong Soviet Union team—the reigning European champions—2–1 in the quarterfinals, with the South American goals coming from Leonel Sánchez and Eladio Rojas. In the next round, Chile faced defending World Cup champions Brazil. Even without Pelé, the Chileans were no match for the outstanding Brazilians, with star winger Garrincha tearing holes in La Roja's defense seemingly at will, scoring twice in the first 30 minutes. Chile pulled a goal back through Jorge Toro in the 42nd minute, but just after halftime, Brazil sealed an insurmountable lead with a goal from Vava. A second Chilean goal by Leonel Sánchez from the penalty spot was to no avail, as Brazil won 4–2 and advanced to the World Cup final, going on to win the competition. Chile moved on to the third-place play-off, winning 1–0 over Yugoslavia—Eladio Rojas scoring the only goal—earning a third-place finish. To date, that remains as Chile's best finish in a World Cup.

Chile advanced to the next World Cup held in England in 1966 thanks to a 2–1 win over Ecuador in a play-off in South American qualifying. La Roja thus advanced to a World Cup in Europe for the first time, under the stewardship of coach Luis Alamos. On foreign soil, Chile could not repeat the success of 1962, failing to win a game in the group stage. A 2–0 defeat to Italy was followed by a 1–1 tie with North Korea, the surprise package of the competition, and elimination at the first stage was confirmed by a 2–1 loss to the Soviet Union.

Chile failed to qualify for the 1970 World Cup in Brazil but did advance to the next World Cup in West Germany. That appearance was marred by political controversy: the Soviet Union had refused to travel to Chile for a qualifying play-off game, as the Soviets refused to play at Estadio Nacional, a stadium that had been used as concentration camp by the military dictatorship led by Augusto Pinochet, who had taken over the country in a coup in 1973. Chile was awarded the game as a walkover to advance to the World Cup finals. In West Germany, still coached by Luis Alamos, Chile began the first-round group stage against the host nation, losing 1–0 to a long-range strike by Paul Breitner, with La Roja's Carlos Caszely sent off in the second half. Chile then earned a point against East Germany, a second-half goal from Sergio Ahumada canceling out Martin Hoffman's earlier goal for the East Germans. However, Chile was again eliminated at the first-round stage following a disappointing 0–0 tie with Australia.

Eight years passed until Chile next appeared at the World Cup, traveling to Spain for the 1982 competition, with a team coached by Luis Alberto Santibáñez and led on the field by veteran defender Elias Figueroa. Chile performed poorly in Spain, losing all three games: a 1–0 loss to Austria was followed by a 4–1 hammering by West Germany and a 3–2 defeat to Austria, eliminated at the bottom of group two in the first round. Controversy then struck Chile again in qualifying for the 1990 World Cup. Chilean goalkeeper Roberto Rojas was found by FIFA to have faked an injury during a qualifying game with Brazil with the score 1–0 to the Brazilians, a result that would have eliminated Chile. Rojas claimed to have been struck by a firework thrown onto the field that video evidence showed had landed some distance from him; Rojas faked injury, and Chile refused to complete the game. FIFA banned Rojas from soccer for life and Chile from qualifying for the 1994 World Cup.

Armed with a lethal strike pair—Marcelo Salas and Iván Zamorano—Chile returned to World Cup action in style with qualification for the 1998 World Cup in France. Coached by Nelson Acosta, Chile faced Italy, Austria and Cameroon in the first-round group stage. Chile began with a 2–2 tie against Italy, Salas scoring twice in a vibrant game, Chile leading 2–1 until the 84th minute, when Roberto Baggio equalized from the penalty spot. Chile again led until late in the game against Austria, thanks to a 70th-minute Salas strike, but conceded a desperately late equalizer deep into stoppage time for a 1–1 tie. For the third consecutive game, Chile conceded a lead against Cameroon, a first-half strike by Jose Sierra equaled by Patrick M'Boma's 56th-minute goal. The 1–1 scoreline was enough to advance Chile to the second round, but a second-place finish in the group meant a matchup with fellow South Americans Brazil, the defending world champions. The game was effectively over by halftime, Brazil scoring three without reply. A strike by Salas in the second half was little consolation, though it did give the Chilean striker four goals for the competition, giving him a record of a goal per game as Chile exited the tournament.

Chile qualified next for the World Cup in 2010, finishing second in South American qualifying. In South Africa, Chile—coached by Argentinean Marcelo Bielsa, a renowned tactician—was placed in group H with Switzerland, Honduras and European champions Spain. Almost 50 years on from Chile's last win in the World Cup finals, Chile secured a victory against Honduras, thanks to a goal from Jean Beausejour. La Roja did not have to wait long for another victory: that came with a 1–0 win over Switzerland, Mark Gonzalez's strike proving to be the difference. Playing open, attacking soccer orchestrated by Bielsa's creative tactics, Chile gave eventual champions Spain a tough game to end the group stage, ultimately succumbing to a 2–1 defeat. Chile qualified for the next round in second place behind Spain and once again faced Brazil in Johannesburg at Ellis Park Stadium. And once again Chile succumbed to Brazil, three unanswered goals coming despite good early possession for La Roja.

During qualification for the 2014 World Cup in Brazil, Chile looked like a side on a mission under Argentinean Claudio Borghi as they rolled to wins in four of their first six games. However, disciplinary problems common to the Chilean national team caused the team's play to suffer. With consecutive 3–1 defeats to Colombia and Ecuador, followed by a 2–1 loss to Argentina, Borghi was fired and replaced with compatriot Jorge Sampaoli. Though Sampaoli's debut was a 1–0 away loss to Peru, that was his only blemish the remainder of the way as Chile finished on a tear, compiling five wins and a draw in their last six matches to qualify for a historic second consecutive World Cup.

Drawn into group B with Spain, Netherlands and Australia, it looked like La Roja had their work cut out for them. The Chileans got off to a perfect start in their first game against Australia (viewed as a must-win by Chilean supporters) when Alexis Sánchez and Jorge Valdívia scored goals two minutes apart to put Chile up 2–0 only 14 minutes into the game. Though a strong header by Tim Cahill in the 35th minute gave Australia momentum, a stoppage-time goal by Jean Beausejour sealed the win for La Roja and set the tone for a crucial game with Spain. Chile's decisive 2–0 win over the defending champions (Chile's first competitive win over Spain in 11 matches) was a result that very few people foresaw. First-half goals from Eduardo Vargas and Charles Aránguiz did the damage, and Spain rarely threatened in either half. Though La Roja now had guaranteed advancement to the round of 16 in consecutive World Cups, their eyes were on finishing first place in a group many thought they would not advance from; unfortunately for Chile, a high-powered Dutch side had their eyes on the same prize. Chile was arguably the stronger side in the first half, but second-half Dutch substitutes Leroy Fer and Memphis Depay were the difference makers, and Chile was relegated to second in their group and a date with host Brazil in the round of 16.

Though seen by many as a favorable matchup for the host side, Brazil found their hands full with a Chilean team brimming with confidence. A Gonzalo Jara own goal (officially credited to David Luiz in the 18th minute) off a Neymar corner got the scoring started, but a clinical Alexis Sánchez finish in the 32nd minute leveled the game. Both teams had their chances in regulation and extra time, but the game was sent to penalty kicks. It was the play of Brazilian goalkeeper Júlio César, who saved shots by Mauricio Pinilla and Sánchez before watching as a pressure-packed shot by Jara rocketed off the post, that ultimately ended Chile's hopes for an upset. Chile finished in ninth place with six goals for and four against.

CHINA. Commonly known as Lóng Zhī Duì (Team Dragon) or Guó Zú (National Football Team). The world's most populous country has only appeared at the World Cup final tournament on one occasion, in 2002. In general, China has enjoyed little international success in men's soccer, never winning Asia's regional international championship, though finishing as runner-up in 1984 and 2004. China's national team had a checkered and difficult history following the founding of the People's Republic of China in 1949, with its actual membership of FIFA a matter of considerable controversy, leaving FIFA in 1958 and rejoining in 1979. Their departure in 1958 followed their first, unsuccessful attempt at qualification for the World Cup. China's next attempt to qualify for the World Cup came for the 1982 competition in Spain, an effort that came agonizingly close to success: after finishing tied in the final-round standings for Asia's second qualification spot with New Zealand, China lost in a play-off held in neutral Singapore on 10 January 1982 to the All Whites. That did not prove to be a springboard for success for China, however, but in 2002, China advanced through Asian qualifying with surprising ease, topping their group in the final round of qualification while only losing one out of eight games played. China's 2002 World Cup squad was made up largely of domestic-based players, such as the vastly experienced midfield pair of Ma Mingyu and Hao Haidong, who each had 90 caps heading into the competition. China also had a sprinkling of players from the highest levels of European soccer, including Sun Jihai of Manchester City in England and Yang Chen of Eintracht Frankfurt in Germany. China did not lack experience in the coaching department, as their Serb coach Bora Milutinović would be leading a fifth different country to the World Cup finals, an all-time record. In Japan and South Korea, China was placed into a difficult group containing Brazil, Turkey and Costa Rica. They kicked off against the latter on 4 June in Gwangju, South Korea. China held firm under unrelenting pressure from Costa Rica for over an hour, but Costa Rica then scored two quick goals, Ronald Gomez curling home a loose ball in the penalty area and Mauricio Wright then stealing in at the near post for a headed goal from a corner, resulting in a 2–0 Costa Rica victory. Four days later in Jeju, China faced Brazil and could do little to contain the South Americans in a 4–0 defeat, who scored through Roberto Carlos, Rivaldo, Ronaldinho and Ronaldo, though China were not overrun, working hard in defeat despite missing two of their best defenders through injury, Sun Jihai and Fan Zhiyi. China's final game came in Seoul against eventual semifinalists Turkey, falling to a 3–0 defeat and this exiting without having scored a goal and having lost all three games. Following the game, Milutinović left his post as China's coach. In qualifying for the 2006 World Cup, China finished behind Kuwait to be disappointingly eliminated in the second-round stage and fared even worse in 2010 qualifying, finishing bottom of their group in the third round. 2014 was only slightly better as China finished third out of four to again miss out on qualification. China, its domestic league still troubled by serious corruption, has yet to develop a consistent international team that can compete on the World Cup stage with any relation to the country's vast population.

CODESAL MÉNDEZ, EDGARDO. B. 2 June 1951, Montevideo, Uruguay. The 1990 World Cup final in Italy between Germany and Argentina was presided over by referee Edgardo Codesal Méndez, a Uruguayan-born official representing his adopted country Mexico at the competition. It was Codesal's third match in charge at the 1990 World Cup. He had also overseen a first-round game between hosts Italy and the United States, a 1–0 win for the Italians, awarding a penalty that Italian forward Gianluca Vialli struck the post with. Codesal then refereed the England–Cameroon quarterfinal, an incident-packed game that went to extra time, England coming out on top with a 3–2 win. England's goals included two penalties awarded by Codesal, while Cameroon converted a penalty of their own, with little doubt raised about any of Codesal's decisions. In the final, a tempestuous affair, Codesal became the first referee to send a player off in the World Cup final, dismissing Argentinean Pedro Monzón after a reckless sliding tackle on German forward Jürgen Klinsmann. Codesal turned down both Argentinean and German penalty claims before finally awarding the Europeans a spot kick in the 83rd minute when Roberto Sensini took down Rudi Völler in the penalty area. The call was controversial as it appeared Sensini won the ball, with Codesal trailing behind play. Vigorous Argentinean protest was waved away by Codesal, Andreas Brehme coolly converting the spot kick that proved to be the winning goal for Argentina. Codesal then sent off a second Argentinean player when Gustavo Dezotti crudely grabbed German defender Jürgen Kohler, who fell theatrically to the floor.

COELHO, ARNALDO. B. 15 January 1943, Rio de Janeiro, Brazil. Arnaldo Coelho became an international referee in the late 1960s and was selected as a referee for both the 1978 and 1982 World Cups, in Argentina and Spain respectively. At the 1978 competition, Coelho took charge of just one game, a group-stage win for France over Hungary. He continued to referee high-profile games in South America ahead of the 1982 World Cup, taking charge of the 1979 Copa América final. At the 1982 World Cup, Coelho was selected to referee England versus West Germany in the second-round group stage, a 0–0 draw. The Brazilian was, somewhat surprisingly, again chosen to take charge of the final, the first non-European to do so, as West Germany faced Italy. Coelho struggled to contain an ugly game filled with niggling fouls but did not lose control, as Italy took charge in the second half and won 3–1. Coelho issued two cautions to the Italians and three to the West Germans. Coelho continued to referee internationally until 1989 but was not selected for any games at the 1986 World Cup in Mexico.

COLLINA, PIERLUIGI. B. 13 February 1960, Viareggio, Italy. Perhaps the 20th century's most recognizable referee, Pierluigi Collina refereed the final of the 2002 World Cup in Yokohama, Japan, among many other high-profile assignments for the distinctive bald Italian official. Collina became an international referee in 1995, taking charge of four games at the 1996 Olympic Games Football Tournament, including the final. He became a regular referee in the UEFA Champions League and also officiated three 1998 World Cup qualifying games, though he was not selected to take charge of any games at the finals in France. Collina's profile continued to rise, refereeing the 1999 UEFA Champions League final, three games at the 2000 European Championship and then three qualifiers for the 2002 World Cup. It was at the latter competition, held jointly in Japan and South Korea, that Collina's profile became global. In the group stage, Collina was assigned to a high-profile matchup between old rivals Argentina and England. Collina controversially awarded England a penalty for Michael Owen, with a questionable amount of contact from a challenge by Mauricio Pochettino causing the Englishman to go down in the penalty area, David Beckham burying the resulting penalty to give England a 1–0 win. Collina was then called on to referee hosts Japan against Turkey, the Europeans squeezing out a 1–0 win. The final, on 30 June 2002, was handled with aplomb by Collina, who issued only two cautions during the game, one to each team. Collina continued as a top-level referee until 2005, when he reached the age of retirement for international referees and was thus ineligible to officiate at the 2006 World Cup in Germany.

COLOMBES STADIUM. In the northwestern suburbs of Paris, France, the third World Cup final took place at Colombes Stadium. It was also known as Stade Olympique de Colombes, having hosted the 1924 Olympic Games, and was originally opened in 1907 and remodeled for the Olympics. Colombes also staged two other games at the 1938 World Cup: France's 3–1 win over Belgium in the first round, 30,454 fans present to see the hosts progress, and then the elimination of France at the quarterfinal stage, 58,455 mostly disappointed spectators watching defending World Cup champions Italy eliminate the French. The final, in which Italy defeated Hungary 4–2 in Colombes, was only attended by a little over 45,000 people. Following the World Cup, Colombes was a frequent host for France's national-team games until the 1970s and was also a prominent rugby venue. With a much-reduced capacity of only a little over 10,000, Colombes suffered from neglect and was close to demolition in 2004, though it was saved, with a redevelopment plan drawn up.

COLOMBIA. Commonly known as Los Cafeteros (The Coffee Growers) or Tricolor. Colombia has made five appearances at the FIFA World Cup finals (1962, 1990, 1994, 1998 and 2014). The furthest Colombia had gone in the World Cup was to the round of 16 in the 1990 competition, until 2014 when, behind the goal scoring of Golden Boot–winner James Rodríguez, they made it to the quarterfinals where they eventually lost 2–1 to host Brazil. Soccer in Colombia was slower to develop than in many other parts of South America, American influence ensuring baseball remained a viable rival in the early decades of the 20th century, and its geography made it difficult for a national sport to develop, soccer restricted to the coastal regions where it was promoted by British sailors and railway workers. In 1909, Colombia's first organized soccer team, Barranquilla FBC, was formed. Colombian soccer began to be organized in the 1920s, with the sport's governing body Federación Colombiana de Fútbol founded in 1924 and affiliating to FIFA in 1936. That was too late for Colombia to participate in the first two World Cup competitions held in 1930 and 1934, and Colombia, like many South American nations, did not travel to France for the 1938 World Cup. Following World War II, Colombia's sudden economic riches—fueled by a coffee export boom, which led to the rapid industrialization of the country—fostered the conditions for a rich professional league to arise. But the political volatility of the country resulted in Colombia's suspension from FIFA; its outlaw league, then drawing in some of South America's greatest players, offered untold riches, a development which did little for the national team, who were not allowed to enter the 1950 or 1954 World Cups by FIFA.

Colombia finally entered qualification for the World Cup in time for the 1958 tournament and, unsurprisingly given the national team's limited international play, finished bottom of their qualification group, not winning a game in a group containing Uruguay and winners Paraguay. For the 1962 World Cup, Colombia was placed in a qualifying group with one other team, Peru, the teams playing one game each at home in April and May 1961 to determine who would travel to Chile next year. Colombia won the first game 1–0 in Bogotá and then traveled to Lima for a 1–1 to advance to the World Cup for the first time. Little was expected of Colombia as they traveled to Chile, placed in group one with two strong European teams—the Soviet Union and

Yugoslavia, who two years earlier had contested the first European Championship final—along with two-time World Cup winners Uruguay. Colombia first faced their fellow South Americans on 30 May in Arica, a mere 7,908 curious fans present for a sunny afternoon kickoff. Colombia took a shocking lead after only 19 minutes, with Francisco Zuluaga driving home a left-footed penalty to the cheers of an unexpectedly excited crowd. Inspired by the grace and power of Germán Aceros and Delio Gamboa at the heart of their team, Colombia held on to the lead until the 56th minute, despite the obvious inexperience of their goalkeeper Efraín Sánchez, Luis Cubilla scoring the equalizer. Colombia then conceded one more for a cruel defeat on their World Cup debut, after a slip by Gamboa in midfield allowed a Uruguayan counterattack ending in José Sasía's winning goal.

Colombia's second game was against the Soviet Union, one of the favorites for the World Cup, the reigning European champions having defeated Yugoslavia in their opening game. The first 20 minutes went as many would have expected when Colombia arrived in Chile, the Soviets' marauding attacks too much for the Colombians to contain, quickly falling to a 3–0 deficit. Colombia, though, did not give up. In the 21st minute, Aceros started a clever passing move in midfield and then burst into the penalty area, Rolando Serrano finding him with a clever pass for Aceros to loft the ball into the back of the net past legendary Soviet goalkeeper Lev Yashin and make it 3–1. Order seemed to be restored 10 minutes after halftime when Viktor Ponedelnik made it 4–1 to the Soviet Union. But then one of the greatest and unlikeliest of World Cup comebacks began. Yashin, all of a sudden, lost his bearings, and a corner kick taken by Marcos Coll rolled into the goal past the Soviet goalkeeper at the near post to make it 4–2 in the 68th minute. Suddenly, Colombia was able to move the ball swiftly past a static Soviet defense, Coll, Marcus Klinger and Hector Gonzalez combining to set up Antonio Rada for a close-range finish four minutes later, the scoreline now reading 4–3 to the Soviets. With only four minutes remaining, Rada collected the ball at the edge of his own area and powered forward on a 40-yard run, then speared the ball through the Soviet defense into the path of the onrushing Klinger, the tricky Colombian forward rounding past Yashin before scoring the equalizing goal. Colombia had achieved a remarkable draw and their first World Cup point, the South American crowd going berserk in response. An exhausted Colombian side proved to be no match for Yugoslavia in their final game of the 1962 World Cup four days later in Arica, losing 5–0 but heading home having surprised on the world stage.

Colombia, though, was unable to build on the platform of 1962 and did not qualify again for the World Cup until 1970. Colombia finished bottom of their group in 1966 World Cup qualifying, third of four teams for 1970, second in their group in 1974 qualifying, bottom in 1978 and 1982 qualifying and lost in the play-offs in 1986 qualifying. Their failure to qualify for 1986 was a small disappointment compared to the greater one surrounding that tournament: Colombia had been awarded the right to host the 1986 World Cup by FIFA in the mid-1970s, but as the country became engulfed in financial and political crises, racked by violence and falling far behind in its stadia-building promises, it withdrew from hosting in November 1982 and was replaced by Mexico. Yet, the country slipped further under the control of narco-fueled cartels in the 1980s, which oddly resulted in a mini-boom for Colombian soccer. The majority of Colombia's first-division clubs were funded by drug cartels by the mid-1980s, and they became highly competitive in South American club tournaments, with resources pumped into youth and infrastructure development—albeit at the massively high price of enmeshment with organized crime. Club officials did not remain immune to the violence sweeping Colombian society. Amid the bloodshed, the 1989 domestic season was canceled before its conclusion. Colombian officials selected to travel to Italy for the World Cup withdrew. Yet the national team itself went, one full of remarkable rising talent, including eccentric goalkeeper René Higuita, gifted playmaker and captain Carlos Valderrama and the talented attacking midfielder Freddy Rincón.

Colombia was placed in group D, alongside West Germany, Yugoslavia and World Cup newcomers the United Arab Emirates. Colombia opened their campaign in Bologna against the United Arab Emirates on 9 June. Bernardo Redín scored his country's first World Cup finals goal for 28 years in the 50th minute, as Colombia beat the offside trap with Leonel Álvarez providing the cross for Redín's header. Valderrama sealed a 2–0 win with a superb goal in the 85th minute, a low right-footed drive from 20 yards out into the bottom right-hand corner. Five days later, Colombia faced a strong Yugoslavian team, again in Bologna, and the South American's defensive ill discipline allowed the Yugoslavs to create a plethora of good opportunities, taking one through Davor Jozić, Higuita saving a late penalty to keep the defeat down to 1–0. Colombia still had a chance to qualify for the next round when they faced West Germany on 19 June in Milan, over 70,000 in attendance. Colombia needed a point and played for the draw, in a negative game that did not see a goal until the Colombians could not contain a West German burst that resulted in an 88th-minute goal for Pierre Littbarski. Over two minutes into injury time, though, Colombian captain Carlos Valderrama—heretofore anonymous in the game—conjured up a superb equalizing goal that guaranteed the South Americans passage to the next round. Receiving the ball just past midfield, Valderrama twisted and turned to find space and then played a left-footed pass that sliced through the West German defense and placed Rincón one-on-one with goalkeeper Bodo Illgner, whom he beat with a shot through the West German's legs. Colombia advanced past the group stage of the World Cup for the first time in their history. In the second round, Colombia would face Cameroon in Naples on 23 June. Ninety minutes of stalemate—with Colombia coming close to scoring when Rincón struck the bar—exploded into life in extra time, to Colombia's disadvantage. Veteran Roger Milla struck twice, first when Colombia's defense allowed Cameroon too much space to carve them open and then thanks to an embarrassing miscue by Higuita, whose trademark insouciance backfired as he gave the ball away 20 yards in front of his penalty area, allowing Milla an easy finish. Colombia clawed one back when Valderrama worked his way superbly into the Cameroonian penalty area and gave the ball to Redín for an easy finish, but it was too little, too late, and Colombia was out of the World Cup.

By the time the 1994 World Cup in the United States began, Colombia had become a dark-horse pick to win the competition, placed in group A with hosts the United States, Romania and Switzerland, a comfortable-looking group. This was largely as a result of their tremendous performance in World Cup qualifying, having topped their group unbeaten and beaten Argentina 2–1 home and 5–0 away in Buenos Aires.

Colombia's squad for the 1994 World Cup contained a mix of 1990 veterans at the peaks of their powers, such as Valderrama (captain for the competition again) and Rincón and talented newcomers Adolfo Valencia and Faustino Asprilla. The coach was still Francisco Maturana. Behind the scenes, though, all was not well. Colombia's drug-racked society and sporting culture piled pressure onto the team traveling to the United States. At the Rose Bowl in California on 18 June, Colombia began their World Cup against Romania, and it almost immediately went disastrously wrong. Colombia began well enough in the opening 15 minutes, Valderrama pulling the strings as the South Americans set up camp in Romania's half. But, Romania took a surprise lead when Romania won the ball and Romanian playmaker Gheorghe Hagi set up forward Florin Răducioiu, who drove past a weak Colombian defense to make it 1–0. Colombia did not seem to recover their composure and confidence. Romania began to control the game, and in the 35th minute, Hagi shocked Oscar Cordoba in the Colombian goal with an unthinkable 35-yard strike into the top corner. Colombia pulled a goal back just before halftime, a corner headed in by Valencia. Colombia could not find the equalizer in the second half, however, and Răducioiu scored a second just before the final whistle to rub salt into Colombia's wound.

It was a wound that was opened further in the days leading up to Colombia's second game against the host United States, who had not won a World Cup finals game since 1950. Murky death threats from Colombia were sent to players and coaches, with defender Gabriel Gomez benched at the request of Colombian officials after shadowy bomb threats were made if he played. Colombia started the game brightly, hitting the post with Antony de Ávila's follow-up shot cleared off the goal line. American pressure grew, though, with Eric Wynalda striking the outside of the post, before disaster struck for Colombia: a speculative cross by John Harkes was deflected inadvertently into his own goal by Colombian defender Andrés Escobar, a moment that would have tragic consequences later. The United States sealed their win with a second goal by Tab Ramos, a consolation goal by Valencia in the 90th minute of no consequence. Colombia's World Cup ended in ignominious fashion in Stanford on 26 June, a depressed team falling 2–0 to Switzerland. Tragedy came only days after the Colombian team's return home. Escobar, scorer of the critical own goal against the United States, was gunned down outside a Medellín nightclub amid circumstances still unclear today.

Colombia, with Asprilla and Valderrama still at the fore, qualified for the 1998 World Cup in France in third place in South American qualifying, behind Brazil and Argentina. Now coached by Hernán Darío Gómez, Colombia headed to France with 36-year-old Valderrama still at the hub of the team, captain for the third successive World Cup. Colombia faced England, Tunisia and Romania in group F. For the second successive tournament, Colombia kicked off against Romania, and once again it was the Europeans who came out on top: on this occasion, an Adrian Ilie goal deep into first-half stoppage time proved to be the difference. Against Tunisia on 22 June in Montpellier, Colombia kept their hopes of qualification to the next round alive, when Valderrama provided an assist for Léider Preciado to give the South Americans a 1–0 win. England, though, snuffed out Colombia's hopes of advancing to the second round on 26 June in Lens, establishing a 2–0 lead in the first half that Gomez's men could not find a response to. Elimination ended the hopes of Colombia's "Golden Generation," and the South American nation did not qualify for another World Cup until 2014, finishing sixth of ten teams in qualifying for both the 2002 and 2006 World Cup finals and seventh of ten teams for the 2010 World Cup.

The qualification for the 2014 World Cup in Brazil began with former Colombian defensive midfielder Leonel Álvarez at the helm, but four points in the first three games spelled disaster and former Argentinean manager José Pékerman was brought in to right the ship. Immediately adding more creativity to the midfield, the goals started to flow, and Colombia scored 14 goals in a torrid four consecutive wins. Headed into Brazil though, questions loomed as Colombia went 2-2-2 over its last six matches.

Placed in group C with Greece, Côte d'Ivoire and Japan, Colombia hoped that their earlier form would return in time for the tournament, and the supporters of Los Cafeteros were rewarded with a resounding 3–0 win over Greece in their first game. With a goal in the fifth minute by Pablo Armero, Colombia was well on its way, and second-half goals by Teófilo Gutiérrez and James Rodríguez made for a comfortable first game and a confident position early atop the group's table. The second game, played at Estádio Nacional de Brasília against Côte d'Ivoire, saw Colombia looking like the more potent team, and two second-half goals within six minutes of each other by Rodríguez and Juan Quintero looked decisive until a 73rd-minute strike from Gervinho put Colombia on their heels. Through to the round of 16, and in control of their own destiny, Los Cafeteros needed only to keep the game close against a reeling Japan side to win their group. An early penalty conversion by Juan Cuadrado looked to seal the deal, but a stoppage-time first-half goal by Shinji Okazaki gave Japan hope. Adding to the World Cup records, a second-half brace by Jackson Martínez gave backup goalkeeper Faryd Mondragón playing time and, with it and his 43 years of age, the distinction of becoming the oldest player ever to play in the World Cup finals. Yet another goal by Rodríguez, this one just before stoppage time, meant a first-place group finish and a date with a Uruguayan side suddenly far less dangerous with the loss of star Luis Suárez.

What was supposed to shape up as a match of two strong South American teams with powerful strikers turned into a showcase for Rodríguez as his two goals thrust him to the top of the tournament's goal scorers while Suárez could do nothing but watch from home, his exclusion the result of a nine game/four month suspension for yet another incident of biting. With five goals in four games, James (as he is affectionately known in his home country) not only led all scorers but also proved that he could do it with flair as his 28th-minute strike (a chest trap and pivot resulting in a full volley just under the bar from 25 yards out) set the bar high for his fellow competitors. The 2–0 win set up a quarterfinal match with host Brazil, a team they had tied four times in four games since 2004.

In a physical battle, Brazil got off to a great start when captain Thiago Silva found himself free on the back post as a result of poor marking and scored in the seventh minute. Though the game went back and forth, a world-class David Luiz free kick from 35 yards out gave the Brazilians some breathing room. Headed into the final 10 minutes down two goals, eventual Golden Boot–winner James's penalty in the 80th minute gave Colombia life, and they found themselves with numerous chances but failed to convert. After not qualifying for 16 years, a historical quarterfinal finish and a Golden Boot winner made Brazil a very successful tournament for Colombia as they finished fifth in the tournament with 12 goals for and four against.

COMBI, GIANPIERO. B. 20 November 1902, Turin, Italy. D. 12 August 1956. Italy's captain and goalkeeper in the 1934 World Cup final, a 2–1 victory over Czechoslovakia, was Gianpiero Combi. The 32-year-old veteran is considered among the greatest Italian goalkeepers of all time, also enjoying an illustrious club career with Juventus of his native Turin, winning five Italian championships with the team. Combi made his debut for Italy at the age of 21 and earned his first international honor in the 1928 Olympic Games Football Tournament, where Italy took the bronze medal, Combi playing in Italy's final four games. Combi captained Italy for the first time in November 1931, replacing his Juventus teammate Umberto Caligaris, as the Italians hosted Czechoslovakia in Rome. The captaincy, though, then went to Virginio Rosetta, another of Combi's teammates at Juventus, who led Italy out for their first game at the 1934 World Cup held in Italy, Combi in goal as Italy strolled to a 7–1 win over an overmatched United States. Rosetta, however, missed Italy's next game, and Combi took over the captaincy again, leading his country to a win over Spain after a replay following a 1–1 tie. Combi then kept a clean sheet in the semifinal, Italy defeating a strong Austrian team 1–0, meaning that with the 2–1 win over Czechoslovakia in the final, he had only conceded three goals in five games at the World Cup. Combi is one of only three players to have both kept goal and captained his side to victory in a World Cup final, along with Dino Zoff in 1982, also for Italy, and Iker Casillas for Spain in 2010. Combi retired from international play after the 1930 World Cup, having made 47 appearances for Italy.

CONEN, EDMUND. B. 10 November 1914, Ürzig, Germany. D. 5 March 1990. Tied for second place in the list of leading goal scorers at the 1934 World Cup was Germany's Edmund Conen, who, along with Angelo Schiavio of Italy, scored four goals in the competition. Both finished one goal behind Oldřich Nejedlý for the Golden Boot. Conen, only 19 years old, had played just one game for Germany when the World Cup began, scoring on his debut in a 2–1 win over Hungary in January 1934. Conen made a dramatic start to his World Cup career: in Germany's first game at the 1934 World Cup against Belgium on 27 May, Conen broke a 2–2 tie in the second half by scoring a hat trick in just 21 minutes, finding the net in the 66th, 70th and 87th minutes. He did not score in either of Germany's next two games, their 2–1 win over Sweden in the quarterfinal or their 3–1 defeat to Czechoslovakia in the semifinal, but did score in Germany's 3–2 defeat in the third-place consolation game on 7 June against Austria. Conen continued to score regularly for Germany following the World Cup until the end of 1935, when illness struck and gravely interrupted his career. He did not return to international play until 1939, missing the 1938 World Cup. Conen continued playing for Germany until 1942 but never took part in another World Cup, with the competition interrupted by World War II. He ended his international career with a tremendous goal-scoring record of 27 goals in 28 games.

CONGO DR. Commonly known as Les Léopards (The Leopards). In 1974, Congo DR—then known as Zaire—became the first nation from sub-Saharan Africa to qualify for the FIFA World Cup finals, that year held in West Germany. Soccer was popularized in Congo in the early 20th century, with the sport's governing body in the country Fédération Congolaise de Football-Association (FECOFA) established in 1919. Congo began international play shortly after the country gained independence from Belgium in 1960, its first game coming in 1963 with a 6–0 win over Mauritania and affiliating to FIFA the following year. Congo quickly developed one of the leading teams in Africa, with victories in the 1968 and 1974 Africa Cup of Nations (in the former as Congo-Kinshasa and in the latter as Zaire, as the country was known from 1971 to 1997). The team had considerable support from President Mobutu Sese Seko, who offered vast rewards for his players and backing, including a private jet for away travel and the hiring of experienced Yugoslavian coach Blagoje Vidinić to manage the team in 1971. Congo qualified for the 1974 World Cup by winning a final qualification group including Morocco and Zambia. The key qualifying game came against Morocco, who were favorites and had been Africa's lone representative at the 1970 World Cup in Mexico, on 9 December 1973 in Congo's capital, Kinshasa. A passionate, at times violent, game ended with a 3–0 win for Congo, the Moroccans protesting the refereeing to FIFA to no avail. The star of the game for Congo was Kembo Uba Kembo, who scored twice to take his tally of goals in the qualifying competition to five in seven games, and he was feted as a national hero.

Congo headed to the 1974 World Cup with high hopes and expectations raised even further after victory in the Africa Cup of Nations in March, with outstanding performances from Adelard Mayanga Maku and Ndaye Mulamba, scorer of nine goals at the competition. President Mobutu made more outlandish promises of rewards for his players, with offers of cars, villas and lavish vacations for the participating players, most of which were never delivered. In West Germany, though, the political pressure from home and the presence of a phalanx of officials created an uncomfortable atmosphere for the team as they prepared to play in a group containing reigning World Cup champions Brazil and fancied teams from Yugoslavia and Scotland. Vidinić's team first faced Scotland at Westfalenstadion in Dortmund on 14 June, with the Scottish entering the game with expectations of winning by a double-digit margin against the unknown Africans. Congo, though, unsettled Scotland early in the game. The breakthrough came, to considerable Scottish relief, in the 26th minute, a free kick leading to a header by Joe Jordan—marked weakly by Mwanza Nel Mukombo—landing perfectly on the foot of Peter Lorimer, the Scottish striker lashing in a volley from 15 yards out. The second goal came after an awful defensive lapse by Congo only eight minutes later, as Joe Jordan ran in on goal completely unmarked from a free kick and headed straight at goalkeeper Kazadi Muamba, who could only fumble it ineptly over the line. Zaire, though, held on for the remainder of the game, a 2–0 defeat disheartening but not devastating.

The devastation, instead, came in Zaire's next game. A 9–0 defeat matched the largest margin of defeat a team had suffered at the World Cup, equaling the ineptness of South Korea against Hungary 20 years earlier. Vidinić made one change to the lineup from the game against Scotland, Mayanga Maku replaced by Kibonge Mafu. From the first whistle, Yugoslavia attacked relentlessly, with Zaire's defensive organization a shambles: a free header from Dušan Bajević past Muamba opened the floodgates, and by halftime, Zaire found themselves down by 6–0, the Europeans scoring with relentless frequency. In a bizarre move, Vidinić replaced Muamba in goal with Tubilandu Ndimbi after Yugoslavia's third goal, even though the goalkeeper himself had done little wrong. Ndimbi conceded a goal within seconds of arriving on the field from a free kick, Vidinić having curiously sent him on for a defensive restart, and he conceded twice more before halftime—at 5 feet 4 inches, he provided an even weaker target for Yugoslavia's shooting practice. Matters deteriorated even further with the dismissal of Ndaye Mulamba, leaving Zaire to play with 10 men for the majority of the game. Things improved only slightly in the second half, and down 7–0, Ndimbi conceded two further goals as Zaire was eliminated and humiliated in the process. Following the game, Vidinić—suspected by some to have colluded with his countrymen—explained that a Ministry of Sport official had ordered the goalkeeping substitution and promised to never again accept such an order.

Zaire then faced the daunting task of facing a Brazil team who had not yet qualified for the next round and knew they would need to score multiple goals to qualify on goal difference past Scotland and keep their hopes of defending their World Cup title alive. Muamba returned to Zaire's goal and put in a fantastic performance, though he could do nothing to stop Jairzinho's superb 12th-minute strike that gave Brazil the lead, though he then made a remarkable double save to keep Zaire in the game in the first half, Maku almost equalizing after a mazy dribble. Zaire held Brazil off until the 66th minute, when Rivelino unleashed an unstoppable drive from 20 yards into the top corner. Muamba then conceded a goal that was cruel given his remarkable efforts, a low, bouncing strike from Valdomiro slipping under his arms and into the goal at the near post with 79 minutes gone, ending the scoring for the day. Zaire could be entitled to feel proud of their efforts under siege, but the game would in fact be remembered for a bizarre incident a few minutes later. Facing a Brazilian free kick from 30 yards out, Zaire defender Mwepu Ilunga inexplicably ran from the wall and kicked the ball downfield before the Brazilians had restarted play. Popular lore has it that Ilunga and Zaire were naive and did not know the rules of the game, but this seems highly unlikely in the closing minutes of their third World Cup game and with most of the team experienced in international competition. Ilunga has instead explained that he struck the ball out of frustration with the situation surrounding the team, who were not receiving the bonuses promised from President Mobutu, as his entourage instead skimmed off the gifts they had been expecting. Ilunga said he had hoped to receive a red card but was instead only cautioned. Regardless, Zaire exited the World Cup with one of the worst records in the tournament's history, having lost all three games and failed to register a goal. It was the end for a glorious generation of players; blamed for humiliating the country, many ended up living in poverty rather than in the villas promised by Mobutu, and as the country slipped deeper into a vicious kleptocracy under his violent rule, Zaire did not even enter World Cup qualification in 1978. Congo has not qualified for another World Cup and has had extremely limited success in the Africa Cup of Nations, the country's terrible warfare having devastated its population since the 1990s.

CORBATTA, OMAR ORESTE. B. 11 March 1936, Daireaux, Argentina. D. 6 November 1991. A gifted right-winger with a remarkable ability to twist and turn past his opponents, Omar Oreste Corbatta played three games for Argentina as a 22-year-old at the 1958 World Cup in Sweden. Corbatta had made his debut two years earlier for Argentina, playing domestically at club level for Racing Club, participating in four of Argentina's games in their successful World Cup qualifying campaign in 1957. He also played a role in Argentina's superb winning campaign at the Copa América. Corbatta opened his World Cup scoring account only two minutes into Argentina's first group game at the 1958 World Cup, against West Germany in Malmö, but Argentina was overrun in a 3–1 defeat. Corbatta scored again in Argentina's second game, a 3–1 win over Northern Ireland, this time from the penalty spot, a skill Corbatta was known for his expertise in. Corbatta struck another penalty in Argentina's final group game, taking his tally to three goals in three games, but it was to no avail for Argentina, who was outclassed in a 6–1 defeat to Czechoslovakia and eliminated from the World Cup as a result. In December 1960, Corbatta played in two of Argentina's World Cup qualifiers for the 1962 competition in Chile, a 6–3 defeat to Ecuador and a 5–0 win in the return game against the same opponent. Those were Corbatta's final games for Argentina, as he was not selected for Argentina's 1962 World Cup team. Corbatta died in 1991 aged 55.

COSTA, FLÁVIO. B. 14 September 1906, Carangola, Brazil. D. 22 November 1999. Brazil's greatest humiliation of the 20th century was their loss to Uruguay in the final game of the 1950 World Cup hosted at their own Maracanã stadium in Rio de Janeiro in front of 200,000 partisan fans and coached by Flávio Costa. The 1950 World Cup was the only World Cup not to feature a knockout stage, but the last game of the final-round group stage between Uruguay and Brazil proved to be the decisive match. Brazil was the heavy favorite to win the trophy and had only to secure a draw against Uruguay on 16 July to do so. Despite taking the lead early in the second half, Brazil conceded two goals to finish as runners-up, the shocking defeat becoming eternally known as the *Maracanazo*. The loss marred the rest of Costa's life and career; he was blamed for the defeat and forever questioned about it. He did, however, return to coach Brazil from 1955 to 1957, leaving a year before Brazil won their first World Cup title in Switzerland. At club level, Costa began his coaching career with Flamengo, a team he had played for, taking them to three consecutive state titles in 1942, 1943 and 1944. He then managed Vasco de Gama, winning further state titles as well as the South American club championship in 1948.

COSTA RICA. Commonly known as Los Ticos. With four appearances in the World Cup, Costa Rica is the most successful Central American nation in the competition. Though Costa Rica began playing international soccer in 1921, almost 70 years passed until Los Ticos appeared at the World Cup. That came in 1990, qualifying after topping the CONCACAF Championship qualifying tournament ahead of the United States in 1989. Led by Serbian coach Bora Milutinović, who had coached Mexico at the 1986 World Cup, Costa Rica opened the competition's first-round group stage with a 1–0 win over Scotland, the goal coming from 29-year-old striker

Juan Arnaldo Cayasso in the 50th minute. Though Costa Rica then succumbed to a 1–0 defeat to three-time world champions Brazil, Los Ticos recovered to record a superb 2–1 win over Sweden to advance to the next round. That result came despite going a goal down to the Europeans after 32 minutes, with a late comeback led by Roger Flores's goal in the 75th minute and a winner from Hernán Medford only three minutes from the end of the game. In Bari, Costa Rica then crashed out of the competition to a strong Czechoslovakia team, losing 4–1, Rónald González's goal for Los Ticos only a consolation.

Costa Rica failed to qualify for the 1994 and 1998 World Cups and next appeared in South Korea and Japan in 2002. Los Ticos were coached by Brazilian-born Alexandre Guimarães, a former Costa Rican national team player, and led by star striker Paulo Wanchope's electrifying pace and finishing. Costa Rica began the competition with a comfortable 2–0 win against China, Ronald Gomez and Mauricio Wright both scoring in the second half. Los Ticos then secured a point against Turkey with a late equalizer, Winston Parks scoring in the 86th minute. However, elimination came at the hands of Brazil in Costa Rica's final group game, a crushing 5–2 defeat despite goals from Wanchope and Gomez.

Once again under the coaching of Guimarães, Costa Rica played at a second successive World Cup in Germany in 2006, with Wanchope still the team's star name. Los Ticos appeared in the competition's opening game, a wide-open affair with six goals scored—four by host nation Germany and only two by Costa Rica, both scored by Wanchope. Costa Rica's defense continued to be porous against Ecuador, a 3–0 defeat against the South Americans preceding a third and final loss to Poland, 2–1, Ronald Gomez scoring the consolation for Los Ticos, who headed home after finishing bottom of group A.

After Costa Rica failed to qualify for the 2010 World Cup (Los Ticos finished in fourth place in CONCACAF qualifying but lost a play-off with the fifth-place finisher in South American qualifying, Uruguay, 2–1 on aggregate), qualification for the 2014 World Cup in Brazil under Colombian Jorge Luis Pinto went much more smoothly. Finishing second in their group behind the United States (a team that they beat 3–1 at home), the team boasted both a solid defensive line that allowed only seven goals in 10 games in the final round and an adequate knack for finding the back of the net when necessary. The only real concern for Pinto's side was that all five of Los Ticos wins came at home.

Placed in group D with England, Uruguay and Italy, Costa Rica needed to play well away from the comforts of home to advance. In their opening game against Uruguay at the Estádio Castelão in Fortaleza, an early Edinson Cavani penalty conversion put Uruguay in a comfortable position, but Los Ticos found a new gear in the second half and two goals within three minutes of each other (Joel Campbell in the 54th and Óscar Duarte in the 57th) gave Costa Rica all of the momentum. From there on through the final whistle, it was all Ticos and a Marco Ureña goal in the 84th minute sealed the first Costa Rican World Cup win since 2002. Game two set up a match with perennial powerhouse Italy, and the Central Americans proved that their win over Uruguay was no fluke. With a favor in possession and control of the match in the first half, Costa Rica proved their mettle when, in the 44th minute,

Júnior Díaz crossed a beautiful ball into a streaking Bryan Ruiz at the far post, who headed in the eventual game winner off the underside of the bar and barely across the line. Italy proved to be outclassed on this day, and Costa Rica secured advancement to the round of 16 for the first time since 1990. A final group game against an England side struggling to find an identity proved to be a mundane 0–0 draw. The point secured a first-place finish for Los Ticos and a matchup with a Greek side many would argue were fortunate to advance out of their group.

This round-of-16 game proved to be all about the resiliency of the Central Americans and the goalkeeping of Keylor Navas, who came through time and time again for Los Ticos. With multiple saves in the first half, Navas was rewarded for his hard work with a Ruiz goal in the 52nd minute. Unfortunately for Costa Rica, Duarte was sloppy on a tackle in the 66th minute and was sent off as the result of his second yellow, which meant playing down a man. Though Navas continued to keep them in the game, a goal in the 91st minute by Sokratis Papastathopoulos sent the game into penalties. Navas again came to his country's rescue as his acrobatic diving save of a Theofanis Gekas penalty and zero misses by his compatriots sent Costa Rica through to the quarterfinals for the first time in their history.

Matched up against a Dutch side dangerous in attack, it was again up to Navas to keep Costa Rica in the game. Though helped by the organization of his defense in front of him (as well as by the woodwork), Navas was forced to make some crucial saves throughout the match to keep his team level. Once in penalties, the clinical skill of the Dutch proved too much as their first four shooters did what Costa Ricans Bryan Ruiz and Míchael Umaña failed to do by finding the back of the net. With five goals scored and only two allowed in five games, the Costa Ricans had much to be proud of in Brazil. Costa Rica finished in eighth place with five goals for and two against.

CÔTE D'IVOIRE. Commonly known as Les Éléphants (The Elephants). West African nation Côte d'Ivoire, sometimes known in English as the Ivory Coast, has appeared in three World Cup finals tournaments, in 2006, 2010 and 2014, reflecting the country's recent rise to the elite in African soccer. The Elephants became a force in continental African soccer in the 1990s, winning the 1992 Africa Cup of Nations. Under French coach Henri Michel, Côte d'Ivoire advanced to the 2006 World Cup with high expectations, featuring elite international talents such as Chelsea's powerful striker Didier Drogba and Paris Saint-Germain attacker Bonaventure Kalou, a team filled with power, pace and technical skill. Côte d'Ivoire, though, did not live up to expectations that they could be a challenger in the elimination phase, knocked out in the first round. That elimination followed two defeats and one win in the group stage, with Côte d'Ivoire placed in what was soon called the "Group of Death" alongside two of the tournament favorites, Argentina and the Netherlands, along with Serbia and Montenegro. First came a 2–1 defeat to Argentina, a 2–0 deficit by halftime only dented by Drogba's 82nd-minute strike. A second 2–1 defeat then followed against the Netherlands, the Elephants again slipping to a 2–0 deficit with Bakary Koné pulling one back. Though Côte d'Ivoire defeated Serbia and Montenegro 3–2, coming from behind to win with those goals from Aruna Dindane (2) and Kalou, it was too little, too late for the West Africans.

The Elephants entered the 2010 World Cup in South Africa with even higher expectations than in 2006, following an unbeaten qualifying campaign, with Drogba and Kalou supported by Barcelona's Yaya Touré and Sevilla's Didier Zokora in midfield, along with Emmanuel Eboué and Kolo Touré in defense. Though Bosnian Vahid Halilhodžić led Côte d'Ivoire through qualifying, experienced Swede Sven-Göran Eriksson took charge of the West Africans for the competition in South Africa. Côte d'Ivoire began the group stage with a marquee matchup against Portugal in Port Elizabeth, though it was one that ended in a hard-fought 0–0 tie. Against Brazil, Côte d'Ivoire fell to a 3–1 defeat that made the West Africans' last group game against North Korea a must-win to advance. However, despite winning 2–0 thanks to goals from Romaric and Yaya Touré, it was not enough for the Elephants to go through to the next round as Portugal secured a point against Brazil to claim second place in the group behind the South Americans.

Qualification for the 2014 World Cup in Brazil proved to be of little concern for the Elephants as they strolled through their opening six matches with four wins and two ties (scoring 15 goals and only conceding 5) on their way to a play-off matchup with Senegal. With a 3–1 home win, all looked secure for the Elephants until the 72nd minute when a goal by Newcastle United striker Papiss Cissé meant that another Senegalese goal would send them home on away goal differential. A stoppage-time goal by Salomon Kalou provided some extra cushion but proved unnecessary as the West Africans were on their way to their third consecutive World Cup finals by way of a 4–2 aggregate win.

Placed in group C with Colombia, Greece and Japan, the Elephants boasted speed and athleticism all around to complement world-class players Didier Drogba and Yaya Touré. In their first-round matchup with Japan at the Arena Pernambuco in Recife, the Elephants fell behind early when, in the 16th minute, Japanese striker Keisuke Honda rocketed a blast into the top corner of the Côte d'Ivoire net. Manager Sabri Lamouchi made a change in the 62nd minute and immediately saw results with goals in the 64th minute by Wilfried Bony and two minutes later by Gervinho to push the Elephants to a desperately needed three points. The second game, played at Estádio Nacional de Brasília against Colombia, saw the Elephants lacking potency. Two second-half goals within six minutes of each other by James Rodríguez and Juan Quintero pushed the game out of reach, in spite of a 73rd-minute strike from Gervinho. Needing at least a tie in their third game to advance, the Elephants found themselves in a battle with a resilient Greek side. After giving up a goal to Andreas Samaris, an Elephant goal by Bony in the 74th minute seemed to seal Côte d'Ivoire's first advancement out of the group stage. It was not to be, however, as, late in stoppage time, Georgios Samaras went to ground inside the 18 and referee Christian Lescano awarded the penalty kick to the Greeks. With no time on the clock, "Africa's hope" was again destined to wait another four years before trying their luck again. Côte d'Ivoire finished in 21st place with four goals for and five against.

CROATIA. Commonly known as Vatreni (The Blazers or The Fiery Ones). The Croatian national team formed in 1991 following the breakup of Yugoslavia and, with a supremely talented group of players available, rapidly became a force in international soccer. The first World Cup that Croatia was able to enter qualifying for was France 1998, and remarkably, the Balkan nation advanced to finish third in the competition. Coached by Miroslav Blažević, the Croatian team featured the supreme talents of playmaker Robert Prosinečki and dynamic forwards Davor Šuker and Zvonimir Bo-ban. Croatia began the first-round group stage by defeating Jamaica 3–1, goals scored by Mario Stanić, Prosinečki and Šuker. A 1–0 win over Japan then secured Croatia's passage to the second round, a 77th-minute Šuker strike proving decisive. A 1–0 loss to Argentina wasn't enough to prevent Croatia from advancing in second place in the group, going on to face Romania in the second round. Another strike from Šuker was again enough as a defense marshaled by Slaven Bilić and Igor Štimac held firm in a 1–0 win. In Lyon, Croatia now faced the daunting task of overcoming Germany, one of the favorites for the competition. Remarkably, Croatia romped to a 3–0 win; Robert Jarni scored the first in stoppage time at the end of the first half, with further goals from Goran Vlaović and Šuker once again in the second half. That win set Croatia up for a semifinal matchup with host nation France in Stade de France on the outskirts of Paris. Croatia took the lead thanks to Šuker's fifth goal of the tournament in the 46th minute, but a Zinedine Zidane–inspired French took the lead and then struck a winner through Lilian Thuram, Croatia's defense crumbling for the first time in the competition. In the third-place play-off, Croatia defeated the Netherlands 2–1—goals from Prosinečki and Šuker, the latter scoring his sixth to lead the competition and claim the Golden Boot.

After opening 2002 World Cup qualifiers with two losses, Blažević stepped down and was replaced by Mirko Jozić, who led the team undefeated through qualifiers. Drawn into group G with Mexico, Italy and Ecuador, Croatia lost a close opening game 1–0 to Mexico before surprising Euro 2000 finalists Italy 2–1. A final group-game loss to first-time participants Ecuador meant a third-place group finish for Croatia.

With Zlatko Kranjčar at the helm for the 2006 qualifiers, Croatia went undefeated and finished atop their group ahead of Sweden and Bulgaria. In Germany, drawn into group F with defending champions Brazil, Japan and Australia, Kranjčar saw his side lose to Brazil in their opener and only managed a tie with both Japan and Australia to again finish third in their group. With defender Slaven Bilić at the helm for 2010, Croatia beat England 3–2 at Wembley Stadium during Euro 2008 qualifying but, four days later, lost their first competitive home match in 14 years to the same side, 4–1 in UEFA's group six. Another 5–1 loss to England, this time back at Wembley, ultimately led to Croatia finishing third in the group and out of South Africa 2010.

Qualification for the 2014 World Cup in Brazil saw turmoil and coaching changes galore for Croatia. After 16 points from five wins and one draw in their first six matches, the Blazers were only able to secure one point out of their next four games and found themselves fortunate to be in second place thanks to their great start. Immediately following the last group game, head coach Igor Štimac resigned from his post and was replaced by former Bundesliga and Croatian national team player Niko Kovač. A two-game play-off against Iceland saw a poor performance from his new charges in their first leg, even while playing a man up for much of the second half. A 2–0 home win pushed Croatia through to Brazil but left many questions to be if they hoped to advance out of group A with Brazil, Mexico and Cameroon.

Kicking off the World Cup against hosts Brazil at the Arena Corinthians in São Paulo, an own goal by Marcelo in the 11th minute was exactly the start Croatia hoped to see. A win was not in the cards, though, as a brace by Neymar gave Brazil life. A brilliant individual effort by Oscar in the 91st minute cemented the win for the home side and left Croatia desperately needing points in their next game against Cameroon. The Croats played well and secured a 4–0 victory, though the game may be remembered more for the reported match fixing, flagrant red cards and player infighting from Cameroon than anything Croatia achieved. With three points, the Blazers were still very much in charge of their own destiny and needed to beat a strong Mexico side to secure their advancement. The first half saw no goals for either side, but Mexico asserted their dominance in the second half with three goals in a 10-minute span that ended any hope of Croatia advancing. Though Ivan Perišić scored a late goal, it was Ante Rebić's straight red in the 89th minute that best summed up the Blazers' frustrations. Croatia finished in 19th place with six goals for and six against.

ČTYŘOKÝ, JOSEF. B. 30 September 1906, Smíchov, Austria-Hungary. D. 11 January 1985. Czechoslovakia's defensive line for the 1934 World Cup final, as they played the hosts Italy, included the experienced Josef Čtyřoký, then starring for Sparta Prague at club level. Čtyřoký played in all four of Czechoslovakia's games at the World Cup, having been an international since his debut against Switzerland in June 1931, going on to play a total of 42 games for his country. Čtyřoký also took part in two World Cup qualifying games: in October 1933, a 2–1 win over Poland that guaranteed Czechoslovakia's place at the 1938 World Cup in France, and in November 1937, a 1–1 tie with Bulgaria. Czechoslovakia qualified for the 1938 World Cup, but Čtyřoký did not travel to the competition. He made his 42nd and final appearance for his country in August 1938 in a 3–1 win over Yugoslavia.

CUBA. Commonly known as Leones del Caribe (Lions of the Caribbean). In 1938, Cuba became the first Caribbean nation to participate in the World Cup final tournament. Cuba's progress to the quarterfinal stage in France remains their sole World Cup appearance. Cuba's progress to the World Cup in 1938 came without having to play a game. They had originally been scheduled to play in a group containing Colombia, Costa Rica, El Salvador and Surinam, but withdrawals by all four nations meant Cuba qualified for the World Cup via a walkover. Cuba traveled to France with only 15 players, 7 short of the maximum 22 allowed and the least in the competition. Cuba sprung a surprise in the first round of the World Cup, facing Romania in Toulouse. A 3–3 tie led to a replay four days later on 9 June, Cuba coming back from 1–0 down at halftime to win 2–1 thanks to goals from Héctor Socorro and Tomás Fernández. Cuba found themselves considerably overmatched at the quarterfinal stage against a strong Swedish side, falling to a comprehensive 8–0 defeat in Antibes on 12 June. The 1938 World Cup was Cuba's second attempt to qualify for the World Cup. The 1930 World Cup came too late for a Cuba team that only played its first international game in March 1930, and they failed to qualify for the 1934 World Cup, losing a three-game series to Mexico by a total of 12 goals to 3. It would again be Mexico who knocked Cuba out of the first World Cup qualifying competition following World War II, this time losing by eight goals to three in a September 1949 qualifying series. With soccer a subservient sport to baseball and the country immersed in revolutionary war, Cuba did not take part again in World Cup qualifying until the 1966 competition in England, where they were eliminated by Jamaica. Cuba did not enter the next two World Cup qualifying competitions and then failed to qualify for both the 1978 and 1982 World Cups, falling to Panama in 1976 and then finishing fifth in the 1981 CONCACAF Championship. Cuba again failed to enter qualifying for the 1986 World Cup and was eliminated early in 1990 qualification by Haiti. Cuba refused to participate in 1994 World Cup qualifying for the competition to be hosted in the United States. Cuba has become more competitive in World Cup qualifying yet has still failed to qualify, an accomplishment made more difficult by the defection of some of its young players when playing overseas.

CUBILLAS, TEÓFILA. B. 8 March 1949, Lima, Peru. Teófila Cubillas is Peru's most outstanding player of all time, participating in three FIFA World Cup finals tournaments for his country, in 1970, 1978 and 1982. In 1970, Peru reached the quarterfinals of the competition, their best performance, going out to Pelé's Brazil, with Cubillas scoring once in a gripping 4–2 defeat, his fifth goal in four games at the competition. A creative attacking midfielder with a deft touch and a powerful shot, Cubillas scored 26 goals in 81 games for his country. In 1976, Cubillas scored two goals in the Copa América as Peru won the South American continental championship. Cubillas was successful in club soccer as well, playing most of his career for his local club Alianza Lima before ending his career in the United States, retiring from playing in 1989.

CZECHOSLOVAKIA. Commonly known as Národná reprezentácia (The National Team) / Naši (The Ours). The national soccer team of Czechoslovakia existed from 1922 to 1993, when the nation dissolved and the Czech Republic and Slovakia formed, both organizing their own national teams. Czechoslovakia enjoyed a substantial record in the World Cup, appearing in eight finals competition and reaching the final itself in the second-ever World Cup held in 1934. In that competition, the Czech team coached by Karel Petrů featured star goalkeeper František Plánička and an attack that included the creative forwards Oldřich Nejedlý and Jiří Sobotka. The 1934 World Cup featured a straight-elimination forward, Czechoslovakia beginning by defeating Romania 2–1, coming back in the second half after a 1–0 deficit at halftime. In the quarterfinal stage, the Czechs again came from behind to defeat Switzerland, thanks to an 82nd-minute winner in a 3–2 win by Oldřich Nejedlý. Sparta Prague star Nejedlý grabbed all three goals in the semifinal, an impressive comprehensive 3–1 win against Germany. That took Petrů's men to the final in Rome, with the daunting opponent the host nation Italy, strongly backed by a partisan crowd and playing on a demand from Italian dictator Benito Mussolini to win the World Cup. The Czech team took the Italians the distance, taking the lead in the 71st minute through a strike by Antonín Puč. Italy, though, equalized 10 minutes later and found a winner in extra time through Angelo Schiavio.

The second-placed finish for Czechoslovakia in 1934 turned out to be the best in the country's history. Four years later, Czechoslovakia reached the quarterfinal stage in France after a 3–0 win over the Netherlands in the first round but lost 1–0 to Brazil in a replay following a 1–1 tie. The Czechs did not advance past the first round again until 1990. Appearances in 1954, 1958, 1970 and 1982 all ended with elimination at the first stage. The country's final appearance in 1990, coached by Jozef Vengloš, was an impressive appearance marked by the Czechs' composure on the ball. The Czechs began in rampant style in the first-round group stage, winning 5–1 over the United States, followed by a 1–0 victory against Austria. Though the Czechs then lost 2–0 to Italy, they secured passage to the second round and crushed Costa Rica 4–1 in Bari, thanks to a hat trick by Tomáš Skuhravý and a long-range strike by Luboš Kubík. The Czech adventure eventually ended in the quarterfinal with a 1–0 defeat to eventual champions West Germany in Milan, a 25th-minute penalty strike by Lothar Matthäus the difference between the two teams. Though Czechoslovakia entered qualifying for the 1994 World Cup, the country dissolved before qualification, and the team failed to qualify for the World Cup in its final attempt.

CZECH REPUBLIC. Commonly known as Národ'ák (The National Team). Following the dissolution of Czechoslovakia in 1992, the Czech Republic formed its own national team, competing at its first international tournament at the European Championships in 1996. In that competition in England, the Czech team finished in second place, an impressive debut. However, the Czech Republic failed to qualify for the 1998 and 2002 World Cup finals, appearing for the first time in 2006 in Germany. Despite an impressive qualification campaign and an opening 3–0 win over the United States, the Czech team was eliminated at the first-round stage following successive 2–0 defeats to Ghana and Italy. The Czech team then failed to qualify for the 2010 World Cup in South Africa.

D

DEL BOSQUE, VINCENTE. B. 23 December 1950, Salamanca, Spain. Spain's first World Cup victory, at the 2010 tournament held in South Africa, came under the astute coaching of Vicente del Bosque. The Spaniard made his name as both a player and a manager with Real Madrid, coaching them to the Champions League title in both 2000 and 2002. He took over as Spain's coach in July 2008, replacing Luis Aragonés, who had led Spain to victory at the 2008 European Championships. Spain won their first 13 games under del Bosque, until a disappointing 2–0 loss to the United States in the 2009 FIFA Confederations Cup in South Africa. Spain then won their next 12 games in the run-up to the 2010 World Cup, qualifying for the competition with ease. In South Africa, del Bosque called up a squad with only a handful of changes from the 2008 European Championship team. Spain's squad was built around a brilliant Barcelona-based fulcrum of Andrés Iniesta and Xavi alongside Real Madrid's Xabi Alonso and a style of play based on possession, rapid, short passes and pressing when without the ball. Typically, Spain lined up in a 4-2-3-1 formation under del Bosque.

At the 2010 World Cup, Spain was drawn into group H, a seemingly weak group, containing Chile, Honduras and Switzerland. On 16 June in Durban, Spain kicked off their World Cup campaign, but del Bosque's team suffered the shock defeat of the round, losing 1–0 to Switzerland. The scoreline flattered the Swiss, Spain having dominated possession, but the Spaniards failed to take advantage when they had the ball, their lack of width an obvious problem for del Bosque to solve in their next game. This he addressed by replacing the injured Iniesta with right-winger Jesús Navas, though it was a superb individual display by David Villa—who scored twice—that made the crucial difference. Villa did, though, miss a penalty won by Navas to leave the score at 2–0. On 25 June, Spain faced Chile needing a win to advance to the second round. Del Bosque brought back Iniesta for Navas, with their midfield now organized with Xavi and Alonso lying deep and Villa and Iniesta cutting in from the right and left to support Fernando Torres. Spain's quality ultimately told as Chile had a man sent off, and del Bosque's men earned a 2–1 win.

Del Bosque named an unchanged team for Spain's second-round game against Portugal on 29 June in Cape Town, and the Spaniards now started to hit their stride facing their neighbors. Despite dominating possession, though, it was only when del Bosque made the critical decision to replace an unfit and ineffective Torres at the center-forward position with Fernando Llorente that the breakthrough came, his hold-up play leading to another goal for Villa that decided the game. Del Bosque continued his faith in starting Torres as Spain faced Paraguay at the quarterfinal stage on 3 July in Johannesburg, naming the same starting 11 for the third successive game. The

Spanish performance was similar to their previous game, ball retention still not leading to a cutting edge until late in the second half, again after the departure of Torres: in this case, the winning goal in a 1–0 win came from Villa in the 83rd minute, both teams having already missed penalties. Del Bosque made a critical decision at the semifinal stage as Spain faced Germany in Durban on 7 July, dropping Torres to the bench, moving Villa to a central forward position and bringing in Pedro to give Spain more width in attack. Spain's possession and pressing game was executed superbly, and Spain sealed a place in the final thanks to Carles Puyol's goal with a header in the 74th minute from a Xavi corner. In the World Cup final on 11 July in Johannesburg, del Bosque made no changes to the team that had defeated Germany, facing a Dutch side who immediately came out attempting to spoil Spain's ball control with frequent fouls, a tactic referee Howard Webb struggled to contain. Del Bosque made two positive substitutions in normal time as he looked to generate a winning goal, Jesús Navas replacing Pedro and Cesc Fàbregas coming for Alonso. It took extra time for Spain to wear the Netherlands down, the Dutch reduced to 10 men after the sending off of defender John Heitinga, but del Bosque and Spain earned their first World Cup title thanks to Iniesta's 116th-minute goal.

As defending World Cup and Euro champions, qualification for the 2014 World Cup in Brazil seemed like a lock, but key injuries to Xabi Alonso and Iker Casillas, among others, meant that separating from a strong French side would not come easily. It took a 1–0 road victory in Saint-Denis to finally gain some breathing room. Placed in group B with the Netherlands, Chile and Australia, defense of their title got off to a rocky start when a del Bosque–led La Roja was dismantled by the Flying Dutchmen 5–1. Spain never looked comfortable against their second-game foes, Chile, and first-half goals from Chileans Eduardo Vargas and Charles Aránguiz did the damage as Spain rarely threatened in either half. The result was a decisive 2–0 loss, a result that very few people foresaw. Against Australia, goals by David Villa, Fernando Torres and Juan Mata gave del Bosque some hope for the future, but after Spain's abysmal performance as reigning World Cup champions, some speculate that this World Cup may be del Bosque's last at the Spanish helm.

DELLA TORRE, JOSÉ. B. 23 March 1906, San Isidro, Argentina. D. 31 July 1979. José della Torre was a defender for Argentina who played in the inaugural World Cup, including in their defeat to Uruguay in the final of the competition. Della Torre played in all five of Argentina's games in the competition, including the semifinal against the United States, during which he became engaged in a scuffle with American forward Jim Brown after the third goal en route to a 6–1 win. At club level, della Torre played most of his career for Racing Club in the Buenos Aires suburbs. His five games at the World Cup proved to be his only five games for his country.

DENMARK. Commonly known as Danish Dynamite or De Rød-Hvide (The Red and White). Though the Danish national team's formation dates back to the early 20th century, it was not until 1986 that the Danes appeared in the World Cup finals, having not entered or failed to qualify for the previous 12 competitions prior to the tournament in Mexico. When Denmark did appear in 1986, under head coach Sepp

Piontek, it was with a roster bursting with talent, including Liverpool's Jan Mølby in midfield, captain Morten Olsen, veteran forward Allan Simonsen and the extravagantly gifted playmaker Michael Laudrup. In the group stage, Denmark dominated group E. The Danes began with a 1–0 win against Scotland and then demolished Uruguay 6–1, including a hat trick by Preben Elkjær Larsen. Denmark secured first place in the group with a hugely impressive 2–0 victory over West Germany, Jesper Olsen and John Eriksen scoring the goals in Querétaro. In the last minute of the game, though, Denmark's creative attacking force Frank Arnesen was sent off for aiming a kick at West German captain Lothar Matthäus. Without Arnesen, Denmark succumbed to a crushing defeat against Spain in the second round, though the 5–1 scoreline hardly reflects how close the first half was, with the scores tied 1–1 at halftime. In the second half, though, the Danes could not contain the Spanish and especially Emilio Butragueño, who scored four.

Denmark did not qualify for the World Cup again until 1998, this time advancing to the quarterfinals with a team that still featured Michael Laudrup along with his talented brother Brian and Manchester United goalkeeper Peter Schmeichel. The core of this team had won the European Championships in 1992. The Danes began the first-round group stage with a 1–0 win over Saudi Arabia, Marc Rieper scoring the only goal of the game, followed by a 1–1 tie with South Africa. A 2–1 defeat to France meant Denmark did not top the group but still moved on to the second stage alongside the French. In the second round, the Laudrup brothers orchestrated an impressive 4–1 win against a lethargic Nigerian team at the Stade de France, with Denmark moving on to the last eight of the competition for the first time. At that stage, Denmark faced defending world champions Brazil in Nantes. The Danes gave the Brazilians an enormous score: Martin Jorgensen gave the Europeans the lead two minutes into the game, though strikes by Bebeto and Rivaldo meant Brazil went into halftime 2–1 up. However, Brian Laudrup equalized in the 50th minute of a riveting affair, and it took a winner from Rivaldo to advance Brazil at Denmark's expense in what turned out to be Michael Laudrup's last international appearance.

In 2002, Denmark again qualified for the World Cup and advanced to the elimination stage at the competition in South Korea and Japan. The Danes won group A in unbeaten style, following wins over Uruguay (2–1) and France (2–0), along with securing a point against Senegal. In the second round, however, the Danes were outclassed by England, losing 3–0 in Niigata, with the English goals all coming in the first half, effectively ending the game as a contest by halftime. A Danish team on the down slope failed to qualify for the 2006 World Cup but did advance to South Africa in 2010. Denmark did not move past the first stage, losing 2–0 to the Netherlands, defeating Cameroon 2–1, but falling short after a 3–1 loss to Japan.

Qualification for 2014 in Brazil saw the Danish Dynamite finish second in their group behind Italy, but their 16 points meant they did not advance to a play-off of the second-place group finishers, and after a successful Euro 2012, Denmark found itself unable to qualify.

DERWALL, JUPP. B. 10 March 1927, Würselen, Germany. D. 26 June 2007. Jupp Derwall coached West Germany at the 1982 World Cup in Spain, leading his country to their fourth World Cup final, where they were defeated by Italy. Derwall had been an assistant of head coach Helmut Schön during the 1970s, including for West Germany's 1974 World Cup victory. Derwall's first major competition in charge of West Germany was a resounding success, as they won the 1980 UEFA European Championship. In the run-up to the 1982 World Cup, West Germany was among the favorites, though with injuries to key players, such as Bernd Schuster and Felix Magath, Derwall was forced to shuffle his lineup and formation as he attempted to build his team around the European Footballer of the Year—Karl-Heinz Rummenigge. Derwall's team had not lost to a European team since he had taken over, with the only defeats coming from Brazil and Argentina. West Germany was placed in group two of the competition, along with Algeria, Austria and Chile. On 16 June in Gijón, West Germany's World Cup campaign began in shocking fashion with a 2–1 defeat to Algeria. The loss opened up divisions in the camp that Derwall was forced to address, but the West Germans got back on track with a 4–1 win over Chile on 20 June and then a controversial 1–0 victory over Austria that suited both teams, qualifying them for the next round at the Algerians' expense, both games again in Gijón. The second-round group stage consisted of four groups, with the winners of each progressing to the semifinal. West Germany was placed with England and Spain in group two. The first game of the group saw West Germany tie 0–0 with England in Madrid, in a tight game with the closest to a goal coming from a venomous 25-yard strike from Rummenigge that struck the crossbar and bounced away. The West Germans' negative play led Horst Hrubesch, not selected by Derwall, to label the West German coach a coward. West Germany next faced hosts Spain, with a hostile home crowd of almost 100,000 cheering on the Spanish at the Santiago Bernabéu Stadium in Madrid. Derwall, though, was able to recall the superb winger Pierre Littbarski, recovered from injury, and he scored in a 2–1 win for the West Germans leading to qualification for the next round when England failed to beat Spain three days later in the final game of the group. In the semifinal, West Germany was outplayed by France—whose forward, Battiston, was brutally fouled by West German goalkeeper Harold Schumacher—but showed their resilience in a dramatic 3–3 tie that went to a penalty shoot-out, won by the West Germans. The West Germans' final successful penalty, ironically, came from Hrubesch, who had entered the game as a substitute. Derwall then led West Germany to their fourth World Cup final, the first since 1974, on 11 July, playing again at the Bernabéu in Madrid. Perhaps fortunate to have progressed so far, Derwall could only select a team hampered by injuries that limited key players such as Rummenigge and Littbarski. Italy deservedly won the final, 3–1, a three-goal burst for the Italians between the 57th and 81st minutes proving decisive, a late consolation goal from Paul Breitner proving irrelevant. Derwall continued as head coach through the 1984 European Championship, but a dismal performance at that competition in France—with West Germany eliminated in the first round—let to his resignation. Derwall went on to coach Galatasaray in Turkey at club level before his retirement in 1987.

DIENST, GOTTFRIED. B. 9 September 1919, Basel, Switzerland. D. 1 June 1998. Gottfried Dienst made one of the most controversial refereeing decisions of all time during the 1966 World Cup final at Wembley Stadium in London, England, when he ruled that Geoff Hurst's shot had crossed the line in the 101st minute of play, awarding England the go-ahead third goal of the game. Dienst later stated he had been unable to determine whether the ball had crossed the line or not and so was relying on Soviet linesman Tofiq Bahramov's judgment call that the ball had crossed the line. This is generally believed to have been an erroneous decision. The Swiss referee was, at the time, one of the most experienced on the international circuit. He had been refereeing at the international level since the mid-1950s, taking charge of the 1961 European Cup final between Benfica and Barcelona and the 1965 European Cup final between Internazionale and Benfica. At the 1962 World Cup in Chile, Dienst officiated three games: two group-stage matchups, Brazil versus Mexico and Mexico versus Czechoslovakia, and the semifinal between Czechoslovakia and Yugoslavia. Dienst awarded a penalty kick in each of the latter two games, though he did not issue any cautions or expulsions in any of the three games. As well as the final of the 1966 World Cup, Dienst also refereed one group-stage game, a 2–0 win for Italy over Chile. Despite the controversy that resulted from Hurst's goal in the final, Dienst was generally considered to have refereed the game fairly and was awarded further high-profile appointments internationally, including the final of the 1968 European Championship between Italy and Yugoslavia, though that game was marred by controversy, with many Yugoslavian observers suggesting Dienst had favored the Italians during the game in Rome. It did, though, make Dienst one of only two men to have refereed both the World Cup and European Championship final. He retired as international referee shortly after.

DIETZ, KÁROLY. B. 21 July 1885, Sopron, Hungary. D. 9 July 1969. Károly Dietz coached his native Hungarian national team from 1934 to 1939, a span of 41 matches that encompassed the 1938 World Cup in France, where he led Hungary to the final, defeated there by defending World Cup champions Italy. Dietz took over management of Hungary from Ödön Nádas after the 1934 World Cup, in which Hungary had been eliminated at the quarterfinal stage. Hungary qualified for the 1938 World Cup with an 11–1 win over Greece in their World Cup qualifying game in March 1938. Dietz was fortunate to have at his disposal a talented generation of players, including prolific goal-scoring forward Gyula Zsengellér and the man he selected as his captain for the 1938 World Cup, the free-roaming György Sárosi. Dietz took to France a squad with a good mix of experience and youth, exactly half of the 22 players having appeared four years earlier at the World Cup in Italy. In France, Hungary's first-round match was a straightforward 6–0 victory over an overmatched side from the Dutch East Indies. Dietz did make a goalkeeping change for Hungary's second game, Antal Szabó replacing József Háda, and also replaced Géza Toldi and István Balogh with Jenő Vincze and Antal Szalay. Hungary defeated Switzerland 2–0 to advance to the semifinal stage, where they would face Sweden. Dietz again made two changes: Géza Toldi and talented winger Pál Titkos came into the team, with Vilmos Kohut and Jenő Vincze sitting out. Hungary had remarkably little trouble brushing aside Sweden 5–1. Vincze, György Szűcs and Gyula Polgár came into Dietz's team for the final against Italy, leaving out Toldi, József Turay and Lajos Korányi. The changes were to no avail, as Italy claimed their second World Cup title with a 4–2 win over Dietz's Hungary. Dietz managed Hungary until the following year.

DONOVAN, LANDON. B. 4 March 1982, Ontario, California, United States. Generally regarded as the best field player in the history of the United States national team, Landon Donovan is the country's all-time leader in goals and assists. After winning the Golden Ball at the 1999 FIFA U-17 World Championships, Donovan moved up to the senior side in 2000 and quickly progressed into a full-time starter. He currently plays at club level for the Los Angeles Galaxy in Major League Soccer and has played for Bayern Munich in Germany's Bundesliga and for Everton in England's Premier League. Donovan has played in three FIFA World Cup finals tournaments (2002, 2006 and 2010) but found himself the center of controversy when he was excluded from the 2014 World Cup in Brazil by men's national-team coach Jürgen Klinsmann. With his 57 career international goals, including 8 in 13 international matches in 2013, Donovan is a quick, creative player able to play in midfield or at forward, with highly accomplished technical skills and an outstanding work rate. Though no one other than Klinsmann will truly ever know why the decision was made, many speculate that it was the tension between Klinsmann's passion to live and breathe soccer and Donovan's decisions to take breaks from the game that created a rift. Following Donovan's criticism of Klinsmann after the United States' round-of-16 exit in Brazil, many speculate he may never suit up for the national team again.

DORADO, PABLO. B. 22 June 1908, Uruguay. D. 18 November 1978. At only 22 years old, Pablo Dorado scored the first-ever goal in a World Cup final, the opening strike for Uruguay on their way to a 4–2 win over Argentina in the inaugural competition held in Dorado's native country. Dorado, usually found attacking from the right wing, played in two other games for Uruguay in the competition, also scoring the opening goal for Uruguay in their 4–0 win over Romania in the group stage and appearing again in their semifinal victory over Yugoslavia.

DUTCH EAST INDIES OR INDONESIA. Commonly known as Merah Putih (The Red and White). Before 1945 and their independence from colonial rule following World War II, Indonesia's national soccer team competed as the Dutch East Indies. As such, they became the first Asian team to compete in the World Cup in 1938. Soccer had advanced rapidly in Indonesia in the 1930s, its governing body established in 1930. Qualifying for the 1938 World Cup became a simple task for the Dutch East Indies merely by organizing a team and being willing to travel to France for the competition: Asia had one place at the final tournament, and when the only other country to enter the qualifying competition—Japan—withdrew, the Dutch East Indies had a walkover. However, the Dutch East Indies did not send their strongest team to the tournament: disagreements between organizers of a team run by Dutch colonial administrators and a more gifted team organized by native Indonesians meant a mostly Dutch team traveled to France, coached by Dutchman Johannes Mastenbroek. The team played under the Dutch flag. They played only one game in France, knocked out in the first round with a heavy defeat to Hungary. Around 9,000 fans watched at the Stade Municipal Velodrome in Reims as the Hungarians, one of the favorites for the World Cup, scored six with no reply against the Dutch East Indies on 5 June 1938. Following independence, Indonesia has yet to qualify for the World Cup, despite the popularity of soccer in the country of over 200 million people.

E

ECUADOR. Commonly known as La Tri (The Tricolor). After a 20th century barren of World Cup finals appearances, Ecuador has since appeared in the competition three times, at South Korea and Japan in 2002, in Germany in 2006 and in Brazil in 2014. Coached by Colombian Hernán Gómez, the South Americans lost both of their first two games in 2002, 2–0 to Italy and 2–1 to Mexico. A 1–0 win over Croatia, thanks to a goal by Édison Méndez, could not prevent Ecuador finishing bottom of group G. Captained by veteran Iván Hurtado, a young Ecuadorian team fared far better in 2006. The South Americans began with a 2–0 win over Poland, goals coming from Carlos Tenorio and Agustin Delgado. Ecuador followed up with a comprehensive 3–0 defeat of Costa Rica, Tenorio and Delgado both finding the net again, along with Iván Kaviedes. Though Ecuador then succumbed 3–0 to Germany in the final group game, passage to the second round was secured for the first time. At that stage, Ecuador lost 1–0 to England in a tight game decided by a David Beckham free kick.

Ecuador failed to qualify for the 2010 World Cup in South Africa after finishing in sixth place in the South American qualifying with 23 points (six wins, five draws and seven losses), one point behind Uruguay for the play-off spot. Qualification for the 2014 World Cup in Brazil saw Ecuador playing with a heavy heart due to the loss of striker Christian Benítez to cardiac arrest in 2013 at the age of 27. Playing inspired at home, where their only blemish was a 1–1 draw with Argentina, La Tri finished in fourth place, tied with Uruguay, but found themselves through to Brazil due to their superior goal differential.

Placed in group E with Switzerland, France and Honduras, Ecuador's hopes of advancing out of the group stage hinged on their ability to play better than their away record showed. Matched up against Switzerland at the Estádio Nacional de Brasília, Ecuador played with energy in the first half and was rewarded with a brilliant header goal by Enner Valencia from a free kick in the 22nd minute. Their lead and energy were not to hold, though, as the sixth-ranked Swiss scored a nearly identical goal shortly after halftime and substitute Haris Seferović scored a stoppage-time goal to steal three full points. In their game versus Honduras, La Tri went down in the 31st minute following poor defending, but Valencia equalized three minutes later and scored the game-winning header off a free kick in the 65th. Sitting on three points, and playing against a French side full of talent, Ecuador needed points to keep their hopes alive. Losing Antonio Valencia in the 50th minute to a studs-up tackle meant playing down a man for the last 40, but Ecuador did what no other team in their group could and kept a clean sheet against the French. Sadly, a Swiss win meant a third-place group finish for Ecuador and their ousting from the tournament in 17th place with three goals for and three against.

EGYPT. Commonly known as the Pharaohs. Despite being the most successful African team in continental championship play—winner of the Africa Cup of Nations on seven occasions—Egypt has only appeared in two World Cup finals tournaments. Egypt's first appearance came as far back as 1934, qualifying for the second World Cup, held in Italy, after overcoming Palestine 11–2 in two games, held in Cairo and Jerusalem respectively. This made Egypt the first African nation to appear in the World Cup—the continent had not been represented four years previously in Uruguay. The team sailed on a ship called the *Helwan* to Italy, a four-day voyage, and was coached by Scotsman James McRea. Egypt's campaign lasted only one game, as the first round of the 1934 World Cup featured a single-elimination format. A renowned Hungarian side was the opponent for Egypt, but though the Africans lost 4–2, they succeeded in giving the Europeans an almighty scare, with the score tied well into the second half, thanks to two goals from Abdel Rahman Fawzi. Egypt seemed to have taken the lead with the score tied, but an apparently legitimate third goal by Fawzi was controversially ruled out for offside by Italian referee Rinaldo Barlassina. Hungary scored two more for the victory.

It would be 56 years before Egypt again qualified for the World Cup. Qualification for the 1990 World Cup in Italy was secured with a 1–0 win over Algeria on 17 November 1989 in front of over 100,000 fans at Cairo Stadium, with the winning goal coming from forward Hossam Hassan. Egypt thus progressed to Italy for a World Cup finals tournament for a second time. In Italy, Egypt was drawn in group F alongside England, the Republic of Ireland and the Netherlands. Coached by former Egyptian national star Mahmoud El-Gohary, Egypt began brightly against the Netherlands, playing fluid soccer that unsettled the Dutch defense on multiple occasions. Though the reigning European champions took the lead in the 58th minute, Egypt found a deserved equalizer in the 83rd minute, a penalty kick converted by Madgi Abdelghani, who had run the midfield with aplomb for the Africans. The game ended 1–1. Egypt followed up that fine performance with a deeply disappointing display against the Irish; apparently unsettled by Ireland's direct play, Egypt was desperately uninventive, and the game petered out into a 0–0 tie. That left Egypt needing a result against England in Cagliari. But the Egyptians again disappointed, losing by a single goal and exiting the tournament. Egypt remains without a victory in World Cup finals tournaments, having failed to qualify again since 1990. Egypt was briefly coached by former U.S. coach Bob Bradley (2011–2013), who won his first six matches to finish atop their group, but a third-round play-off loss to Ghana by a 7–3 aggregate meant he was let go as Egypt again found themselves unable to qualify. Bradley was replaced by former Egyptian national-team player Shawky Gharib.

EKLIND, IVAN. B. 15 October 1905, Stockholm, Sweden. D. 23 July 1981. Swedish referee Ivan Eklind refereed at three different World Cup final tournaments over a span of a remarkable 16 years between 1934 and 1950. He began his career as an international referee at the age of only 25, taking charge of a friendly between Germany and Norway in June 1931. Eklind was the referee for three games at the 1934 World Cup in Italy, only 28 at the time. His first World Cup assignment was a first-round game between Switzerland and the Netherlands, a 3–2 win for the Swiss on 27 May at the San Siro in Milan. Eklind was then selected to take charge of Italy's semifinal against Austria, a 1–0 win for the hosts, again at the San Siro, on 3 June. A week later, Eklind was chosen to officiate the final, a surprising choice given his age and experience. He oversaw Italy's win in extra time over Czechoslovakia in Rome. At the 1938 World Cup in France, Eklind oversaw two extraordinary high-scoring games in the first round: Brazil's 6–5 win against Poland after extra time in Strasbourg on 5 June and Switzerland's 4–2 comeback victory over Germany on 9 June in Paris. With the interruption of World War II, no World Cup was held until 1950, but when the tournament resumed in Brazil, Eklind was selected to be a referee at the age of 44. Co-incidentally, Eklind took charge of a game involving Switzerland for the third straight World Cup, with the only match he refereed their 2–1 first-round win against Mexico in Porto Alegre on 2 July. It was Eklind's final match as an international referee.

ELIZONDO, HORACIO. B. 11 April 1963, Parada Robles, Argentina. An international referee since 1994, Horacio Elizondo took charge of five games at the 2006 World Cup in Germany, including the final between Italy and France, won by the Italians on a penalty shoot-out. Elizondo gained considerable experience at an international level in the late 1990s and early 2000s, taking charge of dozens of games in the Copa Libertadores, Copa América and in World Cup qualifying. He was not, however, selected as a referee for the 2002 World Cup in Japan and South Korea. Elizondo was given the task of officiating three games in the group stage of the 2006 World Cup. On 9 June 2006, he issued one yellow card in a 4–2 win for Germany over Costa Rica in Munich. Elizondo was far busier in his next game in Cologne, the Czech Republic versus Ghana. Elizondo handed out seven yellow cards and one straight red card, to Tomáš Ujfaluši of the Czech Republic. Ujfaluši was sent off after he conceded a penalty in the 65th minute, fouling Matthew Amoah in the Czech penalty area, though Asomoah Gyan missed the resulting penalty kick. Elizondo continued to issue cards liberally in his next game, Switzerland versus South Korea on 23 June in Hanover, handing out five yellow cards to each team in a 2–0 win for the Swiss. He also allowed a controversial goal for Switzerland, overruling his assistant referee who had flagged for offside by ruling the ball had actually come off the leg of a South Korean defender. Following the group stage, Elizondo was assigned to the quarterfinal game between England and Portugal in Gelsenkirchen on 1 July. Elizondo gave out two yellow cards to each team but, most notably, a straight red card to Wayne Rooney for stamping on Ricardo Carvalho. Portugal won the game on penalty kicks. Elizondo's controversial but correct decision was seemingly endorsed by FIFA by his ensuing selection to officiate the World Cup final between Italy and France. In the final, Elizondo once again issued a red card, this time to French superstar Zinedine Zidane for headbutting Italian Marco Materazzi. Elizondo did not spot the offense off the ball but was informed of it by his assistant referee. He also gave out cautions to Gianluca Zambrotta of Italy and Willy Sagnol, Claude Makélélé and Florent Malouda of France during the 1–1 tie that led to an Italian win in a penalty

shoot-out. Horacio retired in 2006 after the 10 December match between Boca Juniors and Lanús, two years before the compulsory retirement age of 45.

EL SALVADOR. Commonly known as La Selecta (The Selected). The smallest nation in Central America, El Salvador can boast of two appearances in the World Cup
finals, in 1970 and 1982. Neither tournament saw El Salvador progress past the first
round, but merely reaching that stage of the competition represents fine achievement
for a country with a population under six million. Soccer in El Salvador dates back to
the late 19th century, introduced by English immigrants, with the country's governing
body of soccer established in 1935 and affiliated to FIFA three years later. El Salvador
regularly played in regional competition, including the CONCACAF Championship,
but did not enter qualification for the World Cup until 1970. First time was a charm for
El Salvador, as a Gregorio Bundio–coached team won their qualification group and
then defeated Haiti in a play-off for a spot in the World Cup finals. It was not achieved
without notable controversy—three qualifying games against Honduras earlier in the
competition, in June 1969, had inflamed political tensions between El Salvador and
Honduras, with fighting breaking out that became known as the "soccer war" due to
the military action that followed El Salvador's 3–2 play-off win on 26 June.

At the 1970 World Cup in Mexico, El Salvador—now coached by Chilean Hernán
Carrasco, who had achieved great success as a domestic coach in the country—lost all
three games, failing to register a single goal. El Salvador's first defeat came against
Belgium, a comprehensive 3–0 defeat that underlined the gap in class the Central
Americans would have to bridge in the tournament. El Salvador's second game saw
a much-stronger effort from kickoff, against the hosts Mexico in front of 100,000
partisan fans at the Azteca Stadium in Mexico City, creating several good chances
and striking the post early on. But it all fell apart just before halftime, when referee
Aly Hussein Kandil allowed a goal for Mexico that ought never to have stood: the official had awarded El Salvador a free kick moments before but did not stop play when
Mexico's Mario Perez instead took the kick, prompting an attack from which Mexico
scored. Despite vehement protest by the El Salvadorians—who punted the ball into
the crowd before restarting play—the goal stood. In the second half, Mexico took control against dispirited opposition and cruised to a 4–0 win. There was no consolation
in El Salvador's final game, as they left the tournament following a 2–0 defeat to the
Soviet Union at the Azteca.

El Salvador's efforts to qualify for the remaining two World Cup finals of the 1970s,
West Germany 1974 and Argentina 1978, proved to be dismal disappointments: the
Central Americans won only 4 of 15 games in the two qualifying campaigns. In 1980,
Mauricio Alonso "Pipo" Rodríguez—a former star player for El Salvador and a part
of the 1970 World Cup team—took charge of the national team and led El Salvador to
the World Cup for the second time. In Spain, though, El Salvador was humiliated on
the world stage. Drawn in a first-round group with Hungary, Argentina and Belgium,
it was imperative that El Salvador should start off strongly against the Hungarians
before playing the more fancied Argentineans and Belgians. Instead, El Salvador
fell two goals down in the first 11 minutes against Hungary in Elche and went on to

concede eight more, scoring just one consolation goal in a 10–1 defeat. That scoreline remains tied for the largest-ever losing margin in a World Cup finals game.

To El Salvador's credit, their team put in a spirited performance against Belgium in the following game (also held in Elche), losing a tightly contested matchup 1–0 to a goal from Ludo Coeck in the 19th minute. Against defending champions Argentina, El Salvador succumbed to a 2–0 defeat, exiting their second World Cup without registering a point. The country's six games without a win or tie remains to date the worst performance in the World Cup finals, with El Salvador having failed to qualify for a World Cup since 1982, in an increasingly competitive CONCACAF region now dominated by much larger countries such as Mexico and the United States.

ENGLAND. Commonly known as the Three Lions. The modern game of soccer was born in England during the mid-19th century, but it was not until 1950—20 years after the inaugural World Cup held in Uruguay in 1930—that the English consented to appear at FIFA's world championship. England's Football Association believed the competition below them and did not take part in any of the first three competitions held in the 1930s, but when they were invited to and appeared at the next World Cup in 1950, a rude awakening awaited. Though England opened their campaign in group one with a 2–0 win over Chile on 25 June, just four days later, a team of unknown Americans defeated an English 11 selected by Arthur Drewry, 1–0, thanks to a goal by Joe Gaetjens in Belo Horizonte. When the whistle blew for full-time, South American fans in the stand burned a funeral pyre made of newspaper for the English. Things did not get any better for England in their third game against Spain at the Maracanã in Rio. After a seemingly valid goal by English forward Jackie Milburn was disallowed for offside, the Spaniards took advantage, and Zarra scored the only goal of the game shortly after halftime to knock England out of the tournament.

In 1954, England sent a strong team—including star domestic players Stanley Matthews, Billy Wright, Nat Lofthouse and Tom Finney—to Switzerland for the country's second World Cup venture. England survived the group stage unbeaten with a wild 4–4 tie with Belgium followed by a 2–0 win over hosts Switzerland, Jimmy Mullen and Dennis Wilshaw grabbing the goals. In the next round—the quarterfinals—England came unstuck against the defending World Cup champions, Uruguay. Despite a fine attacking performance from Matthews and a sturdy defensive display from Wright, Uruguay's Juan Alberto Schiaffino was too much for the English defense to contain—especially with some poor goalkeeping from Gilbert Merrick. England conceded four, and though they scored two, it was not enough.

The 1958 World Cup, in Sweden, proved to be a step back for England compared to the previous tournament. Coached by Walter Winterbottom and captained by Billy Wright, England elected not to bring the aging—but still effective—Stanley Matthews and Nat Lofthouse. Talented newcomers Bobby Robson and Johnny Haynes, both of Fulham, had considerable shoes to fill. England quickly came unstuck at the group stage, drawn alongside the Soviet Union, Brazil and Austria. In England's first game, the Soviets took a 2–0 lead by the 55th minute, and it was only a heroic performance by Tom Finney—who scored the equalizer from the penalty spot in the 85th minute—

that allowed England to escape with a point in a 2–2 tie. England now faced Brazil for the first time in a World Cup, with an unadventurous display resulting in a goal-less game. The English again fell behind against Austria, recovering to tie the score at 2–2 and take a point, thanks to goals from Haynes and Derek Kevan, but it was not enough to ensure England's progress to the next round. Instead, they would have to face the Soviets in a play-off in Gothenburg on 17 June. England struck the post twice, but the Soviets scored the only goal of the game for a 1–0 win that sent England home early in a World Cup for the third successive time.

Four years later, in Chile, England again failed to progress past the quarterfinal stage, again under the guidance of Walter Winterbottom, even with a talented young team including Haynes (now captain), the gifted striker Jimmy Greaves, the smooth and commanding Bobby Moore at the back and the driving force of Bobby Charlton at outside-left. England began their campaign with a poor display against a talented Hungarian team in Rancagua; the pressure of captaincy seemed to strain Haynes, who was no match as an attacking force for his counterpart, Hungary's Flórián Albert—the latter scored the winner in a 2–1 win in the 71st minute. England was much stronger a few days later in their second group game, against Argentina, showing flashes of true potential: Bobby Charlton was in inspired form, creating one and scoring another in a 3–1 win. England proved less inspired in their final group game against Bulgaria, a soporific and at times sloppy display ending in a 0–0 tie, enough at least for England to advance to the quarterfinal stage. Facing Brazil, England could not contain the player of the tournament, the gifted winger Garrincha, who tormented England's defense, scoring twice in a 3–1 win. Once again, England had not been consistently good enough against the best in the world.

With the 1966 World Cup to be hosted in England, Walter Winterbottom's long (1946–1962) reign as England coach came to an end as the country searched for success at home. His replacement—the successful coach of Ipswich Town, Alf Ramsey, who had played under Winterbottom at the 1954 World Cup—demanded and was given greater power than Winterbottom had enjoyed in team selection and developed a strong relationship with many of the key figures among the England players. Ramsey was fortunate to have at his disposal a clutch of extremely gifted players: at the back, the outstanding goalkeeper Gordon Banks and a defensive line marshaled by the impressive captain Bobby Moore; in midfield, the industrious Alan Ball and the gifted goal scorer Bobby Charlton; and upfront, prolific striker Jimmy Greaves. The latter, though, would not be England's forward hero by the end of the tournament, which began with an uninspiring and dour 0–0 draw with Uruguay at Wembley Stadium in London. In England's second group game (also at Wembley, as all of England's games were), Ramsey's men were better against a weak Mexico team, Charlton scoring a fine goal and Roger Hunt adding another for a 2–0 win. England secured qualification to the next round with another 2–0 win in their final group game, against France, but the performance was uninspired, Ramsey chastising his team with the exception of Roger Hunt, who had scored both goals.

Ramsey was moved to make a major change for England's quarterfinal against Argentina at Wembley, replacing Greaves with Geoff Hurst at forward. But the game would be remembered for other reasons, as a clash between South American and European styles of play, amid great controversy. The referee, West Germany's Rudolf Kreitlein, struggled to contain a game punctuated by foul after foul, and he eventually sent off Argentina's captain, Antonio Rattín. Rattín, though, refused to leave the field for a full 10 minutes; Ramsey later, regrettably for Anglo-Argentine relations, called the opposition "animals." Despite being reduced to 10 men, Argentina kept the contest desperately close, and it was only in the 78th minute that Greaves's replacement, Hurst, broke the deadlock when he headed in a cross from Martin Peters. The goal was enough to move England on to the semifinal but with a bitter taste left in everybody's mouths.

England faced a new kind of challenge in the semifinal stage against fellow Europeans Portugal, in the figure of one of the world's best players, the mercurial Eusébio—who would prove to be the leading scorer in the tournament, with nine goals to his credit. He would score only one against England from the penalty spot, though, defended effectively and overshadowed by a virtuoso performance from Bobby Charlton, scoring twice and impressing with tireless attacking effort. England secured a 2–1 win and a place in the World Cup final for the first time; now playing without wingers, Ramsey's men relied on ceaseless effort allied with a solid spine of defense from Banks, Moore and company and the inspiration of Charlton in midfield. Against a West Germany led by the imperious young Franz Beckenbauer in the final, it would take a strong performance backed by a crowd of almost 100,000 partisan fans for England to prevail and not without controversy. The two best players on the field, Beckenbauer and Charlton, effectively neutralized each other in midfield, each following the other so closely neither had the space to inflict their usual level of damage on the opposition. Charlton's teammates, though, proved to be stronger than Beckenbauer's.

Though West Germany struck first, a low drive from Helmut Haller beat Banks with just 13 minutes gone. England equalized only five minutes later, a header from Hurst tying the score. A back-and-forth game stayed deadlocked until just 13 minutes from time, when Hurst's deflected shot was rammed home by Martin Peters. England could not hold the lead, though, Wolfgang Weber scrambling in a second West German goal with only a minute left in play, the score tied 2–2 at full-time. The decisive goal in extra time proved to be one that would be disputed for decades; a ferocious strike from Hurst in the 101st minute crashed back down from the underside of the crossbar and—to English eyes—across the goal line. With the benefit of video replay, it's clear the whole ball did not cross the line, and Swiss referee Gottfried Dienst should not have given a goal—but his assistant referee, Azerbaijani Tofiq Bahramov, informed Dienst the ball had crossed the line. England led despite West German protest and capped the game off in the last minute of extra time when Hurst completed the first hat trick in a World Cup final with a fierce left-footed drive into the net. England had become world champions for the first time.

In Mexico in 1970, England faced the challenge of defending the world championship on another continent and in a culture that Alf Ramsey, still coach, found difficult to deal with in the buildup to the competition. England's preparations were upset when the captain Bobby Moore was falsely accused of stealing from a jewelry store in Bogota, Colombia, ahead of a World Cup warm-up game. Moore managed to brush this aside, and much of England's 1966 core remained intact with Banks, Hurst and

Charlton also headed to Mexico, along with talented newcomers selected for the roster, including Manchester City's Colin Bell and Francis Lee. In Mexico, the winners of the previous three editions of the World Cup—England, 1966, and Brazil, 1958 and 1962—were drawn together in group three, alongside Romania and Czechoslovakia. In Guadalajara, England began strongly against Romania, Lee in particular aggressive on the dribble and drawing fouls. The sole goal of the game came in the 65th minute, when a searching ball into the box by Alan Ball was flicked on by the head of Lee, finding 1966 hero Hurst, who deftly controlled the ball, slipped past a defender and drove it home left-footed. England next faced Brazil in a much-anticipated battle. On a hot day, close to 100 degrees, Brazil attacked England with verve, Jairzinho in particular more than a handful for right-back Tommy Wright. It took one of the greatest saves of all time by Banks, pivoting low to turn aside a header from Pelé, to keep the score level at halftime. England, too, missed chances, Hurst and Lee both culpable in front of goal. A fine contest was settled by Jairzinho, set up neatly by Pelé in the 59th minute, driving home from eight yards out. England came close to tying the game after that when substitute Jeff Astle missed a good chance from close range but were ultimately second best to the team that would go on to the win the World Cup. England still moved on to the next round following a 1–0 win over Czechoslovakia in Guadalajara, though it was not a performance to match their previous effort even in losing against Brazil.

In the quarterfinal stage, England faced West Germany in a rematch of the 1966 final. England was thrown into crisis before the game even kicked off with goalkeeper Gordon Banks ruled out due to sickness, replaced by Bonetti. West Germany had looked strong in the tournament to that point, but England got off to a flying start, with goals from Alan Mullery and Martin Peters giving them a 2–0 lead with 40 minutes to go. But the game unraveled from there for England. Beckenbauer squeezed in a strike under Bonetti to make it 2–1 in the 68th minute; 14 minutes later, Uwe Seeler looped a header over a stranded Bonetti to tie the game at 2–2, and an England–West Germany game once again went to extra time. This time, the West Germans prevailed: the winning goal came 18 minutes into the extra period, Gerd Müller smashing the ball in from close range. England exited the World Cup and lost their title: many question marks hung over Ramsey, who had removed England's driving force in midfield, Bobby Charlton, while England had still led 2–1 with 20 minutes left.

The rest of the 1970s proved to be fallow ground for England's World Cup hopes, with forlorn efforts at qualifying for both the 1974 tournament in West Germany and the 1978 edition in Argentina. England had not needed to qualify for either the 1966 World Cup—as hosts—or the 1970 World Cup—as holders—and for the 1974 competition was placed into a group with Poland and Wales, which they would need to win to head to the finals in West Germany. Ramsey remained as coach, embarking on his first qualifying campaign. It was a campaign that went off the rails in 1973 with an insipid draw against Wales followed by a 2–0 defeat in Poland. In the fall, England's hopes evaporated at Wembley Stadium, only scratching out a draw against Poland. They were out of the World Cup, and Alf Ramsey's tenure as coach was soon over as well.

Four years later, England faced a difficult qualification group for the 1978 World Cup, with only one team to advance alongside Finland, Luxembourg and Italy. Now coached by Don Revie, England struggled to find a rhythm even with talented players, such as Kevin Keegan, who would be the 1978 European Footballer of the Year. England's 2–0 loss in Rome in November 1976 put them on the back foot to Italy. Revie did not even last the duration of the qualifying campaign, leaving in the summer of 1977 for a lucrative contract in the United Arab Emirates. He was replaced by Ron Greenwood, who faced an uphill task catching Italy: England made strides by defeating Italy 2–0 at Wembley and—as Italy did—won all of their other games against Luxembourg and Finland. Though tied on points at the end of the campaign, Italy moved on instead of England due to a superior goal difference—three goals had denied England a spot at the 1978 World Cup.

For the first time since 1962, England successfully qualified for a World Cup by earning passage to the 1982 World Cup in Spain. It was not smooth: England lost three games out of eight but still squeaked through in the second qualification spot in group four, behind Hungary. In Spain, England's base was to be in Bilbao, and Greenwood announced that regardless of the tournament's results, he would step down after its conclusion. England was joined in group four by fellow Europeans, the fancied French and a talented Czechoslovakia, along with Kuwait, about whom the English knew little. England, perhaps to the surprise of their own players, romped through the group: with just 27 seconds gone in the first game against France, England took the lead when the engine of their midfield, Bryan Robson, forced in a goal from a long throw-in. France equalized before halftime, but England pressed on and secured a 3–1 win with another goal from Robson and a third by Paul Mariner. A 2–0 win over Czechoslovakia and a 1–0 victory against Kuwait followed to send England through, which at this World Cup meant taking part in a second group stage. This time, England joined a group containing West Germany and Spain: only one team, the group winner, would advance on to the semifinal stage. In Madrid, West Germany's defensive display could not be cracked by unimaginative England, resulting in a 0–0 tie. That made England's next game against Spain a must-win, already eliminated after losing themselves to West Germany. But for the second successive game, an England bereft of creative ideas could not carve open a resolute defense, a 0–0 result eliminating them.

Following the 1982 World Cup, Greenwood was replaced as head coach by Bobby Robson, who—like Alf Ramsey before him—had made his name taking provincial Ipswich Town to the top of the table. England qualified for the World Cup for the second successive time, reaching Mexico with an unbeaten campaign, though one in which they tied as many games as they won out of the eight qualifiers. England was drawn into what appeared to be a relatively weak group in Mexico, the only previous World Cup finalist alongside Poland, Morocco and Portugal. England had a strong roster, with a talented midfield that included Glenn Hoddle, Bryan Robson (no relation to Bobby), Ray Wilkins and Chris Waddle and predator Gary Lineker at striker. But the group did not turn out to be easy pickings for England. Against Portugal in the opener in Monterrey, early English pressure did not bring a goal, and a late strike on the break by Carlos Manuel gave the Portuguese victory. That result piled on the pressure for England's second game versus Morocco. Robson named an unchanged team, but England could not break down the Africans, and things seemed to go from bad to worse with captain Bryan Robson leaving the game and ultimately the tournament with an injured shoulder. A 0–0 tie meant England had to defeat Poland in order to progress to the next round. Robson made significant changes to the lineup for the crucial game in Monterrey: in came the creative Peter Beardsley at forward in place of target-man Mark Hateley, while midfielders Steve Hodge and Trevor Steven were brought in. It did not take long for the changes to look like the right ones: suddenly, England's midfield linked up superbly, and Lineker struck in the 9th, 14th and 34th minutes, sealing a 3–0 win.

That moved England on to the next round and from Monterrey to Mexico City with a matchup against Paraguay at the Azteca stadium. Robson made only one change in his selection, defender Alvin Martin replacing the suspended Terry Fenwick. Paraguay started brightly, but England soon continued the momentum from the Poland game, with Lineker suddenly in a magical vein of form: two goals from the forward sandwich a strike by his partner up front, Beardsley, in a 3–0 win. England's win paired them against Argentina at the Azteca: a game with politics hanging heavily over it, only four years after the conclusion of war between the two countries over the sovereignty of the Falkland Islands. Such was the drama of the game itself, though, that it would be remembered for events on the field rather than as a proxy drama. In front of 115,000 spectators, the stage was taken by the tournament's best player, Argentina's Diego Maradona. It was by dubious means that Maradona opened the scoring shortly after halftime: breaking through the England defense, he used his hand to punch the ball over the onrushing England goalkeeper, Peter Shilton, into the empty net. It was an offense unseen by the officials, and Maradona would later famously attribute it to the "hand of God." Just four minutes later, Maradona again tore through England's defense but this time by the most magnificent of means: receiving the ball deep in his own half, Maradona dribbled with pace and remarkable balance almost the entire length of the field before slotting past Shilton. It was enough to seal the win despite a strong rally by England, Lineker scoring in the 81st minute, a goal that earned him the Golden Boot as the tournament's top scorer. It was elimination for England and Robson, but a tournament that had started poorly ended with a dignified defeat to the ultimate champions, Argentina.

Robson remained as coach for the 1990 World Cup, despite a disappointing performance by England at the 1988 European Championships, though it was announced he would not continue in charge following the competition in Italy. England qualified for the World Cup finals following an unbeaten campaign, finishing second to Sweden in a group also containing Poland and Albania. In part due to the poor behavior of hooligans who had been following England abroad and creating mayhem on multiple occasions across the European continent, Robson's team was sequestered to a base on the island of Sardinia off the west coast of Italy. England's first-round group included Egypt, the Netherlands and the Republic of Ireland—the latter coached by a 1966 World Cup winner with England, Jack Charlton (brother of Bobby Charlton). England faced Ireland first on 10 June and quickly took the lead when Chris Waddle set up Lineker for an easy finish, but Ireland—playing dour but effective defensive soccer— found an equalizer in the second half when England midfielder Steve McMahon, who had come on as a substitute, lost the ball and Kevin Sheedy pounced for the Irish. It ended 1–1, a poor start that resulted in a media storm back in England. Facing a gifted

Dutch team next, the reigning European champions, Robson brought in Mark Wright to play as a sweeper and shore up the English defense, taking out Peter Beardsley. With greater solidity at the beak, England proved able to build creativity, with Tottenham Hotspur's Paul Gascoigne taking the reins in midfield and proving a consistent menace to the Dutch defense. Neither team was able to score, though, so England recorded a second successive tie. That result meant England would need to secure at least one point against Egypt in the last game of the group stage, and they would have to do it without their captain Bryan Robson, who again left a major tournament with an injury. England secured the win, thanks to a header by Wright from a Gascoigne free kick, and held on for a 1–0 win that meant progression to the next round.

In the second round, England faced Belgium in Bologna. A tight game went into extra time with the score 0–0, and it was only when penalties loomed just a minute away—in the last minute of the added period—that the deadlock was broken: midfielder David Platt, who had entered the game as a substitute, swiveled and volleyed home a magnificent strike from a looping free kick by Gascoigne to earn England the win. England's next opponent was the surprise package of the competition, Cameroon, who had become the first African nation to reach the quarterfinal stage of the World Cup, fired by veteran forward Roger Milla. Platt was rewarded for his goal with a start in the game, and he scored again after only 25 minutes, heading in a Stuart Pearce cross after a bustling run into the box. The score was 1–0 to England at halftime, but the game was wide open. Cameroon equalized with a penalty after a foul by Gascoigne in the 61st minute, and then Milla set up Eugène Ekéké just four minutes later, who beat Shilton to give the Africans a 2–1 lead. With just seven minutes remaining, England equalized from the penalty spot to stay alive and take the game into extra time, Lineker scoring the goal. Gascoigne provided the game-winning moment, playing a perfect pass to Lineker in the penalty area: he was hacked down, resulting in the third penalty of the game, slotted away by Lineker himself again. England progressed 3–2 after a titanic battle.

For the third time at a World Cup, England faced West Germany—having previously met in a final (1966) and a quarterfinal (1970), the old rivals now met at the semifinal stage in Turin. Robson made one change to his lineup, Beardsley coming in for the injured John Barnes. The game was scoreless for an hour, when in unfortunate circumstances, England fell behind—a free kick by Andreas Brehme ballooned off England defender Paul Parker and looped over Shilton in goal. England pressed for an equalizer, and it came 20 minutes later: Parker surged up the right flank and crossed for Lineker, who deftly controlled the ball, turned and struck it past Bodo Illgner in the German goal. It was 1–1 at full-time, and England headed into extra time for the second successive game. A moment all England fans would remember came just 10 minutes into the added period: Gascoigne fouled Thomas Berthold and received a yellow card. Innocuous though it was, it meant Gascoigne would miss the World Cup final if England advanced, and the Englishman broke into tears, creating an iconic moment in itself. There were to be more tears for England soon enough. With no goals to break the deadlock, a penalty shoot-out decided the game, and England was eliminated due to misses by Chris Waddle and Stuart Pearce. England now only had the consolation of a third-place game against hosts Italy, who had lost in the same heartbreaking fashion to Argentina. In a game neither team seemed to want to play, Italy prevailed 2–1 thanks to a winner from Salvatore Schillaci with just a handful of minutes remaining. England finished fourth, Robson's men achieving what is still to date the country's best-ever World Cup result outside of the tournament in England in 1966.

England, though, failed to build on that platform under new coach Graham Taylor and, in fact, did not even qualify for the 1994 edition of the World Cup held in the United States. Taylor appeared out of his depth, England playing a direct style that seemed primitive when matched in qualifying against a dynamic Dutch team. Yet England also failed to best Norway, playing a similar straightforward style, finishing third in the group with only five wins out of ten qualifying games. Taylor was replaced by Terry Venables following intense media criticism of his coaching qualities. Venables led England to the semifinals of the 1996 European Championships held in England but did not stay to lead England's qualifying campaign for the 1998 World Cup in France. That responsibility fell to former England midfielder Glenn Hoddle, and he successfully navigated England through a difficult qualifying campaign, topping a group also containing fellow qualifiers Italy: England's best result of the campaign was a superb defensive display in a 0–0 tie in Rome.

In France for the World Cup, Romania, Colombia and Tunisia were drawn into group G with England. Hoddle's team began amid controversy surrounding Hoddle's selections: he left out Gascoigne from the campaign altogether and then surprisingly omitted young stars David Beckham and Michael Owen from the starting lineup against Tunisia. But England did not miss a beat, Alan Shearer and Paul Scholes both scoring in a comfortable win over the Tunisians. A week later, however, England's performance against Romania proved a major disappointment, succumbing to a 2–1 defeat. That made the final group game against Colombia critical; defeat would mean elimination. Hoddle brought in Owen and Beckham, helping lead to a vibrant 2–0 win. England finished second in the group behind Romania, which meant Hoddle's men traveled to Saint-Étienne to play Argentina in the World Cup for the first time since 1986. The second-round contest was one for the ages: three goals came within the opening 16 minutes, England leading 2–1 thanks to a Shearer penalty and a wondrous run by the lightning-fast Owen. But right before halftime, Javier Zanetti equalized. England's hopes were further dashed just two minutes after the break, when Beckham impetuously kicked Diego Simeone, who had fouled him, and received a straight red card from Danish referee Kim Milton Nielson. England held on with 10 men, both teams creating chances, and the game went to a penalty shoot-out. Heartbreak came in the tiebreaker for England once more, Paul Ince and David Batty with the critical misses on this occasion. England headed home.

Under Swede Sven-Göran Eriksson, England qualified for the 2002 World Cup top of a group containing Germany, including a remarkable 5–1 win over the Germans in Munich. England headed to the World Cup, held jointly by Japan and South Korea, captained by David Beckham, though the Manchester United man was recovering from a broken bone in his foot. England's opponents in group F in the first round were Sweden, Nigeria and old foes Argentina. England began against Sweden with a mediocre display on 2 June, a 1–1 tie in Asian summer heat that left major question marks hanging over the team. But five days later, a goal from a Beckham penalty kick against Argentina gave England an invigorating win and Beckham some vengeance from the events in France four years earlier. England failed to build on the result against Nigeria, however, a drab 0–0 tie meaning England finished second behind Sweden. That meant a game against Denmark in the second round, won comfortably by the English 3–0, thanks to goals from Rio Ferdinand, Michael Owen and Emile Heskey. Brazil, fired by the brilliant trio of Rivaldo, Ronaldinho and Ronaldo, provided the next daunting opposition at the quarterfinal stage. England took the lead thanks to a neat chipped goal by Michael Owen, but before halftime came, Rivaldo equalized. Just five minutes into the second half, Ronaldinho gave Brazil a lead they were not to relinquish with a magnificent long-distance striker that bewildered and dropped in over goalkeeper David Seaman's head. Even though Ronaldinho was sent off shortly after, England created few chances and lost to the better team; Brazil went on to win the World Cup.

Eriksson stayed in charge for the 2006 World Cup in Germany, though it was announced before the tournament began that he would be replaced by Steve McLaren at its conclusion. England topped their qualifying group for the second successive campaign, finishing ahead of Poland with only one defeat in ten games. In Germany, England's group contained Sweden once again, along with Paraguay and Trinidad and Tobago. The opener against Paraguay was settled in only the third minute with the single goal of the game, a Beckham free kick flicked into his own goal by Paraguay's Carlos Gamarra. England followed that with a labored victory over Trinidad and Tobago, only coming to life when Wayne Rooney—like Beckham four years previously, playing while recovering from a broken bone in his foot—came on as second-half substitute and helped forge goals for Peter Crouch and Steven Gerrard in the last 10 minutes of the game. England earned a tie with Sweden in the final group game, 2–2 with goals from Joe Cole and Gerrard, topping the group and advancing to play Ecuador. A brilliant free kick from Beckham settled the game in Stuttgart 1–0 to England. In the quarterfinals, Portugal—featuring Rooney's Manchester United teammate Ronaldo—would be the opposition in Gelsenkirchen. The game had few clear chances, and England's two most notable stars exited in the second half: David Beckham substituted with a leg injury and Wayne Rooney sent off after 62 minutes for stamping on Portuguese defender Ricardo Carvalho. The game petered out into a penalty shoot-out, and for the third time since 1990, it proved the method of England's departure from a World Cup. On this occasion, Steven Gerrard and Jamie Carragher failed to convert their spot kicks.

By the time of the 2010 World Cup, Eriksson's replacement as England boss, Steve McLaren, had himself been replaced by Italian Fabio Capello following a failure to qualify for the 2008 European Championships. Under Capello, England topped their World Cup qualifying group once again, finishing comfortably ahead of Ukraine. In South Africa, England's World Cup first-round group saw them pitted against the United States, Algeria and Slovenia. England began against the Americans in Rustenburg in calamitous fashion: despite taking an early lead from a goal by captain Steven Gerrard, a terrible error by England goalkeeper Robert Green gifted the United States an equalizer, and the game ended 1–1. Capello's team could only manage another tie against Algeria, providing little cutting edge, but qualified for the next round with a

1–0 win over Slovenia thanks to a crucial goal by Jermain Defoe. With the United States topping the group, England had to travel to Bloemfontein to take on Germany once more in the knockout stage. A young and vibrant German team proved far too strong for England, winning 4–1, England's only goal coming from Matthew Upson, though a strike from Frank Lampard was controversially disallowed despite having crossed the line, as replays showed. England exited the World Cup again, the original home of soccer still yet to win a World Cup outside of its own borders.

Under the watchful eye of manager Roy Hodgson, qualification for the 2014 World Cup in Brazil saw England make their way through their group undefeated but in uninspiring fashion. Placed into group D with Uruguay, Costa Rica and Italy, England's hopes of advancing were high. In their opening game against Italy, England found themselves behind in the 35th minute after a Claudio Marchisio goal. Although Daniel Sturridge would score the equalizer just before half, a 50th-minute Mario Balotelli goal meant a 2–1 loss for England in the heat and humidity of Brazil's Amazonian rainforest. It was now a game of catch-up to stay ahead of their next opponent, Uruguay, in the standings. Though Wayne Rooney finally broke his World Cup curse with a much-needed equalizer in the 75th minute, it was an unfortunate misplayed header by Gerrard that sprung Uruguayan Luis Suárez through to goal 10 minutes later. His rocket past goalkeeper Joe Hart for his brace sealed the loss for the Lions and left them desperate for a win. In the end, a dreadful 0–0 draw with Costa Rica in their final game meant a last-place group finish and England's ousting from the tournament in 26th place with only two goals for and four against.

ESTADIO AZTECA. Estadio Azteca is the only stadium to have twice hosted the FIFA World Cup final, at the 1970 and 1986 tournaments hosted by Mexico. It is located in Mexico City, Mexico, and currently has a capacity of 105,000. It is the home stadium for both the Mexico national team and the famous club team Club América. Estadio Azteca's original capacity upon opening in May 1966 was 114,600, and it initially served as the main stadium for the 1968 Olympic Games. The stadium is located 7,200 feet above sea level, considered a considerable local advantage for the Mexican national team, who have a formidable record at the stadium.

ESTADIO DE CENTENARIO. Located in the capital city of Uruguay, Montevideo, Estadio de Centenario played host to the first FIFA World Cup final held in 1930, in which Uruguay defeated Argentina 4–2. It also played host to both semifinals in that inaugural World Cup, along with seven first-round games. It was called a "temple of football" by then Fédération Internationale de Football Association (FIFA) President Jules Rimet and was built specifically for the World Cup. The name, meaning "Centenary Stadium" in English, marked the 100th anniversary of Uruguay's constitution in 1930, and the stadium had an initial capacity of 100,000. Estadio de Centenario remains the home of the Uruguayan national team, with a reduced capacity of 60,000, though the stadium is in need of major renovation. It is also home to Uruguay's two leading club sides, Peñarol and Nacional, though both teams also play some home games at their own smaller stadiums.

ESTADIO DO MARACANÃ. *See* MARACANÃ.

ESTADIO MONUMENTAL. In 1978, the home stadium of Buenos Aires's team Estadio Monumental hosted seven games at the World Cup held in Argentina. Built in the 1930s in the Belgrano area of Buenos Aires, the bowl-shaped stadium—renovated for the World Cup—featured a capacity of just over 70,000 for the competition. Estadio Monumental played host to a total of nine games during the World Cup, with four first-round games including a pair of 2–1 victories for Argentina, over Hungary and France respectively. The stadium was the venue for three further second-stage games, the third-place game between Brazil and Italy and, most notably, the final itself, won by hosts Argentina 3–1 after extra time over the Netherlands. For that game on 25 June 1978, Estadio Monumental was perhaps at its finest, a partisan crowd roaring on Argentina amid a stadium plastered with festive ticker tape that exploded when the hosts claimed victory. Estadio Monumental is still the home venue for River Plate and regularly hosts Argentina's international games, with a current capacity of 64,000.

ESTADIO NACIONAL. Originally built in the 1930s as the national stadium of Chile in the capital Santiago, Estadio Nacional was renovated and expanded to a capacity of over 70,000 ahead of its role as the main stadium for the 1962 World Cup to be held in the South American country. Chile was struck by a severe earthquake ahead of the competition but was able to continue with its hosting duties after a monumental preparation effort. In the competition, Estadio Nacional was the venue for all of the games in group two of the first round, featuring the hosts Chile along with Italy, West Germany and Switzerland. During that stage, Chile's game with Italy infamously became known as the Battle of Santiago. Bad blood had begun before the game even kicked off due to Chilean popular disgust at articles about the country in the Italian press. The game, refereed poorly by Englishman Ken Aston, immediately degenerated into a series of fouls that saw two Italians sent off, bones broken and the police escorting players from the field. In the elimination stage, Estadio Nacional then hosted a 1–0 win for Yugoslavia over West Germany with 63,000 fans present. A capacity crowd of 77,000 watched the next game at the stadium, as hosts Chile took on fellow South Americans Brazil. Fired by two goals each from Vava and Garrincha, Chile was eliminated. A crowd of near 70,000 then watched the seventh World Cup final on 17 June at the Estadio Nacional, Brazil claiming the World Cup for the first time with a 3–1 win over Czechoslovakia.

Estadio Nacional would ultimately become more notorious as a prison camp than as a venue for a World Cup final. Following a coup d'état in September 1973, Chilean president Salvador Allende was deposed and replaced by a military regime who used the stadium as a brutal detention camp, with many prisoners interrogated and tortured in the arena's facilities. This impacted on Chile's qualifying campaign for the 1974 World Cup, as Chile pressed on with plans to host a qualifying game at the stadium against the Soviet Union, who refused to play at the venue due to the reported atrocities. Chile's stance on staging the game at Estadio Nacional was controversially backed by FIFA President Sir Stanley Rous, and when the Soviets boycotted the game, Chile won on a walkover.

Today, Estadio Nacional is a 47,000-capacity venue, home to the Chilean national team and club team Club Universidad de Chile, following a renovation completed in 2010.

ESTADIO SANTIAGO BERNABÉU. Estadio Santiago Bernabéu, commonly known simply as the Bernabéu, is a stadium located in Madrid, Spain, and is home to club team Real Madrid. It played host to the final of the 1982 FIFA World Cup, along with two second-round games in the same tournament. The 1964 UEFA European Football Championship final took place there, and four UEFA Champions League finals have also been played there. It currently has a capacity of 80,354, having undergone significant renovation in recent years.

EUSÉBIO FERREIRA DA SILVA. B. 25 January 1942, Maputo, Mozambique. D. 5 January 2014. Better known simply as Eusébio, Eusébio Ferreira da Silva is Portugal's greatest-ever player and also arguably the greatest African-born player of all time. A mercurial and prolific goal-scoring forward, he led his club Benfica to their second European Cup title in 1962, scoring twice in the final against Real Madrid. Eusébio played for Benfica from 1960 to 1975, scoring a remarkable 320 goals in 313 Portuguese league games. Eusébio was equally deadly at the international level. He was the top scorer for his adopted country, Portugal, at the 1966 FIFA World Cup, where they finished in third place. He scored a total of 41 goals in 64 games for Portugal. Eusébio won the European Footballer of the Year award in 1965 and the European Golden Boot in 1968 and 1973, before spending the final years of his career in the United States.

EVARISTO, JUAN. B. 20 June 1902, Argentina. D. 8 May 1978. Among the starting 11 for Argentina in the first-ever World Cup final was Juan Evaristo, an experienced defender who had won two Copa América titles with his country in 1927 and 1929. Evaristo also played at the 1928 Olympic Games Football Tournament, taking part in the final, a 2–1 defeat to Uruguay. At the 1930 World Cup, Evaristo played in Argentina's opening game win against France but was one of several players dropped for their next match versus Mexico. He returned to the lineup for Argentina's third game, a 3–1 win over Chile, and remained in the first 11 for the rest of the competition, a 6–1 win over the United States and Argentina's 4–2 defeat in the final to Uruguay, the hosts winning in front of a huge partisan crowd at Estadio de Centenario in Montevideo, the capital of Uruguay.

EVARISTO, MARIO. B. 10 December 1908, Buenos Aires, Argentina. D. 30 April 1993. Mario Evaristo played in the 1930 World Cup final for Argentina, in a 2–1 defeat to Uruguay in Uruguayan capital Montevideo. Evaristo was a star player for Buenos Aires–based Boca Juniors, with whom he won the Argentinean club championship on three occasions. He began his international career for Argentina in 1929, appearing for Argentina at the Copa América held in his native city. Evaristo scored in the final as Argentina won 2–0 to be crowned as champions of South America. Evaristo played in four of Argentina's five games at the 1930 World Cup, missing their second game against Mexico, one of several players dropped from the team that had unconvincingly beaten France in Argentina's opening game. Recalled to the lineup for Argentina's game against Chile, Evaristo scored the third goal in a 3–1 win. Evaristo did not play for Argentina again following the 1930 World Cup.

F

FEOLA, VICENTE. B. 20 November 1909, São Paulo, Brazil. D. 6 November 1975. Vicente Feola was a Brazilian soccer coach who led Brazil to the South American nation's first World Cup title in 1958, the same year Pelé debuted at the tournament. Brazil's victory in Sweden marked the first time to date that a non-European team has won a World Cup held in Europe. Feola returned to the World Cup as manager of Brazil in 1966 in England, where he oversaw his team unceremoniously crash out of the tournament in the group stage. His record as manager of Brazil stands at 55 wins, 13 ties and 6 losses.

FERNÁNDEZ, LORENZO. B. 20 May 1900, Redondela, Spain. D. 16 November 1973. Though born in Spain, Lorenzo Fernández won the inaugural World Cup with Uruguay in 1930, playing in the final, a 4–2 win over Argentina. At the time, he was a star player for Peñarol, a leading team in Uruguay's capital, Montevideo, where all the 1930 World Cup games were staged. Fernández played in all four of Uruguay's games in the competition. Alongside José Andrade and Álvaro Gestido, Fernández was at the core of the Uruguayan defense that only conceded three goals in four games at the 1930 World Cup. Fernández had also won a gold medal with Uruguay at the 1928 Olympic Games Football Tournament in Amsterdam, the Netherlands. He played for Uruguay until 1935, also winning the Copa América that year. Fernández was known for his fierce defensive style; he was a bull of a man who intimidated his opponents both physically and verbally.

FERRARI, GIOVANNI. B. 6 December 1907, Alessandria, Italy. D. 2 December 1982. One of an elite group of players to have won two World Cup titles, Giovanni Ferrari was among four Italians to achieve this feat by participating in both the 1934 and 1938 World Cup finals tournaments. Along with Giuseppe Meazza, he was the only Italian to take part in the final of both competitions. Ferrari, a swift inside forward, made his debut for Italy in February 1930 at the age of 22, a 4–2 win over Switzerland in Rome, and was a regular in the Italian team by the time of the 1934 World Cup, selected for the competition by Italian coach Vittorio Pozzo. There he played in five games, including the final, scoring in Italy's first two games, against the United States and Spain respectively. Ferrari continued as a regular for Italy following the 1934 World Cup, playing in Italy's infamous 3–2 defeat to England at Wembley in November of the same year. By the time of the 1938 World Cup, Ferrari was one of the most experienced players on Italy's team, with 38 international appearances under his belt. With Pozzo still at the helm, he was selected for all of Italy's four games, all wins, giving them their second

World Cup title. Ferrari played two further games for Italy, both later in 1938, ending his international career with 14 goals in 44 games. Remarkably, Ferrari was only on the losing side for Italy on three occasions out of those 44 games, taking part in 32 wins and 9 draws. He also enjoyed a remarkable club career, winning no fewer than eight Serie A championships between 1931 and 1941 on three different teams—five with Juventus, two with Internazionale and one with Bologna. After his retirement, Ferrari became a coach and was part of the coaching staff that traveled to the 1962 World Cup in Chile, where Italy was eliminated in the first round.

FERRARIS, ATTILIO. B. 26 March 1904, Rome, Italy. D. 8 May 1947. Among his 28 appearances for Italy, Attilio Ferraris's most glorious moment came with the 1934 World Cup final, as he was one of the Italian 11 who defeated Czechoslovakia 2–1 after extra time to win the World Cup for the first time. Even more marvelously for Ferraris, the game took place in his city of birth, Rome, as Italy hosted the second World Cup. Ferraris, age 30 at the time, did not take part in Italy's first two games of the competition but played in the quarterfinal win over Spain, the semifinal victory against Austria, as well as the final. Ferraris, a right-sided midfielder, played the bulk of his club career for Roma, making his international debut for Italy in 1926. Ferraris quickly made his mark as a creative player who was also brave in the tackle and earned the epithet the "Lion of Highbury" for his performance against England in a famous, hard-fought Italian loss at Arsenal's stadium in 1934 just months before the World Cup began in Italy. He retired from international play in 1935. Ferraris died aged only 43, suffering a heart attack while playing in an informal game.

FERREIRA, MANUEL. B. 22 October 1905, Trenque Lauquen, Argentina. D. 29 July 1983. One of the two captains on the field for the first World Cup final on 30 July 1930 was Manuel Ferreira, who led Argentina out against Uruguay, captained by José Nasazzi. With coaches having less sway over team selection and tactics than in the present day, Ferreira's role as a leader of the team was critical alongside other senior experienced players, such as Luis Monti and Guillermo Stábile. The World Cup was Ferreira's fourth major competition with Argentina since he began his international career in 1927, having been part of the 1927 and 1929 Copa América winning teams and winning a silver medal at the 1928 Olympic Games Football Tournament, with Argentina losing in the final to Uruguay. Ferreira scored six goals in five games at the competition. A dynamic forward, Ferreira played in four of Argentina's five games at the 1930 World Cup, missing one game against Mexico as he had to return across the Río de la Plata to Argentina in order to take a law-school examination. Ferreira led Argentina to a first-half lead in the World Cup final, but in a hostile atmosphere at the Estadio de Centenario in Uruguay's capital, Montevideo, his Argentina team crumbled to defeat in the second half, losing 4–2. The match was Ferreira's last for Argentina, though he continued a successful club career, playing in the Argentinean league for Estudiantes and River Plate.

FILHO, ROMUALDO ARPPI. B. 7 January 1939, Santos, Brazil. A FIFA referee for 29 years, Romualdo Arppi Filho refereed the 1986 World Cup final between

Argentina and West Germany, along with two other games at that World Cup in Mexico. By the time the 1986 World Cup began, Filho, 47 years old, had become one of the best-respected referees in the world and had officiated at three Olympic Games Football Tournaments, in 1968, 1980 and 1984. Filho took charge of his first World Cup game on 5 June 1986, officiating the first-round group-stage game between France and the Soviet Union, issuing four cautions in a 1–1 draw. He then refereed the second-round match between hosts Mexico and Bulgaria, a 2–1 win for the home team, giving out one yellow card in the game. The World Cup final, on 29 June in front of over 100,000 at the Azteca in Mexico City, presented Filho with his toughest test yet, especially with Argentina featuring Diego Maradona, whose mazy dribbles drew tough defensive attention and typically generated a series of difficult refereeing decisions. In the event, Filho handled the game well, balancing a steady stream of cautions in a tense matchup—six yellow cards issued in total—without having to send off any player. Argentina's 3–2 victory was Filho's last World Cup game as a referee.

FONTAINE, JUST. B. 18 August 1933, Marrakech, French protectorate of Morocco. Just Fontaine was a French player who still holds the record for scoring the most goals in a single FIFA World Cup tournament, having tallied 13 during the 1958 World Cup in Sweden. It was the only World Cup that Fontaine played in, participating in six matches for France as they finished third in the tournament. He scored four goals in a single game against West Germany. Fontaine scored a total of 30 goals in 21 international games for France between 1953 and 1960. He retired from playing in 1962 due to injury, having also scored prolifically at club level in France for Nice and Stade Reims. He then went on to have a long and successful career as a coach, most notably managing the national teams of both France and Morocco.

FORLÁN, DIEGO. B. 19 May 1979, Montevideo, Uruguay. A creative forward with a nose for goal—Forlán was the leading scorer in the history of the Uruguayan national team with 33 goals before he was surpassed by Luis Suárez—Forlán received the Golden Ball as the best player at the 2010 World Cup. At that competition, Forlán helped Uruguay to finish in fourth place, scoring five goals in the competition. Forlán is a gifted forward who can both create and score goals and is notably deadly with his delivery from set pieces. He began his senior club career with Independiente in Argentina in 1998, moving to join Manchester United in England in 2002, where he spent two relatively unsuccessful years. Forlán then moved to Spain and played first for Villarreal and then for Atlético Madrid, scoring goals prolifically.

Appearing in his first World Cup in 2002 at the competition in South Korea and Japan, the 23-year-old Forlán scored in his tournament debut against Senegal after entering the game as halftime substitute. He did not appear again in that World Cup, as Uruguay exited the competition at the first stage. In qualifying for the 2006 World Cup, Forlán scored six goals, but Uruguay failed to qualify following defeat to Australia in a play-off. In a successful qualifying campaign for the 2010 World Cup, Forlán was the undisputed fulcrum of the team, scoring seven goals. In South Africa, Forlán scored five goals on his way to leading Uruguay to a fourth-place finish. As the most-capped player in Uruguayan history with 112, Forlán scored twice in World Cup qualifiers but saw limited action in the 2014 World Cup in Brazil, playing 113 minutes in games against Colombia and Costa Rica. Forlán's father, Pablo Forlán, starred for Uruguay at the 1966 and 1974 World Cup finals tournaments.

FRANCE. Commonly known as Les Bleus (The Blues). France has won the World Cup once, as the host nation in 1998, which came on the 60-year anniversary of their first time as hosts. A Frenchman, Lucien Laurent, scored the very first goal in the very first World Cup in 1930 in Uruguay, finding the net in a 4–1 win versus Mexico. France, though, did not advance to the second round after successive 1–0 defeats to Argentina and Chile in the group stage. The French again fell at the first hurdle in 1934 in Italy, losing 3–2 after extra time to a talented Austrian team. France then played host to the next World Cup in 1938, a competition featuring 15 teams playing at 10 venues in 10 host cities, all under the shadow of impending world war. France advanced out of the first round for the first time with a 3–1 win over Belgium but then fell at the quarterfinal stage, losing 3–1 to Italy, and became the first host nation not to win the World Cup held on its own soil. France did not qualify for the next World Cup, held in 1950, and, in 1954, did not advance out of the group stage, a loss to Yugoslavia enough to relegate France to third place in group one, despite a 3–2 win over Mexico.

In 1958, a French team inspired by the brilliant Just Fontaine—who set a record that still stands with 13 goals in the competition—achieved its best finish to date, coming in third place at the competition in Sweden. France began by demolishing Paraguay 7–3 in the first-round group stage, and though that was followed by a 3–2 defeat to Yugoslavia, Les Bleus secured passage to the second round with a 2–1 win over Scotland. In the quarterfinals, Fontaine scored twice in a 4–0 defeat of Northern Ireland. However, despite taking the lead against the host nation Sweden in the semifinal, France's defensive deficiencies were exposed as the Swedes equalized and then scored in the 81st and 88th minutes to knock out the French. Third place was taken by France due to a 6–3 win against West Germany, Fontaine finding the net four times to set his record.

The French failed to qualify in 1962, 1970 and 1974, and though Les Bleus did make it to England in 1966, a first-round exit was on the cards, only securing one point in the group stage from a tie with Mexico, losing 2–1 to Uruguay and 2–0 to the host nation. In the late 1970s, a new generation of French stars emerged led by Michel Platini, who would vie with Diego Maradona for status as the world's best player in the 1980s. France qualified for the World Cup for the first time in 12 years, appearing at the competition in Argentina in 1978, though it did not move beyond the first round in a difficult group containing the host nation along with Italy and Hungary. France lost its opening two games to Italy and Argentina 2–1, and a 3–1 win over Hungary was not enough to advance the French.

Four years later in Spain, the French were captained by Platini, surrounded by a magical midfield also containing Rene Girard, Jean Tigana and Alain Giresse. France lost to England 3–1 in the first game of group three but then defeated Kuwait 4–1 and secured a point with Czechoslovakia to move on to the second group stage. At this stage, the French clicked, winning both games with Austria (1–0) and Northern

Ireland (4–1). France moved to the semifinals, facing West Germany in what became a game for the ages, a 3–3 tie after extra time decided in the West Germans' favor by penalty kicks. The game was marked by a burst of goals in extra time—the score had been 1–1 at full-time—with both teams scoring twice, the French leading 3–1 eight minutes of the extra period before the West Germans pulled two back and went on to win 5–4 in the shoot-out. Yet the game was ultimately remembered for a horrific incident in the 58th minute, when West German goalkeeper Harald Schumacher brutally smashed French forward Patrick Battiston, who had only just come into the game as a substitute and immediately had to exit, with the loss of two teeth and his life even considered to be in danger. Amazingly, the referee, Dutchman Charles Corver, did not even caution Schumacher for his reckless and violent challenge. The French were eliminated with an extremely bitter taste left in their mouths, falling to a 3–2 defeat to Poland in the third-place play-off two days later.

France, inspired by Platini, won the 1984 European Championships and entered the 1986 World Cup in Mexico as one of the competition's favorites under head coach Henri Michel. France qualified from the first round in second place in group B behind the Soviet Union. The French beat both Canada (1–0) and Hungary (3–0) and tied with the Soviets. That advanced France to face defending world champions Italy in Mexico City, and the French team proved clearly superior to the Italians. Platini and Yannick Stopyra scored the goals in a 2–0 win. The French now faced Brazil in Guadalajara, two of the tournament's most free-flowing teams meeting in an engaging encounter ultimately decided in French favor on penalty kicks. Careca opened the scoring for Brazil, but by halftime, the score was deadlocked again at 1–1 thanks to a goal from Platini, and it would remain that way until the end of extra time—though Zico spurned a chance to score from Brazil from the penalty spot, French goalkeeper Joel Bats saving the kick. Bats was also the hero in the shoot-out, saving Brazil's first kick from Socrates and the fourth from Julio Cesar, helping France to a 4–3 shoot-out win, despite Platini missing his kick. France had reached the semifinal again and once more faced West Germany there. Once again, there was dismay for France—beaten this time 2–0, though not without chances crafted by Platini and Tigana, finishing letting the French down. Les Bleus then fell 4–2 to Belgium in the third-place play-off after extra time.

With the magical midfield of Platini, Tigana and Giresse at the tail end of their careers, the French failed to qualify for the 1990 World Cup in Italy and, in painful style, also missed out on the United States in 1994: in the final qualification game, France only needed a tie with Bulgaria to advance, only to concede a last-minute winner scored by Emil Kostadinov after French winger David Ginola gave the ball away. France automatically qualified for the 1998 World Cup as the host nation, with the French—traditionally somewhat reserved toward soccer—ultimately embracing the game as a polyglot team of various ethnic origins came together to win the competition for the first time. Coached by Aimé Jacquet, the French team was studded with talent, a back line containing Marcel Desailly and captain Laurent Blanc anchoring a team constructed around the mercurial genius Zinedine Zidane in midfield. France won all three group-stage games, 3–0, 4–0 and 2–1 against South Africa, Saudi Arabia and Denmark respectively. France then labored to victory over Paraguay in the second round, host nation nerves showing, Laurent Blanc's goal in extra time the difference. France again struggled to score against Italy in the quarterfinal, moving on after a 4–3 penalty shoot-out win. In the semifinal, the French showed more composure in a 2–1 win over Croatia thanks to two goals by defender Lilian Thuram, though it was one marred by a red card for Blanc, the captain forced to sit out the final. There, Zidane orchestrated a 3–0 win over a strangely moribund Brazil in the Stade de France on the outskirts of Paris, scoring twice himself with midfielder Emmanuel Petit scoring the third that capped the game and the tournament for the French in stoppage time at the end of the game. For the first time, the French were world champions, and millions of Parisians appeared on the streets to celebrate.

Roger Lemerre, an assistant of Aimé Jacquet's at the 1998 World Cup, had led France to victory in the 2000 European Championship and brought a team filled with veterans from the reigning world and European title-winning teams to South Korea and Japan for the 2002 World Cup. However, France's appearance was disastrous: Les Bleus were stunned 1–0 in an opening loss to Senegal in group A of the first round and then tied 0–0 with Uruguay and were eliminated following a 2–0 defeat to Denmark. France's dismal display was the worst by a defending champion in World Cup history.

Four years later, a French team still inspired by Zinedine Zidane once again reached the World Cup final in Germany. Led by head coach Raymond Domenech, France began the competition in uninspiring form, tying 0–0 with Switzerland and 1–1 with South Korea in the first two group games, before qualifying to the next round after a 2–0 win against Togo. In the eliminate stage, however, France found form with the 34-year-old Zidane in imperious form supported by the exciting attacking talents of Thierry Henry and Franck Ribéry. The French defeated Spain 3–1 in the second round despite going a goal down and then knocked out defending world champion Brazil 1–0, Henry scoring the only goal of the game. In the semifinal, a Zidane penalty was the difference as France defeated Portugal 1–0 in Munich, moving Domenech's men on to the final against Italy. The French took the lead in the seventh minute when Zidane converted a penalty in cheeky style with a chip down the middle of the goal, though the Italians equalized only 12 minutes later, with a goal from Marco Materazzi. It was Zidane and Materazzi who clashed to create one of the most infamous moments in World Cup history in extra time: after the Italian insulted the Frenchman, Zidane headbutted Materazzi, and after being alerted to the incident by an assistant, referee Horacio Elizondo sent off the French captain. Without their talisman, France fell to defeat on penalty kicks.

Just as 2002 saw the French fall dramatically from the heights of 1998, so the 2010 World Cup brought France back down to earth. A team led by Laurent Blanc fractured, with several players in open revolt, and Les Bleus scored only a single goal, exiting at the first round following a 0–0 tie with Uruguay and 2–0 and 2–1 defeats to Mexico and host nation South Africa respectively.

Led by their 1998 World Cup–winning captain, Didier Deschamps, France finished second in their UEFA qualifying group for the 2014 tournament, three points behind defending world champs Spain (the result of a 1–0 home loss). Placed in group E with Switzerland, Ecuador and Honduras, France saw themselves in a battle with a scrappy Honduran side until Wilson Palacios was issued his second yellow for a sloppy tackle in the box. Karim Benzema finished the ensuing penalty in the 45th minute, and a Noel Valladares own goal in the 48th following a great Benzema strike gave France breathing room. Benzema finished the scoring in the 72nd minute with a blast into the roof of the net. Game two saw France up against sixth-ranked Switzerland, but the game many expected never materialized as France used three first-half goals by Olivier Giroud, Blaise Matuidi and Mathieu Valbuena to gain all of the momentum. Two second-half strikes, by Benzema and Moussa Sissoko, meant a five-goal lead. Two late Swiss goals, by Blerim Džemaili and Granit Xhaka, meant little to the French faithful. With six points and first place secure, France found themselves in a physical battle against an Ecuadorian side needing points to advance. Even with Ecuador losing Antonio Valencia to a studs-up tackle early in the second half, an uninspired French side was unable to convert and drew 0–0.

Through to the round of 16, France was matched up against a Nigerian side determined to make history. Though France was arguably the more skilled side, the pace and athleticism of the Super Eagles gave the French players trouble until the 79th minute, when a miscue by Nigerian keeper Vincent Enyeama left a wide-open net for Paul Pogba's header. With Nigeria pressing, the game was decided when Joseph Yobo misplayed a Valbuena cross into the back of his own net to secure France's advancement to a quarterfinal matchup with Germany.

France was never able to find the magic of their group play against a strong German side, and an early header goal by Mats Hummels in the 13th minute found Les Bleus behind for the first time in the tournament. Though France was able to create some chances on both sides of halftime, the experience and discipline of Germany made it seem like a clean sheet was almost inevitable. In the end, the lone goal was enough for the Germans, and the French were sent home in seventh place with ten goals for and three against.

G

GARRINCHA. B. 28 October 1933, Pau Grande, Brazil. D. 20 January 1983. Born as Manuel Francisco dos Santos, but universally known as Garrincha (the Little Bird), Garrincha is the only rival for Pelé as Brazil's most talented player of all time. Inventive, unpredictable and impudent, Garrincha astonished spectators and humiliated opponents with his devilish dribbling technique, swerving and drifting past defenders seemingly at will. Garrincha overcame considerable obstacles to reach the top of the world's game, growing up in a deprived area and overcoming the physical impediment of having one leg a full two inches shorter than the other. He began his professional career with Botafogo in 1953, staying there for 12 seasons and scoring 232 goals in 581 appearances, winning the Rio de Janeiro state championship three times. It was his performances for Brazil that earned Garrincha worldwide fame, as he played a key part in Brazil's first two FIFA World Cup victories in 1958 in Sweden and 1962 in Chile. He carried a particularly heavy load in the 1962 triumph after injury early in the tournament restricted Pelé's contribution, scoring four goals to finish as joint top scorer. He played 50 times for Brazil, 43 of those games won, 6 drawn and the only loss coming in his final appearance for his country at the 1966 FIFA World Cup in England against Hungary, as a poor Brazil side tumbled out in the first stage. Garrincha's career off the field was as eventful as on it; a heavy drinker not always able to sensibly manage his fame and fortune, he died aged just 49 from cirrhosis of the liver in 1983. He is remembered alongside Pelé as the greatest talent Brazil has produced.

GERMANY. Commonly known as Die Nationalmannschaft (The National Team), Die Nationalelf (The National Eleven), Die Adler (The Eagles), or Die Mannschaft (The Team). Germany, considered by FIFA to be the successor nation to West Germany for its World Cup record, has reached eight World Cup finals and won four competitions (see East Germany for that nation's separate World Cup record). The German team began play in 1908, though it did not compete in the first World Cup held in 1930. At the second World Cup in 1934 in Italy, Germany finished in third place, beating Belgium 5–2 in the first round in large part thanks to an Edmund Conen hat trick, defeating Sweden 2–1 in the quarterfinal and then succumbing 3–1 to Czechoslovakia in the semifinal. Third place was claimed for Germany following a 3–2 win over Austria in the third-place play-off. In 1938 in France, only a year before the outbreak of World War II, Germany was eliminated in the first round, losing to Switzerland on a replayed game following a tie in the first match between the teams.

Both German nations—with West Germany and East Germany now fielding separate teams—were banned from participating in the 1950 World Cup in Brazil, the first held following World War II. In 1954, West Germany returned to action and surprisingly won the World Cup in Switzerland. Coached by Sepp Herberger, Germany won 4–1 against Turkey in first-round group play before being hammered 8–3 by Hungary, fielding a weakened team against the favorite for the competition. The West Germans then crushed Turkey 7–2 to advance to the knockout stage. In the quarterfinals, West Germany beat Yugoslavia 2–0 and, in the semifinal, crushed Austria 6–1, West German captain Fritz Walter claiming two goals. At the final in Bern, the Hungarians—widely regarded as one of the greatest teams to ever play the game—were strong favorites, led by the inimitable Ferenc Puskás. Within eight minutes, Hungary had a 2–0 lead and seemed destined to breeze to victory. However, West Germany struck back twice within 10 minutes, with goals from Max Morlock and Helmut Rahn. In the 84th minute, a left-footed strike by the outside-right Rahn decided the contest in West Germany's favor, to the shock of the world and the joy of a reconstructed West Germany. The game came to be known as the Miracle of Bern and was seen as a signal moment in the nation's restoration following the devastation of World War II.

West Germany reached the last four of the competition again in 1958, at the World Cup held in Sweden, still under the watchful eye of head coach Sepp Herberger. The West Germans did not enjoy smooth sailing to the knockout round, though; after defeating Argentina 3–1, Herberger's men only scraped through in second place in group one behind Northern Ireland after ties with both Czechoslovakia and the Northern Irish. A 1–0 win over Yugoslavia—Helmut Rahn scoring the only goal—sent the West Germans to the semifinal, but host nation Sweden proved too strong with a 3–1 scoreline in the Scandinavians' favor. In the third-place game, Herberger's team was overwhelmed 6–3 by France.

For the third successive World Cup, Sepp Herberger took charge as the West Germans headed to Chile. Though West Germany topped group two after a pair of wins over Switzerland and Chile and a tie with Italy, Herberger's men exited at the quarterfinal stage with a 1–0 defeat to Yugoslavia. Helmut Schön was in charge four years later when West Germany headed to England, with a new star at the helm of the team on the field, the 21-year-old maestro Franz Beckenbauer. The West Germans began in sparkling form with a 5–0 dismissal of Switzerland in the group stage and then moving on after a 0–0 tie with Argentina and a 2–1 win over Spain. West Germany's quality became evident in a 4–0 lathering of Uruguay in the quarterfinal, and Helmut Haller and Beckenbauer scored the goals in the semifinal that put Schön's men into the final with a 2–1 defeat of the Soviet Union at Goodison Park in Liverpool. The West Germans now faced host nation England in the final at Wembley Stadium in London. Beckenbauer and English star Bobby Charlton canceled each other out in midfield in an exciting contest; the West Germans took a lead in the 12th minute from Haller, but Hurst and Peters scored to put England up 2–1 as the final whistle approached. In the 89th minute, Wolfgang Weber equalized to push the game into extra time. Then came controversy in the first additional period: Geoff Hurst's strike cannoned down off the crossbar onto the goal line, though the ball was wrongly adjudged to have crossed the line by the game officials and England took the lead 101 minutes into the game, with Hurst capping off a 4–2 win for England with a goal as time expired, leaving the West Germans feeling mightily aggrieved.

In Mexico four years later, West Germany enjoyed revenge against England, coming from behind in the quarterfinals against the English to claim a 3–2 win after extra time, the team's prolific striker Gerd Müller scoring the winner. The West Germans, coached again by Schön, had reached that stage thanks to wins over Peru, Bulgaria and Morocco in the first round. The semifinal against Italy proved to be an epic affair: 1–0 down until the 90th minute, a goal by Karl-Heinz Schnellinger pushed the game to extra time, and five more goals followed in 30 minutes. The teams exchanged a pair of strikes—Müller scoring twice—before Italy came out on top thanks to a 111th-minute goal by Gianni Rivera.

In 1974, just as 20 years previously, West Germany upset the tournament's favorite team to claim the World Cup, this time with a victory over the Netherlands in the final. This time, the win came on home soil, with West Germany hosting the World Cup. Still coached by Schön, West Germany had won the 1972 European Championships, with Beckenbauer and Müller now at the height of their powers and the brilliant Sepp Maier in goal. West Germany finished second in the group stage; after beating Chile 1–0 and Australia 3–0, the two German nations met in the final group game, and the East came out on top 1–0. In the second group stage, the West Germans won all three games, dismissing Yugoslavia, Sweden and Poland. That took Schön's men to the final, facing Johan Cruyff's heavily favored Dutch team. But though the Netherlands took an early lead from a penalty called by English referee Jack Taylor only two minutes into the game, Paul Breitner equalized from another penalty 25 minutes in, and Müller scored what proved to be the winning goal just before halftime. West Germany claimed a second World Cup title in Munich.

Without Beckenbauer or Gerd Müller, West Germany's run at the 1978 World Cup in Argentina proved to be the nation's worst since 1962. The West Germans only just squeezed through the first round, tying with both Poland and Tunisia 0–0, sandwiching a much-needed 6–0 win against Mexico. In the second group stage, West Germany finished in third place, failing to win a game with draws against Italy and the Netherlands, and a fatal 3–2 loss to Austria eliminated the team coached for the fourth and final time at a World Cup by Helmut Schön. Stewarded by Schön's replacement Jupp Derwall, West Germany reached the World Cup final again in 1982 in Spain, captained by Karl-Heinz Rummenigge. The West Germans began with a disastrous 2–1 defeat to Algeria in the group stage, then defeated Chile 4–1 and advanced thanks to a 1–0 won over Austria, a convenient scoreline that saw both teams advance at Algeria's expense with a slow-paced game presumed by many to have had its scoreline decided in advance of kickoff, with both teams knowing a 1–0 West German win would work for both to go through. In the second group stage, West Germany advanced following a 0–0 tie with England and a 2–1 win over Spain, Pierre Littbarski and Klaus Fischer scoring for the West Germans. That advanced West Germany to a semifinal matchup with France. A game notable for a terrible, unpunished assault by German goalkeeper Harald Schumacher on French forward Patrick Battiston went in favor of the West Germans after a 3–3 tie was settled on penalty kicks. In the final, though, an Italy team playing inspired soccer led by forward Paoli Rossi in the elimination stage overpowered Derwall's men, running out 3–1 winners in Madrid.

1974 World Cup–winning captain Franz Beckenbauer took charge of West Germany at the 1986 World Cup in Mexico and led the team captained by Rummenigge to a second runner-up finish in a row. West Germany finished second in group E to move on to the second round, having tied with Uruguay, beaten Scotland and lost to Denmark. A second-round win over Morocco set up West Germany to face host nation Mexico in Monterrey, and a 0–0 tie was followed by a penalty shoot-out victory for Beckenbauer's team. In the semifinal in Guadalajara, West Germany again bested France, thanks to goals by Andreas Brehme and Rudi Völler. In the final in Mexico City in front of a crowd of 115,000 spectators, West Germany ultimately could not contain an Argentina team inspired by Diego Maradona, losing 3–2 despite coming back from 2–0 down thanks to goals by Rummenigge in the 74th minute and Völler 7 minutes later. A winning goal by Jorge Burruchaga in the 84th minute, set up by Maradona, proved to be the difference.

In 1990, West Germany became the third team to win the World Cup for the third time, taking the crown again in Italy. Still coached by Beckenbauer, West Germany's captain and inspiration was Lothar Matthäus, equally adept at marshalling the defense and prodding attacks, while a strong forward line paired Völler with the equally lethal Jürgen Klinsmann. The West Germans cruised through the group stage top of group D, defeating Yugoslavia 4–1, the United Arab Emirates 5–1 and drawing 1–1 with Colombia. In the second round, a hotly contested 2–1 win in Milan over the Netherlands came courtesy of goals from Klinsmann and defender Andreas Brehme. The Czechs were then defeated 1–0 in the quarterfinals, a Matthäus penalty kick the decider, and a place in the semifinal was secured after a penalty shoot-out win over England following a 1–1 tie, a deflected strike by Brehme canceling out an earlier goal by Gary Lineker. A dour final against Argentina followed; a rematch from 1986, this time a hobbled Maradona was contained, and Argentina was reduced to nine men by the time of the final whistle, though it was only in the 85th minute that Brehme's penalty settled the game. Beckenbauer became the first man to captain and coach his team to World Cup glory, in the last appearance at a World Cup for West Germany.

In the United States in the 1994 World Cup, Germany—now united—was coached by Berti Vogts and put in a relatively weak performance. It began with a 1–0 win over Bolivia in the tournament's opening game, Klinsmann scoring the winner, followed by a 1–1 tie with Spain and a 3–2 win over South Korea that saw the West Germans advance to the second round as group C winners. In the second round, a pair of strikes by Völler and one from Klinsmann saw Germany past Belgium at Soldier Field in Chicago, but in the quarterfinal, the Germans came unstuck despite leading 1–0 just after halftime against Bulgaria in Giants Stadium, New Jersey. Goals from Hristo Stoichkov and Yordan Letchkov stunned Vogts's team, who exited with a 2–1 defeat.

The 1998 World Cup in France again saw Germany exit at the quarterfinal stage, once more under Vogts's leadership, the team this time captained by Klinsmann. The Germans began by defeating the United States 2–0 in Paris, tied 2–2 with Yugoslavia and beat Iran 2–0. In the second round, Klinsmann and Oliver Bierhoff struck twice in the second half as Germany came from behind to defeat Mexico

2–1 in Montpellier. In the quarterfinal, a performance of stunning verve by Croatia wrecked German hopes, beaten 3–0 in Lyon and eliminated.

Germany returned to the form at the 2002 World Cup, reaching the World Cup final for the sixth time, former star striker Rudi Völler now head coach. The Germans began by slaughtering Saudi Arabia 8–0 in the group stage, forward Miroslav Klose netting a hat trick. A 1–1 tie with the Republic of Ireland and a 2–0 defeat of Cameroon was enough to advance Germany to the next round top of group E. Oliver Neuville scored the only goal of the game against Paraguay in the second round for a 1–0 German win. Germany advanced by the same scoreline against both the United States in the quarterfinal and host nation South Korea in the semifinal, Michael Ballack scoring the winning goal in both games, though the team's top performer was goalkeeper and captain Oliver Kahn. In the final, though, Kahn had a poor game as Germany failed to contain Brazil and the explosive Ronaldo, losing 2–0 in Yokohama.

Two consecutive third-place finishes followed for Germany at the 2006 and 2010 World Cups. At home in 2006, hosting the tournament for the second time, a young German team coached by Jürgen Klinsmann played an exciting brand of soccer, winning all three group games with defeats of Costa Rica, Poland and Ecuador. In the second round, a pair of Lukas Podolski strikes saw Klinsmann's team past Sweden in Munich. In the quarterfinal, a late equalizer from Miroslav Klose took Germany to a penalty shoot-out by Argentina, the host nation prevailing 4–2 in the decisive kicks. However, after a 0–0 scoreline at full-time, Italy proved too experienced for the young German team in Dortmund, scoring twice to eliminate the Germans, Klinsmann's men ultimately finishing third after defeating Portugal in the third-place play-off. Another youthful German star lit up the 2010 World Cup in South Africa, with 21-year-old Thomas Müller winning both the Golden Boot and the Best Young Player awards. Germany advanced through the group stage with wins over Australia and Ghana, though the team coached by Joachim Löw also lost 1–0 to Serbia. In the second round, Germany ran over England in the second half of the game between the two old enemies in Bloemfontein, Müller scoring twice and Klose and Podolski netting the others in a 4–1 win. The Germans' fine form continued against Diego Maradona's Argentina in the quarterfinal, with Müller and Friedrich scoring once and Klose twice in a 4–0 win in Cape Town. Germany, though, could not continue that rich rein of form against reigning European champions Spain, losing 1–0 in the semifinal. Third place was claimed by Löw's team with a 3–2 win over Uruguay.

Qualification for the 2014 World Cup in Brazil came easily for a Löw-managed national side loaded with talent. In UEFA group C, Germany won nine of ten matches (their only blemish was a 4–4 draw with Sweden), scoring a German-national-team qualifying record 36 goals while conceding only 10. This dominance meant a World Cup title, not a third consecutive third-place finish, was the new expectation. Placed in group G, the "Group of Death," with Portugal, Ghana and the United States, Germany asserted themselves early with a 4–0 drubbing of fourth-ranked Portugal. Thomas Müller looked like his 2010 Golden Boot award-winning self in the match with the first hat trick of the 2014 tournament, and Mats Hummels added another. Perhaps it was the red card awarded to Portuguese defender Pepe for an ill-advised headbutt, or maybe it was the early Müller penalty, but Portugal could never match Germany's level. Game two, against Ghana at the Estádio Castelão in Fortaleza, saw a first half devoid of goals and a second half that many will recall for years to come. After a Mario Götze goal in the 51st minute, Ghana came roaring back with a goal by André Ayew three minutes later. Now back on their heels, Germany found themselves down a goal when, in the 63rd minute, Asamoah Gyan blasted a screamer past a diving Manuel Neuer. With time running out, Löw turned to his bench and inserted prolific goal scorer Miroslav Klose. Klose did not disappoint, redirecting a flicked corner into the back of the net in the 71st minute on his first touch of the tournament to pull Germany level and tie him atop the list of World Cup goal scorers with Brazil's Ronaldo. With four points, Germany found themselves tied in the group standings with their next opponents, a scrappy United States side, atop a "Group of Death" living up to its name.

A rematch of a thrilling 2002 World Cup quarterfinal played in Korea, this game lived up to the hype as a superior German side found it difficult to break down the U.S. defense, most notably goalkeeper Tim Howard, until the 55th minute when Müller finally capitalized on a tiring U.S. team with a blast from the top left corner of the box following a Howard save. With the one-goal lead, Germany was content to sit back and absorb pressure, and the 1–0 win sent both teams through to the round of 16, Germany in first and the United States in second.

Matched up against an Algerian side looking to make up for the "Disgrace of Gijón" 32 years earlier, for 90-plus minutes of regulation time Algerian goalkeeper M'Bolhi kept Germany scoreless to force extra time. Any Algerian momentum gained from making it to added extra time was short lived, though, as German substitute André Schürrle scored a clever full-speed back-heel flick in the 92nd minute to put Germany up 1–0. The game looked over in the 120th minute when Mesut Özil hammered home a blocked Schürrle shot for a two-goal lead, but Algeria again showed their resolve when, in the 121st minute, Abdelmoumene Djabou rocketed home a cross to close the gap to one. Germany was able to withstand the pressure and was through to the quarterfinals for the ninth consecutive time.

Playing against a French team that dominated its group, Germany's skill proved to be too much. An early header goal by Mats Hummels in the 13th minute put Les Bleus behind for the first time in the tournament, and the experience and discipline of the German side made a fourth consecutive trip to the semifinals an inevitability.

Matched up against a host nation lamenting the loss of captain Thiago Silva to an accumulation of yellow cards and star player Neymar to a broken vertebra, a match that many anticipated as being one of the most entertaining to watch turned into an embarrassment for the home side. An astonishing five goals in the game's first 29 minutes (four coming in a torrid six-minute span) resolutely ended any hopes of a Brazilian comeback, and two second-half goals by André Schürrle meant that Germany was on its way to the greatest semifinal victory in the history of the World Cup.

Through to their eighth final, the matchup of the organization and discipline of Germany versus the skill of Lionel Messi proved to be an entertaining one. Played at Estádio Maracanã in Rio de Janeiro in front of 74,738 spectators, Germany looked to move themselves into a tie with Italy with their fourth World Cup title and become the first European side to win a title on South American soil. Argentina had a couple of good chances but, ultimately, a stout, organized German back line held them to zero shots on target. Though Germany struggled to create chances of their own, in the 113rd minute, German substitute Mario Götze lived up to his Super Mario nickname when he scored a spectacular goal off a chest trap and clinical finish from four yards out. When it was all over, Germany had scored an astonishing 18 goals to go along with only 4 conceded, and German fans finally had another title after 24 years of waiting.

GERMANY, EAST. Commonly known as Weltmeister in Freundschaftsspielen (World Champion in Friendly Games). East Germany appeared in one World Cup finals competition during its existence from 1952 to 1990. The country's lone appearance came in 1974, drawn in group one at the competition in neighboring West Germany, whom the East Germans faced along with Australia and Chile. Coached by Georg Buschner and captained by Bernd Bransch, the East German team surprisingly won the group courtesy of an opening 2–0 win against Australia, a 1–1 tie with Chile and a 1–0 win against West Germany, in the first game between the divided nation, played in Hamburg. In the second-round group stage, East Germany finished third after losing to Brazil and the Netherlands, securing a tie with Argentina but still eliminated.

GERMANY, WEST. *See* GERMANY.

GESTIDO, ÁLVARO. B. 17 May 1907, Montevideo, Uruguay. D. 18 January 1957. A key left-side halfback for leading Uruguayan team Peñarol, Álvaro Gestido played in the first World Cup final for his country, held in his native city, Montevideo, the capital of Uruguay. Uruguay won 4–2 against neighboring Argentina. Gestido was 24 years old at the time. He had become a mainstay of Uruguay's superb team in the late 1920s, winning a gold medal with his country at the 1928 Olympic Games Football Tournament, playing in the final victory over Argentina. Gestido also played at the 1929 Copa América, Uruguay finishing in third place at that competition.

GHANA. Commonly known as the Black Stars. Ghana qualified for the World Cup for the first time in 2006 and has subsequently appeared in each following tournament: 2010 in South Africa and 2014 in Brazil. In 2006 in Germany, a Ghana team coached by Serbian Ratomir Dujković featured numerous world-class talents, including Chelsea's Michael Essien and AS Roma's Samuel Kuffour. Ghana began the group stage by losing 2–0 to Italy but then moved on to the next round following a 2–0 win over the Czech Republic and a 2–1 victory against the United States. In the second round, though, Ghana could not advance past Brazil, losing 3–0 in Dortmund. Four years later in South Africa, Ghana again featured a world-class midfield with Essien, Sulley Muntari and captain Stephen Appiah, along with the exciting forward Asamoah Gyan. The Black Stars began with a 1–0 win over Serbia in the group stage, followed by a 1–1 tie with Australia and a 1–0 defeat to Germany. Despite the loss, Ghana still advanced to the elimination stage. In the second round, at Royal Bafokeng Stadium in Rustenburg, Ghana took an early lead against the United States before conceding an equalizer from the penalty spot midway through the second half. With the scores tied at 1–1 at full-time, Ghana found a winner just three minutes into the extra period, Gyan finishing after a powerful run at the American defense. In the quarterfinals,

Ghana came agonizingly close to becoming the first African nation to reach the World Cup semifinals, losing on penalty kicks after a 1–1 draw with the South Americans. Ghana had a chance to win the game at the end of extra time after Uruguay had been penalized for Luis Suarez stopping a sure goal with his hands on the goal line, but Gyan failed to convert the resulting penalty kick.

Qualification for the 2014 World Cup in Brazil started off well for the Black Stars when they won five of their six matches, losing only to 2012 Africa champions Zambia 1–0. Rolling through their group, Ghana scored 18 goals (conceding only 3) and found themselves in a play-off with seven-time African champion Egypt. What should have been a difficult matchup ended in a 6–1 home win, meaning a 2–1 away defeat was meaningless. Through to their third consecutive World Cup, Ghana was placed in group G, the "Group of Death," with Germany, Portugal and the United States.

Opening their tournament against the United States at the Estádio das Dunas in Natal, Ghana saw themselves quickly behind when, in the first minute, Clint Dempsey tore through the Ghanaian defense and finished with aplomb off the far post for the sixth-fastest goal in World Cup history. Ghana began to assert their dominance and attacked through the flanks as the game went on, but numerous chances, mostly by captain Gyan, never found their target. In the 82nd minute, the pressure paid off, and André Ayew leveled the game at one following some splendid passing and a quality near-post finish. An earned point was not to be for Ghana, as little-used U.S. substitute John Brooks Jr. found himself on the end of a Graham Zusi corner and headed it down and past a flailing Adam Kwarasey for the winner.

In their second group game, Ghana was up against a German side not only favored by many to win it all but also one that was coming off a resounding 4–0 win over Portugal. Played at the Estádio Castelão in Fortaleza, a first half devoid of goals was a bit misleading as the second half proved to be one that many will recall for years to come. After a Mario Götze goal in the 51st minute, Ghana came back with a goal by André Ayew three minutes later. Ghana found themselves up a goal when, in the 63rd minute, Asamoah Gyan blasted a screamer past a diving Manuel Neuer. Had it not been for all-time leading-scorer Miroslav Klose's redirection of a flicked corner in the 71st minute, Ghana may have pulled off the upset of the tournament. Instead, with one point after two games, they now found themselves in a must-win game against Portugal.

Ghana's aggressive play against Portugal backfired when a flailing John Boye inadvertently knocked the ball into the back of his own net 30 minutes in. Though a goal in the 57th minute by Gyan equalized, Portugal's Cristiano Ronaldo calmly tucked away a point-blank gift in the 80th minute for the game winner. The loss sent Ghana packing in last place in their group and 25th overall behind four goals scored and six conceded.

GLÖCKNER, RUDOLF. B. 20 March 1929, Markranstädt, Germany. D. 25 January 1999. Rudolf "Rudi" Glöckner was the first and only East German referee to take charge of a World Cup final, when he officiated the classic 1970 contest in Mexico City between Brazil and Italy, remembered for the South Americans' sauntering style in their 4–1 victory. Glöckner's career as an international referee lasted an impressive 17 years from 1961 to 1978. He established his reputation internationally by overseeing three games at the 1964 Olympic Games Football Tournament, as well as a number of European Cup games. Selected for the 1970 World Cup, Glöckner first took charge of Uruguay's 0–0 tie with Italy in the group stage on 6 June 1970. Glöckner was perhaps a surprising choice for the final given he had never refereed an international match of that caliber before, but his East German nationality made him a preferable choice, with the Italians resisting a South American referee and the Brazilians opposed to a Western European referee. Glöckner issued two cautions in the final, dominated by Brazil without any major controversial incident. Glöckner did not appear at another World Cup but did referee at a high level for several more years, taking charge of games at both the 1972 and 1976 European Championships, along with several World Cup qualifying games and the 1976 UEFA Cup final between Club Brugge and Liverpool.

GOLDEN BALL. Introduced in 1982, the Golden Ball is awarded to the best player at the World Cup finals, as voted for by the media representatives from a short list selected by a FIFA committee. It has never been won more than once by the same player. For a list of winners, see appendix B.

GOLDEN BOOT. Though the top goal scorer has been a statistic kept since the first World Cup in 1930, the award was formally introduced in 1982 as the Golden Shoe. Awarded to the player who scores the most goals in the World Cup finals, the award was renamed the Golden Boot in 2010. To ensure there is only one winner each year, in 1998, it was decided that if two or more players have the same number of goals in the competition, the player with the most assists is awarded the Golden Boot; if there is still a tie after this, it goes to the player with the fewest matches played. No player has won more than one Golden Boot title. Looking back to 1930, and including the top goal scorers, Brazil has produced the most winners, with five. For a full list, see appendix C.

GOLDEN GLOVE. Created in 1994, the award for the best goalkeeper in the World Cup was, until 2010, known as the Lev Yashin award after the great Soviet Union goalkeeper. Like the Golden Ball, the award is selected by the FIFA Technical Study Group. For a list of winners, see appendix D.

GOLDEN SHOE. *See* GOLDEN BOOT.

GREECE. Commonly known as Ethniki (National), Piratiko (The Pirate Ship) or Galanolefki (Sky Blue–White). The Greek national team made its World Cup finals debut in 1994, having either failed to qualify or not entered all of the previous competitions. Greece's appearance at the competition in the United States, coached by Alkis Panagoulias, was disastrous. The Greeks lost all three games, conceding four each to Argentina and Bulgaria and two to Nigeria, without scoring a single goal in the tournament. Greece did not again qualify for the World Cup until 2010, though in the meantime, the European nation did notch up a surprising European Championship win in 2004. In 2010 in South Africa, Greece again exited at the first-round stage, though it did at least register a win with a 2–1 victory over Nigeria, sandwiched by a pair of 2–0 defeats to South Korea and Argentina.

Qualification for the 2014 World Cup in Brazil found Greece tied for second in their group with Bosnia and Herzegovina but forced into a play-off with Romania due to a worse goal differential. With a 3–1 home win and the first goal away, Greece was on their way to Brazil and placed into group C with Colombia, Côte d'Ivoire and Japan. Their first game against Colombia highlighted some Greek weaknesses, and Ethniki were down a goal five minutes in and unable to come back; two second-half goals sealed the loss. Game two, against Japan, saw two sloppy tackles by Kostas Katsouranis and forced Greece to play down a man for much of the match. Fortunately for the Greeks, Japan was unable to truly threaten, and parity among every team in the group, save for Colombia, meant Ethniki still had a shot to advance with a win over Côte d'Ivoire.

After Greek substitute Andreas Samaris scored following a defensive giveaway by Côte d'Ivoire defender Cheick Tioté, the Greeks conceded an equalizer to Wilfried Bony in the 74th minute. Late in stoppage time, Georgios Samaras forced a decision out of referee Christian Lescano when he went to ground in the penalty box. His ensuing finish pushed Ethniki through to a round-of-16 matchup with a Costa Rican side known for defense. After conceding a goal against the run of play to Bryan Ruiz in the 52nd minute, an ill-advised Óscar Duarte tackle produced the player's second yellow. Greece was rewarded again late when a Sokratis Papastathopoulos goal in the 91st minute sent the game into penalties. A clinical finishing display by both teams was abruptly ended when Keylor Navas saved a Theofanis Gekas penalty to send Ethniki home in 13th place with three goals for and five against.

GUAITA, ENRIQUE. B. 11 July 1910, Lucas González, Argentina. D. 18 May 1959. Italy's 1934 World Cup–winning team included the Argentinean-born Enrique Guaita, who scored one goal in four appearances at the competition held in his adopted homeland. Guaita was one of four players in the Italian 1934 World Cup squad who had been born in and previously represented Argentina at the international level, in an era of looser rules on representing multiple nations, though it was an issue that caused considerable controversy for the players known as *oriundo*. Guaita had played for Argentina in 1933, only a year before switching to Italy in time for the 1934 World Cup, having moved to Italian club soccer to play for Roma. He made his debut for Italy in February 1934, scoring in a 4–2 defeat to Austria. He then played in Italy's successful World Cup qualifying game against Greece on 25 March 1934, the last occasion a host nation had to qualify for the World Cup. Guaita did not play in Italy's opening 1934 World Cup game, a 7–1 win over the United States, but played in Italy's final four games of the competition, scoring the winning goal in Italy's 1–0 semifinal defeat of Austria. Guaita returned to Argentina in 1936, playing for Racing Club and Estudiantes and representing his native country once again at the international level in 1937. He retired in 1940 and died at the young age of 48 in 1959.

GUIGUE, MAURICE. B. 8 April 1912, Arles, France. D. 27 February 2011. Frenchman Maurice Guigue was the referee for the sixth World Cup final, held in Stockholm,

Sweden. The second Frenchman to take charge of a World Cup final 20 years after the first, Georges Capdeville, had done so, he oversaw Pelé and Brazil's comprehensive defeat of the hosts Sweden 5–2. He did not issue any cautions in the final. Guigue became an international referee in 1954, taking charge of several European Cup games and World Cup qualifiers before being selected as a referee for the 1958 World Cup. Guigue took charge of three games at the group stage as well as the final, officiating Brazil's 3–0 win against Austria and their 2–0 victory over the Soviet Union, along with Northern Ireland's 2–1 defeat of Czechoslovakia. Guigue continued as an international referee until 1962, taking charge of numerous European Cup games as well as a 1961 World Cup qualifier between Scotland and Ireland.

H

HAITI. Commonly known as Les Grenadiers (The Grenadiers), Le Rouge et Bleu (The Red and Blue), or La Sélection Nationale (The National Selection). The country's first and only World Cup appearance was in 1974, where they lost all three games, including a 7–0 defeat to Poland. Their most recent achievement was in 2007 when they won the 2007 Caribbean Nations Cup.

HALLER, HELMUT. B. 21 July 1939, Augsburg, Germany. D. 11 October 2012. Appearing in three World Cup final tournaments for West Germany, Helmut Haller scored one of his six goals in the competition in the 1966 final, a losing effort for his country in a 4–2 defeat to hosts England at Wembley Stadium. By then, Haller was a star in the Italian league for Bologna at club level, having begun his career at local side FC Augsburg. He later went on to play for Juventus. Haller made his international debut at the age of 19 for West Germany against Denmark, scoring his first international goal nearly two years later in 1960 against Chile. He scored one goal in two World Cup qualifiers ahead of the 1962 World Cup in Chile. At the competition, Haller played in three games but did not score as West Germany was eliminated at the quarterfinal stage. The 1966 World Cup would be by far Haller's best tournament, as he struck twice in West Germany's emphatic opening game victory, 5–0 over Switzerland at Hillsborough Stadium in Sheffield. Haller played in West Germany's next game, a 0–0 tie with Argentina, but missed their final group game, a 2–1 win over Spain. Haller returned to Argentina's lineup for their quarterfinal against Uruguay, again at Hillsborough Stadium, on 23 July. He scored West Germany's first and last goals in a 4–0 win over the two-time World Cup champions, helping propel his team to the semifinal stage. There, at Goodison Park in Liverpool, Haller again started and scored the opening goal against the Soviet Union. Playing in a withdrawn-forward role, Haller received a long pass from Karl-Heinz Schnellinger in the penalty and struck it first time past Lev Yashin in the Soviet goal. Haller then helped West Germany score their second and decisive goal in a 2–1 win, setting up West German captain Franz Beckenbauer on the edge of the area for a finely struck long-distance goal. At Wembley Stadium for the final against England, Haller opened the scoring after only 12 minutes, finishing with a low drive from 12 yards out after a poor defensive clearance, though it was England who ended up 4–2 winners. Haller did not play for West Germany for almost three years following the 1966 World Cup, recalled in April 1969 for West Germany's 1970 World Cup qualifying campaign. He scored twice in three qualifiers, both against Cyprus in a 12–0 win. Haller started Germany's first game at the 1970 World Cup in Mexico against Morocco, but removed at halftime with an injury, he would not appear again in the World Cup or for West Germany internationally again. Haller recorded 13 goals in 33 games for West Germany, though his value was as much in his creative linkup play between midfield and forward as his goal scoring.

HAPPEL, ERNST. B. 29 November 1925, Vienna, Austria. D. 14 November 1992. Ernst Happel is one of the most successful managers of all time, following an excellent playing career with an outstanding coaching record in several countries. As a player, he participated on the Austria team that reached the FIFA World Cup semifinals in 1954. As a manager, Happel won 17 titles with 10 different club and international sides, including winning the European Cup with both Feyenoord in 1970 and Hamburg in 1983. As an international manager, he took the Netherlands to the 1978 World Cup final, where they lost to Argentina, and finally took over his native Austria in 1991 but died the next year of cancer. The largest stadium in Austria was renamed the Ernst-Happel-Stadion in his honor following his death.

HERBERGER, JOSEPH "SEPP." B. 28 March 1897, Mannheim, Germany. D. 28 April 1977. Joseph Herberger, better known as Sepp, was a German player and manager best known for coaching West Germany to victory in the 1954 FIFA World Cup, a seminal event in the history of postwar West Germany. Herberger ran the West German national team for 28 years, spanning the prewar and reconstruction eras from 1936 to 1964. A former amateur player who played three times for the German national team in the early 1920s, Herberger studied for a coaching diploma and worked for four years in the early 1930s at the West Germany Sports Association. He took over the West German team in 1936. Known as an authoritative and disciplined coach, his first major tournament was not a success as the joint Austro-German team (following the annexation of Austria by Nazi Germany) he managed fell in the first round of the 1938 World Cup in France.

The Second World War then ended international play for Germany for over a decade, with Herberger renamed as national team coach of the western side of the divided nation in 1950. Herberger had to build the West Germany team from scratch, playing their first postwar international friendly later that year, and headed to Switzerland for the 1954 World Cup as outsiders. They were crushed 8–3 by the world's most feared team, Hungary, in their second game, as Herberger surprisingly rested several key players. But led by legendary captain Fritz Walter, Herberger's decision paid off as his rested players saw off Turkey 7–2 in the decisive final group game and then reached the final to face Hungary again in the Swiss city of Bern: despite going down 2–0 early on to the favored Hungarians, the Germans came back through goals from Max Morlock and Helmut Rahn, with Rahn scoring again in the dying minutes to make West Germany world champions for the first time. Herberger would forever be immortalized as the orchestrator of what became known in West Germany as the "Miracle of Bern," and the victory would be seen as a key cultural healing moment for West German society in the postwar reconstruction era.

HONDURAS. Commonly known as Los Catrachos. Honduras made its first appearance in the World Cup in 1982. Coached by Jose de la Paz, the Hondurans went 0-2-1 and failed to advance to the second round. In the group stage, the Hondurans faced European giant Spain in their first game. Although the Central Americans took the early lead in the 7th minute on a Héctor Zelaya goal, Honduras conceded a penalty in the 65th minute, and the game ended in a 1–1 tie. The Hondurans' second game of the tournament was against Northern Ireland, and it, too, would finish 1–1. Northern Ireland scored first, but Honduras came back to tie it when Eduardo Laing scored in the 60th minute. Just a few days later, Honduras faced Yugoslavia in their final game of the first round but failed to come away with a victory. Going into the final minutes, it looked like the Hondurans would yet again earn a point, only to lose 0–1 after Yugoslavia scored on a penalty in the 88th minute. With only two points from the group stage, Honduras finished last in their group and was knocked out of the tournament.

Honduras had to wait 28 years before their next appearance in a World Cup. Yet in 2010, under Colombian coach Reinaldo Rueda, they returned to the tournament. In the group stage, Honduras first faced Chile and came away with a 0–1 loss. Their next match was against eventual champions Spain, whose intricate passing style proved to be too much for the Hondurans as they fell 0–2. Their final game was against Switzerland. The Hondurans failed to score a single goal in the entire group stage as they came away with a 0–0 tie and a disappointing showing in the tournament.

Just four years later, Honduras finished atop their group in the third round of CONCACAF qualifying, including a historical win at Azteca over Mexico, to qualify for their third-ever World Cup in 2014. With a world ranking just outside of the top 32 and placed in group E with Switzerland, Ecuador and France, Los Catrachos was seen as an underdog in their group. In their opening group game, Honduras battled with a talented French side. What looked like a great start unraveled when Wilson Palacios was issued his second yellow for a sloppy tackle in the box late in the first half. With Karim Benzema finishing the ensuing penalty and Honduras conceding an early second-half Noel Valladares own goal, their first win remained out of reach. Benzema finished the scoring in the 72nd minute with a blast into the roof of the net. Game two saw Los Catrachos go up in the 31st minute following poor Ecuadorian defending on a long through ball and a brilliant strike by Carlos Costly, but Enner Valencia equalized just three minutes later and then scored the game-winning header off a free kick in the 65th. With zero points and only one goal after the first two games, Honduras faced sixth-ranked Switzerland at the Arena Amazônia in Manaus. A hat trick by Xherdan Shaqiri, the first coming in the sixth minute, means Honduras will have to wait at least another four years before their first World Cup win as they again finished last in their group, this time in 31st place with only one goal scored and eight conceded.

HONG MYUNG-BO. B. 12 February 1969, Seoul, South Korea. Hong Myung-bo is regarded as among the greatest Asian players of all time, playing 136 times for the Republic of Korea and appearing at four consecutive FIFA World Cup competitions, in 1990, 1994, 1998 and 2002. The 2002 tournament was the apex of Hong's career, as he led the joint hosts to a semifinal place and fourth-place finish in the competition. Hong, a consistent and commanding defender, played much of his career for Pohang Steelers, before ending his career in the United States playing for the Los Angeles Galaxy and retiring in 2004.

HÜGI, SEPP. B. 23 January 1930, Riehen, Switzerland. D. 16 April 1995. At the age of 24, Sepp Hügi scored six goals at the 1954 World Cup in his native Switzerland for his county. That made Hügi the joint second leading scorer at the competition, behind Sándor Kocsis, who scored a remarkable 11 goals, and tied with Austria's Erich Probst and West German Max Morlock. Hügi had made his name in the early 1950s playing for FC Basel in the Swiss league, and he would go on to score 244 goals in 320 games for the club. At the 1954 World Cup, Hügi began his World Cup finals career in spectacular fashion by scoring the winning goal in an impressive 2–1 triumph for Switzerland over Italy in Lausanne on 17 June. Switzerland's next game was a disappointment, a 2–0 defeat to England on a sweltering day in Bern, but Hügi then proved to be the difference maker in a play-off against Italy for qualification to the quarterfinal stage: he scored twice in a 4–1 win for the host nation. There would be a hat trick for Hügi in his next game, but in a bizarre seesaw game, Switzerland scored five yet was still eliminated as Austria scored seven in Lausanne on 26 June. Hügi did not play again at the World Cup, taking part in both of his country's failed 1958 and 1962 World Cup qualification attempts.

HUNGARY. Commonly known as the Magical Magyars. Between 1930 and 1986, Hungary enjoyed one of the strongest records in the World Cup, appearing in 9 out of 12 competitions and twice finishing as runners-up. However, Hungary has failed to qualify for a World Cup competition since 1986, the nation's glorious years as a world soccer powerhouse long in the rearview mirror. Hungary's first appearance came in 1934 in Italy, reaching the quarterfinals and knocked out by Austria with a 2–1 defeat. Four years later, at the World Cup in France, Hungary went on an inspired run led by the team's captain György Sárosi, defeating the Dutch East Indies, Switzerland and Sweden to reach the final. In Paris, Hungary fell 4–2 to Italy, the Hungarian goals coming from Sárosi and Pál Titkos.

Following World War II, Hungary did not enter the 1950 World Cup but, by the time the 1954 World Cup in Switzerland rolled around, had become a strong favorite for the title, based off the remarkable "Magical Magyars" team built around the out-standing talent of Ferenc Puskás and coached by the tactical genius Gusztáv Sebes, who had the Hungarians playing a style of fluid soccer few opponents could cope with. Hungary tore through the group stage with a 9–0 drubbing of South Korea and an 8–3 win over West Germany. In the quarterfinals, the Hungarians then tossed aside Brazil 4–2, with goals from Nándor Hidegkuti, Mihály Lantos and two from Sándor Kocsis. The semifinals again saw Hungary defeat South American opposition 4–2, though the defending world champions Uruguay took Puskás's team to extra time before Kocsis twice found the net. The final in Bern was supposed to be the crowning moment for Hungary against an unfancied West German team. Puskás was not fully fit but played anyway and scored after six minutes; Zoltán Czibor added a second for Hungary two minutes later, and victory seemed inevitable for Sebes's men. However, West Germany then struck twice in 10 minutes to equalize the scores, and Hungary could not find the net again. One of the biggest upsets in World Cup history came when West Germany claimed victory following a winning goal by Helmut Rahn six minutes from the end of the game.

At the 1958 World Cup in Sweden, Hungary did not advance past the first round, losing in a play-off game to Wales after the teams had finished level following the first three group games. In both 1962 and 1966, Hungary reached the quarterfinals in Chile and England, losing to Czechoslovakia and the Soviet Union respectively, despite still featuring wonderful talent including István Nagy and Flórián Albert. Hungary's golden era, though, was coming to a close. The Hungarians did not qualify for the 1970 or 1974 World Cups and crashed out at the first-round stage in 1978, 1982 and 1986, failing to qualify for another World Cup finals since.

HURST, GEOFF. B. 8 December 1941, Ashton-under-Lyne, England. The only man to score a hat trick in a World Cup final, England's Geoff Hurst struck the critical goals as the Three Lions defeated West Germany 4–2 in the 1966 final at Wembley Stadium in London. Hurst's inclusion in the team had been controversial, with long-time prolific forward Jimmy Greaves missing out in the latter stages of the competition, but his goals put to rest any potential complaints. Hurst scored the winning goal for England against Argentina in the quarterfinals before his heroics in the final, though his second goal remains controversial to this day, with his shot having struck the underside of the crossbar and bounced onto the line, even though it was ruled a goal by the officials. Hurst appeared again at the 1970 World Cup, scoring once against Romania, and ended his international career with 24 goals in 49 games with England.

I

INTERNATIONAL STADIUM YOKOHAMA. Opened in 1997, International Stadium Yokohama is located around four miles north of Yokohama's downtown. Yokohama itself is a major commercial city located on Tokyo Bay, Japan's second-largest city. International Stadium Yokohama was opened in 1998, and its most prominent day in the global spotlight came on 30 June 2002, when it hosted the 12th World Cup final, contested between Brazil and Germany, with the South Americans winning 2–0. An official attendance of 69,029 was recorded for the game. International Stadium Yokohama hosted three other games at the 2002 World Cup, a competition jointly hosted by Japan and South Korea, all during the group stage of the competition. International Stadium Yokohama was the venue for Japan's second game of the competition on 9 June, a 1–0 win for the hosts over Russia in front of a partisan crowd numbering 66,108. On 11 June, Yokohama hosted Saudi Arabia's 2–0 defeat to the Republic of Ireland, 65,320 in attendance. On 13 June, Ecuador beat Croatia with 65,862 present at International Stadium Yokohama. Ringed by a running track as it was built with a Japanese bid for the Olympic Games in mind, International Stadium Yokohama was opened in March 1998 and is the permanent home for club team Yokohama Marinos in Japan's top division, the J-League. It is the largest stadium in Japan. Before the 2002 World Cup, it hosted the semifinal and final of the warm-up tournament, the FIFA Confederations Cup. Following the World Cup, International Stadium Yokohama has been a frequently used venue for high-profile international club tournaments, first the Intercontinental Cup from 2002 to 2004 and then the FIFA Club World Cup on six occasions between 2005 and 2012.

IRAN. Commonly known as Team Melli (The National Team). The Iranian national team has qualified for the World Cup four times, in 1978, 1998, 2006 and 2014. In Iran's first-ever appearance in the World Cup, they were grouped with Peru, the Netherlands and Scotland for the first round. Their first game was against the Netherlands, who would go on to finish second in the tournament. Conceding two penalties and another goal during the run of play, the Iranians lost 0–3. Their next game—against Scotland—resulted in a 1–1 tie in which the Iranians were unfortunate not to earn a win. Scotland scored first but only from an own goal by Iranian Andranik Eskandarian. Iraj Danayfar brought his team level in the 60th minute. The Iranians fell apart in their following game against Peru, as they conceded two penalties en route to a 4–1 defeat.

Twenty years later, the Iranian national team returned to the World Cup in France in 1998 after winning a tight play-off series with Australia. Coached by Jalal Talebi, the Iranians earned their first World Cup victory against the United States on 21 June 1998. In spite of the notable political tensions between the two countries, the teams presented one another with gifts before kickoff. Goals from Hamid Estili and Mehdi Mahdavikia would prove to be enough as Iran beat the U.S. 2–1. The Iranians failed to earn any additional points in the group stage, losing to Yugoslavia 0–1 and Germany 0–2.

Although Iran did not qualify for the 2002 World Cup, they were back in 2006 for the World Cup in Germany. Their first match was against Mexico, but in spite of a 1–1 score going into halftime, the Iranians would end up losing the game 1–3. Iran faced eventual fourth-place finishers Portugal in the following game. Outshot 18 to 5 and conceding 13 corner kicks to the Portuguese, Iran fell to a score of 2–0. Already eliminated from the tournament, Iran still put in a valiant effort in their third game against Angola, finishing in a 1–1 tie.

Inner turmoil and a struggle to find the right manager found Iran finishing fourth in their qualifying group and out of the 2010 World Cup in South Africa. Under former Portugal and Manchester United manager Carlos Queiroz, qualifying for the 2014 World Cup proved to be easier. Team Melli finished atop their group in each round and secured a berth in Brazil. Iran was placed in group F with Argentina, Bosnia and Herzegovina and Nigeria, and any win would be seen as a success.

After an opening group game against Nigeria ended in a 0–0 draw due to the disciplined and organized Iranian defense, Team Melli had hope going into their next game, against powerhouse Argentina. Played at Estádio Mineirão in Belo Horizonte, Iran put together another strong defensive effort, and had it not been for the fingers of Sergio Romero and a controversial non-call in the Argentinian box, Iran may have pulled off one of the biggest World Cup upsets. Instead, after Iran gave Lionel Messi space for the first time in the game, Messi scored in the 91st minute off a beautiful left-footed shot into the side netting for the Argentine win.

Needing a decisive win in game three against Bosnia and Herzegovina, Iran went down a goal early when Edin Džeko rifled a low screamer from the 18 off the post in the 23rd minute. After the break, the Dragons struck again, this time taking advantage of a rare Iranian defensive error and some superb playmaking to find Miralem Pjanić in the 60th minute. Iran's Reza Ghoochannejhad's goal in the 82nd minute gave Iran life, but a quick counter by Avdija Vršajević a minute later sealed a Dragon win and sent Iran home in 28th place with only one goal scored and four conceded.

IRAQ. Commonly known as the Lions of Mesopotamia. The Iraqi national team made its World Cup finals debut in 1986. The team played well in the group stage, narrowly losing to Paraguay 1–0 in their first match. Iraq scored their first World Cup goal against Belgium in the second game but still came up short, losing 2–1. In Iraq's third game, against Mexico, they had to settle for yet another 1–0 loss, and they were eliminated from the tournament.

Under the Olympic committee leadership of Uday Hussein, 1990–1999 saw a very dark time in Iraqi football and the national team failed to qualify for the 1990, 1994 and 1998 tournaments. After Hussein's ousting, Iraqi football returned to respectability, but despite winning the 2004 AFC Team of the Year award, a gold medal in the 2005 West Asian games and a 2007 AFC Asian Cup title, the Lions have yet to qualify for another World Cup tournament.

IRELAND. *See* REPUBLIC OF IRELAND.

IRIARTE, VICTORIANO. B. 2 November 1902, Montevideo, Uruguay. D. 10 November 1968. Participating in all four of Uruguay's games in their World Cup–winning campaign at the inaugural competition in 1930, Victoriano Iriarte scored two goals to contribute to his country's victory on home soil. Both of his goals came in the knockout stage, one in Uruguay's 6–1 win over Yugoslavia in the semifinal and one in the 4–2 defeat of Argentina in the final. The latter gave Uruguay the lead in the 68th minute, one they held on to, thus making Iriarte the first player to score the winning goal in a World Cup final. A left-sided attacking player, Iriarte played at club level for Racing Club de Montevideo.

ISRAEL. Commonly known as Ha Khoolim Levanim (The Blues and Whites). Israel has played just once in the World Cup, the 1970 competition held in Mexico. Grouped with Italy, Uruguay and Sweden, the Israelis managed a fairly respectable two points from their three games. Although they lost their opening game 2–0 against Uruguay, the team held strong in their remaining two games, tying Sweden 1–1 and Italy 0–0, but it wasn't enough to advance to the next round.

As a result of a proposal by Kuwait to exclude them from AFC competitions, Israel played mostly in Europe during the 1980s and competed in the European stage of qualification for the 1982 FIFA World Cup. For the 1986 and 1990 tournaments, Israel played in Oceania's qualification stage where their best result was an advancement to the CONMEBOL-OFC play-offs where they lost on a 1–0 aggregate to Colombia. In 1991, Israeli clubs began competing in Europe and officially, in 1994, Israel became a full member of UEFA. They have seen sporadic results but have still yet to qualify for another World Cup.

ITALY. Commonly known as Azzurri (The Blues) or La Nazionale (The National Team). Only Brazil has won more World Cup titles than Italy, whose triumphs in 1934, 1938, 1982 and 2006 place them one championship behind the South American's five. The Italians have also appeared in all but two World Cups, not entering the inaugural 1930 competition and failing to qualify for the 1958 World Cup. Italy hosted the second competition in 1934, with Benito Mussolini's regime aiming to take advantage of a global spotlight for propaganda purposes. Games were hosted in eight host cities, broadcast live via radio around Europe. Mussolini demanded victory from a strong Italian team coached by the authoritarian Vittorio Pozzo, who fielded a handful of key South Americans of Italian origin, including Luisito Monti and Raimundo Orsi. The Italians began the single-elimination tournament by crushing the United States 7–1 and then defeated Spain 1–0 in a reply following a 1–1 tie, Giuseppe Meazza scoring the winning goal. In the semifinal, Italy faced Austria, the "Wunderteam" many saw as the Italians' main competition for the title. Pozzo's men claimed victory in a tight, tense game 1–0, thanks to a strike by Enrique Guaita in the

19th minute. The final in Rome with Czechoslovakia did not at first go to plan for the host nation, a long shot from Antonín Puč giving the Czechs the lead with 20 minutes to go. But Italy forced extra time due to a goal by Orsi and, in the additional period, won the game and the world title through Angelo Schiavio's winner.

In France four years later, under the shadow of impending war in Europe, the Italians successfully defended their title. Pozzo again led Italy to victory, with four stars returning from 1934 alongside newcomers such as the gifted forward Silvio Piola. The Azzurri began with a 2–1 victory over Norway, the winning goal scored by Piola in extra time. The host nation, France, proved to be no match for Pozzo's men in the quarterfinal, dismissed 3–1 in Paris, and Italy then defeated Brazil in the semifinal, with goals from Gino Colaussi and Giuseppe Meazza. In the final, Italy faced a strong Hungarian team who were ultimately overwhelmed 4–2, the Italian goals scored by a pair of strikes from Colaussi and Piola. Italy had become the first team to successfully defend the World Cup.

Following World War II, Italy's national team took decades to regain the heights it had struck in the 1930s. The Azzurri exited at the group stage in 1950 and 1954, failed to qualify for the World Cup in 1958 and then did not advance past the first round in either 1962 or 1966. Finally, in 1970 at the World Cup in Mexico, Italian soccer reached the pinnacle of the world game again, as the team coached by Ferruccio Valcareggi built on the strength of Italian club soccer seen by the continental achievements of the likes of Inter Milan reach the final. The Azzurri team was built around a strong defense marshaled by Giacinto Facchetti and a midfield predicated on the playmaking ability of Gigi Riva. The Italians advanced past the first round for the first time since 1938, defeating Sweden and earning ties with Uruguay and Israel to top group two. In the elimination stage, Italy suddenly clicked offensively, scoring four each time in wins over host nation Mexico in the quarterfinal and against West Germany in the semifinal. In the final, however, the Italians' attempt to slam the defensive door shut on a vibrant Brazilian team proved to be a total failure, losing 4–1 to Pelé's outstanding team.

In 1974, Italy did not advance past the group stage at the World Cup in West Germany but did in Argentina in 1978, an Azzurri team led by head coach Enzo Bearzot off the field and by goalkeeper and captain Dino Zoff on it. The Italians won all three games in the group stage, beating Argentina, France and Hungary. In the second group stage, with the winner headed to the final, Italy came in second after a 0–0 tie with West Germany, a 1–0 win over Austria and a 2–1 defeat to the Netherlands that sent the Dutch on at Italian expense. In the third-place play-off, Italy again fell to Brazil, losing 2–1.

The World Cup returned to Europe in 1982, held in Spain, but Italy entered the World Cup under the shadow of the Totonero gambling scandal in Italian domestic soccer in 1980, which saw stars such as forward Paolo Rossi banned from the game. Rossi only returned to play just in time for the World Cup and, along with the rest of the team, seemed sluggish in the opening group stage, scraping on to the next stage only after three ties, scoring only twice. In the second group stage, though, an Italian team fired by a suddenly red-hot Rossi advanced to the final following a 2–1 win over Argentina and a 3–2 victory against Brazil, Rossi claiming a hat trick in the latter game. In the semifinal with Poland, Rossi scored twice more for a 2–0 win in Barcelona. Italy claimed a third World Cup title on 11 July in Madrid, defeating West Germany 3–1 thanks to strikes by Rossi, Marco Tardelli and Alessandro Altobelli.

Qualifying automatically for the 1986 World Cup as the champions, Italy exited at the second-round stage, losing 2–0 to France. In 1990, Italy again qualified automatically as the host nation, welcoming the competition for the second time, with 24 teams playing in 12 host cities. Coached by Azeglio Vicini, Italy featured a typically strong defense with Franco Baresi, Paolo Maldini, Riccardo Ferri and captain Giuseppe Bergomi on the back line and Walter Zenga in goal. The Azzurri advanced through the group stage with three wins and without conceding a goal, defeating Austria and the United States 1–0, and beating Czechoslovakia 2–0. In the second round in Rome, goals by Salvatore Schillaci and Aldo Serena helped the Italians to a 2–0 win over Uruguay, and in the quarterfinal, Schillaci struck again in a 1–0 victory against the Republic of Ireland. Heartbreak came for the Italians in the semifinal against Diego Maradona's Argentina, however. Though Schillaci scored again on his way to winning the Golden Boot, an equalizer by Claudio Caniggia forced the game to extra time and ultimately penalty kicks. Though Baresi, Roberto Baggio and Luigi De Agostini scored the first three Italian penalties, misses by Roberto Donadoni and Serena sent the Italians out. A third-place play-off game in Bari was little consolation, but Italy did at least claim third place following a 2–1 victory over England.

At the 1994 World Cup in the United States, Italy went one better and reached the final, losing there to Brazil. Coached by Arrigo Sacchi, the Italians—led by the creative fulcrum Roberto Baggio in midfield—started off the competition disastrously, slumping to a surprising 1–0 defeat to the Republic of Ireland. Italy recovered with a 1–0 win over Norway, and a 1–1 tie against Mexico allowed the Azzurri to squeak through to the next round in third place in group E as one of the best third-place finishers. In Boston for the second round, Italy seemed primed to exit against Nigeria, who led 1–0 from the 25th to the 88th minute, when Roberto Baggio found an invaluable equalizer. In extra time, Baggio scored again with a penalty to send Italy to the quarterfinals. There, against Spain, a goal by Dino Baggio (no relation to Roberto) gave Italy a lead in the first half, Spain striking back in the 58th minute. Roberto Baggio found the winner once more in the 88th minute. In the semifinal, Baggio's brilliant run of form continued as he scored twice in a 2–1 win over Bulgaria. A seemingly dream final against Brazil in Southern California turned out to be an insipid game, with a few chances in a scoreless game that became the first World Cup final to be decided on penalty kicks. Italy's efforts began poorly with captain Franco Baresi missing his strike, and when Roberto Baggio ballooned Italy's fifth kick over the crossbar, Brazil claimed victory.

In France in 1998, Italy advanced to the quarterfinal stage after topping group A, tying with Chile and beating Cameroon and Austria and winning 1–0 over Norway in the second round, Christian Vieri scoring the lone goal. For the second successive competition, Italy went out on penalty kicks, losing in the quarterfinals to France after a 0–0 tie. The Azzurri did not enjoy a particularly impressive run at the 2002 World Cup in South Korea and Japan, only winning once in the group stage before losing in the second round to South Korea 2–1, the winning goal coming from Ahn Jung-Hwan.

Four years later in Germany, expectations for a relatively old Italian team captained by Fabio Cannavaro and orchestrated by deft playmaker Andrea Pirlo in midfield were low, especially as Italian soccer had recently been struck by another match-fixing scandal. Italy won group D in the opening stage, beating Ghana and the Czech Republic while tying with the United States, and then snuck past Australia in the second round with a goal by Christian Vieri deep into stoppage time of a previously scoreless game. In the quarterfinal, the Italian team coached by veteran Marcello Lippi brushed past Ukraine 3–0, two goals by Luca Toni and one from Gianluca Zambrotta, and then faced Germany in the semifinal. In Dortmund against the host nation, 119 minutes of scoreless action were suddenly transformed by two rapid Italian goals that propelled Lippi's men to the final, Fabio Grosso and Alessandro Del Piero both scoring at the tail end of extra time as a penalty shoot-out loomed. A dramatic final against France in Berlin followed. Zinedine Zidane scored after only 7 minutes for the French, though the Azzurri equalized 12 minutes later through a header by Marco Materazzi from a Pirlo corner. In extra time, Zidane was sent off for headbutting Materazzi, and the game went to a penalty shoot-out. This time, there was joy for the Italians, winning the shoot-out 5–3, with Pirlo, Materazzi, Daniele De Rossi, Del Piero and Grosso all making good on their kicks. For the fourth time, Italy lifted the World Cup.

There was disappointment for the defending champions at the 2010 World Cup in South Africa. Still coached by Marcello Lippi, the Italians failed to win a game in the group stage, tying 1–1 with both Paraguay and New Zealand and losing 3–2 to Slovakia, resulting in elimination at the first stage.

Under new manager Cesare Prandelli, qualification for the 2014 World Cup in Brazil came easy for the Azzurri, and they rolled through their group undefeated, securing a trip to their 14th consecutive World Cup finals with two group games left. Confidence in the team's chances of advancing out of group D with England, Uruguay and Costa Rica was high going into their opening game in Brazil. A game-one matchup with perennial powerhouse England in the heat and humidity of Manaus reinforced the beliefs of the faithful as goals by Claudio Marchisio and "Super Mario" Balotelli bookended a Daniel Sturridge goal for a 2–1 win. In game two, against a Costa Rican side known for its defense, Italy proved to be outclassed. With a favor in possession and control of the match in the first half, Los Ticos took the lead when Júnior Díaz crossed a beautiful ball into a streaking Bryan Ruiz at the far post for the eventual game winner. Needing a win against Uruguay in a game Prandelli called "the most important match of my professional career," Italy not only lost Marchisio to a red card for a studs-up tackle but also the match on a controversial goal in the 81st minute by Diego Godín. Though the goal itself was not controversial, it was Luis Suárez's biting of Italian defender Giorgio Chiellini (arguably one of the strangest moments in World Cup finals history) that caused confusion and a lack of focus for the Italians. Though Suárez was suspended by FIFA for nine games and four months from anything soccer related, this meant little to the Italians, who were sent home in 22nd place with two goals scored and three conceded.

IVANOV, VALENTIN. B. 4 July 1961, Moscow, Soviet Union. D. 8 November 2011. A star forward for the superb Soviet Union teams of the 1950s and 1960s, Valentin Ivanov scored five goals in nine games at the 1958 and 1962 World Cups. Born in Moscow, Ivanov played his entire club career for local team Torpedo Moscow, registering 124 goals in 286 games for the club between 1952 and 1966, one of the leading scorers in the history of the Soviet league. His speed and skill from an inside-forward position quickly led him to the Soviet national team and played a key role on their victorious 1956 Olympic Games Football Tournament team, scoring one goal in four games. This cemented Ivanov's place in the team for the 1958 World Cup held in Sweden. At that competition, Ivanov scored one goal in five games, helping the Soviet Union reach the quarterfinal stage, where they were eliminated by hosts Sweden. His sole goal came against Austria in the group-round stage. Four years later, Ivanov finished as the joint top scorer at the 1962 World Cup in Chile. His four goals led the competition alongside Flórián Albert of Hungary, Dražan Jerković of Yugoslavia, Leonel Sánchez of Chile and Brazil's Vava and Garrincha. All of Ivanov's goals came in the first-round group stage: one against Yugoslavia, two against Colombia and one against Uruguay. He did not score against Chile as the Soviets were eliminated at the quarterfinal stage once again. Ivanov did not play in another World Cup, though he took part in the qualification campaign for the 1966 World Cup in England. Ivanov did claim a major international title in 1960, as the Soviet Union won the inaugural European Championship, scoring twice in the two games of the final stage, and then helped the Soviets reach the final of the same competition again four years later, losing to hosts Spain in the final. Following his retirement from playing, Ivanov spent most of his later career coaching Torpedo Moscow, winning the Soviet championship in 1976.

IVORY COAST. *See* CÔTE D'IVOIRE.

J

JACQUET, AIMÉ. B. 27 November 1941, Sail-sous-Couzan, France. Aimé Jacquet is a French coach and former player. He was the manager of the France national team when they won the 1998 FIFA World Cup, the country's first triumph in the tournament. Previously an assistant coach with the national team, Jacquet took over as head coach of France following the country's failure to qualify for the 1994 FIFA World Cup. He led the country to the semifinals of the 1996 UEFA European Football Championship, where they lost in a penalty shoot-out to the Czech Republic. In the buildup to the 1998 FIFA World Cup, to be held in France itself, Jacquet received considerable media criticism for his perpetual lineup changes. However, once the tournament began in June 1998, a French team inspired by midfielder Zinedine Zidane swept through the first-round group stage. They then beat Paraguay in the second round, Italy in the quarterfinal through a penalty shoot-out and Croatia by two goals to one to meet Brazil in the final. There, Jacquet's team controlled the game from the start, easily beating the surprisingly subdued defending World Cup champions 3–0. Following the 1998 FIFA World Cup, Jacquet stepped down as head coach, taking on a role as France's technical director until 2006, overseeing a further international title win for France at the 2000 UEFA European Football Championship.

JAIRZINHO. B. 25 December 1944, Rio de Janeiro, Brazil. Born as Jair Ventura Filho but universally known as Jairzinho, he was an outstanding force for Brazil's national team from 1964 to 1982. He played a total of 81 games for his country, scoring 33 goals and establishing himself as a winger with the ability to beat defenders with ease and contribute both goals and assists. Jairzinho starred in Brazil's legendary 1970 FIFA World Cup triumph, scoring in every game of the tournament with a total of seven goals to his credit. He also appeared for Brazil at the 1966 and 1974 World Cup finals tournaments. At club level, Jairzinho played most of his career for Botafogo. He retired in 1982. *See also* PELÉ.

JAMAICA. Commonly known as the Reggae Boyz. In 1998, Jamaica became the third Caribbean nation to appear at the World Cup, following Cuba in 1938 and Haiti in 1974 (in 2006, Trinidad and Tobago became the fourth). Jamaica became the first team from the English-speaking former British West Indies to qualify for the World Cup. Soccer gained popularity in Jamaica in the late 19th century, and before its independence in 1962, Jamaica played a series of friendly representative games against fellow Caribbean nations and visiting teams from elsewhere. Jamaica immediately joined FIFA after becoming an independent nation, joining the CONCACAF confederation. They attempted to qualify for the 1966, 1970, 1974 and 1978 World Cups but failed on each occasion. Jamaica was not even able to attempt to qualify for the 1982 or 1986 World Cups due to financial problems. The 1990s, though, saw a new dawn for Jamaican soccer: the "Reggae Boyz," as the men's national team became known as, became far more competitive internationally. With most of the team coming from the black working classes in a sport particularly popular in Jamaica's urban townships, the Reggae Boyz became a symbol for national progress as they qualified for the 1998 World Cup in France by claiming the third and final CONCACAF qualifying spot behind Mexico and the United States. Jamaica's 1998 team was coached by popular Brazilian René Simões, who worked to combine both well-paid English-based Jamaican professionals with homegrown semiprofessional players, a difficult task but one his charismatic approach achieved. Jamaica's team included well-known players such as Frank Sinclair of Chelsea, Deon Burton of Derby County and Marcus Gayle of Wimbledon. Veteran domestic-based goalkeeper Warren Barrett was made captain.

Jamaica's opponents in group H were a difficult trio of Argentina, Croatia and Japan. Jamaica first faced Croatia, who would ultimately finish third in the competition, in Lens on 14 June. Croatia peppered Jamaica's goal with shots early on, though the Reggae Boyz gave Croatia a scare on the counterattack, with a shot cleared off the line. Croatia broke through in the 27th minute, Mario Stanić scoring following a rebound off the crossbar. Croatia struck the crossbar again only minutes later, but Jamaica continued to push forward, and right before halftime, Ricardo Gardener swung in an inch-perfect left-footed cross for Wimbledon's Robbie Earle to thump home a header with and make it 1–1. Jamaica had succeeded in one of their targets for the tournament as a first-time participant in scoring a goal. In the second half, Croatia took the lead somewhat fortuitously, when Robert Prosinečki's intended cross swerved directly into the top corner in unstoppable fashion. Jamaica missed a fine chance to equalize when Deon Burton headed wide from close range, but Croatia confirmed their victory when striker Davor Šuker was given far too much time in the penalty area and his shot took a wicked deflection past Barrett. A week later, in Paris at Parc des Princes, Jamaica gave a much poorer account of themselves in a dismal 5–0 defeat to Argentina, Ariel Ortega scoring two and Gabriel Batistuta three in a battering that eliminated Jamaica from the World Cup. Yet the Caribbean nation still had one group game remaining and an opportunity to return home with pride. Their opponents Japan had lost to both Croatia and Argentina, 1–0 on both occasions, and were themselves also eliminated. The two teams met in Lyon on 26 June, and it was Jamaica who struck first in the 29th minute, Theodore Whitmore pouncing on a loose ball in the penalty area and converting the chance. Whitmore scored his and Jamaica's second 10 minutes into the second half, an excellent individual effort ending with a low drive. Japan pulled one back through Masashi Nakayama, but Jamaica held on for a 2–1 win, returning home having perhaps exceeded expectations by securing their first-ever World Cup win. Jamaica has not qualified for the World Cup since 1998; for the 2002 World Cup in Japan and South Korea, Jamaica was eliminated after finishing fifth in the final round of CONCACAF qualifying. In 2006, results for the Caribbean nation were even worse, eliminated in the third round of qualifying after winning only one of six games in the group stage. In 2010, Jamaica was eliminated at the same stage, though only due to having a poorer goal differential than Mexico after winning three of their six games. In 2014, Jamaica made it past the third round of qualification, finishing second in their group behind the United States, but the Boyz found themselves eliminated after finishing in the sixth and final position in the final round.

JAPAN. Commonly known as Samurai Blues. Though the country did not qualify for its first World Cup until as late as 1998, it has since appeared in each edition for a total of five appearances, reaching the last 16 of the competition in both 2002 and 2010. The former competition was also hosted by Japan jointly with South Korea, the first time the World Cup was held in Asia. Soccer began to be organized on a nationwide scale in Japan during the 1920s, with its governing body, the Japan Football Association, affiliating to FIFA in 1929. It did not appear at any of the pre–World War II tournaments held and was—along with Germany—banned from taking part in the first post–World War II World Cup held in 1950. Japan took part in qualifying for the 1954 World Cup but fell to a comprehensive defeat by South Korea, 7–3 on aggregate over two games, both held in Tokyo. Japan only attempted to qualify one more time before 1970, for the 1962 World Cup in Chile, and again Japan was no match for South Korea, losing both games in a two-game series played in Seoul and Tokyo. From 1970 to 1994, Japan entered Asian qualifying but failed to advance to the final tournament. Japan fell at the final hurdle in 1986 qualifying, losing once again to South Korea, this time in a closer matchup, 3–1 on aggregate over two games. The formation of the professional J-League in Japan in 1992 improved greatly the opportunities for national team players to develop at a high level domestically, and this soon bore fruit internationally. For the 1994 World Cup, Japan again just missed out on qualifying through the final-round group stage of the Asian section, missing out to South Korea on goal difference. Japan's qualification for the 1998 World Cup was thus a historic event and one that they achieved the hard way. Finishing second behind South Korea in group B of the final round of Asian qualifying, Japan advanced to a play-off with Iran to claim Asia's final direct qualification spot to the World Cup. Japan clinched victory in the most dramatic way possible in a single game play-off held on neutral ground, at Larkin Stadium in Malaysia. With the score tied 2–2, the game went to extra time, and Japan sealed their passage to France via a sudden-death "Golden Goal," Masayuki Okano scoring in the 118th minute from eight yards, directing a rebound from the goalkeeper into the net. At the 1998 World Cup in France, Japan was placed into group H, alongside two-time champions Argentina and fellow World Cup newcomers Croatia and Jamaica. Japan's team was drawn entirely from the J-League, with the largest contingent of players drawn from Yokohama Mariners. Japan's coach was Takeshi Okada, a former Japanese international who had taken over the team in 1997, with little prior coaching experience.

Japan's first game was on 14 June in Toulouse at Stade Municipal against Argentina, the South Americans heavy favorites. Japan started brightly, though, and though Argentina scored in the first half through Gabriela Batistuta—a lucky bobble leaving him one-on-one with goalkeeper, Yoshikatsu Kawaguchi, whom he deftly chipped—a 1–0 defeat could easily have been a draw as Japan came close to scoring in the dying seconds. Japan next faced Croatia, six days later, and again fell 1–0 while performing admirably. Croatia, who would eventually finish in third place, had the better of the chances, though Japan had their share too, 20-year-old forward Masashi Nakayama forcing a superb one-handed save from Dražen Ladić in the Croatian goal. Japan's defense held firm until the 77th minute when Davor Šuker poked the ball underneath Kawaguchi, who should have done better with the low shot. Japan's final game against Jamaica, who had also lost both games against Croatia and Argentina, was a dead rubber but resulted in a serious blow to Japanese pride as the "Reggae Boyz" defeated them 2–1. The only bright spot for Japan was that they scored their first-ever World Cup goal, a late consolation by striker Masashi Nakayama.

Despite the final defeat, Japan's performance attracted interest in some of its best players, most notably Hidetoshi Nakata, who moved to Italy to play for Serie A team Perugia. Japan did not need to qualify for the 2002 World Cup as the hosts of the competition. Sharing the World Cup hosting with South Korea, 10 Japanese stadia were utilized in the competition in Ibaraki, Miyagi, Ōita, Osaka, Saitama, Sapporo, Shizuoka and Yokohama—the latter the largest stadium in the competition and the venue for the final. Japan's squad for the 2002 World Cup included, for the first time, foreign-based players: in addition to Nakata, goalkeeper Yoshikatsu Kawaguchi was now on Portsmouth's books in England, Junichi Inamoto was on loan at Arsenal (though he did not make any first team appearances for the London club) and mid-fielder Shinji Ono played for Feyenoord in the Netherlands. Japan's coach was also foreign: well-traveled Frenchman Philippe Troussier had taken charge following the 1998 World Cup. In the interim, Troussier had led Japan's U-20 team to a runner-up position at the 1990 U-20 World Cup and the senior team to first place at the 2000 Asian Cup. Japan had then finished second in the FIFA Confederations Cup a year before the World Cup. Expectation and enthusiasm was thus high as Japan kicked off the World Cup, especially as they had been placed in a relatively easy group containing Belgium, Russia and Tunisia, in group H. Japan's first game took place in Saitama, a partisan home crowd of 55,256 in attendance, as they played Belgium. The first half proved lackluster, and Japan fell behind in the 57th minute to a fine acrobatic goal by Marc Wilmots with an overhead kick. The Belgian goal, though, seemed to inspire Japan, with Inamoto driving the midfield and an equalizer coming only two minutes later, Takayuki Suzuki running onto a long through ball and poking it underneath goalkeeper Geert de Vlieger. Only eight minutes later, Inamoto drove through the Belgian defense after winning the ball in midfield and exchanging passes with Kazuyuki Toda, bursting into the penalty area and firing a left-footed shot past de Vlieger to give Japan the lead. Japan, though, let their concentration slip eight minutes later, Japan's offside trap beaten, allowing Peter Van Der Heyden to lob the ball over Japanese goalkeeper Seigo Narazaki into the net. Japan's World Cup began with a 2–2 draw, earning them their first World Cup point.

There was better to come in Japan's next match against Russia at Yokohama International Stadium, 45,213 officially in attendance. With their midfield, led by Inamoto and Nakata, in fine form and their captain and defensive stalwart Tsuneyasu Miyamoto superb, Japan clinched a 1–0 win. The goal came in the 51st minute when Kōji Nakata's cross was neatly flicked to Inamoto by Takayuki Suzuki, the Arsenal mid-fielder finishing with aplomb. The lead was nearly doubled when Nakata hit the bar with a long-range drive, but 1–0 was enough to give Japan their first World Cup win and send the stadium into raptures. The result left Japan needing only a point against Tunisia in their next game on 14 June in Osaka to qualify for the next round, while a win would seal them first place in the group. Japan began nervously, with no score at halftime. Troussier brought on midfielder Hiroaki Morishima at halftime, replacing Inamoto, a decision that quickly looked inspired as Morishima pounced on a loose ball 12 yards out only three minutes into the second half and steered it into the corner of the net. Morishima then hit the post with a header, but the second goal that confirmed Japan's second victory came after 75 minutes, when another substitute—Daisuke Ichikawa—provided a cross for Nakata to head home.

Japan played their first-ever World Cup knockout game on 18 June in Miyagi, 45,666 at Miyagi Stadium. Japan, though, was unable to put together a head of steam and was deflated as early as the 12th minute when Ümit Davala rose to head in a weakly defended Turkish corner kick. That stood as the lone goal of the game, despite the same pattern of substitutions by Troussier, who left his post as Japanese manager following the defeat.

Japan qualified comfortably for the 2006 World Cup in Germany, topping group B in the final round of Asian qualifying, winning five of six games, though their uninspired performances led to question marks surrounding the team and Brazilian head coach, the legendary Zico, ahead of the start of the tournament. Japan's midfield still looked strong—Inamoto and Nakata were now joined by the gifted Shinji Ono and Celtic's Shunsuke Nakamura—but goal scoring threatened to be an issue, with strikers Naohiro Takahara and Atsushi Yanagisawa out of form at club level. The draw for the final tournament was not particularly kind to Japan, which was placed in group F alongside Brazil, Croatia and Australia. Facing the latter first in Kaiserslautern on 12 June, it was critical Japan began strongly. Japan—fielding the oldest team in the history of their World Cup appearances—took the lead in the 26th minute, when a cross by Nakamura floated directly into the goal, Australian goalkeeper Mark Schwarzer caught up in a melee with the Australians, claiming he had been impeded. Yet with only six minutes remaining in the game, Australia equalized when Tim Cahill pounced on a loose ball in a scramble around the Japanese penalty area. The game unraveled there for Japan: five minutes later, Cahill curled in the winning goal from 20 yards out for the Australians. In injury time, John Aloisi scored a third with embarrassing ease to seal a 3–1 win. That result meant Japan's next game against Croatia was close to a must-win situation, with Zico making two changes from the team that lost to Brazil: Mitsuo Ogasawara and Akira Kaji came into the team, Yūichi Komano and Keisuke Tsuboi making way. In the 21st minute, Japan conceded a penalty when their captain Tsuneyasu Miyamoto brought down Dado Pršo in the penalty area with a clumsy challenge, but Kawaguchi superbly saved the resulting penalty kick. Only seven minutes later, Croatia came even closer to scoring when Niko Kranjčar struck the crossbar from 25 yards out. Nakata—Japan's best player on the day—forced a fine save from Stipe Pletikosa in 36th minute with a long-range drive, but there was no score by halftime. Only six minutes into the second half, Japan should have taken the lead, but Atsushi Yanagisawa somehow missed an open goal from only six yards out, miskicking it wide. The game petered out into a 0–0 draw, a result that did little for Japan's hopes of advancing to the next round. Japan now needed to beat Brazil to stay in the competition, a tough task given Brazil had won their previous nine World Cup finals games heading into the game. Zico again tinkered with the lineup for the game against his compatriots in Dortmund, bringing Inamoto into the midfield, while upfront, Seiichiro Maki and Keiji Tamada came into the team. In defense, Miyamoto did not play due to suspension, the captaincy passing to Yuji Nakazawa. Brazil had the best of the early play, Ronaldo, Juninho and Robinho all coming close to scoring, but Japan surprised the Brazilians on the counterattack with 26 minutes gone, Alex setting up Tamada, who powered a shot into the roof of the net. Japan, though, could not hold on to halftime, Ronaldo scoring in stoppage time with a header, given too much space in the penalty area. The second half was one-way traffic for Brazil, the South Americans scoring three more times for a 4–1 win that eliminated the Japanese. Following the World Cup, Hidetoshi Nakata announced his international retirement, having played in 10 World Cup finals games for Japan. Zico also resigned as coach.

Japan qualified for their fourth straight World Cup in 2010 by claiming the second qualification spot in group A of the final round of Asian qualifying, finishing behind Australia and ahead of Bahrain, Qatar and Uzbekistan. They aimed to win their first World Cup game on foreign turf, their only wins having come at home in Japan during the 2002 World Cup. Back at the helm for Japan was Takeshi Okada, who had coached Japan in the 1998 World Cup. Okada took over from Ivica Osim, Japan's Yugoslavian coach following the 2006 World Cup, who had suffered a stroke in the autumn of 2007. Japan's stars included the 2009 Asian Player of the Year, midfielder Yasuhito Endō, and forward Takayuki Morimoto, then playing for Catania in Italy's Serie A. Most of Japan's squad remained domestic based, though it also included Keisuke Honda of CSKA Moscow in Russia and Makoto Hasebe of VfL Wolfsburg in Germany. Japan was placed in group E at the World Cup in South Africa, along with Cameroon, Denmark and the Netherlands. Japan began their campaign against Cameroon in Bloemfontein on 14 June. A tight game with few chances saw both teams hit the woodwork, but the only goal came for Japan in the 39th minute, Keisuke Honda finishing a cross by Daisuke Matsui at the back post. Cameroon had more shots and more possession, but Japan held firm to claim their first World Cup win on foreign soil. Japan's next game came five days later in Durban, against the Netherlands. Japan put in another disciplined performance but was let down by a goalkeeping error in the 53rd minute, when a snapshot smashed by Dutch midfielder Wesley Sneijder from 25 yards out crept through Eiji Kawashima's hands into the goal. That proved to be the sole goal of the game, with the Dutch dominating possession but largely kept out of dangerous areas by Japan's defensive pressing. Results meant that a draw or a win for Japan in their final group game against Denmark would put them through to the next round. In the event, Japan won a wide-open game in Rustenburg at Royal Bafokeng Stadium. Japan opened the scoring after only 17 minutes, with Keisuke Honda steering a remarkable dipping free kick with his left foot from 30 yards out. Thirteen minutes later, Japan scored from another free kick, this time Yasuhito Endō bending the ball in from 25 yards out. Japan hit the post when another free kick by Endō was mishandled by the Danish goalkeeper, rebounding off the post. Denmark attacked incessantly, striking the crossbar, and finally earned a reward in the 81st minute when

Japanese captain Makoto Hasebe upended Jon Dahl Tomasson in the penalty area, the Danish striker then scoring from a rebound after his penalty kick was saved by Kawashima. Japan, though, sealed a 3–1 win in the 87th minute when Honda cleverly drew out the goalkeeper with a dribble through the Danish defense and squared the ball for Shinji Okazaki to slide into the open goal.

Finishing second in group E, Japan now traveled to Loftus Versfeld Stadium in Pretoria to face Paraguay, the surprise winners of group F. Japan again ceded the majority of possession, but their tight defensive shape and organization ceded few clear chances to the Paraguayans, though Kawashima made a couple of sharp saves in the Japanese goal. Japan almost went ahead after 21 minutes, when Daisuke Matsui struck the crossbar from long range. The game petered out to a 0–0 draw, meaning Japan headed to a penalty shoot-out for the first time in World Cup play. Japan scored their first two penalty kicks, but with the third, Yūichi Komano crashed his shot against the crossbar. Honda converted Japan's fourth kick, but with Paraguay scoring all five of theirs, Japan was eliminated in cruel fashion.

After the resignation of head coach Takeshi Okada following the 2010 tournament, the Japan National Team hired former Juventus and AC Milan coach Alberto Zaccheroni. Though Zaccheroni's campaign started off well (highlighted by a 1–0 win over Argentina), the two-year qualifying campaign for the 2014 World Cup in Brazil proved more difficult a road than expected as the Samurai lost winnable group games. They ultimately righted the ship to seal the points necessary for a fifth successive FIFA World Cup appearance. As with the Japanese World Cup teams of 2006 and 2010, Japan was again the first team to qualify for the 2014 World Cup in Brazil (other than the host country) and drew a favorable grouping in group C with Colombia, Greece and Côte d'Ivoire.

In their first-round matchup with Côte d'Ivoire at the Arena Pernambuco in Recife, the Samurai took control when, in the 16th minute, Japanese striker Keisuke Honda rocketed a blast into the top corner of the Elephants' net. A win was not to be, however, as the Samurai ultimately gave up goals to Wilfried Bony and Gervinho for a 2–1 loss. Game two saw the Japanese playing a man up after a second yellow card was issued to Greek player Kostas Katsouranis following sloppy tackles. Unfortunately for Japanese fans, the Samurai were unable to truly threaten, and the game ended 0–0. Needing a win against Colombia, an early penalty conversion by Juan Cuadrado looked to seal the Samurai's fate, but a first-half stoppage-time goal by Shinji Okazaki gave them hope. It wasn't to be, as a second-half brace by Jackson Martínez and a late goal by James Rodríguez meant Japan's dismissal from Brazil in 29th place with two goals for and six against.

JERKOVIĆ, DRAŽAN. B. 6 August 1936, Šibenik, Yugoslavia. D. 9 December 2008. With four goals in six games for Yugoslavia at the 1962 World Cup in Chile, Dražan Jerković was the joint top scorer at the competition with Flórián Albert of Hungary, Valentin Ivanov of the Soviet Union and Garrincha and Vava of Brazil. By the time of the 1962 World Cup, Jerković was an established international forward, having starred for his country at the 1960 European Championship, scoring twice in two games as Yugoslavia finished runners-up. Jerković played in all six of Yugoslavia's games in Chile, scoring his first goal in their second game against Uruguay and then two further goals against Colombia in their third game. In Yugoslavia's semifinal, Jerković scored his fourth and final goal of the competition, but it was not enough as Czechoslovakia defeated his Yugoslavian team 3–1. Jerković retired from international play in 1964 and went on to be the first coach of Croatia following their independence in 1991.

JUNEK, FRANTIŠEK. B. 17 January 1907, Prague, Czechoslovakia. D. 19 March 1970. Czechoslovakia's right-winger throughout the 1934 World Cup in Italy was František Junek, who played a key role as the Czechs reached the final of the competition hosted by Italy, losing 2–1 after extra time to the host nation. Junek first played for Czechoslovakia in September 1929, making a strong impression early in his international career by scoring 5 goals in 12 games. He did not score at the 1934 World Cup but did set up the first goal for Czechoslovakia in their semifinal win against Germany, his shot parried into the path of Oldřich Nejedlý. Junek played in only two further games for his country following the 1934 World Cup, both later the same year, scoring once against Yugoslavia to end his international career with 7 goals in 32 games, playing in 15 wins, 7 draws and 10 defeats.

K

KAHN, OLIVER. B. 15 June 1969, Karlsruhe, West Germany. Oliver Kahn was an imperious goalkeeper for Bayern Munich at club level and for Germany at the international level. He won the Golden Ball as best player at the 2002 FIFA World Cup, collecting a runners-up medal with Germany after an outstanding tournament. Kahn was the goalkeeper for Germany when they won the 1996 UEFA European Football Championship, playing a total of 86 games for his country between 1994 and 2006. At club level, he began his career for his local team Karlsruher SC, joining German giants Bayern Munich in 1994, with whom he played the rest of his career until retirement in 2008. Kahn won numerous major honors with Bayern Munich, including the German league championship on eight occasions and winners' medals in both the UEFA Champions League and the FIFA Club World Cup in 2001.

KEMPES, MARIO. B. 15 July 1954, Bell Ville, Argentina. Mario Kempes is one of the greatest players ever produced by Argentina, playing for his native country on 43 occasions, scoring 20 goals. A predatory and lethal striker, Kempes appeared in three FIFA World Cup finals tournaments in 1974, 1978 and 1982, scoring 6 goals in 17 games. All six goals came at the 1978 World Cup, where Kempes was the top scorer as Argentina won the World Cup for the first time. He won the South American Footballer of the Year award that year as a result. Kempes also enjoyed a successful career in club soccer, particularly for Valencia in Spain, winning the UEFA Cup Winners' Cup in 1979 and 1980. Since retirement from playing, Kempes has coached teams in Indonesia, Albania, Venezuela and Bolivia.

KLINSMANN, JÜRGEN. B. 30 July 1964, Göppingen, West Germany. Jürgen Klinsmann is a former German National Team and European club player who, as one of the premier strikers of the 1990s, won the 1990 FIFA World Cup and the 1996 UEFA European Championship. Upon hanging up his playing boots, Jürgen went into the coaching ranks, where, as the head coach, he led the German national team to a third-place finish in the 2006 FIFA World Cup in Germany. Following a stint at Bundesliga club Bayern Munich, Jürgen was hired on 29 July 2011 to coach the United States men's national team, a team he ironically scored against in the 1994 FIFA World Cup. Though at the center of controversy when he left team stalwart Landon Donovan off the 2014 roster, Klinsmann proved his coaching mettle by leading the United States to second place in the "Group of Death" with a win over Ghana, a draw with fourth-ranked Portugal and a close 1–0 loss to eventual champs Germany. In the round of 16, the United States lost in added extra time 2–1 to Belgium.

KLOSE, MIROSLAV. B. 9 June 1978, Opole, Poland. Though born in Poland, Miroslav Klose moved to West Germany at the age of eight and is currently the German goal-scoring leader with 71 goals for Germany in international play. With 16 goals in four different World Cups (five in 2002 and 2006, four in 2010 and two in 2014), Klose now holds the record for most goals scored in World Cup finals, passing Brazil's Ronaldo's 15. Notably strong with his head, Klose's five goals at the 2006 World Cup on home soil in Germany won him the Golden Boot as the competition's top scorer. His goals helped Germany to the semifinal stage, though neither Klose nor the Germans could score in a 2–0 defeat there to Italy in Dortmund. A veteran of the team at the 2010 World Cup in South Africa, Klose scored once in the group stage against Austria, once against England in the second round and twice in a 4–0 win over Argentina in the quarterfinal as Germany advanced to the semifinals. The Germans lost 1–0 to Spain at that stage, with Klose and Germany claiming third place following a 3–2 win against Uruguay in the third-place play-off. Coming into the 2014 tournament in Brazil trailing only Ronaldo, Klose's two goals not only gave him the record for most World Cup goals but also equaled him with compatriot Uwe Seeler and Brazilian great Pelé as the only players to score in four World Cup tournaments. His back-to-back five-goal tournaments (tied in 2014 by compatriot Thomas Müller), as well as his back-to-back-to-back four-goal tournaments, are also records.

KOCSIS, SÁNDOR. B. 21 September 1929, Budapest, Hungary. D. 22 July 1979. Sándor Kocsis was a Hungarian player, starring for his national team and for Barcelona in Spain. Kocsis played for the legendary Hungarian side of the 1950s, considered by many to be the best national team ever not to win the FIFA World Cup, appearing alongside the likes of the brilliant Ferenc Puskás in a side nicknamed the "Mighty Magyars." Kocsis was a prolific goal-scoring forward, scoring a remarkable 75 goals in 68 appearances for Hungary and winning a gold medal at the 1952 Olympic Games Football Tournament with his country, as well as a runners-up medal at the 1954 World Cup in Switzerland. At club level, he won three Hungarian league championships playing for Honvéd FC and two Spanish league championships playing for Barcelona, where he scored 151 goals in 235 games. Kocsis retired from playing in 1965, pursuing a brief coaching career cut short by illness, dying in a fall from a fourth-floor hospital window in 1979, aged 49.

KOREA DPR (NORTH KOREA). Commonly known as Chollima (Thousand-Mile Horse). The Democratic People's Republic of Korea, or Korea DPR as it is recognized by FIFA, has qualified for the World Cup twice, in 1966 and 2010. The North Koreans qualified for the 1966 World Cup after beating Australia 6–1 at home and 3–1 in Australia; other Asian and African nations had withdrawn from the tournament in protest of FIFA's decision to allow only one nation to qualify from each continent. North Korea proved to be the surprise of the tournament in England. Although they lost their first game 3–0 to the Soviet Union, the North Koreans began to find their footing with a 1–1 tie against Chile in Middlesbrough. They went on to stun the Italians in their final group match, with Pak Doo-Ik's goal for the North Koreans proving to be the game winner. The 1–0 victory was enough to propel the North Koreans into the quarterfinals, where they would meet eventual third-place finishers Portugal. Twenty-five minutes into the game, the North Koreans looked sure to complete a second consecutive shocking upset in the tournament as they led the Portuguese 3–0. But the North Koreans fell apart as the game progressed, allowing two goals in the first half and three more in the second, with Portuguese star Eusébio running rampant with a hat trick of goals. The final score was 5–3 to the Portuguese, and the North Koreans were sent home.

The North Koreans did not qualify for the World Cup again until 2010. Unfortunately, their success in the 1966 tournament was not repeated 44 years later. Placed in a difficult group with Côte d'Ivoire, Brazil and Portugal, the North Koreans failed to win a single match. They held on for a close 2–1 loss to Brazil but allowed Portugal to score seven goals in the following game and the Côte d'Ivoire to score three, finishing with a grand total of one goal for and twelve goals against in a first-round group-stage exit. Though they won the AFC Challenge Cup in 2010 and 2012, North Korea failed to qualify for the 2014 World Cup in Brazil after finishing third in their qualification group behind Uzbekistan and Japan.

KOREA REPUBLIC (SOUTH KOREA). Commonly known as the Taeguk Warriors. South Korea has participated in 10 World Cup tournaments, making them the most successful team in Asia. Their first appearance in the World Cup was in 1954, during which they lost to Hungary 9–0 and Turkey 7–0. It would be 32 years before their next World Cup appearance, the 1986 World Cup in Mexico. The South Koreans again failed to win a match, as they went 0-1-2. Their one point was earned in a 1–1 draw against Bulgaria. Although South Korea was unable to find success in the 1986 competition, it did mark the start of eight consecutive World Cup appearances. However, South Korea did not get their first win until 2002, going 0-0-3 in 1990, 0-2-1 in 1994 and 0-1-2 in 1998.

South Korea was cohost of the 2002 World Cup tournament with Japan, the first time the competition was held in Asia. South Korea opened the competition against Poland, with goals by Hwang Sun-Hong and Yoo Sang-Chul leading the South Koreans to their first-ever World Cup victory. The following match against the United States ended in a 1–1 draw, and the South Koreans' 1–0 victory against Portugal in the third match put them at the top of their group and into the second round. Their next opponent was Italy. The Italians scored first in the 18th minute, and with the game clock nearing 90 minutes, they looked sure to advance to the quarterfinals. However, a late goal by South Korea's Seol Ki-Hyeon forced the game into extra time, and 27 minutes later, a golden goal by Ahn Jung-Hwan sent the host nation into the final eight for the first time in history. Facing Spain in the quarterfinals, South Korea's defense held the game scoreless throughout regulation and extra time, bringing the match to a penalty shoot-out. South Korea went on to defeat Spain 5–3 on penalties and become the first Asian team to reach the semifinals of the World Cup. Unfortunately, South Korea's amazing run in the tournament was brought to an end by a strong German side, losing 1–0 and finishing fourth in the competition.

Four years later, South Korea returned to the World Cup looking to replicate their success in the previous tournament. Winning their opening match against Togo—

South Korea's first World Cup win outside of Asia—there was hope they could do just that. Their fortunes were not to continue, though, as they drew 1–1 against France and lost 2–0 to Switzerland, ending their World Cup after the opening round.

In the 2010 World Cup, South Korea was placed in a group with Greece, Argentina and Nigeria. Earning a 2–0 win against Greece and a 2–2 draw with Nigeria, the South Koreans made it to the second round for the first time outside of Asia. In the round of 16, they lost 2–1 to Uruguay and were eliminated from the competition.

Qualification for the 2014 World Cup in Brazil saw numerous managerial and lineup changes and left the Warriors needing a 5–1 Uzbekistan win over Qatar to qualify on a greater goal differential. Under 2002 team captain Hong Myung-bo, and placed in group H with Belgium, Algeria and Russia, the turmoil that defined the team during qualification followed them to Brazil. South Korea ultimately finished last in their group on one point. An opening 1–1 draw against a strong Russian team, on goals by Lee Keun-ho in the 68th minute and Aleksandr Kerzhakov in the 74th, gave the Warriors what turned out to be short-lived hope. Against Algeria, Islam Slimani's speed and creativity started off the scoring in the 26th minute, and two minutes later, Rafik Halliche headed home an Abdelmoumene Djabou corner. When Djabou got into the act in the 38th minute, the rout was on. After halftime, Son Heung Min scored for South Korea, but another Algerian goal in the 62nd minute restored the three-goal lead. A 72nd-minute Korean goal by Koo Ja-cheol proved to be too little, too late, and Korea now needed a decisive win against group-favorite Belgium to advance. With Belgium playing like a team that had already moved on, the game itself was unremarkable until the 45th minute, when first-time tournament-starter Steven Defour was issued a straight red for stepping directly on Korean forward Kim Shin-wook after a late challenge. Though down a man, Belgium still looked like the better side, and a late Jan Vertonghen goal sealed South Korea's exit, this time in 27th place with three goals for six goals against.

KOŠT'ÁLEK, JOSEF. B. 31 August 1909, Kročehlavy, Austria-Hungary. D. 21 November 1971. A right-half for the superb Czechoslovakian international team of the 1930s, Josef Košt'álek played seven games in both the 1934 and 1938 World Cups, held in Italy and France respectively. Košt'álek made his debut for Czechoslovakia in May 1932, playing in a 3–2 win over France and scoring the first of only two goals scored for his country. Košt'álek became a regular for his country and was selected for all of Czechoslovakia's four games of the 1934 World Cup, as they reached the final of the competition, meeting but losing to Italy in the final held in Rome. Košt'álek continued to be a mainstay of the Czech team in the run-up to the 1938 World Cup, playing in their successful World Cup qualification game against Bulgaria in April 1938. Košt'álek was one of only four players selected for both the 1934 and 1938 Czech World Cup teams. Czechoslovakia's first round game at the 1938 World Cup came against the Netherlands, and the Dutch held the 1934 finalists to a 0–0 scoreline at the end of 90 minutes. It was Košt'álek who broke the deadlock with his second and final international goal, giving his country the lead in the 93rd minute, in a game that ended with a 3–0 victory. Czechoslovakia, though, exited the competition in the second round, losing in a replay to Brazil, Košt'álek hampered by a stomach injury.

Košťálek played a further three games for Czechoslovakia in 1938 before the political situation ahead of World War II ended international play, with no further games played by the country until 1946. He finished his international career with 2 goals in 42 games, recorded in 23 wins, 12 draws and 9 losses.

KRČIL, RUDOLF. B. 5 March 1906, Trnovany, Austria-Hungary. D. 3 April 1981. Rudolf Krčil, a defensive midfielder, played 20 games for Czechoslovakia, including four at the 1934 World Cup, held in Italy. Krčil was among the starting 11 for Czechoslovakia's losing effort in the final of the competition, as hosts Italy defeated them 2–1 after extra time. At the time, Krčil starred for leading Czech club team Slavia Prague, winning four league championships with them in the 1930s. Krčil retired from international play in 1935, his last game coming in September of that year against Yugoslavia, the same country he had made his debut against in June 1929. He did not record a goal in any of his 20 international appearances. Krčil continued to play at club level until 1943 and later coached several Czech teams.

KUWAIT. Commonly known as Al-Azraq (The Blues). Kuwait made the World Cup just one year, in 1982. Although they managed a 1–1 draw against Czechoslovakia in their first game, they lost both their subsequent games to France and England. Their 4–1 loss to France was not without controversy. At one point in the game, the Kuwaiti players thought they heard a whistle, and when they stopped playing, France scored. The referee, who had not blown his whistle, initially awarded the French the goal, but Kuwait walked off the field in protest. It was not until the referee disallowed the goal that Kuwait returned to the pitch. The Kuwaitis lost their final game to England 1–0 and have not been back to a World Cup since.

L

LANGENUS, JEAN. B. 8 December 1881, Berchem, Belgium. D. 1 October 1952. The referee for the first World Cup final in 1930 was the experienced 48-year-old Belgian Jean Langenus. Langenus was also a referee at the 1934 and 1938 World Cups. Langenus had been a keen player as a youth and, instructed by English referees, began to take charge of games as a referee in the first decade of the 20th century. As international play on the continent became more frequent in the 1920s, Langenus began refereeing internationally. Notably, he oversaw two games at the 1928 Olympic Games Football Tournament held in Amsterdam, a first-round match between the Netherlands and Uruguay and the bronze-medal game between Italy and Egypt. Langenus made an immediate impression, tall, well dressed and calm in his manner, and was selected as a referee by FIFA for the 1930 World Cup in Uruguay. He took charge of four games at the competition, none involving European teams. The first two came in the group stage, Uruguay versus Peru on 18 July and Argentina versus Chile on 22 July. Langenus was then assigned to the first semifinal, Argentina's 6–1 win over the United States, on 26 July. Four days later, Langenus was asked to steward the first-ever World Cup final between hosts Uruguay and Argentina, a bitterly anticipated affair by the rival teams separated by the Río de la Plata. The feverish atmosphere surrounding the game meant many players and Langenus and his officials feared for their safety. Langenus and his team of officials asked for and received an escort to the game and passage out of Uruguay immediately after the final. All accounts record that Langenus refereed a tense and combustuous game fairly. Before kickoff, he solved a dispute about which ball should be used by ruling each team's preferred choice should be used for one half each. Following the 1930 World Cup, Langenus continued to referee internationally across Europe and was selected to officiate at the 1934 World Cup in Italy. He took charge of only one game at the tournament, Czechoslovakia's 1–0 win over Romania in the first round on 27 May. The 1938 World Cup was similar for Langenus, as he was again only chosen to take charge of one game, the first-round game between Switzerland and Germany, a 1–1 draw. In the game, Langenus issued his only expulsion at any World Cup, dismissing Germany's Hans Pesser. Langenus took charge of a handful of further internationals in 1939 before the intervention of World War II ended international play and his career.

LATO, GRZEGORZ. B. 8 April 1950, Malbork, Poland. Grzegorz Lato has the distinction of being the only Polish player to win the Golden Shoe, scoring seven goals in the 1974 World Cup in West Germany. In that competition, Poland finished third place with a deserved win over Brazil courtesy of a Lato goal—the only goal scored in the game. Lato scored his final goal for Poland at the 1982 World Cup in Spain. His 45 goals with the national team are second best in team history, while he remains the most capped player for Poland. Lato was elected president of the Polish Football Association in 2008.

LATYCHEV, NIKOLAJ. B. 22 November 1913, Moscow, Russia. Nikolaj Latychev began his international refereeing career shortly after the end of World War II, eventually going on to officiate at two World Cups, including taking charge of the 1962 World Cup final in Santiago, Chile. The first major tournament Latychev participated in was the 1952 Olympic Games Football Tournament in Melbourne, Australia, overseeing three games, including the bronze-medal game between Bulgaria and India. His reliable performances there and as a referee in a World Cup qualifier between Wales and East Germany in May 1957 saw Latychev selected as a referee for the 1958 World Cup in Sweden. There, Latychev officiated as referee for two first-round games, Sweden versus Mexico and Wales versus Hungary. Latychev would play a larger role at the 1962 World Cup in Chile, assigned to four total games. Two of these came in the first round, and just 17 minutes into his first game, Latychev awarded a penalty to England on their way to a 3–1 win over Argentina on 2 June in Rancagua. Five days later, Latychev took charge of the final game in group two, Italy's comfortable 3–0 win over Switzerland. In the next round, Latychev was selected to oversee Czechoslovakia's 1–0 win over Hungary in Rancagua. On 17 June in Santiago, Latychev became the first Russian to referee the World Cup final. He officiated a 3–1 win for Brazil over Czechoslovakia. That proved to be the final game of Latychev's career as an international referee.

LÁZÁR, GYULA. B. 24 January 1911, Füzesgyarmat, Hungary. D. 27 February 1983. Hungary's 1934 and 1938 World Cup teams both included Gyula Lázár, a defender who played 48 games for his country, scoring one goal. Part of a gifted Hungarian generation, Lázár made his debut in April 1931 in a 6–2 win over Switzerland. At the 1934 World Cup in Italy, Lázár played one game, Hungary's first-round victory over Egypt 4–2. He did not play in Hungary's next game, the quarterfinal defeat against Austria that eliminated them from the competition. Lázár played a large role in Hungary's appearance at the next World Cup, the 1938 competition in France, playing in all four of their games: a 6–0 win over the Dutch East Indies in the first round, a 2–0 win over Switzerland in the quarterfinal, a 5–1 win over Sweden in the semifinal and Hungary's 4–2 defeat to defending World Cup champions Italy in the final on 19 June in Paris. Lázár went on to play a further 11 games for Hungary, his last appearance coming in April 1941.

LEÔNIDAS DA SILVA. B. 6 September 1913, Rio de Janeiro, Brazil. D. 24 January 2004. Leônidas da Silva was a star player for Brazil at two FIFA World Cup finals competition in 1934 and 1938 and the top scorer in the latter tournament with seven goals. He tallied an impressive eight goals in five total World Cup games. Known as the "Black Diamond," Leônidas was the first Brazilian to become a national superstar in his country, presaging the later fame of the likes of Garrincha and Pelé. Unusually agile, Leônidas was reportedly the inventor of the bicycle kick. He retired from international play in 1946, having scored 21 goals in 19 games for Brazil.

LINEKER, GARY. B. 30 November 1960, Leicester, England. Winner of the Golden Boot in 1986 at the tournament in Mexico, England's Gary Lineker was known for his predator finishing inside the penalty area. Lineker struck six goals in Mexico as England reached the quarterfinals before losing to Argentina, including a hat trick in 34 minutes against Poland in England's final group game. Lineker also scored four goals at the 1990 World Cup, helping England to fourth place in the competition.

LIPPI, MARCELLO. B. 12 April 1948, Viareggio, Italy. Marcello Lippi is a highly successful Italian coach at both international and club team levels. He managed Italy to their fourth FIFA World Cup victory in the 2006 World Cup and coached them at the 2010 World Cup, where they were disappointingly eliminated in the first round. A former player for Sampdoria in Italy, Lippi made his name coaching Juventus in the mid-1990s, winning five domestic championships with them in two spells between 1994 and 2004, having spent one season, 1999–2000, as manager of Internazionale in Milan. With Juventus, Lippi won the UEFA Champions League in 1996, also finishing as runners-up in 1997, 1998 and 2003. Lippi then took over the Italian national team in 2004, leading them to their surprising title win in Germany at the 2006 World Cup. Lippi left the job following that competition but returned to the position in 2008, leaving the post again following the 2010 World Cup.

LOCATELLI, UGO. B. 5 February 1916, Toscolano-Maderno, Italy. D. 28 May 1993. Italy's 1938 World Cup–winning team included four players who had also been part of their 1936 Olympic Games Football Tournament winning team, Locatelli one of the talented young players in that group. The coach for both competitions was Vittorio Pozzo. Locatelli made his debut at the Olympic Games in Italy's first game of the competition against the United States, playing in four games at the competition, including the gold medal victory over Austria. He was ever-present for Italy at the 1938 World Cup, playing in all four games, including Italy's win in the final, a 4–2 victory over Hungary. At club level, he enjoyed further honors while with Internazionale of Milan, winning Serie A in 1938 and 1940.

LÓPEZ, JUAN. B. 15 March 1908, Montevideo, Uruguay. D. 4 October 1983. Uruguay was led to its second World Cup title won in 1950 by Juan López, who had begun coaching his country in the late 1940s. He learned his trade at club level assisting Alberto Suppici, who had led Uruguay to their first World Cup title in 1930. At the 1950 World Cup in Brazil, Uruguay qualified past the first round by winning their only group-stage game, as they found themselves in a two-team group paired with Bolivia, who succumbed to a crushing 8–0 Uruguayan victory. Unlike every other World Cup played, 1950 did not end with a final knockout game but with a four-team group stage, with each team playing each other once. Uruguay tied its opening game with Spain 2–2, López naming an unchanged team from the side that faced Bolivia. López made two changes for Uruguay's critical second game against Spain: Roque Máspoli was replaced by Aníbal Paz in goal, while Schubert Gambetta came into the side in place of Juan Carlos Gonzalez. Sweden led 2–1 at halftime, but Uruguay came back strongly in the second half, Óscar Míguez scoring a brace of goals to give the South Americans a 3–2 win and a shot at winning the World Cup. To do so, they would have to defeat hosts and strong favorites Brazil at the legendary Maracanã stadium in Rio de Janeiro in front of 200,000 passionate home fans. Brazil had won their first two games in the final group stage by huge margins, 7–1 over Sweden and 6–1 over Spain, the country in a frenzy as kickoff approached, Uruguay needing to win to take the title. López restored Máspoli as goalkeeper, while Ruben Morán—making his first appearance in the competition—replaced Ernesto Vidal. Brazil took the lead shortly after halftime, but Uruguay equalized through Juan Schiaffino in the 66th minute and then found a winner through Alcides Ghiggia in the 79th minute. López was credited with helping the Uruguayans hand Brazil a tactical defeat, with tight man-marking troubling the Brazilians who were struck on the counterattack by Uruguayan center-half Obdulio Varela, using a similar system that Switzerland had used early on in the competition to stymie the free-scoring Brazilians.

LORENZO, JUAN CARLOS. B. 10 October 1922, Buenos Aires, Argentina. D. 14 November 2001. Argentina was coached at both the 1962 World Cup in Chile and the 1966 World Cup in England by Juan Carlos Lorenzo, winning three, losing two and drawing two in the two competitions. Lorenzo managed Argentina during one of the longest championship-less streaks in its history but is credited as playing a role in the modernization of its approach to the game, emphasizing disciplined teamwork, fitness training and defense rather than individual dribbling. He was selected to coach Argentina based on his experience as a player and coach in Italy and Spain, both countries seen to be ahead of Argentina in their coaching methods at the time, with Argentina having been embarrassed by their first-round exit and performance at the 1958 World Cup. In a long playing career that began in Argentina with Chacarita Juniors and Boca Juniors, Lorenzo then moved to Sampdoria in Italy, playing there from 1947 to 1952. He began as a player-coach at RCD Mallorca, where he won both the Spanish third- and second-division titles, before returning to Argentina to coach San Lorenzo in 1961 before taking over as Argentina coach. The 1962 World Cup began well for Lorenzo and Argentina with a victory in their first group game over Bulgaria, 1–0, but their campaign unraveled with a disappointing 3–1 defeat to England in their second game. A 0–0 draw with Hungary in Argentina's final game was not enough for qualification, but Lorenzo had at least introduced a tougher streak to his country's World Cup play than they had shown in the previous 1958 tournament. In between 1962 and 1966, Lorenzo returned to Italy to coach Lazio and Roma, with the Argentinean coaching job a part-time position.

In 1966, with the World Cup in England, Argentina was drawn in group two with Spain, West Germany and Switzerland. Argentina opened play against Spain, the reigning European champions, and with a backbone of talented defender Roberto Perfumo, the tall and imperious captain and center-half Antonio Rattín, the creativity of Erminio Onega and the finishing of Luis Artime, were able to more than match the favored Spaniards, winning two goals thanks to a pair of strikes by Luis Artime.

In their next game against West Germany, Argentina demonstrated Lorenzo's focus on defensive discipline, holding the eventual finalists to a 0–0 draw. Argentina then needed to defeat Switzerland in their final group game to qualify for the knockout stage and did so thanks to a strong second-half performance led by Onega's brilliance, as he scored one and set up the other for Artime. Lorenzo's team now faced the hosts, England, on 23 July with a partisan home crowd of 90,584 in attendance at Wembley Stadium. It was to be Lorenzo's final match in charge of Argentina, as they succumbed to a 1–0 defeat and one that would be remembered forever due to the controversy that followed the dismissal of Lorzeno's captain Antonio Rattín in the 35th minute. A seven-minute delay followed as Rattín refused to leave the field; players remonstrated with the referee and other officials, and Lorenzo's staff entered the field of play. Lorenzo himself attempted to keep the situation from spiraling entirely out of control, but it was of little use, with Argentina exiting the competition feeling cheated by the referee and branded "animals" by England manager Alf Ramsey. Lorenzo went on to enjoy a highly successful career as a club manager, winning further titles with San Lorenzo and Boca Juniors in Argentina.

M

MARACANÃ. The Estádio Jornalista Mário Filho, commonly known as the Estádio do Maracanã or simply as the Maracanã, is Brazil's best-known stadium and played host to several matches at the 1950 FIFA World Cup, just weeks after its opening. Its official opening capacity was 183,000, making it then the largest soccer stadium in the world by some distance. The Maracanã hosted the final game of the tournament, in which an estimated 220,000 fans crammed into the stadium, far exceeding the official capacity, to see hosts Brazil surprisingly beaten by Uruguay, who as a result won the third FIFA World Cup. Owned by the state government of Rio de Janeiro, the Maracanã plays host to games featuring local club sides Flamengo, Fluminense, Botafogo and Vasco de Gama. It has been the scene of numerous historically noteworthy events, including Pelé's 1,000th goal in 1969, the 1989 Copa América final that saw Brazil beat Uruguay and the inaugural FIFA Club World Cup final in 2000. The Maracanã was one of twelve stadiums used for the 2014 FIFA World Cup in Brazil and hosted the final match, a 1–0 German win in added extra time over Argentina in front of 74,738 spectators. It will also be the venue for the 2016 Summer Olympic Games opening and closing ceremonies.

MARADONA, DIEGO. B. 30 October 1960, Lanús, Argentina. Diego Maradona is Argentina's greatest-ever player and the only rival to Pelé as the greatest player of the 20th century. Maradona played for Argentina from 1977 until 1994, captaining his country to its second FIFA World Cup championship in 1986. Maradona led his country to the World Cup final again four years later in Italy, where they lost to West Germany in a penalty shoot-out. He scored 34 goals in 91 games for his country. Maradona retired in 1997 and later went on to manage Argentina, taking them to the 2010 World Cup finals.

Maradona made his debut for Argentina at the age of 17 on 3 April 1977, but he was not selected by coach César Luis Menotti for the World Cup in 1978, won by Argentina on home soil. Maradona instead led Argentina to victory in the FIFA World Youth Championship in 1979. Maradona did play at the next World Cup in Spain in 1982, scoring twice against Hungary in the first round, but was then sent off against Brazil in the second round as Argentina went out of the competition.

The 1986 World Cup in Mexico would prove to be the peak of Maradona's career internationally. Despite being only 5 feet 5 inches tall, Maradona was able to physically dominate opponents with his strength, while his remarkable ball-control skills allowed him to dribble past opponents with uncanny ease, and these skills were no better demonstrated than at the 1986 World Cup. Famously, Maradona's second goal against England in the 1986 World Cup quarterfinal saw him dribble the ball past half a dozen English players across the length of the field before slotting the ball into the goal. This goal was later crowned in a vote held by the Fédération Internationale de Football Association (FIFA) as the greatest goal of all time in the World Cup. Maradona has also been a highly controversial figure, as his other goal in the same quarterfinal game illustrated: he clearly handballed the ball past England goalkeeper Peter Shilton, an offense unseen by the referee. Maradona later claimed it was the "hand of God." Following the win over England, Argentina went on to score two more as they beat Belgium in the semifinals and then led Argentina to a 3–2 win over West Germany in the final. He ended the tournament with five goals and five assists and as the undoubted best player in the competition.

The mid-1980s were also the peak of Maradona's club career. He had begun his club career in his native country, making his professional debut for Argentinos Juniors at the age of just 15 on 20 October 1976. He moved to Boca Juniors in 1981 and then on to Europe with Barcelona in Spain the next year for a world record fee of almost $10 million. His greatest club success came following a move to Italian club Napoli in 1984: Maradona rejuvenated the southern Italian club, who won the Serie A league championship in 1987 and 1990 and the UEFA Cup in 1989.

Personal problems also began to plague Maradona at this stage of his career, as his cocaine addiction became widely known. He was suspended for 15 months in 1991 for failing a drug test, testing positive for cocaine use. After his suspension, Maradona played for Sevilla in Spain in 1992 and 1993 and then joined Newell's Old Boys back home in Argentina, appearing for his national team again in the 1994 World Cup finals in the United States. Maradona scored in Argentina's opening game against Greece but was then found to have failed a drug test for the use of the illegal drug ephedrine and sent home.

Maradona retired in October 1997, playing his final game for Boca Juniors against River Plate. His personal problems worsened in retirement, as he ballooned in weight, leading to a stomach-stapling surgery in 2005. He became a famous television host in Argentina until he was surprisingly chosen by the Argentinean FA to take over as manager of the national team in 2008. Under his stewardship, Argentina struggled to qualify for the 2010 World Cup finals, with a vitriolic outburst by Maradona against the media leading to a two-month suspension from soccer by FIFA, ending in January 2010. At the 2010 World Cup in South Africa, Maradona's Argentina cruised through the opening round, before a 4–0 defeat to Germany eliminated them, leading to Maradona's departure from the national-team coaching job in August 2010.

MASCHERONI, ERNESTO. B. 21 November 1907, Montevideo, Uruguay. D. 3 July 1984. Ernesto Mascheroni was the second-youngest player on the Uruguayan team that won the inaugural World Cup in 1930 on home turf, only 22 years old during the competition. He played in three of Uruguay's four games at the tournament, starting in Uruguay's final group game against Romania, their semifinal win over Yugoslavia and their 4–2 victory in the final, facing Argentina. A defender, Mascheroni played most of his career at club level in Uruguay for Club Atlético River Plate and

Peñarol, though from 1934 to 1936, he played in Italy for Inter Milan and represented Italy twice at the international level during this period, when rules on representing multiple international teams were more lax than at present. He then returned to Uruguay in 1936. Mascheroni retired in 1940 and was the oldest surviving player from Uruguay's 1930 World Cup–winning team when he died in 1984.

MASCHIO, HUMBERTO. B. 20 February 1933, Avellaneda, Argentina. Despite being regarded as one of the most talented players to have represented two countries, his native Argentina and his adopted nation Italy, Humberto Maschio only played in one FIFA World Cup match. Maschio, born in 1933, was a prolific goal scorer in his native Argentina during the 1950s and came to international prominence with a starring role in Argentina's brilliant and victorious performance at the 1957 Copa América. Maschio scored nine goals in only six games at the tournament in Peru, earning international attention and a financially rewarding move to Italian professional soccer, playing for Bologna, Atalanta, Internazionale and Fiorentina between 1957 and 1966. Maschio's defection, though, ended his involvement with Argentina's national team at 12 goals in 12 games, meaning he missed out on taking part in the 1958 World Cup.

Following his assumption of Italian citizenship, Maschio made his debut for Italy in 1962 and was chosen to start Italy's second game of the group stage on 2 June 1962 in Santiago, after the Italians had drawn 0–0 with West Germany to open their campaign. The game against the World Cup's host nation, Chile, would live in infamy, becoming known as the "Battle of Santiago." Tensions had been heightened ahead of kickoff by crude Italian newspaper reports disparaging Chilean hospitality, while the South American media criticized Italy for the inclusion of the *oriundi*, South American transplants, including Maschio as one of three present, in their team. It was not long into Italy's game with Chile until the tension spilled over onto the pitch, and Maschio ended up at the heart of a violent encounter that English referee Ken Aston was entirely unable to contain. With a swift left hook out of sight of the referee, Chilean Leonel Sánchez broke Maschio's nose, ending his participation in the game, the World Cup and ultimately his international career. The aftermath of the "Battle of Santiago" in Italy saw some blame attached to the *oriundi* for their very existence in the Italian team, and none of the three present in Chile played again for Italy. Maschio returned to Argentina in 1966 to play for Racing Club and went on to coach Argentina's national team briefly in 1969 for a series of friendly games.

MATTHÄUS, LOTHAR. B. 21 March 1961, Erlangen, West Germany. Even for a nation that has produced a stream of World Cup stars, Lothar Matthäus stands out among his peers for his achievements playing in five World Cup competitions between 1982 and 1998, a span in which he played 150 games for West Germany and Germany. Matthäus was a remarkable all-around talent who played in his team's engine room, able to tackle, pass and shoot equally effectively, orchestrating play from anywhere on the field. Most notably, Matthäus captained West Germany to its third World Cup–title win in the 1990 World Cup in Italy, scoring four goals in the competition from his midfield position.

MEAZZA, GIUSEPPE. B. 23 August 1910, Milan, Italy. D. 21 August 1979. One of four Italians to have won two World Cup titles, Giuseppe Meazza starred for Italy at the 1934 World Cup in his native Italy and at the 1938 World Cup in France. He was known for his outstanding technique, ability to read the game, ball-control skills and ability to beat defenders on the dribble, sometimes with seemingly absurd ease. Meazza began his international career for Italy in February 1930, just 19 years old but already an established star at club level for Internazionale in Milan, playing as a striker or attacking midfielder and demonstrating a remarkable eye for goal, Serie A's top scorer in both 1929 and 1930. He scored twice on his Italian debut and quickly became a national star. Meazza played in all five of Italy's games at the 1934 World Cup, mainly as a right-winger, scoring in their first game against the United States, a 7–1 win, and struck the winning goal in their third game against Spain, at the quarter-final stage. In the final against Czechoslovakia, though hampered by injury, Meazza helped create the winning goal for Angelo Schiavio in extra time to earn Italy their first World Cup title.

In 1938, at the age of 27, Meazza captained his country to their second victory in the World Cup, playing every minute of Italy's four games. Meazza scored one goal in the competition, from the penalty spot in Italy's 2–1 semifinal win over Brazil, though he created numerous goals for Italian striker Silvio Piola. He was the only Italian to play in all nine of Italy's World Cup games in the 1930 and 1934 competitions, winning eight and tying one out of the nine total games. Meazza ended his international career with 33 goals for Italy in 53 appearances, his final game for Italy coming in July 1939. The home stadium of Internazionale and AC Milan is named the Stadio Giuseppe Meazza in his honor.

MENOTTI, CÉSAR LUIS. B. 5 November 1938, Rosario, Argentina. César Luis Menotti, nicknamed El Flaco (the Thin One), led Argentina to their first FIFA World Cup title in 1978 on home soil as they hosted the tournament. The victory, with Argentina beating the Netherlands 3–1 in the final, crowned a magnificent career for Menotti. He began his coaching career in 1971, after a successful playing career mainly in Argentina's domestic league. After just two years, he led Huracán to their first-ever league title in 1973, earning the opportunity to manage the Argentinean national team at the age of just 46 after the country's poor showing at the 1974 World Cup. Menotti was fortunate to have at his disposal one of the greatest crops of talent ever seen in world soccer: captain Daniel Passarella and the prolific scoring forward Mario Kempes providing the spine of the team, with Menotti putting together a disciplined team playing attractive, attacking football. Menotti also had at his disposal the remarkable young talent of Diego Maradona, but despite blooding him in Argentina's national team at the age of just 16 in 1977, Menotti controversially left him out of the 1978 World Cup–winning team.

Menotti would manage Maradona the next year at the FIFA World Youth Championship, Argentina claiming their first title in that competition as well, with Maradona leading a team playing swashbuckling football. Menotti would taste failure managing Argentina at the 1982 World Cup, their second-round exit leading to the end of his tenure coaching his national team. He immediately teamed up again with Maradona at club level, coaching Barcelona, but despite some success in Spanish cup competition, the club did not win the league title and Menotti moved on to a meandering career around the world, alternating between broadcasting, coaching and teaching soccer.

MESSI, LIONEL. B. 24 June 1987, Rosario, Argentina. Born Lionel "Leo" Andrés Messi Cuccittini, the man affectionately known as "the Flea" due to his diminutive size, was diagnosed with growth-hormone deficiency at the age of 11. Though local club River Plate showed interest in him at an early age, they were unwilling to foot the $900 per month medical bill necessary for his treatment. Luckily for Messi (and for FC Barcelona), the club's sporting director, Carles Rexach, heard about Messi's talents from relatives in western Catalonia, and after a tryout (and with no paper at hand), Rexach offered Messi a contract on a paper napkin. The contract proved to be a worthwhile investment, as Messi went on to become one of the world's best players. With a soccer résumé far too long to list here, Messi has won the Ballon d'Or, or Golden Ball (merged to become the FIFA Ballon d'Or in 2010), a record four times, La Liga player of the year three times and World Soccer Player of the Year three times to go with his numerous other awards, all before the age of 28.

In 2006, he became the youngest player to represent Argentina at a World Cup when he came on as a substitute in the 74th minute against Serbia and Montenegro. He quickly proved his worth by assisting on a goal within minutes of his arrival and scoring the final goal in a 6–0 victory to make him 2006's youngest goal scorer as well as the sixth-youngest goal scorer all-time in the World Cup. In 2010, forced into a more attacking role, Messi was a part of every Argentine goal on his way to finishing on FIFA's shortlist for the Golden Ball as the tournament's best player, but a Maradona-led Argentina found themselves outclassed by Germany in the quarterfinals. In 2014, after scoring four goals and placing Argentina on his back en route to a 1–0 loss in the final (again to Germany), Messi was the controversial winner of the Golden Ball. Messi himself was surprised, believing that it "meant nothing" after their loss. Gérard Houllier, a respected member of FIFA's Technical Study Group (and former Liverpool and Aston Villa manager), defended the decision, saying that the commission looked at the tournament as a whole, rather than at any one game.

MEXICO. Commonly known as El Tri (The Tricolor). In 1986, Mexico became the first country to host the World Cup twice, having first staged the competition back in 1970 and, on this occasion, replacing the scheduled host nation Colombia, who had been removed due to economic concerns. On the field, Mexico's national team, known as El Tri, has appeared in 14 World Cup finals, the best of any nation from North America. However, it wasn't until 1970 on home soil that Mexico reached the knockout stage of the competition. In that tournament, Mexico qualified in second place in the group stage following a 0–0 tie with the Soviet Union and wins over El Salvador and Belgium. Though Mexico took the lead against Italy in the quarterfinal, Jose Gonzalez scoring after 13 minutes, Italy came back to win 4–1 and eliminate the host nation. Mexico did not qualify for the 1974 World Cup and was eliminated at the first-round stage in 1978 in Argentina and then failed to qualify for the 1982 World Cup. As host nation again in 1986, Mexico reached the quarterfinal stage once more.

Led by the magnificent striker Hugo Sánchez, Mexico advanced past the first round as winners of group B and then defeated Bulgaria in the second round 2–0. In the quarterfinal, neither Mexico nor West Germany could score in regular or extra time, both teams reduced to 10 men, with Javier Aguirre dismissed for Mexico in the 100th minute. A penalty shoot-out decided the game and left the 42,000 fans in Monterrey deeply disappointed, as the West Germans prevailed 4–1. Mexico was banned from taking part in the 1990 World Cup by FIFA for using overage players in a youth tournament but has qualified for every tournament since. That has remarkably resulted in five consecutive defeats in the second round, a hurdle Mexico has been unable to get past except on home soil.

After the Mxican national side won the gold medal in the 2012 London Olympics, expectations were high during qualification for the 2014 World Cup in Brazil. Unfortunately, reality was a bit harsher as Mexico nearly missed out on the tournament entirely when they stumbled in the CONCACAF fourth round, needing a United States win over Panama in the final group game to advance them to a play-off game with New Zealand, where a win finally secured their berth.

Placed in group A with Brazil, Croatia and Cameroon, Mexico began their tournament in a rain-soaked Estádio das Dunas in Natal against Cameroon. After poor officiating led to two Mexican goals being wrongly called back, it was ultimately the goalkeeping of Guillermo Ochoa that kept Mexico in the game. The game winner in the 61st minute on a strike by Oribe Peralta secured three points for Mexico. In a game-two matchup with host Brazil, it was again Ochoa who came up big with arguably the game of his life when he made save upon save, often from point-blank range, to steal a point from the favorites after a 0–0 draw. In their final group game against Croatia, Mexico asserted their dominance in the second half with three goals in a 10-minute span that sent them through to their sixth consecutive round of 16.

Facing a Netherlands side loaded with talent, Mexico hoped to finally break their round-of-16 curse. It looked like a possibility when, in the 48th minute, Giovani dos Santos delivered a 25-yard strike to put Mexico ahead. Wilting in heat that forced FIFA to mandate two cooling breaks, the Dutch looked out of it until the 88th minute, when Wesley Sneijder thumped home a layoff from the top of the penalty box. With the game still in doubt, it was an unnecessary foul by Mexican captain Rafael Márquez on Arjen Robben late in late stoppage time that led to substitute Klaas-Jan Huntelaar's game winner from the penalty spot and yet another round-of-16 exit for El Tri, this time in 10th place with five goals for and three against.

MICHELS, RINUS. B. 9 February 1928, Amsterdam, Netherlands. D. 3 March 2005. Named as the Coach of the 20th Century by world soccer's global governing body, Fédération Internationale de Football Association (FIFA), Rinus Michels was a Dutch player and is best known as a successful, innovative tactician as a manager. Michels began his professional soccer career as a player for Ajax Amsterdam, scoring 121 goals in 269 games for the club and making five appearances for the Dutch national team. A few years after his retirement from playing, in 1965 Michels took over as manager of Ajax Amsterdam, taking a mediocre team and leading them to the Dutch championship in 1966. They would win the title again in 1967, 1968 and 1970 under

Michels and then became the first Dutch team to win the European Cup in 1971, with a team built around the genius of Johan Cruyff within a fluid, attacking structure of team play formulated by Michels that became known as Total Football. That style of play was based on intelligent movement and creative roles for every player on the team, with Michels fortunate to work with players with exceptional talent alongside the inimitable Cruyff at both Ajax Amsterdam and the Netherlands and also including the likes of Johan Neeskens and Johnny Rep.

Following the 1971 European Cup triumph with Ajax Amsterdam, Michels moved to Barcelona (bringing Cruyff with him shortly after), winning the Spanish league in 1974. That same year, Michels coached the Netherlands at the FIFA World Cup in West Germany, comfortably cruising to the final with his team playing at a level rarely before seen in the World Cup. In the final, though, the Netherlands were upset 2–1 by the hosts West Germany. Michels went back to club coaching at several teams but returned as national team manager of the Netherlands for the 1988 UEFA European Football Championship, leading a new golden generation of Dutch players to glory as the country claimed their first international title.

MÍGUEZ, ÓSCAR. B. 5 December 1927. D. 19 August 2006. Uruguay's all-time top scorer in the World Cup is Óscar Míguez, with eight goals in six games at the 1950 and 1954 World Cup finals in Brazil and Switzerland.

MONTI, LUIS. B. 15 May 1901, Buenos Aires, Argentina. D. 9 September 1983. Luis Monti not only played in two different FIFA World Cup finals tournaments for two different countries—Argentina and Italy—but also he has the rare distinction of playing in the final of the competition on each occasion, successively in 1930 and 1934. Born in Buenos Aires, Monti began his career in the 1920s in his native Argentina, primarily for San Lorenzo, with whom he won three Argentinean national championships. Monti made his international debut for Argentina in 1924, playing a key role as his country won the 1927 Copa América and reached the final of the 1928 Olympic Games Football Tournament. Monti played in two of Argentina's three group games at the 1930 World Cup in Uruguay, scoring the winning goal in his country's first game against France and then playing in the 3–1 win over Chile to end the group stage. In the semifinal against the United States, Monti opened the scoring in the 20th minute as Argentina went on to win 6–1 over the Americans. Monti played all 90 minutes in the first World Cup final against hosts Uruguay, but despite holding a 2–1 lead at halftime in Montevideo, Argentina lost 4–2.

Monti's performances, though, attracted Italian scouts, and he signed for Juventus in Italy shortly after the World Cup, the riches of Italian soccer far outstripping the wages on offer in Argentina at the time. Monti, who had Italian citizenship, decided to switch international allegiances to his adopted home and began playing for Italy in 1932. Italy hosted the World Cup two years later, and by then, Monti had become a fixture in the Italian team, playing in seven Italian victories out of his eight appearances in 1932 and 1933. In 1934, Monti appeared in Italy's 4–0 win over Greece in World Cup qualification, the last time a World Cup host nation had to qualify for the World Cup. Italy's World Cup campaign began in Rome on 27 May 1934, with

Italian dictator Benito Mussolini in attendance, Monti starting for the Italians as they defeated the United States by the heady score of 7–1. Monti was one of three players on the Italian squad to have been born in Argentina, alongside Raimundo Orsi and Enrique Guaita. There was no group stage at the 1934 World Cup, so Monti next took part in Italy's quarterfinal game against a strong Spanish side on 31 May. A rough game ended 1–1 after extra time, and the rules determined a deciding game had to be played the next day, Monti taking part in a 1–0 victory for Italy thanks to a goal by Giuseppe Meazza. In the semifinal just two days later in Milan, on 3 June, Monti and Italy won again to advance to the final, defeating a strong Austrian side 1–0 with a robust, physical performance against the cultured Austrians. Monti kept his place in the Italian team for the final against Czechoslovakia in Rome a week later, over 55,000 in attendance in Rome, thus becoming the first player to participate in successive World Cup finals. This time, though, Monti's country—Italy, rather than Argentina—was victorious, defeating Czechoslovakia 2–1 after extra time, the winning goal by Angelo Schiavio in the 95th minute. Monti retired in 1939, playing only two more games for Italy following the 1934 World Cup in 1935 and 1936 and went on to have a career in coaching in both Italy and Argentina.

MONZEGLIO, ERALDO. B. 5 June 1906, Vignale Monferrato, Italy. D. 3 November 1981. Eraldo Monzeglio was one of four Italians to have been part of both the 1934 and 1938 World Cup–winning teams. He made his debut for Italy in 1930 on 11 May in a 5–0 victory over Hungary. Monzeglio played in Italy's World Cup qualifier for the 1934 tournament against Greece in March 1934, the last qualifying game a World Cup host had to play, with automatic qualification the rule thereafter. Italy won the game 4–0. Monzeglio played in four of Italy's five games in the 1934 World Cup, including the final—a 2–1 win over Czechoslovakia—missing out on the Italians' first game of the tournament, a 7–1 win over the United States. Monzeglio continued to play frequently for Italy ahead of the 1938 World Cup and was known to be close to Italian dictator Benito Mussolini, coaching his son's tennis at Mussolini's Rome residence. Monzeglio was selected for Italy's first game at the competition held in France against Norway, a 2–1 win. He did not feature again in the tournament after the Norway game, and it has been suggested that he was removed from the team after Italy's unimpressive performance prompted questions from the fascist authorities in Rome about why Monzeglio, at 32 years old far from the player he had been in 1934, continued to be selected. Monzeglio collected his second World Cup winners' medal as Italy went on to successfully defend their title. His 35th appearance in the game against Norway was his last for Italy, though he continued his club career until 1939, playing for Roma, and then later became a noted coach in the Italian league.

MOREIRA, AYMORÉ. B. 24 April 1912, Miracema, Brazil. D. 26 July 1989. Aymoré Moreira coached Brazil to the nation's second World Cup triumph, a 1962 victory that followed a first title in 1958. Under Moreira, Brazil began playing a 4-3-3 system with the loss of Pelé after the first game, replaced by Amarildo, the only personnel change he would need to make throughout the competition. Brazil, inspired by the brilliance of Garrincha, went through the tournament unbeaten, defeating England, host nation Chile and Czechoslovakia in the final to claim the World Cup. Moreira did not coach Brazil at another World Cup but did take charge of the national team for a second spell in 1967–1968.

MOROCCO. Commonly known as Les Lions de l'Atlas or Al Esoud Al-Atlasiyah (The Lions of the Atlas). Morocco has qualified for the World Cup four times and became the first African and Arab team to finish first in their group in the first round when in 1986 they finished ahead of England, Poland and Portugal. Morocco's first World Cup appearance was in 1970 in Mexico. Although they failed to win a game, the North African nation narrowly lost to Germany 2–1 and tied Bulgaria 1–1.

When the World Cup returned to Mexico in 1986, so did Morocco. In their best World Cup showing to date, the Moroccans went unbeaten in the first round, tying both Poland and England 0–0 before defeating Portugal 3–1 in the third game. In the second round, Morocco faced eventual runner-up West Germany, losing 1–0 to a goal in the 88th minute.

Although Morocco failed to qualify for the 1990 World Cup, they returned to the tournament in 1994. Unfortunately, the success of the 1986 tournament did not follow them to the United States, as they lost all three games in the first round. Four years later, they were back again, this time with a better showing. Grouped with Brazil, Norway and Scotland in the 1998 World Cup in France, the Moroccans opened up the competition with a 2–2 draw against Norway. After losing 3–0 to eventual second-place finishers Brazil in their next game, Morocco pulled together to defeat Scotland 3–0 in their final game of the tournament. Their four points were almost enough to take them to the second round, but a late goal by Norway against Brazil propelled the European nation ahead of Morocco and into second place in the group.

Unfortunately for the Lions, even as champions of the 2012 Arab Nations Cup, they have been unable to qualify for a World Cup since 1998.

MÜLLER, GERHARD. B. 3 November 1945, Nördlingen, Germany. Gerhard Müller, better known as Gerd, is Germany's all-time leading scorer, with 68 goals in 62 games, including 14 goals in FIFA World Cup finals tournaments. Müller was a stocky, strong forward who depended on his power and nose for goal, a prolific scorer in club soccer with 365 goals in 427 games in the German Bundesliga, the vast majority for Bayern Munich. Playing alongside the legendary Franz Beckenbauer, Müller won three German championships and three European Cup titles between 1964 and 1979. Franz Beckenbauer went on to say that "Everything that FC Bayern has become is due to Gerd Müller and his goals." Müller won the European Footballer of the Year award in 1970, after scoring 10 goals for West Germany in the World Cup finals that year, where they were eliminated at the semifinal stage by Italy. Müller scored four goals in the 1974 World Cup finals, including an all-important strike in the final to put West Germany 2–1 up over the Netherlands as they went on to win the World Cup for the third time. Müller ended his playing career in 1981, after spending three years in the United States appearing in the North American Soccer League.

MÜLLER, THOMAS. B. 13 September 1989, Weilheim, West Germany. A product of Bayern Munich's youth system and star for club and country, Thomas Müller won the Golden Boot as the top scorer at the 2010 World Cup at the age of only 20. His five goals—against Australia in the group stage, twice against England in the second round, once against Argentina in the semifinal and another in the third-place consolation game with Uruguay—and three assists helped Germany to a third-place finish. Müller's attacking play from midfield and combination of impressive composure and pace also earned him the Best Young Player award for the competition. With another five goals in 2014—a hat trick against Portugal and the lone goal against the United States in group play as well as the opening goal against Brazil in the semifinals—Müller helped Germany win their fourth World Cup title on his way to a Silver Boot award as the tournament's second-leading scorer. His five goals tied him with compatriot Miroslav Klose as only the second player to ever score five goals in back-to-back tournaments.

N

NASAZZI, JOSÉ. B. 24 May 1901, Montevideo, Uruguay. D. 17 June 1968. The first World Cup–winning captain was José Nasazzi, a stout defender who led Uruguay to victory in the inaugural World Cup in 1930. The first World Cup was held in Montevideo, Nasazzi's city of birth and where he played at club level for Club Atlético Bella Vista as an amateur, cutting marble for a living. The World Cup fell at the peak of Nasazzi's career, aged 29 and already an experienced international known for his inspirational and influential leadership. Nasazzi had made his debut for Uruguay in 1923, playing on his country's victories in the 1923, 1924 and 1926 Copa América competition and winning gold medals at both the 1924 and 1928 Olympic Games Football Tournaments while captaining his country. Nasazzi played and captained all four of Uruguay's games at the 1930 World Cup, all of them victories, over Peru, Romania, Yugoslavia and Argentina respectively. Following the World Cup, Nasazzi became a professional player for Nacional in Montevideo, twice winning the Uruguayan national championship with the club and then leading his country to a further international honor with victory in the 1935 Copa América. He retired in 1937 having recorded 51 appearances for Uruguay, later managing his country's team during World War II.

NEESKENS, JOHAN. B. 15 September 1951, Heemstede, Netherlands. Johan Neeskens appeared at the FIFA World Cup twice as a player for the Netherlands, a member of two of its strongest-ever national teams, reaching the final of the competition in both 1974 and 1978, though losing on both occasions. A skillful attacking midfielder, he scored 5 goals in the 12 games at both competitions and a total of 17 goals in 49 games for his country. At club level, Neeskens starred for Ajax Amsterdam in his native Netherlands in the early 1970s, as the team conquered European soccer, winning three successive European Cup competitions between 1971 and 1973. Neeskens then moved on to play for Barcelona in Spain and then the New York Cosmos in the United States. Since retiring as a player, Neeskens has pursued a career in coaching.

NEJEDLÝ, OLDŘICH. B. 26 December 1909, Žebrák, Austria-Hungary (now Czech Republic). D. 11 June 1990. Oldřich Nejedlý was a skillful forward for the Czechoslovakian national team in the 1930s and was the top scorer at the 1934 World Cup, one of his two appearances in the competition.

Nejedlý had made his name as a forward for Sparta Prague, helping his club to the league championship in 1932, and scored on his international debut in June 1931 during a 4–0 win for Czechoslovakia over Poland. His swift and stylish play was never displayed better than at the 1934 World Cup: in Czechoslovakia's first game, he scored the winning goal against Romania, in their second game, he repeated the trick with the decisive strike late in the game to defeat Switzerland, and in their third, the semifinal against West Germany, he struck a deadly hat trick to take the Czechs to the final—though it was not until 2006 that FIFA officially credited Nejedlý with one of the goals. There, despite an impressive display, he was not to score, and Czechoslovakia fell to a late comeback by the host nation to lose 2–1.

Nejedlý continued his prolific scoring after the 1934 World Cup and struck twice in Czechoslovakia's successful qualifying game for the 1938 World Cup in France, as they defeated Bulgaria 6–0. Nejedlý's remarkable goal-scoring record in World Cup competition continued when the third World Cup got underway in June 1938. Nejedlý and his team faced the Netherlands in Le Havre on 5 June, and he struck the third goal in their 3–0 win, all the goals coming in extra time. Nejedlý scored again a week later against Brazil in a bruising battle—one that essentially ended his career, as he suffered a broken leg in the violent 1–1 tie. Nejedlý was unable to play the next day as Czechoslovakia was eliminated in a replay, and though he recovered to play again for his country later in the year, he never scored again, with Czechoslovakia's international play interrupted by World War II.

Nejedlý ended his career with a total of 28 goals in only 43 games for his country, including a remarkable 7 goals in only 6 World Cup games. At club level, though, Nejedlý continued playing well into his 40s, forming a formidable striking partnership with his son before retiring in 1955.

NETHERLANDS. Commonly known as Oranje (Orange), Clockwork Orange or the Flying Dutchmen. The Dutch are often considered to be the best soccer nation never to win the World Cup, with three appearances in the World Cup finals but defeats in the biggest game of all on all three occasions. The Dutch began slowly in the World Cup, only appearing twice before 1974, exiting in the first round in 1934 and 1938 respectively. But fueled by a sudden rise in the quality of youth development at its premier domestic clubs, such as Ajax Amsterdam, the Dutch team that headed to the 1974 competition in West Germany was favored to excel, led by the unique talent of Johan Cruyff. Playing a style of soccer never before seen for its fluidity and known as "Total Football" under the direction of head coach Rinus Michels, the Dutch topped group three in the first round with wins over Uruguay and Bulgaria and a tie with Sweden. In the second group stage, Cruyff and his team excelled: the Dutch defeated Argentina 4–0, East Germany 2–0 and defending world champions Brazil 2–0, playing bewitching soccer. In the final in Munich against the host nation, the heavily favored Dutch took the lead only two minutes in, Johan Neeskens converting from the penalty spot after Cruyff had been fouled following a surging run. The West Germans, though, struck back after 25 minutes, when Paul Breitner earned a penalty kick and converted it himself. Less than 20 minutes later, the Dutch conceded the winning goal of the game to Gerd Müller, becoming one of the great teams not to win the title.

Four years later in Argentina, lacking Cruyff who refused to play in the competition for personal reasons, the Dutch still reached the final once more. The Dutch were far from convincing in the group stage, only scraping through on goal difference above Scotland following a win against Iran, a tie with Peru and a defeat to the Scottish. In the second-round group stage, the Netherlands found form with a 5–1 demolition of Austria, a 2–2 tie with West Germany and a crucial 2–1 win over Italy that propelled the Dutch to the final. In an intimidating atmosphere soaked in ticker tape and games-manship, the Dutch fought Argentina to a 1–1 tie after extra time, Dick Nanninga equalizing in the 82nd minute to cancel out Mario Kempes's first-half goal for the host nation. In extra time, though, Argentina proved strong, scoring twice to create heartache for the Netherlands once again in the final.

The Dutch did not qualify again for a World Cup until 1990, when another golden generation had arisen, one that won the 1988 European Championships with stars including Ruud Gullit, Frank Rijkaard and Marco Van Basten. In Italy at the 1990 World Cup, the Dutch—coached by Leo Beenhakker—surprisingly failed to excel, drawing all three group games and only advancing to the second round as one of the best third-place teams in the first round. Against West Germany in the second round, the Dutch found form in a pulsating game, though one marred by red cards for Dutchman Frank Rijkaard and West German Rudi Völler. It was a game, though, that was won 2–1 by West Germany, Ronald Koeman's 89th-minute penalty coming too late for the Dutch.

At the 1994 World Cup in the United States, the Netherlands topped group F in the first round, beating both Saudi Arabia and Morocco, though losing to Belgium. In the last 16, the Dutch defeated the Republic of Ireland 2–0, Dennis Bergkamp and Wim Jonk scoring the goals. Against Brazil in Dallas, the Dutch defense at first seemed tired and too slow to cope with the brilliant forwards Bebeto and Romário, who both sliced through to score and give Brazil a 2–0 lead midway through the second half. The Dutch did not wilt, though, and leveled the scores through goals by Bergkamp and Aaron Winter. Brazil restored its lead and claimed victory when fullback Branco struck a searing 30-yard free kick past Ed de Goey in the Dutch goal and eliminated the Netherlands.

The Netherlands returned to the World Cup semifinals in 1998 in France. Coached by Guus Hiddink and with Dennis Bergkamp now the star of the team, the Dutch topped group E in the first round, thanks to ties with Belgium and Mexico and a 5–0 win against South Korea. In the second round, Dennis Bergkamp scored to give the Dutch the lead versus Yugoslavia, though the Balkan nation tied the game before Ed-gar Davids found a Dutch winner deep into added time at the end of the second half. The Dutch again found a late winner in the quarterfinal against Argentina, and this time it was one of the most memorable goals in World Cup history, Bergkamp control-ling a long pass with remarkable grace before turning and converting the chance in the 90th minute. That sent the Dutch to Marseille to face defending world champions Brazil. Once again, the Netherlands relied on late heroics, a Patrick Kluivert strike in the 87th minute leveling the scoreline after the Brazilians had led through a Ronaldo goal. This time, though, there was no happy ending for the Dutch, with a defeat on penalty kicks, strikes missed by Phillip Cocu and Ronald De Boer.

The Dutch then failed to qualify for the 2002 World Cup, returning to the stage in Germany in 2006. Former star striker Marco Van Basten led a Dutch team once again full of talent, including the tricky winger Arjen Robben. The Netherlands successfully negotiated through a difficult first-round group, beating Serbia and Montenegro and Côte d'Ivoire while tying with Argentina. In the second round in Nuremberg, the Dutch became embroiled in a vitriolic, foul-ridden game with Portugal, no fewer than 12 players cautioned and 4 expelled, including Dutchmen Khalid Boulahrouz and Giovanni Van Bronckhorst. The only goal of the game was almost an afterthought, but it was enough to eliminate the Dutch, scored by Portuguese forward Maniche.

South Africa 2010 saw the Dutch reach the World Cup final for the third time, coached by Bert Van Marwijk. His team won all three games in the group stage, defeating Denmark 2–0, Japan 1–0 and Cameroon 2–1. It was not sparkling soccer of the 1970s vintage, but it was effective nonetheless, built around a hard-working midfield and the creative skills of Robben and Wesley Sneijder. In the second round, the Dutch defeated Slovakia 2–1, thanks to strikes by Robben and Sneijder. Despite going a goal down to Brazil in the quarterfinal in Port Elizabeth, Sneijder struck two second-half goals to send the Dutch through to the final four again. A thrilling five-goal affair followed in the semifinal against two-time world champions Uruguay. The Dutch opened the scoring through Giovanni Van Bronckhorst after 18 minutes with a magnificent volley, Diego Forlán equalizing for Uruguay before halftime. The game was decided in Dutch favor in a three-minute spell starting in the 70th minute when Sneijder scored his fifth goal of the competition, a deflected strike from distance, Robben wrapping the game up three minutes later with a header. Though Uruguay pulled one back deep into added time, the Dutch advanced. In the final, the Netherlands faced Spain, who had dominated opponents with mesmeric passing throughout the tournament. The Dutch plan in the final in Johannesburg, as cynical as it could be, became immediately apparent: to foul and disrupt the Spanish rhythm. It seemed to work, as the game was 0–0 after 90 minutes, though Dutch midfielder Nigel de Jong had been lucky to escape a red card in the first half. In extra time, however, the Dutch plan came unstuck: Johnny Heitinga was sent off in the 109th minute for the Dutch when he received a second yellow after a foul on Andrés Iniesta. It was then Iniesta who found the winning goal, his strike condemning the Dutch to a third World Cup final defeat.

Qualification for the 2014 World Cup in Brazil was done in typical Dutch fashion, clinically and in style. Led by the attack, attack, attack style of manager Louis van Gaal, Robin van Persie led the team with 11 goals (almost a third of the team's 34), and only a 2–2 draw with Estonia after the group was decided left a blemish. Placed in a relatively weak group B with Spain, Chile and Australia, advancement out of the group stage (something the Dutch have done in the seven previous World Cup finals they have played in) seemed a foregone conclusion. In game one at the Arena Fonte Nova in Salvador, the Flying Dutchmen exacted revenge for their 2010 finals loss to Spain by dismantling the defending world champions 5–1. Although Spain scored on a 27th-minute penalty by Xabi Alonso, a superb flying-header goal from Van Persie right before half pulled the Dutch level. A second-half Robben brace, Stefan de Vrij header and a late goal by Van Persie meant that the Dutch were well on their way to the top of their group.

The second group game, played at Estádio Beira-Rio in Porto Alegre, saw the Oranje go up early behind another Robben goal, but a minute later, Australian captain

Tim Cahill scored what was surely the goal of the match (if not the tournament) when he first-time volleyed home a cross from eight yards out to pull them level. Australia took the lead in the 54th minute on a Mile Jedinak penalty, but Van Persie knotted the game back up in the 58th minute following some shoddy Aussie defending. A Memphis Depay goal put the game out of reach in the 68th minute with a long strike from 35 yards out.

Though Chile was arguably the stronger side in the first half of the final group game, second-half substitutes Leroy Fer and Memphis Depay were the difference makers as the Dutch edged out a 2–0 win and a spot in another round of 16.

The Dutch faced Mexico in the round of 16, and a Giovani dos Santos 25-yard strike put Mexico ahead in the 48th minute. FIFA mandated two cooling breaks for the tiring players, who were wilting in the heat. The Dutch looked out of it until the 88th minute when Wesley Sneijder thumped home a layoff from the top of the penalty box for the equalizer. With most in attendance expecting penalties, an unnecessary foul by Mexican captain Rafael Márquez on Arjen Robben in the box late in stoppage time led to substitute Klaas-Jan Huntelaar's game winner from the penalty spot and a place in the quarterfinals against Costa Rica. Facing a stingy Costa Rican defense that had given up only two goals in four games, it was goalkeeper Keylor Navas's acrobatic saves and some pesky woodwork that ultimately kept a dangerous Dutch side off the scoreboard. In penalties, a freshly substituted Tim Krul proved to be the difference maker as his two saves and a clinical display from the Dutch proved too much for the Costa Ricans.

Through to their fifth World Cup semifinals, the Oranje faced an Argentina team they have met five times previously in the World Cup. The match was played at the Arena Corinthians, in São Paulo. Argentina was without injured striker Ángel Di María, and it became evident early on that neither coach was willing to take too many risks offensively. The result was a mundane 120 goalless minutes. In the ensuing penalty shoot-out, saves by Argentina goalkeeper Sergio Romero on Ron Vlaar and Wesley Sneijder ultimately made the difference, and the Dutch again had to play for third place rather than the title.

Against a Brazilian side without star Neymar, it seemed the host nation embraced the idea that this game was the "game no team wants to play in." A third-minute penalty by Van Persie, the result of another lumbering tackle by Brazilian captain Thiago Silva, started off the scoring, and 15 minutes later, a crafty settle-and-finish by Daley Blind made the lead two. A stoppage-time goal by Georginio Wijnaldum made the final 3–0 and sent the Dutch home in third place with 15 goals for and only 4 against.

NEUER, MANUEL. B. 27 March 1986, Gelsenkirchen, Germany. Described as a "sweeper-keeper" due to his predilection to play off his line, Neuer is known for his quick reflexes, excellent shot-stopping abilities, command of his area and accurate distribution of the ball. As a club player for Bayern Munich and internationally for Germany, Neuer won the Golden Glove award as the tournament's best goalkeeper at the 2014 World Cup in Brazil when he helped lead Germany to their fourth World Cup title with four clean sheets, including a 1–0 victory over Argentina in the final.

NEW ZEALAND. Commonly known as the All Whites. New Zealand first appeared in the World Cup in 1982, where they were grouped with Scotland, Brazil and the

Soviet Union. Unable to register a win, New Zealand finished with zero points and a −10 goal differential. New Zealand did not appear in another World Cup until 28 years later, when they qualified for the 2010 World Cup in South Africa under coach Ricki Herbert. Although the All Whites still failed to win a single match and suffered a first-round elimination, they finished with three draws and a respectable three points after playing Slovakia, Italy and Paraguay. In 2014, though they won Oceania's qualifying tournament, a 9–3 aggregate against CONCACAF participant Mexico meant the All Whites again missed out on qualifying for the World Cup.

NIGERIA. Commonly known as the Super Eagles. It took until 1994 for Nigeria to qualify for the World Cup for the first time, but since then, the African nation known as the Super Eagles has appeared in every competition except for 2006. Nigeria's debut at the 1994 World Cup in the United States was an explosive one, with a team managed by Hans Westerhof and featuring stars such as Rashidi Yekini and Finidi George topping its first-round group. To achieve that, Nigeria defeated Bulgaria 3–0 and Greece 2–0, though also lost 2–1 to Argentina. There was agony for Nigeria in the nation's first World Cup elimination game against Italy in the second round. Leading through a 25th-minute strike by Emmanuel Amuneke until just two minutes from the end of the game, Roberto Baggio equalized for the Italians to send the game into extra time. In the additional period, Baggio struck again from the penalty spot to eliminate the Nigerians.

For the 1998 World Cup in France, experienced coach Bora Milutinović took charge of a team containing many 1994 veterans, along with the creative talent of Jay-Jay Okocha in midfield. Nigeria again topped the group in the first round, coming back from 2–0 down to defeat Spain 3–2, beating Bulgaria 1–0 and losing to Paraguay. Again, though, there was disappointment in round two, as the Nigerians were comfortably beaten 4–1 by Denmark in the Stade de France on the outskirts of Paris. In 2002, at the World Cup in South Korea and Japan, hopes were high for a strong Nigerian team captained by Okocha and featuring the lanky young talent Nwankwo Kanu. Nigeria, though, flopped: coached by Adegboye Onigbinde, the Super Eagles lost 1–0 to Argentina, 2–1 to Sweden and tied 0–0 with England, finishing bottom of group F.

After failing to qualify for the 2006 World Cup, Nigeria returned to the biggest stage in 2010 in South Africa. Expectations for the Super Eagles were limited, though plenty of explosive, attacking talent was at Swedish head coach Lars Lagerbäck's disposal, including forward Obafemi Martins. Nigeria, though, again failed to win a game, losing 1–0 to Argentina, 2–1 to Greece and earning only a single point in a 2–2 tie with South Korea.

Qualification for the 2014 World Cup in Brazil was a testament to manager Stephen Keshi's philosophy of possession, passing and movement, as the only hiccup was a 1–1 draw with Kenya. A 4–1 aggregate over an improved Ethiopian side in a play-off matchup meant the Eagles were headed to Brazil. Placed into group F with Argentina, Bosnia and Herzegovina and Iran, Nigerian expectations were tempered, but advancement past the group stage was expected back home.

Though they dominated possession in an opening matchup against Iran, Nigeria saw few chances and settled for 0–0 draw. Against Bosnia and Herzegovina, Nigeria was on the fortunate side of bad officiating twice, once on a poorly called offsides and again when Emmanuel Emenike tossed Bosnia defender Emir Spahić down with no call. Emenike found an unmarked Peter Odemwingie for a tap-in from six yards out, and tightening their defense in the second half, the Eagles managed a 1–0 victory. In the final group game, against an Argentinian side already through to the round of 16, the game took a turn early when, three minutes in, Lionel Messi blasted home a rebounded Ángel Di María shot from nine yards out. Needing at least a tie, Nigeria pushed the pace and scored a brilliantly struck screamer from the left corner of the penalty box only a minute later. Tied at 1–1, the game remained wide open until the 46th minute when Messi curled a beautifully struck free kick into the top-right corner from 25 yards out. With their tournament lives at stake, Nigeria took it to the Argentinian defense. Ahmed Musa split the defense with an aggressive run, scoring his second goal of the game in the 47th minute. Five minutes later, Marcos Rojo took advantage of poor defending and an opportune knee placement to knock home a beautifully placed Ezequiel Lavezzi corner in the 50th minute to finalize the scoring. Due to Iran's loss to a previously winless Bosnia and Herzegovina, Nigeria advanced to the round of 16 for the third time.

Determined to make history, Nigeria battled with a French side that was arguably more skilled, but the pace and athleticism of the Super Eagles gave the French players trouble. Nigeria had the run of play in the second half until the 79th minute, when a miscue by keeper Vincent Enyeama left a wide-open net for Paul Pogba's header. With Nigeria pressing, the game was decided when Joseph Yobo unfortunately misplayed a Mathieu Valbuena cross into the back of his own net for a 2–0 final. Nigeria exited in 14th place with three goals scored and five conceded.

NORTHERN IRELAND. Commonly known as the Green and White Army or Norn Iron. Northern Ireland carries the distinction of being the least populous country to qualify for more than one World Cup. They first qualified for the World Cup in 1958, which remains their best performance in the tournament to date. Northern Ireland opened the competition with a 1–0 win over Czechoslovakia, the only goal scored by Wilbur Cush in the 20th minute. The Northern Irish looked to continue their winning ways with a third-minute goal against Argentina in the second match of the tournament, only to fall 3–1 to the Argentines. In the third game against Germany, Northern Ireland yet again led first on a goal by Peter McParland, but the game ended in a 2–2 draw. Their three points left them tied with Czechoslovakia in their group, forcing a play-off between the two teams. Tied at the end of regulation, Northern Ireland scored in the 99th minute to make their way to the quarterfinals. Facing eventual third-place finishers France, Les Bleus proved to be too much for the Northern Irish as they were knocked out of the tournament by a score of 4–0.

Northern Ireland's next appearance at a World Cup was in 1982. The team went 1-2-0 in the first round. Their opening game was against Yugoslavia, and although it ended in a disappointing 0–0 tie, it featured the international debut of Manchester

United star Norman Whiteside, who at 17 became the youngest player to compete in the World Cup finals. Northern Ireland tied 1–1 against Honduras in their next game, making their final game against hosts Spain a must-win. Heading into the second half tied 0–0, Northern Ireland's Gerry Armstrong gave his team the lead with a goal in the 47th minute. When Mal Donaghy was sent off with 30 minutes still left to play, the outcome was still far from certain. Yet, even playing a man down, Northern Ireland was able to hold on to the lead and defeat Spain 1–0, finishing first in their group. In the second round, Northern Ireland was grouped with Austria and France. After a 2–2 tie with Austria, they needed a win to advance to the semifinals. But the French were too strong, and Northern Ireland lost 4–1 and was eliminated from the tournament.

After advancing past the first round in both their previous World Cup appearances, the Northern Ireland squad at the 1986 World Cup failed to replicate the success of their predecessors. Facing Brazil, Spain and Algeria, they did not win a single game and finished with an 0-1-2 record. Northern Ireland's only point came from a 1–1 tie against Algeria in the opening game of the tournament. Since their exit in 1986, Northern Ireland has yet to qualify for another World Cup.

NORTH KOREA. *See* KOREA DPR (NORTH KOREA).

NORWAY. Commonly known as the Drillos. Norway has qualified for three World Cups, the first in 1938. Playing only a single game against Italy, the Norwegians took the game into extra time with the scored tied 1–1 after 90 minutes but lost 2–1 to a winning goal by Silvio Piola in the 94th minute. Their next appearance at the World Cup would not be until 1994 in the United States. Norway scored their opening goal of the tournament in the 84th minute against Mexico, with the strike by Kjetil Rekdal turning out to be the game winner. A 1–0 loss to Italy followed by a 0–0 tie against the Republic of Ireland left Norway with only four points. In spite of the fact that all four teams in their group finished with four points each, Norway finished last and did not advance to the second round, eliminated due to scoring the fewest goals in the group.

Four years later, Norway made the trip to France for the 1998 World Cup. Facing a tough Moroccan side in their opening match, Norway pulled out a 2–2 draw thanks in part to an own goal by the opposition. Norway tied yet again in their next match against Scotland, giving them two points heading into their final match of the group stage against the formidable Brazilians. Scoreless heading into the final minutes of the game, Brazil took the lead with just 12 minutes remaining. Norway refused to back down, as they tied things up in the 83rd minute. The Norwegians looked sure to finish with yet another tie, when in the 89th minute Kjetil Rekdal stepped up and scored on a penalty to win the game for his team. The win propelled them into second place in their group, and Norway advanced to the round of 16 for the first time in the country's history. Norway hung tight with Italy throughout the match, but a goal by Italy's Christian Vieri in the 18th minute proved to be enough to send Norway home. Since the 1998 World Cup, Norway has failed to qualify for the tournament.

OLAZAR, FRANCISCO. B. 10 July 1885, Quilmes, Argentina. D. 21 September 1958. At the inaugural 1930 World Cup held in Uruguay, Argentina—one of the favorites for the title following their 1929 victory in the Copa América, South America's international championship—was coached jointly by two men, Francisco Olazar and the much younger Juan José Tramutola. Olazar had been a star amateur player for Racing Club in the suburbs of Buenos Aires, winning several championships, and had also appeared in 18 international games for Argentina. Olazar began coaching Argentina in June of 1929, losing to Uruguay in his first game in charge, and was then joined by Tramutola for the victorious 1929 Copa América campaign. In Uruguay, Argentina dominated their group in the first-round stage, with a tight win over France followed by strong performances against Mexico (winning 6–3) and Chile (winning 3–1). The decision by Olazar and Tramutola to introduce Guillermo Stábile for the second game onward paid considerable dividends, as the forward notched eight goals in four games to finish as the competition's top scorer. In the next round, the semifinal stage, Argentina dispatched the United States 6–1. Despite a strong start in the first World Cup final against Uruguay, played in front of a raucous home crowd at Estadio de Centenario in Montevideo, Argentina could not hold on to a 2–1 halftime lead and lost 4–2. Olazar would not coach Argentina again.

OLIVIERI, ALDO. B. 2 October 1910, San Michele Extra, Italy. D. 5 April 2001. Italy conceded five goals in four games as they won the World Cup for the second time, and in goal for each game was 28-year-old Aldo Olivieri. He had made his debut for Italy two years earlier against Germany in Berlin and had eight international appearances to his name heading into the 1938 World Cup, as Italy looked to defend their World Cup title, won in Rome in 1934. In Italy's first game at the 1938 World Cup, Olivieri made a famous save to deny Norway's Knut Brynildsen a goal two minutes from the end of the game with the score tied 1–1, a strike that would surely have eliminated Italy from the World Cup. Instead, Silvio Piola scored the winning goal for Italy in extra time, and they advanced to the next round. Olivieri's final game for Italy came in May 1940, a 3–2 win over Germany, and he ended his career having made 24 appearances for Italy, conceding 28 goals in 18 wins, 5 draws and suffering only 1 defeat.

OLYMPIASTADION. Originally built by the Nazi regime for the 1936 Olympic Games, Berlin's Olympiastadion has hosted games at two World Cups—in 1974 and 2006—including the final of the latter competition. The stadium underwent major renovation for the 1974 competition, with roofs added over two stands, and Olympi-astadion hosted three group-stage games. It was drastically reconstructed again three decades later in preparation for the 2006 World Cup, with the lower tier rebuilt and a new roof added. At the 2006 competition, Olympiastadion was the venue for four first-round matches, a quarterfinal won on a penalty shoot-out by Germany over Argentina and the final between Italy and France.

ONEGA, ERMINIO. B. 30 April 1940, Las Parejas, Argentina. Erminio Onega played four games at the 1966 World Cup for Argentina, scoring one goal and playing a critical creative role in Argentina's progression to the quarterfinal stage, where they were defeated 1–0 by England. Onega began and played most of his career for Argentinean giants River Plate, scoring 98 goals in 222 appearances for the club between 1957 and 1968. Onega made his debut for Brazil in 1960 but joined an Argentina side in transition from its former focus on individual dribbling and short passing to an emphasis on more physical play and disciplined defense under coach Juan Carlos Lorenzo. Onega, though, surely would have earned a place on almost any Argentinean team, a midfielder always looking to receive the ball and either play quick give-and-gos or look to curve through balls for running attackers with the outside of his right foot or the inside of the left.

The 1966 World Cup showed both the best and worst of Onega and Argentina. Against Spain, in Argentina's opening game, Onega set up one of Luis Artime's two goals in Argentina's 2–1 win with a pivot in midfield, lofting a perfect ball into Artime's path into the penalty area, from where he struck it first time past José Iribar in the Spanish goal. After a goal-less draw against West Germany, Argentina then defeated Switzerland 2–0 in a taut, physical game, with Onega playing a central role in both Argentinean goals. Onega helped create the first goal for Artime, winning the ball on the edge of the Swiss penalty area and poking it across to the forward, who dribbled it past three defenders and scored with the outside of his right boot. Argentina's second goal showed the full range of Onega's midfield abilities. Picking the ball up just outside his own six-yard box, Onega calmly moved the ball up the entire length of the field in tandem with Alberto Gonzalez, cleverly passing around the retreating Swiss on the counterattack. Onega then surged forward rapidly from the halfway line all the way to the penalty spot leaving several Swiss defenders in his wake, with Gonzalez then picking him out with pinpoint precision: receiving the ball just three yards from the onrushing Swiss goalkeeper Leo Eichmann, Onega flicked the ball first time over the goalkeeper's head into the goal.

Argentina's quarterfinal against England on 23 July at a packed Wembley Stadium produced only disappointment and controversy for Onega and Argentina, despite his own excellent performance, Onega's incisive passing and movement troubling England's midfield repeatedly. But with the dismissal of Argentina's captain Antonio Rattín in the 35th minute, an uphill battle ultimately resulted in a 1–0 defeat for Argentina. Onega would not appear at another World Cup, retiring from international play the next year in 1967, finishing with a record of 11 goals in 30 games for his country. Onega continued playing at club level in Argentina until 1977, dying at the young age of 39 following a car accident. Onega's younger brother, Daniel Onega, also played for Argentina's national team.

ORSI, RAIMUNDO. B. 2 December 1901, Avellaneda, Argentina. D. 6 April 1986. Though born and raised in Argentina, Raimundo Orsi won the World Cup with Italy in 1934, playing in the final in Rome as the Italians hosted the competition. Orsi's career had taken off with Club Atlético Independiente in Argentina in the early 1920s, becoming quickly known as a potent goal scorer and called up for Argentina's Copa América campaign in 1927, scoring one goal as Argentina won the competition. Orsi then played for Argentina at the 1928 Olympic Games in Amsterdam, the Netherlands, where he won a silver medal with his country and scored three goals in five games. Orsi's performance at the Olympics in Europe brought him to the attention of several leading Italian clubs, and he signed for Juventus following the tournament. In an era of looser regulations on playing for multiple international teams, Orsi, granted Italian citizenship, began playing for Italy the next year, making his debut in December 1929 against Portugal and scoring two goals in a 6–1 win. He became a regular in the Italian team on the left-wing, scoring 9 goals in 27 games before his selection for the 1934 World Cup team by Italy's coach Vittorio Pozzo. Orsi struck twice in Italy's opening game rout of the United States, a 7–1 win. In the final, Orsi scored the most important goal of his career, equalizing for the Italians in the 81st minute as they trailed Czechoslovakia 1–0. Orsi collected the ball from Enrique Guaita, dribbled through the Czech defense and curled his shot in. With a goal in extra time by Angelo Schiavio, Orsi and his teammates became world champions. Orsi only played three further international games for Italy, returning to his native Argentina in 1935 and playing one final game for his country of birth again the next year.

OWEN, MICHAEL. B. 14 December 1979, Chester, England. Michael Owen was the European Footballer of the Year in 2001, at the peak of his career after bursting onto the world soccer stage three years earlier at the 1998 FIFA World Cup with a sensational goal against Argentina in the second round of the competition, a long run and finish that showcased Owen's explosive pace playing as an out-and-out striker. He is one of England's all-time leading scorers, with 40 goals in 89 appearances as of August 2010. At club level, Owen began his career as a prolific goal scorer for Liverpool Football Club, before moving to Spain in 2004 to play for Real Madrid. Owen returned to England in 2005 to play for Newcastle United and then joined Manchester United in 2009. In recent years, Owen's goal-scoring record has receded as a series of serious injuries have hampered him physically.

OVERMARS, MARC. B. 29 March 1973, Emst, the Netherlands. Marc Overmars played in two World Cup finals tournaments for the Netherlands, appearing at the 1994 World Cup in the United States and the 1998 World Cup in France. In those two competitions, he played a total of 11 games, scoring 1 goal. Overmars was known for his electric pace, superb balance and ability to strike the ball with either foot, able to play on either the left or right wing. At the 1994 World Cup, Overmars was given the

Best Young Player award for his performances. Overmars had only played 13 times for the Netherlands when the 1994 World Cup began, having made his international debut in February 1993, in a World Cup qualifier against Turkey, aged only 19. Overmars's penetrating pace bamboozled his opponents, tormenting the opposition as the Netherlands won six of the seven qualifying games he took part in, playing a particularly memorable part as the Dutch beat England 2–0 in Rotterdam in October 1993. Overmars started the Netherlands' first game at the 1994 World Cup, against Saudi Arabia, though he was substituted midway through the second half. Dutch coach Dick Advocaat benched Overmars for the Netherlands' next game, a disappointing 1–0 defeat to Belgium at the Rose Bowl in Los Angeles, though he came on for the final 30 minutes. He earned a starting spot as the Netherlands beat Morocco 2–1 in their final first-round group-stage game to qualify for the next round. He again split time with Gaston Taument, who replaced him in the second half. Overmars retained his place for the Netherlands' second-round match against the Republic of Ireland at the Citrus Bowl in Orlando. Overmars broke free in the 11th minute after a poor header by Irish defender Ronnie Whelan laid the ball into his path, and he used his speed to tear into the penalty area and pull the ball back across the goal for an onrushing Dennis Bergkamp to tuck away, giving the Dutch a 1–0 lead. Overmars, playing on the right-wing, played a full 90 minutes for the first time in the World Cup, as the Netherlands progressed with a 2–0 win. At the Cotton Bowl in Dallas, Overmars was selected for the Dutch team taking on Brazil in what would turn out to be a classic World Cup encounter. Brazil took a 2–0 lead, but Dennis Bergkamp pulled one back to make it 2–1, and then, in the 76th minute, Overmars delivered a delightful whipping cross from a corner onto the head of Aaron Winter, who buried it past Brazilian goalkeeper Taffarel to level the scorers. There would, though, be heartbreak for Overmars and the Dutch, as Brazil found a winner late in the game.

The 1994 World Cup had, however, been a breakthrough tournament for Overmars. He continued to star domestically for Ajax Amsterdam until 1997, when he moved to Arsenal in the English Premier League. By the time the 1998 World Cup began in France, Overmars was one of the most experienced players on the Dutch team and his graceful flair feared worldwide. In Paris on 12 June, the Dutch started the World Cup in disappointing fashion, drawing 0–0 with Belgium. It proved to be a prelude to an explosion eight days later in Marseille, however, as the Dutch torched South Korea 5–0. The Dutch simply dominated the game, Overmars playing an advanced left-wing position and frequently drifting to the center, scoring the second goal with a dribble past Choi Sung-Yong, cutting inside and finishing with his right foot. He then created the fourth goal, swerving a right-footed cross from the left-hand side perfectly onto the head of Pierre van Hooijdonk, who headed it down into the goal. The Netherlands' next match ended in a 2–2 draw with Mexico, advancing the Dutch to the second round, where they faced Yugoslavia. The score was tied 1–1 when injury time began in the second half; Overmars almost won the game from a corner, hitting a left-footed drive tipped just wide by Ivica Kralj. The resulting corner, though, led to the winning goal for the Dutch, as Edgar Davids scored from 20 yards out. The quarterfinal in Marseille pitted the Netherlands against Argentina, but Overmars tweaked his hamstring in training the day before the game and was held out of the starting lineup.

When he came into the game in the second half, with 64 minutes gone, Argentina and the Dutch were tied at 1–1. Dutch pressure finally told, though, and Bergkamp struck a winner in the last minute to send the Netherlands to the World Cup semifinal. Unfortunately for Overmars, though, his hamstring worsened, and he was to play no part in the Dutch defeat on penalty kicks. He was only able to return to action in the second half of the Netherlands' third-place play-off against Croatia, a game the crestfallen Dutch lost 2–1. Overmars remained a regular in the Dutch team for a further six years but did not appear at a World Cup again, taking part in the failed Dutch effort to qualify for the 2002 World Cup and retiring from international play before qualification for the 2006 World Cup began. Overmars ended his Dutch international career with 17 goals in 86 games. He retired altogether as a player in 2009.

P

PARAGUAY. Commonly known as Los Guaraníes or La Albirroja (The White and Red). Paraguay was one of thirteen teams to participate in the first-ever World Cup in 1930 in Uruguay. Grouped with the United States and Belgium in the first round, Paraguay lost their opening match 3–0 to the United States and defeated Belgium 1–0 in the second match. With only a single team advancing from each group, Paraguay's one win was not enough for their World Cup to continue, and they were eliminated from the tournament.

Twenty years later, Paraguay returned to the World Cup stage in Switzerland. Paraguay failed to win a match, drawing 2–2 against Sweden and losing 2–0 to Italy. Four years later in the 1958 World Cup held in Sweden, Paraguay went 1-1-1, their lone victory a 3–2 win over Scotland. Finishing third in their group, Paraguay was once again sent home after the first round.

Paraguay failed to qualify for the next six World Cups but returned to the biggest stage in world soccer in 1986. In the first round of the tournament in Mexico, Paraguay earned a 1–0 victory over Iraq, a 1–1 draw against Mexico and a 2–2 draw with Belgium. Their four points were good enough for second place in the group, and Paraguay advanced to the second round for the first time in their nation's history. Paraguay would see their tournament run end in the round of 16 as they lost 3–0 to England.

In the 1998 World Cup in France, Paraguay once again reached the second round, going 1-2-0 in the group stage. Paraguay faced a tough opponent in the round of 16 in hosts and eventual champions France but hung tough through 114 minutes as the game stretched into extra time. Unfortunately for the South Americans, France's captain Laurent Blanc scored the winning golden goal in the second half of extra time, ending Paraguay's tournament. For their strong efforts on defense, Paraguay's central defender Carlos Gamarra and goalkeeper José Luis Chilavert were selected for the all-star World Cup team.

Paraguay would reach the round of 16 yet again in 2002 after going 1-1-1 in the first round against South Africa, Spain and Slovenia. In the second round, Paraguay held Germany scoreless until the 88th minute when Germany's Oliver Neuville scored the game's only goal. Four years later, Paraguay went 1-0-2 in the first round of the 2006 World Cup, losing their first two games against England and Sweden before earning a consolatory win in the third game against Trinidad and Tobago.

Paraguay qualified for their fourth consecutive World Cup when they made it to the 2010 World Cup in South Africa, and it would prove to be their strongest finish to date. Grouped with Italy, New Zealand and Slovakia, Paraguay went 1-2-0 in the first round, tying Italy and New Zealand and defeating Slovakia 2–0. Paired with Japan in the round of 16, the game remained scoreless through regulation and extra time, forcing the game to a penalty shoot-out. Paraguay would reach their first-ever World Cup quarterfinals when they won the shoot-out 5–3. Paraguay faced eventual champions Spain in the next match, and although they kept the game scoreless up to the 83rd minute, Spain's David Villa found the back of the net to send Paraguay home.

Qualification for the 2014 World Cup in Brazil proved to be one of the most unsuccessful campaigns for the Albirroja. With three managers over a 24-month period, Paraguay never went higher than fourth in the CONMEBOL table, ultimately finishing in last place in the group.

PARREIRA, CARLOS ALBERTO. B. 2 February 1927, Rio de Janeiro, Brazil. A fourth World Cup triumph for Brazil in 1994 came with Carlos Alberto Parreira at the helm, though the Brazilians' pragmatic style—a far change from the élan shown in earlier titles—was criticized widely. Parreira has enjoyed a long, itinerant career: along with coaching Brazil in 1994 at the competition in the United States, Parreira has managed four other teams at the World Cup finals, a record shared with Serbian Bora Milutinović. His first two World Cup experiences as head coach came with unfancied Middle Eastern countries, when he took Kuwait to the 1982 World Cup in Spain, gaining one point in a first-round elimination, and with the United Arab Emirates in 1990, losing all three games in Italy. Following his success in 1994, Parreira was again hired to lead a Middle Eastern country, this time Saudi Arabia in 1998, with whom he again secured a lone point, a tie against Tunisia. After an absence in the 2002 World Cup in South Korea and Japan, Parreira returned to the Brazilian national team in 2006 in Germany and led A Seleção to a quarterfinal 1–0 loss to France. In 2010, Parreira was hired to lead the host nation, South Africa. A tough group meant a touch of notoriety as he became the first coach to not lead the host nation out of the group stage. South African's lone point was a 1–1 tie to Mexico.

PATENAUDE, BERT. B. 4 November 1909, Fall River, Massachusetts. D. 4 November 1979. The first hat trick in World Cup history was scored by American Bert Patenaude at the 1930 World Cup in Uruguay. It came in the United States' second game against Paraguay, with goals from Patenaude coming in the 10th, 15th and 50th minutes. Patenaude's second goal was long clouded by doubt over who had actually scored it, but it is now credited by FIFA as belonging to the American, thus earning him a permanent place in the record books. Patenaude also scored in the first round against Belgium, and his four goals in the tournament—as the U.S. claimed third place—remain a record for a single competition by an American player.

PATERNOSTER, FERNANDO. B. 24 May 1903, Buenos Aires, Argentina. D. 6 June 1967. Fernando Paternoster played in the inaugural World Cup final in 1930 on the losing Argentinean side, as they fell 4–2 to hosts Uruguay. It was two times unlucky for Paternoster against Uruguay, as the defensive stalwart had also taken part in Argentina's defeat in the final of the 1928 Olympic Games Football Tournament to their rivals from across the Río de la Plata. At the time of the 1930 World Cup, Paternoster was 27 years old and at the peak of his career, playing domestically for a strong

Racing Club team in a suburb of his native Buenos Aires. Paternoster was not selected for Argentina's first game in the 1930 World Cup, a 1–0 win over France that was so unconvincing several players, including Paternoster, were introduced in Argentina's second game against Mexico. Paternoster remained on the team from there on to the final, participating in the victories over Mexico 6–3, Chile 3–1 and the United States 7–1 in the semifinal. Paternoster did not play for Argentina again following the 1930 World Cup. He became known later in his life as an evangelist for soccer in Colombia, teaching the Argentinean style of play.

PELÉ. B. 23 October 1940, Três Corações, Brazil. Born as Edson Arantes do Nascimento, but known universally as Pelé, the Brazilian is the most legendary player in the history of soccer. Pelé won three FIFA World Cups with Brazil in his international career from 1957 to 1971, scoring 77 goals in 92 games for his country. Pelé played most of his club career for Santos Futebol Club in Brazil, scoring 474 goals in just 438 games. In 2002, he was named joint winner of the FIFA Player of the Century award, sharing the honor with Argentina's Diego Maradona.

Pelé made his professional debut at the age of 15 for Santos and shot to worldwide fame with his international tournament debut for Brazil in the 1958 World Cup finals in Sweden. Aged just 17, Pelé became the youngest scorer in World Cup history in Brazil's quarterfinal against Wales and then scored a hat trick as Brazil beat France 5–2 in the semifinals. In the final against the hosts Sweden, Pelé again scored twice, capping a mesmerizing tournament. Swedish player Sigge Parling said later that "after the fifth goal, I felt like applauding."

At club level, Pelé then led Santos to victorious Copa Libertadores campaigns in 1962 and 1963, followed by back-to-back Intercontinental Cup titles. In the 1962 World Cup finals, Pelé played in only two games due to a groin injury, with Brazil winning the final without him. He was injured again in the group stage of the 1966 World Cup finals as Brazil departed early. The 1970 World Cup finals, though, would prove to be the crowning glory of Pelé's career: the first finals broadcast in Technicolor, Brazil's glorious run to the title included a legendary 4–1 mauling of Italy in the final, including Brazil's 100th FIFA World Cup goal through a powerful header by Pelé.

Pelé would not appear in another World Cup but did achieve further fame in the United States by joining the New York Cosmos in 1975 and playing three seasons in the North American Soccer League (NASL). Pelé retired from playing following the Cosmos' victory in the 1977 NASL Soccer Bowl championship. Unlike many other legendary players of his generation, Pelé has not taken up a coaching career in retirement and has instead pursued commercial activities and an ambassadorial role for world soccer.

PERU. Commonly known as La Blanquirroja (The White and Red). Peru first competed in the World Cup in the inaugural edition of the tournament in 1930 but failed to register a win as they lost to Romania and hosts Uruguay. Forty years later, Peru qualified for the 1970 World Cup in Mexico. This time, Peru found success, finishing with four points in the group stage with wins against Bulgaria and Morocco and advancing to the second round. Peru then found themselves outmatched against eventual champions Brazil and lost 4–2.

Peru failed to qualify for the 1974 World Cup but qualified for the two subsequent World Cups, in 1978 and 1982. In 1978, Peru finished first in their group consisting of the Netherlands, Scotland and Iran with a 2-1-0 record. As in 1970, Peru once again advanced to the second round, this time facing Argentina, Brazil and Poland. Peru was outscored by a total of ten goals to zero and were knocked out of the tournament. Four years later, Peru failed to get past the first stage, finishing fourth in their group without winning a game. Peru has failed to qualify for each subsequent World Cup.

PETRŮ, KAREL. B. 24 January 1891, Austria-Hungary. D. 1949. The coach of Czechoslovakia's World Cup finalist team in 1934, Karel Petrů saw his team fall just short of winning the World Cup, letting slip a 2–1 lead over hosts Italy with less than 10 minutes remaining in the game. Their place in the final, earned with victories over Romania, Switzerland and West Germany respectively, was the best-ever finish for Czechoslovakia at a World Cup competition. Petrů coached Czechoslovakia from 1931 to 1934 and later wrote a history of Czech soccer.

PEUCELLE, CARLOS. B. 13 September 1908, Buenos Aires, Argentina. D. 1 April 1990. One of Argentina's stars in the 1930 World Cup, as they finished runners-up to hosts Uruguay in the inaugural competition, was Carlos Peucelle, a gifted goal-scoring, pacy winger. Only 21 years old at the time, Peucelle had made his national team debut in 1928 and played a key role in Argentina's victory at the 1929 Copa América, scoring one goal in four games. Peucelle began the 1930 World Cup on the bench, however, missing Argentina's unconvincing opening 1–0 win against France. The unsteady performance prompted Peucelle's call-up to start Argentina's next game against Mexico, and he kept his place in the team for the remainder of the tournament. Peucelle opened his goal-scoring account in the World Cup with a brace of goals in the semifinal on 26 July in a 6–1 hammering of the United States. In the final four days later, in front of a raucous crowd supporting the hosts Uruguay at the Estadio de Centenario in Montevideo, it was Peucelle who equalized for Argentina in the 20th minute after Uruguay had taken an early lead, though it was not enough for the Argentineans, who succumbed to a second-half surge from Uruguay and lost 4–2. Peucelle continued to play for Argentina until 1940, totaling 29 appearances with 12 goals for his country, though did not appear in another World Cup, as Argentina refused to enter the 1934 and 1938 competitions. He did, however, make a memorable mark on Argentinean soccer domestically throughout the 1930s, a star player who helped develop River Plate's fluid, fantastic play that built the Buenos Aires team into one of the best in the world. Peucelle retired in 1940.

PIOLA, SILVIO. B. 29 September 1913, Robbio, Italy. D. 4 October 1996. Silvio Piola is perhaps the best striker ever produced by Italy, the all-time top scorer in the top Italian league, Serie A, and scorer of five goals at the 1938 FIFA World Cup for his country, as they won their second World Cup title, Piola scoring twice in the final. He scored a total of 30 goals for Italy, using his height, speed and athleticism to dominate defenders physically. Though Piola's career was interrupted by the Second World War, Piola's goal-scoring record in Serie A remains unbeaten, with the bulk of his strikes coming for Lazio and Novara Calcio.

PIRLO, ANDREA. B. 19 May 1979, Brescia, Italy. An outstanding deep-lying playmaker, Andrea Pirlo was the creative fulcrum of Italy's 2006 World Cup–winning team, producing five assists and awarded the Bronze Ball as the third-best player in the tournament. Though 27 years old at the time, the 2006 World Cup was Pirlo's first. He appeared again at the 2010 World Cup but only played in one game as Italy exited at the first-round stage, having missed the Italians' first two games due to injury. Scoring one goal and assisting on numerous others, Pirlo was again selected to represent the Azzurri in 2014 and wore the captain's armband in the first game due to Gianluigi Buffon's last-minute injury. With his announcement that he would retire from international football following the tournament, Pirlo was probably hoping for a better result as Italy won only one game, 2–1 over England, before consecutive 1–0 group losses meant Italy's exit. Having achieved his 112th cap, against Uruguay, Pirlo retired from the Azzurri tied with Dino Zoff as the fourth-most-capped player in Italian history.

PLÁNIČKA, FRANTIŠEK. B. 2 June 1904, Prague, Austria-Hungary. D. 20 July 1996. Czechoslovakia's goalkeeper and captain for the 1934 World Cup final was František Plánička, a renowned and experienced shot-stopper. Plánička made his debut for Czechoslovakia in 1926 against Italy, having made his name as a goalkeeper for Slavia Prague—the only club he ever played for—winning the Czech championship in 1925. Plánička played a total of 73 games for his country between 1926 and 1938, winning 35, drawing 16 and losing 22. He played in Czechoslovakia's successful World Cup qualifying game against Poland in October 1933. Plánička played in all four of Czechoslovakia's games at the 1930 World Cup, conceding only five goals in four games behind a stout Czech defense. That defense held their opponents in the final, hosts Italy, at bay until the 81st minute, when Raimundo Orsi beat Plánička to score an equalizer for the Italians. The hosts found a winning goal in extra time, handing Czechoslovakia defeat. Plánička had arguably proven himself to be the world's leading goalkeeper, and his reputation was further enhanced at the 1938 World Cup in France. Known for his sportsmanship (never once cautioned by a referee in his career), Plánička's bravery also became apparent during the Czechs' quarterfinal against Brazil, a brutal game that saw two Brazilians and one Czech player sent off by referee Pal von Hertzka. Plánička broke his arm during the mayhem, but—in an era without substitutes—continued all through extra time to earn the Czechs a 1–1 draw and a replay the next day. Unable to play due to his injury, Plánička had to watch from the sidelines as Brazil defeated his country 1–0, ending his international and World Cup career. Plánička retired from soccer altogether the following year.

PODOLSKI, LUKAS. B. 4 June 1985, Gliwice, Poland. A Polish-born German forward, Lukas Podolski is known for his strong left-footed shot and his attacks down the left side of the field. He earned his first cap for Germany in 2004, and his 47 goals currently tie him for third with greats Rudi Völler and Jürgen Klinsmann in the German record books. Podolski was chosen for Germany's 2006 World Cup roster, a tournament his nation hosted. Podolski scored his first World Cup goal in Germany's group match against Ecuador, followed by two goals in Germany's 2–0 win over Sweden in the next round. Although Germany fell short of a World Cup trophy, the team captivated the nation with a new style of attractive, high-tempo attacking soccer. The hosts were the top-scoring team of the tournament with 14 goals—3 from Podolski—and finished in third place following a win over Portugal. Podolski was named the World Cup's Best Young Player.

The Germans found similar success in the 2010 World Cup in South Africa, with another third-place finish. Podolski scored his first goal of the tournament and assisted on another in Germany's opening game against Australia en route to a 4–0 win. Although Podolski struggled to score in a 1–0 loss to Serbia in which the Germans played much of the game down a man, he managed to score against England in the round of 16, helping his team to a 4–1 victory and a place in the quarterfinals. Podolski added two more assists to his tally in the match against Argentina, which the Germans won 4–0. Podolski and his teammates failed to reach the final after a 1–0 loss to Spain but finished on a high note with a win over Uruguay for third place.

Although he played in five qualification matches leading up to Brazil 2014, Podolski saw limited playing time in the tournament. He did not play a full 90 minutes in games versus the United States and Portugal on the way to a fourth German World Cup title.

POGBA, PAUL. B. 15 March 1993, Lagny-sur-Marne, France. After Pogba was named by the *Guardian* as one of the 10 best young players in Europe, Pogba validated their decision in the 2014 World Cup in Brazil. The Juventus star, only 21 years old at the tournament, was named the tournament's best young player following his play in central midfield for the French team. Pogba proved his worth with his 80 percent passing percentage, technical skill and tactical awareness, as well as for his goal against Nigeria in the round of 16. The award comes on the heels of his winning the Golden Ball at the 2013 U-20 World Cup in Turkey.

POLAND. Commonly known as Biało-czerwoni (The White and Reds) or Białe Orły (The White Eagles). The national team of Poland was established in 1919 and made its debut at the 1938 World Cup in France. Poland played only one game in a straight-elimination format, but it was a memorable one in an 11-goal thriller with Brazil. Poland came off on the wrong end of the result, though it was memorable for a four-goal performance by Polish forward Ernst Wilimowski. Poland did not appear again at the World Cup until 1974, though it had by then made its mark internationally, having won a gold medal at the 1972 Olympic Games soccer tournament. The Polish team put on a superb performance at the World Cup held in West Germany, topping group four following wins over Argentina, Haiti and Italy, with forward Grzegorz Lato in prolific form. In the second-round group stage, Poland began with wins over Sweden and Yugoslavia and then faced West Germany knowing the winning team would head to the World Cup final. On a rain-soaked field in Frankfurt, Poland fell to a 1–0 defeat. Third place was secured for Poland with a 1–0 win over Brazil in the third-place playoff, and Lato ended as the tournament's top scorer with seven goals.

At the 1978 World Cup in Argentina, Poland began with a 2–0 defeat to the host nation in group B. A 1–0 win over Peru followed, but a 3–1 defeat to Brazil eliminated Poland at the first stage. The 1982 World Cup in Spain saw a Polish team, featuring the veteran Lato and led by the gifted forward Zbigniew Boniek, excel. Poland topped group one, tying with both Argentina and Cameroon and defeating Peru 5–1. Poland again topped the group in the second stage, beating Belgium 3–0 and drawing with the Soviet Union, advancing to the semifinals. An Italian team inspired by two goals from Paolo Rossi defeated Poland, who settled again for third place after defeating France 3–2 in the play-off game.

Poland reached a fourth successive World Cup in 1986 but could not advance past the first round, tying with Morocco, beating Portugal 1–0 but losing a crucial final group game 3–0 to England. Poland did not qualify for the World Cup again until 2002, advancing to the competition in South Korea and Japan. Coached by Jerzy Engel, Poland lost its first two group games 2–0 to host nation South Korea and 4–0 to Portugal. A 3–1 win over the United States could not prevent Poland from finishing bottom of the group. Poland advanced again to the World Cup in 2006 in neighboring Germany but once more could not move beyond the first-round stage. A 2–0 loss to Ecuador and 1–0 defeat to Germany condemned Poland to elimination in group A, with a 2–1 win over Costa Rica only preventing Poland from finishing bottom of the group. Poland has not since qualified again for either the subsequent 2010 World Cup in South Africa or the 2014 World Cup in Brazil.

POLGÁR, GYULA. B. 8 February 1912, Kistelek, Hungary. D. 26 June 1992. Gyula Polgár played in the 1938 World Cup final for Hungary against Italy, a game his country lost 4–2. It was his 16th appearance for Hungary, having made his debut in 1932 but not having appeared at the 1934 World Cup, where Hungary reached the quarterfinal stage. The final was his only appearance at any World Cup. At the time, he played for Ferencvárosi TC, one of the two leading Hungarian teams based in Budapest. Polgár ended his international career in November 1942, having made 26 appearances with 2 goals to his name.

PORKUYAN, VALERIY. B. 4 October 1944, Kirovohrad, Soviet Union. With four goals in three games at the 1966 World Cup in England, Valeriy Porkuyan was the joint third-highest scorer at the competition. Only 21 years old, Porkuyan had not played for the Soviet Union before the 1966 World Cup began, having recently made his name with FC Chornomorets Odessa at club level in the Soviet league. Porkuyan did not start either of the Soviet Union's first two games at the 1966 World Cup, both wins for the Soviet Union over North Korea and Italy respectively, but came into the team for the Soviets' third and final group game against Chile. Porkuyan made his mark quickly, scoring in the 28th minute to give the Soviets the lead, though the South Americans leveled the score only four minutes later. Late in the second half, with only five minutes remaining, Porkuyan scored his second to win the game for the Soviet Union. The Soviet Union now moved on to the quarterfinal stage, facing Chile, and Porkuyan scored the second goal of the game as they went on to a 2–1 win. West Germany stood between the Soviets and the World Cup final at Goodison Park in Liverpool on 25 July. Porkuyan again struck for the Soviets in the 88th minute, but it was too little, too late, the Soviets down by two goals at that stage. Porkuyan was not selected for the Soviets' third-place play-off against Portugal three days later, a game won 2–1 by the Portuguese. Porkuyan would only go on to play five more games for his country, never scoring again, though he was selected—but did not play—for the 1970 World Cup in Mexico.

PORTUGAL. Commonly known as A Selecção, A Selecção das Quinas (The Selection of the Five), or Os Navegadores (The Navigators). The Iberian nation Portugal has appeared in six World Cup finals competitions, with two finishes in the final four. Portugal did not qualify until 1966 but, in England on its debut, made it all the way to the semifinals. The Portuguese team was led by the superb Mozambique-born forward Eusébio, who scored nine goals in six games at the competition. Portugal blazed through the group stage, scoring three times in each game in defeats of Hungary (3–1), Bulgaria (3–0) and Brazil (3–1). In the quarterfinal, Portugal faced the tournament's surprise package, little-known North Korea, in Liverpool at Goodison Park. The North Koreans took a shocking 3–0 lead after only 25 minutes before Eusébio led a remarkable comeback, scoring four goals in 32 minutes, with a fifth added by José Augusto for a 5–3 scoreline. In the semifinal, Portugal was ousted by the host nation 2–1 at Wembley Stadium in London and then claimed third place by defeating the Soviet Union 2–1 in a play-off.

Portugal did not play again at the World Cup until 1986 in Mexico. This time, the Portuguese team coached by Jose Torres and featuring the talented attacker Paulo Futre did not progress past the group stage. Despite an impressive opening 1–0 win over England, the Portuguese then slumped to a 1–0 defeat to Poland and a 3–1 loss to Morocco to crash out of the competition. A further 16 years passed before Portugal again appeared at the World Cup, but there were high expectations for a new "Golden Generation" of players led by the exciting winger Luís Figo. Shockingly, though, Portugal fell 3–2 to the United States to kick off group D, and though that was followed by a 4–0 win over Poland, they then lost 1–0 to host nation South Korea, resulting in elimination at the first stage. In 2006, Figo—supported by a superb midfield including Ronaldo and Deco—went much closer to fulfilling the vast potential of a technically gifted group of players under the stewardship of Brazilian head coach Luiz Felipe Scolari, reaching the semifinals for the first time since 1966. Portugal rolled comfortably through the group stage, beating Angola 1–0, Iran 2–0 and Mexico 2–1. In the second round, Portugal and the Netherlands played a game that was essentially second fiddle to exchanges of fouls, with 12 players cautioned and two players from each team sent off, including Portugal's Deco and Coutinho. It was Portugal who advanced, though, on the back of a 23rd-minute strike by Maniche. England provided the quarterfinal opposition for Portugal, a game that went 120 minutes without a goal, though not without incident, as the English star striker Wayne Rooney was sent off. On a penalty shoot-out, Portugal prevailed. In Munich, Portugal faced France for a place in the final, but a Zinedine Zidane penalty kick was the only goal of the game. The Portuguese lost the third-place play-off to Germany 3–1.

Portugal qualified for the 2010 World Cup in South Africa and advanced to the second round after 0–0 ties with Côte d'Ivoire and Brazil, along with a crushing 7–0 defeat of North Korea. In the second round, Portugal faced Iberian neighbor and reigning champion Spain in a tense game decided by a 63rd-minute strike by Spanish striker David Villa, eliminating the Portuguese.

Qualification for the 2014 World Cup in Brazil meant yet another play-off in UEFA qualifying for Portugal, this time against Sweden. Thankfully, an away goal and three at home by FIFA Golden Ball winner Cristiano Ronaldo sent Portugal to Brazil, placed in group G, the "Group of Death," with Germany, Ghana and the United States. What was supposed to be a return to the glory days of the 2006 semifinals instead got off to a horrible start when Portugal ran into a German side firing on all cylinders. Perhaps it was the early red card awarded to Portuguese defender Pepe for an ill-advised headbutt, or maybe it was the early Thomas Müller penalty, but Portugal could never match Germany's level. Müller looked like his Golden Boot award–winning self in the match with the first hat trick of the 2014 tournament, and Mats Hummels added another for the 4–0 final score.

Game two against the United States surely meant a necessary three points, and an early goal by Nani in the fifth minute made that result look possible. It wasn't to be, though, as A Selecção's lead evaporated in the 64th minute when Jermaine Jones drilled a ball from 25 yards out past a stationary Beto. In the 81st minute, the Yanks again struck, this time off the chest of captain Clint Dempsey. With their tournament lives at stake, Ronaldo again proved why he is considered one of the best in the world when, in the 95th minute, he found himself one versus one on the right flank and calmly crossed a beautiful ball far post to a streaking Silvestre Varela. The subsequently drilled header past a shocked Tim Howard secured a valuable late point. Needing a big win against a Ghanaian team battling for their own lives, Portugal found themselves up a goal 30 minutes in when Ghanaian defender John Boye inadvertently knocked the ball into the back of his own net. A goal in the 57th minute by Asamoah Gyan equalized, but Cristiano Ronaldo calmly tucked away a point-blank gift in the 80th minute for the game winner. With only three points, Portugal was sent home in 18th place with four goals for and seven against.

POZZO, VITTORIO. B. 2 March 1886, Piedmont, Italy. D. 21 December 1968. An Italian coach, Vittorio Pozzo most famously led Italy to successive FIFA World Cup victories in 1934 and 1938. In 97 games as manager of Italy, spanning from 1929 to 1948, the country won 64 games, drew 17 and lost 16, an outstanding record. An Anglophile, Pozzo had learned the game as a student in England and then went on to play professionally for Grasshopper Club Zürich in Switzerland. In 1906, Pozzo went back to Italy to play for Torino, taking over as manager in 1912. He took charge of the Italian team at both the 1912 and 1924 Olympic Games Football Tournaments, winning a bronze medal at the latter. Five years later, Pozzo took charge of the Italian national team full-time and led Italy to victory in the second World Cup tournament, held in Italy in 1934. A gold medal followed for Italy at the 1936 Olympic Games Football Tournament, and Pozzo became the first and still only coach to win a second World Cup title in 1938 in France, beating a renowned Hungary team in the final. Pozzo's reputation as a soccer manager was impeccable, but postwar Italy looked unkindly on his accommodation to Benito Mussolini's fascist regime, with Pozzo moving on to work in soccer journalism for some years before his death in 1968.

PREUD'HOMME, MICHEL. B. 24 January 1959, Ougrée, Belgium. At the 1994 World Cup in the United States, FIFA awarded the Lev Yashin award to the best goalkeeper of the tournament for the first time. The winner was Belgian goalkeeper Michel Preud'homme. The award came toward the tail end of Preud'homme's long and distinguished career, played domestically in Belgium up to that point (he would then play in Portugal for Benfica until 1999) for Standard Liège and Mechelen. He was named Belgian goalkeeper of the year on five occasions. Preud'homme made his international debut in 1979, appearing in two qualifiers for the 1982 World Cup in Spain, though he was not part of the squad that traveled to the final competition. Preud'homme did not take part in the qualifiers or the Belgium team for the 1986 World Cup in Mexico. His career flourished in the late 1980s as his club side Mechelen excelled in European competition—winning the European Cup Winners' Cup in 1988—and he became a regular starter for the Belgian national team in time for the 1990 World Cup in Italy. Belgium qualified for the second round, Preud'homme conceding three goals in three games at the group stage. Belgium was eliminated in the second round deep into extra time against England, when David Platt struck an unstoppable volley past Preud'homme for a 1–0 win. Preud'homme excelled at the 1994 World Cup, only conceding one goal in the three-group stage as Belgium progressed to the last 16. Belgium lost 3–2 at that stage to Germany, but Preud'homme could do little about any of the goals and made a number of notable saves. Preud'homme retired following the World Cup, moving into coaching.

PROBST, ERICH. B. 5 December 1927, Vienna, Austria. D. 16 March 1998. Austrian forward Erich Probst scored six goals at the 1954 World Cup held in Switzerland, making him the joint second-top scorer in the competition behind Hungarian Sándor Kocsis. At the time, Probst was playing at club level for Rapid Wien, a prolific goal scorer averaging over a goal a game while leading them to league championships in 1951, 1952 and 1954. Probst made his debut for Austria in May 1951. In September 1953, Probst scored five goals in one game as Austria beat Portugal 9–1 to help them qualify for the World Cup. At the ensuing 1954 World Cup, Probst opened his account with the winning goal in Austria's first group-stage game against Scotland. Austria then began scoring with almost absurd ease, with Probst recording the fastest hat trick in World Cup history during their next game against Czechoslovakia, recording goals in the 4th, 21st and 24th minutes in a 5–0 win. Probst then took part in the highest-scoring game in World Cup history as Austria defeated Switzerland 7–5 in a quarterfinal on 26 June in Lausanne. Probst scored the final goal of the game, taking his tally to five goals in three games. Though Probst scored in the semifinal against West Germany, it was to no avail with the West Germans walloping their neighbors 6–1 on their way to winning the World Cup title. Austria won the third-place play-off game versus Uruguay, though Probst did not add to his goal-scoring tally of six for the tournament. Following the 1954 World Cup, Probst played a further five games for Austria, scoring four more goals. He ended his international career in 1960, with a total of 18 goals in 19 games.

PROSINEČKI, ROBERT. B. 12 January 1969, Schwenningen, West Germany. Although Robert Prosinečki was born in West Germany, he played internationally for both Yugoslavia and Croatia. He began his international career with Yugoslavia, competing in the World Youth Championship in 1987 and the World Cup in 1990, where Prosinečki was named the Best Young Player of the tournament. He earned 15 caps and scored 4 goals with Yugoslavia, known for his creative playmaking ability from midfield.

For the 1998 World Cup, Prosinečki suited up for a different country following the breakup of Yugoslavia-Croatia. The team made it to the semifinals, where Croatia fell to France 2–1. The Croatians fought back in their next game to defeat the Netherlands and earn third place. Prosinečki scored two goals in the tournament. In the following World Cup in 2002, Prosinečki made one appearance for Croatia, a 0–1 loss to Mexico in the group stage. In his international career, Prosinečki earned 49 caps for Croatia and scored 10 goals.

With goals in both the 1990 and 1998 World Cups, Prosinečki is the only player in the tournament's history to have scored for two different national teams. He played three World Cup matches for Yugoslavia, scoring one goal, and six for Croatia, scoring three goals. After retiring as a player, Prosinečki became an assistant manager of the Croatian national team. He currently manages a team in the Turkish Super Lig.

PUČ, ANTONÍN. B. 16 May 1907, Jinonice, Austria-Hungary. D. 16 April 1988. Scorer of 35 goals in 61 games for Czechoslovakia, Antonín Puč tallied two of those goals at the 1934 World Cup in France, including one in the final, a 2–1 defeat to hosts Italy. Playing on the left-wing, Puč's 71st-minute goal in Rome against the Italians seemed as if it might give Czechoslovakia the title, but Italy equalized through Raimundo Orsi and then found a winner in injury time. Puč, by the 1934 World Cup, was an established star for his country and at club level for Slavia Prague. He made his international debut in 1926 at only 19 years old, scoring against Yugoslavia, and established a reputation as a deadly finisher. In 1938, toward the end of his career, Puč was selected for Czechoslovakia's team traveling to France for the third World Cup. He was not selected for the Czechs' first-round win over the Netherlands but did play against Brazil as Czechoslovakia exited at the quarterfinal stage. Puč ended his international career after the World Cup.

PUHL, SÁNDOR. B. 14 July 1955, Hungary. The 1994 World Cup final between Brazil and Italy was refereed by the Hungarian, assisted by Paraguayan Venancio Concepción Zarate and Iranian Davoud Fanaei. Puhl became a FIFA referee in 1989 after beginning his career as an assistant referee. He refereed one game at the 1992 UEFA European Championship as well as the 1993 UEFA Cup final. Puhl then took charge of the World Cup qualifying play-off between Argentina and Australia in Sydney in November 1993, a 1–1 draw. At the 1994 World Cup, 39-year-old Puhl took charge of four games in the competition. Three of those games came in the first round, beginning on 19 June as Puhl oversaw Norway's 1–0 win over Mexico at RFK Stadium in Washington DC, issuing three cautions in the game. He then took charge of a 1–1 tie between Brazil and Sweden on 28 June, Puhl giving out two cautions during the game. In the quarterfinal stage, Puhl took charge as Italy defeated Spain 2–1 in a bitterly contested game. Puhl did not see an elbow thrown by Italian Mauro Tassotti that broke the nose of Spanish midfielder Luis Enrique. The incident took place away from the ball, and despite controversy after the game, FIFA deemed that Puhl had been following the play correctly, explaining the missed call. He was then selected to take charge of the World Cup final at the Rose Bowl in Los Angeles. In a poor game with few chances, Puhl gave out two yellow cards to each team in a game won on penalties by Brazil. Puhl became an administrator in Hungarian soccer following his retirement as a referee.

R

RAHN, HELMUT. B. 16 August 1929, Essen, Germany. D. 14 August 2003. The scorer of the winning goal for West Germany in the 1954 World Cup final was Helmut Rahn, inflicting the first defeat on Hungary for over four years and giving the West Germans their first World Cup title in a tournament held in Switzerland. It was West Germany's second game against Hungary at the 1954 World Cup, as they had also met in the group stage, Rahn scoring one in a crushing 8–3 defeat for the West Germans. That game marked Rahn's first appearance in the World Cup, as he was not selected by coach Sepp Herberger for either of West Germany's first two group games. Rahn kept his place in the team for West Germany's quarterfinal on 27 June in Geneva, a 2–0 win in which he scored a late goal. Rahn did not score in West Germany's semifinal, a comprehensive 6–1 victory over Austria in Basel. When the 1954 World Cup final began in Bern on 4 July at Wankdorf Stadium, Hungary was the heavy favorite. Hungary took a quick 2–0 lead after only eight minutes, but it was Rahn who began West Germany's comeback by providing a cross for Max Morlock to finish and make it 2–1 with 10 minutes gone. Rahn then equalized for West Germany in the 18th minute, striking in a goal from close range following a corner kick taken by West German captain Fritz Walter. Rahn then scored the goal that would earn the game infamy in West German lore as the "Miracle of Bern" for the unlikely comeback win, picking up the ball 20 yards out, swerving past a defender as he ran into the penalty area and powered a low drive into the bottom left-hand corner.

Rahn, then 28, played in the 1958 World Cup as West Germany attempted to defend their title in Sweden, though in the intervening period, he had been arrested for drunk driving. Rahn scored in all three of West Germany's games in the first-round group stage, a 3–1 win over Argentina, a 2–2 tie with Czechoslovakia and another 2–2 tie with Northern Ireland. Rahn's scoring streak continued as West Germany faced Yugoslavia at the quarterfinal stage for the second successive World Cup, hitting the winner from a tight angle with the ball squeezing underneath Yugoslavian goalkeeper Srboljub Krivokuća. Rahn had now scored in five successive World Cup finals games. His streak ended in the semifinal, though, as West Germany was beaten 3–1 by hosts Sweden. Rahn scored his final World Cup goal in the consolation game for third place, as France defeated the West Germans 6–3, giving him a record of 10 goals in 10 World Cup finals games. Rahn continued to play for West Germany until 1960, ending his international career with 21 goals in 40 games since his debut in 1951.

RAMSEY, SIR ALF. B. 22 January 1920, London, England. D. 28 April 1999. Sir Alf Ramsey remains the only man to have managed England to victory in the FIFA World

Cup, winning on home soil in 1966. Ramsey was born to a working-class background in London, with a distinguished playing career for Southampton and Tottenham Hotspur, retiring in 1955. He then began his managerial career with Ipswich Town, before moving on the England job, replacing Walter Winterbottom in 1963. He became the first England manager to gain sole control of team selection and training, which previously had been subject to considerable interference from the Football Association's committees. With England, Ramsey managed with discipline but also formed a bond with his players and was unafraid of tactical innovation, introducing a formation known as the "wingless wonders" that proved to be critical to England's success at the 1966 World Cup finals tournament. This was crowned with England's 4–2 win over West Germany at Wembley Stadium after extra time in the final of the World Cup. A small but slow decline followed in the subsequent years of Ramsey's tenure as England's manager. They finished third at the 1968 UEFA European Football Championship, losing to Yugoslavia, and then lost 3–2 to West Germany in the quarterfinals of the 1970 World Cup. Ramsey's England would fall again to West Germany at the 1972 UEFA European Football Championship in the qualifying tournament. Ramsey's tenure would be ended by England's failure to qualify for the 1974 World Cup, the crucial game a failure to beat Poland at home. Ramsey's overall record as England's manager was, however, exceptional: 113 games played, 69 won, 27 drawn and only 17 lost. England, after considerable underachievement in the international game before Ramsey's tenure, established themselves as a world power under his guidance. In 2002, four years after his death, Ramsey was an inaugural inductee into the English Football Hall of Fame.

RÅSUNDA STADIUM. The 1958 World Cup final was played at Råsunda Stadium in Stockholm, Sweden. A sold-out crowd of 51,800 fans was present on 29 June 1958 as Brazil defeated the hosts Sweden to win the World Cup for the first time. The stadium had already hosted seven other games in the World Cup, including a magnificent Brazilian win in the semifinal over France on 24 June featuring a hat trick by a 17-year-old Pelé, though only 27,000 fans were in attendance. A larger crowd had been attracted to the previous game at the Råsunda Stadium, the quarterfinal between Sweden and the Soviet Union on 19 June, a 2–0 win for the hosts. In the first round, Råsunda Stadium was the host stadium for five games in group four, featuring Sweden, Wales, Hungary and Mexico, including a decisive play-off game between Wales and Hungary, the former winning 2–1. Only 2,823 spectators attended the game, with many fans reportedly refusing to attend due to the execution of former Hungarian leader Imre Nagy the previous day. Råsunda Stadium is located in the Solna district of Stockholm, a few miles northwest of downtown. It was opened in 1937 when Sweden hosted England in a friendly game on 17 May. In 1995, the Råsunda Stadium became the first stadium in the world to host both the men's and women's World Cup finals, as Norway defeated Germany to win the second edition of the Women's World Cup (the Rose Bowl in the United States has since also earned that distinction). It also hosted the final of the 1992 European Championship, held in Sweden. Råsunda Stadium was the home for most of Sweden's international games and of club team AIK Fotboll, though, in November 2012, it was closed down and replaced by the newly built Friends Arena about 1 km from the old Råsunda Stadium site.

RAVA, PIETRO. B. 21 January 1916, Cassine, Italy. D. 5 November 2006. In 1938, Pietro Rava became one of the few Italian players to have won both the Olympic Games Football Tournament and the World Cup with his country. A powerful defender playing at club level for Juventus, Rava traveled to the 1936 Olympics at only 20 years old. He was sent off in his first game of the tournament against the United States, his international debut spoiled. He returned to the lineup after serving a one-game suspension and played in all of Italy's remaining games, including the gold-medal-winning triumph over Austria in the final. Rava was selected by Vittorio Pozzo for the World Cup in France two years later, as Italy aimed to defend their World Cup title. He was one of only four players from Italy's triumphant Olympic team to be selected by Pozzo for the World Cup, and he was among the youngest on the team, still only 22 years old. Rava was, though, an automatic selection in defense, playing in all four games and lifting the World Cup in Paris on 19 June 1938. Rava continued his international career until 1946, playing in no further World Cup due to World War II.

RAYNOR, GEORGE. B. 13 January 1907, Hoyland Common, England. D. 24 November 1985. Sweden's coach at the 1958 World Cup held in that country was Englishman George Raynor, who led the hosts to a place in the final, where they lost 5–2 to Pelé's Brazil. Raynor was a former player who began coaching during service in World War II and, in 1946, became the coach of Sweden following a recommendation by the Football Association. He quickly became known for his superb man-management talents and his tactical ability and, in 1948, led Sweden to the gold medal in the Olympic Games Football Tournament. The heart of the team was the superb trio of Gunnar Gren, Gunnar Nordahl and Nils Liedholm, domestic-based players who were quickly poached by professional Italian clubs. This made Raynor's task far more difficult than it might have been as Sweden traveled to Brazil for the 1950 World Cup, as only amateur players were allowed to play for Sweden at the time. Sweden, though, gave a strong account of themselves regardless: facing the defending world champions Italy (though that victory had come a full 12 years earlier due to World War II) in their opening first-round group game, a skillful, tricky performance bamboozled the Italians, and Sweden claimed a 3–2 win, with Raynor's prodigy at center-forward Hasse Jeppson scoring twice. Focused on speed with their lightweight inside forwards, Raynor even encouraged his players to discard their shin guards to maximize their mobility. Sweden secured passage to the final-round group stage with a 2–2 tie against Paraguay, thanks to goals from Stig Sundqvist and Karl-Erik Palmer. Sweden's next opponents were Brazil, and here Raynor was undone, the Brazilians' fluid play unlocking the Swedish defense before they had a chance to break down the Brazilians themselves. With Ademir scoring four goals for the host nation, Sweden went down 7–1 at the Maracanã in Rio de Janeiro. Any hopes of still going on to win the World Cup by topping the final group were lost four days later, as eventual champions Uruguay came back from a 2–1 deficit late in the second half to defeat the Swedes, rather unlucky to lose 3–2. Sweden's final game gave them a chance to claim third place—their highest finish at a World Cup—as they faced Spain, and this they comfortably achieved with a 3–1 win.

After their surprisingly strong showing a the 1950 World Cup, Raynor further illustrated his tactical skills by engineering a 2–2 draw with Hungary in 1952 and only shortly before the brilliant Hungarians went to Wembley and destroyed an arrogant England, who ignored Raynor's advice ahead of the game. Sweden, though, with Raynor little involved, failed to qualify for the World Cup. The Englishman decided it was time to follow the path many of his players had taken and, lured by the lira of Turin-based Juventus, headed to Italy to coach. His one-year spell in Italy, where he ended up coaching Lazio in Rome, ended disastrously, Raynor disillusioned by what he saw as the rampant corruption in the game. He returned to England to manage Coventry City, but his advanced training methods brought only mediocre results. Raynor was then tempted to return to Sweden and take charge of a national team in need of help with the World Cup in Sweden fast approaching.

Shortly before the 1958 World Cup, Sweden allowed professionals into its national team, and Raynor looked to recruit its most gifted players to give itself a better chance of a strong showing on home soil. Negotiations with the Italian clubs that players such as Gren and Liedholm played for proved difficult, however, disrupting Sweden's preparations, with one Italy-based player, Bengt Gustavsson of Atalanta, arriving in Sweden only three days before the competition began. Expectations domestically in Sweden remained low, however, as the games began on 8 June. Those expectations were very quickly raised by Raynor's men: in their opening game against Mexico in Stockholm at Råsunda Stadium, a comprehensive 3–0 win showed that Raynor had somehow gelled his patchwork, talented team together with the utmost speed. Sweden's second group game resulted in a 2–1 win over Hungary, and a 0–0 tie with a strong Welsh side meant Raynor's team topped the group to qualify for the next round. Yet, to many, reigning Olympic champions the Soviet Union were the favorites when Sweden faced them at the Råsunda Stadium on 19 June. The Soviets, though, arrived with tired legs, having played a play-off to qualify for the quarterfinal stage only two days earlier. A tight first half saw Sweden hold off the Soviets successfully, and as their opponents tired, Kurt Hamrin struck shortly after the second half began and then set up an Agne Simonsson goal to seal the win late in the game. Finally, excitement in Sweden for the team's prospects under Raynor hit fever pitch as they prepared to face reigning World Cup winners West Germany on 24 June, playing in Gothenburg for the first time in front of a very partisan home crowd. It was the West Germans, though, who struck first, but Raynor's men kept their nerve, equalizing through Lennart Skoglund and then sealing victory with late goals from Gunnar Gren in the 81st minute and Kurt Hamrin in the 88th minute. What Sweden lacked in pace, they made up for in pluck, and Raynor had led Sweden to their first-ever World Cup final. There, they faced a Brazil team unbeaten in the competition, led by Garrincha, Zito and a 17-year-old Pelé. Raynor faced his toughest test, to attempt to somehow contain the speedy Brazilians with his aging team. It was one he could not succeed at, though Sweden took an early lead, as Brazil ran rampant in the second half, ultimately winning 5–2.

Raynor hoped to take on the England manager's job, but a combination of English reticence to take on new "Continental" methods led to Raynor's disillusionment, and he ended any hope he had of obtaining a prominent job in England with the publication of his autobiography in 1960, containing scathing comments about the

Football Association. Raynor instead worked in Scotland for Skegness before returning to Sweden for one last stint in 1961, an unsuccessful attempt to qualify for the 1962 World Cup in Chile.

READER, GEORGE. B. 22 November 1896, Nuneaton, England. D. 13 July 1978. George Reader is often wrongly believed to have been the first English referee for a World Cup final, at the 1950 competition held in Brazil. But though Reader did referee the decisive final game of the competition between Brazil and Uruguay, it was not in fact a final, as the last round consisted of a round-robin group stage rather than a knockout competition. Reader is one of the oldest referees in the history of the World Cup: aged 53 at the 1950 competition, he had been called out of retirement by FIFA for the competition, given the lack of experienced international referees at the time due to World War II. Reader had taken charge of a number of international games immediately following the war. Reader was a schoolteacher by profession and had been a player before becoming a referee in the 1930s. As well as taking charge of the last game at the 1950 World Cup, he also took charge of the first game, between Brazil and Mexico on 24 June at the Maracanã, receiving praise for his maintenance of order during the game. Reader's second game at the 1950 World Cup was Uruguay against Bolivia in 2 July, an 8–0 win for the Uruguayans. With both teams apparently satisfied with Reader's refereeing, he was selected to take charge of the crucial final game between Brazil and Uruguay.

REPUBLIC OF IRELAND. Commonly known as the Boys in Green or the Green Army. The Republic of Ireland first reached the World Cup finals in 1990, registering draws against England, Egypt and the Netherlands. Coached by Englishman Jack Charlton, the Irish employed a direct, physical style of play that made them very difficult to beat. The three points were enough to send the Irish to the next round, where they faced Romania. With both teams unable to score during regulation, the game went to a penalty shoot-out. The Republic of Ireland was victorious, 5–4. They faced the tournament's host, Italy, in the next round, and Italy's one goal in the first half was the game winner, knocking the Irish out of the tournament.

The Republic of Ireland qualified for the 1994 World Cup in the U.S., still under the stewardship of Jack Charlton. Facing a familiar foe in Italy in their opening game, the Republic of Ireland pulled an upset by coming away with a 1–0 victory thanks to a long-range strike by Ray Houghton. Ireland's loss to Mexico and tie against Norway gave them four points in their group, enough to advance to the second round. In the round of 16, the Irish lost to the Netherlands 2–0 at the Citrus Bowl in Orlando.

Failing to qualify for the 1998 World Cup, the Republic of Ireland returned to the tournament in 2002 in South Korea and Japan. Earning their highest point total for the first round yet, the Irish finished second in their group with five points. Once again, the Republic of Ireland had found a way to make it to the round of 16. This time, the Irish faced Spain, who took an early lead with a goal in the eighth minute. Approaching the end of the match, it appeared that Spain would be the victors, until a penalty goal by Robbie Keane in the 90th minute forced the game to extra time and ultimately a penalty shoot-out. Unlike in 1990, though, the Republic of Ireland failed to put away their penalties, and Spain narrowly won 3–2.

The Republic of Ireland has since lost out on qualification for the 2006, 2010 and 2014 World Cups.

RIVALDO. B. 19 April 1972, Paulista, Brazil. Rivaldo, born as Vítor Borba Ferreira but universally known by that single name, was the FIFA World Player of the Year and the European Footballer of the Year in 1999. He played his first game for Brazil in December 1993 and has made 74 appearances since, scoring 34 goals, last playing for his country in 2003. A tall, hugely talented attacking midfielder, Rivaldo won the FIFA World Cup with Brazil in 2002 in the competition jointly hosted by the Republic of Korea and Japan, playing an important role in his country's winning run despite controversy in the first round, when he was fined for playacting after a dive against Turkey. At club level, Rivaldo's longest and most productive spell of play came for Barcelona in Spain, winning two Spanish league titles between 1997 and 2002 and scoring 136 goals in 253 games. Rivaldo also played for AC Milan, winning the UEFA Champions League with the Italian club in 2003.

RODRÍGUEZ, JAMES. B. 12 July 1991, Cúcuta, Colombia. A Colombian-born striker affectionately known as James to his countrymen, Rodríguez burst onto the international scene at the 2014 World Cup in Brazil when he scored six goals and assisted on two others to win the Golden Boot award as the tournament's most prolific goal scorer. Had there been an award for greatest goal, Rodriguez's 30-yard turn and volley against Uruguay in the round of 16 surely would have given him ample consideration. After winning Man of the Match three times in five games and helping Colombia to its first-ever quarterfinal finish, Rodríguez fulfilled what he called a "life's dream" when he signed a six-year, reported €80 million, contract with Spanish giant Real Madrid on 22 July 2014.

ROMANIA. Commonly known as Tricolorii (The Tricolors). Along with Brazil, France and Belgium, Romania carries the distinction of being one of only four countries that participated in the first three World Cups. However, Romania found little success in the 1930, 1934 and 1938 tournaments, only winning against Peru in 1930. When they returned to the competition in 1970, they finally earned another World Cup win. Although Romania lost their opening match against England, they rebounded with a 2–1 victory over Czechoslovakia. Needing a win against eventual champions Brazil in order to advance, Romania put up a strong fight but still lost 3–2.

There would be another long wait before Romania's next World Cup appearance, as they did not qualify again until the 1990 World Cup in Italy. Grouped with Argentina, Cameroon and the Soviet Union, Romania finished second place in their group with a 1-1-1 record. Facing Ireland in the round of 16, Romania's defense held tight, and the game ended scoreless. The game went to a penalty shoot-out, and although only one player would miss, that player was Romanian Daniel Timofte. Romania was out of the tournament.

Romania built on their second-round appearance four years later in the U.S. Winning both their opening game against Colombia and their third game against the U.S., Romania finished first in their group and moved into the round of 16. There they faced a Maradona-less Argentina and surprised the world with a 3–2 victory in arguably the best game of the tournament, with the Romanians inspired by their superb, creative fulcrum Gheorghe Hagi. In the quarterfinals, Romania played a close match with Sweden. Sweden would take a late lead in the game, only for Romania to answer with a goal of their own in the 88th minute to force the game into extra time. It was then Romania's turn to take the lead with forward Florin Răducioiu scoring his second of the game in the 101st minute, but Sweden struck back to tie the score in the 115th minute. The game finished in a 2–2 draw, and just like in the 1990 World Cup, Romania's future in the tournament would be determined in a penalty shoot-out. Unfortunately, the shoot-out would once again lead to heartbreak, as Sweden won to move on to the semifinals.

Making it three tournaments in a row, Romania qualified for the 1998 World Cup in France. Placed in a group with Colombia, England and Tunisia, Romania went 2-1-0 with victories over Colombia and England and a tie with Tunisia. Their seven points put them in first place in their group, and for the third consecutive World Cup, Romania moved on to the second round. Unfortunately, Croatia would score the lone goal of the game via a penalty kick, and Romania was out. Unfortunately for Romanian fans, despite being competitive in each subsequent World Cup qualification process, Romania has always finished just short and has not been back to the world's stage since 1998.

ROMÁRIO. B. 29 January 1966, Rio de Janeiro, Brazil. Born as Romário de Souza Faria but universally known solely as Romário, he was a Brazilian forward blessed with a remarkable goal-scoring ability, scorer of 55 goals in 70 games for Brazil's national team. He played on the Brazil team that won the 1994 FIFA World Cup, scoring five goals, and was named the tournament's best player. He was named FIFA World Player of the Year in 1994 following the World Cup. Romário's long career in club soccer spanned from 1985 to 2009, appearing for almost a dozen different club teams, most notably for Vasco de Gama in Brazil, PSV Eindhoven in the Netherlands and a prolific spell for Spanish giants Barcelona, where he scored 53 goals in 82 games between 1993 and 1995. In the 1993–1994 season, Romário scored a remarkable 30 goals in 33 league games for Barcelona as the team won the Spanish league championship.

RONALDO. B. 22 September 1976, Rio de Janeiro, Brazil. Commonly known simply as Ronaldo, Ronaldo Luís Nazário de Lima is a Brazilian player and one of only two players to have twice won the FIFA World Player of the Year award. Ronaldo is regarded as one of the best goal scorers in the history of the game, with an unusual combination of pace, power and finesse in his play. Ronaldo has twice won the FIFA World Cup playing with his native Brazil. He did not play in Brazil's victory in the 1994 World Cup in the United States, though he collected a winners' medal as a squad member. In the 2002 World Cup, he scored eight goals to win the Golden Shoe as the tournament's leading scorer, leading Brazil to their record fifth World Cup triumph. At the 2006 World Cup, Ronaldo tallied his 15th goal in World Cup play, setting a new record by passing the previous mark of 14 goals held by Gerd Müller. Between 1994 and 2006, Ronaldo scored a remarkable 62 goals in 97 games in his international career. Ronaldo began his professional club career with Brazilian team Cruzeiro, before moving to Europe and starring for PSV Eindhoven in the Netherlands, Barcelona in Spain, Internazionale in Italy, Real Madrid back in Spain, AC Milan on a return to Italy and, from 2009, Corinthians in Brazil. In 2010, Ronaldo announced that he would retire from playing after the 2011 season in Brazil.

ROSE BOWL. Just outside Los Angeles, the conclusion to the 1994 World Cup—the first held in the United States—took place at the Rose Bowl in the city of Pasadena, California. There were 94,194 spectators watching as Brazil defeated Italy on penalty kicks to win the World Cup. Remarkably, that is not the largest crowd to have attended a soccer game at the Rose Bowl—101,799 attended the final of the 1984 Olympic Games Football Tournament at the stadium. It is also not the only World Cup final hosted at the Rose Bowl, as the 1999 Women's World Cup final also concluded there, 90,185 in attendance to see the United States defeat China, also on penalty kicks. It is, along with Råsunda Stadium in Sweden, the only stadium to have hosted the men's and women's World Cup finals. The Rose Bowl is primarily an American football stadium, the home for UCLA's college football team and a frequent host venue for the Super Bowl. It was also a home stadium for three different soccer clubs, the defunct Los Angeles Wolves and Los Angeles Aztecs of the North American Soccer League and, from 1996 to 2003, before the opening of the Home Depot Center, for the Los Angeles Galaxy of Major League Soccer. The Rose Bowl was originally built in 1922 with a horseshoe shape that accommodated 57,000 spectators, with expansion to the south end taking capacity above 100,000 in the 1950s.

Eight games at the 1994 World Cup were hosted there, with a total attendance of 715,826, an average of 89,478 per game. The Rose Bowl was the most frequently used venue in the competition. The first game played at the Rose Bowl in the World Cup was on 18 June, with Colombia hosting Romania in group A. The Rose Bowl hosted three further games in that group, including two of the United States' three games, including its first FIFA World Cup finals victory since 1950, as the hosts defeated Colombia on 22 June. One round-of-16 game, Romania's victory over Argentina, was hosted at the Rose Bowl on 3 July and proved to be one of the games of the tournament, won 3–2 by the Europeans. Ten days later, it was the venue for the second semifinal, as Brazil defeated Sweden 1–0. On 16 July, the Rose Bowl hosted the third-place consolation game, won by Sweden 4–0 against Bulgaria. The next day, at 12:30 p.m. local time, the World Cup final kicked off in the sunshine, though the game itself proved to be a disappointment.

ROSSI, PAOLO. B. 23 September 1956, Prato, Italy. Italian forward Paolo Rossi was the star player for Italy at the 1982 FIFA World Cup, the tournament's top scorer as his country won the World Cup for the third time. Rossi was also awarded the Golden Ball as the tournament's top player. Rossi's success at that World Cup came as a surprise to many, as he had only recently returned to play before the tournament after serving a two-year ban from soccer for his involvement in an Italian match-fixing scandal. Rossi had made his name at the previous World Cup tournament in 1978, scoring three goals, as Italy finished in fourth place. In the 1982 World Cup, despite a slow start in the early matches, Rossi scored six goals to win the Golden Shoe as the tournament's top scorer, including scoring one in the final as Italy defeated West Germany 3–1 to win the World Cup for the third time. Following the tournament, Rossi won the 1982 European Football of the Year award. At club level, Rossi then went on to achieve spectacular success playing for Juventus, with whom he won the Italian championship in 1982 and 1984 and the European Cup in 1985, playing alongside the brilliant Frenchman Michel Platini. Physically, Rossi was not endowed with outstanding pace or strength but was an intelligent goal-poaching striker, always ready to pounce on any opportunity around the goal. Rossi retired in 1987.

RUMMENIGGE, KARL-HEINZ. B. 25 September 1955, Lippstadt, Germany. Karl-Heinz Rummenigge is best known as a star player for Bayern Munich at club level and for West Germany internationally, with a goal-scoring record matched by very few in the European game. He was named European Footballer of the Year in both 1980 and 1981. He began his professional career with Bayern Munich in 1974, going on to score 162 goals in 310 appearances in the German league for the club, winning two European Cup titles and two German league championships. In 1984, Rummenigge moved to Internazionale in Italy, playing three seasons without winning a major honor. Rummenigge enjoyed extraordinary success playing for West Germany, scoring 45 goals in 95 international games, winning the UEFA European Football Championship in 1980 and twice finishing as a runner-up with his country at FIFA World Cup finals tournaments, in 1982 in Spain and 1986 in Mexico. Following retirement from playing in 1987, Rummenigge entered a successful career in soccer administration and is currently the chairman of Bayern Munich and of the European Clubs Association. He also sits on the board of the German Football League.

RUSSIA. Commonly known as Sbornaya (The National Team). When Russia qualified for the 1994 World Cup in the United States, it marked the first time they had competed as an independent country, rather than as part of the Soviet Union. The Russians were placed in a group with Cameroon, Sweden and Brazil. Playing in their opening match against the eventual champions Brazil, Russia lost 2–0. The Russians found Sweden just as difficult to handle, as they fell 3–1 in the following game. The team found their footing in their third game. Facing Cameroon in what would be their last game of the tournament, Russia won 6–1, with Oleg Salenko scoring five of the six goals for Russia. His five goals in a single match set a World Cup record.

After failing to qualify for the 1998 World Cup, Russia returned to the finals in 2002. Although placed in what was considered an easier group than in 1994, the Russians finished with an identical 1-0-2 record. Opening the tournament with a positive 2–0 win over Tunisia, Russia struggled in their following games and lost 1–0 to Japan and 3–2 against Belgium. Their three points were once again not enough to send them to the second round.

After failing to qualify for the 2006 or 2010 tournaments, qualification for the 2014 World Cup in Brazil began with low expectations. A perfect start (including a 1–0 home win over Portugal) quickly shifted the expectations for Fabio Capello's group. Though they stumbled midway through, Sbornaya recovered to finish atop their group and secure a group H placement in Brazil with Belgium, Algeria and South Korea, where, with the vast rubles of the Russian Premier league paving the way for many of its players, Russian hopes of advancement out of a relatively weak group were high.

An opening 1–1 draw against a Korean team they expected to beat served notice that maybe the pressure of being back on the world's stage was something this group would struggle with. In a second-group chess match between Capello and his Belgian counterpart, Marc Wilmots, the end result was a boring game (as evidenced by cameras catching fans asleep in the stands) until the 88th minute when 19-year-old Belgian substitute Divock Origi played a give-and-go with Eden Hazard for the game winner. With a win over Algeria in their final game a necessity, a favored Russian side found themselves up a goal early when Aleksandr Kokorin headed home a Dmitri Kombarov cross in the sixth minute. Ahead by one and in a position to advance, Russia gave up a controversial equalizer in the 60th minute (video evidence clearly showed a green laser light shining on the Russian goalkeeper just before the kick) to Islam Slimani and couldn't find the net again in a tense final 30 minutes. With just two points in their group, Russia exited in 24th place with two goals for and three against.

S

SACCHI, ARRIGO. B. 1 April 1946, Fusignano, Italy. Arrigo Sacchi coached Italy to the final of the 1994 FIFA World Cup, losing at that stage on a penalty shoot-out to Brazil. Unlike many top-level coaches, Sacchi did not play professional soccer before beginning his management career, instead starting out his career coaching at lower levels and working his way up to take over AC Milan in 1987, leading the club to the Serie A domestic championship in 1988. He then led AC Milan to two consecutive European Cup titles in 1989 and 1990. In 1991, Sacchi took over Italy, the year after they had lost at the semifinal stage of the 1990 World Cup on home soil.

SALENKO, OLEG. B. 25 October 1969, Saint Petersburg, Russia. In his international career playing for Russia, forward Oleg Salenko played in only eight games, scoring six goals. However, five of those goals came in a game against Cameroon in the first round of the 1994 World Cup, a record earning Salenko—along with one other goal against Sweden—the Golden Boot as top scorer, even though he only played in three games, with Russia knocked out in the first round. Plagued by injury problems, Salenko did not appear in another international game after 1994.

SÁNCHEZ, LEONEL. B. 25 April 1936, Santiago, Chile. Appearing at two FIFA World Cup final tournaments for Chile, Leonel Sánchez was the joint top scorer at the 1962 competition, one of six players to score four goals. Sánchez made his debut for Chile at 19 years old against Brazil in 1955, then going on to take part in Chile's unsuccessful qualifying campaign for the 1958 World Cup. As hosts, Chile did not have to qualify for the 1962 World Cup, and they were placed in a difficult group alongside Italy, Switzerland and West Germany. A crowd of 65,006 at Estadio Nacional was ecstatic as Sánchez scored twice in a 3–1 win for the hosts, the first a low left-footed drive from eight yards out and the second from even closer in with his right foot. Sánchez played but did not score in either of Chile's next two games, an impressive 2–0 win over Italy and a 2–0 defeat to West Germany. Chile's two wins were enough to advance them to the knockout stage, and in their quarterfinal on 10 June in Arica against the Soviet Union, Sánchez scored the opening goal, firing in a direct free kick from the edge of the penalty area and helping his country to a 2–1 win. In the semifinal against Brazil, Sánchez converted a penalty kick in Chile's 4–2 defeat, his fourth goal of the competition. Sánchez also played in Chile's victory in their third-place play-off game against Yugoslavia, helping them to their best-ever World Cup finish. Sánchez then took part in Chile's successful qualifying campaign for the 1966 World Cup in England.

SÁROSI, GYÖRGY. B. 5 August 1912, Budapest, Hungary. D. 20 June 1993. The captain of Hungary in the 1938 World Cup final was György Sárosi, one of the stars of the tournaments, scoring five goals in four games to finish as the joint second-highest scorer in France behind Brazilian Leônidas da Silva. Sárosi had made his debut for Hungary over seven years earlier and was selected for Hungary's team at the 1934 World Cup in Italy. He played one game at that competition, scoring one goal from the penalty spot in Hungary's 2–1 defeat to Austria at the quarterfinal stage. Sárosi became increasingly critical to Hungary's team as the 1938 World Cup approached, scoring prolifically, including seven goals in one game against Czechoslovakia in September 1937. When the 1938 World Cup began in France, Sárosi continued his goal-scoring streak, scoring twice against the Dutch East Indies in Hungary's first-round game and following up with a goal in both the quarterfinal victory over Switzerland and the semifinal win against Sweden. In the final, Sárosi struck again, but it was not enough for Hungary, who lost 4–2 to defending World Cup champions Italy. He ended the tournament, though, having scored in every round and in seven straight games for Hungary overall—a streak that would end at eight games, after a goal in Hungary's next game against Scotland. With the intervention of World War II meaning no World Cup was held again until 1950, Sárosi did not participate in another world championship but did continue playing for Hungary until 1943. He totaled a remarkable tally of 42 goals in 62 games for his country. He continued playing at club level for Ferencvárosi TC, the only other team he ever played for, until 1948, ending with over 300 goals for the club and 5 Hungarian championship honors. He later went on to coach at several clubs in Italy.

SAS, FERENC. B. 1 January 1915, Budapest, Hungary. D. 3 September 1988. As a 23-year-old right-winger, Ferenc Sas played in all four of Hungary's games at the 1938 World Cup in France. Sas had made his debut for Hungary in April 1936, playing in a 5–3 defeat to Austria, and quickly became established on the team, taking part in their successful World Cup qualifying effort, with an 11–1 win over Greece in March 1938. At the 1938 World Cup, he played in Hungary's victories over the Dutch East Indies (6–0), Switzerland (2–0) and Sweden (5–1) that took his country to the World Cup final for the first time. In the final, on 19 June in Paris, Hungary faced defending World Cup champions Italy. The Italians struck first in the sixth minute, but it was Sas who helped Hungary get back on level terms only two minutes later, providing the cross that led to Pál Titkos's equalizer. Italy, though, soon proved to be too strong for the Hungarians, claiming a 4–2 win. The World Cup final was Sas's last game for Hungary, as he took the unusual route of immigrating to Argentina, going on to play for Boca Juniors and Argentinos Juniors at club level.

SAUDI ARABIA. Commonly known as Al Sogour Al Akhdar (The Green Falcons). Starting in 1994, Saudi Arabia qualified for four consecutive World Cups, with their last appearance being in 2006. In their inaugural tournament, they went 2-0-1, finishing second in their group. Their opening match was against the Netherlands. Fuad Amin got Saudi Arabia off to a strong start with a goal in the 18th minute, but the Dutch came back to score two second-half goals and win 2–1. The Saudi Arabian team then won their next two games against Morocco and Belgium. The six points earned from those wins proved enough to put them through to the next round where they faced a tough Sweden team. Although Fahad al Ghesheyan scored for Saudi Arabia in the 85th minute, the final score was 3–1 to the Swedes.

Their second-round finish would prove to be the best in World Cup history for the Saudi Arabians. In each subsequent tournament, the Middle Eastern nation has failed to win a single match, going 0-1-2 in 1998, 0-0-3 in 2002 and 0-1-2 in 2006. They have since failed to qualify for another tournament, missing out on both South Africa in 2010 and Brazil in 2014.

SCARONE, HÉCTOR. B. 26 November 1898, Montevideo, Uruguay. D. 4 April 1967. One of Uruguay's creative forces in their victory in the 1930 World Cup was Héctor Scarone, who scored one goal in three games at the competition held in his native country. Scarone had starred for Uruguay throughout the 1920s after making his debut in 1917 at just 18 years old, a glorious period for himself and his native country on the field, playing eight games at the Olympic Games Football Tournaments of 1924 and 1928, scoring eight goals and winning two gold medals. He also played on the 1917, 1923, 1924 and 1926 Copa América winning teams, scoring 13 goals in the four competitions. At club level, Scarone played the majority of his career for Nacional in Uruguay, though he also enjoyed brief but successful spells at Barcelona in Spain and Inter Milan and Palermo in Italy. Scarone was known for his improvising play and, despite not being particularly tall, his ability to win and score with headers. Scarone played in only one of Uruguay's three first-round group-stage games at the 1930 World Cup, scoring in a 4–0 win over Romania, but played a full part in both the semifinal victory over Yugoslavia and the final, as Uruguay defeated Argentina 4–2 to claim the inaugural World Cup title. Scarone retired from international play after the game, though he continued to play at club level until 1939. His record of 31 goals in 52 games for Uruguay was a goal-scoring tally for his country unmatched until Diego Forlán surpassed that total in 2011.

SCHIAVIO, ANGELO. B. 15 October 1905, Bologna, Italy. D. 17 April 1990. Angelo Schiavio was an Italian forward who played for Italy at the 1934 FIFA World Cup, scoring four goals, including the winning strike in the final against Czechoslovakia, as his country won the World Cup for the first time on home soil. A strong and powerful forward, Schiavio scored 15 goals in 21 total games for Italy, while playing his entire career for his hometown team Bologna Football Club 1909, scoring over 200 goals for the club between 1922 and 1939, the year of his retirement. Schiavo began his international career in 1925 and established his international reputation with a fine performance at the 1928 Olympic Games Football Tournament, scoring four goals in four games as Italy won a bronze medal. Schiavo took the honor of scoring Italy's first-ever World Cup goal during their opening game at the 1934 World Cup in the 18th minute of their game with the United States, going on to score two more in the same game to record a hat trick in Italy's 7–1 win over the Americans. Schiavio did not score again until extra time in the final against Czechoslovakia, later attributing that World Cup–winning finish to the "strength of desperation."

SCHILLACI, SALVATORE. B. 1 December 1964, Palermo, Italy. Salvatore Schillaci was the top scorer at the 1990 FIFA World Cup with six goals, playing for his native Italy, who finished third at the competition. It was Schillaci's only appearance at the World Cup, and he played a mere six further times for Italy, finishing his national team career with 16 appearances and 7 goals. His club career lasted from 1982 to 1999, notably playing for Juventus and Internazionale, earning a reputation as a potent poacher around the goal.

SCHÖN, HELMUT. B. 15 September 1915, Dresden, Germany. D. 23 February 1996. In the early 1970s, a remarkable spell of success for West Germany's national team was shepherded by Helmut Schön, a former national-team player who joined the West German coaching setup as an assistant in the mid-1950s, taking over sole control in 1964. He led West Germany to the 1966 World Cup final, losing there to England, and to third place at the 1970 World Cup, defeated at the semifinal stage by Italy. Two years later, Schön's team won the European Championship and followed that up in 1974 by winning the World Cup on home soil, becoming the first team to be both European and world champions at the same time. Schön's outstanding period in charge ended on a low note, as West Germany were eliminated from the 1978 World Cup by a shock upset defeat to Austria. His tenure with West Germany ended with an impressive record of 87 wins in 139 international games as coach.

SCIFO, ENZO. B. 19 February 1966, Haine-Saint-Paul, Belgium. Scifo made his professional debut in 1983, aged 17, for Belgian giants Royal Sporting Club Anderlecht, going on to play for eight different clubs before retirement in 2001. Scifo won the Belgian league four times with Anderlecht and the French league once with Monaco. From 1984 to 1998, Scifo played 84 times for Belgium, scoring 18 goals and winning acclaim for his technical ability as a midfield maestro. Since retirement, he has pursued a managerial career without notable success.

SCOLARI, LUIZ FELIPE. B. 9 November 1948, Passo Fundo, Brazil. A talented Brazilian team—featuring the likes of Ronaldo and Rivaldo—was led to the World Cup title by Scolari in 2002. He had only taken over the national-team coaching job a year earlier, firming up a shaky Brazilian effort to qualify for the competition. At the 2002 World Cup, a Brazil inspired by Ronaldo romped to its fifth World Cup victory, winning all seven games. Scolari left Brazil by the end of 2002, taking charge of Portugal. He took Portugal to the final of Euro 2004 on home soil, upset in the final to Greece, and then led the Portuguese to the semifinals of the 2006 World Cup in Germany, losing at that stage to France. In 2012, Scolari again took charge of the Brazilian national team ahead of the 2014 World Cup, to be hosted in Brazil. With "a duty" to win on home soil, Scolari led A Seleção to the semifinals, but the loss of star Neymar to injury and Thiago Silva to an accumulation of yellow cards led to the worst World Cup semifinal loss ever, a 7–1 thumping by eventual champions Germany. It also ended Brazil's 39-game home unbeaten streak, doubled the previous record for defeats by a host country and went down as the worst World Cup loss ever for Brazil. With the return of Silva for the third-place game, hope of a recovery quickly abated as Brazil gave up a third-minute goal and eventually lost 3–0 to the Netherlands. Immediately following the tournament, Scolari and the Confederação Brasileira de Futebol came to a mutual understanding, and three weeks later, he returned to Grêmio, a Brazilian first-division team where he previously won six titles in three years.

SCOTLAND. Commonly known as the Tartan Terriers. Scotland has qualified for the World Cup eight times but has yet to make it past the group stage. They first qualified in 1954 but lost to Austria and Uruguay in the first round at the tournament in Switzerland. Four years later in Sweden, Scotland earned their first point in a World Cup tournament when they drew against Yugoslavia 1–1, but after losing to Paraguay and France in their following two games, the Scots were out of the competition.

Scotland earned their first World Cup victory in 1974 under coach Willie Ormond. Grouped with Yugoslavia, Zaire and Brazil, the team went unbeaten with a 2–0 win over Zaire and ties against Yugoslavia and Brazil. Although Scotland finished with the same number of points as Brazil and Yugoslavia, they were sent home with the weakest goal difference in the group.

Four years later in Argentina, Scotland improved with each game and finished the group stage with a 1-1-1 record. After losing their first game against Peru and tying the second match against Iran, Scotland went out with style. Facing eventual runners-up Holland, Scotland fought back after falling behind in the 34th minute and won 3–2. The win was not enough for second place in their group, and Scotland was eliminated once again based on goal differential.

In their third consecutive World Cup in 1982, Scotland found themselves in a familiar place after three games. After going 1-1-1 in their three first-round matches, they were once again tied for second place. And again, goal differential would eliminate Scotland from the tournament.

Scotland would go on to qualify for three more World Cups—1986, 1990 and 1998—but did not progress beyond the group stage. Their one win in the last three tournaments was against a winless Swedish team in 1990. They have yet to qualify since.

SEBES, GUSZTÁV. B. 22 January 1906, Hungary. D. 30 January 1986. A renowned coach and administrator, Gusztáv Sebes was best known as the tactical genius behind his native Hungary's brilliant national team of the early 1950s. The "Magical Magyars," as they were nicknamed, transformed the future of world soccer with their visionary dynamic fluidity, presaging the Dutch mastery of Total Football. Hungary's most stunning international performance came in November 1953, in a much-hyped friendly game against England, who had never been beaten on home soil by a national team from overseas: at Wembley Stadium, Sebes's Hungary outclassed and humiliated the English 6–3, their graceful yet incisive play mesmerizing their opponents and the crowd, especially from the unstoppable Ferenc Puskás. A return match in Budapest the next year saw Hungary confirm their superiority with a 7–1 win over England. These famous victories came in the midst of a brilliant four-year unbeaten streak for Hungary under Sebes, the competitive highlight a gold medal at the 1952 Olympic Games Football Tournament. Sebes's Hungary continued the unbeaten streak into the 1954 FIFA World Cup, where they easily beat West Germany, the Republic of

Korea, Brazil and Uruguay on their way to the final. Yet it was there that Hungary's unbeaten streak was finally broken, and Sebes was denied his greatest triumph, as West Germany surprisingly took revenge on Hungary with a 3–2 win in a muddy, ugly game unsuited to the Hungarians' grace. Sebes went on to manage several Hungarian club sides and play an important role as the vice president of the Union of European Football Associations (UEFA) from 1954 to 1960.

SERANTONI, PIETRO. B. 11 December 1906, Venice, Italy. D. 6 October 1964. At the 1934 World Cup in France, midfielder Pietro Serantoni played in all four of Italy's games as the Italians successfully defended their World Cup title. At the age of 27, the triumph made up for Serantoni's disappointment in 1934, when he missed out on selection for Italy's World Cup triumph at home, despite having become a regular in the Italian side following his international debut in 1933. Serantoni played in Italy's successful qualifying game for the 1934 World Cup, a 4–0 win over Greece that was the last occasion a World Cup host nation had to earn its place at the World Cup. Following success at the 1938 World Cup, Serantoni played three further international games for Italy in 1938 and 1939, his career then interrupted by World War II. At club level, Serantoni starred in the 1930s for Internazionale in Milan, Juventus and Roma.

SERBIA. Commonly known as Beli Orlovi (The White Eagles). Serbia has been a member of FIFA since 2006, when Montenegro declared its independence from the former nation Serbia and Montenegro. They qualified for the 2010 World Cup in South Africa and were grouped with Ghana, Germany and Australia in the first round. After a hard-fought 1–0 defeat to Ghana, Serbia had to face eventual third-place finishers Germany. German star Miroslav Klose was shown his second yellow card late in the first half, forcing his team to play down a man for over 45 minutes. Serbia made the most of the man advantage and scored just minutes later. Although Serbia was outshot by Germany, they held on to their lead and stunned their opponents with a 1–0 victory thanks to a strike by midfielder Milan Jovanovič. Needing only a point in their next game against Australia to advance to the second round, Australia's two second-half goals doomed the Serbs, with a 2–1 loss resulting in elimination. With hopes for a return to Brazil in 2014 high, poor results during the qualification process meant that Serbia would have to wait at least four more years before playing in another World Cup.

SERBIA AND MONTENEGRO. Commonly known as Plavi (The Blues). Up until 2003, Serbia and Montenegro were known as the Federal Republic of Yugoslavia and competed as such in previous World Cups. Their first World Cup campaign as Serbia and Montenegro began with an undefeated record in their qualifying group, a first-place finish and a place in the 2006 World Cup in Germany. Just prior to the competition, however, Montenegro declared independence from Serbia. It was decided that the "combined" team that had qualified for the World Cup would stay together for the tournament but would split immediately after their elimination. Placed in a group with the Netherlands, Argentina and Côte d'Ivoire, Serbia and Montenegro went 0-0-3 and were outscored 12–2. Their only appearance as a unified nation would end after just three games.

SLOVAKIA. Commonly known as Repre (Representation) or Národný tím (National Team). Up until 1993, Slovakia was represented in the World Cup by the Czechoslovakian team. When the state disbanded and became two distinct nations, Slovakia and the Czech Republic, the two countries competed separately in the World Cup. Following independence, Slovakia failed to qualify for the competition until 2010 in South Africa. Grouped with New Zealand, Paraguay and Italy, Slovakia finished the first round with a 1-1-1 record. It was enough to put them into the second round, where they lost to eventual runners-up Holland, 2–1.Qualifying for 2014 saw Slovakia finish third in their group behind Greece and Bosnia and Herzegovina and out of the World Cup in Brazil.

SLOVENIA. Commonly known as the Dragons or Fantje (The Boys), the national team is without a true nickname. Slovenia was officially recognized by FIFA in 1991 after it split from Yugoslavia. Although the nation would have to wait over 10 years before it qualified for a World Cup, it achieved this success in 2002. Grouped with Spain, Paraguay and South Africa in the first round, Slovenia failed to win a match and finished last in their group.

Slovenia did not qualify for the 2006 World Cup but returned in 2010 in South Africa. There, the team bested their previous showing with a 1-1-1 record in the first round. In spite of their win against Algeria and tie with the United States, Slovenia was once again eliminated after the first round when a stoppage-time goal by American Landon Donovan meant the United States and England had secured one more point than Slovenia. During the 2014 qualifying campaign, Slovenia finished in third place in UEFA group E, behind Iceland and Switzerland.

SOBOTKA, JIŘÍ. B. 6 June 1911, Prague, Austria-Hungary. D. 20 May 1994. At the 1934 World Cup, Jiří Sobotka scored one goal for Czechoslovakia as he played in all four games of their outstanding campaign that ended with defeat in the final to hosts Italy. Sobotka had only made his debut internationally in March 1934, scoring twice in three games ahead of the World Cup to cement his place in the team. Sobotka's lone goal came in the second round against Switzerland in a 3–2 win. He had made his mark in the first round, though, winning the ball in a melee that ended with Oldřich Nejedlý scoring the winning goal for the Czechs against Romania. In the final, however, Sobotka missed an easy chance to seal victory for Czechoslovakia. Sobotka went on to play a further 16 games for his country, ending his international career in August 1937, having scored 8 goals in 23 games, 11 of them wins, 5 of them draws and suffering 7 defeats.

SOCCER CITY. Both the first World Cup finals game and the first World Cup final itself held on the African continent took place at Soccer City stadium in Johannesburg, South Africa, in 2010. The venue was initially constructed in the late 1980s but received a major renovation for the 2010 World Cup, upgraded to feature a capacity of 95,000 to become the largest stadium in Africa. As well as the opening game and the final, Soccer City also hosted four group games, a second-round victory for Argentina over Mexico and a quarterfinal between Uruguay and Ghana, won by the

South Americans in a penalty shoot-out. Its current design was created by American architects Populous, its shape similar to a traditional African pot. It now hosts Johannesburg club team the Kaizer Chiefs and national team games by South Africa.

SOUTH AFRICA. Commonly known as Bafana Bafana (Boys Boys). In 2010, South Africa became the first African nation to host the World Cup, holding the tournament's 64 games in 10 venues across 9 cities. Over three million fans attended the competition, with the final held at Soccer City stadium in Johannesburg, a crowd of almost 85,000 watching Spain defeat the Netherlands 1–0. For the South African team itself, its appearance at the 2010 competition was its third. Bafana Bafana did not advance past the first round, finishing third in group A behind Uruguay and Mexico. On their home soil, South Africa earned four points by tying with Mexico 1–1 and beating France 2–1, but a final group-game loss to Uruguay 3–0 meant a poorer goal differential to Mexico and the dubious distinction of being the first host nation not to advance out of the group stage. South Africa's two previous World Cup appearances took place in 1998 and 2002. Bafana Bafana's 1998 debut in France saw a team starring striker Benni McCarthy and captain Lucas Radebe finish third in group C, losing 3–0 to France but earning ties with both Denmark and Saudi Arabia. In 2002, in South Korea and Japan, South Africa also finished third in the group stage, failing to advance to the next round. Bafana Bafana tied with Paraguay 2–2, beat Slovenia 1–0 but fell short of moving on following a 3–2 defeat to Spain.

Prior to 1998, South Africa failed to qualify for the 1994 World Cup and, for over two decades before that, had been banned from playing at the World Cup due to the racially discriminatory policies in South African soccer instigated by the country's apartheid regime. With a second-place finish behind Ethiopia in the group stage of African qualifying for the 2014 tournament, the Boys Boys will have to wait before playing in another World Cup.

SOUTH KOREA. *See* KOREA REPUBLIC (SOUTH KOREA).

SOVIET UNION. Commonly known as the Red Army. Since the Soviet Union first competed in the World Cup in 1958, they failed to reach the final tournament only two times, in 1974 and 1978, until the dissolution of the Soviet Union in 1991. In the 1958 World Cup in Sweden, the Soviet Union went 1-1-1 in their first three games, tying England for second place in their group with three points each. In the play-off match between the two teams, the Soviet Union's Anatoli Ilyin scored the only goal to eliminate England from the tournament and advance the Soviet Union to the second round. Paired with the hosts and eventual runners-up Sweden in the quarterfinals, the Soviet Union's run in the tournament came to an end after losing 2–0. The Soviet Union advanced to the quarterfinals for the second consecutive World Cup in 1962 in Chile. Grouped with Yugoslavia, Colombia and Uruguay, the Soviet Union finished first in their group with five points, only to lose to host nation Chile 2–1 in the quarterfinals.

The 1966 World Cup in England resulted in the best finish for the Soviet Union in the nation's history, with the team anchored by legendary goalkeeper Lev Yashin. After winning all three games in the first round against Korea, Italy and Chile, the

Soviet Union beat Hungary 2–1 in the quarterfinals. Although the Soviet Union would go on to lose to Germany 2–1 in the semifinals, it would be the only time their nation advanced to the final four of the competition. The Soviet Union finished fourth after losing 2–1 to Portugal in the third-place game.

In the 1970 World Cup, the Soviet Union continued their streak of advancing past the first round when they finished first in their group with a 2-1-0 record, beating Belgium and El Salvador at the competition in Mexico. Unfortunately, a single goal by Uruguay in extra time of the quarterfinals was enough to end the Soviet Union's tournament. After missing the next two World Cups, in 1982 the Soviet Union once again advanced to the second round. Although the Soviet Union defeated Belgium and tied Poland in round two, they finished in second place due to goal differential and were eliminated. The 1986 World Cup saw the Soviet Union go 2-1-0 in the first round to finish first in their group, but they lost to Belgium 4–3 in the round of 16.

In the Soviet Union's final World Cup in 1990, the nation failed for the first time to advance to the second round. They went 1-0-2 against Argentina, Romania and Cameroon, with their only win a 4–0 victory over Cameroon.

SPAIN. Commonly known as La Roja (The Red), La Furia Roja (The Red Fury) or La Furia (The Fury). For most of the 20th century, Spain's national team was considered the greatest underachiever on the international stage. While the country's club teams, such as Real Madrid and Barcelona, dominated continental honors, Spain claimed only a single European Championship in the 20th century, and La Roja failed even to reach the World Cup final. In the 21st century, though, that record has been turned around, Spain twice winning the European Championship and claiming its first World Cup title in 2010.

Spain competed in its first World Cup in 1934 at the competition in Italy, winning its first game 3–1 over Brazil in the first round, coached by Amadeo García Salazar and captained by legendary goalkeeper Ricardo Zamora. In the second round, though, Spain lost in a replay to host nation Italy, falling to a lone goal by Giuseppe Meazza. Spain withdrew from the 1938 World Cup in the midst of civil war but reappeared at the first World Cup following World War II, claiming fourth place at the competition in Brazil. La Roja cruised through the group stage, defeating the United States, Chile and England. In the final-round group stage—with this World Cup not featuring an elimination stage—Spain struggled. A creditable 2–2 draw with Uruguay was followed by a crushing 6–1 defeat to Brazil and a 3–1 loss to Sweden that placed Spain at the bottom, though still claiming fourth place overall, a finish that would prove to be the Iberian nation's best of the century.

Spain did not qualify for either the 1954 or 1958 World Cups, and group-stage exits followed at the 1962 and 1966 World Cups, followed by further failures to qualify for the 1970 and 1974 competitions. In 1978, Spain did advance to the competition in Argentina but, once again, fell at the group stage. Four years on, Spain had a chance to make amends for past disappointments as the competition's host nation. José Santamaría coached a team that underwhelmed in the group stage, only winning one game and advancing to the second-round group stage behind group winners Northern

Ireland. Spain failed to win a game in the second stage, losing 2–1 to West Germany and tying 0–0 with England for another disappointing exit. Spain continued to under-achieve through the remainder of the 20th century, not advancing past the last eight at any World Cup competition: reaching the quarterfinals in Mexico in 1986 and the United States in 1994, the second round in Italy in 1990 and exiting at the group stage in France in 1998. A similar pattern was followed at the start of the 21st century, Spain exiting in the quarterfinals in 2002 in South Korea and Japan and in the second round in Germany in 2006.

At the 2010 World Cup, though, Spain—by then reigning European champions—vanquished past champions with a magnificent series of performances predicated on intricate possession soccer modeled similarly to the club success enjoyed by Barce-lona, who provided the core of the team's midfield, Xavi and Andrés Iniesta, coached by Vicente del Bosque. Spain began the group stage with an awkward 1–0 defeat to Switzerland, despite enjoying the lion's share of possession, but recovered with a 2–0 win against Honduras and a 2–1 victory over Chile. In the elimination rounds, Spain's remarkable dominance of the ball allowed opponents precious few chances, and a defense marshaled by goalkeeper Iker Casillas did not concede a goal in four consecutive victories that saw Spain claim a first World Cup title. That came with four straight 1–0 wins over Portugal, Paraguay, Germany and, in the final, the Netherlands. Forward David Villa scored the winners against Portugal and Paraguay, while defen-sive stalwart Carles Puyol struck the decisive goal against Germany. The final itself in Johannesburg was a taut affair marked by a Dutch strategy to foul the Spaniards and disrupt the team's rhythm, one that proved ultimately unsuccessful thanks to the game's only goal scored by Andrés Iniesta deep into extra time.

As defending World Cup and Euro champions, qualification for the 2014 World Cup in Brazil seemed like a lock, but key injuries to Xabi Alonso and Iker Casillas, among others, meant qualification would not come easily. It took a 1–0 road victory in Saint-Denis to finally gain some breathing room. Placed in group B with the Nether-lands, Chile and Australia, defense of their title got off to a rocky start when La Roja were dismantled by the Flying Dutchmen 5–1. A 27th-minute penalty by Xabi Alonso momentarily gave Spain life, but a superb diving goal off a flying header right before half by Robin van Persie pulled the Dutch level. Looking out of their element, La Roja saw the floodgates open in the second half behind a Robben brace, Stefan de Vrij header and a late-second goal by Van Persie. Perhaps it was the 5–1 drubbing at the hands of the Netherlands, but Spain never looked comfortable in their second group game against Chile. First-half goals from Eduardo Vargas and Charles Aránguiz did the damage as Spain rarely threatened in either half, giving Chile its first competi-tive win over Spain in 11 matches. In Spain's final game against Australia, with Tim Cahill sitting out due to an accumulation of yellow cards, the Spanish side everyone expected to see finally came to play. In the 36th minute, a poorly marked David Villa cheekily back flicked the ball for the first goal, and the game was put out of reach with goals by Fernando Torres and Juan Mata late in the second half. Too little, too late, the 3–0 win meant a consolatory three points but also an exit from Brazil in 23rd place with four goals for and seven against.

STÁBILE, GUILLERMO. B. 17 January 1906, Buenos Aires, Argentina. D. 27 December 1966. Guillermo Stábile was a leading player and coach from Argentina and was the top scorer at the inaugural FIFA World Cup, held in 1930, finishing with eight goals in four games. Argentina reached the final of that competition, though lost to hosts Uruguay, Stábile scoring once in a 4–2 defeat. Stábile played the first half of the 1930s at club level, playing in Italy for Genoa and Napoli, before retiring in 1939 after spending three years in France playing for Red Star Paris and even appearing for the French national team. Stábile then began a very successful coaching career, taking charge of Argentina from 1939 to 1960 and winning an impressive six Copa América titles in that period.

STADE DE FRANCE. In the Parisian suburb of Saint-Denis, the 1998 World Cup final was played at the Stade de France, a 70,000-capacity venue built for the competition. Without a stadium with a capacity over 50,000, Stade de France was a critical development for the competition, with construction beginning in 1995. It hosted nine games in the World Cup, including the opener between the defending champions Brazil and Scotland and three successive games for France in the elimination stage, the quarterfinal against Italy, semifinal against Croatia and the final versus Brazil, as France won the World Cup for the first time. Stade de France now serves as the national stadium for the French soccer and rugby teams.

STADIO NAZIONALE PNF. Originally built in 1911 but majorly renovated for a reopening in 1927, Rome's Stadio Nazionale PNF lived a relatively short life for a stadium, demolished only 26 years later in 1953. By then, it had already become part of World Cup history as the host venue for the 1934 World Cup final between Italy and Czechoslovakia, won by the host nation in front of 50,000 fans. Games at the 1934 World Cup were marked by the presence of propaganda for Benito Mussolini's fascist regime, and the stadium's name literally meant "Stadium of the Fascist Party." It also hosted two other games at the 1934 World Cup: Italy's 7–1 victory over the United States in the first round and Czechoslovakia's 3–1 win against Germany in the semifinal.

STADIO OLIMPICO. Originally built under the fascist regime of Benito Mussolini, Rome's Stadio Olimpico underwent a massive renovation for the 1990 World Cup in Italy, with the addition of a roof and a new capacity of 74,000 for the competition. The stadium hosted six games, five of them involving Italy: all of three of the nation's group-stage games, along with Italy's second round and quarterfinal games. Most prominently, Stadio Olimpico hosted the final of the World Cup on 8 July, a capacity crowd present as West Germany defeated Argentina 1–0. Today, the stadium serves as the home for Rome clubs AS Roma and SS Lazio, while also hosting rugby, athletics and other events. It was recently renovated and hosted the 2009 UEFA Champions League final.

STOICHKOV, HRISTO. B. 8 February 1966. Hristo Stoichkov is a former star player for Bulgaria and was named European Footballer of the Year in 1994. Combining a combustible temper with formidable power and skill, Stoichkov was a prolific goal scorer and creative forward for his country and for his clubs. His peak came in the early 1990s, leading Bulgaria to fourth place at the 1994 FIFA World Cup in the United States and winning the Spanish league with Barcelona in Spain on five occasions, along with one UEFA Champions League victory in 1992, forming an impressive and productive striking partnership at Barcelona with Brazil's Romário. Stoichkov ended his playing career in the United States, playing in Major League Soccer with the Chicago Fire and DC United, before embarking on a peripatetic coaching career with less success than his playing days.

SUBIABRE, GUILLERMO. B. 25 February 1903, Osorno, Chile. D. 1964. An outstanding goal scorer, Guillermo Subiabre scored two goals in three games for Chile at the inaugural 1930 World Cup, held in Uruguay. Subiabre had a considerable reputation entering the competition, having scored three goals in three games at the 1928 Olympic Games Football Tournament in Amsterdam, the Netherlands. In Uruguay at the World Cup two years later, Subiabre played in all three of Chile's games as they were eliminated at the first-round group stage. Subiabre did not score in Chile's opening-game win, 3–0 over Mexico, but did score the decisive goal in Chile's second successive win over France, finding the net in the 65th minute. In Chile's crucial third game against Argentina on 22 July in Montevideo, Subiabre scored in the 15th, but at that stage, Chile was already two goals down to Argentina and exited the competition with a 3–1 defeat. Subiabre did not appear in another World Cup competition, as Chile did not appear again in the World Cup until 1950, long after his retirement.

ŠUKER, DAVOR. B. 1 January 1968, Osijek, Croatia. The strongest appearance by Croatia in the World Cup to date, third place in the 1998 World Cup, was inspired in considerable part by the goals from lethal striker Davor Šuker, who scored six times in seven games to claim the Golden Ball as the competition's top scorer. Šuker's achievement came at the tail end of a career where he made his name playing for Sevilla and Real Madrid in Spain. In France at the 1998 World Cup, Šuker found the net in the group stage against Jamaica and Japan but really found his form in the elimination stage: Šuker scored the winner against Romania in the second round, found the net again in a stunning 3–0 quarterfinal win over Germany and opened the scoring against host nation France in the semifinal, though the French came back to claim a 2–1 victory. In the consolation third-place matchup with the Netherlands, Šuker scored the winner. At the age of 34, Šuker's 2002 World Cup in South Korea and Japan was far less successful. Šuker, captaining the team, was withdrawn after only 64 minutes of Croatia's first game and did not return to the field as Croatia went on to be eliminated at the first-round stage. His World Cup career ended with Šuker recording 6 goals in 8 finals appearances and a further 6 goals in 12 qualifying games.

SUPPICI, ALBERTO. B. 20 November 1898, Colonia del Sacramento, Uruguay. D. 21 June 1981. The first man to win the World Cup as a coach was Alberto Suppici, who led hosts Uruguay to the inaugural title on 30 July 1930 with a 4–2 victory over Argentina. He remains the youngest coach to win the World Cup, only 31 years old at the time. Suppici began coaching Uruguay in 1928 following the country's victory in the Olympic Games Football Tournament that year. Taking over an immensely talented team, Suppici led Uruguay to a disappointing third-place finish at the 1929 Copa América. Suppici redeemed himself the next year at the World Cup, though he began the tournament in controversial fashion by dropping starting goalkeeper Andrés Mazali for breaking curfew in the lead-up to the competition. Uruguay's preparations—as with all the other teams at the competition—were vastly different from those used by modern-day teams. The focus was not on tactics, which were barely discussed, but on physical fitness, with Suppici working his team, mostly amateurs, to get in shape to play 4 games in only 12 days. Tactical adjustments on the field were made by the team captain, in this case José Nasazzi, rather than by Suppici. Uruguay won all four games at the World Cup; as well as defeating Argentina in the final, they also beat Peru 1–0 in the first round, Romania 4–0 in the second round and Yugoslavia 6–1 in the semifinal. Estadio Suppici, a 12,000-capacity stadium in Suppici's hometown of Colonia del Sacramento, is named after the World Cup–winning coach.

SVOBODA, FRANTIŠEK. B. 5 August 1906, Vienna, Austria-Hungary. D. 6 July 1948. František Svoboda made his debut for Czechoslovakia in June 1926 against Hungary, with the peak of his international career coming eight years later at the second World Cup hosted by Italy, as Czechoslovakia reached the final, losing to the hosts after extra time. A forward with a tremendous goal-scoring record for club team Slavia Prague, with whom he spent 14 seasons, Svoboda scored on goal at the 1934 World Cup. Svoboda's goal came in Czechoslovakia's second game (Svoboda was not selected for their opening game) against Switzerland, the second goal in a 3–2 win. In the final, Svoboda almost made the difference for Czechoslovakia, striking the post shortly after Antonín Puč had given the Czechs a 1–0 lead, but it was not to be for Svoboda or his country on that day in Rome. Svoboda played a further four games for Czechoslovakia following the 1934 World Cup, his final appearance coming in May 1935 against Scotland. He ended his international career with 22 goals in 43 matches, 19 of them wins, 12 draws and 11 defeats.

SWEDEN. Commonly known as Blågult (The Blue and Yellow). Sweden has appeared in 11 World Cups and was the host nation in 1958. Their first appearance was in 1934 in Italy, where the Swedes won their opening match against Argentina 3–2 but lost to Germany 2–1 in the second round. In 1938, in France, Sweden advanced to the semifinals where they lost to Hungary, finishing in fourth place after losing to Brazil in the third-place game.

In the 1950 World Cup, Sweden improved on their previous fourth-place finish. After defeating Italy 3–2 and tying Paraguay 2–2 in the first round, Sweden advanced to the final round, featuring four teams in a round-robin format to determine the World Cup champions. Their first game was against hosts Brazil, which ended in a humbling 7–1 loss for the Swedes. Playing Uruguay in the following match, Sweden again lost, this time by a score of 3–2. Although Sweden was now out of the running for first place, they came back in their third game to defeat Spain 3–1 and finish third.

Sweden failed to qualify for the 1954 World Cup but had the honor of hosting the 1958 World Cup. Grouped with Mexico, Hungary and Wales, Sweden did not lose a game in the first round, defeating Mexico and Hungary and tying Wales. Advancing to the quarterfinals, Sweden played the Soviet Union to a surprise 2–0 victory and moved on to face Germany in the semifinals. There, the Germans took a first-half lead on a Hans Schaefer goal in the 24th minute. Enjoying strong home-crowd support, Sweden stayed in the game and tied things up just eight minutes later. Starting the second half tied 1–1, things took a surprise turn to the advantage of the Swedes when Germany's Erich Juskowiak was given a red card. A man up for over 30 minutes, Sweden took control of the game and won 3–1. The final against Brazil would start well for Sweden when Nils Liedholm scored just four minutes in. Unfortunately, the strength of the Brazilian side would prove to be too much for Sweden, as they lost 5–2. Sweden's second-place finish is their best World Cup result to date.

Sweden's next World Cup appearance was in 1970 in Mexico. In the first round, they went 1-1-1 against Italy, Uruguay and Israel, finishing third in their group and failing to advance to the second round. Four years later, Sweden fared better, finishing second in their group with Uruguay, the Netherlands and Bulgaria and moving on to the second group stage. Placed with Germany, Poland and Yugoslavia, Sweden lost their first game against Poland 1–0. Needing a win against Germany in their next game, Sweden scored first in the 24th minute. Unfortunately, they weren't unable to hold on to the lead and lost 4–2. Knowing they could not advance to the finals or the third-place game, Sweden still managed a 2–1 victory over Yugoslavia, ending their tournament on a positive note.

Sweden would not find success in their next two World Cups, failing to earn a win in either 1978 or 1990. The 1994 World Cup in the United States would prove to be one of their most successful tournaments, as they advanced as far as the semifinals, led by tricky forward Tomas Brolin. After defeating Saudi Arabia 3–1 in the second round, Sweden played Romania to a 2–2 tie and advanced to the semifinals when they won 5–4 in a penalty shoot-out. In the semifinals, Sweden would face Brazil for the second time in the tournament, having tied them 1–1 in the group stage. For the first time in the competition, Sweden was unable to find the back of the net, losing 1–0 and moving into the third-place game. Playing Bulgaria, Sweden rediscovered their scoring ways and won 4–0.

Although Sweden advanced to the round of 16 in both the 2002 and 2006 World Cups, they failed to make it any further in either tournament. Losses to Portugal in the ensuing 2010 and 2014 qualifications meant Sweden will have to wait at least 12 years before returning to the World Cup.

SWITZERLAND. Commonly known as Schweizer Nati or La Nati (The National Team). The Swiss have qualified for the World Cup 10 times through 2014. They have reached the quarterfinals three times, in 1934, 1938 and 1954. Switzerland hosted the World Cup in 1954, finishing first in their group ahead of England, Italy and Belgium. The Swiss faced neighbors Austria in the quarterfinals, in what would prove to be a high-scoring affair. Although Switzerland scored five goals, their defense was unable to stop the Austrians, and they lost 7–5.

The Swiss found little success in their following two World Cup appearances, going 0-0-3 in both the 1962 and 1966 competitions, in Chile and England respectively. It would be another 28 years before they returned to the World Cup, and though they advanced to the round of 16 in 1994 in the United States, they were eliminated at that stage by Spain, 3–0.

In the 2006 World Cup, Switzerland gained the dubious distinction of being the only team in the history of the competition to be eliminated without conceding a goal during the run of play. In the group stage, they tied their opening match against France 0–0, defeated Togo 2–0 and won against Korea by the same score. In the round of 16, they held Ukraine scoreless, but in the penalty shoot-out, they failed to score a single penalty and were eliminated.

Four years later, Switzerland failed to advance to the second round, although they did defeat the eventual champions Spain 1–0 in the group stage.

Qualification for the 2014 World Cup in Brazil saw a couple of minor hiccups, but a team built around the 2009 U-17 World Cup winners finished atop their group seven points clear of Iceland. Placed in group E with Ecuador, France and Honduras, advancement out of the group was expected by German manager Ottmar Hitzfeld. Matched up against Ecuador in their first match at the Estádio Nacional de Brasília, Switzerland found themselves down a goal midway through the first half to an energetic Ecuadorian side when Enner Valencia headed home a free kick in the 22nd minute. Playing with more energy to start the second half, Switzerland quickly found the equalizer when Admir Mehmedi finished a well-placed corner. Against a tiring Ecuadorian side, a late switch-and-cross to a streaking Haris Seferović in the final seconds of stoppage time meant a 2–1 win. Game two, against 17th-ranked France, was supposed to be a coming-out party of sorts for the 6th-ranked Swiss; instead, the game many expected never materialized as France used three first-half goals to gain all of the momentum. Sitting on three points, Switzerland found themselves needing a win and help from the French to guarantee advancement. In their final game against Honduras, a hat trick by Xherdan Shaqiri—the first goal coming in the sixth minute—and a French tie with Ecuador meant advancement to the round of 16.

At the Arena Corinthians in São Paulo, the Swiss side sat back on defense and forced the Argentinians to attempt to break through a host of red shirts while looking to counter. It almost worked, too, when, in the 45th minute, Argentine goalkeeper Sergio Romero had to parry wide a Granit Xhaka blast. With neither team able to break through in full time, it looked as though the Swiss were content to play for penalties—until Lionel Messi had other ideas. After an Argentinian win at midfield, Messi quickly found the ball at his feet in the middle of the field and tore toward goal. With a quick leap over a diving Fabian Schär flailing to stop him, Messi found a wide-open Ángel Di María for the game winner. La Nati was sent home in 11th place with seven goals for and seven against.

SZABÓ, ANTAL. B. 4 September 1910, Hungary. D. 21 April 1958. Among his 42 appearances for Hungary's national team, Szabó's most prominent day came on 19 June 1938, when he kept goal for his country in the World Cup final against Italy in Paris, France. It was to end in disappointment, Hungary and Szabó conceding four goals in a defeat to the defending World Cup champions. Until that point, Szabó and his Hungarian defenders had kept an extremely tight ship, only allowing one goal in their first three games at the competition and that in a 5–1 win over Sweden in the semifinal. Szabó's experience, having been a regular starter for Hungary since 1931, proved invaluable. He also had World Cup experience, having played two games at the 1934 World Cup, where Hungary exited at the quarterfinal stage, Szabó having conceded twice in a 2–1 defeat to Austria.

SZALAY, ANTAL. B. 12 March 1912, Hungary. D. 1960. At the 1934 and 1938 World Cups, Antal Szalay played a total of six games. A defender, Szalay starred domestically for Hungarian giants Újpest FC. At the 1934 World Cup, held in Italy, Szalay played one game. He did not feature in Hungary's first game against Egypt, a 4–2 win, but came into the team for their quarterfinal matchup against Austria. Hungary was eliminated at that stage with a 2–1 defeat. Szalay played a fuller part in the 1938 competition held in France, though he was again on the bench for their first-round victory, this time a 6–0 win over the Dutch East Indies. Szalay was picked in the first 11 for Hungary's quarterfinal game against Switzerland, a 2–0 victory, and stayed in the Hungarian team as they beat Sweden 5–1 in Paris to reach the final. In the French capital, Szalay took part in Hungary's defeat to Italy, their fellow Europeans winning the World Cup for the second consecutive occasion.

SZŰCS, GYÖRGY. B. 23 April 1912, Budapest, Hungary. D. 10 December 1991. Defender György Szűcs appeared for Hungary at both the 1934 World Cup in Italy and the 1938 World Cup in France. He made his debut for his country in January 1934, earning selection for the World Cup by playing in games against Germany, Bulgaria and England in the lead-up to the 1934 competition. Szűcs started for Hungary in their first-round victory versus Egypt and then in Hungary's next game, a quarterfinal stage defeat to Austria. Szűcs remained a regular in the Hungarian team in the years leading up to the 1938 World Cup. However, he did not start for Hungary until the final of that competition, as Hungary lost 4–2 to Italy in Paris. Szűcs played only one further game for Hungary in 1939 before his international retirement, giving him a total of 25 appearances for his country, with no goals scored. At club level, Szűcs starred for the great Budapest-based Újpest FC team of the 1950s, winning numerous honors.

T

TAYLOR, JACK. B. 21 April 1930, Wolverhampton, England. D. 27 July 2012. In the 1974 World Cup final between West Germany and the Netherlands, referee Jack Taylor awarded a penalty to the Dutch within a minute of the game kicking off. The penalty is not only remembered for how early it came in the game but also for being the first ever awarded in a World Cup final. It was also not the last penalty Taylor awarded that day, as he also gave a penalty to West Germany after 25 minutes. Both penalty decisions were, by most accounts, fair decisions. In the first case, Dutch captain Johan Cruyff was clearly fouled by German defender Uli Hoeneß as he surged into the penalty area, though there is some argument the first contact in the challenge came just outside the penalty area. For the second penalty, Wim Jansen was adjudicated to have tripped Bernd Hölzenbein in the Dutch penalty box, and it appears that clear contact—albeit exaggerated by Hölzenbein—did bring the German down. Both penalties were scored, and West Germany ultimately won the final 2–1. Taylor also issued four cautions in the game, three to the Netherlands and one to West Germany. As well as the final, Taylor also refereed the 1–1 draw between Bulgaria and Uruguay in the first-round group stage and another 1–1 tie between Argentina and East Germany in the second-round group stage. By the time of the 1974 World Cup, Taylor was a vastly experienced referee who had been officiating internationally since 1963. His experience included refereeing at the 1964 European Championship quarterfinal stage and taking charge of the 1971 European Cup final. Taylor was also selected as a referee for the 1970 World Cup in Mexico, overseeing one game, Italy's 1–0 victory over Sweden in the group stage. Following the 1974 World Cup, Taylor continued as an international referee until 1978, his last assignment a World Cup qualifying game in May 1977 between the Soviet Union and Hungary.

THIRD-PLACE GAME. A third-place play-off has taken place at almost every World Cup final tournament to determine the finishing order for third and fourth in the competition between the losers of each semifinal. The first World Cup held in 1930 did not feature a third-place game. In 1934, at the World Cup held in Italy, the first third-place play-off took place, won by Germany 3–2 over neighbors Austria. Continuing what would be a trend of high scoring third-place games, in 1938, Brazil beat Sweden 4–2 to take third place at the World Cup in France. In 1950, the World Cup—for the only time in its history—did not feature a decisive knockout stage at the tournament staged in Brazil but instead used a round-robin group to determine the final standings, thus rendering a third-place play-off unnecessary. The 1954 World Cup in Switzerland saw a return of the third-place game, won by Austria 3–1 over

Uruguay. A record nine goals were scored at the 1958 third-place play-off in Sweden, as France defeated West Germany 6–3. In 1966, Portugal claimed third place at Wembley Stadium in London with a 2–1 victory over the Soviet Union. The 1970 World Cup saw a record attendance, still standing today, of 104,403 spectators for the third-place game at the Azteca in Mexico City, won by West Germany over Uruguay. Four years later, Brazil lost 1–0 to Poland in the lowest-scoring third-place game to date at the Olympistadion in Munich. Brazil appeared again in the next third-place game at the 1978 World Cup in Argentina, this time defeating Italy 2–1 at El Monumental, 69,659 fans in attendance. Five goals were scored in the 1982 third-place play-off, a small crowd of 28,000 in Alicante, Spain, as Poland defeated France 3–2. The scoring continued in 1986 again in Mexico, six goals in an extra-time thriller between France and Belgium, the former winning 4–2. Only 21,000 fans watched the game in Puebla. Hosts Italy appeared in the 1990 World Cup third-place game, against England, both teams having lost on penalty kicks at the semifinal stage. The Italians won 2–1, 51,426 present at the game in Bari. The third-place play-off at the 1994 World Cup in the United States proved to be a one-sided affair for the 91,500 spectators at the Rose Bowl in California, as Sweden crushed Bulgaria 4–0. The next third-place play-off in 1998, at the World Cup in France, was a much tighter affair, as Croatia defeated the Netherlands 3–1 in front of 45,500 fans at the Parc des Princes in Paris. In 2002, one of the two host nations appeared in the third-place game, as South Korea—the cohost along with Japan—lost 3–2 to Turkey in Daegu, 63,483 at Daegu World Cup Stadium. The hosts also appeared in the 2006 World Cup third-place play-off, Germany beating Portugal 3–1 in Stuttgart, 52,000 present. Nelson Mandela Bay Stadium in Port Elizabeth was the venue for the 2010 World Cup's third-place play-off, 36,254 in the 41,000-capacity stadium. Two records were set, as Germany won the game to finish third for the fourth time, while Uruguay lost to finish fourth for the third time. In 2014, the host nation again saw itself in the third-place game, this time at Nacional in Brasília. Unfortunately for the majority of the 68,034 fans in attendance, the Netherlands rolled to a 3–0 win, meaning a second loss in as many games for Brazil.

THURAM, LILIAN. B. 1 January 1972, Pointe-à-Pitre, Guadeloupe. As outspoken off the field in addressing issues such as racism as he was dominating as a defender on it, Lilian Thuram was not born in France, but is one of the nation's greatest-ever players. He played a key role in helping France win the World Cup for the first time in 1998, an anchor at right-back in a defense that conceded just two goals in seven games. Thuram even contributed offensively as well, scoring twice in France's semifinal victory over Croatia—though he had been partially responsible for allowing the first goal of the game to the Croatians, Thuram struck a minute later, finishing neatly from a Youri Djorkaeff through ball. He added a second with a left-footed drive from the edge of the penalty area to take France to the final, where they easily defeated Brazil. Thuram was awarded the Bronze Ball as the third-best player in the tournament.

Four years later, Thuram was part of a French team that suffered a nightmare meltdown in the World Cup held in Japan and South Korea. Thuram played in all three games as France failed to win or score a goal, eliminated at the first stage. Thuram had briefly retired from international play following that debacle but was persuaded to return in time for the 2006 World Cup. At center-back, Thuram, now 34, helped lead France to the final and, at the same tournament, broke the French record for international appearances. He retired following the 2008 European Championships, his World Cup record encompassing 16 games, 9 of them wins.

TITKOS, PÁL. B. 8 January 1908, Budapest, Hungary. D. 8 October 1988. Pál Titkos scored one of Hungary's two goals in the 1938 World Cup final, a losing effort for his country in their 4–2 defeat to Italy. Titkos was a veteran player for Hungary by the time of the 1938 World Cup, having made his debut almost a decade earlier in February 1929, though he was not part of Hungary's team at the 1934 World Cup in Italy. Titkos played in two games at the 1938 World Cup, not selected for their first two games but joining the starting 11 at the semifinal stage and scoring his first World Cup goal against Sweden in a 5–1 win. In the final, Titkos scored after eight minutes, firing the ball into the roof of the net past Aldo Olivieri in the Italian goal to equalize for Hungary in the eighth minute. But though Titkos, playing on the left-wing, continued to trouble the Italian defense, it would not be enough as Italy won 4–2. Titkos played one final game for Hungary in December 1938 against Scotland, as he finished his international career having scored 13 goals in 48 games.

TOGO. Commonly known as Les Eperviers (The Sparrowhawks). The small West African nation Togo gained independence from France in 1960, and the governing body of soccer in the country, Fédération Togolaise de Football, affiliated to FIFA in 1964. It has since appeared in one World Cup finals tournament, in 2006. Togo first attempted to qualify for the World Cup in 1974, falling on that occasion to the eventual lone African qualifier, Zaire, 4–0 on aggregate over two games. Togo failed to qualify for the next World Cup in 1978, losing at the second-round stage, but did achieve their first World Cup victory by beating Senegal, with a 1–0 victory at home in the capital of Togo, Lomé, followed by a 1–1 tie in Senegal. In the second round, Togo was eliminated by Guinea 4–1 over two games. During qualification for the 1982 World Cup, Togo achieved their second win in the history of the competition and their first away from home, beating Niger 1–0 in Niamey. Disappointingly, though, Togo lost 2–1 at home in Lomé in the return fixture and was thus eliminated on the away-goals rule. Due to organizational problems, Togo did not take part in either the 1986 or 1990 World Cup qualifying competitions. Togo returned to the qualification process for the 1994 World Cup but, desperately short of experience, lost all five games in the first-round group stage, conceding 11 goals and only scoring twice. Togo showed improvement in qualification for the 1998 World Cup, defeating Senegal 3–2 on aggregate in the first round. They were eliminated in the second-round group stage, with one win, one draw and four defeats. Togo continued a trend of improvement in 2002 World Cup qualifying, reaching the final-round group stage, winning two, drawing three and losing three games as they were eliminated. In 2006, Togo's qualification for the World Cup surprised many, as they topped a final-round group in African qualifying containing Senegal, Zambia, Congo, Mali and Liberia, only losing one out of ten games and winning seven.

Togo's squad for the 2006 World Cup in Germany was almost entirely foreign based, with the exception of goalkeeper Kodjovi Obilalé. The largest contingents of Togo's players were based in France, though their best-known player was Arsenal forward Emmanuel Adebayor, the top scorer in African qualifying. The buildup to Togo's first World Cup appearance was troubled by the unexpected departure of their coach Stephen Keshi during qualifying, after Togo struggled at the 2006 Africa Cup of Nations in February, losing all three games. Keshi was replaced by veteran German coach Otto Pfister. Togo was drawn into group G, along with France, South Korea and Switzerland, each with far more experience in the World Cup than the Africans. In Germany, Togo's preparations were disrupted by a dispute over player bonuses, and Pfister's standing as coach was unclear right until kickoff of their opening game against South Korea in Frankfurt on 13 June. Togo, though, took the lead in the first half, when Mohamed Kader struck a right-footed drive sweetly into the bottom corner from the edge of the penalty area in the 31st minute. Togo nearly doubled their lead in the 41st minute, Yao Junior Sènaya sending a dipping free kick from 25 yards out that the South Korean goalkeeper Lee Woon-Jae was just able to tip over the crossbar. Togo's surprising lead was derailed in the second half, however, when Togo's captain Jean-Paul Abalo was dismissed for receiving his second yellow card, tripping Park Ji-Sung in the 53rd minute. This opened up the game for South Korea, who scored from the resulting free kick 25 yards out to equalize and then found a winner in the 72nd minute from Ahn Jung-Hwan. Togo's next game against Switzerland began poorly, Alexander Frei scoring after only 17 minutes, but Togo then created several good chances, with a penalty claim turned down when Adebayor appeared to be fouled by Swiss defender Patrick Müller. Switzerland, though, sealed victory late on and eliminated Togo with an 88th-minute strike. That left Togo playing for pride against eventual finalists France, and though the Africans held the score to 0–0 at halftime, French domination eventually resulted in two goals for the Europeans. Togo did not qualify for the 2010 World Cup, eliminated in the third round after finishing behind Cameroon and Gabon, and failed again in 2014 after falling in the second round.

TRAMUTOLA, JUAN JOSÉ. B. 21 October 1902, La Plata, Argentina. D. 30 November 1968. Aged just 27 when he coached Argentina at the inaugural 1930 World Cup in Uruguay, Juan José Tramutola led his country to second place in the competition. Tramutola was younger than seven of the Argentinean players on the roster and remains the youngest coach in the history of the World Cup. In 1929, Tramutola had led Argentina to victory in the Copa América, South America's international championship, his first games as coach. From the Copa América to the World Cup, Tramutola was part of a coaching duo for Argentina with Francisco Olazar. Argentina, favorites for the 1930 World Cup alongside hosts Uruguay, strolled through their first-round group after a tough first game against France, won 1–0, followed by comfortable 6–3 and 3–1 victories over Mexico and Chile respectively. Tramutola and Olazar juggled their lineup considerably during the group stage, with the critical introduction of forward Guillermo Stábile for his international debut in Argentina's second game against Mexico proving to be an inspired choice: he went on to be the top scorer in the World

Cup with eight goals in four games. Two of those goals came against the United States in the semifinal on 26 July at Estadio de Centenario, a 6–1 for Argentina that flattered the South Americans, the scoreline only 1–0 at halftime and the Americans hampered in the second half by an injury to their goalkeeper Jimmy Douglas. As had been expected, Argentina faced Uruguay in the final, but Tramutola and Olazar could not find a way to contain the home team playing in front of a large six-figure crowd in Montevideo. Despite leading at halftime, thanks to goals from Carlos Peucelle and Guillermo Stábile, Argentina lost 4–2 in the first World Cup final. It was the only game in charge of Argentina that Tramutola lost, with a record of seven wins, one loss and one draw during his nine games in charge from 1929 to 1930. Tramutola did not coach Argentina again, managing sporadically at club level in Argentina before his death, aged 66, in 1968.

TRINIDAD AND TOBAGO. Commonly known as the Soca Warriors. In 2006, the Caribbean nation Trinidad and Tobago qualified for the World Cup for the first and only occasion in its history. In doing so, it became the smallest nation (in both size and population) to ever qualify. Though eliminated in the first round, Trinidad and Tobago did earn their first World Cup point in a draw with Sweden. It was almost a century earlier, in 1908, that Trinidad and Tobago's Football Federation was established, though it was not until the 1960s that they first attempted to qualify for the World Cup, affiliating to FIFA in 1964. Trinidad and Tobago first came close to reaching the World Cup finals for the 1974 competition in West Germany. CONCACAF's sole qualification spot was guaranteed to the winner of the 1973 CONCACAF Championship held in Haiti. Trinidad and Tobago finished in second place behind Haiti, but there was heated controversy surrounding Haiti's decisive victory over Trinidad and Tobago, as the latter had no fewer than five goals disallowed in a 2–1 defeat, with the referee later banned for life by FIFA. Trinidad and Tobago came just as close to qualification 16 years later for the 1990 World Cup in Italy. Hosting the United States, who had not qualified for a World Cup themselves since 1950, Trinidad and Tobago needed only a draw at home to advance to Italy. Yet a looping shot by American Paul Caligiuri proved to be the only goal of the game, shocking Trinidad and Tobago.

Following failures to qualify for the 1994, 1998 and 2002 World Cups, qualification for the 2006 World Cup was a long process for Trinidad and Tobago. Their campaign began with a second round win in CONCACAF qualifying over the Dominican Republica, 6–0, and then qualified for the fourth-round stage by finishing second in their group at the third-round stage. In the fourth round, Trinidad and Tobago's fourth-place finish earned them a play-off against the fifth-placed team from the Asian zone of qualifying with the winner over a home-and-away contest to gain direct entry to the World Cup. Trinidad and Tobago faced Bahrain, who held them to a 1–1 draw at home. In Bahrain, though, Trinidad and Tobago secured a 1–0 win when a cross by Manchester United's Dwight Yorke led to a powerful headed goal by Dennis Lawrence. The game ended in chaos when Colombian referee Óscar Ruiz ruled out an equalizer by Bahrain, with Bahrain having a man sent off for accosting the referee. The result meant Trinidad and Tobago would become the fourth Caribbean country to appear at the World Cup, joining Cuba in 1938, Haiti in 1974 and Jamaica in 1998.

Trinidad and Tobago's coach during qualification and at the 2006 World Cup was veteran Dutch manager Leo Beenhakker, who most famously coached Real Madrid and the Netherlands in the late 1980s and early 1990s. Beenhakker's squad, drawing from the smallest population of any of the 32 teams in Germany, was composed of players outside the elite European teams, with the majority playing in Scotland or lower-league English soccer. Beenhakker's team was drawn in group B, alongside England, Sweden and Paraguay. The Caribbean team surprised Sweden with a stout defensive performance against Sweden. Though the Europeans dominated possession, they could only muster six shots on Shaka Hislop's goal, Hislop having only played due to a last-minute injury to first-choice Kelvin Jack. Trinidad and Tobago's performance was all the more remarkable for playing almost the entire second half with 10 men, Avery John sent off shortly after the break following a second yellow card for a reckless challenge on Christian Wilhelmsson. Trinidad and Tobago next faced England in Nuremburg, and another fine defensive performance caused an unimaginative England team problems as it took until the 83rd minute for English forward Peter Crouch to break the deadlock. Steven Gerrard added a second for England in stoppage time. Trinidad and Tobago still had an outside chance of qualification for the next round as they faced Paraguay in Kaiserslautern on 20 June but fell 2–0 after an own goal by Brent Sancho in the first half and a second by Paraguayan winger Nelson Cuevas late in the second half. Eliminated, Trinidad and Tobago went home with their first World Cup point.

TUNISIA. Commonly known as Les Aigles de Carthage (The Eagles of Carthage). In their inaugural appearance at the World Cup in 1978 in Argentina, Tunisia opened with a 3–1 win over Mexico. With the win, Tunisia became the first African team to win a World Cup match. Although they lost their second game to Poland, they managed a 0–0 draw against West Germany, the defending champions. Tunisia's 1-1-1 record put them in third place in their group, and they were eliminated from the tournament.

Tunisia would go another 20 years before they qualified for another World Cup but then appeared in three consecutive competitions: 1998, 2002 and 2006. Unfortunately, their dream start in the 1978 tournament did not continue the following years. Tunisia would go all three World Cups without registering a single win and therefore did not advance past the first round. The team failed to qualify for the 2010 and 2014 competitions.

TURKEY. Commonly known as Ay Yıldızlılar (The Crescent Stars) or the Comeback Kings. Although Turkey first qualified for the World Cup in 1950, their team was forced to withdraw due to financial issues. Four years later, they qualified yet again and this time were able to compete in the finals. In the 1954 World Cup in Switzerland, Turkey was grouped with Hungary, Germany and the Korean Republic. They finished with a 1-0-2 record and did not advance to the second round.

Turkey failed to qualify for the next 11 World Cups but would eventually make it back to the finals in 2002. Facing eventual champions Brazil in their opening match, Turkey was defeated 2–1. Things looked grim for Turkey after a 1–1 tie with Costa

Rica in their second game, but a 3–0 win against China snuck them into the second round ahead of Costa Rica on goal difference. In the round of 16, Turkey defeated co-hosts Japan by a score of 1–0 and were suddenly in the quarterfinals. There, they beat Senegal 1–0 on a golden goal and surprised everyone by advancing to the semifinals. Facing a familiar foe in Brazil, Turkey found themselves once again unable to defeat the strong Brazilian side and lost 1–0. However, they ended the tournament on a high note as they beat South Korea in the bronze-medal match by a score of 3–2. Unfortunately for Turkish fans, this amazing finish did not translate into future success, and the Comeback Kings have yet to qualify for another World Cup finals since.

U

UKRAINE. Commonly known as Zbirna or Sbirna (The Team) or Yellow-Blue. The Ukrainian team first qualified for the World Cup in 2006, which was also their first-ever appearance in the finals of a major competition. In Germany, their opening match against Spain finished in a 4–0 loss, but Ukraine turned things around in their subsequent matches, beating Saudi Arabia 4–0 and Tunisia 1–0. The two wins put Ukraine into second place in their group, and they advanced to the second round. Facing a tough Swiss team in the round of 16, Ukraine refused to let their World Cup end. The game remained scoreless through regulation and extra time, with Ukraine finally pulling out a 3–0 win in a penalty shoot-out. Unfortunately, their good fortunes did not continue. Paired with eventual champions Italy in the quarterfinals, Ukraine fell 3–0 and was sent home. During qualifying for the 2010 and 2014 World Cup finals, Ukraine twice made it to the UEFA play-off stage, losing in 2010 to Greece on a 1–0 aggregate and to France in 2014 on a 3–2 aggregate.

UNITED ARAB EMIRATES. Commonly known as Al-Abyad (The White) or Eyal Zayed (Zayed's Sons). The United Arab Emirates appeared in their first and only World Cup in 1990 in Italy. Facing Colombia, West Germany and Yugoslavia in the first round, they lost all three games when they scored only 2 goals and allowed 11 and finished last in their group. Since 1990, Zayed's Sons have not qualified for another World Cup finals, their only successes as a national side coming in the AFC Asian Cup, Kirin Cup, the Asian Games and the Gulf Cup of Nations.

UNITED STATES. Commonly known as the Americans, the Stars and Stripes, the Yanks, or Team USA. Out of 10 appearances at the World Cup, the United States' best finish remains the third place achieved at its very first appearance in the inaugural 1930 World Cup. The American national team's most famous result, a 1–0 win over England in the 1950 World Cup, preceded a 40-year barren spell in which the United States did not qualify for the World Cup. Yet since then, the American team has appeared in every World Cup. The ups and downs of the United States national team reflect the rocky story of professional soccer in the country; while much of the rest of the world embraced soccer with unabashed enthusiasm during the 20th century, Americans proved the exception with embraces of an American version of football, baseball and basketball. Despite the establishment of promising, popular professional leagues in the 1920s and 1970s, neither proved enduring, and it was only in the aftermath of staging the World Cup itself in 1994 that a professional league, Major League Soccer, would become a significant and permanent presence on the American sports scene.

The American national team played its first official game in 1916, on a tour of Scandinavia, under the auspices of the country's governing body of soccer today known as the United States Soccer Federation (US Soccer or the USSF), founded in 1913 and affiliated to FIFA in the same year. By the time of the first World Cup in 1930, the U.S. had played in both the 1924 and 1928 Olympic Games soccer tournaments and, at the time, had a strong domestic professional league—the American Soccer League—to pick its roster from for the tournament in Uruguay. An American roster of 16 players boarded the SS *Munargo* for the competition, entirely held in the Uruguayan capital Montevideo. Of the 16 players, 6 had been born in Britain, whose immigrants still dominated American soccer, though only one had come to America to play professionally—the team was a selection of the best talent the country itself had produced. As one of four teams seeded in Uruguay, the Americans received a favorable draw, paired in group four with Paraguay and Belgium. In the opener against Belgium, with a comfortable 3–0 win, the U.S. showed their strength and speed was a force to be reckoned with, the goals coming from Bart McGhee, Tom Florie and Bert Patenaude. Against a highly rated Paraguayan team, the U.S. roared to a 2–0 lead within 15 minutes, Patenaude scoring twice. The Americans' third goal came from Patenaude, completing the first hat trick in World Cup history, though it would be decades before FIFA would acknowledge the achievement due to some doubt over whether Patenaude or Florie had scored one of the goals. The U.S. secured a second straight 3–0 victory and moved on as the group winner to the semifinal stage.

Both of the Americans' previous games had been held at the 20,000-capacity venue Parque Central in Montevideo, as the stadium intended as the tournament's center-piece, Estadio Centenario, had not been completed in time. For the semifinal, the U.S. met Argentina at the now-completed Centenario. Suddenly, the American players appeared in front of 80,000 fans, many thousands of them from across the Río de la Plata cheering for their opponents. The field itself was also considerably larger than at Parque Central. In the first half, the Americans were hobbled by injuries to goalkeeper Jimmy Douglas and center-half Raphael Tracy, neither of whom could be replaced in an era before substitutions. Argentina took a 1–0 lead into halftime, a game considered even to that point, but in the second half, the Americans were overwhelmed, conceding five further goals and only scoring a single consolation goal, through Jim Brown, in the 89th minute.

A 6–1 defeat was harsh on the U.S. team, who had shown that, while they lacked the flair of the South American teams at the competition, they did have a professional level of organization and fitness to compete internationally. Unfortunately, with the collapse of the American Soccer League in the 1930s, it was not a platform that could be built on. The U.S. did qualify for the next World Cup, held in Italy in 1934. Qualification came in curious circumstances: only three days before the World Cup proper began, the U.S. played Mexico in a one-game qualifier held in Rome to decide who would represent the North and Central American region in the competition. Under the watching eyes of Mussolini at Nazionale PNF Stadium, "Buff" Donelli scored all four goals for the Americans in a 4–2 win. It earned the U.S. what would prove to be a short and less-than-sweet shot in the 1934 World Cup finals. With the final tournament beginning with a knockout stage rather than the round-robin group stage used at the previous tournament, America's World Cup ended swiftly at the hands of the host nation and ultimate World Cup champion Italy. A U.S. team now made up mostly of amateurs was no match for the talented Italians, who won 7–1 at a canter.

American professional soccer had made few strides forward by the time of the nation's next World Cup appearance in 1950. Qualification had been secured via a second-place finish in the 1949 North American championship held in Mexico. The U.S. team for the 1950 World Cup in Brazil featured talented players, including captain Walter Bahr, though several of the star Americans from Mexico the previous year did not make the trip for various reasons—striker Benny McLaughlin of Philadelphia, for example, could not arrange for time off work, illustrating the downside of entering a team not made up of professionals. One unusual inclusion was Haitian-born forward Joe Gaetjens, who had studied at Columbia University in New York and was awaiting American citizenship; more importantly for U.S. soccer, he had scored prolifically for Brookhatten in the (third) American Soccer League in the most recent season. As was often the case for the American team, preparation for the trip was haphazard, with the team's coach, Bill Jeffrey, only appointed two weeks before the team set out for Brazil. Jeffrey was well respected, though, as a successful college coach for Penn State.

The U.S. began the competition in Brazil by taking on Spain in Curitiba. The Americans took a surprising early lead thanks to a goal from St. Louis–born forward Gino Pariani and surprised everyone further by holding on to a 1–0 scoreline until the 81st minute. Spain, though, equalized and added two more for a 3–1 win. Still, a strong performance for so long emboldened the Americans for their next game against England, the founder nation of modern soccer making its World Cup debut and armed with world-class talents, including Stanley Matthews and Nat Lofthouse. Amazingly, the U.S. defeated the English 1–0 in Belo Horizonte. The game winner came early in the second half: Bahr's long shot was deflected in by Gaetjens. England pushed for an equalizer, but stout defense by the U.S. team kept their frustrated opponents at bay. The Americans had claimed a famous victory, though it was one hardly noticed back home, a country almost entirely uninterested in international soccer. The U.S. team returned home following a 5–2 defeat to Chile that eliminated them in the group stage to little fanfare following a famous victory.

There would be no more fanfare about the World Cup in the United States for 40 years. The U.S. team, strapped for resources in a sport marooned in obscurity compared to baseball, basketball, football and ice hockey, failed to qualify for the 1954, 1958, 1962, 1966, 1970, 1974, 1978, 1982 and 1986 World Cup finals. The Americans became peripheral even in the North and Central American region, as Mexico became the powerhouse nation in the area's competitions. Even the relative success of a professional league operating in the United States between 1967 and 1984, the North American Soccer League, did little to improve the national team, largely reliant on overseas talent. An attempt to include a team of all-American national-team players in the league during the 1983 season, known as Team America, was a dismal failure, the team finishing last.

By the late 1980s, though, a boom in participation in youth soccer across the U.S. since the 1970s began to pay dividends for the national team, with a collection of talented players who would go abroad to make their livings in the era between the demise of the NASL in 1984 and the launch of a new, professional, top-tier outdoor league, Major League Soccer, in 1996. With new talents on the team, including John Harkes, Peter Vermes, Tony Meola and Tab Ramos, the U.S. qualified for the 1990 World Cup in dramatic fashion. On 19 November 1989, the U.S. played at Trinidad and Tobago's National Stadium in Port of Spain knowing a win was needed to qualify for the World Cup; a draw would see Trinidad and Tobago advance. The U.S. had not won a qualifying game on the road for 21 years. But thanks to a goal after half an hour by Paul Caligiuri, a looping long-distance strike that became known as "the Shot," the U.S. secured a remarkable victory. In part, it had come due to stronger organizing by the U.S. Soccer Federation, who during the qualification campaign began employing a pool of players directly to allow them to train and play on a more professional basis, given the absence of a professional-league option domestically.

Coached by Bob Gansler, at the 1990 World Cup, the U.S. was drawn in group A for the first round, with Czechoslovakia, Austria and host nation Italy. Gansler headed to Italy with a youthful team: the team's oldest player was 27 and was filled with up-and-coming stars, including Meola (21 years old), Ramos (23), Marcelo Balboa (22) and Eric Wynalda (20). The team's inexperience was exposed as soon as the Americans' first game of the tournament in Florence against a strong and battle-hardened Czechoslovakia. By the 50th minute, the U.S. had already conceded three goals and, shortly after, was reduced to 10 men with Wynalda expelled for a shove on Jozef Chovanec. The U.S. pulled back a goal through Caligiuri, but the Czechs scored twice more for a 5–1 win that humbled the American team, who had been confident before kickoff. Facing the host nation next, Gansler packed the defense to avoid another humiliation. The tactic employed at the Olympic Stadium in Rome succeeded in its limited aim: the Italians found it difficult to break the Americans down, succeeding only once through a left-footed blast by Giuseppe Giannini in the 11th minute. Vermes almost scrambled in an equalizer from one of the few U.S. attacks after Gianluca Vialli missed a penalty in a 1–0 game much closer than almost everyone had anticipated. Things got little better for the U.S. in the country's final group game, a disappointing 2–1 defeat to Austria in a tempestuous game; despite being up a man from the 33rd minute on following a red card issued to Austrian midfielder Peter Artner, the U.S. conceded twice in the 49th and 63rd minutes and only scored the team's lone goal of the competition through a Bruce Murray strike, set up by a jinking Ramos run and cross. At its first World Cup in 40 years, the U.S. exited after a difficult set of games but had gained valuable experience.

That experience was deemed crucial as the U.S. was to host the next World Cup in 1994, and a more competitive appearance at home was seen as important for the future of soccer in America. Nine venues were selected to host the first World Cup to be held in the United States: the Rose Bowl in Pasadena, California; the Citrus Bowl in Orlando, Florida; Soldier Field in Chicago, Illinois; the Pontiac Silverdome in Detroit, Michigan; Stanford Stadium in Stanford, California; Giants Stadium in New Jersey; the Cotton Bowl in Dallas, Texas; Foxboro Stadium in Foxborough, Massachusetts; and RFK Stadium in Washington DC. On the field, the Americans were prepared by new coach Bora Milutinović, an idiosyncratic Serbian who had coached Mexico at the 1986 World Cup and Costa Rica at the 1990 World Cup.

Those preparations included the addition of three experienced European-based players who had not been born in the U.S. but qualified to play for the U.S. team by parentage: Roy Wegerle, a forward in England; Thomas Dooley, a regular in Germany's Bundesliga; and Earnie Stewart, a goal scorer in the Dutch league. Only eight players remained from the 1990 World Cup roster, including the flourishing Harkes, Ramos and Wynalda, with talented newcomers born and bred in the U.S. also added, including Alexi Lalas and Claudio Reyna.

Seeded as the host nation, the U.S. team received a favorable draw, placed in group A for the first round along with Switzerland, Colombia and Romania. The host's first game, against Switzerland, was the first World Cup to take place at an indoor venue—the Pontiac Silverdome outside Detroit, on grass carted in for the occasion. The Americans were cheered on by a raucous crowd of 73,000, but the air was deflated by Georges Bregy giving the Swiss the lead 39 minutes in. The goal came direct from a free kick after Dooley had slid in from behind and taken away the legs of talented midfielder Alain Sutter, Bregy curling it beautifully past the American captain Meola in goal. The U.S., though, equalized only five minutes later with a magnificent goal also direct from a free kick, Wynalda striking in from 25 yards, striking in off the crossbar. In the second half, both teams spurned chances to claim a winner, Ramos particularly noticeable for failing to hit the target when clear on goal, while the U.S. stoutly defended, Lalas a particular standout—as much for his ability to clear the lines as for his striking red hair and goatee. A 1–1 tie with the Swiss meant the U.S. would need to push for a result against Colombia, considered dark horses for the tournament, at the Rose Bowl near Los Angeles. A crowd of 93,000 packed the stadium, and by halftime, the U.S. led when a cross by Harkes was deflected into his own goal by Colombia's Andrés Escobar. Seven minutes into the second half, the U.S. wrapped an unexpected victory when Earnie Stewart finished from a Ramos pass, a Colombian goal in stoppage time counting for little. There would be a tragic postscript to the game, as Escobar was murdered only two weeks later back home in Colombia following the South Americans' elimination.

The U.S. momentum stalled four days after the Colombia game at the Rose Bowl, losing 1–0 to Romania thanks to a goal by defender Dan Petrescu. The Americans limped into the second round as one of the best third-placed teams in the group stage. The result also meant the U.S. faced the daunting task of beating three-time champions Brazil to advance. The game was set for 4 July in front of 84,000 in Stanford, ensuring a suitably patriotic occasion. Brazil, though, proved too strong for the U.S., the Brazilian strike pair of Romário and Bebeto proving too elusive for the U.S. defenders to track, even though it was 10 Americans versus 11 Brazilians for 60 minutes after a vicious elbow by Brazilian defender Leonardo on Ramos led him to be sent off. Bebeto found the breakthrough and the only goal of the game with 15 minutes left of the 90, set up by Romário and finishing with a low shot that squeezed through Lalas's legs, past Meola's dive and into the far corner of the goal. The U.S. was eliminated, but losing to the Brazilians—who went on to win the competition—was a respectable way to depart, and the tournament as a whole proved a success, with record attendances providing a springboard that helped establish an outdoor professional league again in the U.S. two years later, with the 1996 launch of Major League Soccer.

Bora Milutinović was replaced as coach, slightly surprisingly, by one of his assistants, the young and inexperienced Utah native Steve Sampson. His reign began well, with a strong showing at the 1995 Copa América, the U.S. playing as a guest in the South American championship and reaching the semifinal stage after victories. Sampson led the U.S. through qualification for the 1998 World Cup, the team's two defeats coming at Costa Rica's intimidating Saprissa Stadium, also earning a creditable point in a hard-fought 0–0 draw at the Azteca in Mexico City, where the Americans had lost in 17 previous competitive games.

Heading to France for the World Cup, Sampson made several controversial decisions, leaving captain John Harkes off the roster while drafting in David Regis, a defender from Martinique who spoke almost no English, fast-tracked to U.S. citizenship in time for the tournament. Drawn into group F alongside strong German and Yugoslavian teams as well as a politically charged matchup with Iran, the U.S. faced a daunting task that Sampson proved unable to adequately manage. Facing Germany in Paris at the Parc des Princes, Sampson opted for a 3-6-1 formation with seven World Cup newcomers, building the team around the gifted but inconsistent midfielder Claudio Reyna. The Americans were outclassed, Andreas Möller scoring for Germany after 10 minutes and Jürgen Klinsmann adding another during the second half for a 2–0 German win. The result piled pressure on the U.S. ahead of playing Iran in Lyon, a game already brimming with attention due to the political overtones. Sampson made a handful of changes to the lineup, dropping Wynalda, Stewart and Mike Burns, bringing in Joe Max-Moore, Brian McBride and Tab Ramos as starters. It was to little avail, as the Iranians scored twice before McBride netted a consolation with three minutes left, a desperately disappointing defeat for the U.S. Already eliminated, the U.S. slumped to one more defeat in the last group game against Yugoslavia 1–0 and finished 32nd out of the 32 teams at the competition.

Sampson's tenure came to a predictable end following the debacle in France. The U.S. Soccer Federation plucked Bruce Arena from D.C. United as Sampson's replacement. The U.S. progressed to the World Cup for the fourth straight occasion, though not without some nervous moments in qualification. Arena selected an experienced team for the World Cup in South Korea and Japan, with an average age of 29, with veterans like Meola, Reyna and Stewart joined by talented, young newcomers Landon Donovan and DaMarcus Beasley. Exactly half of the roster plied their trade in MLS, including mercurial forward Clint Mathis, expected to make a splash in the competition. In group D, the Americans were placed with hosts South Korea, Poland and Portugal. Arena's team opened its tournament against the much-admired Portuguese—featuring world-class talents including Luís Figo, Vítor Baía and Joao Pinto—and shocked everyone by winning 3–2. Indeed, the U.S. led 3–0 after only 36 minutes: a Stewart corner led to a poacher's goal by John O'Brien, a cross by Donovan was deflected into his own net by Jorge Costa, and McBride added a third with a diving header from a sweeping Tony Sanneh cross. Portugal pulled two back by the end of the 90 minutes, but the U.S. had still claimed a famous victory. The U.S. then faced host nation South Korea in front of over 60,000 partisan fans in Daegu; thanks to tremendous goalkeeping from Brad Friedel, who saved a penalty from the Koreans, the Americans ground out a valuable 1–1 draw, having taken the lead through Clint

Mathis, scoring with a fine low strike following a superb left-footed through ball from O'Brien. Despite two good results, the U.S. followed it up with a poor 3–1 defeat to Poland in Daejeon—down 2–0 after only five minutes to the Poles—and qualified for the next round only thanks to a 1–0 defeat to Portugal by South Korea.

The U.S. faced regional rivals Mexico in the second round. The Americans raced out to the lead thanks to an 8th-minute goal from McBride, scoring emphatically from 15 yards out, and Landon Donovan doubled the lead in the 65th minute, finishing with a close-range header from an Eddie Lewis cross. Despite plenty of Mexican pressure and possession, the U.S. held on for a deserved and significant victory, moving on further in the World Cup finals than the nation had since 1930. At the quarterfinal stage, the U.S. faced a stern test against Germany. It proved a step too far, with the Germans winning 1–0 through a 39th-minute Michael Ballack header. The U.S., though, had hardly been outclassed, creating two early chances Donovan was unable to capitalize on. The Americans felt robbed when a clear handball by German defender Torsten Frings on his own goal line was not spotted by Scottish referee Hugh Dallas, and they wasted an opportunity to equalize with just minutes remaining when Tony Sanneh planted a close-range header the wrong side of the post. Arena's team had lay to rest the ghosts of the 1998 World Cup and established the United States as a competitive force in the World Cup.

Arena remained in charge of the U.S. for the 2006 World Cup cycle and qualified in first place with only 2 losses in 16 games. That helped the U.S. enter the World Cup in Germany ranked fifth in the world by FIFA, feeding expectations that the team would go at least as far as in 2006 as it had in 2002, especially as the likes of Beasley, Donovan and McBride had established themselves at elite levels of European soccer. It all began to go wrong only five minutes into the first game for the U.S. in Gelsenkirchen against the Czech Republic when Jan Koller planted a powerful header past Kasey Keller in the American goal. Two more goals without reply came for the Czechs through Tomás Rošický. The U.S. regrouped against Italy in Kaiserslautern in a game that saw three men sent off for only the fourth time in World Cup history: on the American side, Pablo Mastroeni and Eddie Pope were both dismissed by the 47th minute, while Daniele De Rossi's elbow that had bloodied McBride earned him a straight red card. By then, the score was already 1–1, Alberto Gilardino having opened the scoring for Italy before an own goal by Cristian Zaccardo tied the game, and the U.S. put in a hard-working performance to earn a point by keeping the scores level in the second half despite being down a man.

In order to qualify for the next round, the U.S. team took on Ghana in Nuremberg knowing that they would have to beat Ghana while, simultaneously, Italy would also need to defeat the Czech Republic. The latter result occurred, but Arena's 11 fell behind to Ghana after the 22nd minute, and though Clint Dempsey provided an equalizer, the African team took the honors and eliminated the Americans with a penalty kick converted by Stephen Appiah. The U.S. vociferously objected to the penalty decision, awarded for Oguchi Onyewu's seemingly innocuous challenge on Razak Pimpong. It was only one of numerous decisions the American team objected to both during and after the game, but the 2–1 defeat meant the U.S. headed home—and Arena's tenure as coach ended—on a sour note at the first-round stage.

To replace Arena, the U.S. Soccer Federation again looked to MLS, selecting Bob Bradley, most recently of the MetroStars but best known for winning the MLS Cup with the Chicago Fire in 1998. Bradley had twice been an assistant to Arena, at the University of Virginia and at DC United, providing a continuity the U.S. had rarely enjoyed in the past. The U.S. again topped the CONCACAF region in qualifying, finishing ahead of Mexico by one point in the final round, led by six goals from young forward Jozy Altidore and five from Clint Dempsey, a starter in the Premier League for Fulham. Also from the Premier League was Tim Howard of Everton in goal, though the team's fortunes would depend to a large degree on Landon Donovan of MLS's LA Galaxy and Bob Bradley's son, midfielder Michael Bradley of Germany's Borussia Mönchengladbach.

Drawn with England, Algeria and Slovenia in group C, Bradley's men began their campaign against the English in Rustenburg. The U.S. got off to a dreadful start, allowing England to take the lead through Steven Gerrard only four minutes into the game, the English midfielder left with too much space to burst through into the penalty area. The U.S. equalized by halftime, albeit via a mistake by the other team—Dempsey's tame 25-yard strike crept through the hands of England goalkeeper Robert Green in the 40th minute. In the second half, England and the U.S. both enjoyed chances, with Altidore coming close to scoring twice for the Americans, but both teams settled for a point. In Johannesburg at Ellis Park Stadium, the second group game of the competition for the U.S. began disastrously against Slovenia, with Bradley's team conceding twice in the first half, Valter Birsa firing past Tim Howard from 25 yards, who was beaten a second time when Zlatan Ljubijankić slipped through the American defense. The second half saw a reverse of fortunes; Donovan got the U.S. back in the game three minutes after halftime, racing in from the right flank and smashing the ball into the top corner of the near side of the goal. The coach's son, Michael Bradley, claimed a precious point for the U.S. with an equalizer eight minutes from time, bursting into the penalty and finishing with a drive from an Altidore knockdown. Maurice Edu almost claimed a winner for the Americans, but his apparent goal was ruled out for offside by referee Koman Coulibaly. Against Algeria in Pretoria, the U.S. secured qualification for the next stage in the most dramatic fashion possible. After 90 frustrating minutes had passed, the score remained tied, a result that would have seen the U.S. eliminated and Algeria progress. But in stoppage time, Donovan found the net after a rapid breakaway started by a throw from Howard, sending the U.S. through.

The 2–1 win over Algeria secured the U.S. top place in group C, earning a trip back to Rustenburg to face Ghana. Bradley's team conceded an early goal once more, with Ghana scoring after only five minutes, Kevin-Prince Boateng taking advantage of a mistake in midfield by Ricardo Clark to give the Africans the lead. Clark was substituted after only half an hour, and with the score still 1–0 to Ghana at halftime, Bradley made another change with Benny Feilhaber coming on to replace Robbie Findley. Feilhaber almost scored not long after the switch, and American pressure paid off in the 62nd minute, when Dempsey was brought down in the penalty area and Landon Donovan converted the spot kick to tie the score. The U.S. had chances to take the lead during the remainder of the second half, but Ghana's goalkeeper Richard Kingson denied opportunities for Altidore and Bradley. In extra time, though, Ghana immediately seized the initiative, when Asamoah Gyan broke clear and ripped the ball past Howard for a 2–1 lead. The U.S., seemingly drained of energy, created few chances to equalize and departed at the second-round stage with the defeat.

Bradley remained as U.S. coach until the summer of 2011, when he was replaced by German coach Jürgen Klinsmann. Qualification for the 2014 World Cup in Brazil under the new coach's leadership saw some early American struggles. After losing an away game to Honduras, Klinsmann tweaked and adjusted the American lineups repeatedly during the six games of the CONCACAF semifinal round. Klinsmann's approach fostered confidence and competition within the team, and the result was an astounding seven wins in ten games and a Hexagonal-high 15 goals (with only eight conceded) to finish four full points above runners-up Costa Rica in the final standings.

Though confidence was high after qualifications, the Americans were placed in group G, the "Group of Death," with Germany, Portugal and Ghana, and advancing into the round of 16 was now seen as a success. Opening their tournament against a Ghanaian team that had beaten them in the group stage in 2006 and sent them home in the round of 16 in 2010, the United States was a team on a mission. At the Estádio das Dunas in Natal, the Stars and Stripes played with aggression. In the first minute, Clint Dempsey tore through the Ghanaian defense and cleverly tucked the ball just inside the far post for the sixth-fastest goal in World Cup history. Yet, just as the United States was gaining even more momentum, forward Jozy Altidore went down in a heap with a pulled hamstring, ultimately forcing him out of the remainder of the tournament. It wasn't until the 82nd minute that Ghana's pressure paid off when André Ayew leveled the game at one following some splendid passing and a quality near-post finish. Now tied and pressing for the lead again, the American answer came in the form of little-used substitute John Brooks Jr., who found himself on the end of a brilliant Graham Zusi corner. Brooks headed it down and past a flailing Adam Kwarasey for the winner and redemption.

Game two against fourth-ranked Portugal immediately put the Americans to the test after an early goal by Nani in the fifth minute. The United States came out strong in the second half, and a Jermaine Jones rocket from 25 yards out left goalkeeper Beto frozen in his tracks with no chance to do anything but watch as the equalizer flew past him. A battle of wills, the game went back and forth until the 81st minute, when the Yanks struck again, this time off the chest of captain Clint Dempsey. With three points and guaranteed advancement within the Americans' grasp, Ronaldo again proved why he is considered one of the best in the world. In the 95th minute, Ronaldo found himself one versus one on the right flank versus DaMarcus Beasley and calmly crossed a beautiful ball far post to a streaking Silvestre Varela. The subsequent drilled header past a shocked Tim Howard and a 2–2 Ghana/Germany result meant that every team in group G was still mathematically alive.

Sitting on four points and facing a German side many considered a favorite to win it all, the United States needed to keep the game close, and fans found themselves rooting for a Portuguese team that had just broken their hearts. A rematch of the thrilling 2002 World Cup quarterfinal played in Korea, this final group game lived up to the hype as a superior German side found it difficult to break down the U.S. defense, most notably the goalkeeping of Tim Howard. It wasn't until the 55th minute when Germany finally got on the board, Thomas Müller capitalizing on a tiring U.S. team with a blast from the top-left corner of the box. With the one-goal lead, Germany was content to sit back and absorb pressure, and the ensuing 1–0 win sent both teams through to the round of 16, Germany in first and the United States in second.

In the elimination round against a Belgium side full of stars, Tim Howard proved time and again why he is considered one of the best in the world with tremendous play after tremendous play. Even though they were against the run of play for most of the 90-plus minutes, the United States clearly had the best chance to win it when, in the 91st minute, a flicked header by Jermaine Jones saw Chris Wondolowski alone at the six with a tap in. Inexplicably, Wondolowski sent the ball high and wide over the bar. Given life, Belgium dominated from the start of extra time, and Kevin De Bruyne scored the first goal after clinically settling a deflected cross, beating two defenders and blasting a right-footed shot past a diving Howard into the far-post side netting. Sensing victory, the Belgians continued to apply pressure, and in the 105th minute, De Bruyne found a streaking Lukaku, who blasted a first-time rocket near post. Trailing by two goals with one 15-minute period to play, the Americans provided their fans hope when substitute Julian Green volleyed a brilliant Michael Bradley through ball past a stunned Thibaut Courtois. Back on their heels, Belgium weathered a close miss by Jones and a brilliant free kick in the final seconds to send the United States home in 15th place with five goals for and six against.

URUGUAY. Commonly known as La Celeste (The Sky Blue). For a country with fewer than four million citizens, Uruguay has had outsized success in the World Cup since the inaugural competition was held in the Uruguayan capital, Montevideo, in 1930. By the 1920s, Uruguay—where the sport of soccer had taken hold in the late 19th century after being brought over by British immigrants—had become one of the leading teams in the world, winning the gold medal at both the 1924 and 1928 Olympic Games. Along with a promise to build a new stadium for the occasion, Uruguay's success on the field prompted FIFA to award the 1930 World Cup to the South American nation. Though the country's grand, new stadium, Estadio Centenario, was not completed until after the first few games took place in July 1930, Uruguay staged the competition with aplomb and to enthusiastic crowds that helped ensure the tournament's future success. On the field, Uruguay—coached by Alberto Suppici and captained by José Nasazzi—strolled to the final, defeating Peru and Romania in the group stage and Yugoslavia 6–1 in the semifinal. In the final, Uruguay met bitter rival Argentina, who brought thousands of traveling fans across the Río de la Plata for the game, held in front of an official attendance of 68,346 in the Centenario, a number that in actuality was far higher. A back-and-forth first half saw Uruguay take an early lead through Pablo Dorado, before two strikes for Argentina by Carlos Peucelle and Guillermo Stábile saw the host nation enter halftime 2–1 down. In the second half, though, Uruguay came out inspired, scoring through Pedro Cea in the 57th minute, Victoriano Iriarte in the 68th minute and Héctor Castro in the 89th minute, capping off a 4–2 win that saw Uruguay crowned as the first world champions and a nation celebrate ecstatically.

Uruguay did not defend its world title at the next World Cup in Italy in 1934. The Italians had snubbed Uruguay by not traveling to the competition in 1930, so the South

Americans returned the favor four years later. Uruguay did not enter the World Cup in 1938, returning to the stage in 1950 when the tournament resumed following World War II. Remarkably, Uruguay won the World Cup, producing a stunning upset in the final game of the competition to beat host nation Brazil and take the title. A stunned Maracanã stadium, filled with more than 100,000 fans expecting a Brazilian victory, saw Uruguay claim the final group-stage victory (the 1950 World Cup did not feature an elimination stage), inspired by captain Obdulio Varela and goals from Juan Schiaffino and Alcides Ghiggia.

Uruguay entered the 1954 World Cup in Switzerland unbeaten since the tournament's inception. Defeat finally came but not until the semifinal stage, Uruguay having won a group containing Austria, Czechoslovakia and Scotland and then beaten England 4–2 in the quarterfinal. In the final four, Uruguay faced tournament-favorite Hungary, the two playing an epic game won 4–2 after extra time by the Hungarians. Uruguay's second defeat in the competition swiftly followed, as the South Americans lost 3–1 to Austria in the third-place play-off.

Needing to qualify for the World Cup in 1958, Uruguay failed to do so and next appeared at the 1962 competition in Chile, failing to progress out of the group stage. In 1966 in England, Uruguay advanced to the quarterfinal stage, losing there 4–0 to a Franz Beckenbaur–inspired West Germany. In 1970, Uruguay again made it to the final four as the competition was held in Mexico. The Uruguayans, coached by Juan Hohberg, beat the Soviet Union in the quarterfinal stage 1–0 with an extra-time winner scored by Víctor Espárrago in the 117th minute. A brilliant Brazil team proved too strong for Uruguay in the semifinal; even though the Uruguayans took an early lead, Brazil scored three more without reply to advance to the final. Uruguay lost the third-place game, defeated 1–0 by West Germany.

A barren spell followed for Uruguay, knocked out in the group stage at the 1974 World Cup in West Germany and failing to qualify for the 1978 and 1982 competitions. Back in Mexico at the 1986 World Cup, Uruguay did advance to the last 16, losing 1–0 to eventual champion Argentina. Uruguay fell at the same stage in Italy in 1990, this time defeated 2–0 in the second round by host nation Italy. The Uruguayans then did not qualify for the 1994 or 1998 World Cups. An appearance at the 2002 World Cup was brief, with the Uruguayans eliminated at the group stage, and Uruguay then failed to qualify for the 2006 World Cup.

In 2010, led by forward and captain Diego Forlán, coached by Óscar Táberez, who had previously led Uruguay at the 1990 World Cup, the Uruguayans began with a 0–0 draw with France, then brushed host nation South Africa aside 3–0, Forlán scoring twice along with a goal from Alvaro Pereira. Uruguay moved on to the second round following a 1–0 win over Mexico, Luis Suarez scoring the lone goal. In the second round, two goals from Suarez saw Uruguay sweep aside South Korea in Port Elizabeth. Controversy came in Uruguay's quarterfinal with Ghana, with the score tied 1–1 in extra time after Diego Forlán canceled out Sulley Muntari's earlier strike. With only seconds remaining before a penalty shoot-out, Luis Suarez handled a shot on the line, deliberately preventing a goal. Suarez was shown a red card, but Asamoah Gyan missed the resulting penalty, and the game went to a shoot-out, with Uruguay prevailing 4–2 on spot kicks. In the semifinal, Uruguay faced the Netherlands in Cape

Town and fell behind in the 18th minute before equalizing through Forlán shortly before halftime. Halfway through the second half, a pair of Dutch goals extinguished Uruguayan hopes, only raised briefly with a stoppage-time strike by Maximiliano Pereira for a 3–2 defeat. Uruguay once again lost a third-place game, going down 3–2 to Germany, though Forlán scored his fifth goal of the competition and was awarded the Golden Ball as the tournament's best player.

Coming off their fourth-place finish in South Africa and a Copa America triumph a year later, qualifying for the 2014 World Cup in Brazil started off with three wins and two losses. With only two points in the next six games, Uruguay used late wins over Colombia and Argentina to force their way into a play-off with Jordan. A decisive 5–0 win in the first leg meant a group D placement in the World Cup finals with England, Costa Rica and Italy. With their past success at the World Cup, expectations for greatness remained high, even with the recent struggles.

In their opening game against Costa Rica at the Estádio Castelão in Fortaleza, an early Edinson Cavani penalty conversion put Uruguay in a comfortable position. Los Ticos found a new gear in the second half, and two goals within three minutes of each other (Joel Campbell in the 54th and Óscar Duarte in the 57th) gave Costa Rica all of the momentum. From there on through the final whistle, it was all Ticos, and a Marco Ureña goal in the 84th minute sealed the first Costa Rican World Cup win since 2002. In game two, against perennial powerhouse England, Luis Suárez, playing in his first match, put Uruguay up in the 39th minute with a brilliant header. Though Wayne Rooney finally broke his World Cup curse with a much-needed equalizer in the 75th minute, it was an unfortunate misplayed header by Steven Gerrard that sprung Suárez through to goal 10 minutes later. His rocket past goalkeeper Joe Hart for his second goal of the game sealed the win. With only three points, Uruguay found themselves needing a win to secure placement in the round of 16; in their way stood an Italian side fighting for their lives as well. In a brutally physical game that saw four yellow cards and one red among numerous fouls, it was one of the strangest moments in World Cup finals history. In the 80th minute, cameras clearly show Luis Suárez inexplicably biting down on Italian defender Giorgio Chiellini and then attempting to claim Chiellini hit him. With Chiellini showing off the bite marks and pleading with the ref, the ensuing confusion and a lack of focus on the part of the Italians led directly to the Diego Godín header that ended all Italian hope and pushed Uruguay into the round of 16.

Through to the elimination stage, a FIFA investigation into the Suárez incident found that Suárez had indeed bitten the Italian, and Uruguay was without their star striker (suspended by FIFA for nine games and four months from anything soccer related) for their next match against Colombia. What was supposed to shape up as a match of two powerful South American teams with gifted strikers turned into a showcase for Golden Boot winner James Rodríguez, as his two goals thrust him to the top of the tournament's goal scorers. With the loss, Uruguay went home in 12th place with four goals for and six against.

V

VALCAREGGI, FERRUCCIO. B. 12 February 1919, Trieste, Italy. D. 2 November 2005. Ferruccio Valcareggi, a former player in Serie A during the 1940s, coached Italy at the World Cup in both 1970 in Mexico and 1974 in West Germany, leading them to the final in the former tournament, defeated there by Brazil. Valcareggi took charge of Italy following his country's poor performance at the 1966 World Cup in England, where they were eliminated at the first-round stage following an embarrassing defeat to North Korea. Valcareggi was originally appointed alongside Helenio Herrera, a strong-minded domestic coaching legend, as part of a two-man technical team beginning with a friendly against the Soviet Union in November 1966. The partnership only lasted four games, however, and Valcareggi took sole responsibility for the team in Italy's first competitive game following the World Cup in June 1967, a qualifying game for the 1968 European Championship against Romania, a 1–0 win. Valcareggi led Italy to victory in that competition, held on home soil, making Italy champions of Europe for the first time following a controversial victory in a replay of the final against Yugoslavia. Italy then began their qualification road to the ninth World Cup with a 1–0 win over Wales in October 1968 and went on to qualify unbeaten, topping a group also containing East Germany. At the 1970 World Cup in Mexico, Italy was placed into group two, a comparatively weak group, with Uruguay, Sweden and Israel. For his captain, Valcareggi selected Giacinto Facchetti, the influential attacking defender for Internazionale. Italy began the World Cup with a less-than-convincing 1–0 over Sweden, followed by a stale 0–0 tie with Uruguay. In the third game, Valcareggi attempted to solve one of his selection dilemmas: Gigi Riva had been chose as his playmaker for the first two games, but he had left out the equally gifted Gianni Rivera. Against Israel, Valcareggi took off Riva at halftime and replaced him with the equally gifted Gianni Rivera. Though the tactic produced little against Israel—another 0–0 draw secured Italy's passage to the next round—it would reap dividends in the knockout stage, though it would now be Sandro Mazzola who gave way for Rivera at halftime, in a relay tactic that became known as the *staffetta*. Facing hosts Mexico in the quarterfinal in Toluca with the score tied 1–1 at halftime, Rivera scored once and Riva twice in the second half as they took the field together for the first time, leading Italy to a 4–1 win. Italy had suddenly found their creative powers and won a dramatic semifinal against West Germany at the Azteca in Mexico City on 17 June. With the score tied 1–1 at full-time, Karl-Heinz Schnellinger having scored a last-minute equalizer for the West Germans, five goals were scored in extra time, and it was again Rivera and Riva who proved to be the difference, scoring Italy's two final goals for a 4–3 win. In the final, though, Rivera only came on for the final six minutes as Italy was beaten 4–1 by Brazil, whose flowing soccer Italy was unable to contain.

Valcareggi remained in charge of Italy following the 1970 World Cup, taking them to the quarterfinal stage of the 1972 European Championship, eliminated there by Belgium in a replay. Valcareggi then led Italy through qualifying for the 1974 World Cup with ease, Italy topping a group containing Turkey, Switzerland and Luxembourg without losing a game. Valcareggi's team for the 1974 World Cup in West Germany was made up largely of aging veterans from the 1970 World Cup, including Facchetti as captain again, with Rivera, Riva and Mazzola all now together in the starting 11. Yet Valcareggi was undermined before the competition began: notorious "fixer" Italo Allodi was installed as general manager for the competition, undermining Valcareggi's authority and clouding the situation. Allodi was accused of attempting to bribe Italy's group-stage opponents without Valcareggi's knowledge. Italy almost began disastrously, trailing 1–0 to tiny Haiti halfway through their first game. Though Italy came back to win 3–1, the team's ill discipline was illustrated by forward Giorgio Chinaglia's open dissent to Valcareggi when he was substituted in the second half. Italy then drew with Argentina but crashed out of the competition with a 2–1 defeat to Poland. This ended Valcareggi's tenure with Italy.

VALDERRAMA, CARLOS. B. 2 September 1961, Santa Marta, Colombia. During their three appearances at the FIFA World Cup in the 1990s, Colombia was captained in every game by Carlos Valderrama, the country's playmaker from central midfield and best player of the decade. His extravagant curly hairstyle matched his passion, vision and creativity. Valderrama made his debut for Colombia in October 1985 during Colombia's unsuccessful attempt to qualify for the 1990 World Cup. He then played for Colombia as they finished in third place at the 1987 Copa América, winning the South American Footballer of the Year award that year. In 1989, Valderrama was part of the Colombian team that successfully qualified for the 1990 World Cup, in what would be their first appearance in the finals since 1962. By the time the World Cup began in Italy in June 1990, Valderrama had already made his name in Europe, having moved to the French first division to Montpelier in 1988.

Valderrama, 28 years old and at the height of his powers, was named Colombia's captain for the competition. Colombia's first game was in Bologna against the United Arab Emirates on 9 June, with Valderrama sealing a 2–0 win with a superb goal in the 85th minute, striking a low right-footed drive from 20 yards out into the bottom right-hand corner. Five days later, Colombia faced a strong Yugoslavian team, again in Bologna, but Valderrama and Colombia could do little as they were outclassed in a 1–0 defeat. Colombia retained a chance to qualify for the next round when they faced West Germany on 19 June in Milan. Playing for a draw, Valderrama was almost anonymous in a negative game that did not see a goal until the Colombians could not contain a West German attack that ended in an 88th-minute goal for Pierre Littbarski. Over two minutes into injury time, though, Valderrama suddenly emerged to conjure up a superb equalizing goal that guaranteed the South Americans qualification to the next round. Receiving the ball just past midfield, Valderrama twisted and turned to find space and then played an accurate left-footed pass that sliced through the West

German defense and placed Freddy Rincón one-on-one with goalkeeper Bodo Illgner, who he beat with a shot through the West German's legs. In the second round, Colombia faced Cameroon in Naples on 23 June. No goals were scored in normal time, but Colombia's defense collapsed in extra time, Cameroon scoring twice. Colombia clawed one back when Valderrama worked his way superbly into the Cameroonian penalty area and gave the ball to Redín for an easy finish, but it was too little, too late, and Colombia was out of the World Cup—though Valderrama left the competition with his reputation enhanced, having scored or set up three of Colombia's four goals and played a central role with his range of passing on show.

In qualifying for the 1994 World Cup, Valderrama led Colombia to the tournament in the United States that raised considerable expectations of what the team might achieve. Their South American qualifying campaign included unexpected victories over Argentina 2–1 at home and by an unlikely 5–0 margin away in Buenos Aires orchestrated by Valderrama for midfield. Once the 1994 World Cup began, however, Colombia's dream quickly crumbled, and the fallout for Valderrama as captain of the team was painful. Despite displaying his range of neat passing, Valderrama could do little as Colombia lost 3–1 to Romania and 2–1 to the United States, a 2–0 win over Switzerland no consolation as Colombia was shockingly eliminated in the first round. On their return to Colombia, Valderrama was hounded for his supposed ineffectiveness, but events took an even more tragic turn when his teammate Andrés Escobar was shot and killed, apparently stemming from his own goal against the United States.

Valderrama led Colombia to qualification for the 1998 World Cup, as Colombia finished in third place in the South American zone, behind Argentina and Paraguay. In France, Colombia was drawn in a first-round group alongside Romania, Tunisia and England. Once again, Colombian began a World Cup with defeat to Romania, 1–0. Against Tunisia on 22 June in Montpellier, Colombia kept their hopes of qualification to the next round alive, when Valderrama provided an assist for Léider Preciado to give the South Americans a 1–0 win. But Valderrama's 111th and last international appearance came in Colombia's final group-round game, a 2–0 defeat to England eliminating the South Americans from the World Cup, Valderrama choosing to end his international career as the holder of a record number of appearances for his country. He continued playing at club level in Major League Soccer until 2002 and is now a youth coach in Florida.

VARALLO, FRANCISCO. B. 5 February 1910, La Plata, Argentina. D. 30 August 2010. The last surviving player from the inaugural 1930 World Cup in Uruguay to die was Francisco Varallo, who was 100 years old when he passed away in 2010. A bullish center-forward known as "Cañoncito" by fans for his fearsome, cannonball-like shooting, Varallo was the youngest player selected on Argentina's team for the World Cup at 20 years old, scoring one goal against Mexico in Argentina's group-round games. Varallo sustained a knee injury that kept him out of Argentina's semi-final win over the United States, and he looked to miss the final against Uruguay until he was cleared to play by the senior members of his team after an examination of his knee on the morning of the game. Varallo struck the bar in the second half, but his injury severely limited his movement, and Argentina fell 4–2 to Uruguay despite leading at halftime. Following the World Cup, Varallo turned professional with Boca Juniors in the Argentinean league, refusing larger offers to play in Italy, and scored prolifically for the Buenos Aires club, leading them to several championships. He scored three goals at the 1937 Copa América for Argentina as they won the South American championship.

VAVA. B. 12 November 1934, Recife, Brazil. D. 19 January 2002. Though Vava only played in 20 international games for Brazil, he is one of the country's most legendary and successful players, despite the steep competition. It was Vava's goals that proved critical to Brazil's first two World Cup triumphs in 1958 in Sweden and 1962 in Chile. Twenty-four years old and then a star for Vasco de Gama, Vava scored five goals in the four games he played at the 1958 competition. He scored twice against the Soviet Union in the group stage, though he did not appear in Brazil's quarterfinal win over Wales, Mazzola preferred by Brazilian coach Vicente Feola, but returned for the semifinal and scored just two minutes in, setting up a 5–2 victory. Brazil won 5–2 again in the final on the outskirts of Stockholm; with his teammates Pelé and Garrincha in devastating form, Vava took full advantage by scoring Brazil's first two goals on their way to lifting the World Cup for the first time. In between the 1958 and 1962 World Cups, Vava added to his global reputation with an impressive spell at Atlético Madrid in Spain. Yet his 1962 World Cup did not start strongly: Vava failed to score in Brazil's first three games, only finding the net for the first time against England in the quarterfinals, the second strike in a 3–1 win. Brazil proved unstoppable in the semifinal, crushing Chile 4–2, with Vava scoring twice with his head. His fourth goal of the competition came in his last World Cup appearance, as Brazil defeated Czechoslovakia in the final 3–1. Vava's World Cup career ended with the Brazilian having notched nine goals in ten games, a remarkable ratio that reflected both his efficient finishing and the fortune of playing alongside some of the most creative attackers of all time, including the geniuses Pelé and Garrincha.

VIDINIĆ, BLAGOJE. B. 11 June 1934, Skopje, Yugoslavia. D. 29 December 2006. Blagoje Vidinić managed two different African teams in successive World Cups, 1970 in Mexico and 1974 in West Germany, leading Morocco and DR Congo (then known as Zaire) respectively. Before his career in coaching, Vidinić was a well-traveled player who played in Yugoslavia, Switzerland and the United States in the 1950s and 1960s, as well as representing his country at the 1956 and 1960 Olympic Games Football Tournaments, winning a gold medal in the latter competition. In 1970, Vidinić led Morocco in their first appearance at the World Cup, where they were placed in a group with 1966 World Cup finalists West Germany, Peru and Bulgaria. In their first game, Morocco shocked the West Germans by taking an early lead through a goal by Houmane Jarir, leading until 11 minutes into the second half when Uwe Seeler equalized and then Gerd Müller found a late winner, the game ending 2–1 to West Germany. Morocco again looked well drilled by Vidinić in their next game, holding a talented Peru team scoreless for 65 minutes, though a trio of goals quickly coming to end Morocco's hopes of advancing any further in the competition. They did, at least, earn their first-ever World Cup goal and point in their final game against Bulgaria, a 1–1 tie.

Vidinić, a consummate politician, proved able to handle the particular political pressures that came with Morocco, resisting demands from the king of Morocco to dictate his team selection. The next year, in 1971, Vidinić took over DR Congo, who had only begun playing international soccer in 1963 and had never qualified for a World Cup or come close to doing so. They did, though, have a talented team: Hungarian coach Ferenc Csandai had led them to their first international honor with victory in the 1968 Africa Cup of Nations. But the team had not performed well at the 1970 Africa Cup of Nations, improving under Vidinić by taking fourth place at the same competition in 1972 and instilling confidence and greater understanding of the game's tactics. Vidinić led Congo to qualification for the 1974 World Cup with victory over his former team, Morocco, sealing their place with a 3–0 win in Kinshasa in December 1973. In the lead-up to the World Cup, Vidinić oversaw Congo's victory at the 1974 Africa Cup of Nations in Egypt.

When the World Cup began in West Germany in June of 1974, the world knew little of Vidinić's team, though the Yugoslavian was quietly confident Congo would not prove to be a walkover for their opponents, placed in a difficult group with defending World Cup champions Brazil, a much-ballyhooed Scotland team and his native Yugoslavia. Congo began their World Cup in Dortmund against Scotland, surprising the Europeans with their aggressive play early on, but lax defending and poor goalkeeping allowed the Scots to take a 2–0 win. The next game, against Yugoslavia in Gelsenkirchen on 18 June, proved to be the nadir of Vidinić's coaching career. Congo appeared completely unable to organize defensively or contain the Yugoslavians from the kickoff, who scored three times in the first 18 minutes. Vidinić then made a decision still questioned today, removing goalkeeper Kazadi Muamba—who had, in fact, performed adequately and had been at no fault for the goals conceded—in the 20th minute. His diminutive replacement, Tubilandu Ndimbi, only made matters worse, conceding a goal within seconds and a further five more before the final whistle blew on a 9–0 defeat, tying the worst result in World Cup history. To make matters worse, Congo had a man sent off with Ndaye Mulamba given his marching orders by referee Omar Delgado in the 23rd minute. After the game, many questioned whether Vidinić had been aiming to assist his countrymen, especially in light of his curious substitution: an allegation denied both by his players and by the Yugoslavian, who later revealed that he taken Muamba off on the orders of an official representative from Zaire's Ministry of Sport. It was only the latest instance of official interference making Vidinić's position almost untenable, as the team had threatened to boycott their game against Yugoslavia, after officials traveling with the team were found to have pocketed substantial gifts intended for the players. Vidinić now had the unenviable task of holding together the team for their final game against Brazil, which ended in a 3–0 defeat. The African nation left the World Cup with one of the poorest records in competition history, having lost all three games, failed to score a goal and conceded 14 goals. It was the end for Vidinić's tenure with the team and his last direct involvement with the World Cup.

350 • VIERI, CHRISTIAN

VIERI, CHRISTIAN. B. 12 July 1983, Bologna, Italy. A tall, powerful striker, Christian Vieri registered a prolific goal-scoring record for Italy at the 1998 and 2002 World Cups. In France in 1998, Vieri scored four times. His first strike came against Chile in Italy's first game, a 1–1 draw, and twice more in Italy's next game, a 3–0 win over Cameroon. His fourth goal of the competition came against Austria's in Italy's third group game, the Italians winning 2–1. Vieri continued his streak in the second round, scoring in his fourth consecutive game, a 1–0 win over Norway. However, neither Vieri nor any of his teammates could find the net in Italy's quarterfinal versus France: it went to penalty kicks, and though Vieri converted his spot kick, the Italians were eliminated. At the age of 29, Vieri appeared in his last World Cup four years later in South Korea and Japan. He scored twice in Italy's opener against Ecuador, a 2–0 win, and then again in Italy's next game versus Croatia, though his goal could not prevent a 2–1 defeat. In the second round, Vieri scored his fourth of the competition as Italy crashed out 2–1 to South Korea. That left Vieri with an impressive total of nine goals in nine World Cup appearances. He would not add to the tally, injured for the 2006 World Cup—as Italy reached the final—and retired before the 2010 World Cup.

VILLA, DAVID. B. 3 December 1981, Langreo, Spain. The all-time top scorer for the Spanish national team, David Villa scored five goals to lead his country in scoring at the 2010 World Cup in South Africa, as Spain claimed the championship for the first time. It was Villa's second appearance at the World Cup, as the forward also struck three times in 2006 for his country in Germany. On that occasion, Spain was eliminated in the second round, even though Villa had given his country the lead with a 28th-minute penalty kick. In the 2010 World Cup, Villa opened his scoring account against Honduras, scoring both the goals in a 2–0 win—though he missed a penalty kick in the last minute that could have completed his hat trick, rolling the ball wide of the net. Villa scored again against Chile in Spain's third game, progressing his team to the third round with a 2–1 win, a 40-yard strike beating the Chilean goalkeeper, Claudio Bravo, who had raced out of his goal. Facing neighbors Portugal in the second round, Villa's fourth goal of the competition proved to be the difference in a 1–0 win. His strike came in the 63rd minute, prodding the ball home from 10 yards out with his right foot after his initial left-footed effort had been blocked, illustrating Villa's predatory instinct. Villa scored in a fourth consecutive game in the quarterfinal, the only goal of the game against Paraguay, scoring on a rebound with only seven minutes remaining. Villa did not score again in the tournament even though he played in both the semifinal and the final, ending the competition with five goals, tied for the lead in the Golden Boot, though it was awarded to Germany's Thomas Müller, who also had two more assists than Villa. In the 2014 competition in Brazil, Villa saw no time in opening losses to the Netherlands and Chile. Once Spain was officially unable to advance, Villa was given the start in the final group game against Australia where he promptly scored his 59th all-time goal in a 3–0 win. He announced his retirement following the tournament and retired as Spain's all-time leading scorer in the World Cup with nine total goals. At club level, the former FC Barcelona star now plays for New York City FC in the MLS.

VINCZE, JENŐ. B. 20 November 1908, Versec, Austria-Hungary. D. 20 November 1988. Making three total appearances for Hungary at World Cup finals tournaments, forward Jenő Vincze appeared at both the 1934 and 1938 World Cup competitions in Italy and France respectively. He made his international debut in June 1930, only 21 years old, but did not turn out again for Hungary until January 1934, winning a place in the squad for the 1934 World Cup. He scored in his only game at the World Cup in a 4–2 win over Egypt at the first-round stage. Vincze became a more regular selection for Hungary in the run-up to the 1938 World Cup, now starring domestically for Újpest FC in Budapest, scoring in Hungary's 11–1 win over Greece in their March 1938 World Cup qualifying game. Vincze did not play in Hungary's opening game at the World Cup in France but did take part in their quarterfinal victory over Switzerland as well as the final, a 4–2 defeat to Italy, where he was unable to make much impact. Vincze played one further game for Hungary in November 1939, ending his international career with 25 games played and 8 goals scored.

VÖLLER, RUDI. B. 13 January 1960, Hanau, West Germany. Germany's Rudi Völler played in three FIFA World Cup finals tournaments for his country, in 1986, 1990 and 1994. West Germany won the 1990 World Cup with Völler scoring three goals in the competition. Völler was a predatory striker who also scored prolifically in Germany, Italy and France at club level between 1977 and 1996, winning the UEFA Champions League with French club Olympique de Marseille in 1993. Since retirement from playing, Völler has managed at club level and also coached Germany's national team at the 2002 World Cup, leading his country to the final of the competition, losing there to Brazil. He resigned from the post in 2004 after a disappointing performance at the UEFA European Football Championship that year. *See also* MATTHÄUS, LOTHAR.

VYTLAČIL, RUDOLF. B. 9 February 1912, Schwechat, Austria-Hungary. D. 1 June 1977. Czechoslovakia's greatest run in the World Cup came under the astute tactical coaching of Rudolf Vytlačil, as they reached the final of the 1962 World Cup. Though born in what is now Austria, Vytlačil became best known as a player for Slavia Prague and played an international game for Czechoslovakia in 1936. Following World War II, he took up a coaching career that led him to take over as Czechoslovakia's coach in 1958. At the 1962 World Cup, Vytlačil took a talented group of players and molded them into a hard-to-beat team, leading them out of group three in second place, behind Brazil but ahead of Spain and Mexico. Czechoslovakia defeated Hungary and Yugoslavia in the quarterfinal and semifinal stages respectively, but though they held Brazil to a 1–1 score at halftime of the final, Zito and Vava scored in the second half to deny Vytlačil's team. By the time of the 1966 World Cup, Vytlačil was coaching Bulgaria instead of Czechoslovakia, though this experience—his last in the World Cup—proved to be dismal: the Bulgarians lost all three games, only scoring one and conceding eight against Portugal, Hungary and Brazil.

WALES. Commonly known as Y Dreigiau (The Dragons). Wales has qualified for only one major international tournament, the 1958 World Cup in Sweden. Featuring stars such as John Charles, Wales was placed in a group with Hungary, Mexico and Sweden in the first round and drew each match. Their three points were enough to force a play-off match against Hungary, which they subsequently won 2–1 and advanced to the second round. Unfortunately, Wales was matched against eventual champions Brazil. The game remained close throughout, but a goal by a 17-year-old called Pelé was the difference maker as Wales lost 1–0.

WANKDORF STADIUM. The "Miracle of Bern," an infamous victory for West Germany over favored Hungary in the 1954 World Cup final, took place at Wankdorf Stadium in Bern, Switzerland. Wankdorf Stadium hosted four other games at the 1954 World Cup, beginning on 16 June in the first-round group stage, as reigning World Cup champions Uruguay defeated Czechoslovakia 2–0, with only a little over 20,000 present in the 60,000-capacity stadium. The next day, a crowd of 39,000 attended Wankdorf as West Germany beat Turkey 4–1. Wankdorf hosted its final group-stage game on 20 June, the first game at the stadium featuring the hosts Switzerland, over 50,000 attending as England defeated the host nation 2–0. Wankdorf hosted one further game before the final, an exciting quarterfinal matchup between Brazil and Hungary, a capacity crowd watching the Hungarians defeat the 1950 finalists. On 4 July 1954, Wankdorf Stadium was packed to the rafters for the World Cup final as West Germany shocked Hungary with a 3–2 win. Originally opened in 1925, Wankdorf Stadium went on to host a number of further major international games, including the 1962 European Cup final and the 1989 European Cup Winners' Cup final. It was also the home ground for Swiss club team BSC Young Boys from 1925 until its demolition in 2001. Stade de Suisse, a 2008 European Championships venue, was built on the grounds of the Wankdorf Stadium.

WEBB, HOWARD. B. 14 July 1971, Rotherham, England. Refereeing the 2010 World Cup final in South Africa was Howard Webb, issuing no fewer than 14 yellow cards in the game, a record for a World Cup final. Those cards included two for Dutch defender Johnny Heitinga, who became the fifth player to be sent off in a World Cup final. Following the game, Webb was criticized by both the Dutch and Spanish coaches for his apparent lenient treatment of the opposing team. Webb, though, was placed in a difficult situation in a game that featured a litany of fouls almost from kickoff, with a total of 47 committed during the game. Of the 14 cards, 9 were issued to the Dutch, 5 to Spanish players. Webb, the son of a referee, became a Premier League referee in 2003 and, in 2005, took charge of his first international game under FIFA auspices. The next year, Webb's first experience at a major senior international tournament came as he took charge of two games at the 2006 European Championships. Webb received the call for numerous further high-profile games, including the 2009 FA Cup final in England and the 2010 UEFA Champions League final in Madrid, Spain. Apart from the final of the competition, Webb also took charge of three other games: two first-round group-stage games, Spain versus Switzerland on 16 June in Durban and Slovakia versus Italy on 24 June in Johannesburg, along with Brazil's 3–0 win over Chile in the round of 16 on 28 June, also in Johannesburg. When the World Cup final began on 11 July 2010, Webb became the first man to referee both the UEFA Champions League final and the World Cup final in the same year. Webb admitted after the World Cup final that had he seen a high kick by Dutch player Nigel de Jong on Spaniard Xabi Alsono from a better angle, he would have issued a straight red card instead of only cautioning the player.

WEMBLEY STADIUM. Located in London, England, Wembley Stadium is the 90,000-all-seater-capacity home of England's national team and all other flagship events of its owner, the Football Association, including the Football Association Cup final and semifinals. It is arguably the most famous soccer stadium in the world. Wembley Stadium is a multipurpose venue that has also hosted rugby, American football, motor racing and musical concerts. The current stadium was opened in 2007, after a long and expensive rebuilding project. The stadium was designed by acclaimed architect Sir Norman Foster, with its most striking feature being a 133-meter-tall arch above the northern half of the stadium.

The original Wembley Stadium, built in just 300 days, was opened on 23 April 1923. It was initially known as the Empire Stadium, as it was built for the British Empire Exhibition in the Wembley Park Leisure Grounds. The stadium quickly became famous for its distinctive "twin towers" at the entrance to the stadium. The first event at the stadium was the 1923 Football Association Cup final between Bolton Wanderers and West Ham United, which became infamously known as the White Horse Final. This name came about because the stadium's 127,000 capacity was massively overrun by an estimated 200,000 fans cramming in for the first Football Association Cup final held in London, causing scenes of considerable disorder and danger. Order was successfully restored and the final played following intervention by mounted police, with one light gray horse immortalized due to the black-and-white photos of the event published after, and it has become known forever in popular imagination since as the White Horse Final. Football Association Cup finals and England internationals have produced the most memorable moments in the stadium's history, including the 1966 World Cup final, where hosts England defeated West Germany 4–2 after extra time.

WORLD CUP QUALIFYING. The qualification process has evolved enormously since the first qualification competition took place for the 1934 World Cup—the second World Cup was the first to require qualification, as the inaugural 1930 World Cup in Uruguay was contested by finalists invited by FIFA. The World Cup hosts,

Italy, had to qualify for the World Cup—the first and last time this has been required. The Italians achieved this by taking part in one game, a 4–0 win over Greece on 25 March 1934 at the San Siro Stadium in Milan, with Greece withdrawing from the return game. Italy was 1 of 32 teams to enter the qualification tournament to earn 1 of the 16 places at the finals, though only 27 eventually participated in the process. The teams were divided into 12 groups on a geographic basis. Of the entering countries, 21 were European. Four entries came from South America, but only two actually took part, with many not entering at all in response to the refusal of most European countries to travel to the previous 1930 World Cup in Uruguay. Argentina and Brazil thus qualified without having to play a game following the withdrawals of Peru and Chile. North and Central America provided four entrants: Cuba, Haiti, Mexico and the United States. Africa and Asia were represented by Egypt, the British Mandate of Palestine and Turkey, the latter of whom withdrew before playing a game. Egypt became the first African nation to qualify for the World Cup, with the second not coming until the 1970 World Cup.

The first-ever World Cup qualifying game took place on 11 June 1933, less than a year before the start of the 1934 World Cup the next May. The final qualifying game took place on 24 May 1934, a mere three days before the World Cup began. It was a play-off between the United States and Mexico, with the Americans having submitted their entry too late to take part in the original qualifying competition. The United States won the game in Rome 4–2.

The number of entrants for the 1938 World Cup, to be held in France, rose from the previous number of 32 in 1934 to 37. The draw was seeded for the first time, with Germany, France, Czechoslovakia, Hungary, Italy, Cuba and Brazil the seeds. While the European contingent grew to 26 nations, the South American number fell, with only Argentina and Brazil entering; when the former withdrew from qualifying, Brazil qualified automatically, Argentina refusing to play due to continued pique at having been passed over to host the tournament. Africa, meanwhile, had no entrants, while Asia only had two: Japan withdrew, leaving the Dutch East Indies as automatic qualifiers. They were one of four nations to qualify for the World Cup for the first time, alongside Cuba—who advanced out of seven entrants from North and Central America, the other six having withdrawn—Norway and Poland. The hosts, France, qualified automatically, as did Italy, who became the first defending champions to play in the following World Cup. Europe's worsening political situation in the run-up to World War II played havoc with the qualification process. Spain was refused entry as civil war raged. Austria qualified but no longer existed as an independent nation once the World Cup began (England was offered their place but refused). Only 21 out of the 37 countries who entered the competition actually participated. Japan pulled out, busy with war.

International war prevented the staging of the next World Cup until 1950, with the 1946 FIFA Congress deciding it would be held in Brazil. Yet the impact of devastating conflict around the world meant few countries had the means and inclination for sporting competition so soon after war; while a new Cold War further impacted on the number of entries, with the entire Eastern bloc boycotting. Only 34 countries submitted an application to FIFA, and a mere 19 actually played a qualifying game, both numbers down from 1938. Nineteen European nations took part, but two of the qualifiers, Scotland and Turkey, both withdrew after qualifying—Portugal and France were invited to take their places yet refused to travel to South America. Eight South American countries entered, the largest contingent from the continent yet, though none actually played any qualification games: Bolivia, Chile, Paraguay and Uruguay qualified automatically, following the withdrawals of Argentina (in dispute with Brazil's soccer federation), Ecuador and Peru. All four Asian teams to enter withdrew before a ball had been kicked. From North and Central America, Mexico and the United States qualified ahead of Cuba. England was the sole team to qualify for the World Cup for the first time. In December 1949, FIFA requested that qualifying be sped up for completion by the end of January 1950.

The 1954 World Cup, to be held in Switzerland, attracted a record number of entries: 45 teams entered, and 33 actually played in the qualification tournament, with 57 games taking place. There was an African applicant for the first time in two decades: Egypt lost to Italy. The Italians were 1 of 29 European nations to enter, with several Eastern European countries rejoining. Scotland qualified for the second time in a row but for the first time actually took part in the World Cup finals. Turkey was the other team from Europe to qualify and play in the World Cup for the first time. West Germany and Japan had recently joined FIFA, the former qualifying, the latter losing to South Korea, still in the throes of civil war but qualifying for the World Cup for the first time. There were only four South American entrants accepted by FIFA, but with just one withdrawal this time (Peru), a qualifying contest was needed for the first time—Brazil qualified ahead of Paraguay and Chile.

The 1958 World Cup qualification had more than 50 entries submitted to FIFA for the first time, 55 applying, 46 actually playing in 89 matches. Defending champions West Germany qualified automatically along with World Cup hosts Sweden. In the qualification tournament, 17 countries made their debuts, including Argentina, both Germanys, the Soviet Union and two-time World Cup winners Uruguay. For the first time, FIFA delegated the qualification process to its continental confederations, as the foundation of UEFA in 1954 meant every region now had its own governing authority. From the European zone, Northern Ireland, Wales and the Soviet Union all qualified for the World Cup for the first time. Northern Ireland topped a group containing two-time World Cup winners Italy, eliminated after a tense game in Belfast. Nine countries took part in South American qualification, a record, and were divided into three groups of three teams, with Paraguay, Argentina and Brazil advancing to Sweden. FIFA allotted one qualification place to North and Central America, taken by Mexico out of the six entrants. Africa and Asia, between them entering 11 teams, also fought for one place at the finals; after a series of withdrawals, Israel became the only remaining team from the region without even playing a game. FIFA intervened and ruled Israel could not qualify without playing a game, and they were forced to play Wales, who had already been eliminated in European qualifying: the Welsh beat Israel 2–0, both home and away, to become the first and still only eliminated team to take part in a World Cup.

In qualifying for the 1962 World Cup, 92 matches were played, a record, with one more country entering the competition than in 1958, 56. Defending champions Brazil and World Cup hosts Chile qualified automatically. One change to the process taken to simplify matters was that instead of play-offs being used to determine the qualifier between teams tied in points in their group, the team with best average of goals scored per game would advance. Growing independence in Africa meant that continent provided several newcomers to the World Cup qualifying competition, including Ethiopia, Ghana, Nigeria, Tunisia and Morocco. But no African nation advanced to the World Cup: the winner of its zone had to play off against a UEFA runner-up, and Morocco lost to Spain 4–2 over two games. Similarly, the winner of the Asian zone had to play off against a European runner-up, with Yugoslavia dispatching South Korea. The North and Central American regional winner, meanwhile, had to beat a South American runner-up, and in this case, Mexico succeeded, defeating Paraguay thanks to a 1–0 win in Mexico City and a 0–0 tie in Asunción. From Europe, Bulgaria qualified for the first time, surprisingly eliminating France. In South American qualifying, Colombia advanced for the first time, alongside Argentina and Uruguay.

The difficult process for African and Asian nations to qualify for the World Cup produced controversy ahead of the 1966 World Cup, as the number of independent nations and members of FIFA from Africa and Asia grew in an era of rapid decolonization but were collectively dismayed that only one country from the two vast continents could qualify for the World Cup in England. FIFA had decided that the winners of the Asian and African zones of qualifying would face a play-off to determine which advanced to the finals, resulting in a mass boycott as 16 of 21 entrants from Africa, Asia and Oceania withdrew. South Africa was not admitted to the qualification process due to apartheid, while French Congo and the Philippines were deemed unable to take part. That left only Australia and North Korea (both debutants) in the qualification process from all three continents, and the Asian nation defeated the Australians to qualify for the first time. A record 31 European countries entered, and 1 achieved qualification for the first time, a Eusébio-inspired Portugal. Czechoslovakia and Yugoslavia, 1962 semifinalists, were surprisingly eliminated. Reigning champions Brazil qualified automatically, as did hosts England. Nine South American nations took part in qualifying, with Uruguay, Chile and Argentina advancing. Mexico, meanwhile, became North America's sole representative, qualifying for their fifth successive World Cup finals.

The same number of countries entered 1970 World Cup qualifying for the finals in Mexico as had entered in 1966, 75, but far more took part as FIFA had allayed African and Asian concerns by allotting each region one direct qualification spot. From Africa, Morocco qualified, becoming the first African nation to appear at the World Cup since 1934 and making their debut in it. From Asia and Oceania, Israel advanced to Mexico, beating Australia in the final round of qualifying, heading to the World Cup for the first time. Israel had originally been in the European zone but was moved to Asia for political reasons, triggering the withdrawal of North Korea, who refused to play the Israelis. Eight teams made their debuts in qualifying: Algeria, Bermuda, Cameroon, El Salvador, Libya, New Zealand, Rhodesia and Zambia. European competition saw 1966 quarterfinalists Portugal and Hungary eliminated, with Belgium, Bulgaria, Czechoslovakia, West Germany, Italy, Romania, Sweden and the Soviet Union advancing to join defending champions England, who qualified automatically. Also qualifying automatically were hosts Mexico, with the North and Central American qualifying spot taken by El Salvador, who made their World Cup finals debut. South America's three places were contested by a record ten teams, Argentina surprisingly eliminated, with Peru, Brazil and Uruguay heading to Mexico.

For the 1974 World Cup, 99 teams entered qualification, easily a record, with 226 games actually taking place featuring 90 teams eventually taking part—23 of them making their debuts. No fewer than 33 European nations attempted to claim one of UEFA's nine guaranteed places, with one further spot available in a play-off with the fourth-placed team in South American qualifying. The automatic spots went to Bulgaria, East Germany (the only European nation to make their World Cup debut), Italy, the Netherlands, Poland, Scotland and Sweden, with hosts West Germany also qualifying automatically. England missed out on the World Cup for the first time since the end of World War II, after being bested by Poland in their qualification group. The Soviet Union faced Chile in the intercontinental play-off between Europe and South America, but politics meant that the former withdrew, unwilling to play against a country that had just seen a violent right-wing coup d'état overthrow the elected rule of Salvador Allende. That advanced Chile, who joined qualifiers Uruguay and Argentina along with Brazil (automatically qualified as defending champions) from South America in West Germany. From Africa, Zaire qualified for the first time, finishing ahead of Zambia and Morocco in the final round of qualifying. Australia, meanwhile, also made history with their first World Cup appearance, advancing from the Asian and Oceanic zone by defeating South Korea in the final round.

More than 100 entries for the 1978 World Cup were received by FIFA, 107 nations applying and 95 actually taking part in the qualification rounds, with a record 252 games played. Qualification began earlier than ever ahead of the World Cup, to be played in Argentina, kicking off on 30 October 1975 with Sierra Leone between Niger 5–1. No fewer than 26 African countries were competing for only one qualification spot, and it was Tunisia who emerged from an epic process, finishing ahead of Egypt and Nigeria in the final round. Asian and Oceanic qualifying was almost as competitive with 22 countries entering, Iran ultimately emerging to qualify for the World Cup for the first time, edging South Korea who again just missed out. Mexico made up for the disappointment of missing out in 1974 by winning the North and Central American qualification spot. West Germany qualified automatically as defending champions, joined from Europe by Austria, France, Hungary, the Netherlands, Poland, Scotland, Spain and Sweden—with England failing to qualify for the second successive time in a barren decade. From South America, hosts Argentina advanced automatically, joined by Brazil and Peru, with Uruguay surprisingly eliminated. Bolivia lost their chance to qualify in a play-off with a UEFA runner-up, Hungary, the Europeans advancing with a comfortable 9–2 win over two games.

In a record 306 games, 797 goals were scored in 1982 World Cup qualification, 109 teams having entered the competition and 103 actually playing. The expansion of the World Cup from 16 to 24 teams meant 22 places were available to qualifiers, with hosts Spain and defending champions Argentina qualifying automatically. Battling for 13 automatic places were 34 European countries, claimed by Austria, Belgium, Czechoslovakia, England, France, West Germany, Hungary, Italy, Northern Ireland, Poland, Scotland and Yugoslavia. A record 15 countries attempted to qualify from the CONCACAF zone, which was now awarded two places: surprisingly, Mexico was eliminated with El Salvador and Honduras advancing, the latter making their World Cup debut. Africa, now given two direct places in the finals, also advanced two World Cup debutants, Algeria and Cameroon, out of 29 entrants. Cameroon's passage was sealed by a defeat of Morocco in the capital of Cameroon, Yaoundé, over 100,000 jubilant fans present. The Asian and Oceanic zone sent the final qualifier to Spain, joining Kuwait who had won the zone's final qualification round, as the play-off on 10 January 1982 was won by New Zealand over China 2–1 on neutral ground in Singapore. Both New Zealand and Kuwait made their World Cup finals debuts in Spain.

The qualification process continued its inexorable expansion for the 1986 World Cup in Mexico: this time, 121 countries entered, 110 actually playing in 308 games that saw 801 goals scored. The hosts qualified automatically along with defending champions Italy. Europe's qualifying zone was headed by the only unbeaten team, England, who advanced along with Belgium, Bulgaria, Denmark, France, West Germany, Hungary, Northern Ireland, Poland, Portugal, Scotland, Spain and the Soviet Union. The Netherlands missed out, defeated by Belgium in a tremendous play-off contest. Denmark's qualification meant they would make their World Cup debut in Mexico. South America's four qualification places were taken by Argentina, Brazil, Uruguay and Paraguay, the latter of whom defeated Chile in a play-off. Eighteen nations from CONCACAF contested to claim the one place on offer for their region, Canada coming through to reach the World Cup for the first time, finishing ahead of Honduras and Costa Rica in the final-round group. Morocco and Algeria advanced as the African representatives, while Asia now sent two qualifiers automatically as well, Iraq making it for the first time, accompanied by South Korea. The winner of the Oceanic zone—Australia—now faced a UEFA runner-up for the final place at the World Cup, Scotland advancing 2–0 on aggregate after games in Glasgow and Melbourne in November and December 1985.

The number of entrants for the 1990 World Cup declined slightly, down 5 teams to 116, with 314 games played by 103 teams. Three countries made their qualifying debuts: Gabon, Oman and Pakistan. CONCACAF sent a new team to the World Cup finals, Costa Rica qualifying along with the United States, who had not been to the finals since 1950, after beating Trinidad and Tobago in a dramatic game settled by Paul Caligiuri's "shot heard around the world." Their passage had been eased by the absence of perennial CONCACAF qualifiers Mexico, suspended by FIFA for falsifying the age of players at a youth competition. Asian qualifying also produced a World Cup finals debutant, the United Arab Emirates, who advanced along with South Korea. Cameroon and Egypt both qualified from the African zone. The Oceania region's winner, Israel (who was not actually part of the OFC but was placed in that zone for qualifying by FIFA), faced a play-off against the third-best South American team in qualifying, Colombia. The South Americans advanced after beating Israel 1–0 over two games. The other two South American nations to qualify were Brazil, continuing their perfect record of attendance at the World Cup finals, along with two-time champions Uruguay. Europe's 33 entrants were divided into 7 groups by UEFA, the biggest surprise proving to be France's failure to qualify, finishing behind Yugoslavia and Scotland in group 5. The other 11 European qualifiers were Belgium, Czechoslovakia, England, West Germany, the Netherlands, the Republic of Ireland (qualifying for the first time), Romania, Scotland, Soviet Union, Spain, Sweden and Yugoslavia.

The year 1994 saw a dramatic increase in the size of the qualifying competition. The number of entrants jumped from 116 in the previous edition to 147, with 132 actually taking part in 497 matches. The World Cup took place in the United States, the Americans qualifying automatically along with defending champions Germany. Africa was now granted three places, up from their previous high of two, and these were taken by Cameroon, Morocco and Nigeria out of a record-high 40 African entrants—the Nigerians achieving their first World Cup qualification. South Korea and Saudi Arabia (who would make their World Cup debut) became the 2 qualifiers from the 29 Asian entrants. Europe's 39 applicants ended up divided into 6 groups, with Belgium, Bulgaria, Greece, Italy, the Netherlands, Norway, the Republic of Ireland, Romania, Russia, Spain, Sweden and Switzerland advancing. England, semifinalists at the 1990 World Cup, and France surprisingly failed to qualify, the latter losing their place by conceding an injury-time goal to Bulgaria in their final qualifying game. A dramatic period in European history meant Russia was now an independent state, while a united Germany appeared at the World Cup for the first time since 1938. Greece, meanwhile, qualified for their first World Cup. From the CONCACAF zone, Mexico advanced to the World Cup for their 10th appearance at the finals. Second-place Canada went to a play-off with the winner of the Oceania zone, Australia. In a dramatic matchup, both teams won 2–1 at home, Australia earning their passage to the United States with a penalty shoot-out win.

The number of World Cup finals places increased to 32 at the 1998 World Cup in France, up from 24 in 1994, and 174 nations attempted to claim one of 30 places available through the qualifying competition—hosts France and reigning champions Brazil qualifying automatically—resulting in 643 games featuring 168 teams actually taking part, watched by a total of over 15 million fans. A total of 31 countries joined the qualifying process for the first time, from places as small as the Cook Islands to as large as Ukraine. The additional places on offer meant three CONCACAF nations now qualified. Mexico and the United States unsurprisingly finished first and second, while Jamaica claimed the third qualifying spot, becoming the first Caribbean nation to qualify since Cuba in 1934 and making their World Cup debut in France. African qualifying provided another World Cup newcomer, South Africa, who qualified alongside Cameroon, Morocco, Nigeria and Tunisia. A third World Cup debutant qualified from the Asian zone, Japan, along with Saudi Arabia and South Korea. Iran, meanwhile, also qualified after beating Oceanic winner Australia, stunning Melbourne in the second leg with a two-goal burst in the second half to qualify on the away-goals rule. European qualification advanced a further World Cup newcomer, Croatia, qualifying along with Austria, Belgium, Bulgaria, Denmark, England, Germany, Italy, the Netherlands, Norway, Romania, Scotland, Spain and Yugoslavia advancing out of a record pool of 50 European nations. Remarkably, 31 countries made their first appearance in World Cup qualifying.

The number of entrants for 2002 World Cup qualifying rose from 1998, with 199 countries applying to FIFA, 193 actually taking part. That resulted in a record 777 matches played, those games attended by over 17 million spectators. It was a competition that also saw other World Cup qualifying records broken: Australia crushed American Samoa 31–0 for the biggest-ever win; Togo's Souleymane Mamam took the field aged just 13 years and 310 days to become the youngest player to participate; and the fastest hat trick ever took place when Egypt's Abdelhamid netted his in only 177 seconds. Each FIFA confederation also had a record number of entries. There were 51

European nations entered, with France qualifying automatically as World Cup hosts, and 14 countries earned direct berths in the finals from the UEFA zone: Belgium, Croatia, Denmark, England, Germany, Italy, Poland, Portugal, the Republic of Ireland, Russia, Slovenia, Spain, Sweden and Turkey. Of those, all but Slovenia had previously taken part in the World Cup. For the first time, Africa tied Europe in the number of countries entering its qualification competition, with only one withdrawal, Burundi. The five African qualifiers were Cameroon, Nigeria, Senegal, South Africa and Tunisia. Senegal was the only first-time qualifier of the bunch, the other four all playing in their second successive World Cup finals tournament. In the Asian zone, Saudi Arabia was joined in qualifying by China, the world's most populous nation heading to Japan and South Korea for their World Cup debut. The third-placed Asian team faced the best runner-up from the UEFA zone, the Republic of Ireland, in a play-off for qualification: the Irish advanced with a 2–1 win over two games in Dublin and Tehran. The winner of the Oceania zone also faced a play-off against the fifth-placed South American team: Australia won the first game over Uruguay 1–0 at home in Melbourne but lost 3–0 away in Montevideo, the Uruguayans thus advancing to the World Cup for the first time since 1990. The other South American countries to qualify were Argentina, Brazil, Ecuador and Paraguay. From CONCACAF, a now familiar trio of World Cup participants advanced: Costa Rica, Mexico and the United States.

Out of 198 entries for the 2006 World Cup, to be held in Germany, 194 actually played in the qualifying competition, a record. Three entrants dropped out, while hosts Germany automatically qualified—a change in the rules by FIFA meant the defending champions now had to qualify, in this case Brazil. Two teams took part in qualifying for the first time: Afghanistan and New Caledonia. The latter joined the Oceanic zone, which saw the last appearance in it for Australia, who moved to the Asian confederation in time for 2010 qualifying. Australia claimed top spot in Oceanic qualifying, seeing off the Solomon Islands 9–1 on aggregate in the final, to earn a play-off against South America's fifth-place team, two-time champions Uruguay. In the first leg, played at the 1930 World Cup final venue, Estadio de Centenario in Uruguayan capital Montevideo, the home nation claimed a 1–0 win. Roared on by over 80,000 fans in Sydney for the return fixture, Australia defeated Uruguay 1–0 at home and the qualifying spot was decided by a penalty shoot-out won by Australia, who thus qualified for the World Cup for the second time. In Asia, continuity was the watchword: from group one in the final round, South Korea qualified for their sixth straight World Cup and Saudi Arabia for their fourth straight World Cup. Group two saw Japan reach their third straight World Cup and Iran qualify for the third time in their history. Bahrain advanced to a play-off against CONCACAF's fourth-placed qualifier, Caribbean nation Trinidad and Tobago, the latter winning 2–1 over two games to qualify for the first time. The top three CONCACAF qualifiers were the unsurprising trio of the United States, Mexico and Costa Rica. Mexico's Jared Borgetti scored 14 goals in qualifying, unmatched worldwide. There was also little surprise in South American qualifying: the top four qualifiers were Brazil, Argentina, Ecuador and Paraguay. There was, however, plenty of excitement in African qualifying, as four of the five qualifying teams had never before appeared at a World Cup: Angola, Ghana, Côte d'Ivoire and Togo were the newcomers, joining Tunisia, who would be making its fourth appearance. European qualifying provided one World Cup newcomer, Ukraine, who finished ahead of 2002 semifinalists Turkey, the latter losing in the play-offs to Switzerland, returning to the World Cup for the first time since 1994. Perennial qualifiers Russia and Bulgaria also failed to make it, but most of Europe's powerhouses did succeed. Joining Ukraine and Switzerland were repeat qualifiers Croatia, Czech Republic, England, France, Italy, the Netherlands, Poland, Portugal, Serbia and Montenegro, Spain and Sweden.

The number of entrants and participants for 2010 World Cup qualifying surpassed 200 for the first time, with 206 entering and 200 actually playing. Hosts South Africa automatically qualified for the competition. No fewer than 853 matches were played in qualifying, with 2,344 goals scored and almost 20 million fans attending the games. All previous World Cup winners qualified for the first World Cup to be held in Africa. In Europe, former winners England, France, Germany and Italy were joined in qualifying by Denmark, Greece, the Netherlands, Portugal, Serbia, Slovakia, Slovenia, Spain and Switzerland. A record number of African nations would appear at the World Cup, with host nation South Africa accompanied by Algeria, Cameroon, Côte d'Ivoire, Ghana and Nigeria. The Algerians qualified in dramatic fashion, defeating Egypt in a heated play-off game. In Asia, Japan became the first country to qualify for the World Cup, joined in group A by Australia, the latter having moved from Oceanic qualifying. In group B, both Koreas qualified, North Korea for the first time since 1966, South Korea for the seventh consecutive time. Australia's absence from Oceania eased the passage for New Zealand, the All Whites not having made it to the World Cup since 1982 but taking the confederation's now automatic qualifying place. In South America, Argentina left it late to qualify under the coaching of Diego Maradona, only sealing their place with their final qualifying game. They advanced to South Africa automatically along with Brazil, Chile and Paraguay. In the CONCACAF zone, the United States and Mexico once again finished first and second in qualifying, with the third automatic place going to Honduras, who had not qualified since 1982. Costa Rica finished fourth and thus had to face a play-off against fifth-placed South American team Uruguay. The latter won 2–1 on aggregate, meaning they would make their 11th appearance at a World Cup in South Africa.

In the qualifying competition for the 2014 FIFA World Cup, 203 countries entered, a record number, with 31 of the 32 places at the finals in Brazil allocated to qualifying teams. The host nation, in this case Brazil, qualified automatically. The qualification spots were divided among the six regional FIFA confederations. Each confederation does not receive an equal number of places in the final tournament; for the 2014 World Cup, Europe provided the most countries with 13 qualifiers. Africa had five qualifying nations. Asia had four, and South America five (for six total nations, including Brazil). South America's final qualifying nation, Uruguay, qualified after defeating Jordan, Asia's fifth-placed nation, in a play-off match. North and Central America and the Caribbean (CONCACAF) had four teams qualify, as their fourth-placed team, Mexico, defeated New Zealand, the winner of Oceanic zone qualifying, in their intercontinental play-off match. The 203 entrants for the 2014 qualifying contest is a record, up from the previous record of 200 set for the 2010 World Cup in South Africa. The growth of the qualifying competition's intensity and importance is illustrated by a record number of 19.3 million fans attending the 853 qualifying games at a record average attendance of just under 23,000 spectators per game.

Y

YUGOSLAVIA. Commonly known as Plavi (The Blues) or the Brazilians of Europe. Yugoslavia competed in nine World Cups before the country dissolved in the 1990s, first becoming Serbia and Montenegro, then just Serbia in 2006. They took part in the first World Cup in 1930, where they went 2-0-0 in the first round but lost to host nation Uruguay in the semifinals. Twenty years later in the 1950 World Cup, held in Brazil, the Yugoslavians finished second in their group, but with only the first-place teams from each group advancing to the next round, Yugoslavia was eliminated. Yugoslavia would advance to the quarterfinals in the 1954, 1958 and 1962 World Cups, playing West Germany in each match. Although West Germany got the better of Yugoslavia in the first two quarterfinals, in 1962 Yugoslavia defeated West Germany 1–0 and advanced to the semifinals for the first time since 1930. There they lost to Czechoslovakia, and after losing to Chile in the third-place game, as well, Yugoslavia finished fourth in the competition.

Yugoslavia failed to qualify for the 1966 and 1970 World Cups but returned in 1974 in West Germany. Finishing first in their group consisting of Brazil, Scotland and Zaire, Yugoslavia did not find the same success in the second round. There they lost to West Germany, Poland and Sweden and were eliminated. Eight years later, Yugoslavia went 1-1-1 in the group stage and did not advance out of their group at the World Cup in Spain. In 1990, at the World Cup in Italy, Yugoslavia defeated Spain 2–1 in the round of 16, but lost to Argentina in a penalty shoot-out in the quarterfinals. The year 1998 was the final World Cup for a national team known as Yugoslavia, representing the Federal Republic of Yugoslavia, and it ended in the round of 16 after a 2–1 loss to the Netherlands.

Z

ZAGALLO, MÁRIO. B. 9 August 1931, Maceió, Brazil. An enormously successful Brazilian player and coach, Mário Zagallo played a key role in four of Brazil's first five FIFA World Cup triumphs. As a player, Zagallo won several titles with Flamengo and Botafogo in his native Brazil. Zagallo played for Brazil in the 1950s and 1960s, making 37 appearances and scoring 4 goals, including a goal against Sweden in the 1958 World Cup final, which Brazil went on to win. Again featuring Zagallo, Brazil won the next World Cup in 1962 held in Chile as well.

After retirement from playing, Zagallo took over coaching at Brazilian club Botafogo in the late 1960s, before taking over as Brazilian national-team manager in 1970. Zagallo inherited a team with remarkable talent, and he molded them into one of the greatest attacking sides the world has ever seen: with Pelé playing a starring role, Brazil romped to their third World Cup victory in the 1970 finals in Mexico, winning all six games, with Zagallo becoming the first man to win a World Cup as both a player and a manager. Brazil was less successful at the next World Cup in 1974, finishing fourth in West Germany under Zagallo's guidance. He then had a peripatetic career as both a club and international coach, with spells in Kuwait, Saudi Arabia and the United Arab Emirates at the international level and with several clubs, his most notable success being a Brazilian national championship with Flamengo in 1986.

Zagallo won his fourth FIFA World Cup medal as an assistant coach for Brazil at the 1994 tournament in the United States. He then took over as head coach of Brazil once again, leading them to victory in the 1997 Copa América and then to a runners-up spot at the 1998 World Cup in France. Despite some success, his second spell in charge of Brazil did not live up to his first, and Brazil's pragmatic approach received some criticism in contrast to the fluid style of the 1970s team Zagallo coached. After further short managerial spells at Portuguesa and Flamengo, Zagallo appeared again on the Brazil bench at the 2006 World Cup in Germany, this time as a technical director, but on this occasion, they got no further than the quarterfinals.

ZAIRE. *See* CONGO DR.

ŽENÍŠEK, LADISLAV. B. 7 March 1904, Vinohrady, Austria-Hungary. D. 14 May 1985. Ladislav Ženíšek was a defender for Czechoslovakia at the 1934 World Cup in Italy, part of a miserly back line that conceded four goals in the three games Ženíšek took part in. That included the final of the competition, a painful 2–1 defeat to the host nation even though Czechoslovakia led with just 10 minutes remaining in the game. Ženíšek was 30 years old in 1934 and had led a meandering career to that point, including a five-year spell playing in Chicago for the Czechoslovakian ethnic team Sparta Chicago in the late 1920s. He returned to his homeland and, in the early 1930s, shone for Slavia Prague as they dominated the Czech league in that period, winning the championship with the club for five successive seasons. Ženíšek retired from international play in 1935. He later coached several club teams and the Czechoslovakian national team in 1950 and 1951, though they took no part in the World Cup held in 1950 in Brazil.

ZICO. B. 3 March 1957, Rio de Janeiro, Brazil. Perhaps the greatest Brazilian player of his generation, Zico's international career did not result in the same triumphs as his predecessor as Brazil's best, Pelé, did prior to him, but some still whisper his name in the same breath when considering the respective talents of the two. Born Arthur Antunes Coimbra, he began his career with local club Flamengo in 1971, staying with the Brazilian club until 1983 and earning a reputation as one of Brazil's best attacking players, a goal scorer particularly deadly at taking free kicks. In that period, Flamengo claimed six São Paulo state titles, three national Brazilian championships and, in 1981, won both the Copa Libertadores and the Intercontinental Cup.

Zico made his international debut for his country in 1976 and represented Brazil at the 1978, 1982 and 1986 FIFA World Cup tournaments. Zico was unfortunate to play for Brazil during a period of frustrating underachievement: despite their flowing, fantastic play—with Zico as the fulcrum of the side—they failed to live up to the impossible standard set by the previous generation of Brazilians who had won three World Cup victories between 1958 and 1970. Zico came closest to glory with Brazil in the 1978 World Cup, reaching the semifinal stage. The 1982 Brazil team, though it did not go as far in the competition, is regarded as one of the best in World Cup history, with Brazil winning all three of their group-stage games, Zico scoring three goals. In the second group stage, Brazil beat reigning champions Argentina 3–1, with Zico scoring again, but exited the tournament after a surprising defeat to hosts Italy. The next year, Zico moved to Italy itself to play for Udinese in Serie A, a successful sojourn that ended in 1985 with a return to Flamengo in Brazil, retiring from play in 1994 and going on to have a successful managerial career in Japan.

ZIDANE, ZINEDINE. B. 23 June 1972, Marseille, France. Zinedine Zidane's only rival for recognition as France's greatest-ever player is Michel Platini, though Zidane went a step further than his predecessor from the 1980s by leading his country to their first and only FIFA World Cup triumph in 1998, on home soil. Zidane also led France to victory in the 2000 UEFA European Football Championship, in the midst of a five-year period of glory that saw him named as FIFA World Player of the Year three times. At club level, he also reached the pinnacle of the game starring for Real Madrid in their victorious 2002 UEFA Champions League run.

Born in Marseille in Southern France, Zidane's Algerian heritage and leadership of France's multicultural 1998 team saw him become a national icon for reasons beyond his phenomenal talent with the ball. Still, it was his magical mastery of the ball that took him out of poverty in childhood to a professional career with Cannes, making his debut in 1988, before moving on to Girondins de Bordeaux in 1992. Zidane's impressive play turned Bordeaux into a title contender and led to a move to Italian giants Juventus in 1996, winning the league championship in his first season with the club. This was followed by impressive runs to, but disappointing defeats in, two consecutive UEFA Champions League finals in 1997 and 1998. It was following a world-record transfer fee move to Real Madrid that Zidane finally won the UEFA Champions League, scoring the winning goal for his Spanish club with a superb volley in a 2–1 win over Bayer Leverkusen from Germany.

At the international level, the 1998 World Cup finals in Zidane's native France saw him earn worldwide fame, as the creative hub of his country's first World Cup victory. Zidane scored twice in the final against Brazil in a 3–0 victory for France. He then led his country to an unprecedented back-to-back sequence of victories in international tournaments, scoring two goals in France's winning run in the 2000 UEFA European Football Championship. But struggling with injury, Zidane was able to do little to help his country defend their World Cup title in 2002, as France exited in the first round of the finals tournament. The 2004 UEFA European Football Championships was almost as disappointing, with France losing to Greece in the quarterfinals. Zidane briefly retired from international soccer before returning in time for the 2006 World Cup tournament in Italy, earning the FIFA Golden Ball as player of the tournament as he drove France to the final once again. Yet it was there that Zidane would earn global infamy for the wrong reasons, despite his seventh-minute goal from the penalty spot: taunted by Italian midfielder Marco Materazzi in extra time with the score tied at 1–1, Zidane headbutted him in the chest in response and was sent off. France went on to lose the game in a penalty shoot-out. That moment illustrated most vividly that behind Zidane's placid appearance, a temperamental passion flamed. Zidane retired following the final, a controversial ending to one of the greatest careers in the game's history.

ŻMUDA, WŁADYSŁAW. B. 6 June 1954, Lublin, Poland. Władysław Żmuda is a four-time World Cup participant, playing a total of 21 matches in the 1974, 1978, 1982 and 1986 tournaments, the third-most appearances of all competitors. A defender, he earned 91 caps with Poland and scored 2 goals. In the 1974 World Cup, Poland placed third and Żmuda was named the Best Young Player of the tournament. He earned another third-place finish with Poland in the 1986 World Cup. His appearances in four World Cup tournaments are second-most all-time, behind only Antonio Carbajal and Lothar Matthäus.

ZSENGELLÉR, GYULA. B. 27 December 1915, Cegléd, Hungary. D. 29 March 1999. With five goals in four appearances at the 1938 World Cup for Hungary, Gyula Zsengellér finished as the joint second-highest scorer at the third World Cup, along with compatriot György Sárosi and Italy's Silvio Piola, behind Brazil's Leônidas da Silva, who scored eight goals. Zsengellér played a crucial role as Hungary progressed to the final of the competition, losing there to defending champions Italy, Zsengellér unable to get on the score sheet as Hungary lost 4–2. Zsengellér scored his first two goals at the World Cup in Hungary's opening game, a straightforward 6–0 win over the Dutch East Indies in their only World Cup appearance.

In the second round, Zsengellér scored again, adding the second for Hungary's 2–0 win against Switzerland. In the semifinal, Zsengellér scored for the third consecutive game, recording a brace of goals in a 5–1 victory for Hungary over Sweden to advance to the World Cup final. Zsengellér was only 22 during the 1938 World Cup, having made his debut for Hungary in 1936, quickly making his mark internationally and scoring five goals in one World Cup qualifier as Hungary defeated Greece 11–1. Zsengellér continued to play for Hungary through World War II, making his final appearance internationally in August 1947. He finished his career with an impressive goal-scoring ratio of 32 goals in 39 international games for his country. Zsengellér was even more prolific as a goal scorer for Hungarian team Újpest FC at club level, scoring over 300 goals at a ratio of more than one goal per game. Following his retirement from playing, Zsengellér enjoyed a long coaching career at a dozen other clubs around Europe.

Appendix A

The FIFA World Cup: Dates, Hosts, Winners and Runners-Up

	Host Nation	*Dates*	*Winners*	*Runners-Up*
1930	Uruguay	13–30 July	Uruguay	Argentina
1934	Italy	27 May–10 June	Italy	Czechoslovakia
1938	France	4–19 June	Italy	Hungary
1950	Brazil	24 June–16 July	Uruguay	Brazil
1954	Switzerland	16 June–4 July	West Germany	Hungary
1958	Sweden	8–29 June	Brazil	Sweden
1962	Chile	30 May–17 June	Brazil	Czechoslovakia
1966	England	11–30 July	England	West Germany
1970	Mexico	31 May–21 June	Brazil	Italy
1974	West Germany	13 June–7 July	West Germany	Netherlands
1978	Argentina	1–25 June	Argentina	Netherlands
1982	Spain	13 June–11 July	Italy	West Germany
1986	Mexico	31 May–29 June	Argentina	West Germany
1990	Italy	8 June–8 July	West Germany	Argentina
1994	United States	17 June–17 July	Brazil	Italy
1998	France	10 June–12 July	France	Brazil
2002	South Korea / Japan	31 May–30 June	Brazil	West Germany
2006	Germany	9 June–9 July	Italy	France
2010	South Africa	11 June–11 July	Spain	Netherlands
2014	Brazil	12 June–13 July	Germany	Argentina

Appendix B
Golden Ball Winners

	Winner	Second Place	Third Place
1982	Paolo Rossi (Italy)	Falcão (Brazil)	Karl-Heinz Rummenigge (West Germany)
1986	Diego Maradona (Argentina)	Harald Schumacher (West Germany)	Preben Elkjær Larsen (Denmark)
1990	Salvatore Schillaci (Italy)	Lothar Matthäus (West Germany)	Diego Maradona (Argentina)
1994	Romário (Brazil)	Roberto Baggio (Italy)	Hristo Stoichkov (Bulgaria)
1998	Ronaldo (Brazil)	Davor Šuker (Croatia)	Lilian Thuram (France)
2002	Oliver Kahn (Germany)	Ronaldo (Brazil)	Hong Myung-Bo (South Korea)
2006	Zinedine Zidane (France)	Fabio Cannavaro (Italy)	Andrea Pirlo (Italy)
2010	Diego Forlán (Uruguay)	Wesley Sneijder (Netherlands)	David Villa (Spain)
2014	Lionel Messi (Argentina)	Thomas Müller (Germany)	Arjen Robben (Netherlands)

Appendix C

Golden Boot Winners

1930	Guillermo Stabile (Argentina), 8 goals
1934	Oldřich Nejedlý (Czechoslovakia), 5 goals
1938	Leônidas (Brazil), 7 goals
1950	Ademir (Brazil), 8 goals
1954	Sándor Kocsis (Hungary), 11 goals
1958	Just Fontaine (France), 13 goals
1962	Flórián Albert (Hungary), 4 goals
1966	Eusébio (Portugal), 9 goals
1970	Gerd Müller (West Germany), 10 goals
1974	Grzegorz Lato (Poland), 7 goals
1978	Mario Kempes (Argentina), 6 goals
1982	Paolo Rossi (Italy), 6 goals
1986	Gary Lineker (England), 6 goals
1990	Salvatore Schillaci (Italy), 6 goals
1994	Oleg Salenko (Russia), 6 goals
1998	Davor Šuker (Croatia), 6 goals
2002	Ronaldo (Brazil), 8 goals
2006	Miroslav Klose (Germany), 5 goals
2010	Thomas Müller (Germany), 5 goals
2014	James Rodríguez (Colombia), 6 goals

Appendix D

Golden Glove Winners

1994	Michel Preud'homme (Belgium)
1998	Fabian Barthez (France)
2002	Oliver Kahn (Germany)
2006	Gianluigi Buffon (Italy)
2010	Iker Casillas (Spain)
2014	Manuel Neuer (Germany)

Appendix E

Best Young Player

2006   Lukas Podolski (Germany)
2010   Thomas Müller (Germany)
2014   Paul Pogba (France)

Appendix F
FIFA Fair Play Trophy

1970	Peru
1974	*
1978	Argentina
1982	Brazil
1986	Brazil
1990	England
1994	Brazil
1998	England, France
2002	Belgium
2006	Brazil, Spain
2010	Spain
2014	Colombia

*No award given by FIFA

Bibliography

Alegi, Peter, and Chris Bolsmann, eds. *Africa's World Cup: Critical Reflections on Play, Patriotism, Spectatorship, and Space*. Ann Arbor: University of Michigan Press, 2013.

Bondi, Filip. *Chasing the Game: America and the Quest for the World Cup*. New York: De Capo, 2010.

Cantor, Andrés. *Goooal: A Celebration of Soccer*. New York: Touchstone, 1997.

Cottle, Eddie, ed. *South Africa's World Cup: A Legacy for Whom?* Scottsville, South Africa: University of KwaZulu-Natal Press, 2011.

Crouch, Terry. *The World Cup: The Complete History*. 3rd ed. London: Aurum, 2010.

Douglas, Geoffrey. *The Game of Their Lives*. New York: Holt, 1996.

Dubois, Laurent. *Soccer Empire: The World Cup and the Future of France*. Berkeley: University of California Press, 2010.

Freddi, Cris. *Complete Book of the World Cup 2006*. London: HarperSport, 2006.

Galeano, Eduardo. *Soccer in Sun and Shadow*. London: Verso, 1998.

Glanville, Brian. *The Story of the World Cup*. London: Faber and Faber, 1997.

Goldblatt, David. *The Ball Is Round: A Global History of Soccer*. New York: Viking, 2006.

Harvey, Adrian. *Football: The First Hundred Years: The Untold Story*. New York: Routledge, 2005.

Jawad, Hyad. *Four Weeks in Montevideo: The Story of World Cup 1930*. London: Seventeen Media, 2009.

Jennings, Andrew. *Foul! The Secret World of FIFA: Bribes, Vote Rigging and Ticket Scandals*. London: HarperCollins, 2007.

Kuper, Simon. *Soccer against the Enemy: How the World's Most Popular Sport Starts and Fuels Revolutions and Keeps Dictators in Power*. New York: Nation Books, 2006.

Lanfranchi, Pierre, Christiane Eisenberg, Tony Mason, and Alfred Wahl, eds. *100 Years of Football: The FIFA Centennial Book*. London: Weidenfeld and Nicolson, 2004.

Lisi, Clemente Angelo. *A History of the World Cup: 1930–2006*. Lanham, MD: Scarecrow, 2007.

Martinez, D. P., and Projit Bihari Mukharji. *Football: From England to the World*. London: Routledge, 2009.

McIlvanney, Hugh. *McIlvanney on Football*. London: Mainstream, 1999.

McIlvanney, Hugh, and John Arlott. *World Cup '66*. London: Eyre and Spottiswood, 1966.

Murray, Bill. *The World's Game: A History of Soccer*. Urbana: University of Illinois Press, 1998.

Rous, Stanley. *Football Worlds: A Lifetime in Sport*. London: Faber and Faber, 1978.

Spurling, John. *Death or Glory: The Dark History of the World Cup*. London: Vision Sports, 2010.

Sugden, John Peter, and Alan Tomlinson. *Badfellas: FIFA Family at War*. Edinburgh, UK: Mainstream, 2003.

——. *FIFA and the Contest for World Football: Who Rules the People's Game*. Cambridge: Polity, 1998.

——. *Hosts and Champions: Soccer Cultures, National Identities and the USA World Cup*. Aldershot, UK: Arena, 1994.

Tomlinson, Alan, and Christopher Young. *National Identity and Global Sports Events: Culture, Politics, and Spectacle in the Olympics and the Football World Cup*. Albany: State University of New York Press, 2006.

Weiland, Matt, and Sean Wilsey, eds. *The Thinking Fan's Guide to the World Cup*. London: Harper Perennial, 2006.

WEBSITES

British Broadcasting Corporation: www.bbc.com
ESPN soccer website: www.espnfc.com
Official website of FIFA: www.fifa.com
Forbes online: www.forbes.com
Goal.com: www.goal.com
Guardian online: www.theguardian.com
Los Angeles Times online: www.latimes.com
New York Times online: www.nytimes.com

Index

About the Authors

Tom Dunmore is a soccer writer and executive originally from Brighton, England. Dunmore moved to Chicago in 2001 and began his career in soccer as the publisher of the award-winning global soccer culture blog, www.pitchinvasion.net, winner of a gold-medal award from *When Saturday Comes* magazine in 2009. In 2010 and 2011, Dunmore served as the chairman of Section 8 Chicago, the Independent Supporters' Association for the Chicago Fire Soccer Club. In 2012, Dunmore cofounded *XI Quarterly*, a print periodical exploring soccer in North America. He lives in Indianapolis with his wife, Monika, and infant son, Jack, and is currently serving as the vice president of marketing and operations for Indy Eleven in the North American Soccer League.

Andrew Donaldson is an ex-collegiate and semiprofessional soccer player who found that the old adage "those who can no longer do, coach" rang a bit too true. Currently a middle-aged, fading athlete who can't quite bend it like Beckham residing in Corvallis, Oregon, Donaldson received a master's degree in sport psychology at the same time he traded his playing boots in for coaching ones. He transitioned to a life of teaching the game of soccer to collegiate, high school, club and ODP kids around the state of Oregon. An ex-physical-activity-course instructor, Donaldson now spends his days coaching and working to improve his writing.

CPSIA information can be obtained at www.ICGtesting.com
Printed in the USA
BVOW08*1711050115

381668BV00004B/5/P

9 780810 887428